CRIMINAL PROCEDURE
(SCOTLAND) ACT 1995

AUSTRALIA
LBC Information Services—Sydney

CANADA and USA
Carswell—Toronto

NEW ZEALAND
Brooker's—Auckland

SINGAPORE and MALAYSIA
Sweet & Maxwell Asia
Singapore and Kuala Lumpur

CRIMINAL PROCEDURE (SCOTLAND) ACT 1995

Third Edition

Annotated by

Iain Bradley
Solicitor and member of the Procurator Fiscal Service

and

Robert S. Shiels
Solicitor and member of the Procurator Fiscal Service

*   *   *   *   *

Appeal provisions annotated by

Ann Ogg
Solicitor Advocate

Mental health provisions annotated by

Petra Collins
Advocate

EDINBURGH
W. GREEN/Sweet & Maxwell
2001

First Published 1996
Second Edition 1999

© 2001
W. Green & Son Ltd

ISBN 0 414 01415 4

A CIP catalogue record for this book is available from the British Library

Typeset by Mendip Communications Ltd, Frome, Somerset
Printed and bound in Great Britain by MPG Books, Bodmin, Cornwall

CRIMINAL PROCEDURE (SCOTLAND) ACT 1995*

(1995 c. 46)

ARRANGEMENT OF SECTIONS

PART I

CRIMINAL COURTS

JURISDICTION AND POWERS

The High Court

PART II

POLICE FUNCTIONS

Lord Advocate's instructions

---

* Annotations by Iain Bradley, Solicitor in Scotland and Robert S. Shiels, Solicitor in Scotland.

PART VI

MENTAL DISORDER

PART VII

SOLEMN PROCEEDINGS

PART VIII

APPEALS FROM SOLEMN PROCEEDINGS

PART IX

SUMMARY PROCEEDINGS

General

Complaints

Citation

Children

Companies

First diet

Pre-trial procedure

Criminal Procedure (Scotland) Act 1995

Certain rights of accused

290. Accused's right to request identification parade.
291. Precognition on oath of defence witnesses.

Mode of trial

292. Mode of trial of certain offences.

Art and part and attempt

293. Statutory offences: art and part and aiding and abetting.
294. Attempt at crime.

Legal custody

295. Legal custody.

Warrants

296. Warrants for search and apprehension to be signed by judge.
297. Execution of warrants and service of complaints, etc.

Trial judge's report

298. Trial judge's report

Correction of entries

299. Correction of entries.
300. Amendment of records of conviction and sentence in summary proceedings.

Rights of audience

301. Rights of audience.

Fixed penalties

302. Fixed penalty: conditional offer by procurator fiscal.
303. Fixed penalty: enforcement.
303A. Transfer of rights of appeal of deceased person.

Part XIV

General

304. Criminal Courts Rules Council.
305. Acts of Adjournal.
306. Information for financial and other purposes.
307. Interpretation.
308. Construction of enactments referring to detention etc.
309. Short title, commencement and extent.

SCHEDULES:
Schedule 1—Offences Against Children Under the Age of 17 Years to which Special Provisions Apply.
Schedule 2—Examples of Indictments.
Schedule 3—Indictments and Complaints.
Schedule 4—Supervision and Treatment Orders.
    Part I—Preliminary.
    Part II—Making and Effect of Orders.
    Part III—Revocation and Amendment of Orders.
Schedule 5—Forms of Complaint and Charges.
Schedule 6—Discharge of and Amendment to Probation Orders.
Schedule 7—Supervised Attendance Orders: Further Provisions.

11

Schedule 8—Documentary Evidence in Criminal Proceedings.
Schedule 9—Certificates as to Proof of Certain Routine Matters.
Schedule 10—Certain Offences Triable only Summarily.

An Act to consolidate certain enactments relating to criminal procedure in Scotland.   [8th November 1995]

PARLIAMENTARY DEBATES
Hansard, H.L. Vol. 565, col. 14; Vol. 566, cols. 384, 581, 894. H.C. Vol. 265, col. 181.

INTRODUCTION AND GENERAL NOTE
It has been said that it takes lawyers five years to change a habit: if that is correct then the memory of the Criminal Procedure (Scotland) Act 1975 will linger on for some time, most probably in the reference to the very familiar sections. The Criminal Procedure (Scotland) Act 1995 is a consolidating provision so that much of the legal landscape remains the same even though the reference to individual parts has changed.

The Criminal Procedure (Scotland) Act 1995 has to be seen as part of a substantial Government policy to consolidate Scots criminal law, evidence and procedure. The Criminal Justice (Scotland) Act 1995 amended some aspects of the law of evidence and procedure and made new provisions in relation to attacking the proceeds of crime.

Once the Criminal Procedure (Scotland) Act 1975 (c.21) had been amended the law was consolidated in the Criminal Procedure (Scotland) Act 1995. The complete package of contemporary legislation must be seen to include also the Criminal Law (Consolidation) (Scotland) Act 1995 (c.39), the Criminal Law (Consequential Provisions) (Scotland) Act 1995 (c.40) and the Proceeds of Crime (Scotland) Act 1995 (c.43). The mechanics of the application of much of the law is to be found in the Act of Adjournal (Criminal Procedure Rules) 1996.

Consideration of the new law is restricted in this note to the Criminal Procedure (Scotland) Act 1995. Comprehensive annotations follow and those should help practitioners round the details of Act but there is benefit in knowing the structure of the Act itself: the parts are set out with general reference to some of the interesting sections.

Part I
Sections 1 to 11 make various provisions in regard to the jurisdiction and powers of the criminal courts of Scotland. There is virtually nothing new in this Part, merely a re-ordering of existing powers.

Part II
Sections 12 to 22 make provision for police functions. The power of the Lord Advocate to issue instructions to a chief constable in regard to the reporting of matters continues to provide an important constitutional safeguard, especially when seen in the context of the proviso to s.17(3) of the Police (Scotland) Act 1967 (c.77). The additional provisions reflect the original provision in law resulting from the Criminal Justice (Scotland) Act 1980 (c.62) as interpreted in subsequent case law.

Part III
Sections 23 to 33 consolidate the law of bail: it is the result of this consolidation that several Acts are no longer required, including the Bail etc. (Scotland) Act 1980 (c.4).

Part IV
Sections 34 to 40 deal with the peculiarly Scottish procedure of judicial examination. Sheriff Gerald Gordon referred to the pre-1980 judicial examination as an "empty ritual": see *The Criminal Justice (Scotland) Act 1980* (1981) (W. Green, Edinburgh) p. xviii. Whether very much more is now achieved is debatable but it is nevertheless the start of criminal proceedings leading for many to trial in a criminal court.

Part V
Sections 41 to 51 are provisions dealing with children and young persons in the capacity of offenders. Reference might also be made to the Children (Scotland) Act 1995 (c.36) which forms an important additional part of current legislation.

Part VI
Sections 52 to 63 make provision for various aspects of mental disorder. Perhaps the most substantial change in the whole of this Act is the introduction in s.55 of examination of facts.

This permits evidence to be led (by either party) in order that the court can determine whether it is satisfied beyond reasonable doubt that the accused did the act or made the omission constituting the offence, and if it is satisfied on the balance of probabilities that there are no grounds for acquitting him. This procedure can only follow where an accused is found to be insane: s.54(1). However, it now allows for an examination of circumstances where hitherto no trial would have taken place.

Part VII

Sections 64 to 102 set out the procedural stages and requirement for trial by jury. By s.12 of and Sched. 4 to the Criminal Justice (Scotland) Act 1980 there was abolished the mandatory diet in solemn proceedings and in its place there was established as required the preliminary diet. The new provision includes a first diet for solemn procedure in the sheriff court and a preliminary diet as required for solemn procedure in the High Court of Justiciary. Another change in nomenclature is the demise of the "section 102 letter"; the procedure where the accused desires to plead guilty is now found in s.76.

Part VIII

Sections 103 to 132 deal with appeals from solemn proceedings. Undoubtedly the major reform in this regard is the need to receive the grant of leave to appeal from a single judge in chambers: see s.105. The pressure that this rule puts on getting the ground of appeal stated correctly at the outset cannot be over-emphasised. Carefully thought-out appeals against conviction are unlikely to be weeded out early on, but speculative appeals against summary sentences may be much reduced.

Part IX

Sections 133 to 172 replicate generally the rules for summary prosecutions that apply for solemn prosecutions. In the Criminal Procedure (Scotland) Act 1975 the division between solemn and summary procedure was more marked than under this Act, *e.g.* the various latitudes and implied terms are now contained in Sched. 3 and apply equally to indictments and complaints by ss.64(6) and 138(4) respectively.

Part X

Sections 173 to 194 replicate generally the rules for summary appeals that apply for solemn appeals. Those familiar with the work of appellate judges will know that numerically the heaviest burden is, or was until the passing of this Act, the appeals against summary sentences. The single judge shift will undoubtedly affect the volume but the concession that two judges may deal with this class of case will be welcomed: s.173(2).

Part XI

Sections 195 to 254 deal with a wide range of post-conviction issues. On occasions the detail of the sections overwhelms the inherent excitement. However, practitioners may look forward to the implementation of s.197 which requires courts at first instance to have regard to sentencing opinions pronounced on statutory authority. It would be crass merely to offer a percentage discount on sentence for a guilty plea but explicit recognition for an acceptance of responsibilities may have a marked effect on summary business.

Part XII

Sections 255 to 286 make provision for evidential matters. There is no attack on the general requirement for a sufficiency of evidence but it is clear from the wide range of provisions that those advising accused persons will require at the earliest opportunity after receiving instructions to narrow the issues and agree evidence accordingly. That is especially the case for routine evidence of the type covered by certificates in terms of s.281 of and Sched. 9 to this Act.

Part XIII

Sections 287 to 303 cover a wide variety of matters. The fixed penalty system, under ss.303 and 304, will probably and properly keep out of court a wide variety of minor infringements at the least serious end of criminal behaviour.

Part XIV

Sections 304 to 310 deal with general points but mention must be made of the establishment of the Criminal Courts Rules Council. It is true that many other bodies take an interest in criminal law but this body has the function of keeping under general review the procedures and practices of the courts exercising criminal jurisdiction in Scotland and that in itself is progress: see s.304(9).

Sched. 1

Section 21 and Sched. 1 give constables powers to take offenders into custody in relation to the offences against children under the age of 17 years.

Sched. 2

Petitions and indictments may be in a form set out in Sched. 2: see ss.34(1)(a) and 64(2)(a) respectively. The Schedule sets out examples of indictments. Given that the changes are discretionary in regard to the contents of the Schedule, the real question with a variance from an example is whether a change is relevant, not whether it coincides with such an example. Reference may also be made to Sched. 5.

Sched. 3

The structure of the 1975 Act was such that identical provisions were made for solemn proceedings and summary proceedings respectively. This duplication was felt to be unnecessary and by ss.64(6) and 138(4) the contents of Sched. 3 have effect as regards indictments and complaints. This Schedule will repay careful reading regularly by court practitioners because of the complexity of the provisions that frequently render pleas to the relevancy, for example, unnecessary and assist with more efficient pleading.

Sched. 4

The regime of supervision and treatment orders was introduced by s.50 of and Sched. 2 to the Criminal Justice (Scotland) Act 1995. The development is simply repeated in this Act.

Sched. 5

This Schedule provides forms of change in addition to those in Sched. 2. Questions may be raised as to why the Schedules are separate or what benefit is conferred by them in any event. Further, several of the forms are clearly anachronistic, for example by reference to assault "to the great effusion of blood".

Sched. 6

By s.231(1), this Schedule has effect in relation to the discharge and amendment of probation orders.

Sched. 7

Supervised attendance orders have been developed as an alternative to imprisonment and such orders have been extended by s.235 and Sched. 7.

Sched. 8

This Schedule makes provision regarding the admissibility in criminal proceedings of copy documents and of evidence contained in business documents. It should be noted that the Schedule has, by para. 8, definitions of terms that are not contained in the main interpretation section.

Sched. 9

Proof of routine or incontrovertible evidence is tedious and expensive and this Schedule provides for the increased use of certificates as to these matters. The consolidating nature of this legislation is such that this Schedule has a far wider range of subject-matters that may be covered by certificates.

Sched. 10

This Schedule must be read in the context of s.292 and the effect is to establish a narrow range of offences triable only summarily.

ABBREVIATIONS

The 1975 Act : Criminal Procedure (Scotland) Act 1975 (c.21).
The 1980 Act : Bail (Scotland) Act 1980 (c.4).
The 1984 Act : Mental Health (Scotland) Act 1984 (c.36).
The 1993 Act : Prisoners and Criminal Proceedings (Scotland) Act 1993 (c.9).
The 1995 Act : Criminal Procedure (Scotland) Act 1995 (c. 46).

The 1996 Act of Adjournal : Act of Adjournal (Criminal Procedure Rules) 1996 (S.I. 1996 No. 513).

PART I

CRIMINAL COURTS

JURISDICTION AND POWERS

The High Court

Judges in the High Court

1.—(1) The Lord President of the Court of Session shall be the Lord Justice General and shall perform his duties as the presiding judge of the High Court.

(2) Every person who is appointed to the office of one of the Senators of the College of Justice in Scotland shall, by virtue of such appointment, be a Lord Commissioner of Justiciary in Scotland.

(3) If any difference arises as to the rotation of judges in the High Court, it shall be determined by the Lord Justice General, whom failing by the Lord Justice Clerk.

(4) Any Lord Commissioner of Justiciary may preside alone at the trial of an accused before the High Court.

(5) Without prejudice to subsection (4) above, in any trial of difficulty or importance it shall be competent for two or more judges in the High Court to preside for the whole or any part of the trial.

DEFINITIONS
    "High Court": s.307(1).
    "Lord Commissioner of Justiciary": s.307(1).

GENERAL NOTE
    With one exception, the origins of this section are probably more a matter of legal history than a concern for practitioners. Section 1(5), reflecting the collegiate nature of Scottish judges, permits in any trial of difficulty or importance that it shall be competent for two or more judges in the High Court of Justiciary to provide for the whole or any part of the trial. Such problems tend to arise at short notice and while judges are on circuit but there are still a number of instances of this happening: see *H.M. Advocate v. Cairns*, 1967 J.C. 37; *H.M. Advocate v. MacKenzie*, 1970 S.L.T. 81; *MacNeil v. H.M. Advocate*, 1986 S.C.C.R. 288 and *Copeland v. H.M. Advocate*, 1987 S.C.C.R. 232.

Fixing of High Court sittings

2.—(1) The High Court shall sit at such times and places as the Lord Justice General, whom failing the Lord Justice Clerk, may, after consultation with the Lord Advocate, determine.

(2) Without prejudice to subsection (1) above, the High Court shall hold such additional sittings as the Lord Advocate may require.

(3) Where an accused has been cited to attend a sitting of the High Court, the prosecutor may, at any time before the commencement of his trial, apply to the Court to transfer the case to another sitting of the High Court; and a single judge of the High Court may—
    (a) after giving the accused or his counsel an opportunity to be heard; or
    (b) on the joint application of all parties,
make an order for the transfer of the case.

(4) Where no cases have been indicted for a sitting of the High Court or if

15

it is no longer expedient that a sitting should take place, it shall not be necessary for the sitting to take place.

(5) If any case remains indicted for a sitting which does not take place in pursuance of subsection (4) above, subsection (3) above shall apply in relation to the transfer of any other such case to another sitting.

DEFINITIONS
  "High Court": s.307(1).
  "order": s.307(1).
  "prosecutor": s.307(1).

Solemn courts: general

Jurisdiction and powers of solemn courts

3.—(1) The jurisdiction and powers of all courts of solemn jurisdiction, except so far as altered or modified by any enactment passed after the commencement of this Act, shall remain as at the commencement of this Act.

(2) Any crime or offence which is triable on indictment may be tried by the High Court sitting at any place in Scotland.

(3) The sheriff shall, without prejudice to any other or wider power conferred by statute, not be entitled, on the conviction on indictment of an accused, to pass a sentence of imprisonment for a term exceeding three years.

(4) Subject to subsection (5) below, where under any enactment passed or made before 1st January 1988 (the date of commencement of section 58 of the Criminal Justice (Scotland) Act 1987) an offence is punishable on conviction on indictment by imprisonment for a term exceeding two years but the enactment either expressly or impliedly restricts the power of the sheriff to impose a sentence of imprisonment for a term exceeding two years, it shall be competent for the sheriff to impose a sentence of imprisonment for a term exceeding two but not exceeding three years.

(5) Nothing in subsection (4) above shall authorise the imposition by the sheriff of a sentence in excess of the sentence specified by the enactment as the maximum sentence which may be imposed on conviction of the offence.

(6) Subject to any express exclusion contained in any enactment, it shall be lawful to indict in the sheriff court all crimes except murder, treason, rape and breach of duty by magistrates.

DEFINITIONS
  "crime": s.307(1).
  "offence": s.307(1).
  "sentence": s.307(1).

GENERAL NOTE
The maximum sentence of imprisonment that a sheriff may impose after conviction on indictment is, for most practical purposes, three years: s.3(3). However, that power must be read with the terms of s.219(8) in mind for that requires a sheriff to remit a case to the High Court of Justiciary for sentence where a period of imprisonment in default of payment is in contemplation and that period exceeds three years. In *Torres v. H.M. Advocate*, 1997 S.C.C.R. 491, the Appeal Court declined to review the competence of a search warrant granted by the Canadian authorities to search a vessel commanded by the appellant noting that, in any event, there had been nothing to suggest that Canadian officials had not acted in good faith.

The sheriff

Territorial jurisdiction of sheriff

4.—(1) Subject to the provisions of this section, the jurisdiction of the sheriffs, within their respective sheriffdoms shall extend to and include all navigable rivers, ports, harbours, creeks, shores and anchoring grounds in or adjoining such sheriffdoms and includes all criminal maritime causes and proceedings (including those applying to persons furth of Scotland) provided that the accused is, by virtue of any enactment or rule of law, subject to the jurisdiction of the sheriff before whom the case or proceeding is raised.

(2) Where an offence is alleged to have been committed in one district in a sheriffdom, it shall be competent to try that offence in a sheriff court in any other district in that sheriffdom.

(3) It shall not be competent for the sheriff to try any crime committed on the seas which it would not be competent for him to try if the crime had been committed on land.

(4) The sheriff shall have a concurrent jurisdiction with every other court of summary jurisdiction in relation to all offences competent for trial in such courts.

DEFINITIONS
"court of summary jurisdiction": s.307(1).
"crime": s.307(1).
"offence": s.307(1).

GENERAL NOTE
The ancient lineage of this provision has not been tested much in court: however, in *Lewis v. Blair* (1858) 3 Irv. 16 the sheriff had jurisdiction to try a foreign sailor for an offence committed by him aboard a foreign vessel lying within the sheriff's territory, upon a seaman engaged on that vessel. *Shields v. Donnelly*, 2000 S.L.T. 147; 1999 S.C.C.R. 890 indicates that while papers may be signed outwith his jurisdiction, a sheriff can only deal with any procedural aspects while within the jurisdiction, and not elsewhere.

A more contemporary example is to be found in *Friel v. McKendrick*, 1996 G.W.D. 1–8 in which a passenger appeared at Paisley Sheriff Court on a complaint charged with breach of the peace following his misconduct on an aircraft flying between New York and Glasgow. No objection was taken to the competency of the charge.

The Sexual Offences (Conspiracy and Incitement) Act 1996, s.6 which brings criminal liability to persons within Scotland who assist in procuring sexual acts abroad involving children raises wide jurisdictional issues.

The sheriff: summary jurisdiction and powers

5.—(1) The sheriff, sitting as a court of summary jurisdiction, shall continue to have all the jurisdiction and powers exercisable by him at the commencement of this Act.

(2) The sheriff shall, without prejudice to any other or wider powers conferred by statute, have power on convicting any person of a common law offence—

(a) to impose a fine not exceeding the prescribed sum;
(b) to ordain the accused to find caution for good behaviour for any period not exceeding 12 months to an amount not exceeding the prescribed sum either in lieu of or in addition to a fine or in addition to imprisonment;
(c) failing payment of such fine, or on failure to find such caution, to award imprisonment in accordance with section 219 of this Act;
(d) to impose imprisonment, for any period not exceeding three months.

(3) Where a person is convicted by the sheriff of—
(a) a second or subsequent offence inferring dishonest appropriation of property, or attempt threat; or
(b) a second or subsequent offence inferring personal violence,
he may, without prejudice to any wider powers conferred by statute, be sentenced to imprisonment for any period not exceeding six months.

(4) It shall be competent to prosecute summarily in the sheriff court the following offences—

(a) uttering a forged document;
(b) wilful fire-raising;
(c) robbery; and
(d) assault with intent to rob.

DEFINITIONS
"caution": s.307(1).
"court of summary jurisdiction": s.307(1).
"fine": s.307(1).
"offence": s.307(1).
"prescribed sum, the": s.225(8) [*i.e.* £5,000].

GENERAL NOTE
The enhanced penalty competent on conviction by a sheriff of a second or subsequent offence inferring personal violence has led to challenges as to what is meant by "inferring personal violence". Section 5(3) repeats the terms of s.290 of the 1975 Act against which several appeals were taken.

The appellate judges have construed the term strictly and in favour of appellants so that threats or hints of violence are insufficient: see *Adair v. Morton*, 1972 S.L.T. (Notes) 70; *Sharp v. Tudhope*, 1986 S.C.C.R. 64; *Hemphill v. Donnelly*, 1992 S.C.C.R. 770; and *McMahon v. Lees*, 1993 S.L.T. 593 and *Youngson v. Higson*, 2000 S.L.T. 1441, a libel of breach of the peace which had contained no suggestion of violence. In addition to the maximum sentences for common law offences set out in subs. (2) for a first, or subsequent offence inferring personal violence or dishonesty, it will be noted that subs. (2) operates without prejudice to the maximum sentences imposed by other statutes. The most common examples of the operation of subs. (1) are to be found in the Police (Scotland) Act 1967, s.41, and the Misuse of Drugs Act 1971, s.5 which, summarily, permit sentences of up to 9 months' and one year's imprisonment respectively. However the summary tariff for a statutory contravention ordinarily has no bearing upon the sentencing powers available to a sheriff sitting in solemn proceedings; in that situation s.3(3) of the 1995 Act provides that a sheriff can impose a sentence of up to 3 years' imprisonment, unless the statute enacts a different tariff specifically in relation to solemn proceedings (see generally *Howard v. H.M. Advocate*, 1997 S.L.T. 575).

The previous convictions which in effect authorise the enhanced penalty set out in subs. (3), must be libelled by the Crown in the Notice of Previous Convictions and laid before the court: *Sim v. Lockhart*, 1994 S.L.T. 1063. *McPhail v. Crowe*, 1997 G.W.D. 17–779 is a rare instance of an incompetent sentence, in breach of subs. (2)(d), being imposed on conviction of a first offence of dishonesty. Provided that the statutory maximum period of imprisonment is not exceeded when subs. (3)(a) is invoked, any combination of concurrent or consecutive sentences can be imposed (*Hepburn v. Howdle*, 1998 G.W.D. 18–910).

Since Scots law does not require a *nomen juris* to constitute a competent criminal libel, the court has to have regard to the facts proved or admitted, not simply the terms of the libel, to ascertain whether or not it is dealing with an offence inferring personal violence; *Sproull v. McGlennan*, 1999 S.L.T. 402; 1999 S.C.C.R. 63. See the discussion at A4.348.

Starrs and Chalmers v. Ruxton, 1999 S.C.C.R. 1052 settles that a temporary sheriff cannot, in terms of Art. 6 of the European Convention of Human Rights, be regarded as an independent and impartial tribunal for the purpose of determining a trial notwithstanding appointment in accordance with the Sheriff Courts (Scotland) Act 1971 (c. 58). Note that in *Starrs and Chalmers* the Appeal Court remitted the case back to the presiding temporary sheriff and directed that he discharge the trial and fix a new trial diet to be heard before a permanent sheriff. This judgment serves to confirm first, that it is entirely compatible with Convention rights for temporary judges to deal with procedural matters and preliminary matters, but not with the determination of a trial itself (see also *Gibbs v. Ruxton*, 2000 S.L.T. 310); and secondly, that devolution issues should be adjudicated upon within the existing framework of first and preliminary diets in solemn proceedings, or by debate in summary cases.

District courts

District courts: area, constitution and prosecutor

6.—(1) Each commission area shall be the district of a district court, and the places at which a district court sits and, subject to section 8 of this Act, the days and times when it sits at any given place, shall be determined by the local authority; and in determining where and when a district court should sit, the local authority shall have regard to the desirability of minimising the expense and inconvenience occasioned to those directly involved, whether as parties or witnesses, in the proceedings before the court.

(2) The jurisdiction and powers of the district court shall be exercisable by a stipendiary magistrate or by one or more justices, and no decision of the court shall be questioned on the ground that it was not constituted as required by this subsection unless objection was taken on that ground by or on behalf of a party to the proceedings not later than the time when the proceedings or the alleged irregularity began.

(3) All prosecutions in a commission area shall proceed at the instance of the procurator fiscal.

(4) The procurator fiscal for an area which includes a commission area shall have all the powers and privileges conferred on a district prosecutor by section 6 of the District Courts (Scotland) Act 1975.

(5) The prosecutions authorised by the said Act of 1975 under complaint by the procurator fiscal shall be without prejudice to complaints at the instance of any other person entitled to make the same.

(6) In this section—

"commission area" means the area of a local authority;

"justice" means a justice of the peace appointed or deemed to have been appointed under section 9 of the said Act of 1975; and

"local authority" means a council constituted under section 2 of the Local Government (Scotland) Act 1994.

DEFINITIONS

"commission area": s.6(6).
"complaint": s.307(1).
"district prosecutor": s.26(1) of the District Courts (Scotland) Act 1975.
"justice": s.6(6).
"local authority": s.6(6).
"procurator fiscal": s.307(1).

GENERAL NOTE

This section is derived from several parts of the District Courts (Scotland) Act 1975 which brought about very substantial change to the existing system of lay courts of summary criminal jurisdiction. The extensive commentary on the District Courts (Scotland) Act 1975 by Dr Enid A. Marshall in Current Law Statutes Annotated, encapsulated the details of the then old system which was to replace it. This section consolidates these matters.

In *Shields v. Donnelly*, 2000 S.L.T. 147 a conviction was quashed where the District Court had temporarily moved to an adjacent local authority district while the court building was being refurbished. The Appeal Court emphasised that the powers of District Court judges were restricted to the territorial area over which they had jurisdiction and could not be exercised elsewhere unless statute created a specific exception.

Parliament could modify that rule, but had not modified that general rule when it enacted s.6(1) which simply gave the local authority the power to determine where and when the district was to sit within its jurisdiction; that since there was no other statutory provision to support the competency of the justice sitting outwith her district the subsequent proceedings were tainted by a fundamental nullity; and the appeal was allowed.

In *Clark v. Kelly*, 2000 S.L.T. 1038; 2000 S.C.C.R. 821, where the role of the assessor was challenged (following *Starrs v. Ruxton*, 2000 S.L.T. 42; 1999 S.C.C.R 1052), it was held that the assessor was not a member of the court; his function was confined to advising the court on applicable law. The Appeal Court found nothing incompatible with the terms of Art.6(1) of the European Convention on Human Rights in the common practice of justices and assessors retiring from the court—and being outwith the presence of the accused—during deliberations. The court recognised that issues which arose during those deliberations which might merit further submissions by parties should be made known to the parties for any additional submissions they might then have.

District court: jurisdiction and powers

7.—(1) A district court shall continue to have all the jurisdiction and powers exercisable by it at the commencement of this Act.

(2) Where several offences, which if committed in one commission area could be tried under one complaint, are alleged to have been committed in different commission areas, proceedings may be taken for all or any of those offences under one complaint before the district court of any one of such commission areas, and any such offence may be dealt with, heard, tried, determined, adjudged and punished as if the offence had been wholly committed within the jurisdiction of that court.

(3) Except in so far as any enactment (including this Act or an enactment passed after this Act) otherwise provides, it shall be competent for a district court to try any statutory offence which is triable summarily.

(4) It shall be competent, whether or not the accused has been previously convicted of an offence inferring dishonest appropriation of property, for any of the following offences to be tried in the district court—

(a) theft or reset of theft;

(b) falsehood, fraud or wilful imposition;

(c) breach of trust or embezzlement,

where (in any such case) the amount concerned does not exceed level 4 on the standard scale.

(5) A district court when constituted by a stipendiary magistrate shall, in addition to the jurisdiction and powers mentioned in subsection (1) above, have the summary criminal jurisdiction and powers of a sheriff.

(6) The district court shall, without prejudice to any other or wider powers conferred by statute, be entitled on convicting of a common law offence—

(a) to impose imprisonment for any period not exceeding 60 days;

(b) to impose a fine not exceeding level 4 on the standard scale;

(c) to ordain the accused (in lieu of or in addition to such imprisonment or fine) to find caution for good behaviour for any period not exceeding six months and to an amount not exceeding level 4 on the standard scale;

(d) failing payment of such fine or on failure to find such caution, to award imprisonment in accordance with section 219 of this Act,

but in no case shall the total period of imprisonment imposed in pursuance of this subsection exceed 60 days.

(7) Without prejudice to any other or wider power conferred by any enactment, it shall not be competent for a district court, as respects any statutory offence—

(a) to impose a sentence of imprisonment for a period exceeding 60 days;

(b) to impose a fine of an amount exceeding level 4 on the standard scale; or

(c) to ordain an accused person to find caution for any period exceeding six months or to an amount exceeding level 4 on the standard scale.

(8) The district court shall not have jurisdiction to try or to pronounce sentence in the case of any person—

(a) found within its jurisdiction, and brought before it accused or suspected of having committed any offence at any place beyond its jurisdiction; or

(b) brought before it accused or suspected of having committed within its jurisdiction any of the following offences—

(i) murder, culpable homicide, robbery, rape, wilful fire-raising, or attempted wilful fire-raising;

(ii) theft by housebreaking, or housebreaking with intent to steal;

(iii) theft or reset, falsehood fraud or wilful imposition, breach of trust or embezzlement, where the value of the property is an amount exceeding level 4 on the standard scale;

(iv) assault causing the fracture of a limb, assault with intent to ravish, assault to the danger of life, or assault by stabbing;

(v) uttering forged documents or uttering forged bank or banker's notes, or offences under the Acts relating to coinage.

(9) Without prejudice to subsection (8) above, where either in the preliminary investigation or in the course of the trial of any offence it appears that the offence is one which—

(a) cannot competently be tried in the court before which an accused is brought; or

(b) in the opinion of the court in view of the circumstances of the case, should be dealt with by a higher court,

the court may take cognizance of the offence and commit the accused to prison for examination for any period not exceeding four days.

(10) Where an accused is committed as mentioned in subsection (9) above, the prosecutor in the court which commits the accused shall forthwith give notice of the committal to the procurator fiscal of the district within which the offence was committed or to such other official as is entitled to take cognizance of the offence in order that the accused may be dealt with according to law.

DEFINITIONS

"fine": s.307(1).
"level 4": s.225(2) [*i.e.* £2,500].
"offence": s.307(1).
"procurator fiscal": s.307(1).
"prosecutor": s.307(1).
"sentence": s.307(1).
"standard scale": s.225(1).
"stipendiary magistrate": s.5 of the District Courts (Scotland) Act 1975.

GENERAL NOTE

This section provides for the jurisdictions and powers of the District Court. It is worth asserting that the additional jurisdiction conferred on a stipendiary magistrate by s.7(5) allows for the prosecution of more serious matters in the District Court.

The problems peculiar to Glasgow District Court, where both lay and stipendiary magistrates sit, are highlighted in *Graham v. Normand*, 1996 S.C.C.R. 371: an accused after being remanded in custody for trial pled guilty before a lay magistrate and had sentence deferred for reports. He next appeared before a stipendiary magistrate, who refused to continue the case further for sentence to be imposed by a lay magistrate, and imposed sentences exceeding those competent to a lay magistrate. On appeal the sentence was upheld as being neither incompetent nor oppressive. Compare the approach however in *Halleron v. Vannet*, 2000 S.C.C.R. 50 where the accused's failure to pay a fiscal fine led to a summary complaint being placed before a lay magistrate and, following a plea being tendered and the case continued for reports, three months imprisonment was imposed by a stipendiary magistrate; the Appeal Court regarded the original forum as being a highly relevant factor in the sentencing process and substituted a sentence of 60 days imprisonment. See also *Main v. Normand*, 1996 S.C.C.R. 256. *Maclean v. City of Glasgow Council*, 1997 G.W.D. 34–1737 resolved that stipendiary magistrates enjoy the same tenure of office as sheriffs, *ad vitam aut culpam*.

It has been held not to be oppressive for a District Court to hear proceedings initiated by the local education authority, a separate arm of the local authority (*Matts v. Cumming*, 2000 S.L.T. 220). It is doubted, in the light of the decision in *Starrs and Chalmers v. Ruxton* (1999 S.C.C.R. 1052), that *Matts* now would be upheld. In any event, see now s.11 of the Bail, Judicial Appointments etc. (Scotland) Act 2000 (asp 9).

The whole status of the legal assessor in the District Court was the subject of challenge in a devolution issue: see *Clark v. Kelly*, 2000 S.L.T. 1038. It was held that the clerk to the District Court was confined to acting as a legal adviser to the Justices of the Peace who acted as decision-maker and the clerk was therefore not a member of the court. Further, that there was nothing objectionable in the practice of private communications between clerks and Justices of the Peace provided that these were restricted to the provision of legal advice and that they recognised and raised in open court any matter on which the defence or prosecution might wish to make material comment.

Sittings of sheriff and district courts

8.—(1) Notwithstanding any enactment or rule of law, a sheriff court or a district court—

    (a) shall not be required to sit on any Saturday or Sunday or on a day which by virtue of subsection (2) or (3) below is a court holiday; but

    (b) may sit on any day for the disposal of criminal business.

(2) A sheriff principal may in an order made under section 17(1)(b) of the Sheriff Courts (Scotland) Act 1971 prescribe in respect of criminal business not more than 10 days, other than Saturdays and Sundays, in a calendar year as court holidays in the sheriff courts within his jurisdiction; and may in the like manner prescribe as an additional court holiday any day which has been proclaimed, under section 1(3) of the Banking and Financial Dealings Act 1971, to be a bank holiday either throughout the United Kingdom or in a place or locality in the United Kingdom within his jurisdiction.

(3) Notwithstanding section 6(1) of this Act, a sheriff principal may, after consultation with the appropriate local authority, prescribe not more than 10 days, other than Saturdays and Sundays, in a calendar year as court holidays in the district courts within his jurisdiction; and he may, after such consultation, prescribe as an additional holiday any day which has been proclaimed, under section 1(3) of the said Banking and Financial Dealings Act 1971, to be a bank holiday either throughout the United Kingdom or in a place or locality in the United Kingdom within his jurisdiction.

(4) A sheriff principal may in pursuance of subsection (2) or (3) above prescribe different days as court holidays in relation to different sheriff or district courts.

Territorial jurisdiction: general

Boundaries of jurisdiction

9.—(1) Where an offence is committed in any harbour, river, arm of the sea or other water (tidal or otherwise) which runs between or forms the boundary of the jurisdiction of two or more courts, the offence may be tried by any one of such courts.

(2) Where an offence is committed on the boundary of the jurisdiction of two or more courts, or within the distance of 500 metres of any such boundary, or partly within the jurisdiction of one court and partly within the jurisdiction of another court or courts, the offence may be tried by any one of such courts.

(3) Where an offence is committed against any person or in respect of any property in or on any carriage, cart or vehicle employed in a journey by road or railway, or on board any vessel employed in a river, loch, canal or inland navigation, the offence may be tried by any court through whose jurisdiction the carriage, cart, vehicle or vessel passed in the course of the journey or voyage during which the offence was committed.

(4) Where several offences, which if committed in one sheriff court district could be tried under one indictment or complaint, are alleged to have been committed by any person in different sheriff court districts, the accused may be tried for all or any of those offences under one indictment or complaint before the sheriff of any one of such sheriff court districts.

(5) Where an offence is authorised by this section to be tried by any court, it may be dealt with, heard, tried, determined, adjudged and punished as if the offence had been committed wholly within the jurisdiction of such court.

"complaints": s.307(1).
"indictment": s.307(1).
"offence": s.307(1).
"sheriff court districts": s.307(1).

GENERAL NOTE
There seem to have been few modern authorities on the issue of jurisdiction, although the older cases may still provide assistance should doubts arise: see *Lewis v. Blair*, (1858) 3 Irv. 16; *Witherington*, (1881) 4 Couper 475; *Mortensen v. Peters*, (1906) 5 Adam 121 and *Lipsey v. Mackintosh*, (1913) 7 Adam 182.

Crimes committed in different districts

10.—(1) Where a person is alleged to have committed in more than one sheriff court district a crime or crimes to which subsection (2) below applies, he may be indicted to the sheriff court of such one of those districts as the Lord Advocate determines.

(2) This subsection applies to—
   (a) a crime committed partly in one sheriff court district and partly in another;
   (b) crimes connected with each other but committed in different sheriff court districts;
   (c) crimes committed in different sheriff court districts in succession which, if they had been committed in one such district, could have been tried under one indictment.

(3) Where, in pursuance of subsection (1) above, a case is tried in the sheriff court of any sheriff court district, the procurator fiscal of that district shall have power to prosecute in that case even if the crime was in whole or in part committed in a different district, and the procurator fiscal shall have the like powers in relation to such case, whether before, during or after the trial, as he has in relation to a case arising out of a crime or crimes committed wholly within his own district.

DEFINITIONS
"crime": s.307(1).
"procurator fiscal": s.307(1).
"sheriff court district": s.307(1).

Certain offences committed outside Scotland

11.—(1) Any British citizen or British subject who in a country outside the United Kingdom does any act or makes any omission which if done or made in Scotland would constitute the crime of murder or of culpable homicide shall be guilty of the same crime and subject to the same punishment as if the act or omission had been done or made in Scotland.

(2) Any British citizen or British subject employed in the service of the Crown who, in a foreign country, when acting or purporting to act in the course of his employment, does any act or makes any omission which if done or made in Scotland would constitute an offence punishable on indictment shall be guilty of the same offence and subject to the same punishment, as if the act or omission had been done or made in Scotland.

(3) A person may be proceeded against, indicted, tried and punished for an offence to which this section applies—
   (a) in any sheriff court district in Scotland in which he is apprehended or is in custody; or
   (b) in such sheriff court district as the Lord Advocate may determine, as if the offence had been committed in that district, and the offence shall, for all purposes incidental to or consequential on the trial or punishment thereof, be deemed to have been committed in that district.

(4) Any person who—

(a) has in his possession in Scotland property which he has stolen in any other part of the United Kingdom; or

(b) in Scotland receives property stolen in any other part of the United Kingdom,

may be dealt with, indicted, tried and punished in Scotland in like manner as if he had stolen it in Scotland.

[[1](5) Where a person in any part of the United Kingdom outside Scotland—

(a) steals or attempts to steal any mail-bag or postal packet in the course of its transmission by post, or any of the contents of such a mail-bag or postal packet; or

(b) in stealing or with intent to steal any such mail-bag or postal packet or any of its contents commits any robbery, attempted robbery or assault with intent to rob,

he is guilty of the offence mentioned in paragraph (a) or (b) as if he had committed it in Scotland and shall be liable to be prosecuted, tried and punished there without proof that the offence was committed there.

(6) Any expression used in subsection (5) and in the Postal Services Act 2000 has the same meaning in that subsection as it has in that Act.]

DEFINITIONS
   "crime": s.307(1).
   "offence": s.307(1).
   "sheriff court district": s.307(1).

NOTE
   [1]Prospectively inserted by the Postal Services Act 2000 (c.26), s.127(4) and Sched. 8, para. 24.

Conspiracy to commit offences outside the United Kingdom

11A.—(1) This section applies to any act done by a person in Scotland which would amount to conspiracy to commit an offence but for the fact that the criminal purpose is intended to occur in a country or territory outside the United Kingdom.

(2) Where a person does an act to which this section applies, the criminal purpose shall be treated as the offence mentioned in subsection (1) above and he shall, accordingly, be guilty of conspiracy to commit the offence.

(3) A person is guilty of an offence by virtue of this section only if the criminal purpose would involve at some stage—

(a) an act by him or another party to the conspiracy; or

(b) the happening of some other event,

constituting an offence under the law in force in the country or territory where the act or other event was intended to take place; and conduct punishable under the law in force in the country or territory is an offence under that law for the purposes of this section however it is described in that law.

(4) Subject to subsection (6) below, a condition specified in subsection (3) above shall be taken to be satisfied unless, not later than such time as the High Court may, by Act of Adjournal, prescribe, the accused serves on the prosecutor a notice—

(a) stating that, on the facts as alleged with respect to the relevant conduct, the condition is not in his opinion satisfied;

(b) setting out the grounds for his opinion; and

(c) requiring the prosecutor to prove that the condition is satisfied.

(5) In subsection (4) above "the relevant conduct" means the agreement to effect the criminal purpose.

(6) The court may permit the accused to require the prosecutor to prove that the condition mentioned in subsection (4) above is satisfied without the prior service of a notice under that subsection.

(7) In proceedings on indictment, the question whether a condition is satisfied shall be determined by the judge alone.

(8) Nothing in this section—

(a) applies to an act done before the day on which the Criminal Justice (Terrorism and Conspiracy) Act 1998 was passed, or

(b) imposes criminal liability on any person acting on behalf of, or holding office under, the Crown.

GENERAL NOTE

This section was inserted by section 7 of the Criminal Justice (Terrorism and Conspiracy) Act 1998 (c. 40). Although it was explained under reference to terrorism during the parliamentary debates, it in fact applies to all offences and all countries the approach originally taken to "sex tourism" cases in s.16A of the Criminal Law (Consolidation) (Scotland) Act 1995 (c. 39), which section is now amended so as to restrict its ambit to incitement. Conspiracy in Scotland to commit an offence in a country or territory outside the U.K. is now dealt with under the present section.

Subs. (1)

Any act. Subsection (8) excludes any act done before the Criminal Justice (Terrorism and Conspiracy) Act 1998 (c. 40) was passed.

Which would amount to conspiracy to commit an offence but for the fact that the criminal purpose is intended to occur ... outside the United Kingdom. This subsection states the preconditions for the section as a whole to have effect. The case must be one in which there is conduct which, in Scots law would amount to a conspiracy except for the fact that the agreement is to do or achieve something outside the U.K.

The section was not discussed in Parliament in its own right. Rather, it was taken along with ss.5 and 6, which make equivalent provision for England and Wales and Northern Ireland. Lord Williams of Mostyn, speaking for the Government, explained the policy intention as follows: "Conspiracy is dealt with in Clause 5 and subsequent clauses. These provisions are designed to close off a gap which has been recognised for some time in our response to international terrorism and other international crime. In our country it is not always an offence to conspire to commit criminal acts outside this country. This section of the Bill deals with those people who try to use our country as a safe place to plot the commission of terrorist offences or other crimes abroad. Terrorism and other forms of organised crime cannot be contained by a line on a map. Crime in one country is often instigated and planned in another. We think that there should not be a hiding place in our jurisdiction for terrorists, those who traffic in arms, drug smugglers, money launderers or counterfeiters ... Some powers already exist in this field. Extra-territorial jurisdiction is available for some offences such as computer misuse and sexual offences against children. Other offences are covered, but only in relation to certain countries, under the Suppression of Terrorism Act ... Your Lordships will find no prohibition of incitement in this Bill. That is deliberate as we did not wish to interfere with a tradition which remains valid, noble and distinctive to our country; that is, that political dissent is important and should be allowed, even when it is disagreeable; in fact, particularly when it is disagreeable ... We have included safeguards in Clause 5 and subsequent clauses. The principle of dual criminality—in other words, the conspiracy to commit the unlawful act—depends on the act being unlawful in the foreign country and also in our own domestic jurisdiction" (*Hansard*, H.L. Debs, September 3, 1998, Col. 14).

Lord Williams' remark that "In our country it is not always an offence to conspire to commit criminal acts outside this country" was made against the background of the English case of *Board of Trade v. Owen* [1957] A.C. 602, in which Lord Tucker held that, since the purpose of the criminal law is to protect the Queen's peace and maintain order within the realm, conspiracy to do something in another country is not criminal in English law. This was an essentially nineteenth-century view, reflecting the isolationist approach taken by English courts to jurisdiction over crimes with cross-frontier aspects. That approach has been much criticised in the literature (see, for example, Geoff Gilbert, "Crimes Sans Frontiers: Jurisdictional Problems in English Law" (1992) 63 *British Yearbook of International Law* 415 and Matthew Goode, "Two New Decisions on Criminal 'Jurisdiction': The Appalling Durability of Common Law", 20 *Criminal Law Journal* 267 (1996) (Australia); but for a contrary view, see Peter Alldridge, "Sex Offenders Act 1997—Territoriality Provisions" [1997] Crim.L.R. 655).

The question whether conspiracy in Scotland to commit crime in a foreign jurisdiction is criminal at common law in Scotland seems never to have been judicially considered. The legislation seems simply to assume that the law of Scotland was as isolationist as that of England and Wales. Since the legislation has now been enacted, the accuracy of that assumption is unlikely ever to be determined. It may, however, be commented that there is no particular reason to suppose that the High Court of Justiciary would have been quite so parochial as its counterparts south of the border, especially since there are in any event material differences between the approaches which the two systems take to jurisdiction in general (see P. W. Ferguson, "Jurisdiction and Criminal Law in Scotland and England", in Robert F. Hunter (ed.), *Justice and Crime*, 1993, 96).

Under the Suppression of Terrorism Act 1978 (c. 26), jurisdiction already exists in relation to conspiring within the U.K. to commit crimes in other Council of Europe countries, India and the United States. This reflects the U.K.'s particular treaty relationships.

Subs. (2)
 An act to which this section applies. See subs. (1).

Subs. (3)
 This subsection applies a "double" or "dual" criminality test. The acts or events to be carried out in the foreign jurisdiction in pursuance of the criminal purpose which, by subs. (1) must be of a sort which would be criminal in Scotland if carried out here, must also be such as to be criminal by the law of the place where they are intended to take place. There would, for obvious reasons, be difficulties about criminalising in the U.K. an agreement to do something in a foreign country if that act would be perfectly lawful in the country where it was to be carried out.

 The concept of the double criminality test has been developed most fully in relation to extradition law, where in general the conduct for which it is intended to prosecute the fugitive must be criminal in both the state in which he is to be prosecuted and that in which he is found before extradition can take place. The emphasis is always placed on the acts complained of and precise equivalence in the offence creating provisions is not necessary. Nothing in this subsection suggests that a different approach is intended here.

Subs. (4)
 A condition specified in subs. (3) above. That is, the double criminality requirement.
 Shall be taken to be satisfied. There is a rebuttable presumption that the double criminality requirement is satisfied.
 Unless, not later than such time as the High Court of Justiciary may … prescribe. Notwithstanding this, subs. (6) gives the court a discretion to permit the accused to require the prosecutor to prove that the double criminality requirement is satisfied without service of a notice.
 A notice. By contrast with notices under, for example, s.280(6)(b) of the present Act, the notice contemplated here cannot simply put the Crown to the proof. The notice must not only state that in the opinion of the accused the double criminality requirement is not satisfied and require the prosecutor to prove it; to be effective it must also state the *grounds* for the accused's opinion. This is likely to involve investigation of foreign law.

Subs. (6)
 Since the exercise of the discretion given to the court by this subsection will almost certainly involve the leading of evidence as to the content of foreign law, it seems likely that an adjournment will be required. It might therefore be that the court, in deciding whether to exercise that discretion, will have in mind the three interests which, in terms of *Skene v. McLaren*, 1976 S.L.T. (Notes) 14, it should consider in relation to motions to adjourn (namely that of the accused, that of the prosecutor and the possibility of prejudice to the public interest).

Subs. (8)
 Speaking for the Government, Lord Dubs explained that the purpose of this subsection is "not to give minor civil servants carte blanche to pursue criminal careers. It applies to actions which might have to be taken in the course of official duty where there is no exemption. There is a range of circumstances in which technical breaches of the new provisions might otherwise arise. For example, if the police or Customs were planning an undercover operation involving infiltration of an organised crime group, a consignment of drugs or weapons might be tracked to a number of different transit countries, each with a different legal system. There would obviously be no question of prosecution here in those circumstances" (*Hansard*, H.L. Debs, September 3, 1998, Col. 91).

Part II

Police Functions

Lord Advocate's instructions

Instructions by Lord Advocate as to reporting of offences

12. The Lord Advocate may, from time to time, issue instructions to a chief constable with regard to the reporting, for consideration of the question of prosecution, of offences alleged to have been committed within the area of such chief constable, and it shall be the duty of a chief constable to whom any such instruction is issued to secure compliance therewith.

Definition
"offence": s.307(1).

General Note
This section repeats the terms of s.9 of the 1975 Act which, in turn, derived from the Criminal Justice (Scotland) Act 1949 (c. 94), s.33. The Lord Advocate's authority to appoint or remove procurators fiscal and delineate their territorial jurisdictions, is found in the Sheriff Courts and Legal Officers (Scotland) Act 1927 (c. 35), s.1(2). By s.12 of that Act the Lord Advocate may also after consultation with the Treasury, by Order direct, notwithstanding the terms of any Act of Parliament, that any sheriff court proceedings for contraventions thereof shall proceed at the instance of the procurator fiscal. The Sheriff Courts (Prosecutions for Poaching) Order 1938 is the only instance in which this power has been exercised.

The Lord Advocate's power to amend or rescind policy, or change the instructions or guidance issued by his predecessors in that office is unfettered; see *MacDonald v. H.M. Advocate*, 1997 S.C.C.R. 408 for its discussion of the constitutional standing of that office.

Detention and questioning

Powers relating to suspects and potential witnesses

13.—(1) Where a constable has reasonable grounds for suspecting that a person has committed or is committing an offence at any place, he may require—
  (a) that person, if the constable finds him at that place or at any place where the constable is entitled to be, to give his name and address and may ask him for an explanation of the circumstances which have given rise to the constable's suspicion;
  (b) any other person whom the constable finds at that place or at any place where the constable is entitled to be and who the constable believes has information relating to the offence, to give his name and address.

(2) The constable may require the person mentioned in paragraph (a) of subsection (1) above to remain with him while he (either or both)—
  (a) subject to subsection (3) below, verifies any name and address given by the person;
  (b) notes any explanation proffered by the person.

(3) The constable shall exercise his power under paragraph (a) of subsection (2) above only where it appears to him that such verification can be obtained quickly.

(4) A constable may use reasonable force to ensure that the person mentioned in paragraph (a) of subsection (1) above remains with him.

(5) A constable shall inform a person, when making a requirement of that person under—

(a) paragraph (a) of subsection (1) above, of his suspicion and of the general nature of the offence which he suspects that the person has committed or is committing;

(b) paragraph (b) of subsection (1) above, of his suspicion, of the general nature of the offence which he suspects has been or is being committed and that the reason for the requirement is that he believes the person has information relating to the offence;

(c) subsection (2) above, why the person is being required to remain with him;

(d) either of the said subsections, that failure to comply with the requirement may constitute an offence.

(6) A person mentioned in—

(a) paragraph (a) of subsection (1) above who having been required—

    (i) under that subsection to give his name and address; or

    (ii) under subsection (2) above to remain with a constable,

fails, without reasonable excuse, to do so, shall be guilty of an offence and liable on summary conviction to a fine not exceeding level 3 on the standard scale;

(b) paragraph (b) of the said subsection (1) who having been required under that subsection to give his name and address fails, without reasonable excuse, to do so shall be guilty of an offence and liable on summary conviction to a fine not exceeding level 2 on the standard scale.

(7) A constable may arrest without warrant any person who he has reasonable grounds for suspecting has committed an offence under subsection (6) above.

DEFINITIONS

"constable": s.307(1) and s.51(1) of the Police (Scotland) Act 1967 (c. 77).
"offence": s.307(1).

GENERAL NOTE

The provisions of s.1 of the 1980 Act, after minor re-numbering of subsections, are re-enacted to form s.13. This section deals with the preliminary stages of police enquiries many of which will never develop into criminal proceedings. It gives a general power to police officers, when they have reasonable cause to suspect that an offence either has occurred or is in the course of commission, to demand information from certain members of the public. Two distinct categories of person are affected by these provisions, those who may have committed an offence, and those who are potential witnesses to an offence.

Powers In Relation To Suspects

Subsection (1)(a) relates to any person whom the officer suspects is guilty of such an offence (whether it is an arrestable offence or not), and empowers the constable to demand that person's particulars and an explanation for the conduct which has given rise to suspicion. Note that at this early stage no caution of any sort need be administered and it seems likely that any reply would be admissible subject to the ordinary rules of evidence.

The criteria governing a citizen's right to arrest and search a suspect were discussed by the Appeal Court in *Wightman v. McFadyen*, 1999 S.C.C.R. 664.

If however, suspicions were sufficiently tangible for the constable to feel a caution to be appropriate, then the s.13 procedure would not be appropriate; the proper approach would be to caution with a view to charging (in the case of non-arrestable offences) or, where the offence could attract a sentence of imprisonment, to consider whether the circumstances would justify the use of the power of detention now specified in s.14 of the Act (the statutory successor to s.2 of the 1980 Act), or arrest.

In the exercise of his power under subs. (1)(a) an officer must first explain the nature of his suspicion and may then require the potential suspect to remain while the veracity of his particulars is established (provided this can be done quickly) and any explanation given may be noted. It will be observed that in terms of subs. (6) failure to provide particulars or to remain while the explanation given is noted by the officer constitutes an offence which attracts arrest without warrant; nonetheless a suspect is under no more of an obligation to give an explanation than an officer is to note it.

Doubtless a suspect's failure to offer an account may well serve to heighten the constable's existing suspicions. On an equally pragmatic level an officer's failure to note an explanation given in response to a s.13 requirement would no doubt attract adverse comment in any subsequent proceedings.

Unlike s.14 below (which has re-enacted the provisions of s.2 of the 1980 Act), where strict adherence to the six hour detention period is demanded, no time limit is stipulated in s.13 for the completion of these initial enquiries, except that the procedure for verifying personal particulars must be capable of being completed quickly (see subs. (3)). While a suspect can be caused to remain for that verification to be made rapidly, it must be emphasised that he cannot be restrained under s.13 while his explanation is examined—that is the role of statutory detention.

What then is the status of the suspect who is required to remain in terms of s.13(2) or, worse, restrained at the scene by a constable using his powers under s.13(4)? It might reasonably be felt, not least by the hapless suspect, that he is not at liberty to go and is in the officer's custody. However, reference to s.295 of the Act suggests that legal custody or detention only occurs when a person is required to be taken, or is held for the purpose of being taken, to a place for the purposes of the Act. It is notable that s.13(2) studiously avoids use of the word "detain" and the meaning of being required "to remain" for the limited purposes of the section must surely be something more dilute than detention. It is submitted that the precise status of the suspect is by no means clearly established.

Powers In Relation To Potential Witnesses

Subsection (1)(b) applies to persons whom the officer has reason to believe may, wittingly or unwittingly, have information to offer about the offence. It seems that this could extend to the circumstances in which the officer exercised his powers in relation to the suspect under subs. (1)(a): for example, the witness could be a bystander at the time when the suspect gave an explanation to the constable, given if he had not witnessed the offence giving rise to the enquiry.

First however, a general explanation of the nature of the alleged offence being investigated must be given by the officer to the potential witness. The officer is also obliged to inform the other party of the belief that he or she possesses information relevant to that investigation and that failure to provide personal particulars in those circumstances is an offence.

Police powers in pursuit of requirements under subs. (1)(b) are more limited than those applicable to suspects, for subs. (4) allows the use of reasonable force to ensure that a suspect remains until the enquiries specified in subs. (2) are quickly completed or noted as the case may be. No force may be employed to cause a witness to remain at the scene. All that can lawfully be demanded of a witness is that he provides his name and address, albeit failure to give these particulars will render him liable to immediate arrest (subs. (7)).

Restrictions On Use Of Section 13 Powers

Most obviously an officer can only resort to using his powers under s.13 when he has reasonable cause to suspect that an offence has been committed or is ongoing.

The Act does not attempt to define what would constitute "reasonable cause" and nor need it do so. The phrase has been minutely examined by the courts, albeit usually in the context of the Road Traffic Acts. Suffice to say that the suspicions formed by the officer need not rest upon personal ocular observation; they can stem from the observations of other persons, from "information received" or from prior knowledge of the suspect's habits and background, as well as general knowledge of the area being policed.

It will be appreciated that some of the factors giving rise to cause to suspect, may well be inadmissible as evidence, but that would not disentitle the officer from forming his suspicion. The general considerations are discussed in *McNicol v. Peters*, 1969 S.L.T. (J.) 261, notably in Lord Wheatley's judgment at pp.265 and 266, from which it can also be seen that even an ill-founded suspicion can still constitute reasonable cause to suspect. Lord Wheatley returned to this topic in *Dryburgh v. Galt*, 1981 S.C.C.R. 27 at p.29 noting:

" ... the fact that the information on which the police officer formed his suspicion turns out to be ill-founded does not in itself necessarily establish that the police officer's suspicion was unfounded. The circumstances known to the police officer at the time he formed his suspicion constitute the criterion, not the facts as subsequently ascertained."

Nonetheless the Crown will have to establish objectively that the factors which exercised the constable's suspicions would reasonably create a cause to suspect an offence without, at that stage, amounting to sufficient grounds for detention or arrest or charge.

The section is equally silent on the question of defining "any place" or "a place where the constable is entitled to be". The phrases serve to differentiate between the locus of the offence (where the officer can proceed on his enquiries armed with his suspicions) at the time of the offence or later, and elsewhere, in which latter case a right to information may depend upon the legitimacy of the officer's presence there. For example, the constable may be in a public place, or in a private place where access has been gained by warrant, by invitation or for an unrelated legitimate purpose: each of these different situations may subtly impinge upon the ability of the constable to exercise his powers under s.13. It will also be borne in mind that the degree of restraint used to ensure that the suspect remains, must be reasonable.

If it is established that the force employed was unreasonable, *i.e.* excessive or inappropriate, or both, then that might well nullify any subsequent evidence and constitute a criminal assault upon the suspect.

There is a dearth of case authorities dealing with this section, a fact which serves to underline its preliminary nature in the scale of proceedings.

Detention and questioning at police station

14.—(1) Where a constable has reasonable grounds for suspecting that a person has committed or is committing an offence punishable by imprisonment, the constable may, for the purpose of facilitating the carrying out of investigations—

(a) into the offence; and

(b) as to whether criminal proceedings should be instigated against the person,

detain that person and take him as quickly as is reasonably practicable to a police station or other premises and may thereafter for that purpose take him to any other place and, subject to the following provisions of this section, the detention may continue at the police station or, as the case may be, the other premises or place.

(2) Detention under subsection (1) above shall be terminated not more than six hours after it begins or (if earlier)—

(a) when the person is arrested;

(b) when he is detained in pursuance of any other enactment; or

(c) where there are no longer such grounds as are mentioned in the said subsection (1),

and when a person has been detained under subsection (1) above, he shall be informed immediately upon the termination of his detention in accordance with this subsection that his detention has been terminated.

(3) Where a person has been released at the termination of a period of detention under subsection (1) above he shall not thereafter be detained, under that subsection, on the same grounds or on any grounds arising out of the same circumstances.

(4) Subject to subsection (5) below, where a person has previously been detained in pursuance of any other enactment, and is detained under subsection (1) above on the same grounds or on grounds arising from the same circumstances as those which led to his earlier detention, the period of six hours mentioned in subsection (2) above shall be reduced by the length of that earlier detention.

(5) Subsection (4) above shall not apply in relation to detention under section 41(3) of the Prisons (Scotland) Act 1989 (detention in relation to introduction etc. into prison of prohibited article), but where a person was detained under section 41(3) immediately prior to his detention under subsection (1) above the period of six hours mentioned in subsection (2) above shall be reduced by the length of that earlier detention.

(6) At the time when a constable detains a person under subsection (1) above, he shall inform the person of his suspicion, of the general nature of the offence which he suspects has been or is being committed and of the reason for the detention; and there shall be recorded—

(a) the place where detention begins and the police station or other premises to which the person is taken;

(b) any other place to which the person is, during the detention, thereafter taken;

(c) the general nature of the suspected offence;
(d) the time when detention under subsection (1) above begins and the time of the person's arrival at the police station or other premises;
(e) the time when the person is informed of his rights in terms of subsection (9) below and of subsection (1)(b) of section 15 of this Act and the identity of the constable so informing him;
(f) where the person requests such intimation to be sent as is specified in section 15(1)(b) of this Act, the time when such request is—
  (i) made;
  (ii) complied with; and
(g) the time of the person's release from detention or, where instead of being released he is arrested in respect of the alleged offence, the time of such arrest.

(7) Where a person is detained under subsection (1) above, a constable may—
(a) without prejudice to any relevant rule of law as regards the admissibility in evidence of any answer given, put questions to him in relation to the suspected offence;
(b) exercise the same powers of search as are available following an arrest.

(8) A constable may use reasonable force in exercising any power conferred by subsection (1), or by paragraph (b) of subsection (7), above.

(9) A person detained under subsection (1) above shall be under no obligation to answer any question other than to give his name and address, and a constable shall so inform him both on so detaining him and on arrival at the police station or other premises.

DEFINITIONS
"constable": s.307 and s.51(1) of the Police (Scotland) Act 1967.
"offence": s.307(1).
"offence punishable by imprisonment": s.307(6).
"prison": s.307(1).

GENERAL NOTE
This section regulates the practice of removing persons to, and detaining persons at police stations, for the purposes of questioning in relation to specified allegations of criminal conduct prior to charge.

The provisions were originally contained in s.2 of the Criminal Justice (Scotland) Act 1980 (c.62) and followed upon the recommendations of the Thomson Committee (II Chap. 3, recs. 3 to 13). A fixed six hour period of detention was then introduced along with a statutory form of caution distinct from the familiar common law caution. The intention was to allow time for further enquiry by the police where there was reasonable cause to suspect the commission of a crime but insufficient evidence immediately available to press charges. Detention was not, and should not be, regarded as a means of delaying arrest and charge; as soon as it is clear that sufficient evidence exists to arrest a suspect, detention has to be terminated. Note that while detention must be terminated at the point when a sufficiency of evidence is obtained, or within six hours (whichever is earlier), neither the 1980 Act nor this Act require that arrest must follow. However as a safeguard against oppressive use of detention powers it remains the case that only one period of detention will be permitted on the same or related grounds (see subs. (3)).

One of the benefits of s.2 detention was that it introduced both clarity and flexibility to the previously grey area between voluntary attendance, when (in theory at least) a person being interviewed was free to leave the police station at any time, and arrest. Deprivation of liberty is unlikely to be an individual's preferred option; nonetheless it should be appreciated that statutory detention in the form provided by s.14 has the merit of establishing a suspect's legal status beyond doubt both in his mind and in the minds of those responsible for his detention.

Lawful Detention
The elements needed to constitute a lawful detention are not presented chronologically in s.14 but for convenience this course has been followed in the discussion below.

Grounds for Detention

Subsection (1) requires that the constable detaining a suspect must have reasonable grounds for suspecting that he has committed, or is in the course of committing, an imprisonable offence (for discussion of the factors underpinning "reasonable cause to suspect" see note to s.13 above), see *Wilson and Nolan v. Robertson*, 1986 S.C.C.R. 700. *Houston v. Carnegie*, 2000 S.L.T. 333 is an example of a situation in which the detaining officer had neither sufficient direct knowledge nor information upon which to form reasonable grounds for suspicion. Compare *Stark v. Brown*, 1997 S.C.C.R 382. In contrast to s.13 powers (the right to require personal particulars from suspects and potential witnesses, and an explanation of circumstances from suspects) which can be exercised in relation to any offence, s.14 detention is only permissible when the offence under investigation can attract a term of imprisonment on conviction.

It will be seen that the section is not a preventative one, *i.e.* detention cannot be used to inquire into an offence which has yet to occur. In reality this distinction may be more apparent than real; often matters may have advanced sufficiently to consider that contemplation has blossomed into preparation and, accordingly, an attempt at the suspected offence can be established.

Secondly, the only valid purpose of the detention is to assist in the investigation of the matter at hand. If those inquiries can be shown objectively to have been capable of completion without the necessity of detaining the suspect, then logically, procedures should be regarded as vitiated—that is a determination which commonsense suggests it would be difficult for a court to reach.

Information To Be Given To A Detainee

Subsection (6) requires the constable to outline to the suspect the grounds for detention, namely the nature of his suspicions and general details of the offence suspected. It is certain that these steps must be taken at the time when the suspect is detained though, in practice, the grounds will undoubtedly be repeated when the place of detention is reached.

Subsection (9) obliges the officer, before undertaking any questioning of the detainee, to administer the statutory form of caution both when initially detaining the suspect and when presenting him at the place of detention. The statutory caution requires a detainee to furnish his name and address; otherwise he is under no obligation to answer any further questions. Note that in *Tonge v. H.M. Advocate*, 1982 S.C.C.R. 313 the Appeal Court stressed the desirability of administering a common law caution prior to interviews conducted during the six hour detention period.

Best practice also dictates that the statutory caution described above should be administered at the earliest opportunity although failure to do so will not inevitably damage a Crown case fatally. In *Scott v. Howie*, 1993 S.C.C.R. 81 the appellant was detained under s.2 of the 1980 Act on suspicion of housebreaking and conveyed to a police office. No statutory caution in terms of s.2(7) (the statutory precursor of s.14(9)), was administered but such a caution was given at the office, as was a common law caution, following which the appellant made a statement whose contents the Crown founded upon. The admitted absence of a statutory caution at the time of detention in the street was not fatal in this instance. However, there can be no doubt that any effort to lead evidence of statements made by the detainee between being stopped by the officers and his arrival at the police office would have foundered on the grounds of inadmissibility.

Reasonable force may be used to effect detention and at that time, or later, to search the suspect's person (see subss. (1), (7) and (8)).

From the moment of detention a suspect is to be regarded as being in legal custody (see s.295 below).

Reference should be made to *Ucak v. H.M. Advocate*, 1999 S.L.T. 392, in which the detention of the accused, a Turk who spoke no English, was held to be lawful although an interpreter was not available during the six hour statutory period; the police had done all that they could to comply.

Removal To A Police Office Or Other Premises

Once detained, the objective has to be to ensure the swift removal of the suspect to a police station or other premises (usually detention will be continued at a police station but that is not demanded by s.14(1)). One of the operational limitations of s.2 of the 1980 Act was that the detainee could only be taken to either a police station or other premises and, once there, could not be removed elsewhere. This could create practical difficulties, for example, in organising a swift identification parade or in detaining individuals for an offence which had been investigated by another officer or had occurred in another police division or area.

European Convention on Human Rights

The Appeal Court was sceptical that detention in terms of the section could properly be regarded as being "charged with an offence", the starting point for application of art. 6 (*H.M. Advocate v. Robb*, 1999 G.W.D. 32–1524). The issue of access to a solicitor during the detention period was raised in *Paton v. Ritchie* (High Court of Justiciary, avizandum, October 22, 1999). Crown reliance on the terms of a police interview in which the accused was not given access to a solicitor was ruled upon in *Murray v. United Kingdom* (1996) 22 E.H.R.R. 29; note however that in the Northern Ireland case an adverse inference could be drawn by the court from an accused's silence, a rule which has no general application in Scots procedure.

It will be remembered also that these powers of detention can only be exercised by "a constable", and are not available to other law enforcement agencies whose powers, if any, are derived on the basis of individual statutory provisions.

Section 14(1) incorporates amendments which were made to s.2 of the 1980 Act by the Criminal Justice and Public Order Act 1994 (c. 33), s.129(1). These go some way to answering the logistical difficulties mentioned above. It is now permissible to remove a suspect from the establishment where he has originally been detained to another police office, or other place, for the purpose of facilitating the investigation. So a suspect could be moved between police offices or, say, from a local trading standards office once detained, to a police office for photographing and fingerprinting. A valuable degree of flexibility has been created, but it will be borne in mind that a record of the detention procedures and times, sufficient to comply with the provisions of s.15 has to be maintained (see the notes to s.15 below) and all such inquiries are subject to the six hour time limit stipulated in s.14(2).

Different considerations apply to removal of detainees between jurisdictions in Great Britain and these are examined below.

The requirement to take the accused "as quickly as is reasonably practicable" does not mean that an accused must be conveyed to the closest police station. Operational factors may make detention at a more distant station appropriate. See *Menzies v. H.M. Advocate*, 1995 S.C.C.R. 550 (suspect detained near Airdrie conveyed to Dunfermline).

The Time Factors

Subsection (2) provides that the period of detention shall not exceed six hours. The 1980 Act contained provisions identical to those now found in subss. (a) and (c) but subs. (b), which re-enacts provisions contained in s.129 of the Criminal Justice and Public Order Act 1994, represents a significant alteration to the old six hour rule.

Generally the period of detention (six hours or less) will end with the suspect being arrested and charged or, alternatively, released without charge at that time if the grounds of suspicion have not been made out in that time. In the latter case the police or the Crown would not be barred subsequently from preferring charges arising from the grounds of detention: they would in terms of s.14(3) be unable to detain again using the statutory detention to be found in s.14. In theory, at the conclusion of the six hour detention period a suspect could remain voluntarily at the police office (or other premises used) when not then arrested and charged—it may fairly be assumed that this is, at best, an improbable scenario.

The end of the six hour detention clearly represents a procedural watershed, for at that point (subject to subs. (b) discussed later) the suspect's status must change to that of a prisoner or a citizen free to return to his own affairs. If procedures laid out in s.14 are complied with, then it would seem that evidence collected during that time will be admissible, despite any subsequent want of procedure; see *Grant v. H.M. Advocate*, 1990 S.C.C.R. 618 where arrest did not occur till some twenty minutes after the end of detention and replies made within the six hours were objected to. The Appeal Court held that subsequent laxity in compliance with formal requirements would not in themselves vitiate what had gone before.

It should not be forgotten that the cross-border enforcement provisions contained in Pt. X of the Criminal Justice and Public Order Act 1994 introduce in s.138(6)(a) an allowable period of four hours detention calculated from the time of arrival at a police station outside Scotland, in circumstances described in s.137 of that Act, *i.e.* where a person is detained in England or Wales for an offence previously committed (or attempted) in Scotland.

So far as Northern Ireland is concerned, quite different provisions, found in s.137(7)(d) apply. A suspect found there and detained in connection with an offence in Scotland can either be taken to the nearest convenient police station in Scotland, or to the nearest designated police station in Northern Ireland, as soon as reasonably practicable (on arrest elsewhere in Great Britain in relation to a Scottish crime, the arresting officer's duty is to take the arrested person either to the nearest convenient police station in Scotland or to a police station within the sheriffdom where the offence is being investigated).

When recourse is had to these cross-border provisions, it should be stressed that it is only competent to convey the detainee to a police office, or to police offices; the references in s.14 of the 1995 Act to "other premises" must then be disregarded.

Lastly, it is worthy of note that the powers of cross-border enforcement bear a surprising, and doubtless unintended, resemblance to the doctrine of hot pursuit which operated in the Scottish and English Borders during the times of the reivers.

Section 14 Detention And Other Statutory Powers

As has been mentioned, the inclusion of subs. (b) has substantially affected the previously clear cut operation of s.14. Now detention under the Act may be only a prelude to further statutory periods of detention. The provisions of the Prevention of Terrorism (Temporary Provisions) Act 1989 (c. 4) and the Customs and Excise Management Act 1979 (c. 2) as augmented by the Criminal Justice (Scotland) Act 1987 (c. 41), ss.48 to 50, spring to mind. Indeed it will be noted that the Customs legislation cited is a refinement of the 1980 Act's detention provisions and is generally directed against drug smuggling offences.

Subsection (4) requires that a period of detention under any other enactment upon the same grounds, shall be deducted from the six hour period ordinarily available under s.14. A like provision is made specifically in regard to the Prisons (Scotland) Act 1989 (c. 45). Section 41(3) of that Act permits temporary detention within a prison for the purpose of investigating the introduction (*i.e.* smuggling) of forbidden materials by persons into prisons.

Details To Be Recorded

In addition to the obligation upon the detaining officer to disclose the nature of his suspicions and the reason for detention, subs. (6) stipulates other requirements which must be complied with by the officer and other police officers who become involved in the detention process later. It is an absolute requirement that (i) the time and place at which detention began, (ii) the general nature of the suspected offence, (iii) the time of arrival at the police office or other premises used for detention, (iv) the time, or times, at which the detainee was informed of his right to refuse to answer questions except those requiring his personal particulars (pursuant to subs. (9)) and his right to request that his solicitor and another person be advised of the fact of his detention as provided by s.15 of the Act, and the particulars of the officer who intimates this information, (v) the times when the above requests were made by the detainee and fulfilled by the police, and (vi) the time when detention terminated and/or the time of arrest should be recorded. All of these requirements simply echo the provisions contained in s.2(4) of the 1980 Act; it should be noted however that the corollary of the new power in subs. (1) of this Act to remove the detainee from the police office to "any other place", is that subs. (6)(b) demands that the "other place" should be specified in the record if such a power is exercised (although not statutorily required, it would be prudent to record fully the times of removal to that "other place" and return to the police office).

The practice adopted by Scottish police forces is for the detention forms which constitute the record of detention (stipulated now in subs. (6)), to be raised and maintained at police offices from the moment a detainee arrives there. It follows of course that initially the forms raised will necessarily have a retrospective effect since the detention process will have been initiated elsewhere: consequently it is sound practice for the detaining officer to note the time of initiating detention in his notebook.

In *Cummings v. H.M. Advocate*, 1982 S.C.C.R. 108 the only record produced to show that a statutory caution had been administered was contained in the officer's notebook. This was held to constitute a record sufficient for the purposes of s.2(4) of the 1980 Act. Nevertheless it is sound practice to ensure that the terms of the statutory caution in subs. (9) are repeated at the police office when documentation is raised.

Purpose Of Detention

While s.2(5) of the 1980 Act did broadly specify the avenues of inquiry which could be followed during detention, reference now has to be made to ss.18 and 19 of the 1995 Act to appreciate the wide-ranging powers which can be exercised (see notes to ss.18 and 19 below). Subsection (7) preserves the right to question and search the detainee. The power of search was held in *Skirving v. Russell*, 1999 G.W.D. 15–701 to include a search of a woman's handbag as well as any pockets in her clothing.

Rights of person arrested or detained

15.—(1) Without prejudice to section 17 of this Act, a person who, not being a person in respect of whose custody or detention subsection (4) below applies—

(a) has been arrested and is in custody in a police station or other premises, shall be entitled to have intimation of his custody and of the place where he is being held sent to a person reasonably named by him;

(b) is being detained under section 14 of this Act and has been taken to a police station or other premises or place, shall be entitled to have intimation of his detention and of the police station or other premises or place sent to a solicitor and to one other person reasonably named by him,

without delay or, where some delay is necessary in the interest of the investigation or the prevention of crime or the apprehension of offenders, with no more delay than is so necessary.

(2) A person shall be informed of his entitlement under subsection (1) above—

(a) on arrival at the police station or other premises; or

(b) where he is not arrested, or as the case may be detained, until after such arrival, on such arrest or detention.

(3) Where the person mentioned in paragraph (a) of subsection (1) above requests such intimation to be sent as is specified in that paragraph there shall be recorded the time when such request is—

(a) made;

(b) complied with.

(4) Without prejudice to the said section 17, a constable shall, where a person who has been arrested and is in such custody as is mentioned in paragraph (a) of subsection (1) above or who is being detained as is mentioned in paragraph (b) of that subsection appears to him to be a child, send without delay such intimation as is mentioned in the said paragraph (a), or as the case may be paragraph (b), to that person's parent if known; and the parent—

(a) in a case where there is reasonable cause to suspect that he has been involved in the alleged offence in respect of which the person has been arrested or detained, may; and

(b) in any other case shall,

be permitted access to the person.

(5) The nature and extent of any access permitted under subsection (4) above shall be subject to any restriction essential for the furtherance of the investigation or the well-being of the person.

(6) In subsection (4) above—

(a) "child" means a person under 16 years of age; and

[1](b) "parent" includes guardian and any person who has the care of a child.

DEFINITIONS
"child": s.307(1) as restricted by subs. (6) below.
"constable": s.307(1) and Police (Scotland) Act 1967 (c.77), s.51(1).
"parent": subs. (6) below.

NOTE
[1]Substituted by the Crime and Punishment (Scotland) Act 1997 (c. 48) s.62(1) and Sched. 1, para. 21 with effect from August 1, 1997 by the Crime and Punishment (Scotland) Act 1997 (Commencement and Transitional Provisions) Order 1997 (S.I. 1997 No. 1712) para. 3.

GENERAL NOTE
This section specifies the extent to which arrested or detained persons are entitled to have other persons informed of their circumstances and whereabouts. This must be intimated to the subject as soon as he is presented at the station charge bar or at whatever other place he is being lawfully held in custody. Note that the entitlement does not extend to those attending voluntarily. Section 14(6) requires that the procedure be properly documented at the time of arrival at the police station or "other place", not before.

There are some important differences in the obligations the police are placed under by this section when dealing with arrested, as distinct from detained, persons.

Arrested Persons

In the case of arrested persons, subs. (1)(a) only deals with the right to have friends or relatives told this information and, while the arrested person has to be advised of his right to have a named person told of his circumstances, the police can, when there are legitimate grounds for doing so, delay such a notification. Section 17 makes it mandatory for the arrested person to be advised immediately of his right to have a legal representative (whether personally nominated by the person or acting as the duty solicitor under the Legal Aid Scheme) informed of his status and whereabouts. While that section stipulates that the arrested person must be informed of this right immediately on arrest, it does not demand immediate intimation to the solicitor who is named. Nevertheless an unexplained delay in notification would risk an unfavourable interpretation in subsequent proceedings. There is no obligation upon the solicitor to attend the police station (or other named premises) when notification is received from the police.

It should be noted that separate, more extensive, provisions are made in regard to children, and these are discussed below.

Detained Persons

Subsection (1)(b) relates to suspects detained in terms of s.14. Their rights to intimation differ from those applicable to arrested persons. At the time of detention at a police office or other place, the detainee must be informed of his entitlement to have his circumstances made known to a reasonably named person and to a solicitor. This right applies equally to situations where the subject is held at a police office or elsewhere but greater latitude is permitted in delaying the implementation of the detainee's demands. Informing either the detainee's reasonably named person or his solicitor, or both, can be delayed. Normally notifications requested by the suspect must be acted upon swiftly, in order to comply with the spirit of the Act unless, as subs. (1) stipulates, there are plausible grounds relative to the matter under investigation or affecting the prospects of apprehending others or relating to the prevention of crime (this last being an undefined catch-all) which justify a temporary withholding of notification.

There is no automatic right of access to a solicitor either prior to, or during a detention interview, but the admissibility of evidence obtained from the accused during the interview must still meet a general test of fairness. See *Paton v. Ritchie*, 2000 S.L.T. 239; 2000 S.C.C.R. 151 (following *H.M. Advocate v. Fox,* 1947 J.C. 30) where the accused's appeal was based upon a purported breach of his Art. 6 rights: the Appeal Court accepted that Art. 6 could apply even at this early investigative stage in proceedings.

Section 15 As Applied To Children

These provisions apply to children aged between eight and 16 years since s.41 statutorily repeats the common law concept of nonage; see also *Merrin v. S*, 1987 S.L.T. 193 and the general discussion there of the absence of dole in children under eight years.

In the context of s.15 it will be observed that the definition of "child" found in subs. (6) is narrower than that contained in the Interpretation section (s.308), which in turn refers back to the provisions of the Children (Scotland) Act 1995 (c. 36). The narrower definition in subs. (6) has the effect of ensuring that identical provisions apply to all those aged 16 years or more. That section apart, the 1995 Act and Pt. II of the Children (Scotland) Act 1995, s.93(2)(b) adhere to the definition of a "child" as either a person less than 16 years old, or a person over the age of 16 years and less than 18 years old who is subject to a supervision requirement.

Subsection (4) places a positive onus upon the police when they think that the person in custody is a child, to take active steps to contact the child's parent or guardian and allow access to the child. This is the case even when it is suspected that the parent or guardian was involved in the offence which gave rise to the child's detention in the first place: subs. (5) allows access to the child to be limited (and, arguably, even refused) where this is essential to the further investigation of the offence under scrutiny or for the safety of the parent or guardian, or both. It is submitted that the grounds for any restriction upon, or refusal of, access in these circumstances should be fully noted by the officers involved. Failure to adhere to these requirements arose in the case of *H.M. Advocate v. G.B. and D.J.M.*, 1991 S.C.C.R. 533 and a confession obtained by the police was withheld from the jury.

Generally the Act proceeds on the basis that children arrested for offences shall be liberated to appear at court rather than being detained in custody. See s.43 below which sets out the procedures following the arrest of a child.

Observations

Curiously while s.15 demands that the suspect be informed of these rights and (together with s.14(6)(e) and (f)) that a record of the person and solicitor named be kept along with the times of notification, it is not necessary to record when notification is wilfully delayed or the reasons for so doing. It is submitted that where a departure from the usual practice of notification occurs, this should only be done when the following factors are *all* present; (a) the suspect has been informed of his rights of intimation, and (b) has elected names which are deemed unreasonable or as inexpedient (broadly not in the interests of justice for the reasons expressed in subs. (1)) at that time, and (c) has been informed that such intimation will not be made and advised of the grounds for that decision. The suspect cannot simply be left in the dark if the spirit of s.15 is to have any meaning. As was remarked earlier, it would be expedient, with an eye to later proceedings, that the grounds for delaying notification to the suspect's solicitor or friend be recorded along with the other details stipulated in s.14(6) and subs. (3). Failure to comply with the terms of this section would taint any admissions, prints or samples subsequently obtained from the accused. Adapting the *ratio* in *Grant v. H.M. Advocate*, 1989 S.C.C.R. 618 (see notes to s.14 above) suggests that evidence obtained from the accused beforehand would still be admissible.

Drunken persons: power to take to designated place

16.—(1) Where a constable has power to arrest a person without a warrant for any offence and the constable has reasonable grounds for suspecting that that person is drunk, the constable may, if he thinks fit, take him to any place designated by the Secretary of State for the purposes of this section as a place suitable for the care of drunken persons.

(2) A person shall not by virtue of this section be liable to be detained in any such place as is mentioned in subsection (1) above, but the exercise in his case of the power conferred by this section shall not preclude his being charged with any offence.

DEFINITIONS
"constable": s.307(1) and s.51(1) of the Police (Scotland) Act 1967.
"offence": s.307(1).

GENERAL NOTE
More in hope than expectation this section repeats the provisions, word for word, of s.5 of the 1980 Act. The original intention of the section was to enable drunken persons to be dealt with other than by criminal prosecution and it gave the police the option of conveying the offender to a designated place for detoxification. The section can only be applied where such designated places exist and to date only pilot schemes have operated.

While a constable may choose to exercise his powers to deliver a drunkard to a designated place, neither he nor the staff there have any power to compel the subject to remain there. It will also be noted that conveyance to a place is entirely without prejudice to any further proceedings arising from the arrest. It is of interest that this section does not require the offence giving rise to arrest to be one specifically of drunkenness, or to have been committed in a public place, only that the offender offended while apparently drunk. That said, the scope of the powers of arrest for common law offences committed by a drunken offender remains hazy: plainly a common law offence witnessed by a constable would qualify, but what is the position when the suspicion of an offence stems from *ex parte* statements?

Certain statutory powers of arrest of drunken persons do exist. For example, the Civic Government (Scotland) Act 1982 (c. 45), s.50(1) created an offence of being drunk and incapable, suggesting a more advanced state of intoxication and incapacity than mere drunkenness, while s.50(5) relates to possession of a firearm or crossbow in a public place while drunk.

The Criminal Justice (Scotland) Act 1980 confined itself to dealing with drunkenness: s.69(c) related to drunken persons on public passenger vehicles en route to designated sporting events; s.74 to drunkenness at a designated sports ground during the currency of a designated sporting event. These provisions are now to be found in Pt. 2 of the Criminal Law (Consolidation) (Scotland) Act 1995 (c. 39). In the absence of local or centrally funded provision of designated places s.16 is destined to be moribund.

Arrest: access to solicitor

Right of accused to have access to solicitor

17.—(1) Where an accused has been arrested on any criminal charge, he shall be entitled immediately upon such arrest—

(a) to have intimation sent to a solicitor that his professional assistance is required by the accused, and informing the solicitor—
    (i) of the place where the person is being detained;
    (ii) whether the person is to be liberated; and
    (iii) if the person is not to be liberated, the court to which he is to be taken and the date when he is to be so taken; and
(b) to be told what rights there are under—
    (i) paragraph (a) above;
    (ii) subsection (2) below; and
    (iii) section 35(1) and (2) of this Act.

(2) The accused and the solicitor shall be entitled to have a private interview before the examination or, as the case may be, first appearance.

GENERAL NOTE

It is mandatory that an accused person, following arrest, must be informed (i) of his right to have a solicitor informed of this development and that the solicitor's services are required (ii) of his right to a private interview with his solicitor which is to be accorded to him prior to the first court appearance on the charges and (iii) where applicable, of his right to have a solicitor of his choosing present at judicial examination and, if need be, for that examination to be delayed up to 48 hours to permit the attendance of that solicitor.

There is no obligation upon the solicitor to attend immediately or, indeed, at all but legal advice must be available before the accused's court appearance.

It will be noted that while a request by the accused to have a solicitor informed of his arrest must be acted upon by the police, there is no similar entitlement to have friends or relatives told of his circumstances though this should ordinarily be permitted; see the discussion in Notes to s.15 above regarding "Arrested Persons".

Grounds sufficient to merit arrest can be less than would be needed to prefer charge (*Hay v. H.M. Advocate*, 1998 G.W.D. 35–1780). There is no prohibition on interview by the police after arrest (*Johnston v. H.M. Advocate*, 1994 S.L.T. 300).

See also *Van Lierop v. McLeod*, 2000 S.L.T. 291 in relation to the extent of admissibility of answers to questions after arrest.

Prints and samples

Prints, samples etc. in criminal investigations

[4]**18.**—(1) This section applies where a person has been arrested and is in custody or is detained under section 14(1) of this Act.

[1,5](2) A constable may take from the person, or require the person to provide him with, such relevant physical data as the constable may, having regard to the circumstances of the suspected offence in respect of which the person has been arrested or detained, reasonably consider it appropriate to take.

[2](3) Subject to subsection (4) below, all record of any relevant physical data taken from or provided by a person under subsection (2) above, all samples taken under subsection (6) below and all information derived from such samples shall be destroyed as soon as possible following a decision not to institute criminal proceedings against the person or on the conclusion of such proceedings otherwise than with a conviction or an order under section 246(3) of this Act.

(4) The duty under subsection (3) above to destroy samples taken under subsection (6) below and information derived from such samples shall not apply—
(a) where the destruction of the sample or the information could have the effect of destroying any sample, or any information derived therefrom, lawfully held in relation to a person other than the person from whom the sample was taken; or
(b) where the record, sample or information in question is of the same kind as a record, a sample or, as the case may be, information lawfully held by or on behalf of any police force in relation to the person.

(5) No sample, or information derived from a sample, retained by virtue of subsection (4) above shall be used—

(a) in evidence against the person from whom the sample was taken; or

(b) for the purposes of the investigation of any offence.

(6) A constable may, with the authority of an officer of a rank no lower than inspector, take from the person—

(a) from the hair of an external part of the body other than pubic hair, by means of cutting, combing or plucking, a sample of hair or other material;

(b) from a fingernail or toenail or from under any such nail, a sample of nail or other material;

(c) from an external part of the body, by means of swabbing or rubbing, a sample of blood or other body fluid, of body tissue or of other material;

(d) from the inside of the mouth, by means of swabbing, a sample of saliva or other material.

(7) A constable may use reasonable force in exercising any power conferred by subsection (2) or (6) above.

[3](7A) For the purposes of this section and sections 19 and 20 of this Act "relevant physical data" means any—

(a) fingerprint;

(b) palm print;

(c) print or impression other than those mentioned in paragraph (a) and (b) above, of an external part of the body;

(d) record of a person's on an external part of the body created by a device approved by the Secretary of State.

(7B) The Secretary of State by order made by statutory instrument may approve a device for the purpose of creating such records as are mentioned in paragraph (d) of subsection (7A) above.

(8) Nothing in this section shall prejudice—

(a) any power of search;

(b) any power to take possession of evidence where there is imminent danger of its being lost or destroyed; or

(c) any power to take prints, impressions or samples under the authority of a warrant.

DEFINITIONS

"constable": s.307(1) and Police (Scotland) Act 1967 (c. 77), s.51(1).

"in custody": s.295.

"relevant physical data": s.18(7A) of the 1995 Act.

NOTES

[1]Substituted by the Crime and Punishment (Scotland) Act 1997 (c. 48), s.47(1))(a) with effect from August 1, 1997 in terms of the Crime and Punishment (Scotland) Act 1997 (Commencement and Transitional Provisions) Order 1997 (S.I. 1997 No. 1712) para. 3.

[2]Substituted by the Crime and Disorder Act 1998 (c. 37), Sched. 8, para. 117(1) and (2) (effective August 1, 1997: S.I. 1998 No. 2327).

[3]Inserted by s.47(1)(d) of the 1997 Act with effect from August 1, 1997 in terms of the Order above.

[4]Prospectively amended by the Terrorism Act 2000 (c. 11), s.47 and Sched. 8, para. 20(1).

[5]Prospectively substituted by the Terrorism Act 2000 (c. 11), s.47 and Sched. 8, para. 20(2).

GENERAL NOTE

This section is derived from the Prisoners and Criminal Proceedings (Scotland) Act 1993 (c. 9), s.28, which gave effect to the recommendations of the Scottish Law Commission's *Report on Evidence: Blood Group Tests, DNA Tests and Related Matters*, Paper No. 120, 1989. The current provisions were intended to give clearer expression to the extent of police powers (those contained in s.2(5)(c) of the 1980 Act being somewhat indeterminate) and to apply equally to arrested suspects and to those detained under s.14 of the 1995 Act. Section 18 does give more extensive sampling powers to the police in subs. (6) than were previously available under the

1980 Act, but note that these can only be exercised after authorisation by a senior police officer, *i.e.* an officer of inspector rank or higher. The tenor of the Act might suggest that the authorising officer should not be involved in the investigation but this is not expressly stated.

The section stops short of permitting the procuring of evidence by methods which case law has defined as invasive, for example, internal physical examinations, endoscopic or colono-scopic examinations. It remains the case that such extreme invasions of bodily privacy, which involve entering the suspect's body, still require the authority of a sheriff's warrant which has to be obtained by the procurator fiscal. An application for a warrant of this kind can be made at any time, but the court will take account of the nature of the examination or sampling proposed, the degree of physical invasion involved (when set against the public interest in the detection of crime), the stage which proceedings have reached and whether, at that time, there is a *prima facie* justification for the application. (See *Hay v. H.M. Advocate*, 1968 S.L.T. 334; *Advocate, H.M. v. Milford*, 1973 S.L.T. 12; *McGlennan v. Kelly*, 1989 S.L.T. 832; *Smith v. Cardle*, 1993 S.C.C.R. 609; *Hughes v. Normand*, 1993 S.L.T. 113). The extension of this section to entitle the police to recover "relevant physical data" (as defined in subs. (7A)) primarily reflects the technological advances in the field of fingerprinting brought about by electronic "livescan" fingerprinting. "Livescan" is expected to produce higher-definition print quality (improving detection rates) and to deliver an instantaneous comparison of data on file to enable immediate confirmation of an offender's identity on completion of scanning.

Approval for the use of the Digital Biometrics Incorporation (DBI) Tenprinter 1133S, with palmprint option, was given by the Secretary of State with effect from August 8, 1997 by the Electronic Fingerprinting etc. Device Approval Order 1997 S.I. 1997 No. 1939 (S.140).

Subs. (1)
This stipulates that the section applies to all persons arrested or detained by the police.

Subs. (2)
The reference to an "external part of the body" suggests that physical measurement of a suspect (as in *Smith v. Cardle*), would be permissible using s.18 powers but the obtaining of dental impressions (as in *Hay v. H.M. Advocate*) would not and would normally demand a sheriff's warrant. However subs. (8)(b) by implication permits urgent steps to be taken in situations where delay would create a real risk of evidence being irretrievably lost; the legitimacy, or otherwise, of such steps would fall to be considered in any subsequent proceedings.

Subss. (3) and (4)
Superficially, subs. (3) re-enacts the terms of s.2(1)(c) of the 1980 Act which provided for the destruction of fingerprint forms in the event either of their being no proceedings against the accused, or his acquittal following such proceedings. It will be noted that a decision not to proceed against an accused person will not always be because there is an insufficiency of evidence: the Crown may in broad terms decide that prosecution would not be in the public interest for a variety of reasons, or might opt to deal with the matter by way of a warning. It is in these situations, especially where proceedings are maintained against other accused, that intractable problems arise now because of the interaction of subss. (3) and (4).

Subsection (3) refers to "all information derived from such samples" and would seem to be more rigorous than the earlier provisions of s.2(1)(c) of the 1980 Act. The later provision suggests that data obtained as a result of such samples, which could arguably have been retained even after the destruction of the sample material under the 1980 Act, must also be destroyed. Yet while subs. (3) might momentarily be viewed as clarifying the law in this grey area, the terms of subs. (4) serve to qualify and obscure the position.

Subsection (4)(a) permits the retention of the samples, or the information derived from them, where to destroy such would itself "destroy" similar information obtained in relation to a person still accused. Presumably then, sample evidence gathered at an early stage in proceedings from suspect A against whom charges are later dropped, could still be preserved for use as evidence against suspect B now to be prosecuted. In such a situation there would be no obligation upon the police to destroy A's samples at all: they would only be precluded from using them as evidence in any other proceedings against A (see subs. (5) below).

Subsection 4(b) also militates against the general requirement to destroy samples when no proceedings are to follow. In this case both samples and the data derived from them could be preserved to update existing data held by the police about the person concerned, albeit these could not be deployed *directly* in evidence or in the investigation of crime. Since the technology now exists to extract DNA from body samples of the sort specified in subs. (6), this is an issue of no small importance.

There has of course been no judicial interpretation as yet of these subsections.

Subs. (5)

The implications of this provision are discussed above in the Notes to subss. (3) and (4). This appears to open the way to the preservation of databanks derived from samples of previously convicted persons.

Subs. (6)

The samples which can be taken by a police officer, are those deemed to be of a non-invasive nature. In practice these are generally obtained by police casualty surgeons and while subs. (7) permits the use of reasonable physical force to recover the necessary samples, it is likely that doctors would assist in the procedures in the absence of the suspect's consent, only when a sheriff's warrant had been obtained by the procurator fiscal.

Prints, samples etc. in criminal investigations: supplementary provisions

19.—(1) This section applies where a person convicted of an offence—
[1](a) has not, since the conviction, had taken from him, or been required to provide, any relevant physical data or had any impression or sample taken from him; or
[1](b) has at any time had—
  (i) taken from him or been required (whether under paragraph (a) above or under section 18 or 19A of this Act or otherwise) to provide any physical data; or
  (ii) any impression or sample taken from him,
which was not suitable for the means of analysis for which the data were taken or required or the impression or sample was taken or, though suitable, was insufficient (either in quantity or in quality) to enable information to be obtained by that means of analysis.

(2) Where this section applies, a constable may, within the permitted period—
[2](a) take from on require the convicted person to provide him with such relevant physical data as he reasonably considers it appropriate to take or, as the case may be, require the provision of;
(b) with the authority of an officer of a rank no lower than inspector, take from the person any sample mentioned in any of paragraphs (a) to (d) of subsection (6) of section 18 of this Act by the means specified in that paragraph in relation to that sample.

(3) A constable—
(a) may require the convicted person to attend a police station for the purposes of subsection (2) above;
(b) may, where the convicted person is in legal custody by virtue of section 295 of this Act, exercise the powers conferred by subsection (2) above in relation to the person in the place where he is for the time being.

(4) In subsection (2) above, "the permitted period" means—
(a) in a case to which paragraph (a) of subsection (1) above applies, the period of one month beginning with the date of the conviction;
[3](b) in a case to which paragraph (b) of that subsection applies, the period of one month beginning with the date on which a constable of the police force which instructed the analysis receives written intimation that the relevant physical data were or the sample was unsuitable or, as the case may be, insufficient as mentioned in that paragraph.

(5) A requirement under subsection (3)(a) above—
(a) shall give the person at least seven days' notice of the date on which he is required to attend;
(b) may direct him to attend at a specified time of day or between specified times of day.

(6) Any constable may arrest without warrant a person who fails to comply with a requirement under subsection (3)(a) above.

DEFINITION
"constable": s.307(1) and s.51(1) of the Police (Scotland) Act 1967.
"relevant physical data": s.18(7A) of the 1995 Act.

NOTES
[1]Substituted by the Crime and Punishment (Scotland) Act 1997 (c. 48) s.47(2)(a) with effect from August 1, 1997 in terms of the Crime and Punishment (Scotland) Act 1997 (Commencement and Transitional Provisions) Order 1997 (S.I. 1997 No. 1712) para. 3.
[2]Substituted by the above Act s.47(2)(b) with effect from August 1, 1997 as provided by the Order above.
[3]Amended by the above Act s.47(2)(c) with effect from August 1, 1997 as provided by the Order above.

GENERAL NOTE
This section gives the police a general power in the course of investigations or after the conviction of an accused, within the permitted period of one month specified in subs. (4), to obtain relevant physical data as defined in s.18A. (See the General Note at p.39 above.) The power can be utilised within that time in two distinct situations; (i) when no such samples have been taken since conviction (subs. (1)(a)) and (ii) when the materials obtained in the course of detention or arrest of the person have been either insufficient or deficient for the purposes of analysis (subs. (1)(b)). This section operates without prejudice to the Crown's own rights to petition the court for relevant physical data by way of Incidental Application or petition warrant.
As with s.18 a proposal to seek samples of head hair, mouth swabs, nail clippings or scrapings can only proceed after clearance from a senior police officer.

The Permitted Period (subs. (4))
The timescale in the event of conviction is unambiguous—one month from the date of that conviction. This would apply equally in the cases of the imposition of a money fine or caution, probation as defined in s.228 below or a deferment of sentence. Subsection (4)(a) provides for an opportunity to correct acts of omission.
Subsection (4)(b), which applies to suspects under investigation and to those convicted of offences, is by its nature much less precise; the one month timescale is effective from the date upon which the police force instructing a forensic or fingerprint examination of samples previously obtained from the suspect, receives written intimation of their unsuitability. Note that a verbal report to the same effect would not start the clock ticking. It should also be appreciated that subs. (4)(b) does not provide a remedy for situations where no samples had been taken from the suspect; the subsection only operates when samples taken are later found to be defective.

Police Powers Under s.19
The police are entitled, within the permitted period, to require that the accused makes himself available for sampling purposes if he is at liberty or to have access to him for those purposes if he is in custody. No notice need be given to a remand or serving prisoner of the police intention to exercise such powers, but subs. (3)(b) curiously makes it clear that the sampling procedures must be executed, "in the place where he is for the time being": this suggests that the sampling must be carried out in the penal establishment in which the accused is serving his sentence.
A person at large is entitled to no less than seven days notice of the requirement that he attend at a specified place and may also be directed to attend on a particular day and time (or days and times).
Failure to attend the nominated police station as demanded under s.19(3) renders the subject liable to arrest without warrant, but the Act does not treat such a failure as an offence. A further issue which is unresolved in the Act is the position when a suspect does attend as required, but samples are not sufficient for analysis or indeed no samples are taken at all. It is submitted that in the former case the whole procedure in subs. (4)(b) could be invoked anew, but in the latter, the suspect would have fulfilled his obligation and could not be subjected to the procedure again. Note also that subs. (5) is peremptory and is not qualified by any reasonableness test.
It will be necessary if the power of arrest in subs. (6) is to be invoked, that the police can demonstrate that notice of the requirement has been lawfully served upon the subject.

Use of prints, samples etc.

20. Without prejudice to any power to do so apart from this section, relevant physical data, impressions and samples lawfully held by or on behalf of any police force or in connection with or as a result of an investigation of an offence and information derived therefrom may be checked against other such data, impressions, samples and information.

DEFINITION
"relevant physical data": s.18(7A) of the 1995 Act.

GENERAL NOTE
This section preserves the existing rights of the police to collate and compare fingerprint impressions of accused persons and authorises such operations in relation to other samples lawfully obtained by the police (see the notes to s.18(3) and (4) above). In *H.M. Advocate v. Shepherd*, 1997 S.C.C.R. 246 the Court of Appeal upheld the use of a fingerprint form, lawfully obtained from an accused following arrest in regard to a later offence, to prove earlier offences in which no fingerprint form had been obtained before the accused's full committal. The Court noted that carefully framed questions could avoid revealing that the accused had apparently been involved in another offence, and that the formal evidence of the taking of fingerprints had been incorporated into a statement of uncontroversial evidence. It may be that suitably circumspect questioning could validate the use of a fingerprint form lawfully obtained, but predating the offence libelled. Further, following *Lawrie v. Muir*, 1950 S.L.T. 37 and *Namyslak v. H.M. Advocate*, 1995 S.L.T. 528 it will be noted that even irregularly or unlawfully obtained fingerprint forms could be admissible as evidence, provided there was no unfairness to the accused. The 1997 Act has extended these rights to the retention and collation of relevant data which has been gathered in the course of investigation of an offence. On one reading this could entitle the police to retain data garnered from persons other than suspects or accused during an investigation.

Schedule 1 offences

Schedule 1 offences: power of constable to take offender into custody

21.—(1) Without prejudice to any other powers of arrest, a constable may take into custody without warrant—
  (a) any person who within his view commits any of the offences mentioned in Schedule 1 to this Act, if the constable does not know and cannot ascertain his name and address;
  (b) any person who has committed, or whom he had reason to believe to have committed, any of the offences mentioned in that Schedule, if the constable does not know and cannot ascertain his name and address or has reasonable ground for believing that he will abscond.
(2) Where a person has been arrested under this section, the officer in charge of a police station may—
  (a) liberate him upon a written undertaking, signed by him and certified by the said officer, in terms of which that person undertakes to appear at a specified court at a specified time; or
  (b) liberate him without any such undertaking; or
  (c) refuse to liberate him, and such refusal and the detention of that person until his case is tried in the usual form shall not subject the officer to any claim whatsoever.
(3) A person in breach of an undertaking given by him under subsection (2)(a) above without reasonable excuse shall be guilty of an offence and liable to the following penalties—
  (a) a fine not exceeding level 3 on the standard scale; and
  (b) imprisonment for a period—
      (i) where conviction is in the district court, not exceeding 60 days; or
      (ii) in any other case, not exceeding 3 months.
(4) The penalties provided for in subsection (3) above may be imposed in addition to any other penalty which it is competent for the court to impose,

notwithstanding that the total of penalties imposed may exceed the maximum penalty which it is competent to impose in respect of the original offence.

(5) In any proceedings relating to an offence under this section, a writing, purporting to be such an undertaking as is mentioned in subsection (2)(a) above and bearing to be signed and certified, shall be sufficient evidence of the terms of the undertaking given by the arrested person.

DEFINITION
"constable": s.307(1) and s.51(1) of the Police (Scotland) Act 1967.

GENERAL NOTE
This section repeats the provisions contained in ss.18(1) and 294(1) of the 1975 Act relating to offences against children under the age of 17 years. The relevant offences are found in Sched. 1 to the 1995 Act which now reflects the consolidating amendments contained in the Criminal Law (Consolidation) (Scotland) Act 1995 (c. 39).

Section 136(2) preserves the six month timebar provision in relation to statutory proceedings which are prosecuted summarily. It is often forgotten that common law offences involving bodily injury to a child, or lewd, indecent or libidinous practices towards a child (specified in paras. 2 and 3 of Sched. 1) must also be commenced within six months of the contravention. Powers to liberate persons charged with a Sched. I offence are vested in the officer in charge of the police station to which the accused has been brought. The powers, and penalties for failure to comply with the terms of any undertaking imposed, are identical to those contained in s.22 below, but note that liberation can be utilised for potentially more serious charges under s.21: liberation under s.22 is only competent if the charges preferred could be tried summarily.

Evidential Provisions
In proceedings for breach of the terms of a written undertaking made under s.21(2)(a) or the more commonplace provision under s.22(1)(a) below, the Act provides that a copy thereof certified and signed by the liberating officer, shall suffice as proof of the facts contained in it. In entering into such an undertaking an accused person is, in effect, placing himself in a special capacity. Once the court is satisfied as to the terms of the undertaking and that the accused failed to obtemper them, the onus of proof then falls upon an accused to make out reasonable grounds on the balance of probabilities for his failure to attend.

Penalties
Ordinarily the statutory maximum penalties of imprisonment or fine are laid down in s.3 (Sheriff Solemn), s.5(2) (Sheriff summary) and s.7(7) (District Courts) and cannot be exceeded *in cumulo*. Exceptions to this generality are provided in ss.21(4) and 22(4) in relation to breach of written undertakings and s.27(5) in regard to breach of bail conditions. In either case the sentence imposed can be added to that imposed for the substantive matter, even if this results in a cumulative sentence or fine higher than that which the Court could normally impose. See *Kelso v. Crowe*, 1992 S.C.C.R. 415—sentencing principles where contravention of bail conditions occur.

Police liberation

Liberation by police

22.—(1) Where a person has been arrested and charged with an offence which may be tried summarily, the officer in charge of a police station may—
  (a) liberate him upon a written undertaking, signed by him and certified by the officer, in terms of which the person undertakes to appear at a specified court at a specified time; or
  (b) liberate him without any such undertaking; or
  (c) refuse to liberate him.

(2) A person in breach of an undertaking given by him under subsection (1) above without reasonable excuse shall be guilty of an offence and liable on summary conviction to the following penalties—
  (a) a fine not exceeding level 3 on the standard scale; and
  (b) imprisonment for a period—
      (i) where conviction is in the district court, not exceeding 60 days; or

(ii) where conviction is in the sheriff court, not exceeding 3 months.

(3) The refusal of the officer in charge to liberate a person under subsection (1)(c) above and the detention of that person until his case is tried in the usual form shall not subject the officer to any claim whatsoever.

(4) The penalties provided for in subsection (2) above may be imposed in addition to any other penalty which it is competent for the court to impose, notwithstanding that the total of penalties imposed may exceed the maximum penalty which it is competent to impose in respect of the original offence.

(5) In any proceedings relating to an offence under this section, a writing, purporting to be such an undertaking as is mentioned in subsection (1)(a) above and bearing to be signed and certified, shall be sufficient evidence of the terms of the undertaking given by the arrested person.

General Note

This section permits the officer in charge of a police station, at his discretion, to liberate an accused person pending the submission of a report to the procurator fiscal, or to liberate him to appear at a named court on a specified future occasion, or to hold the person in custody for appearance at court on the next lawful day. These powers only apply when the charges preferred are capable of being prosecuted summarily, but the fact that a written undertaking has been entered into in no way commits the Crown to proceed summarily. Since a suspect has to consent to abide by the specified terms of an undertaking, it is equally open to him to refuse them and in that event it would be incompetent to proceed in terms of subs. (1)(a). The accused would either have to be detained in custody or be liberated for report.

Evidential Provisions

These are identical to those contained in s.21. See the notes on "Evidential Provisions" in that section.

Penalties (subs. (4))

The implications of this provision mirror those in s.21. Refer to the notes on "Penalties" in that section.

Part III

Bail

Consideration of bail on first appearance

[1]**22A.**—(1) On the first occasion on which—

(a) a person accused on petition is brought before the sheriff prior to committal until liberated in due course of law; or

(b) a person charged on complaint with an offence is brought before a judge having jurisdiction to try the offence,

the sheriff or, as the case may be, the judge shall, after giving that person and the prosecutor an opportunity to be heard and within the period specified in subsection (2) below, either admit or refuse to admit that person to bail.

(2) That period is the period of 24 hours beginning with the time when the person accused or charged is brought before the sheriff or judge.

(3) If, by the end of that period, the sheriff or judge has not admitted or refused to admit the person accused or charged to bail, then that person shall be forthwith liberated.

(4) This section applies whether or not the person accused or charged is in custody when that person is brought before the sheriff or judge.

Definitions

"complaint": s.307(1)

"offence": s.307(1)

"prosecutor": s.307(1)

"bail": s.307(1)

NOTE
[1]Inserted by the Bail, Judicial Appointments etc. (Scotland) Act 2000 (asp 9), s.1.

GENERAL NOTE
The contents of the Bail, Judicial Appointments etc. (Scotland) Act 2000 (asp 9) represent a legislative response to problems which arose following the advent of the European Convention on Human Rights into Scots law in the Scotland Act 1998 (c. 46).

On the first appearance of a person from custody, whether on complaint or on petition, the court is automatically obliged to consider his admission to bail. Thus it would not be necessary at that stage in proceedings to make a formal application on behalf of the accused until the court had first deliberated on the question. Subsection (2) permits the court to continue its consideration of bail for up to 24 hours but subs.(3) provides that if the question is not settled within that time then the accused must be liberated. That does not, of course, bar a prosecution but there would be no bail domicile for the accused. Subsection (5) applies these provisions whether or not the accused is in custody in respect of a separate matter.

Bail applications

23.—[1](1) Any person accused on petition of a crime shall be entitled immediately, on any (other than the first) occasion on which he is brought before the sheriff prior to his committal until liberated in due course of law, to apply to the sheriff for bail, and the prosecutor shall be entitled to be heard against any such application.

(2) The sheriff shall be entitled in his discretion to refuse such application before the person accused is committed until liberated in due course of law.

(3) Where an accused is admitted to bail without being committed until liberated in due course of law, it shall not be necessary so to commit him, and it shall be lawful to serve him with an indictment or complaint without his having been previously so committed.

(4) Where bail is refused before committal until liberation in due course of law on an application under subsection (1) above, the application for bail may be renewed after such committal.

[2](5) Any sheriff having jurisdiction to try the offence or to commit the accused until liberated in due course of law may, at his discretion, on the application of any person who has been committed until liberation in due course of law for any crime or offence, and having given the prosecutor an opportunity to be heard, admit or refuse to admit the person to bail.

[3](6) Any person charged on complaint with an offence shall, on any (other than the first) occasion on which he is brought before a judge having jurisdiction to try the offence, be entitled to apply to the judge for bail and the prosecutor shall be entitled to be heard against any such application.

(7) An application under subsection (5) or (6) above shall be disposed of within 24 hours after its presentation to the judge, failing which the accused shall be forthwith liberated.

(8) This section applies whether or not the accused is in custody at the time he appears for disposal of his application.

DEFINITIONS
"bail": s.307(1).
"complaint": s.307(1).
"judge": s.307(1).
"offence": s.307(1).
"prosecutor": s.307(1).

NOTES
[1]As amended by the Bail, Judicial Appointments etc. (Scotland) Act (asp 9), s.12 and Sched., para. 7(1)(a).

[2]As amended by the Bail, Judicial Appointments etc. (Scotland) Act (asp 9), s.12 and Sched., para. 7(1)(b).
[3]Substituted by the Bail, Judicial Appointments etc. (Scotland) Act (asp 9), s.12 and Sched., para. 7(1)(c).

GENERAL NOTE

Subs. (1)
"*On petition*": This makes it clear that s.23(1) to (5) applies only to those accused at the outset of solemn procedure.
"*A crime which is by law bailable*": By s.24(1) all crimes are bailable except murder, treason and any others for which the Lord Advocate or the High Court admit the accused to bail. In *Boyle, Petr,* 1993 S.C.C.R. 251 an accused on a murder charge was admitted to bail.
"*On any occasion on which he is brought before the sheriff*": This makes it certain that the accused must be present at the time of the application to the sheriff.
"*Prior to his committal until liberated in due course of law*": An application for bail cannot be after such committal on this wording.
"*The prosecutor shall be entitled to be heard*": The Crown attitude is crucial but not conclusive, having regard to s.23(2). For examples, see *H.M. Advocate v. Saunders,* (1913) 7 Adam 76 and *Mackintosh v. McGlinchey,* 1921 J.C. 75.

Subs. (2)
"*His discretion*": The decision is one for the sheriff although the Crown attitude is crucial. There is no presumption in favour of the Crown on this question. The decision is based on attitude and is not amenable to proof. *Burn, Petr,* 2000 S.L.T. 538 requires the Crown to furnish some information to justify refusal of bail even at the first calling of the petition when moving for committal for further examination . Further the court indicated that as soon as practicable on the completion of the Crown's further enquiries an accused ought to be brought back before the sheriff.
There are important aspects to which, broadly, the court will have regard when exercising this discretion: (1) the more serious the crime the less willing the court is to allow bail, unless the Crown offers no objection: *Rennie v. Dickson,* (1907) 5 Adam 372; (2) the previous record of the accused is an important factor: *MacLeod v. Wright,* 1969 J.C. 12; (3) the attitude of the Crown; (4) no fixed abode weighs heavily but is not in itself sufficient to determine the question: *H.M. Advocate v. Docherty,* 1958 S.L.T. (Notes) 50; (5) breach of earlier bail, which tends to suggest a contempt for earlier judicial fairness; (6) evidence that the accused will intimidate or threaten witnesses if released.

Subs. (3)
Ordinarily, committal for further examination is followed thereafter by committal until liberated in due course of law. This provision makes it clear that the latter need not necessarily follow the former.

Subs. (4)
A single application for bail is not provided for by this section: an application may be made at the stage of committal for further examination and may be renewed later when the accused next appears. Such an appearance may be for committal until liberated in due course of law or it may be for the purpose of such an application by arrangement.

Subs. (5)
"*Jurisdiction*": This may be territorial or in terms of statutory powers: see ss.4 and 5.
In *Love, Petr,* 1998 S.L.T. 461, L. failed to appear for trial while on bail following committal until liberated in due course of law, and was refused bail on arrest. His application for bail had been made by petition to the nobile officium and L. appealed the refusal to the High Court. His appeal by that route was held to be incompetent, the Court noting that s.32(1) was the appropriate avenue for such appeals.

Subs. (6)
"*On complaint*": This extends shrieval discretion referred to in earlier subsections to "any judge having jurisdiction for the offence". For a definition of "judge", see s.308(1).

Subs. (8)

This subsection rehearses the provision in s.28(3) of the 1975 Act.

Bail and liberation where person already in custody

[1]**23A.**—(1) A person may be admitted to bail under section 22A or 23 of this Act although in custody—

(a) having been refused bail in respect of another crime or offence; or

(b) serving a sentence of imprisonment.

(2) A decision to admit a person to bail by virtue of subsection (1) above does not liberate the person from the custody mentioned in that subsection.

(3) The liberation under section 22A(3) or 23(7) of this Act of a person who may be admitted to bail by virtue of subsection (1) above does not liberate that person from the custody mentioned in that subsection.

DEFINITIONS

"bail": s.307(1).
"crime": s.307(1).
"offence": s.307(1).
"imprisonment": s.307(1).

NOTE

[1]Inserted by the Bail, Judicial Appointments etc. (Scotland) Act 2000 (asp 9), s.1.

GENERAL NOTE

The intention of this reform to long-standing legislation governing bail applications is to enable those serving terms of imprisonment, or on remand for other matters, to make formal application for bail. Hitherto the practice has been that bail applications could only be made when the petitioner was in an immediate position to be liberated on bail, otherwise the application had to be dismissed as incompetent. In the future the court will be obliged to consider a bail application even if the grant of bail cannot be given immediate effect.

In *Monterroso v. H.M. Advocate,* 2000 S.C.C.R. 974, the Appeal Court applied a purposive interpretation to subs. (1) and rejected the Crown's efforts to read the provision literally. *M* had been arrested on arrival in the United Kingdom and was remanded in custody on petition charges following a successful Crown bail appeal. Simultaneously the Home Secretary had refused *M* entry to the country as a result of these criminal allegations, a decision which led to a concurrent remand under the Immigration Act 1971 (c. 7). *M* sought judicial review of this remand, and bail in relation to the criminal charges. The Crown contended that subs. (1) did not competently apply to *M*'s peculiar circumstances. The Appeal Court held it competent to apply for bail but refused bail on the merits. (The civil proceedings are reported as *Monterroso v. Secretary of the Home Department,* 2000 G.W.D. 33–1295.)

Bail and bail conditions

24.—[1](1) All crimes and offences are bailable.

(2) Nothing in this Act shall affect the right of the Lord Advocate or the High Court to admit to bail any person charged with any crime or offence.

(3) It shall not be lawful to grant bail or release for a pledge or deposit of money, and—

(a) release on bail may be granted only on conditions which subject to subsection (6) below, shall not include a pledge or deposit of money;

(b) liberation may be granted by the police under section 21, 22 or 43 of this Act.

(4) In granting bail the court or, as the case may be, the Lord Advocate shall impose on the accused—

(a) the standard conditions; and

(b) such further conditions as the court or, as the case may be, the Lord Advocate considers necessary to secure—

(i) that the standard conditions are observed; and

(ii) that the accused makes himself available for the purpose of participating in an identification parade or of enabling any print, impression or sample to be taken from him.

(5) The standard conditions referred to in subsection (4) above are conditions that the accused—

(a) appears at the appointed time at every diet relating to the offence with which he is charged of which he is given due notice;

(b) does not commit an offence while on bail;

(c) does not interfere with witnesses or otherwise obstruct the course of justice whether in relation to himself or any other person; and

(d) makes himself available for the purpose of enabling enquiries or a report to be made to assist the court in dealing with him for the offence with which he is charged.

(6) The court or, as the case may be, the Lord Advocate may impose as one of the conditions of release on bail a requirement that the accused or a cautioner on his behalf deposits a sum of money in court, but only where the court or, as the case may be, the Lord Advocate is satisfied that the imposition of such condition is appropriate to the special circumstances of the case.

(7) In any enactment, including this Act and any enactment passed after this Act—

(a) any reference to bail shall be construed as a reference to release on conditions in accordance with this Act or to conditions imposed on bail, as the context requires;

(b) any reference to an amount of bail fixed shall be construed as a reference to conditions, including a sum required to be deposited under subsection (6) above;

(c) any reference to finding bail or finding sufficient bail shall be construed as a reference to acceptance of conditions imposed or the finding of a sum required to be deposited under subsection (6) above.

(8) In this section and sections 25 and 27 to 29 of this Act, references to an accused and to appearance at a diet shall include references respectively to an appellant and to appearance at the court on the day fixed for the hearing of an appeal.

DEFINITIONS

"bail": s.307(1).
"crime": s.307(1).
"diet": s.307(1).
"High Court": s.307(1).
"offences": s.307(1).
"standard conditions, the": s.24(5).

NOTE

[1]As amended by the Bail, Judicial Appointments etc. (Scotland) Act 2000 (asp 9), s.3(1).

GENERAL NOTE

Until the advent of the Bail, Judicial Appointments etc. (Scotland) Act 2000 (asp 9), bail in murder cases could only be obtained either at the behest of the Lord Advocate (whose refusal to admit to bail could not be challenged) or by petition to the Lord Advocate; otherwise murder was a non-bailable offence (see for example *H.M. Advocate v. Renwicks,* 1998 S.C.C.R. 417; 1999 S.L.T. 407). All crimes are now bailable, but it will be noted that the factors which would previously have justified opposition to bail—the risk of absconding, interference with witnesses, danger to public safety, the risk of further offending and the nature or gravity of the offence—remain valid grounds (see *Monterroso v. H.M. Advocate,* 2000 S.C.C.R. 974). The right of the Lord Advocate to admit persons to bail even after it has been refused, or not sought, at earlier points in proceedings, is preserved.

Ordinarily a bail order granted by the court will echo the terms of subs.(5) but additional conditions can be imposed, including where circumstances warrant, the imposition of money bail as caution, albeit this is unusual (see for example, *Adam v. Kirichenko,* 1995 G.W.D. 26–1373).

Bail conditions: supplementary

25.—(1) The court shall specify in the order granting bail, a copy of which shall be given to the accused—
(a) the conditions imposed; and
(b) an address, within the United Kingdom (being the accused's normal place of residence or such other place as the court may, on cause shown, direct) which, subject to subsection (2) below, shall be his proper domicile of citation.
(2) The court may on application in writing by the accused while he is on bail alter the address specified in the order granting bail, and this new address shall, as from such date as the court may direct, become his proper domicile of citation; and the court shall notify the accused of its decision on any application under this subsection.
(3) In this section "proper domicile of citation" means the address at which the accused may be cited to appear at any diet relating to the offence with which he is charged or an offence charged in the same proceedings as that offence or to which any other intimation or document may be sent; and any citation at or the sending of an intimation or document to the proper domicile of citation shall be presumed to have been duly carried out.

DEFINITIONS
"bail": s.307(1).
"order": s.307(1).
"proper domicile of citation": s.25(3).

GENERAL NOTE
The importance for the Crown of this provision lies in the terms of s.25(2) which allows service of the citation to appear at any diet on the accused at the "proper domicile of citation". The importance for the accused lies in his release but there is a balancing factor of providing such a domicile of citation: change is possible on application but failure to observe the requirements has serious consequences, or may have: *McMahon v. MacPhail*, 1991 S.C.C.R. 470. Further, the evidence of the points in this section is routine evidence under s.280(1) of and Sched. 9 to this Act and may thus be embodied in a certificate for service on the accused.

Bail: circumstances where not available

26.—[*Deleted by s.4 of the Bail, Judicial Appointments etc. (Scotland) Act 2000 (asp 9)*]

GENERAL NOTE
This section previously contained an absolute prohibition upon the grant of bail where an accused charged with attempted murder, culpable homicide, rape or attempted rape had a previous conviction for such an offence, or murder or manslaughter. The imperative nature of the section is plainly at odds with an accused's Art. 6 rights under the European Convention. Grounds for opposition to bail are discussed at p. 49.

Breach of bail conditions: offences

27.—(1) Subject to subsection (7) below, an accused who having been granted bail fails without reasonable excuse—
(a) to appear at the time and place appointed for any diet of which he has been given due notice; or
(b) to comply with any other condition imposed on bail,
shall, subject to subsection (3) below, be guilty of an offence and liable on conviction to the penalties specified in subsection (2) below.
(2) The penalties mentioned in subsection (1) above are—
(a) a fine not exceeding level 3 on the standard scale; and
(b) imprisonment for a period—
(i) where conviction is in the district court, not exceeding 60 days; or
(ii) in any other case, not exceeding 3 months.

(3) Where, and to the extent that, the failure referred to in subsection (1)(b) above consists in the accused having committed an offence while on bail (in this section referred to as "the subsequent offence"), he shall not be guilty of an offence under that subsection but, subject to subsection (4) below, the court which sentences him for the subsequent offence shall, in determining the appropriate sentence or disposal for that offence, have regard to—

    (a) the fact that the offence was committed by him while on bail and the number of bail orders to which he was subject when the offence was committed;

    (b) any previous conviction of the accused of an offence under subsection (1)(b) above; and

    (c) the extent to which the sentence or disposal in respect of any previous conviction of the accused differed, by virtue of this subsection, from that which the court would have imposed but for this subsection.

(4) The court shall not, under subsection (3) above, have regard to the fact that the subsequent offence was committed while the accused was on bail unless that fact is libelled in the indictment or, as the case may be, specified in the complaint.

[1](4A) The fact that the subsequent offence was committed while the accused was on bail shall, unless challenged—

    (a) in the case of proceedings on indictment, by giving notice of a preliminary objection under paragraph (b) of section 72(1) of this Act or under that paragraph as applied by section 71(2) of this Act; or

    (b) in summary proceedings, by preliminary objection before his plea is recorded,

be held as admitted.

(5) Where the maximum penalty in respect of the subsequent offence is specified by or by virtue of any enactment, that maximum penalty shall, for the purposes of the court's determination, by virtue of subsection (3) above, of the appropriate sentence or disposal in respect of that offence, be increased—

    (a) where it is a fine, by the amount for the time being equivalent to level 3 on the standard scale; and

    (b) where it is a period of imprisonment—

        (i) as respects a conviction in the High Court or the sheriff court, by 6 months; and

        (ii) as respects a conviction in the district court, by 60 days,

notwithstanding that the maximum penalty as so increased exceeds the penalty which it would otherwise be competent for the court to impose.

(6) Where the sentence or disposal in respect of the subsequent offence is, by virtue of subsection (3) above, different from that which the court would have imposed but for that subsection, the court shall state the extent of and the reasons for that difference.

(7) An accused who having been granted bail in relation to solemn proceedings fails without reasonable excuse to appear at the time and place appointed for any diet of which he has been given due notice (where such diet is in respect of solemn proceedings) shall be guilty of an offence and liable on conviction on indictment to the following penalties—

    (a) a fine; and

    (b) imprisonment for a period not exceeding two years.

(8) At any time before the trial of an accused under solemn procedure for the original offence, it shall be competent—

    (a) to amend the indictment to include an additional charge of an offence under this section;

    (b) to include in the list of witnesses or productions relating to the original offence, witnesses or productions relating to the offence under this section.

(9) The penalties provided for in subsection (2) above may be imposed in addition to any other penalty which it is competent for the court to impose, notwithstanding that the total of penalties imposed may exceed the maximum penalty which it is competent to impose in respect of the original offence.

(10) A court which finds an accused guilty of an offence under this section may remit the accused for sentence in respect of that offence to any court which is considering the original offence.

(11) In this section "the original offence" means the offence with which the accused was charged when he was granted bail or an offence charged in the same proceedings as that offence.

DEFINITIONS
   "bail": s.307(1).
   "indictment": s.307(1).
   "level 3": s.225(2) [*i.e.* £1,000].
   "offence": s.307(1).
   "original offence, the": s.27(11).
   "sentence": s.307(1).
   "standard scale": s.225(1).
   "subsequent offence, the": s.27(3).

GENERAL NOTE

Subss. (1) and (2)
   These subsections create the main offences of breaching bail conditions and to the extent that they replicate s.3(1) and (2) of the Bail, etc. (Scotland) Act 1980 they are not new. What is new is the increase in the maximum fine to level three on the standard scale; *i.e.* from £200 to £1,000.
   There has been an extensive number of decisions in regard to bail. Some of these are of a general nature.

Subs.(4)
   In *Boyd v. H.M. Advocate,* 2000 S.L.T. 1358 the libelling, as an aggravation of the substantive offence, the fact that it was committed while the accused was already on bail, was submitted to infringe Art.6(1) of the European Convention. *Boyd* contended that this would unfairly colour the jury's consideration of the merits: the court rejected this argument and held that a properly directed jury's impartiality would not be tainted by inclusion of a bail aggravation.

Subs. (4A)
   Prior to the coming into force of the Criminal Procedure (Scotland) Act 1995 it had been judicially determined that bail was a special capacity and, that in the absence of a timeous challenge to that capacity, the Crown did not require to prove that a bail order was in force (*Aitchison v. Tudhope,* 1981 J.C. 65; 1981 S.C.C.R. 1). However the cumulative effect of subss. (3) and (4) is that offending while subject of an earlier bail order now falls to be disposed of as an aggravation of the substantive offence; an enhanced sentence may only be imposed where the prosecutor has specifically libelled the existence of the bail order in the body of the substantive charge itself. When sentencing upon the substantive offence aggravated by being committed while on bail, the court shall impose one all-embracing sentence and minute (but apparently not pronounce) the element of sentence attributable to the aggravation (*Hill v. H.M. Advocate,* 1997 S.C.C.R. 376). Where separate offences are prosecuted on distinct complaints, and each offence has been aggravated by being committed while on bail, it is perfectly competent to impose consecutive sentences in relation to both the substantive offences and the aggravations (*Connal v. Carmichael,* 1996 G.W.D. 30–1807).
   An effect of the draftmanship of the 1995 Procedure Act, possibly unintended, was that bail ceased to be a special capacity and would henceforth have to be proved by the Crown. It will be noted that s.73 of the Criminal Procedure and Investigations Act 1996 (c. 25) has introduced the provisions now found in subs. (4A) which, by statute, reintroduce bail as a special capacity.
   These provisions apply only to bail contraventions arising after July 4, 1996 when that Act came into force. It will be appreciated that transitional problems of the sort highlighted in *Hamilton v. Robertson,* 1996 S.C.C.R. 539 are by no means at an end and that for some time to come there will be several narrow, but important, distinctions to be drawn before bail contraventions can competently be libelled and proved.
   Being subject of a bail order granted prior to March 31, 1996 (the date upon which the

52

Criminal Procedure (Scotland) Act 1995

Criminal Justice (Scotland) Act 1995, s.2, the statutory precursor of the 1995 Procedure Act, came into force) falls to be regarded as a special capacity in accordance with case law (*Aitchison v. Tudhope, supra*) and contraventions of that bail order should be libelled under s.3(1)(b) of the Bail etc. (Scotland) Act 1980 since it was under that legislation that bail was granted.

Different considerations apply where an accused person has been admitted to bail in terms of ss.24 and 25 of the Criminal Procedure (Scotland) Act 1995 after April 1, 1996 (or more rarely, on March 31, 1996 in terms of s.1 of the Criminal Justice (Scotland) Act 1996). In some situations (*i.e.* where such a bail order is contravened between March 31, 1996 and July 4, 1996) this will be an aggravating feature of the later offence, if the Crown elects to specify the existence of the earlier s.24 bail order in the libel, but will not be a special capacity; however where there are contraventions of any s.24 bail order libelled as having occurred after July 4, 1996 (the date when the provisions which now appear as s.27(4A) of the 1995 Procedure Act took effect) the existence of that bail order will be both a special capacity and an aggravating factor in sentencing any subsequent substantive offence.

Subs. (5)

The maximum penalty which may be imposed upon a summary complaint which incorporates a bail aggravation will ordinarily be one of nine months in the Sheriff Court and eight months in the District Court. The maximum penalty can increase in the Sheriff Court when the accused has cognate prior convictions as provided in subs. 5(3) of the Act. See *Hamilton v. Heywood*, 1998 S.L.T. 133.

Subs. (6)

The court's minute of the sentence imposed state the total sentence and then specify the period of the sentence attributed to the bail offence (*Cochrane v. Heywood*, 1998 G.W.D. 13–662).

Subs. (7)

It is commonplace to libel a contravention of s.27(7) as an additional charge in the indictment, indeed subs.(8) permits such a charge to be added by amendment up until the trial starts. In *Slater v. H.M. Advocate*, (High Court of Justiciary, November 22, 2000, unreported) this factor, and the *ratio* in *Boyd* (discussed in the Notes to subs.(4) above), caused the Appeal Court to refuse a motion for separation of the s.27(7) charge from others on the indictment. It remains the case that in order to advance a reasonable excuse for failing to appear, an accused may have to give evidence to explain his earlier absence and thus render himself liable to cross-examination on the substantive charges.

Subs. (8)

It has to be observed however that the terms of subs. (4A), as applied to solemn proceedings, obviously cannot operate in circumstances where the Crown makes use of the concession contained in subs. (8) and adds a bail offence to the original libel prior to the jury being sworn unless the amendment is made at least two days prior to the first (or the preliminary) diet. Such timeous amendment will preserve the Crown's right to treat the extant bail order as a fact of special capacity and, equally, afford the defence an opportunity to challenge that capacity by preliminary plea. Later amendment would deny the defence that preliminary plea and compel the Crown to prove the existence of the bail order alleged to have been contravened. (At the risk of complicating matters yet further, for the sake of completeness it has to be stressed that subs. (4A) is of no application to s.27 bail offences committed before July 4, 1996; in such cases the applicability of a bail order will always have to be proved.)

The court minutes must refer to grants of bail; see *MacNeill v. Smith* 1984 S.L.T.(Sh.Ct.) 63. Any special conditions imposed by the court must be stipulated expressly on the face of the copy bail order served upon the accused (*H.M. Advocate v. Crawford*, 1985 S.L.T. 242). It is clear that the currency of a bail order is not affected by whether any subsequent proceedings are solemn or summary (*McGinn v. H.M. Advocate*, 1991 S.L.T. 266) while in *Mayo v. Neizer*, 1994 S.L.T. 931 it was held that bail orders continue for so long as the accused is at liberty even if, as an appellant, he abandons an appeal against sentence and awaits arrest on a consequent warrant. In *Fitzpatrick v. Normand*, 1994 S.L.T. 1263 it was held that recall or modification of a bail order must be the subject of an express decision by the court.

It will be observed that s.31 *infra* entitles the prosecutor to apply for a review of bail or the conditions of bail.

Subs. (9)

It is a general rule where one substantive offence involves contravention of a number of separate bail orders, that sentences for the bail offences should be consecutive to any sentence imposed for the substantive offence but concurrent with each other: *Milligan v. Normand*, 1996 G.W.D. 24–1367, *Appleton v. Vannet*, 1996 G.W.D. 12–698 and *Stuart v. Heywood*, 1997 G.W.D. 31–1563. It is not incompetent to impose consecutive sentences for each bail offence (*Whyte v. Normand*, 1988 S.C.C.R. 465) and the onus for proving that such an exercise of judicial discretion was inappropriate seems to rest with the appellant rather than requiring justification by the sentencing judge. See *Nicholson v. Lees*, 1996 S.C.C.R. 551 (at 561B) which summarises the general principles governing the imposition of concurrent and consecutive sentences and note also *Connal v. Carmichael*, 1996 G.W.D. 30–1807. Generally backdating of a sentence to take account of time on remand awaiting trial is usual, and the reasons for refusal of backdating should be specified in the minutes. However in the case of a failure to appear for trial, particularly on indictment, it cannot be presumed that backdating will occur even where an acquittal is obtained on the original substantive charges (*Bowers v. H.M. Advocate*, 1997 G.W.D. 31–1562).

Act of Adjournal
   Refer to Chap. 5 of the Act of Adjournal (Criminal Procedure Rules) 1996 (S.I. 1996 No. 2147) in relation to alteration (or opposing the alteration) of the address specified in a bail order.

NOTE
   [1]Inserted by the Criminal Procedure and Investigations Act 1996 (c. 25), s.73(2).

Breach of bail conditions: arrest of offender, etc.

   28.—(1) A constable may arrest without warrant an accused who has been released on bail where the constable has reasonable grounds for suspecting that the accused has broken, is breaking, or is likely to break any condition imposed on his bail.
   (2) An accused who is arrested under this section shall wherever practicable be brought before the court to which his application for bail was first made not later than in the course of the first day after his arrest, such day not being, subject to subsection (3) below, a Saturday, a Sunday or a court holiday prescribed for that court under section 8 of this Act.
   (3) Nothing in subsection (2) above shall prevent an accused being brought before a court on a Saturday, a Sunday or such a court holiday where the court is, in pursuance of the said section 8, sitting on such day for the disposal of criminal business.
   (4) Where an accused is brought before a court under subsection (2) or (3) above, the court, after hearing the parties, may—
   (a) recall the order granting bail;
   (b) release the accused under the original order granting bail; or
   (c) vary the order granting bail so as to contain such conditions as the court thinks it necessary to impose to secure that the accused complies with the requirements of paragraphs (a) to (d) of section 24(5) of this Act.
   (5) The same rights of appeal shall be available against any decision of the court under subsection (4) above as were available against the original order of the court relating to bail.
   (6) For the purposes of this section and section 27 of this Act, an extract from the minute of proceedings, containing the order granting bail and bearing to be signed by the clerk of court, shall be sufficient evidence of the making of that order and of its terms and of the acceptance by the accused of the conditions imposed under section 24 of this Act.

Bail: monetary conditions

   29.—(1) Without prejudice to section 27 of this Act, where the accused or a cautioner on his behalf has deposited a sum of money in court under section 24(6) of this Act, then—

(a) if the accused fails to appear at the time and place appointed for any diet of which he has been given due notice, the court may, on the motion of the prosecutor, immediately order forfeiture of the sum deposited;

(b) if the accused fails to comply with any other condition imposed on bail, the court may, on conviction of an offence under section 27(1)(b) of this Act and on the motion of the prosecutor, order forfeiture of the sum deposited.

(2) If the court is satisfied that it is reasonable in all the circumstances to do so, it may recall an order made under subsection (1)(a) above and direct that the money forfeited shall be refunded, and any decision of the court under this subsection shall be final and not subject to review.

(3) A cautioner, who has deposited a sum of money in court under section 24(6) of this Act, shall be entitled, subject to subsection (4) below, to recover the sum deposited at any diet of the court at which the accused appears personally.

(4) Where the accused has been charged with an offence under section 27(1)(b) of this Act, nothing in subsection (3) above shall entitle a cautioner to recover the sum deposited unless and until—

(a) the charge is not proceeded with; or

(b) the accused is acquitted of the charge; or

(c) on the accused's conviction of the offence, the court has determined not to order forfeiture of the sum deposited.

(5) The references in subsections (1)(b) and (4)(c) above to conviction of an offence shall include references to the making of an order in respect of the offence under section 246(3) of this Act.

Bail review

30.—(1) This section applies where a court has refused to admit a person to bail or, where a court has so admitted a person, the person has failed to accept the conditions imposed or that a sum required to be deposited under section 24(6) of this Act has not been so deposited.

(2) A court shall, on the application of any person mentioned in subsection (1) above, have power to review its decision to admit to bail or its decision as to the conditions imposed and may, on cause shown, admit the person to bail or, as the case may be, fix bail on different conditions.

(3) An application under this section, where it relates to the original decision of the court, shall not be made before the fifth day after that decision and, where it relates to a subsequent decision, before the fifteenth day thereafter.

(4) Nothing in this section shall affect any right of a person to appeal against the decision of a court in relation to admitting to bail or to the conditions imposed.

DEFINITION
"bail": s.307(1).

GENERAL NOTE
This section applies in a number of separate circumstances: *e.g.* the court may have refused to admit a person to bail. For the general guidelines as to the allowance or refusal of bail, see *Smith v. M.*, 1982 S.L.T. 421. Alternatively, a court may have so admitted a person but the person has failed to accept the conditions imposed: for a special condition that was challenged see *Brawls v. Walkingshaw*, 1994 S.C.C.R. 7. Also, a court may have required the deposit of a sum of money but that has not been done. In any or all of these circumstances, a person may seek to have the original decision reviewed within modest statutory time-limits and yet otherwise appeal the original decision.

In *Ogilvie v. H.M. Advocate*, 1998 G.W.D. 9–438, O's petition for review of refusal of bail was rejected by the sift judge considering O's appeal who was unaware that leave to appeal had been granted by the trial judge and had not seen the trial judge's report. At the full hearing the Court held that review was competent given the terms of s.30 but that leave to appeal a conviction did not automatically infer that an application for bail pending appeal should be granted. See also s.112 below.

Bail review on prosecutor's application

31.—(1) On an application by the prosecutor at any time after a court has granted bail to a person the court may, where the prosecutor puts before the court material information which was not available to it when it granted bail to that person, review its decision.

(2) On receipt of an application under subsection (1) above the court shall—
(a) intimate the application to the person granted bail;
(b) fix a diet for hearing the application and cite that person to attend the diet; and
(c) where it considers that the interests of justice so require, grant warrant to arrest that person.

(3) On hearing an application under subsection (1) above the court may—
(a) withdraw the grant of bail and remand the person in question in custody; or
(b) grant bail, or continue the grant of bail, either on the same or on different conditions.

(4) Nothing in the foregoing provisions of this section shall affect any right of appeal against the decision of a court in relation to bail.

DEFINITIONS
"bail": s.307(1).
"diet": s.307(1).
"prosecutor": s.307(1).

GENERAL NOTE
This section enables the prosecutor to apply to the court to reconsider a decision to grant bail. Application must be made on the basis of information relevant to the decision to grant bail which was not available to the court when the decision was taken. Subsection (2) describes the procedure to be followed on receipt of an application by a prosecutor. Subsection (3) specifies the options available to the court on hearing the prosecutor's application. In the absence of this provision under the 1980 Act one reported solution was to petition the court for warrant to apprehend the accused; see *Lockhart v. Stokes*, 1981 S.L.T.(Sh.Ct.) 71 where efforts to serve an indictment foundered because the domicile given had ceased to be a proper domicile of citation.

Bail appeal

32.—[1](1) Where, in any case, bail is refused or where the accused is dissatisfied with the amount of bail fixed, he may appeal to the High Court which may, in its discretion order intimation to the Lord Advocate or, as the case may be, the prosecutor.

[3](2) Where, in any case, is granted, or, in summary proceedings an accused is ordained to appear, the public prosecutor, if dissatisfied—
(a) with the decision allowing bail;
(b) with the amount of bail fixed; or
(c) in summary proceedings, that the accused has been ordained to appear,
may appeal to the High Court, and the applicant shall not be liberated, subject to subsection (7) below, until the appeal by the prosecutor is disposed of.

(3) Written notice of appeal shall be immediately given to the opposite party by a party appealing under this section.

(4) An appeal under this section shall be disposed of by the High Court or any Lord Commissioner of Justiciary in court or in chambers after such inquiry and hearing of parties as shall seem just.

[2](5) Where an accused in an appeal under this section is under 21 years of age, section 51 of this Act shall apply to the High Court or, as the case may be, the Lord Commissioner of Justiciary when disposing of the appeal as it applies to a court when remanding or committing a person of the accused's age for trial or sentence.

(6) In the event of the appeal of the public prosecutor under this section being refused, the court may award expenses against him.

[2](7) When an appeal is taken by the public prosecutor either against the grant of bail or against the amount fixed, the accused to whom bail has been granted shall, if the bail fixed has been found by him, be liberated after 72 hours from the granting of the bail, whether the appeal has been disposed of or not, unless the High Court grants an order for his further detention in custody.

(8) In computing the period mentioned in subsection (7) above, Sundays and public holidays, whether general or court holidays, shall be excluded.

(9) When an appeal is taken under this section by the prosecutor in summary proceedings against the fact that the accused has been ordained to appear, subsections (7) and (8) above shall apply as they apply in the case of an appeal against the granting of bail or the amount fixed.

(10) Notice to the governor of the prison of the issue of an order such as is mentioned in subsection (7) above within the time mentioned in that subsection bearing to be sent by the Clerk of Justiciary or the Crown Agent shall be sufficient warrant for the detention of the applicant pending arrival of the order in due course of post.

DEFINITIONS
  "bail": s.307(1).
  "Clerk of Justiciary": s.307(1).
  "complaint": s.307(1).
  "governor": s.307(1).
  "High Court": s.307(1).
  "Lords Commissioner of Justiciary": s.307(1).
  "order": s.307(1).
  "prison": s.307(1).
  "prosecutor": s.307(1).

NOTES
  [1]Subsituted by the Bail, Judicial Appointments etc. (Scotland) Act 2000 (asp 9), s.4.
  [2]As amended by the Bail, Judicial Appointments etc. (Scotland) Act 2000 (asp 9), s.12 and Sched., para. 7(2)(a).
  [3]As amended by the Bail, Judicial Appointments etc. (Scotland) Act 2000 (asp 9), s.12 and Sched., para. 7(2)(b).

GENERAL NOTE
  The essence of this section in the most general of terms is that, by subs. (1), the accused may appeal a refusal of bail and by subs. (2) the Crown may appeal the grant of bail. Each party appealing must give written notice to the other side, by subs. (3). Disposal of the appeal may be by the High Court or a single judge in court or in chambers: subs. (4).
  Section 32(1) affords the means for an appeal against refusal of bail: see *Love, Petr*, 1998 G.W.D. 11–528, discussed at p.47 above.

Bail: no fees exigible

33. No clerks fees, court fees or other fees or expenses shall be exigible from or awarded against an accused in respect of a decision on bail under section 22A above, an application for bail or of the appeal of such a decision or application to the High Court.

DEFINITIONS
  "bail": s.307(1).
  "High Court": s.307(1).

NOTE
  [1]As amended by the Bail, Judicial Appointments etc. (Scotland) Act (asp 9), s.12 and Sched., para.7(3)(a) and (b).

PART IV

PETITION PROCEDURE

Warrants

Petition for warrant

34.—(1) A petition for warrant to arrest and commit a person suspected of or charged with crime may be in the forms—
  (a) set out in Schedule 2 to this Act; or
  (b) prescribed by Act of Adjournal,
or as nearly as may be in such form; and Schedule 3 to this Act shall apply to any such petition as it applies to the indictment.

(2) If on the application of the procurator fiscal, a sheriff is satisfied that there is reasonable ground for suspecting that an offence has been or is being committed by a body corporate, the sheriff shall have the like power to grant warrant for the citation of witnesses and the production of documents and articles as he would have if a petition charging an individual with the commission of the offence were presented to him.

GENERAL NOTE
  Solemn proceedings are generally initiated by the presentation of a petition to a sheriff in chambers. The petition may be put before the court along with the person accused of the crime, or the Crown may petition for a warrant to arrest the accused: on occasion where several accused are involved the petition may take both forms. In *Hamilton v. H.M. Advocate* 1997 S.L.T. 31, a prosecution under the Trades Description Act 1968, it was held that in contrast to England where proceedings were deemed to commence with service of an indictment (an event which would affect calculation of the time-bar on proceedings), in Scotland proceedings commenced with the obtaining of a petition warrant by the prosecutor or by service of an indictment when no initiating petition had been obtained. Offences committed by corporate bodies can in terms of subs. (2) also be initiated by way of the same petition procedure and, when granted by the court, give the same powers to the Crown as would a petition against an individual accused. Prior to the enactment of s.74(7) of the 1975 Act the form of petition used for offences committed by such bodies was derived from the Criminal Justice (Scotland) Act 1949, s.40(7); indeed until the Second World War solemn proceedings against companies or other corporate bodies were unknown.
  The crimes charged are narrated in the third person and s.40 of the 1995 Act requires that the principal petition must be signed by the prosecutor (normally a fiscal or a fiscal depute) and by a sheriff, both of whom must have a jurisdiction derived from one or more of the charges libelled. Subsection (1) refers to the forms of indictments set out in Sched. 2 to the Act. It will be noted that these charges originated in the Criminal Procedure (Scotland) Act 1887 (c.35) and many are arcane, obsolescent or obsolete (it has to be doubted that the Crown would ever libel a crime euphemistically as an "attempt to ravish" or "ravish" now—the charge would be one of attempted rape or rape).
  As a matter of course the warrant granted by the court will authorise (i) the arrest of the accused and require that he be brought before the court for examination, (ii) the search of his abode or other premises for the purpose of such arrest and to gather evidence, (iii) the citation of witnesses and the production to the Crown of documentary and label productions, and (iv) after examination, his committal for further examination or until liberated in due course of law (technically the first-mentioned step is unnecessary in situations where the petition is of even

date with the first appearance of the accused or where the accused is a body corporate). In order to fulfil the Crown's obligations under the European Convention on Human Rights, arts 5 and 6, a fuller narration of the circumstances which the prosecutor alleges justify the charges libelled in the petition is now routinely served on the accused when the Crown moves for committal for further examination. A fuller outline of the Crown case is likely to follow at full committal. It is usual for this additional information to be put in a paper apart, rather than within the body of the petition itself. Either approach would be acceptable (*Brown v. Selfridge*, 2000 S.L.T. 437). See also *Hamilton v. Vannet*, 1999 G.W.D. 8–406.

In the absence of voluntary provision by the accused, or the securing by the police of bodily samples by way of the powers contained in section 18 of the Act, a separate warrant would have to be craved by the prosecutor to obtain blood or other body fluid samples where invasive means were to be used. See *Mellors v. Normand*, 1996 G.W.D. 14–817 and the authorities cited in the Notes to s.18 above.

Judicial examination

Judicial examination

35.—(1) The accused's solicitor shall be entitled to be present at the examination.

(2) The sheriff may delay the examination for a period not exceeding 48 hours from and after the time of the accused's arrest, in order to allow time for the attendance of the solicitor.

(3) Where the accused is brought before the sheriff for examination on any charge and he or his solicitor intimates that he does not desire to emit a declaration in regard to such a charge, it shall be unnecessary to take a declaration, and, subject to section 36 of this Act, the accused may be committed for further examination or until liberated in due course of law without a declaration being taken.

(4) Nothing in subsection (3) above shall prejudice the right of the accused subsequently to emit a declaration on intimating to the prosecutor his desire to do so; and that declaration shall be taken in further examination.

(5) Where, subsequent to examination or further examination on any charge, the prosecutor desires to question the accused as regards an extrajudicial confession, whether or not a full admission, allegedly made by him to or in the hearing of a constable, which is relevant to the charge and as regards which he has not previously been examined, the accused may be brought before the sheriff for further examination.

(6) Where the accused is brought before the sheriff for further examination the sheriff may delay that examination for a period not exceeding 24 hours in order to allow time for the attendance of the accused's' solicitor.

(7) Any proceedings before the sheriff in examination or further examination shall be conducted in chambers and outwith the presence of any co-accused.

(8) This section applies to procedure on petition, without prejudice to the accused being tried summarily by the sheriff for any offence in respect of which he has been committed until liberated in due course of law.

DEFINITIONS
"constable": s.307(1) and s.51(1) of the Police (Scotland) Act 1967.
"procurator": s.307(1).
"sheriff": s.4(1) and (4).

GENERAL NOTE
The process of judicial examination is often a part of petition procedure and its origins can be found in the Criminal Procedure (Scotland) Act 1887. After the passing of the Criminal Evidence Act 1898 (c.36) the practice of making "no plea; no declaration" became almost universal and while it remains competent for an accused to make a judicial declaration, it is now a rare event.

As with all petition procedure, judicial examination is held in private, outwith the presence of any co-accused or their agents.

The right of an accused person to emit a judicial declaration is preserved by s.35(4) of the 1995 Act and this can be made at any time before service of the indictment. The terms of a previously prepared statement can be declared by an accused provided that the words used are truly his own; it is not permissible for another person, even his solicitor, to edit or style the declaration since this may alter its sense or character (see *Carmichael v. Armitage*, 1982 S.C.C.R. 475).

A rare modern example of a declaration being made and not properly recorded either to meet the statutory requirements of s.20B of the 1975 Act or even the common law standards which prevailed prior to the 1980 Act is found in *Robertson v. H.M. Advocate*, 1995 S.C.C.R. 153, discussed in the notes to s.37 below.

Subsection (5) affords the prosecutor an opportunity then, or at a later time, to question the accused either about the contents of such a declaration or about any new admission made to, or heard by, a police officer which is deemed relevant to the charge libelled on the petition.

The prosecutor's right to examine upon any new material certainly can be exercised at any time before service of the indictment and arguably, by inference from *Frame v. Houston*, 1995 S.C.C.R. 436, up until the trial commences.

Section 17(2) of the 1995 Act stipulates that the accused shall be entitled to a private interview with his solicitor prior to judicial examination or court appearance and s.35(2), in effect, places the court under an obligation to ensure that access to legal advice has been offered. There is no requirement that an accused person must have had such a private interview or be legally represented at his judicial examination, but the court has to draw the accused's attention to his right to such services. Failure to do so may vitiate any admissions made in the course of the declaration by an accused without benefit of legal representation: see *H.M. Advocate v. Goodall*, (1888) 2 White 1.

Subsection (6) gives the sheriff a discretion to delay the first examination for a further 24 hours to allow for the attendance of the agent nominated by the accused. Until the first examination has been concluded it is not competent for the accused to apply for bail.

There is no obligation upon the Crown to seek to judicially examine an accused in any petition case; the procedure for conduct of judicial examinations is laid out in s.36 of the Act and ss.37 and 38 specify the form of the record of proceedings. Additional provisions are found in the Act of Adjournal (Criminal Procedure Rules 1996), Chaps. 5 and 25.

Judicial examination: questioning by prosecutor

36.—(1) Subject to the following provisions of this section, an accused on being brought before the sheriff for examination on any charge (whether the first or a further examination) may be questioned by the prosecutor in so far as such questioning is directed towards eliciting any admission, denial, explanation, justification or comment which the accused may have as regards anything to which subsections (2) to (4) below apply.

(2) This subsection applies to matters averred in the charge, and the particular aims of a line of questions under this subsection shall be to determine—

(a) whether any account which the accused can give ostensibly discloses a defence; and

(b) the nature and particulars of that defence.

(3) This subsection applies to the alleged making by the accused, to or in the hearing of a constable, of an extrajudicial confession (whether or not a full admission) relevant to the charge, and questions under this subsection may only be put if the accused has, before the examination, received from the prosecutor or from a constable a written record of the confession allegedly made.

(4) This subsection applies to what is said in any declaration emitted in regard to the charge by the accused at examination.

(5) The prosecutor shall, in framing questions in exercise of his power under subsection (1) above, have regard to the following principles—

(a) the question should not be designed to challenge the truth of anything said by the accused;

(b) there should be no reiteration of a question which the accused has refused to answer at the examination; and

(c) there should be no leading questions,

and the sheriff shall ensure that all questions are fairly put to, and understood by, the accused.

(6) The accused shall be told by the sheriff—

(a) where he is represented by a solicitor at the judicial examination, that he may consult that solicitor before answering any question; and

(b) that if he answers any question put to him at the examination under this section in such a way as to disclose an ostensible defence, the prosecutor shall be under the duty imposed by subsection (10) below.

(7) With the permission of the sheriff, the solicitor for the accused may ask the accused any question the purpose of which is to clarify any ambiguity in an answer given by the accused to the prosecutor at the examination or to give the accused an opportunity to answer any question which he has previously refused to answer.

(8) An accused may decline to answer a question under subsection (1) above; and, where he is subsequently tried on the charge mentioned in that subsection or on any other charge arising out of the circumstances which gave rise to the charge so mentioned, his having so declined may be commented upon by the prosecutor, the judge presiding at the trial, or any co-accused, only where and in so far as the accused (or any witness called on his behalf) in evidence avers something which could have been stated appropriately in answer to that question.

(9) The procedure in relation to examination under this section shall be prescribed by Act of Adjournal.

(10) Without prejudice to any rule of law, on the conclusion of an examination under this section the prosecutor shall secure the investigation, to such extent as is reasonably practicable, of any ostensible defence disclosed in the course of the examination.

(11) The duty imposed by subsection (10) above shall not apply as respects any ostensible defence which is not reasonably capable of being investigated.

DEFINITIONS

"constable": s.307(1) and s.51(1) of the Police (Scotland) Act 1967.

"prosecutor": s.307(1).

GENERAL NOTE

Section 35(7) provides that judicial examination is to be conducted in chambers outwith the presence of any other accused. It is not mandatory that the accused be legally represented at his judicial examination but it is the norm.

In terms of s.39, charges arising from other sheriff court jurisdictions can competently be included in the petition before the sheriff and the accused can be examined upon all charges.

The procedures specified in s.36 are recognisably derived from s.20A of the 1975 Act but the 1995 Act incorporates the amendments introduced by s.10(1) of the Criminal Justice (Scotland) Act 1995 (c.20): in summary these allow more direct questioning of the accused, require the Crown to make reasonable enquiry into any defence tendered by an accused in the course of his examination and, accordingly, oblige the presiding sheriff to impart additional information to the accused in the course of the judicial admonition which must precede any examination.

The prosecutor is not obliged to conduct a judicial examination at either the first or the further examination stage, but if he elects to do so he must adhere to the provisions laid down in s.36.

The role of the defence solicitor is still a reactive one; he may only consult with his client when the accused requests advice or intervene through the sheriff, as provided by subs. (7), to clarify ambiguities or to solicit answers to questions previously unanswered by the accused. Regulation of the proceedings remains the responsibility of the presiding sheriff.

At no time is an oath administered to the accused and nor can he be cross-examined, facts which following *Morrison v. H.M. Advocate*, 1990 S.C.C.R. 235 at 248E, the trial judge should make known to the jury at trial.

Subs. (1)

The revised terms of subs. (1) now make reference to the prosecutor's function to be able to question the accused about the charge with a view to securing any "admission" as well as any "denial, explanation, justification or comment" the accused may offer. On a strict interpretation of the 1980 Act's provisions the Crown could not directly ask an accused whether he admitted the charge in whole or part, only whether he denied the allegations entirely or not. Such a literal reading hardly lent clarity to the proceedings; indeed one means of complying with such a rigourous interpretation was to question the accused using a double negative ("Is there any part of the charge you do not deny?") then relieve the confusion with the obvious question ("Do you admit the charge or any part of it?"). Such circumlocutions should now be unnecessary but the radical nature of this apparently small amendment should not be under-estimated: an accused may now be asked questions which are directly aimed to achieve his self-incrimination, and his failure to answer (as subs. (8) provides) can be commented upon if he leads evidence at trial. Moreover his position can be still worse if he simply declines to answer any question put at judicial examination and fails to lead evidence at his trial, since s.32 of the Criminal Justice (Scotland) Act 1995, which repealed s.141(1)(b) of the 1975 Act and now effectively entitles the prosecutor to comment upon such a failure.

Subs. (2)

The scope of the prosecutor's questions in relation to the charge itself are restricted to eliciting whether the accused will advance any sort of defence at the examination. A greater (but still limited) latitude is available to the procurator fiscal when the accused is alleged to have uttered an extrajudicial admission: see the discussion relative to subs. (3) below.

It is of note that subs. (2) is explicitly drafted more broadly than was s.20A(1)(a) of the 1975 Act. As well as the generally understood defences of self-defence, alibi, incrimination and consent it could be argued that temporary insanity, certain forms of automatism, lawful authority or coercion could each equally constitute a defence.

Once a possible defence is stated at judicial examination subs. (10) below places a limited obligation upon the Crown to investigate its substance. Note however that there is no *compulsitor* upon the Crown, and no timescale specified for the conduct of these enquiries or even a duty to report findings to the court. Nonetheless it would be imprudent to ignore this provision if only because it would then be open to the accused at his trial to found upon any lack of diligence in investigating the defence tendered. It is submitted that in terms of subs. (2)(b) the fiscal can justifiably question the accused to obtain sufficient information to allow the Crown to fulfil the statutory duty imposed by subs. (10), namely, investigation of the defence revealed by the examination. During the Committee stage of the Bill the Lord Advocate reiterated that if the procurator fiscal discovered evidence at this stage of proceedings which might assist the accused, then it would be the Crown's duty to make the fact known to the defence (*Hansard*, January 12, 1995, Vol. 560, col. 369).

In the absence of a statutory duty to disclose the outcome of an investigation of any stated defence, or any sanction upon the Crown for failing to investigate, the Appeal Court held in *McDermott v. H.M. Advocate*, 2000 S.L.T. 366 that the provisions in subss. (2) and (10) were administrative in character. The obligation upon the Crown to disclose to the defence evidence which is potentially favourable to an accused's case is stated in *McLeod, Petr*, 1998 S.L.T. 233. In *McDermott* the trial judge was criticised for reaching the view, in the absence of evidence one way or the other, that the Crown had not complied with s.37, and for leaving the jury to resolve whether the prosecutor's conduct had been prejudicial.

Subs. (3)

In addition to questions about the charge itself and any defence which the accused may then wish to tender as provided by subs. (1) and (2), the fiscal may also examine the accused upon any extrajudicial utterance made by him to, or within earshot of, a police officer. Note that the Crown may choose whether or not to put these alleged words to the accused and may elect not to do so, particularly when the reply is either mixed, self-serving or discloses previous convictions or references to matters not libelled. See *H.M. Advocate v. Cafferty*, 1984 S.C.C.R. 444.

The 1996 Act of Adjournal stipulates that examination about such extrajudicial admissions can only occur if the presiding sheriff has first received a copy of the text of admissions already served on the accused; this does no more than codify the existing practice.

Although the usual procedure is for the procurator fiscal to examine initially upon the charges on the petition and any appropriate defences before questioning about any alleged replies, there is no statutory necessity to follow this chronology; the only requirements are that the "confession", partial or full, must be served upon the accused in written form prior to the examination for questioning to be permitted and the rules of the 1996 Act of Adjournal are obeyed.

Normally the statement of extrajudicial confessions is annexed to the copy petition served on the accused, though this is not a mandatory requirement. It will have to (i) specify the wording averred to have been used by the accused; (ii) identify the police officer in whose hearing the words were uttered and, by inference, the time and place of the event in order to qualify as legitimate material for the purposes of subs. (3). Where the accused has been interviewed on tape by the police this is usually indicated on the statement of extrajudicial admissions. When the accused has made a voluntary statement which is incriminating, it is the practice to annex a copy of it to the petition and question him about its contents and the circumstances in which it was made.

All of this raises the intractable issue of what does, or does not, constitute an extrajudicial confession: this is particularly problematical when the statement made is in part self-serving or is a veiled attack on the complainer's character (see *Morrison v. H.M. Advocate*, 1990 S.C.C.R. 235 discussed in the notes to subs. (8) below).

In *McKenzie v. H.M. Advocate*, 1982 S.C.C.R. 544 objection was taken by the agent at the examination, to a reply attributed to the accused on the grounds that it was not a confession. The sheriff allowed questioning by the fiscal and permitted the agent to clarify at the conclusion of the questioning. It is submitted that there is no *locus* for such an objection by the agent at this stage in proceedings; it is then solely a matter for judicial discretion. The appropriate time for objection is if, or when, either party (or a co-accused) seeks to found upon the transcript of judicial examination at the trial. The fairness and admissibility of the transcript can be properly weighed then and, in any event, such an approach excludes the possibility of the trial judge being called upon to review the earlier decision of the sheriff who presided at the examination. See also *Moran v. H.M. Advocate*, 1990 S.C.C.R. 40; 1990 S.L.T. 756.

Subss. (5), (6) and (7)

Judicial examination is not an opportunity for the Crown to cross-examine the accused. Subsection (5) underlines the role of the sheriff to ensure the fair conduct of proceedings. The accused must be informed by the sheriff (i) of the right to consult the solicitor appearing with him prior to answering questions and (ii) that the Crown will be under an obligation to investigate, so far as practicable, any defence disclosed during the examination. It is submitted that a judicial failure to admonish the accused with due regard to subss. (6), (8) and (10) would render the resultant transcript of proceedings inadmissible.

Note however that the solicitor's role in the examination is reactive; he may not initiate a consultation with his client during questioning by the fiscal and may only ask questions of his client as permitted by subs. (7). While that subsection does not expressly stipulate it, the practice has developed of giving leave to the defence solicitor to question at the conclusion of the fiscal's examination.

Subs. (8)

The object of judicial examination is to cause the accused at the earliest stage in proceedings to state his defence both as a means of focusing the issues and as a deterrent to the introduction of spurious lines of defence at the trial. While the accused is entitled to keep his own counsel at the examination, this may work to his disadvantage at his trial when other parties can utilise the provisions of subs. (8) to undermine his defence case. However the 1996 Act of Adjournal rule 5.5(4) imposes possible limits upon the freedom of others to comment upon contrasts in the accused's position at judicial examination and in his evidence at trial. It is now a matter for the trial judge to consider whether such comments can be made to the jury by other parties, or the judge himself, having regard to the terms of the original petition charges and the libel now before the court. To assist in the judge's deliberations, the prosecutor must be able to provide the original petition or a certified copy.

A number of issues flow from this reform; first, it would seem to be good practice for the Crown as a matter of course to include a certified copy of the petition and, by implication, a certified copy of the written record of any extrajudicial admissions referred to during the examination. Secondly the provision suggests that before either the prosecutor or other accused invoke the right to comment under s.36(8), they should seek the authority of the presiding judge to do so. Thirdly, if the judge resolves to comment it would seem sensible, to say the least, to refer to the original petition and canvass the views of the parties, including the co-accused, before hand and outwith the presence of the jury.

Support for this reading can be found in Chap. 25 of the 1996 Rules, for rule 25.1(3) permits the trial judge to release copies to the jury of any written record of confession (appropriately edited) referred to during judicial examination.

It must be stressed that subs. (8) only comes into play when the accused leads evidence, from himself or other witnesses, at his trial. An accused who has declined to comment at examination and has not led evidence at trial is outwith the subsection's scope. See *Walker v. H.M. Advocate*, 1985 S.C.C.R. 150 and *Dempsey v. H.M. Advocate*, 1995 S.C.C.R. 431.

In *Walker* it was held on appeal that the statutory provisions of the 1975 Act, s.20A(5) were wrongly applied, the accused having maintained silence throughout and left the Crown to prove its case. Even then note, that while it was conceded that the trial judge had misdirected the jury, this did not in the circumstances, constitute a miscarriage of justice. Nonetheless where the judge does direct the attention of the jury to the operation of subs. (8) this must be done with restraint and without undue emphasis; see *McEwan v. H.M. Advocate*, 1990 S.C.C.R. 401.

It is common for an accused during examination to decline to answer questions and to state that this has been done on the advice of his solicitor. This stock reply does not protect an accused from unfavourable comment should he choose to lead evidence at his trial. Thus the judge's direction in *Gilmour v. H.M. Advocate*, 1982 S.C.C.R. 590 at 604, that such conduct at judicial examination could not be considered as relevant evidence is much too favourable to the accused. See *Alexander v. H.M. Advocate*, 1988 S.C.C.R. 542.

Subsection (8) does not deal with the potentially intractable situation where an accused, at judicial examination, responds to questioning by providing a self-serving account and founds upon it at trial without leading further evidence. Just such a situation arose in *Morrison*, above, a seven judge decision, which deals (it is hoped) definitively with the approach to mixed statements, or qualified admissions, including extrajudicial confessions. The law is stated at 247F to 248E and is discussed fully by Dr D.B. Griffiths, in *Confessions* (Edinburgh 1994) at pp.90 to 97: Dr Griffiths' comment that *Morrison* "is a difficult case and is always going to remain so", defies contradiction.

Prudence dictates that at trial the presiding judge would do well simply to echo and endorse the "Morrison formula" cited above. See *Smith v. H.M. Advocate*, 1994 S.C.C.R. 72; *Pickthall v. H.M. Advocate*, 1998 S.L.T. 117 (conviction quashed), *MacLeod v. H.M. Advocate*, 1995 S.L.T. 145, *Harley v. H.M. Advocate*, 1995 S.C.C.R. 595 *Geddes v. H.M. Advocate*, 1997 S.L.T. 392 (convictions upheld despite failure to follow *Morrison* explicitly). *Hoy v. H.M. Advocate* 1997 S.L.T. 26 in which the trial judge consciously declined to make a *Morrison* direction, authority was granted for a retrial. Opinion has been reserved however as to whether founding upon exculpatory answers given in the course of a judicial examination would be sufficient to meet the burden of proof resting upon an accused in charges under the Prevention of Corruption Act 1906 (c. 34) (*Ridler v. H.M. Advocate*, 1995 S.C.C.R. 655).

Section 32 of the Criminal Justice (Scotland) Act 1995 which repealed s.141(1)(b) of the 1975 Act now entitles the prosecutor, but not co-accused, to comment upon the accused's failure to lead evidence. The removal of this long-standing prohibition introduces a much more telling weapon into the prosecutor's armoury than s.36(8) of the 1995 Act allows. The long-recognised right of the trial judge to comment upon the accused's failure to give evidence under oath was upheld in *Handley v. H.M. Advocate*, 1998 S.L.T. 1104.

Subss. (10) and (11)
See the discussion in the notes to subs. (2) above.

Act of Adjournal
Additional provisions are found in the Act of Adjournal (Criminal Procedure Rules) 1996, Chaps. 5 and 25. See particularly r.5.5.

Judicial examination: record of proceedings

37.—(1) The prosecutor shall provide for a verbatim record to be made by means of shorthand notes or by mechanical means of all questions to and answers and declarations by the accused in examination, or further examination, under sections 35 and 36 of this Act.

(2) A shorthand writer shall—

(a) sign the shorthand notes taken by him of the questions, answers and declarations mentioned in subsection (1) above and certify the notes as being complete and correct; and

(b) retain the notes.

(3) A person recording the questions, answers and declarations mentioned in subsection (1) above by mechanical means shall—

(a) certify that the record is true and complete;

(b) specify in the certificate the proceedings to which the record relates; and

(c) retain the record.

(4) The prosecutor shall require the person who made the record mentioned in subsection (1) above, or such other competent person as he may specify, to make a transcript of the record in legible form; and that person shall—

(a) comply with the requirement;

(b) certify the transcript as being a complete and correct transcript of the record purporting to have been made and certified, and in the case of shorthand notes signed, by the person who made the record; and
(c) send the transcript to the prosecutor.
(5) A transcript certified under subsection (4)(b) above shall, subject to section 38(1) of this Act, be deemed for all purposes to be a complete and correct record of the questions, answers and declarations mentioned in subsection (1) above.
(6) Subject to subsections (7) to (9) below, within 14 days of the date of examination or further examination, the prosecutor shall—
(a) serve a copy of the transcript on the accused examined; and
(b) serve a further such copy on the solicitor (if any) for that accused.
(7) Where at the time of further examination a trial diet is already fixed and the interval between the further examination and that diet is not sufficient to allow of the time limits specified in subsection (6) above and subsection (1) of section 38 of this Act, the sheriff shall (either or both)—
(a) direct that those subsections shall apply in the case with such modifications as to time limits as he shall specify;
(b) subject to subsection (8) below, postpone the trial diet.
(8) Postponement under paragraph (b) of subsection (7) above alone shall only be competent where the sheriff considers that to proceed under paragraph (a) of that subsection alone, or paragraphs (a) and (b) together, would not be practicable.
[1](9) Any time limit mentioned in subsection (6) above and subsection (1) of section 38 of this Act (including any such time limit as modified by a direction under subsection (7) above) may be extended, in respect of the case, by the High Court; and an application to the High Court for any such extension shall be disposed of by the High Court or any Lord Commissioner of Justiciary in court or in chambers.
(10) A copy of—
(a) a transcript required by paragraph (a) of subsection (6) above to be served on an accused or by paragraph (b) of that subsection to be served on his solicitor; or
(b) a notice required by paragraph (a) of section 38(1) of this Act to be served on an accused or on the prosecutor,
shall be served in such manner as may be prescribed by Act of Adjournal; and a written execution purporting to be signed by the person who served such transcript or notice, together with, where appropriate, the relevant post office receipt shall be sufficient evidence of service of such a copy.

DEFINITION
"prosecutor": s.307(1).

NOTE
[1]As amended by the Act of Adjournal (Extension of Time Limit for Service of Transcript of Examination) 1998 (S.I. 1998 No. 2635: effective December 1, 1998).

GENERAL NOTE
This section provides that the record of proceedings at any judicial declaration or judicial examination is to be noted in shorthand or mechanically recorded. In either case it then becomes the responsibility of the prosecutor to effect service upon the accused and his agent of a transcript of the proceedings duly certified as complete and accurate by the person appointed to transcribe the record by the prosecutor. Service must be effected within 14 days of the hearing unless as subs. (7) allows, a trial diet occurs within that time or either the prosecutor or the accused have in terms of s.38 sought rectification of the transcript: in either of these events the sheriff has power to modify the timescale laid out in subs. (6) or, alternatively, postpone the trial diet. The High Court can review the sheriff's decision.
The Act of Adjournal (Criminal Procedure Rules) Chap. 5 regulates the use of both shorthand and tape transcription; applications for rectification of transcripts are to be in the form specified in these Rules.

In *Robertson v. H.M. Advocate*, 1994 S.C.C.R. 152 the previous provisions under s.20B of the 1975 Act were considered. The appellant by Minute of Notice took objection to the competency of proceedings following failure by the Crown either to record his declaration or to serve it upon him prior to the trial diet: he alleged that this could prejudice his case and nullified any proceedings.

While it is of note that the charge which had formed the subject matter of the petition had not been libelled in the subsequent indictment, and the likelihood of prejudice would be slim, the Appeal Court considered the much more fundamental issue of whether or not the provisions of the section were obligatory (in which event the Crown's non-compliance must result in a nullity) or directory in character.

The court in a majority decision took the latter view but it has to be said that even then that conclusion was reached with little common agreement on either the approach or terminology to be adopted. The best that can be said is that while some statutory provisions are so fundamental that failure to comply creates a nullity, s.20B (or its statutory successor) s.37 of the 1995 Act are not such provisions.

For completeness, following conviction Robertson persisted with claims before the Appeal Court that his defence had been prejudiced by the unavailability of his declaration at trial. Following remit to the Sheriff Principal to investigate it was concluded that the declaration did not relate to the subject matter of the indictment, was entirely exculpatory in nature, and the matter could have been, but had not been, raised in the course of the trial and accordingly could not appropriately be raised on appeal. See *Robertson v. H.M. Advocate*, 1996 S.C.C.R. 243; 1996 G.W.D. 5–254.

Refer to s.278 below which deals with the principles to be applied to use of judicial examination transcripts at any trial.

Act of Adjournal
See the Act of Adjournal (Criminal Procedure Rules) 1996 r.5.2 and Form 5.2 which deal with the record of proceedings. The form to be used for intimation where a trial diet has been postponed for the purpose of s.37(7) is found at Form 5.8.

Judicial examination: rectification of record of proceedings

38.—(1) Subject to subsections (7) to (9) of section 37 of this Act, where notwithstanding the certification mentioned in subsection (5) of that section the accused or the prosecutor is of the opinion that a transcript served under paragraph (a) of subsection (6) of that section contains an error or is incomplete he may—
  (a) within 10 days of service under the said paragraph (a), serve notice of such opinion on the prosecutor or as the case may be the accused; and
  (b) within 14 days of service under paragraph (a) of this subsection, apply to the sheriff for the error or incompleteness to be rectified,
and the sheriff shall within 7 days of the application hear the prosecutor and the accused in chambers and may authorise rectification.
  (2) Where—
  (a) the person on whom notice is served under paragraph (a) of subsection (1) above agrees with the opinion to which that notice relates the sheriff may dispense with such hearing;
  (b) the accused neither attends, nor secures that he is represented at, such hearing it shall, subject to paragraph (a) above, nevertheless proceed.
  (3) In so far as it is reasonably practicable so to arrange, the sheriff who deals with any application made under subsection (1) above shall be the sheriff before whom the examination or further examination to which the application relates was conducted.
  (4) Any decision of the sheriff, as regards rectification under subsection (1) above, shall be final.

DEFINITION
  "prosecutor": s.307(1).

The procedure for the rectification of errors in, or addition of materials omitted from, the transcript of judicial examination or any declaration are found in this section. If the partiesconcur that such rectification or amendment is required, then no hearing is necessary; otherwise the prosecutor is obliged to be represented at any hearing though an accused or his agent need not attend.

Act of Adjournal
See the Act of Adjournal (Criminal Procedure Rules) 1996 particularly r.5.6 and Forms 5.6–A to 5.6–C.

Judicial examination: charges arising in different districts

39.—(1) An accused against whom there are charges in more than one sheriff court district may be brought before the sheriff of any one such district at the instance of the procurator fiscal of such district for examination on all or any of the charges.

(2) Where an accused is brought for examination as mentioned in subsection (1) above, he may be dealt with in every respect as if all of the charges had arisen in the district where he is examined.

(3) This section is without prejudice to the power of the Lord Advocate under section 10 of this Act to determine the court before which the accused shall be tried on such charges.

DEFINITIONS
"procurator fiscal": s.307(1).
"sheriff court district": s.307(1).

GENERAL NOTE
The Lord Advocate's discretion to select which sheriff court shall exercise jurisdiction over offences arising from more than one jurisdiction is preserved by this section.

Committal

Committal until liberated in due course of law

40.—(1) Every petition shall be signed and no accused shall be committed until liberated in due course of law for any crime or offence without a warrant in writing expressing the particular charge in respect of which he is committed.

(2) Any such warrant for imprisonment which either proceeds on an unsigned petition or does not express the particular charge shall be null and void.

(3) The accused shall immediately be given a true copy of the warrant for imprisonment signed by the constable or person executing the warrant before imprisonment or by the prison officer receiving the warrant.

GENERAL NOTE
The petition should correspond with the forms prescribed in Scheds. 2 and 3 of the Act or as near as may be; see s.34 above and the general note thereto.

In *Mellors v. Normand*, 1996 S.C.C.R. 500 a bill of suspension was taken against full committal on a petition which had charged M. with attempting to defeat the ends of justice by his failure to provide blood and saliva samples and dental impressions in compliance with an earlier warrant; while the bill was refused on its merits as being premature, it is noted that the Crown did not challenge its competency. There is no doubt that if an essential feature of a petition charge (designation of accused, a charge and sufficient information in support of the petition) is absent then a bill to suspend a committal warrant would be competent. No such deficiencies were evident in M.'s case.

PART V

CHILDREN AND YOUNG PERSONS

Age of criminal responsibility

41. It shall be conclusively presumed that no child under the age of eight years can be guilty of any offence.

DEFINITION
"child": s.307(1) and s.93(2)(b) of the Children (Scotland) Act 1995.

GENERAL NOTE
This provision repeats the presumption of nonage found in the Children and Young Persons (Scotland) Act 1937 (c.37), s.55. See also Macdonald (5th ed., Edinburgh 1948), p. 271.
Consequently proceedings against a child aged less than eight years are incompetent and should be disposed of by means of a plea in bar of trial at a first diet in sheriff and jury proceedings or a preliminary diet in the High Court (refer to ss.71 to 73 below).

Prosecution of children

42.—(1) No child under the age of 16 years shall be prosecuted for any offence except on the instructions of the Lord Advocate, or at his instance; and no court other than the High Court and the sheriff court shall have jurisdiction over a child under the age of 16 years for an offence.

(2) Where a child is charged with any offence, his parent or guardian may in any case, and shall, if he can be found and resides within a reasonable distance, be required to attend at the court before which the case is heard or determined during all the stages of the proceedings, unless the court is satisfied that it would be unreasonable to require his attendance.

(3) Where the child is arrested, the constable by whom he is arrested or the police officer in charge of the police station to which he is brought shall cause the parent or guardian of the child, if he can be found, to be warned to attend at the court before which the child will appear.

(4) For the purpose of enforcing the attendance of a parent or guardian and enabling him to take part in the proceedings and enabling orders to be made against him, rules may be made under section 305 of this Act, for applying, with the necessary adaptations and modifications, such of the provisions of this Act relating to summary proceedings as appear appropriate for the purpose.

(5) The parent or guardian whose attendance is required under this section is—

   (a) the parent who has parental responsibilities or parental rights (within the meaning of sections 1(3) and 2(4) respectively of the Children (Scotland) Act 1995) in relation to the child; or

   (b) the guardian having actual possession and control of him.

(6) The attendance of the parent of a child shall not be required under this section in any case where the child was before the institution of the proceedings removed from the care or charge of his parent by an order of a court.

(7) Where a child is to be brought before a court, notification of the day and time when, and the nature of the charge on which, the child is to be so brought shall be sent by the chief constable of the area in which the offence is alleged to have been committed to the local authority for the area in which the court will sit.

(8) Where a local authority receive notification under subsection (7) above they shall make such investigations and submit to the court a report which shall contain such information as to the home surroundings of the child as appear to them will assist the court in the disposal of his case, and the report shall contain information, which the appropriate education authority

shall have a duty to supply, as to the school record, health and character of the child.

(9) Any child detained in a police station, or being conveyed to or from any criminal court, or waiting before or after attendance in such court, shall be prevented from associating with an adult (not being a relative) who is charged with any offence other than an offence with which the child is jointly charged.

(10) Any female child shall, while detained, being conveyed or waiting as mentioned in subsection (9) above, be kept under the care of a woman.

DEFINITIONS

"child": s.307(1) and s.93(2)(b) of the Children (Scotland) Act 1995.
"constable": s.307(1) and s.51(1) of the Police (Scotland) Act 1967.
"High Court": s.307(1).
"local authority": s.307(1).
"parent or guardian": s.42(5) below and in relation to "guardian" only, note also s.307(1).

GENERAL NOTE

While it is theoretically the case that reports of criminal offences committed by children will be submitted to the procurator fiscal in the first instance, administrative directions from the Lord Advocate instruct that such reports involving child offenders aged under 16 years will, ordinarily, be referred to the principal reporter for his consideration. Even where there are factors which merit the submission of a report to the procurator fiscal, the police are still required in terms of s.38(2) of the Social Work (Scotland) Act 1968 (c.49) to furnish a copy of the report to the appropriate reporter. Thereafter it is a matter for discussion between the procurator fiscal and the reporter whether the case should be retained for criminal prosecution or dealt with under the previously-mentioned Act.

When the case is retained by the procurator fiscal to initiate a prosecution, it is mandatory in terms of subs. (1) that any proceedings must occur in the sheriff court or a higher court. Rule 6.3 of the 1996 Act of Adjournal enacts that criminal proceedings can only be raised by the procurator fiscal who is, of course, required to comply with the Lord Advocate's directions. The spirit of s.15 of the 1995 Act (which enacts special provisions in regard to the detention of a child, and parental access to a child held in custody) is echoed in s.54: subss. (9) and (10) contain provisions to segregate children from adult offenders while remanded in custody or awaiting trial at court. Oddly, it is not deemed necessary to separate the child entirely from adult accused. Subsection (9) stops short of this and permits detention in custody, or in the court precincts, and transportation to or from court appearances, in the company of adult co-accused or relatives (whether the relatives are, or are not, accused persons).

In a similar spirit, s.142 of the Act stipulates that summary proceedings against a child must be held in private and in different rooms, or on different days, from the criminal courts in which adults appear. The sole exception to this rule is when the child appears on the same complaint or petition as an adult accused; in that event the case has to proceed in the usual "adult" court. The corollary of these provisions so far as an adult co-accused is concerned, is that when charged along with a child on a summary complaint he will necessarily appear in the sheriff, not the district, court.

The scope of s.142 (which replaces s.366(1) of the 1975 Act) extends to appearances from custody, cited diets and trials but it has been held to be directory rather than mandatory in character: failure by the court to obtemper its provisions would not nullify any subsequent conviction; see *Heywood v. B.*, 1993 S.C.C.R. 554. It is likely that the provisions of s.42 would equally be construed as being directory in nature. Similarly the 1996 Act of Adjournal, Rule 6.8 indicates that steps should be taken by the court to avoid children attending hearings from mixing with each other by appropriate scheduling of cases and providing suitable supervision of waiting facilities.

Subss. (3), (7) and (8)

Subsection (3) instructs the police to notify the parent or guardian of the child of the impending court appearance and, wherever practicable, to require parental attendance at the court on the appropriate date. Unreasonable failure to attend the court by a parent or guardian after receipt of such notice can attract criminal penalties and, accordingly, the police should warn of this fact when giving notice of the court date.

Where the child is already in the care of the local authority or has a guardian as a result of a court order, the police are under no duty to advise the parent (defined in subs. (5)(a)) of the proceedings. The date and time of the child's court appearance, and the nature of charges must also be communicated by the police to the local authority within whose boundaries the court is situated. In the event of a finding of guilt, that authority will be responsible for preparing background reports about the child's circumstances for the court.

Act of Adjournal
   Refer to Chap. 6 of the Act of Adjournal (Criminal Procedure Rules) 1996 for procedural guidance.

Arrangements where children arrested

43.—[1](1) Where a person who is apparently a child is apprehended, with or without warrant, and cannot be brought forthwith before a sheriff, a police officer of the rank of inspector or above or the officer in charge of the police station to which he is brought, shall inquire into the case, and, subject to subsection (3) below, may liberate him—
   (a) on a written undertaking being entered into by him or his parent or guardian that he will attend at a court and at a time specified in the undertaking; or
   (b) unconditionally liberate him on a written undertaking being entered into by him or his parent or guardian that he will attend at the hearing of the charge.
   (2) An undertaking mentioned in subsection (1) above shall be signed by the child or, as the case may be, the parent or guardian and shall be certified by the officer mentioned in that subsection.
   (3) A person shall not be liberated under subsection (1) where—
   (a) the charge is one of homicide or other grave crime;
   (b) it is necessary in his interest to remove him from association with any reputed criminal or prostitute; or
   (c) the officer has reason to believe that his liberation would defeat the ends of justice.
   (4) Where a person who is apparently a child having been apprehended is not liberated as mentioned in subsection (1) above, the police officer referred to in that subsection shall cause him to be kept in a place of safety other than a police station until he can be brought before a sheriff unless the officer certifies—
   (a) that it is impracticable to do so;
   (b) that he is of so unruly a character that he cannot safely be so detained; or
   (c) that by reason of his state of health or of his mental or bodily condition it is inadvisable so to detain him,
and the certificate shall be produced to the court before which he is brought.
   (5) Where a person who is apparently a child has not been liberated as mentioned in subsection (1) above but has been kept under subsection (4) above, and it is decided not to proceed with the charge against him, a constable shall so inform the Principal Reporter.
   [2,3](6) Any person, who without reasonable excuse fails to appear at the court and at the time specified in the undertaking entered into by him or on his behalf under subsection (1) above, shall be guilty of an offence, and liable on summary conviction of any charge made against him at the time he was liberated under that subsection in addition to any other penalty which it is competent for the court to impose on him, to a fine not exceeding level 3 on the standard scale.
   (7) In any proceedings relating to an offence under this section, a writing, purporting to be such an undertaking as is mentioned in subsection (1) above and bearing to be signed and certified, shall be sufficient evidence of the undertaking given by the accused.

DEFINITIONS
   "child": s.307(1) and s.93(2)(b) of the Children (Scotland) Act 1995.
   "parent or guardian": s.42(5) and in relation to "guardian" only also refer to s.307(1).

"place of safety": s.307(1) and s.93(1) of the Children (Scotland) Act 1995.
"Principal Reporter": s.93(1) of the Children (Scotland) Act 1995.

NOTES
[1]Substituted by the Crime and Punishment (Scotland) Act 1997 (c. 48) s.55(2) with effect from August 1, 1997 in terms of the Crime and Punishment (Scotland) Act 1997 (Commencement and Transitional Provisions) Order 1997 (S.I. 1997 No. 1712) para. 3.
[2]Substituted by the 1997 Act s.55(3) with effect from August 1, 1997 by the above Order.
[3]Inserted by s.55(3) of said Act with effect from August 1, 1997 as above.

GENERAL NOTE
This section repeats the provisions previously contained in ss.295 and 296 of the 1975 Act with account being taken of the introduction of the Children (Scotland) Act 1995 and small, but significant, changes wrought by the Crime and Punishment (Scotland) Act 1997. It is still to be assumed generally that a child arrested for a criminal offence will be brought before a court without delay, or be liberated on his undertaking, or that of his parent or guardian, to appear at court on a specified date. Subs. (1) as now enacted gives greater discretion to the police to withhold an undertaking. Once an undertaking is entered into, failure to appear at the designated time and place becomes an offence but only in the event of conviction of the original charge which gave rise to the undertaking. The terms of the undertaking can be proved in any proceedings by production of a certified copy of the original form and, it is submitted, that the signatory is in a position of special capacity. While the Act does not specify the form the undertaking should take, subs. (7) clearly envisages that it should be in writing.
In more serious cases as defined in subs. (3), the first effort should be to bring the child before a sheriff forthwith. If that is not practicable, then the senior police officer involved must first endeavour to obtain accommodation for the child in a place of safety, namely a local authority residential establishment, a community home, a hospital, surgery or "other suitable place" whose occupier is willing to take in the child.
Note that while the statutory definition of "a place of safety" in the Children (Scotland) Act, s.93(1) includes a police station, this does not hold good for the purposes of s.43(4) of the 1995 Act—police stations are expressly excluded as acceptable accommodation for this purpose. The reason for this apparent anomaly is found later in subs. (4) which stipulates the conditions which must prevail before a child can be held in police custody pending his appearance before the court: broadly, if it is not practical to convey the child to a suitable place of safety or such a place is not available, or the child's character is unruly and militates against his safe detention in an available place of safety, or there are medical grounds which raise concern for his well-being, then continued detention in a police station will be justified. The senior police officer must then certify the reasons for resorting to detention of the child in police custody rather than the preferred option of a place of safety and that certificate must be produced to the court when the child first appears. It will be noted that during such a period of detention, the police are still obliged to keep the child segregated from adult prisoners (see the notes to s.42(9) above).
If the procurator fiscal decides not to proceed with charges against the child, subss. (6) and (7) contain saving provisions to enable the child to be detained pending initial investigation by the principal reporter (see s.56(1) and (6) of the Children (Scotland) Act 1995) and consideration if necessary by a children's hearing within seven days.

Detention of children

44.—(1) Where a child appears before the sheriff in summary proceedings and pleads guilty to, or is found guilty of, an offence to which this section applies, the sheriff may order that he be detained in residential accommodation provided under Part II of the Children (Scotland) Act 1995 by the appropriate local authority for such period not exceeding one year as may be specified in the order in such place (in any part of the United Kingdom) as the local authority may, from time to time, consider appropriate.

(2) This section applies to any offence in respect of which it is competent to impose imprisonment on a person of the age of 21 years or more.

(3) Where a child in respect of whom an order is made under this section is detained by the appropriate local authority, that authority shall have the same powers and duties in respect of the child as they would have if he were subject to a supervision requirement.

[1](4) Where a child in respect of whom an order is made under this section is also subject to a supervision requirement ... the supervision requirement

shall be of no effect during any period for which he is required to be detained under the order.

(5) The Secretary of State may, by regulations made by statutory instrument subject to annulment in pursuance of a resolution of either House of Parliament, make such provision as he considers necessary as regards the detention in secure accommodation of children in respect of whom orders have been made under this section.

[1](6) ...

[1](7) ...

[1](8) ...

[1](9) ...

[1](10) Where a local authority consider it appropriate that a child in respect of whom an order has been made under subsection (1) above should be detained in a place in any part of the United Kingdom outside Scotland, the order shall be a like authority as in Scotland to the person in charge of the place to restrict the child's liberty to such an extent as that person may consider appropriate having regard to the terms of the order.

(11) In this section—

"the appropriate local authority" means—

(a) where the child usually resides in Scotland, the local authority for the area in which he usually resides;

(b) in any other case, the local authority for the area in which the offence was committed; and

"secure accommodation" has the meaning assigned to it in Part II of the Children (Scotland) Act 1995.

DEFINITIONS

"appropriate local authority": s.44(11).

"child": s.307(1) and s.93(2)(b) of the Children (Scotland) Act 1995.

"offence": s.307(1).

"residential accommodation": s.307(1).

"secure accommodation": s.44(11) and s.93(1) of the Children (Scotland) Act 1995.

"supervision requirement": s.307(1) and s.70(1) of the Children (Scotland) Act 1995.

NOTE

[1]Deleted by the Crime and Punishment (Scotland) Act 1997 (c. 48) s.62(1) and Sched. 1, para. 21(3) with effect from August 1, 1997 in terms of the Crime and Punishment (Scotland) Act 1997 (Commencement and Transitional Provisions) Order 1997 (S.I. 1997 No. 1712) para. 3.

GENERAL NOTE

This section enables a sheriff sitting summarily to impose a term of detention in residential accommodation of up to one year when an offence, for which imprisonment could competently be imposed upon an adult, is held or admitted to have been committed by a child. The sheriff may then consider immediate use of his powers under s.44 or, in the first instance (and more usually), refer the case under s.49 of the Act to the Principal Reporter for the advice of a children's hearing: when the child is already under a supervision requirement, s.49(3)(b) stipulates that the advice of a children's hearing must be obtained.

Only a minority of cases will be likely to merit a disposal in terms of s.44 without first obtaining the advice of a children's hearing. The use of s.44 powers is perhaps an indication that the paramount consideration in sentencing has been public safety and the preservation of good order rather than the well-being of the child. Most cases involving juveniles found guilty of offences will continue to require the advice of a children's hearing.

Statutory duties of local authority

When the sheriff either with, or less usually without, advice of a children's hearing imposes detention under s.44, it is then the duty of the Scottish local authority within whose area the child lives, to provide such accommodation at a place within the United Kingdom selected by the authority. However if the child is not ordinarily resident in Scotland then this responsibility falls upon the local authority within whose area the offence was committed. It is not explicitly stated in the Act, but it seems reasonable to assume that, in the event of offences being committed in a number of jurisdictions, responsibility for providing suitable accommodation would rest with the local authority within whose area the sheriff court making the order was situated.

Subsection (3) provides that the powers and responsibilities of a local authority given charge of such a child will be the same as those regulating supervision requirements and reference to s.70(4) of the Children (Scotland) Act shows that this includes such restrictions on the child's liberty as are deemed appropriate.

Where supervision requirements are imposed by a children's hearing, the hearing can direct that the child resides in residential accommodation or (in more extreme cases) in such accommodation but under secure conditions (see s.70(3) and (8) of the Children (Scotland) Act 1995). Subsection (1) of the 1995 Act states that the court can order that the child "be detained" in residential accommodation, while subs. (5) deals with the regulation of secure accommodation. It is unfortunate that the same phraseology has not been employed consistently in both pieces of legislation, but the provisions of subs. (6) suggest that what is envisaged is placement of the child in secure accommodation and not simply local authority residential care.

Subsection (10) permits the Scottish local authority exercising jurisdiction to remit the child into the custody of persons elsewhere in the United Kingdom when this is felt appropriate. The persons then assuming responsibility for the charge of the child have the same duties and powers as would be vested in an individual under s.44 in Scotland.

Early release provisions and effect of further offences

In a manner similar to s.16 of the Prisoners and Criminal Proceedings (Scotland) Act 1993 (c.9) (which deals with the commission of offences by released prisoners during remission), subs. (6) affords a child an opportunity of remission of at least half of the period of detention. This concession can be rescinded if it is established that a further offence has been committed during the remission period and the timescale of the original detention order has not expired (in practice it may be difficult to re-apply the unexpired portion of the detention period since the sentence imposed under s.44 by the sheriff may have been relatively short).

In the event of re-offending being established the court can apply a full range of disposals but subs. (8) makes it competent to return the child to the residential accommodation from which he was earlier released there to serve the unexpired portion of that earlier detention, calculated according to subs. (8). This re-imposition of the order can be instead of, or in addition to, any disposal resulting from the later offence which had been committed during the early release period. Subsection (9) adds that the remaining portion of the original detention order may be served prior to, or concurrent with, the period of detention imposed for the later offence.

Section 44 and existing supervision requirements

Where the child appearing before the court is already the subject of a supervision requirement made by a children's hearing, subs. (4) provides for the suspension of that requirement until the appropriate period of detention has been served by the child.

On release from detention (either at the expiry of the full term of detention imposed by the court, or earlier in accordance with subs. (6)(a)), the pre-existing supervision requirement can be resumed. However, even when detention has been imposed by the court, the local authority still has a statutory duty to review the case of any child subject to a supervision requirement (see s.72(6) of the Children (Scotland) Act 1995) and has a discretionary power under the 1995 Act to conduct such a review for children detained by way of a s.44 order—see subs. (6)(b). Indeed, theoretically, such a s.44 review could constitute the first contact between the hearing and the child offender since, as was noted earlier, the statutory obligation upon the sentencing sheriff to seek the advice of a children's hearing before imposing a period of detention upon the child only applies to children who were already subject to a current supervision requirement.

When reviewing the case of a child detained under a s.44 order, the hearing may, following subs. (6) discharge it altogether or vary its terms once due regard has been paid to both the interests of the child and the protection of the public.

Security for child's good behaviour

45.—(1) Where a child has been charged with an offence the court may order his parent or guardian to give security for his co-operation in securing the child's good behaviour.

(2) Subject to subsection (3) below, an order under this section shall not be made unless the parent or guardian has been given the opportunity of being heard.

(3) Where a parent or guardian has been required to attend and fails to do so, the court may make an order under this section.

(4) Any sum ordered to be paid by a parent or guardian on the forfeiture of any security given under this section may be recovered from him by civil diligence or imprisonment in like manner as if the order had been made on the conviction of the parent or guardian of the offence with which the child was charged.

(5) In this section "parent" means either of the child's parents, if that parent has parental responsibilities or parental rights (within the meaning of sections 1(3) and 2(4) respectively of the Children (Scotland) Act 1995) in relation to him.

Definitions
"child": s.307(1) and s.93(2)(b) of the Children (Scotland) Act 1995.
"offence": s.307(1).
"parent": s.45(5) and ss.1(3), 2(4) and 3(5) of the Children (Scotland) Act 1995.
"guardian": s.307(1).

General Note
This section permits the court to require caution to be found by the parent or *de facto* guardian of the child as a surety for parental co-operation in assuring the future good conduct of the child. Such a condition can only be imposed after the parent or guardian has been given an opportunity to be heard by the court, but it has been ruled unnecessary for a formal citation to attend there to have been served upon him; notification made by a police officer would probably suffice. See *White v. Jeans* (1911) 6 Adam 489 and *Montgomery v. Grey* (1915) 7 Adam 681. Note that subs. (2) does not stipulate that the parent must have been heard, only that the opportunity to be heard has been given. The court under subs. (3) can order attendance by the parent or guardian and require a finding of security, even in the absence of the person concerned. Failure by the parent or guardian to ensure the orderly conduct of the child can result in forfeiture of the amount of security. This can be recovered by civil diligence or by the imprisonment of the guarantor.

Presumption and determination of age of child

46.—[1](1) Where a person charged with an offence whose age is not specified in the indictment or complaint in relation to that offence is brought before a court other than for the purpose of giving evidence, and it appears to the court that he is a child, the court shall make due enquiry as to the age of that person, and for that purpose shall take such evidence as may be forthcoming at the hearing of the case, and the age presumed or declared by the court to be the age of that person shall, for the purposes of this Act or the Children and Young Persons (Scotland) Act 1937, be deemed to be the true age of that person.

(2) The court in making any inquiry in pursuance of subsection (1) above shall have regard to the definition of child for the purposes of this Act.

[1](3) Without prejudice to section 255A of this Act, where in an indictment or complaint for—
- (a) an offence under the Children and Young Persons (Scotland) Act 1937;
- (b) any of the offences mentioned in paragraphs 3 and 4 of Schedule 1 to this Act; or
- (c) an offence under section 1, 10(1) to (3) or 12 of the Criminal Law (Consolidation) (Scotland) Act 1995,

it is alleged that the person by or in respect of whom the offence was committed was a child or was under or had attained any specified age, and he appears to the court to have been at the date of the commission of the alleged offence a child, or to have been under or to have attained the specified age, as the case may be, he shall for the purposes of this Act or the Children and Young Persons (Scotland) Act 1937 or Part I of the Criminal Law (Consolidation) (Scotland) Act 1995 be presumed at that date to have been a child or to have been under or to have attained that age, as the case may be, unless the contrary is proved.

(4) Where, in an indictment or complaint for an offence under the

Children and Young Persons (Scotland) Act 1937 or any of the offences mentioned in Schedule 1 to this Act, it is alleged that the person in respect of whom the offence was committed was a child or was a young person, it shall not be a defence to prove that the person alleged to have been a child was a young person or the person alleged to have been a young person was a child in any case where the acts constituting the alleged offence would equally have been an offence if committed in respect of a young person or child respectively.

(5) An order or judgement of the court shall not be invalidated by any subsequent proof that—

  (a) the age of a person mentioned in subsection (1) above has not been correctly stated to the court; or

  (b) the court was not informed that at the material time the person was subject to a supervision requirement or that his case had been referred to a children's hearing by virtue of regulations made under the Children (Scotland) Act 1995 for the purpose of giving effect to orders made in different parts of the United Kingdom.

(6) Where it appears to the court that a person mentioned in subsection (1) above has attained the age of 17 years, he shall for the purposes of this Act or the Children and Young Persons (Scotland) Act 1937 be deemed not to be a child.

(7) In subsection (3) above, references to a child (other than a child charged with an offence) shall be construed as references to a child under the age of 17 years; but except as aforesaid references in this section to a child shall be construed as references to a child within the meaning of section 307 of this Act.

DEFINITIONS

    "child": s.307(1) and s.93(2)(b) of the Children (Scotland) Act 1995. Note that a more restricted definition is employed in relation to subs. (3) only by virtue of subs. (7).
    "offence": s.307(1).

NOTE

    [1]Inserted by the Crime and Punishment (Scotland) Act 1995 (c. 48) s.62(1) and Sched. 1, para. 21(4) with effect from August 1, 1997 by the Crime and Punishment (Scotland) Act 1997 (Commencement and Transitional Provisions) Order 1997 (S.I. 1997 No. 1712) para. 3.

GENERAL NOTE

    This section repeats the provisions found in the 1975 Act as amended and, in effect, contains saving provisions to prevent proceedings in which children are involved either as witnesses or as accused, being invalidated on account of error as to a child's age. The savings only operate to cure a want of procedure and cannot cure a nullity (note that in addition to the provisions of s.46 which relate specifically to children, the 1995 Act, s.307(7) contains a general saving presumption covering adult persons whose age becomes a material factor during criminal proceedings).

Subss. (1), (5) and (6)

    The subsections relate to the age of child offenders appearing before the court and extend to children aged under 16 years, and to any youth up to 18 years of age who at the time of appearing before the court was already the subject of a supervision requirement.

    The court should if possible question the child as a means of establishing his age and assess the age by reference to his appearance. Additionally if evidence is led, that too can be scrutinised for indications of the offender's age. The court can then legitimately hold the offender's age to be established and consider the options for disposal of the case if the offence is admitted or proved. Note that if it is concluded on the basis of all the available material that the offender is 17 years old and it is not disclosed that he is subject to local authority supervision, the court can lawfully treat him as a young offender. Subsection (5) enacts that findings or orders pronounced by the court in circumstances where the court has had to deduce the child's age will not be voided if it is subsequently discovered that the court was misled.

Subss. (3) and (7)

These subsections apply when a child is either accused of an offence or is the victim of an offence. The effect of subs. (7) is to distinguish between those who meet the statutory definition of a "child" as promulgated by the 1995 Act and those who fulfil the narrower statutory definition of a "child" found in the Children and Young Persons (Scotland) Act 1937. In relation to the offences specified in Sched. 1 to the 1995 Act: in the first case an offender can be aged 17 years or more and continue to be treated as a "child" within the meaning of the 1995 Act provided he is still the subject of a supervision order. However, as a victim the complainer is to be regarded as a child only until his seventeenth birthday is attained. A rebuttable presumption exists that the complainer in the statutory offences specified in subs. (3) was a child at the time of the incident libelled. Similarly where it is averred in a libel that the accused was a "child" in terms of the 1995 Act's statutory definition at the time of committing an offence, and this allegation appears to be confirmed by his bearing and physical appearance, it will be presumed that the offender's age has been established.

Subs. (4)

This subsection prevents the introduction of purely technical defences in cases involving victims who are either children or young persons.

When charged with contravening either of the statutory provisions specified in relation to a child or a young person, an accused cannot base a defence upon a discrepancy between the age of the victim, as stated in the libel, and the actuality when, in either case, an offence would have been committed.

The amendment introduced to subs. (1) by the Crime and Punishment (Scotland) Act 1997 has the effect of removing the court's duty to enquire into the age of a child when his age has been specified in the complaint or indictment. A further presumption as to proof of age, of broader application to witnesses, has been introduced into the 1995 Act as s.255A.

Restriction on report of proceedings involving children

47.—(1) Subject to subsection (3) below, no newspaper report of any proceedings in a court shall reveal the name, address or school, or include any particulars calculated to lead to the identification, of any person under the age of 16 years concerned in the proceedings, either—

(a) as being a person against or in respect of whom the proceedings are taken; or

(b) as being a witness in the proceedings.

(2) Subject to subsection (3) below, no picture which is, or includes, a picture of a person under the age of 16 years concerned in proceedings as mentioned in subsection (1) above shall be published in any newspaper in a context relevant to the proceedings.

(3) The requirements of subsections (1) and (2) above shall be applied in any case mentioned in any of the following paragraphs to the extent specified in that paragraph—

(a) where a person under the age of 16 years is concerned in the proceedings as a witness only and no one against whom the proceedings are taken is under the age of 16 years, the requirements shall not apply unless the court so directs;

(b) where, at any stage of the proceedings, the court, if it is satisfied that it is in the public interest so to do, directs that the requirements (including the requirements as applied by a direction under paragraph (a) above) shall be dispensed with to such extent as the court may specify; and

(c) where the Secretary of State, after completion of the proceedings, if satisfied as mentioned in paragraph (b) above, by order dispenses with the requirements to such extent as may be specified in the order.

(4) This section shall, with the necessary modifications, apply in relation to sound and television programmes included in a programme service (within the meaning of the Broadcasting Act 1990) as it applies in relation to newspapers.

(5) A person who publishes matter in contravention of this section shall be guilty of an offence and liable on summary conviction to a fine not exceeding level 4 of the standard scale.

(6) In this section, references to a court shall not include a court in England, Wales or Northern Ireland.

DEFINITION
"witness": s.307(1).

GENERAL NOTE
There is a general prohibition upon identifying anyone involved in criminal proceedings as a victim, a witness or an accused when that person is aged less than 16 years of age. The prohibition is intended to prevent the publication or broadcasting of the person's particulars, home address or educational background as well as any details of the circumstances of the case which would be sufficient to establish this information. It extends to photographs of the child, but not of other persons however closely related to the child. Such prohibitions remain in force until the child reaches 16 years of age. See *Caledonian Newspapers, Petrs*, 1995 S.C.C.R. 576 and the general discussion there of the scope of s.169 of the 1975 Act, whose terms are echoed by s.47 of the 1995 Act.

Subsection (3) permits a relaxation of this prohibition where; (i) the accused is older than 16 years and the child appears as a witness only, not as a victim, though even here it must be noted that the court can direct that the provisions of subs. (1) are to apply; (ii) the court decides during the proceedings that it is in the public interest to identify the person concerned and stipulates the extent of material which may be published or broadcast; (iii) the Secretary of State decides after proceedings are concluded that it is in the public interest for such information, as specified, to be disseminated.

Note that the Act of Adjournal (Criminal Procedure Rules) 1996 r.6.9 requires the court to specify the persons whose identities are to be protected or, alternatively may be revealed, along with suitable directions in that regard.

Extent
These provisions do not extend to reports of proceedings arising outwith Scotland. The section does apply to any report of such Scottish proceedings published or broadcast in Scotland or elsewhere in Great Britain. The penalties for contravening s.47 are found in subs. (5).

Act of Adjournal
See the Act of Adjournal (Criminal Procedure Rules) 1996, r.6.7 for procedural directions.

Power to refer certain children to reporter

48.—(1) A court by or before which a person is convicted of having committed an offence to which this section applies may refer—
(a) a child in respect of whom an offence mentioned in paragraph (a) or (b) of subsection (2) below has been committed; or
(b) any child who is, or who is likely to become, a member of the same household as the person who has committed an offence mentioned in paragraph (b) or (c) of that subsection or the person in respect of whom the offence so mentioned was committed,
to the Principal Reporter, and certify that the offence shall be a ground established for the purposes of Chapter 3 of Part II of the Children (Scotland) Act 1995.

(2) This section applies to an offence—
(a) under section 21 of the Children and Young Persons (Scotland) Act 1937;
(b) mentioned in Schedule 1 to this Act; or
(c) in respect of a person aged 17 years or over which constitutes the crime of incest.

DEFINITIONS
"offence": s.307(1).

"Principal Reporter": s.93(1) of the Children (Scotland) Act 1995.

GENERAL NOTE

Section 48 entitles the court before which a person is convicted of an offence specified in subs. (2) to take immediate account of the harm done to the child victim, or the risk, or potential risk, of harm to any child who stays or may stay in the same household as the offender. This power also extends to the households of persons convicted of incest.

With a view to preserving the moral and physical well-being of such children, the court is empowered to certify the grounds for a supervision order to be established, without there being any need for a children's hearing to be constituted to consider the matter. The task of the hearing is confined to consideration in terms of ss.69 and 70 of the Children (Scotland) Act 1995, of the measures necessary to safeguard the welfare of the child or children.

Reference or remit to children's hearing

49.—(1) Where a child who is not subject to a supervision requirement pleads guilty to, or is found guilty of, an offence the court—

(a) instead of making an order on that plea or finding, may remit the case to the Principal Reporter to arrange for the disposal of the case by a children's hearing; or

(b) on that plea or finding may request the Principal Reporter to arrange a children's hearing for the purposes of obtaining their advice as to the treatment of the child.

(2) Where a court has acted in pursuance of paragraph (b) of subsection (1) above, the court, after consideration of the advice received from the children's hearing may, as it thinks proper, itself dispose of the case or remit the case as mentioned in paragraph (a) of that subsection.

(3) Where a child who is subject to a supervision requirement pleads guilty to, or is found guilty of, an offence the court dealing with the case if it is—

(a) the High Court, may; and

[2](b) the sheriff or district court, shall,

request the Principal Reporter to arrange a children's hearing for the purpose of obtaining their advice as to the treatment of the child, and on consideration of that advice may, as it thinks proper, itself dispose of the case or remit the case as mentioned in subsection (1)(a) above.

[1](4) Subject to any appeal against any decision to remit made under subsection (1)(a) or (7)(b) below, where a court has remitted a case to the Principal Reporter under this section, the jurisdiction of the court in respect of the child shall cease, and his case shall stand referred to a children's hearing.

(5) Nothing in this section shall apply to a case in respect of an offence the sentence for which is fixed by law.

(6) Where a person who is—

(a) not subject to a supervision requirement;

(b) over the age of 16; and

(c) not within six months of attaining the age of 18,

is charged summarily with an offence and pleads guilty to, or has been found guilty of, the offence the court may request the Principal Reporter to arrange a children's hearing for the purpose of obtaining their advice as to the treatment of the person.

(7) On consideration of any advice obtained under subsection (6) above, the court may, as it thinks proper—

(a) itself dispose of the case; or

(b) where the hearing have so advised, remit the case to the Principal Reporter for the disposal of the case by a children's hearing.

DEFINITIONS

"child": s.307(1) and s.93(2)(b) of the Children (Scotland) Act 1995.

"children's hearing": s.93(1) of the Children (Scotland) Act 1995.

"High Court": s.307(1).

"offence": s.307(1).
"Principal Reporter": s.93(1) of the Children (Scotland) Act 1995.
"supervision requirement": s.307(1) and ss.70(1) and 93(1) of the Children (Scotland) Act 1995.

NOTES
[1]Inserted by s.23(a) of the Crime and Punishment (Scotland) Act 1997 with effect from August 1, 1997 in terms of the Crime and Punishment (Scotland) Act (Commencement and Transitional Provisions) Order 1997 (S.I. 1997 No. 1712) Art. 3.
[2]Inserted by the Crime and Disorder Act 1998 (c. 37), Sched. 8, para. 118 (effective September 30, 1998: S.I. 1998 No. 2327).

GENERAL NOTE
When a child not currently the subject of a supervision requirement admits, or is held to have committed an offence, the court effectively has three options; proceeding to an immediate disposal of the case, or remitting the case to a children's hearing either for their advice or for their consideration and disposal. Subsections (6) and (7) extend these provisions to youths aged up to 17½ years who are convicted on summary complaint. Once the case is remitted to a hearing for disposal, the court's involvement ceases.
In cases where the child is the subject of a supervision requirement, and thus can be aged up to 17½ years old, admits or is found guilty of an offence in the sheriff or (following the amendment introduced by the 1998 Act in relation only to children already the subject of supervision) the district court, the court must obtain the advice of a children's hearing. On receipt of the hearing's advice the court can dispose of the case or remit the child to the hearing for their decision and disposal. Note that as subs. (3)(b) reads, this procedure would apply equally to summary or solemn cases but that the provisions of s.44 of the Act (which empower a sheriff sitting summarily to order detention of up to one year's duration in residential accommodation) derogate from this general requirement.
Section 208 of the Act empowers solemn courts to impose periods of detention following conviction on indictment.
When the child is convicted before the High Court it is in the discretion of the court to obtain the advice of a children's hearing except where the conviction is for murder since, in that event, the sentence provided by s.205 is a mandatory one of life imprisonment.

Children and certain proceedings

50.—[1](1) No child under 14 years of age (other than an infant in arms) shall be permitted to be present in court during any proceedings against any other person charged with an offence unless his presence is required as a witness or otherwise for the purposes of justice or the Court consents to his presence.
(2) Any child present in court when, under subsection (1) above, he is not to be permitted to be so shall be ordered to be removed.
(3) Where, in any proceedings in relation to an offence against, or any conduct contrary to, decency or morality, a person who, in the opinion of the court, is a child is called as a witness, the court may direct that all or any persons, not being—
    (a) members or officers of the court;
    (b) parties to the case before the court, their counsel or solicitors or persons otherwise directly concerned in the case;
    (c) *bona fide* representatives of news gathering or reporting organisations present for the purpose of the preparation of contemporaneous reports of the proceedings; or
    (d) such other persons as the court may specially authorise to be present,
shall be excluded from the court during the taking of the evidence of that witness.
(4) The powers conferred on a court by subsection (3) above shall be in addition and without prejudice to any other powers of the court to hear proceedings *in camera*.
(5) Where in any proceedings relating to any of the offences mentioned in Schedule 1 to this Act, the court is satisfied that the attendance before the

court of any person under the age of 17 years in respect of whom the offence is alleged to have been committed is not essential to the just hearing of the case, the case may be proceeded with and determined in the absence of that person.

(6) Every court in dealing with a child who is brought before it as an offender shall have regard to the welfare of the child and shall in a proper case take steps for removing him from undesirable surroundings.

DEFINITIONS
"child": as defined in subs. (1).
"witness": s.307(1).

NOTE
[1]As amended by the Access to Justice Act 1999 (c. 22), s.73(2) (effective September 27, 1999).

GENERAL NOTE
The provisions of this section are of a directory character and non-compliance would not render the proceedings null.

It will be noted that ss.271 and 272 of the 1995 Act allow for applications to be made for a child's evidence to be taken by a commissioner, relayed to the court by means of a remote closed-circuit television link, or to be taken in court while the child is screened from sight of the accused.

Remand and committal of children and young persons

51.—(1) Where a court remands or commits for trial or for sentence a person under 21 years of age who is charged with or convicted of an offence and is not released on bail or ordained to appear, then, except as otherwise expressly provided by this section, the following provisions shall have effect—

[1](a) subject to paragraph (b) below, if he is under 16 years of age the court shall, instead of committing him to prison, commit him to the local authority which it considers appropriate to be detained—

(i) where the court so requires, in secure accommodation within the meaning of Part II of the Children (Scotland) Act 1995; and

(ii) in any other case, in a suitable place of safety chosen by the authority;

[2](aa) if the person is over 16 years of age and subject to a supervision requirement, the court may, instead of committing him to prison, commit him to the local authority which it considers appropriate to be detained as mentioned in sub-paragraphs (i) or (ii) of paragraph (a) above;

[3](b) if he is a person of over 16 years of age to whom paragraph (aa) above does not apply, or a child under 16 years of age but over 14 years of age who is certified by the court to be unruly or depraved, and the court has been notified by the Secretary of State that a remand centre is available for the reception from that court of persons of his class or description, he shall be committed to a remand centre instead of being committed to prison.

(2) Where any person is committed to a local authority or to a remand centre under any provision of this Act, that authority or centre shall be specified in the warrant, and he shall be detained by the authority or in the centre for the period for which he is committed or until he is liberated in due course of law.

(3) Where any person has been committed to a local authority under any provision of this Act, the court by which he was committed, if the person so committed is not less than 14 years of age and it appears to the court that he is unruly or depraved, may revoke the committal and commit the said person—

(a) if the court has been notified that a remand centre is available for the reception from that court of persons of his class or description, to a remand centre; and

(b) if the court has not been so notified, to a prison.

[4](4) Where in the case of a person under 16 years of age who has been committed to prison or to a remand centre under this section, the sheriff is satisfied that his detention in prison or a remand centre is no longer necessary, he may revoke the committal and commit the person to the local authority which he considers appropriate to be detained—

(a) where the court so requires, in secure accommodation within the meaning of Part II of the Children (Scotland) Act 1995; and

(b) in any other case, in a suitable place of safety chosen by the authority.

[5](4A) The local authority which may be appropriate in relation to a power to commit a person under paragraphs (a) or (aa) of subsection (1) or subsection (4) above may, without prejudice to the generality of those powers, be—

(a) the local authority for the area in which the court is situated;

(b) if the person is usually resident in Scotland, the local authority for the area in which he is usually resident;

(c) if the person is subject to a supervision requirement, the relevant local authority within the meaning of Part II of the Children (Scotland) Act 1995 in relation to that requirement.

DEFINITIONS

"commits for trial": s.307(1).

"local authority": s.307(1).

"place of safety": s.307(1) of the 1995 Act and, in relation to children see s.93(1) of the Children (Scotland) Act 1995.

"prison": s.307(1).

"remand": s.307(1).

"remand centre": s.307(1).

"secure accommodation": s.93(1) of the Children (Scotland) Act 1995.

"supervision requirement": s.307(1) of the 1995 Act and the Children (Scotland) Act 1995 ss.70(1) and 93(1).

NOTES

[1]Substituted by the Crime and Punishment (Scotland) Act 1997 (c. 48) s.56(2)(a) with effect from August 1, 1997 in terms of the Crime and Punishment (Scotland) Act 1997 (Commencement and Transitional Provisions) Order 1997 (S.I. 1997 No. 1712) para. 3.

[2]Inserted by s.56(2)(b) of the above Act with effect from August 1, 1997 in terms of the above Order.

[3]Inserted by s.56(2)(c) of the above Act and in terms of the above Order.

[4]Substituted by s.56(3) of the above Act and in terms of the above Order.

[5]Inserted by s.52(4) of the above Act and in terms of the above Order.

GENERAL NOTE

Section 51 applies equally to summary or solemn proceedings and specifies the forms of remand facilities which are to be utilised when persons under 21 years of age are held in custody awaiting trial or remanded for sentence by the court. The aim, so far as practicable, is not to resort to use of remand facilities either before or after any trial unless the circumstances of the case, or the offender, make this unavoidable. The provisions introduced by the 1997 Act reflect the changes brought about by local government reorganisation and give the courts a degree of flexibility when nominating the local authority to provide suitable remand facilities for children and young offenders. It no longer follows that this function must necessarily be met by the local authority within whose boundaries the court is situated; it is now being left to the court to decide the most appropriate authority in the case of each offender.

In discussing s.43 of the Act it was noted that when it was felt that ordaining or liberating a child to appear at the first diet of the case was considered inappropriate, the options available to the police thereafter would be to remand a child to a place of safety, unless his conduct or circumstances militated against that form of detention. The more stringent restrictions upon the child's liberty, produced by detaining him in police cells pending his appearance before the court from custody could only be justified by the production to the court, on first appearance, of an unruly certificate. A similar philosophy is applied by the courts when it is felt that a child or young person must be remanded in custody for trial or sentence; the broad objective is then to remand the offender to an establishment most suited to the offender's circumstances and so far as possible, to minimise the rigour of the remand regime.

Children Under 16 Years

Prior to the child's appearance from custody before the sheriff, the procurator fiscal and the principal reporter (or their deputes) should already have considered whether such an appearance is necessary or whether the child can instead be referred to the reporter in custody or liberated for the reporter to arrange a later children's hearing. Such a consultation process also applies when the offender is aged between 16 and 17 years and six months old and is the subject of a supervision requirement, but failure on the part of the procurator fiscal to consult with the reporter in these circumstances would not vitiate proceedings: see s.46(5) above.

Section 51 only takes effect when the procurator fiscal, having weighed the interests of the child and the broad public interest, elects to retain the case. If the child has been detained in police cells, the procurator fiscal will receive the unruly certificate from the police and has to produce it to the sheriff when the child appears from custody (following s.142 of the 1995 Act it will be observed that in summary proceedings such an appearance should not occur in an adult court (unless there is an adult co-accused) and must be held in private).

Should the procurator fiscal decide that bail will be opposed because of the nature of the offence or the unruliness of the child, he should have established with the local authority before the case is called, whether suitable remand facilities are available. This information should be put before the court in conjunction with a motion to remand the child in custody. In the absence of suitable accommodation, the court, if it refuses bail, will have no option but to consider whether the child is unruly, and if so, certify the child unruly and remand him to a remand institution or an adult prison albeit subs. (4) does permit later variation of the order. It is submitted that while the nature of the offence may well point to the child being unruly or depraved that is not the test; it is the nature of the child himself which should be assessed by the court. See however *R.M., Pet.*, 1996 S.C.C.R. 92 and the editor's commentary thereon in regard to the implications of a lack of suitable secure accommodation.

It ought to be clearly established whether the child is or is not in custody pending trial, since the warrant issued by the court will specify either the centre to which the child is remanded or identify the local authority into whose charge he is placed and (following subs. (1)(a)) the nature of the accommodation to be provided—a place of safety, residential or secure accommodation. The important factor is whether the child is granted bail, and is at liberty, or remanded in custody, since this has an obvious bearing upon the timescale and competency of later proceedings; see ss.65 and 147 of the 1995 Act which re-enact the familiar provisions of ss.101 and 331A of the 1975 Act regarding prevention of delay in proceedings, *i.e* the 110 day and 40 day rules respectively. The warrant issued by the court will not conclusively determine whether a child is in custody or not, that is ultimately an issue of fact in each case, but the warrant will assuredly be a highly persuasive determining factor. The court must be furnished with comprehensive and accurate information about the precise circumstances of the child and the basis upon which he is held. In *X., Petr.*, 1996 S.C.C.R. 436 the Crown was criticised for making representations which were based upon inaccurate information provided by the local authority. The court observed that the Crown had a duty to verify the accuracy of such information for itself and should seek an adjournment for that purpose if necessary.

These comments apply with even greater force when the child appearing before the court is already the subject of a residential supervision order: it is then vital that it is determined whether the child is bailed, and returns to the care of the local authority to continue the current supervision order, or is remanded to secure accommodation provided by the local authority as a preferred alternative to a remand or prison place. It is also essential that the local authority seek a review of the case in terms of subs. (4), should the circumstances of the offender change.

The complications which can arise are amply illustrated in *K. v. H.M. Advocate*, 1991 S.C.C.R. 343, where the child was "bailed" to reside at a List D school which in fact contained both secure and residential accommodation. K was bailed to reside in the school's secure unit, instead of being either remanded into the care of the local authority or certified unruly and remanded. The court's well-meant intention was to substitute an earlier warrant which had remanded K to an adult prison with a more suitable regime but, on any view, K was not at liberty and the provisions (then) of s.110 applied, since the bail order had had no practical effect (the solution would have been for the local authority, if it was in agreement, to seek review of the warrant as subs. (4) provides in the 1995 Act).

See also *X., Petr.*, 1996 S.C.C.R. 436; following a petition appearance upon a rape charge and refusal of bail, C was held in custody in a remand institution. A review hearing later allowed bail subject to residence in a List D school; although the bail order did not stipulate it, C was kept in secure accommodation by staff solely in execution of the order, and only the issue of instructions by the procurator fiscal for the child's liberation (which were acted upon on the 109th day) stopped the 110 days running. A petition to the *nobile officium* was refused since *de facto* liberty had been obtained before the expiry of the 110 days.

Note that once a child has been certified unruly by the sheriff it is doubtful whether it can be revoked by anyone, even the certifying sheriff, or formally appealed. In *X., Petr., supra*, the child was certified unruly and remanded in a remand institution after absconding from the local authority home to which he had earlier been bailed. A petition to the *nobile officium* for revocation of the certification was lodged, but the High Court doubted that such an order would be competent; in the absence of Crown opposition the court used its inherent equitable powers to grant a bail order specifying residence in a secure unit. The principles which prompted this decision appear in conflict with the *ratio* in *K. v. H.M. Advocate* above.

A similar situation arose in *Y., Petr.*, 1995 S.C.C.R. 457, with the court ruling that a petition to the *nobile officium* was not a competent means for review of an unruly certificate.

Nevertheless the court substituted a bail order requiring Y to reside in the secure unit of a List D school.

PART VI

MENTAL DISORDER

Committal of mentally disordered persons

Power of court to commit to hospital an accused suffering from mental disorder

52.—(1) Where it appears to the prosecutor in any court before which a person is charged with an offence that the person may be suffering from mental disorder, it shall be the duty of the prosecutor to bring before the court such evidence as may be available of the mental condition of that person.

(2) Where a court remands or commits for trial a person charged with any offence who appears to the court to be suffering from mental disorder, and the court is satisfied that a hospital is available for his admission and suitable for his detention, the court may, instead of remanding him in custody, commit him to that hospital.

(3) Where an accused is committed to a hospital as mentioned in subsection (2) above, the hospital shall be specified in the warrant, and if the responsible medical officer is satisfied that he is suffering from mental disorder of a nature or degree which warrants his admission to a hospital under Part V of the Mental Health (Scotland) Act 1984, he shall be detained in the hospital specified in the warrant for the period for which he is remanded or the period of committal, unless before the expiration of that period he is liberated in due course of law.

(4) When the responsible medical officer has examined the person so detained he shall report the result of that examination to the court and, where the report is to the effect that the person is not suffering from mental disorder of such a nature or degree as aforesaid, the court may commit him to any prison or other institution to which he might have been committed had he not been committed to hospital or may otherwise deal with him according to law.

(5) No person shall be committed to a hospital under this section except on the written or oral evidence of a registered medical practitioner.

(6) Without prejudice to subsection (4) above, the court may review an order under subsection (2) above on the ground that there has been a change of circumstances since the order was made and, on such review—

    (a) where the court considers that such an order is no longer required in relation to a person, it shall revoke the order and may deal with him in such way mentioned in subsection (4) above as the court thinks appropriate;

    (b) in any other case, the court may—

(i) confirm or vary the order; or
(ii) revoke the order and deal with him in such way mentioned in subsection (4) above as the court considers appropriate.
(7) Subsections (2) to (5) above shall apply to the review of an order under subsection (6) above as they apply to the making of an order under subsection (2) above.

DEFINITIONS
"commits for trial": s.307(1).
"hospital": s.307(1).
"offence": s.307(1).
"order": s.307(1).
"prison": s.307(1).
"prosecutor": s.307(1).
"registered medical practitioner": s.2 of the Medicine Act 1968.
"responsible medical officer": s.307(1).

GENERAL NOTE
This section amends and consolidates the existing provisions of the court to commit to a specified hospital at the pre-trial stage an accused who appears to be suffering from a mental disorder. The section makes express provision for review of that committal. The committal to hospital is an alternative to remanding such an accused in custody pending trial. Thus the committal to hospital is subject to the maximum remand time limits of 40 days in summary proceedings and 110 days in solemn proceedings. Before the court can make the hospital committal order three criteria must be met. First the court must be satisfied on the written or oral evidence of a registered medical practitioner that the accused appears to be suffering from mental disorder, although at this stage it is not necessary for the nature or degree of mental disorder to be established. Secondly, the court must be satisfied that a hospital is *available* for the accused's admission, and thirdly the court must be satisfied that the hospital is *suitable* for the accused's detention pending trial. Accordingly the registered medical practitioner should confirm to the court that a suitable hospital is prepared to admit the accused.
It should be noted that it is open to anyone with an interest in the case to raise the possibility of an accused's mental disorder with the court. Such interested parties would include the prosecutor, the police, the defence agent and the judge.

Subs. (1)
The breadth of the definition of the word "prosecutor" should be noted for in solemn proceedings it includes Crown counsel. The flexibility implied by this is such that relevant evidence may be brought at what would otherwise be the trial diet in the High Court of Justiciary. The procedure is not contingent on a conviction because of the phrase "is charged with": see *Herron v. McCrimmon*, 1969 S.L.T.(Sh.Ct.) 37 for circumstances in which a summary complaint was deserted *pro loco et tempore* to place the accused on petition and yet the phrase was still satisfied.
The provision of a psychiatric report by the Crown in compliance with this section's provisions is to be regarded as the fulfilment of a statutory duty which has been placed on the prosecutor for the protection of the accused, and not as an element of the Crown's investigation in furtherance of its case against the accused. Thus in *Sloan v. Crowe*, 1996 S.C.C.R. 200 an objection to the competency of proceedings was repelled, and refused on appeal, the defence having asserted that information provided to the Crown in a psychiatric report on the accused unfairly made reference to the offence itself. In *MacDonald v. Munro*, 1996 S.C.C.R. 595 where the psychiatrist had interviewed both the accused and his mother (the complainer) about the circumstances of the offence in compiling his report, it was observed that any prejudicial material would fall to be ignored by the judge and that any attempt by the Crown to found on such material would likely be objectionable.
Whether a person may be suffering from "mental disorder" is a medical question for those qualified to answer the question but that is frequently the most difficult point: in *Allan v. H.M. Advocate*, 1983 S.C.C.R. 183 four psychiatrists divided on precisely that aspect and, if the accused was so suffering, what the best method of disposal would be.
A similar division is apparent in *Jessop v. Robertson*, 1989 S.C.C.R. 600 (Sh.Ct.) where it was held by a sheriff that: (1) a written report that had been produced by the prosecutor but was not spoken to by a witness at the proof was not admissible; (2) there was an onus on any person alleging unfitness by reason of insanity to satisfy the court of that allegation by corroborated evidence on a balance of probabilities; and (3) in the circumstances of medical division the unfitness had not been proved; and the accused was called upon to plead.

Subs. (2)

Where ultimately a sentence of imprisonment or detention is to be imposed, the Court is obliged to have regard to any period of time spent in hospital at the pre-trial stage by virtue of an order made under subs. (2) (see s.210 as amended by s.12 of the Crime and Punishment (Scotland) Act 1997, with effect from August 1, 1997).

Subs. (5)

The evidence required for committal should be the "written or oral" evidence of a registered medical practitioner. Given that a proof is held then on *Jessop v. Robertson*, above, the meaning of that phrase would seem to be "oral evidence supplemented, if necessary, by written evidence".

Subs. (6)

Subsection (3) permits the receiving hospital to have the accused examined and if the responsible medical officer is satisfied that the accused is suffering from mental disorder of the requisite degree then the accused is detained. If the responsible medical officer is not so satisfied then the standard criminal procedures are resumed. Thus under subs. (4) the accused can be committed by the court to any prison or other institution, or otherwise dealt with according to law, *e.g.* by the court granting bail pending trial.

Subsection (6) introduces a degree of flexibility into the system. Under the previous law there was no express provision to permit any variation of the committal to hospital or for its revocation except in the circumstances identified in subs. (4), that is, immediately following initial examination. The new flexibility provides for fluctuating degrees of mental disorder and for a change of hospital to meet the requirements of the accused. Review, variation and revocation may be by the court at any time.

Interim hospital orders

Interim hospital orders

53.—[1,3](1) Where, in the case of a person to whom this section applies the court is satisfied on the written or oral evidence of two medical practitioners (complying with section 61 of this Act)—

    (a) that the offender is suffering from mental disorder within the meaning of section 1(2) of the Mental Health (Scotland) Act 1984; and

    (b) that there is reason to suppose—

        (i) that the mental disorder from which the offender is suffering is such that it may be appropriate for a hospital order to be made in his case; and

        (ii) that, having regard to section 58(5) of this Act, the hospital to be specified in any such hospital order may be a State hospital,

the court may, before making a hospital order or dealing with the offender in some other way including imposing a sentence of imprisonment and making a hospital direction, make an order (to be known as "an interim hospital order") authorising his admission to and detention in a state hospital or such other hospital as for special reasons the court may specify in the order.

    [3](2) . . .

    [2](3) An interim hospital order shall not be made in respect of an offender unless the court is satisfied that the hospital which is to be specified in the order, in the event of such an order being made by the court, is available for his admission thereto within 7 days of the making of such an order.

    [1](4) Where a court makes an interim hospital order it shall not at that time make any other order for detention or impose a fine or pass sentence of imprisonment or make a probation order or a community service order in respect of the offence, but may make any other order which it has power to make apart from this section.

    [2](5) The court by which an interim hospital order is made may include in the order such direction as it thinks fit for the conveyance of the offender to a place of safety and his detention therein pending his admission to the hospital within the period of 7 days referred to in subsection (3) above.

    [1](5A) Subsections (1) and (4) of section 60 of the Mental Health

(Scotland) Act 1984 shall apply to an interim hospital order as they apply to a hospital order.

^{1,3}(6) An interim hospital order—

(a) shall be in force for such period, not exceeding 12 weeks, as the court may specify when making the order; but

(b) may be renewed for further periods of not more than 28 days at a time if it appears to the court on the written or oral evidence of the responsible medical officer that the continuation of the order is warranted,

but no such order shall continue in force for more than twelve months in all and the court shall terminate the order if it makes a hospital order in respect of the offender or decides, after considering the written or oral evidence of the responsible medical officer, to deal with the offender in some other way including imposing a sentence of imprisonment and making a hospital direction.

(7) An interim hospital order may be renewed under subsection (6) above without the offender being brought before the court if he is represented by counsel or a solicitor and his counsel or solicitor is given an opportunity of being heard.

(8) If an offender absconds from a hospital in which he is detained in pursuance of an interim hospital order, or while being conveyed to or from such a hospital, he may be arrested without warrant by a constable and shall, after being arrested, be brought as soon as practicable before the court which made the order; and the court may thereupon terminate the order and deal with him in any way in which it could have dealt with him if no such order had been made.

(9) When an interim hospital order ceases to have effect in relation to an offender the court may deal with him in any way (other than by making a new interim hospital order) in which it could have dealt with him if no such order had been made.

(10) The power conferred on the court by this section is without prejudice to the power of the court under section 200(1) of this Act to remand a person in order that an inquiry may be made into his physical or mental condition.

(11) This section applies to any person—

(a) convicted in the High Court or the sheriff court of an offence punishable with imprisonment (other than an offence the sentence for which is fixed by law);

(b) charged on complaint in the sheriff court if the sheriff is satisfied that he did the act or made the omission charged but does not convict him; or

(c) remitted to the sheriff court from the district court under section 58(10) of this Act if the sheriff is satisfied as mentioned in paragraph (b) above.

(12) In this section "the court" means—

(a) the High Court, as regards a person—

(i) convicted on indictment in that court; or

(ii) convicted on indictment in the sheriff court and remitted for sentence to the High Court; and

(b) the sheriff court, as regards a person—

(i) convicted in the sheriff court and not remitted as mentioned in paragraph (a)(ii) above; or

(ii) referred to in paragraph (b) or (c) of subsection (11) above.

<small>DEFINITIONS</small>
"constable": s.307(1).
"court": s.53(12).
"fine": s.307(1).
"hospital direction": s.59A(1).
"interim hospital order": s.53(1).

"medical practitioner": s.61(1).
"mental disorder": s.1(2) of the Mental Health (Scotland) Act 1984.
"probation order": s.307(1).
"responsible medical officer": s.307(1).
"sentence": s.307(1).
"State hospital": s.307(1).

NOTES

[1]As amended by the Crime and Punishment (Scotland) Act 1997 (c. 48) s.62(1) Sched. 1, and para. 21(5) with effect from January 1, 1998 by the Crime and Punishment (Scotland) Act 1997 (Commencement No. 2 and Transitional Provisions) Order 1997 (S.I. 1997 No. 2323) para. 3.
[2]Substituted by the Act and Order above mentioned.
[3]Amended by the Crime and Punishment (Scotland) Act 1997 (c. 48) ss.10 and 11 with effect from January 1, 1998 by the Crime and Punishment (Scotland) Act 1997 (Commencement No. 2 and Transitional Provisions) Order 1997 (S.I. 1997 No. 2323) art. 4, Sched. 2.

GENERAL NOTE

An interim hospital order is a temporary order whereby the court may remand the offender to the State Hospital or other appropriate hospital prior to disposal, in order to allow sufficient time for a thorough assessment of his mental condition. Such an order can only be made when the court is provided with medical evidence that the offender suffers from mental disorder of a degree that detention in the State Hospital may ultimately be warranted (see ss.53(1) and 58(5)). It should be noted that the definition of "mental disorder" in s.1(2) of the Mental Health (Scotland) Act 1984 has been extended to include "personality disorder" (see s.3 of the Mental Health (Public Safety and Appeals) (Scotland) Act 1999, effective from September 1, 1999). The interim nature of an order under this section is emphasised by the time limits specified in s.53(6) and no interim hospital order shall continue in force for more than twelve months in total. Initially the medical evidence can be given in writing or orally, and at least one of the two medical practitioners involved must be employed in the proposed receiving hospital. This requirement is presumably intended to ensure that facilities will be available at that hospital to cater for the offender. It will be noted that an identical standard of medical evidence is required for insanity in bar of trial (s.54(1)(c)), for a hospital or guardianship order (s.58), and for the newly introduced hospital direction (s.59A(3) as inserted by s.6 of the Crime and Punishment (Scotland) Act 1997, with effect from January 1, 1998).

Note that an interim hospital order is not a sentence pronounced by the court, merely a preliminary to sentence. However, where a sentence of imprisonment or detention is ultimately imposed the court is obliged to have regard to the period of detention spent in the hospital by virtue of such an order, in determining the length of sentence (see s.210 as amended by s.12 of the Crime and Punishment (Scotland) Act 1997, with effect from August 1, 1997).

Insanity in bar of trial

Insanity in bar of trial

54.—(1) Where the court is satisfied, on the written or oral evidence of two medical practitioners, that a person charged with the commission of an offence is insane so that his trial cannot proceed or, if it has commenced, cannot continue, the court shall, subject to subsection (2) below—

(a) make a finding to that effect and state the reasons for that finding;

(b) discharge the trial diet and order that a diet (in this Act referred to as an "an examination of facts") be held under section 55 of this Act; and

(c) remand the person in custody or on bail or, where the court is satisfied—

  (i) on the written or oral evidence of two medical practitioners, that he is suffering from mental disorder of a nature or degree which warrants his admission to hospital under Part V of the Mental Health (Scotland) Act 1984; and

  (ii) that a hospital is available for his admission and suitable for his detention, make an order (in this section referred to as a "temporary hospital order") committing him to that hospital until the conclusion of the examination of facts.

(2) Subsection (1) above is without prejudice to the power of the court, on an application by the prosecutor, to desert the diet *pro loco et tempore.*

(3) The court may, before making a finding under subsection (1) above as to the insanity of a person, adjourn the case in order that investigation of his mental condition may be carried out.

(4) The court which made a temporary hospital order may, at any time while the order is in force, review the order on the ground that there has been a change of circumstances since the order was made and, on such review—

(a) where the court considers that such an order is no longer required in relation to a person, it shall revoke the order and may remand him in custody or on bail;

(b) in any other case, the court may—
   (i) confirm or vary the order; or
   (ii) revoke the order and make such other order, under subsection (1)(c) above or any other provision of this Act, as the court considers appropriate.

(5) Where it appears to a court that it is not practicable or appropriate for the accused to be brought before it for the purpose of determining whether he is insane so that his trial cannot proceed, then, if no objection to such a course is taken by or on behalf of the accused, the court may order that the case be proceeded with in his absence.

(6) Where evidence is brought before the court that the accused was insane at the time of doing the act or making the omission constituting the offence with which he is charged and he is acquitted, the court shall—

(a) in proceedings on indictment, direct the jury to find; or
(b) in summary proceedings, state,

whether the accused was insane at such time as aforesaid, and, if so, to declare whether he was acquitted on account of his insanity at that time.

(7) It shall not be competent for a person charged summarily in the sheriff court to found on a plea of insanity standing in bar of trial unless, before the first witness for the prosecution is sworn, he gives notice to the prosecutor of the plea and of the witnesses by whom he proposes to maintain it; and where such notice is given, the court shall, if the prosecutor so moves, adjourn the case.

(8) In this section, "the court" means—

(a) as regards a person charged on indictment, the High Court or the sheriff court;
(b) as regards a person charged summarily, the sheriff court.

DEFINITIONS
"bail": s.307(1).
"court": s.54(8).
"examination of facts": s.307(1).
"medical practitioner": s.61(1).
"temporary hospital order": s.54(1)(c).

GENERAL NOTE
It is interesting to note, by way of a preliminary, that s.52 is concerned with "mental disorder", s.53 is concerned with "mental disorder within the meaning of s.1(2) of the Mental Health (Scotland) Act 1984" and s.54 is concerned with "insanity".

The broad question in a plea-in-bar on grounds of insanity is whether the accused has the capacity to instruct his legal representatives as to his defence and to follow proceedings at his trial. The case of *Stewart v. H.M. Advocate (No. 1)*, 1997 S.C.C.R. 330, where such a plea was taken at a preliminary diet in relation to a mentally handicapped accused, emphasises that it is for the Judge to decide on assessing the medical evidence whether the plea is made out. See also the case of *McLachlan v. Brown*, 1997 S.C.C.R. 457, which confirms that s.54(1) applies not only to cases where the accused is unfit to plead due to mental illness, but also to cases where the accused is unfit to plead due to some mental impairment or handicap. It is conceivable that such a plea-in-bar could also extend to extreme physical defects (see *H.M. Advocate v. Wilson*, 1942 J.C. 75; 1942 S.L.T. 194 approved in *Stewart (No. 1)* above). Also worthy of note is *Stewart v. H.M. Advocate (No. 2)*, 1997 S.C.C.R. 430 where it was held, *inter alia*, that there is nothing in the legislation to exclude the right of an accused to renew a plea of insanity in bar of trial at a preliminary diet following service of a fresh indictment, despite the fact that such a plea was unsuccessful in respect of the original indictment. The decision recognises the fact that an accused's mental condition may fluctuate, and that accordingly insanity for the purposes of s.54 includes not only insanity by reason of some permanent condition but also insanity by reason of a condition which may alter from time to time.

Subsection (6) of s.54 deals with the special defence of insanity at the time of the offence, as distinct from insanity in bar of trial. Insanity as a defence rests upon alienation of reason at the time of the wrongful act, such that there can have been no *mens rea* for its commission. Acquittal as a result of a finding of insanity at the time of the offence may arise after trial (s.54(6)) or as a conclusion of an EOF (discussed below and see s.55(4)). In either case the court moves to disposal under s.57 of the Act.

Section 54 requires a court in both solemn and summary proceedings, following a finding that a person is insane so that a trial cannot proceed or continue, to hold an examination of the facts ("EOF") relating to the charges. The section further provides for the court to remand in custody or on bail, or to commit such a person to hospital under a temporary hospital order, until the conclusion of the EOF.

The new procedure very much contrasts with the previous law under which, when a person was found insane in bar of trial, no attempt was made by the court to examine the evidence as to whether the accused did the act with which he is charged. The new procedure requires that there be an examination of the relevant facts. It gives effect to certain recommendations contained in the Second Thomson Report on Criminal Procedure (Cmnd. 6218 (1975)). The only circumstances in which an EOF cannot be held are when the Crown applies for and the court agrees to the diet being deserted *pro loco et tempore*.

The novelty of these proceedings is accentuated by the possibility that the hearing to determine insanity may in some circumstances proceed in the absence of the accused: see s.54(5); but it should be borne in mind that the hearing is to be conducted along the lines of a trial in so far as possible, and accordingly proof of the material fact of identification requires to be considered and addressed.

In relation to solemn proceedings, s.54 should be read together with s.67. The latter section sets out the statutory requirements on the Crown for the witnesses and for intimation in writing of the details of the witnesses and where they can be contacted for the purposes of precognition. For that reason the accused or those advising him should have clear intimation of the availability of the two medical practitioners who may give evidence for the Crown of insanity. If the illness has developed immediately prior to the trial then such medical practitioners may be called with leave of the court: see s.67(5). If the defence seek to raise the issue then they must intimate the details of the two medical practitioners: see s.78(4).

In relation to summary proceedings, the approach to the issue is necessarily different. There appears to be no duty on the Crown to intimate the issue in advance of the trial although one would hope that such an important matter would be intimated in the interests of justice. In any event, an adjournment for inquiry at the first calling in terms of s.145(1) would undoubtedly follow where there had been no intimation. The accused or those advising him are under a clear duty to give notice: see s.54(7).

Finally, it should be noted that for the purposes of s.54(1) a report in writing purporting to be signed by a medical practitioner may, subject to the provisions of s.61, be received in evidence without proof of the signature or qualifications of the practitioner: but the court may, in any case, require the practitioner by whom such a report was signed be called to give oral evidence; s.61(3).

Examination of facts

Examination of facts

55.—(1) At an examination of facts ordered under section 54(1)(b) of this Act the court shall, on the basis of the evidence (if any) already given in the trial and such evidence, or further evidence, as may be led by either party, determine whether it is satisfied—

    (a) beyond reasonable doubt, as respects any charge on the indictment or, as the case may be, the complaint in respect of which the accused was being or was to be tried, that he did the act or made the omission constituting the offence; and

(b) on the balance of probabilities, that there are no grounds for acquitting him.

(2) Where the court is satisfied as mentioned in subsection (1) above, it shall make a finding to that effect.

(3) Where the court is not so satisfied it shall, subject to subsection (4) below, acquit the person of the charge.

(4) Where, as respects a person acquitted under subsection (3) above, the court is satisfied as to the matter mentioned in subsection (1)(a) above but it appears to the court that the person was insane at the time of doing the act or making the omission constituting the offence, the court shall state whether the acquittal is on the ground of such insanity.

(5) Where it appears to the court that it is not practical or appropriate for the accused to attend an examination of facts the court may, if no objection is taken by or on behalf of the accused, order that the examination of facts shall proceed in his absence.

(6) Subject to the provisions of this section, section 56 of this Act and any Act of Adjournal the rules of evidence and procedure and the powers of the court shall, in respect of an examination of facts, be as nearly as possible those applicable in respect of a trial.

(7) For the purposes of the application to an examination of facts of the rules and powers mentioned in subsection (6) above, an examination of facts—

(a) commences when the indictment or, as the case may be, complaint is called; and

(b) concludes when the court—

      (i) acquits the person under subsection (3) above;

      (ii) makes an order under subsection (2) of section 57 of this Act; or

      (iii) decides, under paragraph (e) of that subsection, not to make an order.

DEFINITIONS

"examination of facts": s.54(1)(b).
"offence": s.307(1).

GENERAL NOTE

Section 54 establishes the competency of an examination of facts ("EOF") and s.55 specifies the procedure and powers of the court, its findings, and a number of detailed ancillary matters. An EOF is to be held along the lines of a trial as far as possible and, again emphasising the novelty, it may proceed in certain circumstances in the absence of the accused.

It seems important to stress that an EOF need not necessarily be a matter wholly separate from a trial in the conventional sense. Section 54(1) refers to "a person charged with the commission of an offence" being insane "so that his trial cannot proceed or, if it has commenced, cannot continue". On that approach it is easy to imagine under solemn procedure a trial commencing in the ordinary way and after the jury has heard some evidence the defence lawyers (or others) intimating that there is concern about the accused's health. Thereafter, a medical examination might produce the necessary evidence leading the court to make the essential finding (s.54(1)(a)) and the trial diet being discharged and an EOF then being held (s.54(1)(b)). Indeed, the citation of the accused and any witnesses to the trial diet is valid citation to the EOF: see s.56(1) and (2). It follows from the discharge of the trial diet and the terms of s.55 that the jury is released.

Thereafter, at the EOF the court must consider both any evidence already given in the trial and the evidence led at the EOF itself, by either party. The court must then determine whether it is satisfied that the accused did the act or made the omission constituting the offence and that there are no grounds for his acquittal. The standard for the first determination is beyond reasonable doubt and for the second it is on a balance of probabilities (s.55(1)(a) and (b)).

If the court is not satisfied that these standards have been made out the accused is acquitted (s.55(3)). However, if the court is satisfied that the accused did the act or made the omission constituting the offence, but on a balance of probabilities it appears to the court that the accused was insane at the time, acquittal on that ground may competently be determined and stated by the court (s.55(4)).

Examination of facts: supplementary provisions

56.—(1) An examination of facts ordered under section 54(1)(b) of this Act may, where the order is made at the trial diet, be held immediately following the making of the order and, where it is so held, the citation of the accused and any witness to the trial diet shall be a valid citation to the examination of facts.

(2) Where an examination of facts is ordered in connection with proceedings on indictment, a warrant for citation of an accused and witnesses under section 66(1) of this Act shall be sufficient warrant for citation to an examination of facts.

(3) Where an accused person is not legally represented at an examination of facts the court shall appoint counsel or a solicitor to represent his interests.

(4) The court may, on the motion of the prosecutor and after hearing the accused, order that the examination of facts shall proceed in relation to a particular charge, or particular charges, in the indictment or, as the case may be, complaint in priority to other such charges.

(5) The court may, on the motion of the prosecutor and after hearing the accused, at any time desert the examination of facts *pro loco et tempore* as respects either the whole indictment or, as the case may be, complaint or any charge therein.

(6) Where, and to the extent that, an examination of facts has, under subsection (5) above, been deserted *pro loco et tempore*—

    (a) in the case of proceedings on indictment, the Lord Advocate may, at any time, raise and insist in a new indictment; or

    (b) in the case of summary proceedings, the prosecutor may at any time raise a fresh libel,

notwithstanding any time limit which would otherwise apply in respect of prosecution of the alleged offence.

(7) If, in a case where a court has made a finding under subsection (2) of section 55 of this Act, a person is subsequently charged, whether on indictment or on a complaint, with an offence arising out of the same act or omission as is referred to in subsection (1) of that section, any order made, under section 57(2) of this Act shall, with effect from the commencement of the later proceedings, cease to have effect.

(8) For the purposes of subsection (7) above, the later proceedings are commenced when the indictment or, as the case may be, the complaint is served.

DEFINITIONS

    "complaint": s.307(1).
    "diet": s.307(1).
    "examination of facts": s.54(1)(b).
    "indictment": s.307(1).
    "order": s.307(1).
    "prosecutor": s.307(1).

GENERAL NOTE

    This section makes supplementary provisions for examinations of facts ("EOF"): the most important aspects that arise are probably that existing powers of citation for the trial diet are valid for citation for the EOF (s.56(1) and (2)) and that any time-limits that might constrain the Crown following an EOF being deserted *pro loco et tempore* are disapplied (s.56(6)).

    If at the EOF a finding is delivered to the effect that the accused did the act charged as the main offence, thus paving the way for the EOF to move to disposal under s.57, the prosecutor may not wish to prolong the EOF and move to desert the remaining charges under s.56(5). The effect of such desertion *pro loco et tempore* is to terminate the present proceedings, but reserve the Crown's right to reraise proceedings should the accused recover his sanity sufficiently to stand trial. Any disposal order made under s.57 in relation to the previous finding of insanity ceases to have effect from the commencement of the new proceedings, namely when the new indictment or complaint is served (see s.56(7) and (8)). Thus on an accused person sufficiently recovering his sanity, he may be prosecuted in exactly the same terms as those contained in the original indictment or complaint against him, except of course for those charges where he has been acquitted by the court at the EOF. In other words, insanity is no longer a bar to trial. This is in line with case law to the effect that a person found to be insane in bar of trial has not tholed his assize and may be tried upon recovering his sanity or upon it being discovered that he was not insane: see *H.M. Advocate v. Bickerstaff*, 1926 J.C. 5 followed in *H.M. Advocate v. Graham* (High Court of Justiciary, February 16, 1996, unreported).

Disposal in case of insanity

Disposal of case where accused found to be insane

¹**57.**—(1) This section applies where—
(a) a person is, by virtue of section 54(6) or 55(3) of this Act, acquitted on the ground of his insanity at the time of the act or omission; or
(b) following an examination of facts under section 55, a court makes a finding under subsection (2) of that section.
(2) Subject to subsection (3) below, where this section applies the court may, as it thinks fit—
(a) make an order (which shall have the same effect as a hospital order) that the person be detained in such hospital as the court may specify;
(b) in addition to making an order under paragraph (a) above, make an order (which shall have the same effect as a restriction order) that the person shall, without limit of time, be subject to the special restrictions set out in section 62(1) of the Mental Health (Scotland) Act 1984;
(c) make an order (which shall have the same effect as a guardianship order) placing the person under the guardianship of a local authority or of a person approved by a local authority;
(d) make a supervision and treatment order (within the meaning of paragraph 1(1) of Schedule 4 to this Act); or
(e) make no order.
(3) Where the offence with which the person was charged is murder, the court shall make orders under both paragraphs (a) and (b) of subsection (2) above in respect of that person.
(4) Sections 58(1), (2) and (4) to (7) and 59 and 61 of this Act shall have effect in relation to the making, terms and effect of an order under paragraph (a), (b) or (c) of subsection (2) above as those provisions have effect in relation to the making, terms and effect of, respectively, a hospital order, a restriction order and a guardianship order as respects a person convicted of an offence, other than an offence the sentence for which is fixed by law, punishable by imprisonment.
(5) Schedule 4 to this Act shall have effect as regards supervision and treatment orders.

Definitions
"examination of facts": s.54(1)(b).
"medical practitioner": s.61(1).
"new supervising officer": Sched. 4, para. 7(1)(b).
"order": s.307(1).
"relevant sheriff court": Sched. 4, para. 3(2)(b).
"supervised person": Sched. 4, para. 1(1).
"supervising officer": Sched. 4, para. 1(1).
"supervision and treatment order": Sched. 4, para. 1(1).

Note
¹Prospectively amended by the Adults with Incapacity (Scotland) Act 2000 (asp 4), s.88 and Sched. 5, para. 26.

This section specifies the disposals available to a court at an examination of facts ("EOF") in both solemn and summary proceedings, and to a court acquitting a person on the grounds of insanity at the time of the commission of the offence charged. It provides for the making of a hospital order, with or without a restriction order, a guardianship order, a new disposal (the Supervision and Treatment Order) in which the recipient resides in the community under the supervision of a social worker and for the purposes of treatment under a medical practitioner, and, finally, the making of no order at all. The power to specify a hospital contained in subs. (2)(a) includes a power to specify a hospital unit, but only where the court also makes an order in terms of subs. (2)(b), subjecting the person to the special restrictions set out in s.62(1) of the Mental Health (Scotland) Act 1984. The power to specify a hospital unit was introduced by s.9 of the Crime and Punishment (Scotland) Act 1997 with effect from January 1, 1998, and thus allows a measure of flexibility in placing patients at distinct, possibly specialist, mental health units.

Section 57 thus provides a court with a wider range of disposals than was available under the previous law when dealing with an accused who is unfit to plead. Only two observations need to be made in regard to these disposals. First, the new disposal of a Supervision and Treatment Order is only new to Scotland as it has been provided for in the Criminal Procedure (Insanity and Unfitness to Plead) Act 1991 (c.25) for England and Wales. The extensive arrangements for the new disposal are set out in Sched. 4 to this Act. Secondly, in only one disposal is the discretion of the court restricted. When the charge is one of murder the court must impose a hospital order and a restriction order without limit of time (s.57(3)).

Hospital orders and guardianship

Order for hospital admission or guardianship

[3]**58.**—(1) Where a person is convicted in the High Court or the sheriff court of an offence, other than an offence the sentence for which is fixed by law, punishable by that court with imprisonment, and the following conditions are satisfied, that is to say—
  (a) the court is satisfied, on the written or oral evidence of two medical practitioners (complying with section 61 of this Act) that the grounds set out in—
      (i) section 17(1); or, as the case may be
      (ii) section 36(a),
  of the Mental Health (Scotland) Act 1984 apply in relation to the offender;
  (b) the court is of the opinion, having regard to all the circumstances including the nature of the offence and the character and antecedents of the offender and to the other available methods of dealing with him, that the most suitable method of disposing of the case is by means of an order under this section,
subject to subsection (2) below, the court may by order authorise his admission to and detention in such hospital as may be specified in the order or, as the case may be, place him under the guardianship of such local authority or of such other person approved by a local authority as may be so specified.
  (2) Where the case is remitted by the sheriff to the High Court for sentence under any enactment, the power to make an order under subsection (1) above shall be exercisable by that court.
  (3) Where in the case of a person charged summarily in the sheriff court with an act or omission constituting an offence the court would have power, on convicting him, to make an order under subsection (1) above, then, if it is satisfied that the person did the act or made the omission charged, the court may, if it thinks fit, make such an order without convicting him.
  [1](4) An order for the admission of a person to a hospital (in this Act, referred to as "a hospital order") shall not be made under this section in respect of an offender or of a person to whom subsection (3) above applies unless the court is satisfied that that hospital, in the event of such an order

being made by the court, is available for his admission thereto within 7 days of the making of such an order.

(5) A State hospital shall not be specified in a hospital order in respect of the detention of a person unless the court is satisfied, on the evidence of the medical practitioners which is taken into account under paragraph (a) of subsection (1) above, that the offender, on account of his dangerous, violent or criminal propensities, requires treatment under conditions of special security, and cannot suitably be cared for in a hospital other than a State hospital.

(6) An order placing a person under the guardianship of a local authority or of any other person (in this Act referred to as "a guardianship order") shall not be made under this section unless the court is satisfied—

    (a) after taking into consideration the evidence of a mental health officer, that it is necessary in the interests of the welfare of the person that he should be placed under guardianship; and

    (b) that that authority or person is willing to receive that person into guardianship.

[2](7) A hospital order or guardianship order shall specify the form of mental disorder, being mental illness (including personality disorder) or mental handicap or both, from which, upon the evidence taken into account under paragraph (a) of subsection (1) above, the offender is found by the court to be suffering; and no such order shall be made unless the offender is described by each of the practitioners, whose evidence is taken into account as aforesaid, as suffering from the same form of mental disorder, whether or not he is also described by either of them as suffering from the other form.

(8) Where an order is made under this section, the court shall not pass sentence of imprisonment or impose a fine or make a probation order or a community service order in respect of the offence, but may make any other order which the court has power to make apart from this section; and for the purposes of this subsection "sentence of imprisonment" includes any sentence or order for detention.

[1](9) The court by which a hospital order is made may give such directions as it thinks fit for the conveyance of the patient to a place of safety and his detention therein pending his admission to the hospital within the period of 7 days referred to in subsection (4) above; but a direction for the conveyance of a patient to a residential establishment shall not be given unless the court is satisfied that the authority is willing to receive the patient therein.

(10) Where a person is charged before the district court with an act or omission constituting an offence punishable with imprisonment, the district court, if it appears to it that that person may be suffering from mental disorder, shall remit him to the sheriff court in the manner provided by section 7(9) and (10) of this Act, and the sheriff court shall, on any such remit being made, have the like power to make an order under subsection (1) above in respect of him as if he had been charged before that court with the said act or omission as an offence, or in dealing with him may exercise the like powers as the district court.

(11) Section 58A of this Act shall have effect as regards guardianship orders made under subsection (1) of this section.

DEFINITIONS

    "guardianship order": s.58(6).
    "High Court": s.307(1).
    "hospital order": s.58(4).
    "local authority": s.307(1).
    "medical practitioner": s.61(1).
    "offence": s.307(1).

"sentence": s.307(1).
"sentence of imprisonment": s.58(8).
"State hospital": s.307(1).

NOTES

[1]Amended by the Crime and Punishment (Scotland) Act 1997 (c. 48), s.62(1) and Sched. 1 para. 21(6), with effect from January 1, 1998 in terms of the Crime and Punishment (Scotland) Act 1997 (Commencement No. 2 and Transitional and Consequential Provisions) Order 1997 (S.I. 1997 No. 2323) Art. 4, Sched. 2.)

[2] As amended by the Mental Health (Public Safety and Appeals) (Scotland) Act 1999 (asp 1), s.3(b) (effective September 13, 1999).

[3]Prospectively amended by the Adults with Incapacity (Scotland) Act 2000 (asp 4), s.88 and Sched. 5, para. 26.

[4]Prospectively inserted by the Adults with Incapacity (Scotland) Act 2000 (asp 4), s.88 and Sched. 5, para. 26.

GENERAL NOTE

This section provides for the making of orders for hospital admission or guardianship and to the extent that it re-enacts s.175 of the 1975 Act nothing new is set out here: some parts of this section have been taken from other parts of the 1975 Act.

The section is in the generality for the admission of a person to a hospital but there is a requirement (s.58(7)) that an order made under the section specifies the form of mental disorder "being mental illness or mental handicap or both", from which the person is suffering and each medical practitioner must give evidence that the person is "suffering from the same form of mental disorder, whether or not he is also described by either of them as suffering from the other form". It should be noted that the definition of "mental disorder" in s.1(2) of the Mental Health (Scotland) Act 1984 has been extended to include "personality disorder" (see s.3 of the Mental Health (Public Safety and Appeals) (Scotland) Act 1999, effective from September 1, 1999). Of the medical practitioners whose evidence is taken into account under s.58(1)(a)(i) at least one shall be employed at the hospital which is to be specified in the order (see s.61 as amended by s.10(2) of the Crime and Punishment (Scotland) Act 1997, with effect from January 1, 1998).

The section is specific in regard to a State hospital not being named in a hospital order unless the court is satisfied on medical evidence that the accused "on account of his dangerous, violent or criminal propensities, requires treatment under conditions of special security, and cannot suitably be cared for in a hospital other than a State hospital" (see s.58(5)).

A hospital order shall not be made under s.58 unless the court is satisfied that the hospital is available for the person's admission within seven days of the making of the order. The court's power to specify a hospital order under s.58 includes the power to specify a hospital unit, and thus tailor the order to meet the needs of the patient, but only where the court also makes a restriction order in terms of s.59 of the 1995 Act (see s.9 of the Crime and Punishment (Scotland) Act 1997, in force as from January 1, 1998).

Finally, it should be noted that for the purposes of s.58(1)(a) a report in writing purporting to be signed by a medical practitioner may, subject to the provisions of s.61, be received in evidence without proof of the signature or qualifications of the practitioner; but the court may, in any case, require the practitioner by whom such a report was signed be called to give oral evidence: s.61(3).

For a recent case which highlights the difficulties inherent in diagnosing mental illness, see *Jackson v. H.M. Advocate*, 1998 S.C.C.R. 539, where a sentence of life imprisonment imposed in 1984 was quashed on appeal in 1998, it being found that the appellant was mentally ill at the time of the original offences and sentence. A hospital order in terms of this section, restricted in terms of s.59, was substituted.

Once a restriction order has been imposed on the basis of valid reports it is not appropriate for the order to be rescinded because one of the doctors has changed his opinion; see the discussion at A4.136 below.

[1]Application of Adults with Incapacity (Scotland) Act 2000

58A.—(1) Subject to the provisions of this section, the provisions of Parts 1, 5, 6 and 7 of the Adults with Incapacity (Scotland) Act 2000 (asp 4) ("the 2000 Act") apply—

(a) to a guardian appointed by an order of the court under section 57(2)(c), 58(1) or 58(1A) of this Act (in this section referred to as a "guardianship order") whether appointed before or after the coming into force of these provisions, as they apply to a guardian with powers relating to the personal welfare of an adult appointed under section 58 of that Act;

(b) to a person authorised under an intervention order under section 60A of this Act as they apply to a person so authorised under section 53 of that Act.

(2) In making a guardianship order the court shall have regard to any regulations made by the Scottish Ministers under section 64(11) of the 2000 Act and—

(a) shall confer powers, which it shall specify in the order, relating only to the personal welfare of the person;

(b) may appoint a joint guardian;

(c) may appoint a substitute guardian;

(d) may make such consequential or ancillary order, provision or direction as it considers appropriate.

(3) Without prejudice to the generality of subsection (2), or to any other powers conferred by this Act, the court may—

(a) make any order granted by it subject to such conditions and restrictions as appear to it to be appropriate;

(b) order that any reports relating to the person who will be the subject of the order be lodged with the court or that the person be assessed or interviewed and that a report of such assessment or interview be lodged;

(c) make such further inquiry or call for such further information as appears to it to be appropriate;

(d) make such interim order as appears to it to be appropriate pending the disposal of the proceedings.

(4) Where the court makes a guardianship order it shall forthwith send a copy of the interlocutor containing the order to the Public Guardian who shall—

(a) enter prescribed particulars of the appointment in the register maintained by him under section 6(2)(b)(iv) of the 2000 Act;

(b) unless he considers that the notification would be likely to pose a serious risk to the person's health notify the person of the appointment of the guardian; and

(c) notify the local authority and the Mental Welfare Commission of the terms of the interlocutor.

(5) A guardianship order shall continue in force for a period of 3 years or such other period (including an indefinite period) as, on cause shown, the court may determine.

(6) Where any proceedings for the appointment of a guardian under section 57(2)(c) or 58(1) of this Act have been commenced and not determined before the date of coming into force of section 84 of, and paragraph 26 of schedule 5 to, the Adults with Incapacity (Scotland) Act 2000 (asp 4) they shall be determined in accordance with this Act as it was immediately in force before that date.]

NOTE
[1]Prospectively inserted by the Adults with Incapacity (Scotland) Act 2000 (asp 4), s.84.

Hospital orders: restrictions on discharge

[1]**59.**—(1) Where a hospital order is made in respect of a person, and it appears to the court—

(a) having regard to the nature of the offence with which he is charged;

(b) the antecedents of the person; and

(c) the risk that as a result of his mental disorder he would commit offences if set at large,

that it is necessary for the protection of the public from serious harm so to do, the court may, subject to the provisions of this section, further order that the person shall be subject to the special restrictions set out in section 62(1) of the Mental Health (Scotland) Act 1984, without limit of time.

(2) An order under this section (in this Act referred to as "a restriction order") shall not be made in the case of any person unless the medical practitioner approved by the Health Board for the purposes of section 20 or section 39 of the Mental Health (Scotland) Act 1984, whose evidence is taken into account by the court under section 58(1)(a) of this Act, has given evidence orally before the court.

(3) Where a restriction order is in force in respect of a patient, a guardianship order shall not be made in respect of him; and where the hospital order relating to him ceases to have effect by virtue of section 60(3) of the Mental Health (Scotland) Act 1984 on the making of another hospital order, that order shall have the same effect in relation to the restriction order as the previous hospital order, but without prejudice to the power of the court making that other hospital order to make another restriction order to have effect on the expiration of the previous such order.

DEFINITIONS
    "hospital order": s.58(4).
    "mental disorder": s.1(2) of the Mental Health (Scotland) Act 1984.
    "offence": s.307(1).
    "restriction order": s.59(2).

NOTE
    [1]Prospectively amended by the Adults with Incapacity (Scotland) Act 2000 (asp 4), s.88 and Sched. 6.

GENERAL NOTE
    Section 59 makes provision to restrict the discharge of hospital orders made under s.58. As a court may make a further hospital order that amounts to a person being subject to statutory special restrictions without limit of time, the tests to be met are suitably high. Indeed, the aspects of risk and protection in s.59(1) are redolent of the concerns latent in the terms of s.58(5).
    In *M v. H.M. Advocate*, 1998 G.W.D. 24–1231, an appeal against the making of a restriction order founding upon a change of opinion by one of the examining psychiatrists subsequent to the sheriff's determination, the Appeal Court held that the only relevant material for the purposes of appeal was that which had been laid before the sheriff; *M's* case might be considered administratively by the Secretary of State.
    The making of a restriction order is ultimately a matter for the Court in the circumstances of each particular case—see *Thomson v. H.M. Advocate*, 1999 S.C.C.R. 640 where the necessary criteria under section 59(1) was held made out and a restriction order made, despite psychiatric evidence that a restriction order was not necessary.
    Reference is made in passing to the Mental Health (Public Safety and Appeals) (Scotland) Act 1999 which received Royal Assent on September 13, 1999 and is effective from September 1, 1999. This Act, *inter alia*, adds public safety to the criteria to be taken into account on an appeal under section 64 of the Mental Health (Scotland) Act 1984 by a person subject to a restriction order. Accordingly, it is provided that the sheriff shall refuse such an appeal if satisfied that the patient is suffering from a mental disorder the effect of which is such that it is necessary, in order to protect the public from serious harm, that the patient continue to be detained in a hospital, "whether for medical treatment or not". The definition of "mental disorder" in s.1(2) of the 1984 Act has been extended to include "personality disorder" (see s.3 of the Mental Health (Public Safety and Appeals) (Scotland) Act 1999, effective from September 1, 1999). This radical provision is subject to a right of appeal to the Court of Session. It is expected that in future greater use will be made of the hospital direction under section 59A of the 1995 Act which allies a period of remedial hospitalisation to a custodial sentence, but of course this hybrid disposal has only been available to the solemn court since January 1, 1998.

Hospital directions

[1]**59A.**—(1) Subject to subsection (2) and (3) below, where a person is convicted on indictment in the High Court or in the sheriff court of an offence punishable by imprisonment, the court may, in addition to any

sentence of imprisonment which it has the power or the duty to impose, by a direction under this subsection (in this act referred to as a "hospital direction") authorise his admission to and detention in such hospital as may be specified in the direction.

(2) Subsection (1) above shall not apply where the person convicted is a child.

(3) A hospital direction shall not be made unless—

(a) the court is satisfied on the written or oral evidence of two medical practitioners complying with section 61 of this Act) that the grounds set out in section 17(1) of the Mental Health (Scotland) Act 1984 apply in relation to the offender;

[2](b) the medical practitioners mentioned in paragraph (a) above each describe the person as suffering from the same form of mental disorder, being mental illness (including personality disorder) or mental handicap, whether or not he is also described by either of them as suffering from the other form; and

(c) the court is satisfied that the hospital to be specified in the direction can admit the person in respect of whom it is to be made within 7 days of the direction being made.

(4) A State hospital shall not be specified in a hospital direction in respect of the detention of a person unless the court is satisfied, on the evidence of the medical practitioners which is taken into account under paragraphs (a) and (b) of subsection (3) above, that the person—

(a) on account of his dangerous or violent or criminal propensities requires treatment under conditions of special security; and

(b) cannot suitably be cared for in a hospital other than a State hospital.

(5) A hospital direction shall specify the form of mental disorder from which, upon the evidence taken into account under paragraphs (a) and (b) of subsection (3) above, the person in respect of whom it is made is found to be suffering.

(6) The court by which a hospital direction is made may give such additional directions as it thinks fit for the conveyance of the person in respect of whom it is made to a place of safety and for his detention in that place pending his admission to hospital within the period mentioned in paragraph (c) of subsection (3) above.

(7) The court shall not make an additional direction under subsection (6) above directing the conveyance of the person concerned to a place of safety which is a residential establishment unless it is satisfied that the managers of that establishment are willing to receive him in the establishment.

DEFINITIONS
"child": s.307(1).
"High Court": s.307(1).
"hospital": s.307(1) and s.9(3) of the Crime and Punishment (Scotland) Act 1997.
"hospital direction": s.307(1) and s.6(5) of the Crime and Punishment (Scotland) Act 1997.
"indictment": s.307(1).
"medical practitioner": s.61(1).
"mental disorder": s.1(2) of the Mental Health (Scotland) Act 1984.
"offence": s.307(1).
"place of safety": s.121A of the Mental Health (Scotland) Act 1984.
"sentence": s.307(1).
"State hospital": s.307(1).

NOTES
[1]Inserted by the Crime and Punishment (Scotland) Act 1997 (c. 48) s.6 with effect from January 1, 1998 by the Crime and Punishment (Scotland) Act 1997 (Commencement No. 2 and Transitional and Consequential Provisions) Order 1997 (S.I. 1997 No. 2323) Art. 4, Sched. 2.

Criminal Procedure (Scotland) Act 1995

[2] As amended by the Mental Health (Public Safety and Appeals) (Scotland) Act 1999 (asp 1), s.3(b) (effective September 13, 1999).

GENERAL NOTE

This section was inserted by s.6 of the Crime and Punishment (Scotland) Act 1997, with effect from January 1, 1998. It introduces a new power, the hospital direction, as a sentencing disposal in the solemn court. Following conviction on indictment for an offence punishable by imprisonment, the convicted person can be sentenced to imprisonment allied to a hospital direction provided that the requirements of subs. (3) are fulfilled. The intention is to provide a sentencing disposal for those offenders well enough to stand trial but suffering from a mental disorder which is amenable to treatment, thus combining a hybrid sentence, a custodial disposal with an immediate period of remedial hospitalisation.

In order to impose such a direction the court must be presented with written or parole evidence from two medical practitioners, at least one of whom is recognised as having special experience in the diagnosis or treatment of mental disorder and at least one of whom must be employed in the hospital nominated in their reports (see s.61). The medical practitioners must concur that (i) the offender suffers from an identified mental illness, impairment or severe mental impairment, (ii) his condition necessitates hospitalisation for treatment to alleviate it or prevent further deterioration, and (iii) detention is felt necessary to protect his health and safety or to protect other persons. It should be noted that the definition of "mental disorder" in s.1(2) of the Mental Health (Scotland) Act 1984 has been extended to include "personality disorder" (see s.3 of the Mental Health (Public Safety and Appeals) (Scotland) Act 1999, effective from September 1, 1999.

Subsection (3) underlines that the practitioners must identify the same mental illness or impairment (irrespective of the number of conditions or illnesses which afflict the offender), since the direction must stipulate the disorder expressly, and that the court must be persuaded that a named hospital can accommodate him within seven days of the making of the direction. In the interim, if the convicted person cannot be taken to that hospital immediately, the court may designate a temporary place of safety and issue additional directions concerning his removal there, and his care, pending the availability of the identified hospital place. Subsection (7) requires the court to be satisfied that any residential place of safety designated by it will receive the convicted person.

The court's power to specify a hospital includes a power to specify a "hospital unit" by virtue of s.9 of the Crime and Punishment (Scotland) Act 1997 (in force from January 1, 1998), and thus to focus the hospital direction to the particular needs of the accused. "Hospital unit" means any part of a hospital which is treated as a separate unit (s.9(3) of the 1997 Act).

It should be noted that the provisions in relation to hospital directions have no application to any child (subs. (2)).

Section 7 of the Crime and Punishment (Scotland) Act 1997 inserts a new section, s.62A, into the Mental Health (Scotland) Act 1984 with effect from January 1, 1998, to accommodate procedures for the actual implementation and operation of a hospital direction within the ambit of the 1984 Act.

Appeals against hospital orders

[1]**60.** Where a hospital order, interim hospital order (but not a renewal thereof), guardianship order, a restriction order or a hospital direction has been made by a court in respect of a person charged or brought before it, he may without prejudice to any other form of appeal under any rule of law (or, where an interim hospital order has been made, to any right of appeal against any other order or sentence which may be imposed), appeal against that order or, as the case may be, direction in the same manner as against sentence.

DEFINITIONS

"guardianship order": s.58(6).
"hospital direction": s.59A(1).
"hospital order": s.58(4).
"interim hospital order": s.53(1).
"restriction order": s.59(2).

"sentence": s.307(1).

NOTE
[1]As amended by the Crime and Punishment (Scotland) Act 1997 (c. 48) s.6(2) with effect from January 1, by the Crime and Punishment (Scotland) Act 1997 (Commencement No. 2 and Transitional Provisions) Order 1997 (S.I. 1997 No. 2323) Art. 4, Sched. 2.

GENERAL NOTE
This section conjoins the right of appeal formerly to be found in ss.280 and 443 of the 1975 Act. The right of appeal against these orders is treated as an appeal against sentence so that, for example, an appeal against a finding on fact under s.55(2) by the court cannot be appealed under s.60. Appeals against findings and orders are dealt with by ss.62 and 63.
The right of appeal against the making of a hospital direction was inserted into s.60 by virtue of s.6(2) of the Crime and Punishment (Scotland) Act 1997, with effect from January 1, 1998.

Appeal by prosecutor against hospital orders etc.

[1, 2]**60A.**—(1) This section applies where the court, in respect of a person charged or brought before it, has made—
  (a) an order under any of paragraphs (a) to (d) of subsection (2) of section 57 of this Act or such a decision as is mentioned in paragraph (e) of that subsection; or
  (b) a hospital order, guardianship order, restriction order or a hospital direction.
    (2) Where this section applies, the prosecutor may appeal against any such order, decision or direction as is mentioned in subsection (1) above—
  (a) if it appears to him that the order, decision or direction was inappropriate; or
  (b) on a point of law,
and an appeal under this section shall be treated in the same manner as an appeal against sentence under section 108 of this Act.

NOTES
[1]Inserted by the Crime and Punishment (Scotland) Act 1997 (c. 48) s.22 with effect from January 1, 1998 by the Crime and Punishment (Scotland) Act 1997 (Commencement No. 2 and Transitional and Consequential Provisions) Order 1997 (S.I. 1997, No. 2323) Art. 4, Sched. 2.
[2]Prospectively amended by the Adults with Incapacity (Scotland) Act 2000 (asp 4), s.88 and Sched. 5, para. 26.

GENERAL NOTE
This section was inserted by s.22 of the Crime and Punishment (Scotland) Act 1997, with effect from January 1, 1998. It extends the right of appeal of the prosecutor found in s.63 of this Act, to include a right to appeal against hospital orders, etc. made where an accused is found to be insane.

Medical evidence

Requirements as to medical evidence

[3]**61.**[1]—(1) Of the medical practitioners whose evidence is taken into account in making a finding under section 54(1)(a) of this Act or under any of the relevant provisions, at least one shall be a practitioner approved for the purposes of section 20 or section 39 of the Mental Health (Scotland) Act 1984 by a Health Board as having special experience in the diagnosis or treatment of mental disorder.
[2](1A) Of the medical practitioners whose evidence is taken into account under section 53(1), 54(1)(c), 58(1)(a)(i) or 59A(3)(a) and (b) of this Act, at least one shall be employed at the hospital which is to be specified in the order or, as the case may be, direction.

[1](2) Written or oral evidence given for the purposes of any of the relevant provisions shall include a statement as to whether the person giving the evidence is related to the accused and of any pecuniary interest which that person may have in the admission of the accused to hospital or his reception into guardianship.

[1](3) For the purposes of making a finding under section 54(1)(a) of this Act or of any of the relevant provisions a report in writing purporting to be signed by a medical practitioner may, subject to the provisions of this section, be received in evidence without proof of the signature or qualifications of the practitioner; but the court may, in any case, require that the practitioner by whom such a report was signed be called to give oral evidence.

(4) Where any such report as aforesaid is tendered in evidence, otherwise than by or on behalf of the accused, then—

(a) if the accused is represented by counsel or solicitor, a copy of the report shall be given to his counsel or solicitor;

(b) if the accused is not so represented, the substance of the report shall be disclosed to the accused or, where he is a child under 16 years of age, to his parent or guardian if present in court;

(c) in any case, the accused may require that the practitioner by whom the report was signed be called to give oral evidence, and evidence to rebut the evidence contained in the report may be called by or on behalf of the accused,

and where the court is of the opinion that further time is necessary in the interests of the accused for consideration of that report, or the substance of any such report, it shall adjourn the case.

(5) For the purpose of calling evidence to rebut the evidence contained in any such report as aforesaid, arrangements may be made by or on behalf of an accused person detained in a hospital or, as respects a report for the purposes of the said section 54(1), remanded in custody for his examination by any medical practitioner, and any such examination may he made in private.

[2](6) In this section the "relevant provisions" means sections 53(1), 54(1)(c), 58(1)(a) and 59A(3)(a) and (b) of this Act.

DEFINITIONS
"hospital": s.307(1).
"medical practitioner": s.61(1).
"mental disorder": s.58(7).

NOTES
[1]As amended by the Crime and Punishment (Scotland) Act 1997 (c. 48) s.10(2) with effect from January 1, 1998 by the Crime and Punishment (Scotland) Act 1997 (Commencement No. 2 and Transitional and Consequential Provisions) Order 1997 (S.I. 1997 No. 2323) Art. 4, Sched. 2.
[2]As inserted by the above in Note 1.
[3]Prospectively amended by the Adults with Incapacity (Scotland) Act 2000 (asp 4), s.88 and Sched. 5, para. 26.

GENERAL NOTE
Section 61 specifies requirements as to medical evidence in respect of (i) a finding of insanity in bar of trial (s.54(1)(a)), (ii) the making of an interim hospital order (s.53(1)), (iii) the making of a temporary hospital order (s.54(1)(c)), (iv) the making of a hospital or guardianship order (s.58(1)(a)), and (v) the newly introduced hospital direction (s.59A(3)(a) and (b) as inserted by s.6 of the Crime and Punishment (Scotland) Act 1997 as from January 1, 1998).

One of the purposes of this section is to ensure that medical practitioners who give evidence on the mental health of the person in question do so in the capacity of skilled witnesses, or at least one of them must to meet the terms of s.61(1). In addition, by virtue of subs. 1(A) at least one of the medical practitioners involved must be employed in the proposed receiving hospital. This requirement is presumably intended to ensure that facilities will be available at that hospital and that at an early stage a practitioner experienced in the treatment of mental illness has had an input to the case.

Appeals under Part VI

Appeal by accused in case involving insanity

62.—(1) A person may appeal to the High Court against—

(a) a finding made under section 54(1) of this Act that he is insane so that his trial cannot proceed or continue, or the refusal of the court to make such a finding;

(b) a finding under section 55(2) of this Act; or

(c) an order made under section 57(2) of this Act.

(2) An appeal under subsection (1) above shall be—

(a) in writing; and

(b) lodged—

    (i) in the case of an appeal under paragraph (a) of that subsection, not later than seven days after the date of the finding or refusal which is the subject of the appeal;

    (ii) in the case of an appeal under paragraph (b), or both paragraphs (b) and (c) of that subsection, not later than 28 days after the conclusion of the examination of facts;

    (iii) in the case of an appeal under paragraph (c) of that subsection against an order made on an acquittal, by virtue of section 54(6) or 55(3) of this Act, on the ground of insanity at the time of the act or omission, not later than 14 days after the date of the acquittal;

    (iv) in the case of an appeal under that paragraph against an order made on a finding under section 55(2), not later than 14 days after the conclusion of the examination of facts,

or within such longer period as the High Court may, on cause shown, allow.

(3) Where the examination of facts was held in connection with proceedings on indictment, subsections (1)(a) and (2)(b)(i) above are without prejudice to section 74(1) of this Act.

(4) Where an appeal is taken under subsection (1) above, the period from the date on which the appeal was lodged until it is withdrawn or disposed of shall not count towards any time limit applying in respect of the case.

(5) An appellant in an appeal under this section shall be entitled to be present at the hearing of the appeal unless the High Court determines that his presence is not practicable or appropriate.

(6) In disposing of an appeal under subsection (1) above the High Court may—

(a) affirm the decision of the court of first instance;

¹(b) make any other finding, order or other disposal which that court could have made at the time when it made the finding or order which is the subject of the appeal; or

(c) remit the case to that court with such directions in the matter as the High Court thinks fit.

(7) Section 60 of this Act shall not apply in relation to any order as respects which a person has a right of appeal under subsection (1)(c) above.

DEFINITIONS

  "examination of facts": s.54(1)(b).

  "High Court": s.307(1).

  "order": s.307(1).

NOTE
[1]As amended by the Crime and Punishment (Scotland) Act 1997 (c. 48) Sched. 1, para. 21(7) with effect from January 1, 1997 (Commencement No. 2 and Transitional and Consequential Provisions) Order 1997 (S.I. 1997 No. 2323) Art. 4, Sched. 2.

GENERAL NOTE
Under the previous law, ss.174(1) and 375(2) of the 1975 Act enabled a court to find a person insane in bar of trial. An accused person had no right of appeal either against such a finding or against the refusal of any plea or motion that such a finding should be made. The only exception was where the finding was made at a preliminary diet in solemn proceedings in which event the accused had a right of appeal by s.76A(1) of the 1975 Act.

The new section provides the accused under solemn or summary procedure with rights of appeal in relation to any findings, or the refusal to make a finding, that the accused is insane in bar of trial and against findings made by, and orders made at, examinations of fact. Although such appeals must be made in comparatively short periods of time, longer periods may be allowed by the High Court of Justiciary on cause shown. The appellate judges have a broad range of powers to affirm or vary decisions and orders appealed against and to remit cases with directions.

Appeal by prosecutor in case involving insanity

63.—(1) The prosecutor may appeal to the High Court on a point of law against—
(a) a finding under subsection (1) of section 54 of this Act that an accused is insane so that his trial cannot proceed or continue;
(b) an acquittal on the ground of insanity at the time of the act or omission by virtue of subsection (6) of that section;
(c) an acquittal under section 55(3) of this Act (whether or not on the ground of insanity at the time of the act or omission); or
[2](d) ...
(2) An appeal under subsection (1) above shall be—
(a) in writing; and
(b) lodged—
(i) in the case of an appeal under paragraph (a) or (b) of that subsection, not later than seven days after the finding or, as the case may be, the acquittal which is the subject of the appeal;
(ii) in the case of an appeal under paragraph (c) of that subsection, not later than seven days after the conclusion of the examination of facts,
or within such longer period as the High Court may, on cause shown, allow.
(3) Where the examination of facts was held in connection with proceedings on indictment, subsections (1)(a) and (2)(b)(i) above are without prejudice to section 74(1) of this Act.
(4) A respondent in an appeal under this subsection shall be entitled to be present at the hearing of the appeal unless the High Court determines that his presence is not practicable or appropriate.
(5) In disposing of an appeal under subsection (1) above the High Court may—
(a) affirm the decision of the court of first instance;
[1](b) make any other finding, order or disposal which that court could have made at the time when it made the finding [2]or acquittal which is the subject of the appeal; or
(c) remit the case to that court with such directions in the matter as the High Court thinks fit.
(6) In this section, "the prosecutor" means, in relation to proceedings on indictment, the Lord Advocate.

DEFINITIONS
"examination of facts": s.54(1)(b).
"High Court": s.307(1).

"order": s.307(1).
"prosecutor": s.63(6).

NOTES
[1] As amended by the Crime and Punishment (Scotland) Act 1997 (c.48) Sched. 1, para. 21(8) with effect from January 1, 1998 by the Crime and Punishment (Scotland) Act 1997 (Commencement No. 2 and Transitional and Consequential Provisions) Order 1997 (S.I. 1997 No. 2323) Art. 4, Sched. 2.
[2] As repealed by the above in Note 1.

GENERAL NOTE
Under the previous law, ss.174(1) and 375(2) of the 1975 Act enabled a court to find a person insane in bar of trial. The Crown had no right of appeal against such a finding unless it had been made at a preliminary diet in solemn proceedings, in which event the Crown had a right of appeal by s.76A(1) of the 1975 Act.

This section now provides the Crown with a right of appeal similar to those given to the accused under s.62. The Crown may appeal against a finding of insanity in bar of trial, against a trial verdict of acquittal on the ground of insanity, and against any acquittal at an examination of facts. In each of these the appeal may be only on a point of law. Note also s.60A which allows the prosecutor a right of appeal against hospital orders, etc. made where an accused is found to be insane.

PART VII

SOLEMN PROCEEDINGS

The indictment

Prosecution on indictment

64.—(1) All prosecutions for the public interest before the High Court or before the sheriff sitting with a jury shall proceed on indictment in name of Her Majesty's Advocate.

(2) The indictment may be in the forms—
(a) set out in Schedule 2 to this Act; or
(b) prescribed by Act of Adjournal,
or as nearly as may be in such form.

(3) Indictments in proceedings before the High Court shall be signed by the Lord Advocate or one of his deputes.

(4) Indictments in proceedings before the sheriff sitting with a jury shall be signed by the procurator fiscal, and the words "By Authority of Her Majesty's Advocate" shall be prefixed to the signature of the procurator fiscal.

(5) The principal record and service copies of indictments and all notices of citation, lists of witnesses, productions and jurors, and all other official documents required in a prosecution on indictment may be either written or printed or partly written and partly printed.

(6) Schedule 3 to this Act shall have effect as regards indictments under this Act.

DEFINITIONS
"High Court": s.307(1).
"indictment": s.307(1).
"procurator fiscal": s.307(1).

GENERAL NOTE
The provisions dealing with the latitudes as to time, place, capacity and implied terms previously contained in ss.43 to 67 of the 1975 Act, in relation to solemn proceedings, and s.311 relative to summary proceedings, are now incorporated in Sched. 3 to the 1995 Act. It remains a moot point what practical benefit is derived from preserving the indictment styles of the 1887 Act as Sched. 2 does.

Section 287 of the 1995 Act makes provision for the maintenance of indictment proceedings

leath of, or demission of office by, the Lord Advocate. Even where the
rcised his powers in terms of s.287(2) following the resignation of the Lord
ry 2000, it is of note that conform to subs.(4) above, sheriff and jury
d to have the words "By Authority of Her Majesty's Advocate" upon
is mandatory in its terms and probably reflects the fact that a procurator
s protected in terms of s.1 of the Sheriff Courts and Legal Officers
c.35). See also the discussion in *Hester v. MacDonald*, 1961 S.C. 370; 1961
88 below entitles the Lord Advocate to be advised of, and be heard in
)sed private prosecution: see *X. v. Sweeney*, 1982 S.C.C.R. 161 which
Criminal Letters, the Lord Advocate not objecting, following formal
___wn to the accused of no further proceedings.

It is well-understood that no *nomen juris* is required in any indictment or complaint; it is
sufficient that the facts set out in the libel would, if proved, constitute a crime in Scots law (see
Lippe v. Wilson, 1997, G.W.D. 17–766 following *Angus v. H.M. Advocate* (1905) 8 F.(J) 10 and
at para. A4.348).

The incorporation into one charge of a series of offences, as in a fraudulent scheme, should
not itself preclude a submission of no case to answer on any one of those offences (*H.M.
Advocate v. Young*, 1997 G.W.D. 33–1669 following *Cordiner v. H.M. Advocate*, 1993 S.L.T. 2).

Prevention of delay in trials

65.—(1) Subject to subsections (2) and (3) below, an accused shall not be
tried on indictment for any offence unless the trial is commenced within a
period of 12 months of the first appearance of the accused on petition in
respect of the offence; and, failing such commencement within that period,
the accused
[1](a) shall be discharged forthwith from any indictment as respects the
offence; and
(b) shall not at any time be proceeded against on indictment as respects
the offence.

(2) Nothing in subsection (1) above shall bar the trial of an accused for
whose arrest a warrant has been granted for failure to appear at a diet in the
case.

(3) On an application made for the purpose, the sheriff or, where an
indictment has been served on the accused in respect of the High Court, a
single judge of that court, may on cause shown extend the said period of 12
months.

[1](3A) An application under subsection (3) shall not be made at any time
when an appeal made with leave under s.74(1) of this Act has not been
disposed of by the High Court.

(4) Subject to subsections (5) to (9) below, an accused who is committed
for any offence until liberated in due course of law shall not be detained by
virtue of that committal for a total period of more than—
(a) 80 days, unless within that period the indictment is served on him,
which failing he shall be liberated forthwith; or
(b) 110 days, unless the trial of the case is commenced within that period,
which failing he shall be liberated forthwith and thereafter he shall be
for ever free from all question or process for that offence.

(5) Subject to subsection (6) below, a single judge of the High Court, may,
on an application made to him for the purpose, for any sufficient cause
extend the period mentioned in subsection (4)(a) above.

(6) An application under subsection (5) above shall not be granted if the
judge is satisfied that, but for some fault on the part of the prosecution, the
indictment could have been served within the period of 80 days.

(7) A single judge of the High Court may, on an application made to him
for the purpose, extend the period mentioned in subsection (4)(b) above
where he is satisfied that delay in the commencement of the trial is due to—
(a) the illness of the accused or of a judge;

(b) the absence or illness of any necessary witness;

(c) any other sufficient cause which is not attributable to any fault on the part of the prosecutor.

(8) The grant or refusal of any application to extend the periods mentioned in this section may be appealed against by note of appeal presented to the High Court; and that Court may affirm, reverse or amend the determination made on such application.

(9) For the purposes of this section, a trial shall be taken to commence when the oath is administered to the jury.

(10) In calculating the period of 12 months specified in subsections (1) and (3) above there shall be left out of account any period during which the accused is detained, other than while serving a sentence of imprisonment or detention, in any other part of the United Kingdom or in any of the Channel Islands or the Isle of Man in any prison or other institution or place mentioned in subsection (1) or (1A) of section 29 of the Criminal Justice Act 1961 (transfer of prisoners for certain judicial purposes).

DEFINITIONS
"High Court": s.307(1).
"indictment": s.307(1).
"offence": s.307(1).
"prison": s.307(1).

NOTE
[1]Inserted by the Crime and Punishment (Scotland) Act 1997 Sched. 1, para. 21(9) with effect from August 1, 1997 in terms of the Crime and Punishment (Scotland) Act 1997 (Commencement and Transitional Provisions) Order 1997 (S.I. 1997 No. 1712) para. 21(9).

GENERAL NOTE
The provisions of this section restate the terms of s.101 of the 1975 Act and impose time-limits upon the commencement of solemn proceedings. Failure on the part of the Crown to take proper account of these mandatory provisions can, on rare occasions, be cured retrospectively, but generally the section's terms are strictly construed. Existing case law, of which there is, unsurprisingly, a substantial volume given the mandatory finality of s.101 of the 1975 Act, will still be authoritative.

Two distinct time scales are specified by s.65: the rules applicable to custody proceedings on indictment which demand service of any indictment within 80 days of full committal and the commencement of those proceedings within 110 days (subs. (4)); and the prescriptive one year period within which those persons liberated on petition bail must be brought to trial (subs. (1)). If the relevant time-limits are not met by the Crown, proceedings will ordinarily fall.

Subss. (1), (2) and (3)
It is hard to believe that this provision against delay in solemn cases where the accused has been admitted to bail was introduced as recently as 1980 by s.6 of the Criminal Justice (Scotland) Act of that year.

Service of any indictment should be effected not less than 29 days before the assigned diet of trial (see s.66(6) below) unless the accused has opted to plead guilty by way of an accelerated plea under s.76 of the 1995 Act. Such accelerated proceedings apart, for practical purposes sheriff and jury proceedings are now activated by the calling of the indictment at the first diet, a mechanism introduced by ss.66 and 71 of the 1995 Act. Until this formal step has been taken the Crown has not begun to comply with the terms of s.65(1) in those proceedings.

Note that the one year period commences from the date of the accused's first appearance on the relative petition, whether he is committed for further examination, as is usual, or fully committed and halts, in terms of subs. (9), when the jury is put on oath at the trial diet (by contrast, calculation of the 80 and 110 day periods in solemn custody cases only runs from the date of full committal). It will be seen that s.66 does not make mandatory provision of first diets in proceedings before the High Court, but that a preliminary diet can be fixed by way of the procedures laid out in s.72. It has been held that the furnishing of incorrect information about the current domicile of citation to the prosecutor by the sheriff clerk (it being the practice to make a final check before indicting) which resulted in a failure to effect service of the indictment would justify an extension of the 12 month period (*Anderson v. H.M. Advocate*, 1996 S.C.C.R. 487). In *H.M. Advocate v. Brodie*, 1996 G.W.D. 33–1963 in which several extensions had been granted previously, a further Crown motion for extension was allowed, B having appeared on petition in this case charged with murder and having disappeared after his release; it was noted that extradition proceedings might be necessary to secure his appearance and these would only be competent if there were live proceedings.

In *H.M. Advocate v. Sorrie*, 1996 G.W.D. 30–1795 it was held on appeal that fault did not lie with the Crown where banknotes seized by the police and lodged with the procurator fiscal, had after forensic tests, been stolen. Note that the sheriff had already upheld a plea in bar of trial on the basis that the accused had thus been denied the opportunity of examining the notes listed as productions in the indictment. (See also the notes to s.68(2).)

Application for an extension of the one year period can be made by either the prosecutor or the defence and is considered by the judge of first instance (a sheriff or in High Court cases a High Court judge sitting alone), whose decision can be appealed to the High Court by way of note of appeal. Many of the issues referred to in the case law are likely to be aired at first or preliminary diets rather than at the trial diet itself in future.

Applications for extension of the 12 month period can be made, and granted, more than once and can be made prospectively and retrospectively; in *Ashcroft v. H.M. Advocate*, 1996 S.C.C.R. 608 two applications for extension were made and only on the second occasion was opposition expressed by the accused. In that case the Crown's aim in seeking a second period of extension was to allow the trial of both accused on a charge of indecently assaulting a 14-year-old girl to occur at one diet and avoid the need for the girl to testify twice. As a matter of policy in such a case the Appeal Court regarded the nature of the allegations as suficient cause for extending the period.

The grant of a warrant following upon a failure to appear by the accused has the effect of interrupting the 12 month period specified in subs. (1). This is so even where the failure to appear which gave rise to the warrant is later found to have occurred inadvertently rather than wilfully (see *H.M. Advocate v. Taylor*, 1996 S.C.C.R. 510). Once the warrant is granted the accused will be remanded in custody to await trial in due course of law, bail not being competent. It is questionable what remedy (if any) is open to a hapless accused in the absence of a statutory power of review of the grant of a warrant under subs. (3): practice suggests that a petition to the nobile officium is appropriate. The issue is discussed in "Suspension of Arrest Warrants" by Peter W. Ferguson in 1996 J.L.S.S. 358.

In *Leckie v. Crowe*, 1997 G.W.D. 3–90 the Appeal Court declined to quash a conviction where the appellant had tendered a plea following execution of a warrant which, he claimed, had been granted wrongly at a diet, the case having been called earlier than the hour stipulated when the indictment was served.

Extension of the one year time bar (subs. (3))

Any such motion will be considered by a single judge and can be granted on cause shown, a less strict test than is applied to motions to extend the 110 day period in custody; see subss. (6) and (7) which in custody cases requires that any delay shall not be the fault of the prosecutor. Compare *Langan v. H.M. Advocate*, 1997 G.W.D. 13–551, where the Appeal Court could not divine any basis for the sheriff's grant of a retrospective extension to proceedings, they reduced the matter to a summary complaint.

The judge does not have an absolute discretion when considering a motion to extend the 12 month period; in *H.M. Advocate v. Brown*, 1984 S.C.C.R. 347 it was held that the sheriff acted unreasonably in granting a defence motion to adjourn the trial, but refusing an unopposed Crown motion for an extension. *McCulloch v. H.M.Advocate,* 2000 G.W.D. 36–1357 (discussed at A4–513 below) in which an extension of the year was allowed to enable re-indictment of the case, perhaps surprisingly since the Crown had commented upon the failure of a spouse to give evidence, illustrates the competing interests which must be weighed in the balance when considering applications for extension. Note that an application for extension in terms of subs. (3) can only be made to the High Court once an indictment has been served for trial in the High Court; otherwise the application should be made to a sheriff in advance of any indictment or once an indictment for sheriff and jury proceedings has been served (*H.M. Advocate v. Caulfield*, 1999 G.W.D. 19–872).

A degree of fault on the part of the Crown would not be fatal to an application for extension of the year period (*Mallison v. H.M. Advocate*, 1987 S.C.C.R. 320 and *McGill v. H.M. Advocate*, 1997 S.C.C.R. 230), but certainly failure to serve an indictment at a domicile of citation would attract particularly rigorous scrutiny (*H.M. Advocate v. Swift*, 1984 S.C.C.R. 216; 1985 S.L.T. 26) while a libel which constituted a nullity would not generally warrant an extension; *Stenton v. H.M. Advocate*, 1999 S.L.T. 255. Similarly adjournment of a trial to a non—existent sitting, and efforts to constitute a sitting to overcome the error, led to refusal of a last—minute motion for extension of the year (see *Willoughby v. H.M. Advocate,* 2000 S.C.C.R. 73). *Rennie v. H.M. Advocate*, 1998 S.L.T. 191, is probably an extreme example of the excusal of Crown fault, and may have been not unrelated to the fact that the complainer in what had begun life as an allegation of rape and had been indicted as shameless indecency, was mentally backward;

objection to the libel, which the Crown did not defend, was taken just four days prior to trial—the lateness of this challenge being a factor which the Appeal Court felt had wrongly been taken into consideration by the sheriff. Accordingly the Appeal Court reviewed the decision to extend the time bar, held the fault on the part of the Crown in serving an indictment which they later conceded to be irrelevant was not entirely inexcusable and paid due regard to the seriousness of the allegations. The extension was upheld on appeal but, whether it accurately reflected the anticipated evidence or not, it could be said that the Crown had been too hasty in conceding that the libel was irrelevant. However, failure on the part of the police to execute service of an indictment timeously or to comply with express instructions are not faults of the prosecutor; see *Welsh v. H.M. Advocate*, 1985 S.C.C.R. 404; *H.M. Advocate v. Davies*, 1993 S.C.C.R. 645; *Coutts v. H.M. Advocate*, 1992 S.C.C.R. 87. Even where the Crown instructed service of an indictment on the last available day with unclear instructions and in the knowledge that the accused had no proper domicile of citation, the Appeal Court felt able to uphold the grant of an extension; it was observed that the terms of the indictment were known to him some days before service and that no claim of prejudice had been advanced (*Finlay v. H.M. Advocate*, 1998 S.L.T. 1235). It is clear that failure to intimate a change of domicile which results in service being unsuccessful at the accused's former address will not count against the Crown (*Black v. H.M. Advocate*, 1990 S.C.C.R. 609); similarly the provision of an incomplete or imprecise address as domicile when seeking bail will not benefit an accused when service at that address proves to be defective (*Brown v. H.M. Advocate*, 1998 S.L.T. 971).

In *Forrester v. H.M. Advocate* 1997, S.C.C.R. 9 the year had been extended twice already, on Crown motion, due to the prolonged illness of an essential witness. Before applying for a third extension the prosecutor had intimated to the defence, that if a further extension was opposed the Crown intended to lead the evidence of that witness, through use of the hearsay provisions of s.259 of the 1995 Act. The Crown then sought a last extension arguing that the illness of a vital witness was not its fault. A defence appeal against the grant of that third extension, founding *inter alia* upon the unwillingness of the Crown to lead evidence by means of s.259 for tactical reasons, was refused by the Appeal Court, which distinguished between the technical sufficiency of evidence available using the provisions in s.259 and the desirability of the jury hearing the testimony of such vital witness and any cross-examination. More unusually the sheriff's decision to desert proceedings *pro loco et tempore* and to extend the year time bar were upheld on appeal in a case where both he, and the prosecutor, had gone too far in comforting a child witness who had broken down in the course of her evidence (see *McKie v. H.M. Advocate*, 1997 S.L.T. 1018, discussed more fully at A4.527 below).

An extension of time has been permitted to enable the Crown to indict an offence committed by the accused late during the year after his petition appearance. In *Campbell v. Ritchie*, 1999 S.C.C.R. 914 it was of particular significance that *Moorov* could be applied to both groups of offences.

Pressure of business alone will not justify an extension and even when administrative difficulties are founded upon, the court is under an obligation to make enquiry into their nature (see *Dobbie v. H.M. Advocate*, 1986 S.L.T. 648; *Fleming v. H.M. Advocate*, 1992 S.C.C.R. 575). Note that in *Rudge v. H.M. Advocate*, 1989 S.C.C.R. 105 a Crown motion in such circumstances was granted and one persuasive factor was the lack of real prejudice being demonstrated. In *Beattie v. H.M. Advocate*, 1995 S.C.C.R. 606 where a Crown motion to extend the 110 day period was granted, the Court of Appeal disfavoured the view that the non-availability of the trial judge was itself sufficient cause for extending the statutory time-limits. The court was critical of the lack of enquiry made by the trial judge as to possible alternatives and emphasised that the tests involved in extending the 110 day period are more exacting than those applicable to extending the one year period. An extension was granted to the Crown in *H.M. Advocate v. McNally*, 1999 S.L.T 1377 where insufficient jurors were available to deal with the remaining cases in the sitting but the Appeal Court (at p.1381F) was at pains not to give the Crown *carte blanche* in the event of a repetition. In *Warnes v. H.M.Advocate*, 2000 G.W.D. 36–1356 a Crown motion for extension of the year time-bar was refused following an appeal by the accused. The Crown, which had given precedence to cases which did not time-bar in the sitting over *Warnes* whose case did, had cited pressure of business in a sitting already shortened by Easter holidays. The court was critical of the resources made available by the Scottish Executive and noted that the pressure in the sitting was entirely predictable but had been ignored by the Crown.

Miscalculation of the time bar period on the Crown's part was rejected by the Appeal Court as a valid ground for extension in *Lyle v. H.M. Advocate*, 1992 S.L.T. 467 and *Bennett v. H.M. Advocate*, 1998 S.C.C.R. 23 (but see *Millar v. H.M. Advocate*, 1994 S.L.T. 461 and *Duke v. Lees*, 1997 G.W.D. 15–659 discussed below), as has a realisation too late that essential corroborative evidence had not been secured; see *Stewart v. H.M. Advocate*, 1994 S.L.T. 518 where a successful Crown application for extension was overturned on appeal when it was conceded that such additional evidence could have been obtained within the statutory year. Correction of a misnumbered production on the indictment by the Crown without this being made known to the defence or the court was held in *Brown v. H.M. Advocate*, 1999 S.L.T. 1369 to justify refusal of an extension. Detention in England and consequent absence which necessitated an extension was, on the facts, regarded as attributable to the accused, not the Crown (*Duffy v. H.M. Advocate*, 1991 S.C.C.R. 685). Subsection (10) provides some statutory clarification in this area, by enacting that periods of remand served elsewhere in the United Kingdom shall interrupt the advance of the year time bar, an issue which had surfaced (and caused judicial calls for just such a reform) in *H.M. Advocate v. Rowan*, 1994 S.C.C.R. 801. In *Rowan* the Court of Appeal considered a Crown appeal against a refusal of extension of the year period where R was in custody in England on other matters, and the English authorities lacked any powers to transfer him to Scotland; the appeal was allowed and this anomalous situation resulted in the amendment of the Criminal Justice (Scotland) Act 1995, s.15 at the Report Stage (*Hansard*, H.L. Vol. 561, col. 39). However, detention as a serving prisoner in Scotland on other charges is not a factor, which can properly be taken into account by the court, when considering an application for extension (*McGill v. H.M. Advocate*, 1997 S.C.C.R. 230).

While an application for extension may be presented orally to the court, the defence are entitled to be heard (*Sandford v. H.M. Advocate*, 1986 S.C.C.R. 573) and to have warning of the motion to be made, albeit no formal notice is necessary (*Ferguson v. H.M. Advocate*, 1992 S.C.C.R. 480; *Cation v. H.M. Advocate*, 1992 S.C.C.R. 480). These last two cases also serve as warnings to the Crown of the risks associated with excusing witnesses without first securing the agreement of the defence: in both cases appeals against extensions of the year period were successful. By contrast see *Berry v. H.M. Advocate*, 1989 S.L.T. 71 where delays in notifying the Crown that a witness on the indictment could not be excused, or his evidence be agreed, resulted in an extension of time which was upheld on appeal. Equally where adjournment of the trial was on defence motion and, in an oversight, the Crown failed to seek the necessary time-bar extension to preserve the proceedings, the Appeal Court was unimpressed by defence opposition to extension (*McGinlay v. H.M. Advocate*, 1999 S.C.C.R. 779).

Persistent illness or absence of co-accused may not justify extensions if the Crown have not considered proceeding against the accused who is present on his own (*Mejka v. H.M. Advocate*, 1993 S.L.T. 1321; 1993 S.C.C.R. 978).

Where an accused has appeared on successive petitions, the court has to look to each petition individually in order to determine the effective date of the year time bar (*Ross v. H.M. Advocate*, 1990 S.C.C.R. 182). Thus in *H.M. Advocate v. Muir*, 1998 S.L.T. 1296 where M. had been remanded on petition and was later released at the trial diet following the failure to appear of a co-accused, only to fail to appear himself at a later trial resulting in a further period of remand after arrest, it was held on appeal that s.65(4) required that both periods of imprisonment had to be added together in calculating the 80 and 110 day periods; appropriate extensions had to be obtained.

It is possible for the time-bar to be extended retrospectively (*H.M. Advocate v. M.*, 1986 S.C.C.R. 624) and as subs. (2) provides the accused's failure to appear at a first or preliminary diet, or a trial diet, immediately stops the operation of the time-bar. Prospective extension of the time-bar is competent even where no indictment has yet been served is competent (*H.M. Advocate v. Caulfield*, 1999 G.W.D. 19–872).

While the provisions of s.65 do not apply directly to private prosecutions by way of a Bill of Criminal Letters, in *G.M.C. v. Forsyth*, 1995 S.C.C.R. 553, the court had regard to the spirit of the statutory provisions in refusing a Bill presented 14 months after proceedings were deserted by the Crown.

In computing the time-scale of any extension, the natural interpretation of such a motion is that the extended period runs from the expiry of the original 12 month period, not from the date upon which the motion for extension is made. This applies equally to applications made under subs. (3) and to cases begun on petition and later reduced to summary complaint (see *Millar v. H.M. Advocate*, 1994 S.L.T. 461 and *Duke v. Lees*, 1997 G.W.D. 15–659).

The Note of Appeal in relation to an application for extension of the 12 month period should be on Form 8.1–A of the Act of Adjournal (Criminal Procedure Rules).

Subs. (3A)

This new provision necessarily clarifies the position where an appeal has been taken to the High Court upon a preliminary point under s.74. An application cannot be made under s.65(3) while such an appeal is pending. Consideration of such an application can however be pursued before the High Court at the time of its hearing of parties on the issues raised in that appeal.

Subss. (4) to (7)

Unlike the 12 month time bar in solemn bail cases which runs from the date of the first appearance on the petition, calculation of the 80 and 110 day time limits begins from the date of full committal. The 80 and 110 day rules are vigorously enforced by the courts and applications for extension of either period will not succeed if failure to serve the indictment, or delay in starting the trial, was occasioned by a fault of the Crown. Failure to serve the indictment timeously in custody cases will not itself bar proceedings; the Crown can either apply to the court for an extension of the 80 day period or elect to liberate the accused as soon as possible thereafter and certainly before the 110th day. It is difficult to envisage circumstances which would merit extension of the 80 days to allow service of an indictment except perhaps illness of the accused, but see *Farrell v. H.M. Advocate*, 1985 S.L.T. 58.

It is well-decided that a period of remand beyond 80 days without an indictment being served will not *per se* preclude proceedings until the provisions of subs. (4)(b) become operative (see *H.M. Advocate v. McCann* 1977 S.L.T.(Notes) 19, and *X., Petr*, 1995 S.C.C.R. 407, which is discussed in notes to s.51 above).

The 80 day limit is peremptory, can be interrupted by a custodial sentence or liberation of the accused and, exceptionally, may be extended. The 110 day period can be interrupted either by such liberation or by the imposition of a term of imprisonment: to count towards calculation of the 110 days, the period spent in custody has to be referable solely to the committal order giving rise to the indictment charges (*H.M. Advocate v. Boyle*, 1972 S.L.T.(Notes) 16; *Harley v. H.M. Advocate*, 1970 S.L.T.(Notes) 6); and where two or more petitions are conjoined on an indictment, the dates of each committal have to be weighed separately in any calculation (*Ross v. H.M. Advocate*, 1990 S.C.C.R. 182). Similarly where the 110 days are interrupted by a term of imprisonment, they recommence at the prisoner's earliest release date and not by reference to the working practices of the prison authorities which, in the past, released prisoners whose liberation date fell during a weekend, on the Friday before (*Brown v. H.M. Advocate*, 1988 S.C.C.R. 577).

The fact that an indictment has been served after the lapse of 80 days does not vitiate the proceedings or undermine the validity of any indictment served after that time, though the period of detention in excess of the statutory 80 days may give rise to a civil claim against the Crown (see *McCluskey v. H.M. Advocate*, 1993 S.L.T. 897).

Extension of the 110 day period (subs. (7))

Applications for such extensions can only be considered by a High Court judge and, as subs. (7) indicates, can only be granted where no fault for the delay attaches to the Crown. See *Beattie v. H.M. Advocate*, 1995 S.C.C.R. 606 discussed above.

So in *H.M. Advocate v. McTavish*, 1974 S.L.T. 246 a Crown motion for extension, to enable the completion of further forensic tests and to allow further treatment of the accused's mental illness, in circumstances where the Crown was admittedly able to proceed to trial upon the matters libelled in the petition was rejected. In *H.M. Advocate v. Bickerstaff*, 1926 J.C. 65 where trial had been unable to proceed due to the accused's supervening insanity, a Full Bench held the delay as being attributable to the accused, not the Crown. Illness of the judge and of co-accused permitted three extensions (upheld on appeal) in *Young v. H.M. Advocate*, 1990 S.C.C.R. 315, the High Court itself admitting the accused to bail on a murder charge. Two extensions of time, once on the motion of a co-accused and once on Crown motion because of illness of a witness, were allowed in *Johnston (R.) v. H.M. Advocate*, 1993 S.C.C.R. 295. Perhaps the most contentious use of these provisions in which no fault was felt to lie with the Crown is found in *Gildea v. H.M. Advocate*, 1983 S.C.C.R. 144 where an extension was granted on account of a case scheduled earlier in the assize having taken longer than could reasonably be foreseen.

Particular difficulty can arise in cases involving children who are remanded into the custody of the local authority pending trial or who are already subject of supervision requirements. It is essential to establish whether bail has been refused, if the child has been bailed into the care of local authority accommodation be in secure or open accommodation, and whether the residential regime has been altered as a result of the petition appearance or at the initiative of the local authority exercising separate powers under the Children (Scotland) Act 1995. Refer to the Notes "Children Under 16 Years" at p. 82 and the cases of *X., Petr*, 1996 S.C.C.R. 436 and *M., Petr*, 1996 S.C.C.R. 92.

Subs. (8)

It may seem tautological but an appeal against the grant or refusal of an extension of the periods of 80 or 110 days, or 12 months, can only be competently taken where there has *de facto* been such a grant or refusal. See *McKnight v. H.M. Advocate*, 1996 G.W.D. 20–1151 where an appeal to the nobile officium was ruled incompetent, the sheriff having refused to consider an application for extension at an earlier diet (the case being adjourned through lack of time) and there being no decision to appeal statutorily and no judicial acting to justify recourse to the nobile officium.

Act of Adjournal

Appeals from decisions from subss. (5) or (6) proceed in terms of subs. (8) and r.8.1 and Form 8.1–B of the Act of Adjournal (Criminal Procedure Rules) 1996.

Form 8.1–A in the Rules is used for appeals arising from applications to extend the 12 month period (subs. (3)).

NOTE

[1] Substituted by the Criminal Procedure and Investigations Act 1996 (c. 25), s.73(3).

Service and lodging of indictment, etc.

66.—(1) When a sitting of the sheriff court or of the High Court has been appointed to be held for the trial of persons accused on indictment—

(a) where the trial diet is to be held in the sheriff court, the sheriff clerk; and

(b) where the trial diet is to be held in the High Court, the Clerk of Justiciary,

shall issue a warrant to officers of law to cite the accused, witnesses and jurors, in such form as may be prescribed by Act of Adjournal, or as nearly as may be in such form, and such warrant authenticated by the signature of such clerk, or a duly certified copy thereof, shall be a sufficient warrant for such citation.

(2) The execution of the citation against an accused, witness or juror shall be in such form as may be prescribed by Act of Adjournal, or as nearly as may be in such form.

(3) A witness may be cited by sending the citation to the witness by ordinary or registered post or by the recorded delivery service and a written execution in the form prescribed by Act of Adjournal or as nearly as may be in such form, purporting to be signed by the person who served such citation together with, where appropriate, the relevant post office receipt shall be sufficient evidence of such citation.

(4) The accused shall be served with a copy of the indictment and of the list of the names and addresses of the witnesses to be adduced by the prosecution.

(5) Except in a case to which section 76 of this Act applies, the prosecutor shall on or before the date of service of the indictment lodge the record copy of the indictment with the clerk of court before which the trial is to take place, together with a copy of the list of witnesses and a copy of the list of productions.

(6) Except where the indictment is served under section 76(1) of this Act, a notice shall be served on the accused with the indictment calling upon him to appear and answer to the indictment—

(a) where the case is to be tried in the sheriff court, at a first diet not less than 15 clear days after the service of the indictment and not less than 10 clear days before the trial diet; and

(b) at a trial diet (either in the High Court or in the sheriff court) not less than 29 clear days after the service of the indictment and notice.

(7) Service of the indictment, lists of witnesses and productions, and any notice or intimation to the accused, and the citation of witnesses, whether for precognition or trial, may be effected by any officer of law.

(8) No objection to the service of an indictment or to the citation of a witness shall be upheld on the ground that the officer who effected service or executed the citation was not at the time in possession of the warrant of citation, and it shall not be necessary to produce the execution of citation of an indictment.

(9) The citation of witnesses may be effected by any officer of law duly authorised; and in any proceedings, the evidence on oath of the officer shall, subject to subsection (10) below, be sufficient evidence of the execution of the citation.

(10) A court shall not issue a warrant to apprehend a witness who fails to appear at a diet to which he has been duly cited unless the court is satisfied that the witness received the citation or that its contents came to his knowledge.

(11) No objection to the competency of the officer who served the indictment to give evidence in respect of such service shall be upheld on the ground that his name is not included in the list of witnesses served on the accused.

(12) Any deletion or correction made before service on the record or service copy of an indictment shall be sufficiently authenticated by the initials of the person who has signed, or could by law have signed, the indictment.

(13) Any deletion or correction made on a service copy of an indictment, or on any notice of citation, postponement, adjournment or other notice required to be served on an accused shall be sufficiently authenticated by the initials of any procurator fiscal or of the person serving the same.

(14) Any deletion or correction made on any execution of citation or notice of other document requiring to be served shall be sufficiently authenticated by the initials of the person serving the same.

DEFINITIONS
  "Clerk of Justiciary": s.307(1).
  "diet": s.307(1).
  "High Court": s.307(1).
  "indictment": s.307(1).
  "officer of law": s.307(1).
  "prosecutor": s.307(1).
  "sheriff clerk": s.307(1).
  "witness": s.307(1).

GENERAL NOTE
  The provisions relating to service of indictments, citations and proof of service were spread over ss.58, 69 to 73, 75 and 78 in the 1975 Act but are now brought together in s.66 of the 1995 Act.
  Service of the indictment upon the accused is the event which dictates the timetable for the proceedings and, as subs. (6) indicates, must be effected not less than 29 clear days before the assigned trial diet in High Court cases, and not less than 15 days before the now mandatory first diet in sheriff and jury cases. It is difficult to see what practical purpose is achieved by the lodging of the record copy of the indictment with the clerk of court, as subs. (5) requires other than confirming the expectation of a forthcoming first diet or trial; this is still contingent upon lawful and timeous service of the indictment upon the accused. In dealing with the statutory predecessor of subs. (5), s.78(1) of the 1975 Act (which stipulated lodging of the record copy of the indictment not less than 10 clear days before trial), in *H.M. Advocate v. Graham*, 1985 S.L.T. 498, the High Court in an appeal from a preliminary diet held that the provision was directory, not mandatory, in nature and that a failure by the Crown to comply with the section's provisions did not nullify the proceedings. Nonetheless the case of *Willoughby v. H.M. Advocate,* 2000 S.C.C.R.73 (discussed at p. 110 above) does underline the fundamental importance of the existence of a warrant for a sitting to be competently constituted.
  It is competent, though unusual, to run two identical indictments simultaneously against an accused. So in *H.M. Advocate v. Dow*, 1992 S.L.T. 577 where a minute of postponement had been lodged by the defence, and granted by the court, and the Crown was given authority under s.77A(2) of the 1975 Act to serve notice of a new trial diet (the equivalent procedure is now contained in s.80(3) of the 1995 Act) but did not do so, service of a fresh indictment in identical terms was held to be neither oppressive nor incompetent. (See also the notes to s.80 *infra*.)
  In *Smith v. H.M. Advocate*, 1996 G.W.D. 29–1731 it was discovered, before a preliminary diet, that an error in the minute of notice meant that an incorrect address had been given for the High Court sitting, and a second identical indictment was served. The High Court on appeal held that as the master of the instance it was a matter within the discretion of the Crown which indictment would be called. This suggests that the terms of the indictments themselves (be they identical or

not) are not of moment since the Court also indicated that the service of a second indictment implied that the Crown were deserting the first and proceeding on the later indictment.

Provisions relating to service of indictments

Rule 2.2.–(2) of the 1996 Act of Adjournal specifies a number of acceptable methods of service of indictments including in subpara. (2)(d) a means of service for accused who have no proper domicile of citation, a useful provision to deal with the circumstances described in the notes to s.65(4) to (7) above or where an accused has never appeared on petition at all.

Subsection (8) enacts that it is unnecessary for the officer serving the indictment to have seen the warrant to cite mentioned in subs. (1). However, failure to serve an indictment is undoubtedly fatal to any proceedings on that indictment (*McAllister v. H.M. Advocate*, 1985 S.C.C.R. 36; 1985 S.L.T. 399) and cannot be cured by the accused's appearance (*Hester v. MacDonald*, 1961 S.C. 370). In such circumstances the warrant for committal of an accused would not fall and nor would any bail order granted earlier to the accused albeit, in custody cases, the provisions of s.65(4) against delay in proceedings would still have to be obtempered by the Crown (see *Jamieson v. H.M. Advocate*, 1990 S.C.C.R. 137; 1990 S.L.T. 845).

In *Bryson v. H.M. Advocate*, 1961 S.L.T. 289, an accused bailed to a domicile was subsequently remanded in custody for further charges, but the indictment was served at his original domicile not at the prison, a procedure which was upheld. Service of an indictment without giving the requisite 29 clear days notice stipulated in subs. (6) would not create a nullity and in the absence of an objection to service, which should be taken at a preliminary diet (or at the first diet in Sheriff and jury cases), trial could proceed: furthermore the *induciae* can be waived and it can be argued that this has occurred in the absence of a preliminary challenge (see *H.M. Advocate v. McDonald*, 1984 S.L.T. 426).

Proof of service

An indictment must be served by an officer of law in the presence of a witness in one of the manners specified in Rule 2.2 of the 1996 Act of Adjournal, namely; (i) by personal service; (ii) by leaving it in the hands of a member of the accused's family, an inmate or employee at the domicile of citation; or (iii) by delivery through, or affixing to the door of the domicile. Similar provisions apply in situations where the accused has no domicile of citation in which event service can be effected at the address which the officer has reasonable cause to believe is occupied by the accused or by personal service.

The execution of service completed by the officer should comply with Form 2.6–A shown in the Appendix to the 1996 Act of Adjournal and be returned to the prosecutor: the execution will in all likelihood require to be produced to the court if the accused fails to appear at any diet before an arrest warrant will be granted. In *Welsh v. H.M. Advocate*, 1986 S.L.T. 664 a dispute arose as to whether the police could have served the indictment as claimed, since (it was alleged) the building had been demolished. The claim was refuted by the officers but the court noted that even if the accused's assertion had been correct, there would have been a failure to inform the court of a change of domicile.

It is competent in terms of subs. (8) and (11) for the officers effecting service of the indictment to be heard in evidence without their particulars being added to the indictment, a useful provision in the event of later additional charges for failure to appear at a lawful diet.

Witnesses for precognition or trial can be cited in conformity with subs. (3) but in the event of a failure to appear at trial, it may be difficult to persuade the court to grant an arrest warrant, as subs. (10) allows, unless an execution of personal service conforming to Form 2.6–E of the 1996 Act of Adjournal can be exhibited. However the same Act of Adjournal has introduced a new Form 8.2–D, a reply form to be returned by witnesses cited in indictment cases acknowledging citation and this should be a factor to be taken into account in the event of non-appearance and, incidentally, may alert the Crown at an early stage to any potential shortcomings in citation (it must be doubted that precognition mentioned in subs. (7) can be regarded as "a diet" for the purposes of subs. (10); it is submitted that a warrant for arrest could not properly be sought following failure to appear for precognition, except precognition on oath. The relevant forms of petition for authority to precognosce on oath, are Forms 29.1–A and 29.1–B in the above Act of Adjournal).

For purposes of computation of time, note that in the case of the time limits specified in subs. (6), s.75 enacts that where the final day falls on a *dies non*, the effective date for calculation is the next working day.

Witnesses

67.—(1) The list of witnesses shall consist of the names of the witnesses together with an address at which they can be contacted for the purposes of precognition.

(2) It shall not be necessary to include in the list of witnesses the names of any witnesses to the declaration of the accused or the names of any witnesses to prove that an extract conviction applies to the accused, but witnesses may be examined in regard to these matters without previous notice.

(3) Any objection in respect of misnomer or misdescription of—

(a) any person named in the indictment; or

(b) any witness in the list of witnesses,

shall be intimated in writing to the court before which the trial is to take place, to the prosecutor and to any other accused, where the case is to be tried in the sheriff court, at or before the first diet and, where the case is to be tried in the High Court, not less than ten clear days before the trial diet; and, except on cause shown, no such objection shall be admitted at the trial diet unless so intimated.

(4) Where such intimation has been given or cause is shown and the court is satisfied that the accused making the objection has not been supplied with sufficient information to enable him to identify the person named in the indictment or to find such witness in sufficient time to precognosce him before the trial, the court may grant such remedy by postponement, adjournment or otherwise as appears to it to be appropriate.

(5) Without prejudice to—

(a) any enactment or rule of law permitting the prosecutor to examine any witness not included in the list of witnesses; or

(b) subsection (6) below,

in any trial it shall be competent with the leave of the court for the prosecutor to examine any witness or to put in evidence any production not included in the lists lodged by him, provided that written notice, containing in the case of a witness his name and address as mentioned in subsection (1) above, has been given to the accused not less than two clear days before the day on which the jury is sworn to try the case.

(6) It shall be competent for the prosecutor to examine any witness or put in evidence any production included in any list or notice lodged by the accused, and it shall be competent for an accused to examine any witness or put in evidence any production included in any list or notice lodged by the prosecutor or by a co-accused.

DEFINITIONS

"diet": s.307(1).
"High Court": s.307(1).
"indictment": s.307(1).
"prosecutor": s.307(1).
"witness": s.307(1).

GENERAL NOTE

Section 67 anticipates that the identity and particulars of most witnesses will be known to the Crown sufficiently early for inclusion in the indictment served upon the accused. Experience suggests otherwise; in custody cases particularly, increasing reliance has been placed upon the use of the provisions in s.67(5) of the Act both for adding witnesses and productions to the indictment.

Generally the inclusion of a witness on the indictment will entitle the defence to expect that the witness will be made available, if required, at the trial diet (following *Dickson v. H.M. Advocate*, Crown Office Circular A22/83) and the absence, or unavailability, of a Crown witness should be made known before the trial begins. In *Mellors v. H.M. Advocate*, 1999 G.W.D. 32–1530 the Crown advised the defence that a witness had not appeared but failed to disclose that the witness had not been cited at all, an omission, severely criticised by the Appeal Court, which ordered the witness' evidence to be heard by a single judge during the appeal against conviction.

The introduction of first diets in sheriff and jury cases and optional preliminary diets in High Court cases now means that any objection to inadequate identification, or misdescription of witnesses must be notified in writing to the prosecutor and co-accused, (a) at or prior to the first diet, or (b) 10 days before the High Court trial diet. Section 75 provides that where the last day of the period falls on a *dies non*, the effective date for calculation purposes will be the next working day (this provision is quite separate from the matters which can be raised by way of provisional diet in the High Court in terms of s.72(1) and (6)). Failure to give such notice timeously will have to be justified to the court at the trial diet but it has to be said that it would be difficult for a court to refuse an objection under subs. (4), even at that late stage, in view of the potential for prejudice to an accused. The remedy is adjournment of the trial or postponement if necessary in the interests of justice (*Vetters v. H.M. Advocate*, 1944 J.C. 138), but the court might well have to consider extending the time-limits upon proceedings dictated by s.65 and, *in extremis*, consider whether the Crown should be held at fault (see s.65(3) and (7) above).

Subs. (5)
As was noted above, the provisions of s.81 in regard to late intimation of witnesses and productions have been preserved in s.67(5) of the 1995 Act: provided due notice has been given to the accused, such evidence can be added to the indictment with leave of the court. However while an error in describing a witness in a s.67 notice is probably capable of being remedied by amendment in the course of proceedings, given the grounds of amendment in s.96 of the Act, a misdescription of a production either in the list of productions or, later, in a s.67 notice, cannot be so remedied. In *H.M. Advocate v. Swift*, 1983 S.C.C.R. 204 an error in the original list of productions was corrected in a s.81 notice which itself misdescribed the production. The sheriff held the terms of s.81 to be peremptory and held evidence arising from the production, a tape, to be inadmissible. It is observed that it would still be open to parties to have such evidence admitted by way of a Minute of Agreement in the course of the trial if they were so minded.

Subsection (5)(a) entitles the prosecutor to examine certain witnesses without having given intimation to the accused. The most obvious categories of witnesses covered by this concession are co-accused whose pleas have been accepted prior to, or during trial, or even by way of an accelerated plea following service of a common indictment (see *Monaghan v. H.M. Advocate*, 1984 S.L.T. 262), witnesses cited by any of the accused, witnesses led in replication in accordance with s.269 of the 1995 Act, police officers proving service of an indictment (s.66(11)), and the officials specified in subs. (2) above.

[1]**67A.**—(1) This section applies where a prosecutor has obtained a warrant to cite a witness for precognition and has served a citation for precognition on the witness.

(2) Where this section applies, a witness who—

(a) fails without reasonable excuse, after receiving at least 48 hours notice, to attend for precognition by a prosecutor at the time and place mentioned in the citation served on him; or

(b) refuses when so cited to give information within his knowledge regarding any matter relative to the commission of the offence in relation to which such precognition is taken,

shall be guilty of an offence and shall be liable on summary conviction to a fine not exceeding level 3 on the standard scale or to a term of imprisonment not exceeding 21 days.

DEFINITIONS
"fine": s.307(1) of the 1995 Act.
"offence": s.307(1) of the 1995 Act.
"prosecutor": s.307(1) of the 1995 Act.
"standard scale": s.225(1) of the 1995 Act.
"witness": s.307(1) of the 1995 Act.

NOTE
[1]Inserted by the Crime and Punishment (Scotland) Act 1997 (c. 48) s.57(1) with effect from August 1, 1997 in terms of the Crime and Punishment (Scotland) Act 1997 (Commencement and Transitional Provisions) Order 1997 (S.I. 1997 No. 1712) para. 5.

GENERAL NOTE
This section relates to solemn proceedings and restates the Crown's *compulsitor* to require cited witnesses to attend for precognition. This is a distinct procedure from precognition on oath which statutorily, in s.291 of the 1995 Act relates only to defence applications. This new

provision, replacing s.140A of the 1995 Act, deals with the more routine citing of witnesses for precognition and the (all too common) failure by cited witnesses to attend. The petition warrant granted by the court ordinarily includes a warrant to cite witnesses, but s.67A's provisions can be used at the pre-petition stage if the prosecutor first makes a formal application to the court for a warrant to cite witnesses.

The section creates two criminal offences both of which depend in the first instance upon proving the fact of valid citation for precognition. Subsection (2)(a) makes it a criminal offence to fail without reasonable excuse to attend for precognition after valid citation, a crime which it should be relatively easy to establish corroboratively.

Subsection (2)(b) makes it an offence for a cited witness to fail at precognition to disclose information within his knowledge in relation to the offence under investigation. Corroboration of this offence may be less easy; two contrasting subs. (2)(b) offences can be distinguished: the first simply being the withholding of evidence in one's possession (an offence which could extend to documents identified to the witness as pertinent, since the statutory definition of "witness" in s.307 of the 1995 Act includes haver); the second being where the witness's account is found to be at odds with other reliable and credible evidence. In the latter situation above it is questionable how far precognition (which involves what are, in effect, privileged communications) can then truly be regarded as confidential. It is a matter of interpretation whether the subs. (2)(b) offence is committed only at the time of precognition or both then and *ex post facto* under reference to evidence given by others at a trial. It is submitted that the second reading appears more likely, particularly when it is considered that, as a result of misleading or undisclosed information, a potential witness cited for precognition might not then be called to give evidence at the trial at all and, in that situation, could not by definition be charged with perjury. It might be argued that a wilful failure to disclose pertinent information could be viewed as an attempt to pervert the course of justice, a much graver offence than the new statutory offence with its Level 3 penalty. In the final analysis it seems that the prime purpose of this new section is to bring home to cited witnesses the seriousness of their responsibilities when they are cited for precognition; it is likely that these offences and penalties will be mentioned in future citations to encourage witnesses to attend.

Note that s.57(2) of the 1997 Act amends s.140 of the 1995 Act and now empowers the Crown to apply for a warrant to cite in cases under investigation but where no one has appeared before the court. Section 140, which was also slightly amended by s.57 of the 1997 Act, is the statutory basis for citing both an accused and witnesses to appear at court.

Paragraph 5 of the Commencement Order (S.I. 1997, No. 1712) stipulates that the provisions of s.67A only apply to citations served on or after August 1, 1997.

Productions

68.—(1) The list of productions shall include the record, made under section 37 of this Act (incorporating any rectification authorised under section 38(1) of this Act), of proceedings at the examination of the accused.

(2) The accused shall be entitled to see the productions according to the existing law and practice in the office of the sheriff clerk of the district in which the court of the trial diet is situated or, where the trial diet is to be in the High Court in Edinburgh, in the Justiciary Office.

(3) Where a person who has examined a production is adduced to give evidence with regard to it and the production has been lodged at least eight days before the trial diet, it shall not be necessary to prove—

(a) that the production was received by him in the condition in which it was taken possession of by the procurator fiscal or the police and returned by him after his examination of it to the procurator fiscal or the police; or

(b) that the production examined by him is that taken possession of by the procurator fiscal or the police,

unless the accused, at least four days before the trial diet, gives in accordance with subsection (4) below written notice that he does not admit that the production was received or returned as aforesaid or, as the case may be, that it is that taken possession of as aforesaid.

(4) The notice mentioned in subsection (3) above shall be given—

(a) where the accused is cited to the High Court for the trial diet, to the Crown Agent; and

(b) where he is cited to the sheriff court for the trial diet, to the procurator fiscal.

DEFINITIONS

"diet": s.307(1).
"High Court": s.307(1).
"procurator fiscal": s.307(1).
"sheriff clerk": s.307(1).

GENERAL NOTE

The list of productions must include the judicial examination (if any) and by implication the executions of service, to show compliance by the Crown with the terms of s.37(6) and (10). In *H.M. Advocate v. Cafferty*, 1984 S.C.C.R. 444, the terms of s.78(2), the identical provision in the 1975 Act were held to be mandatory and when objection was taken to the competency of the proceedings during the trial, the sheriff deserted the diet *pro loco et tempore*, reserving the right of the Crown to re-raise proceedings. Failure by the Crown to lodge the transcript of judicial examination is a matter which should be raised timeously at the first diet in sheriff and jury cases or by way of a preliminary diet in cases indicted before the High Court (the problems associated with the late lodging or misdescription of productions are discussed in the notes to s.67 above).

Subsection (3) contains presumptions that, (i) productions examined after their recovery by the police or lodging with the procurator fiscal were produced to the witness in the same condition as when recovered or lodged and (ii) that the articles produced to the witness were those seized by the police or the procurator fiscal. The presumption only applies to productions lodged not less than eight days prior to trial. Notice of a challenge to the presumption must be served in accordance with subs. (4) not less than four days before the trial.

Note that in *Livingston v. H.M. Advocate*, 1991 S.C.C.R. 350 examination of productions and their comparison against the accused's fingerprint forms, which necessitated a motion for the removal of articles from the court during the course of a trial for that purpose, was upheld on appeal. This was viewed as a matter within the discretion of the trial judge, albeit an exceptional procedure. In that case the Lord Justice General (at 356C) echoed the view expressed in *William Turner Davies, Petr*, 1973 S.L.T. (Notes) 36 by the Lord Justice Clerk at p. 37, that after service of an indictment:

"the productions ... are lodged with the sheriff clerk who has a duty to retain them in his custody and make them available at the trial. At that stage, the only body with the authority to allow the productions to be inspected and examined is the court, and the proper procedure is to make application to the court thereanent. It is then for the court to decide whether the application should be granted or refused."

Davies had petitioned the *nobile officium* for authority for a defence expert to examine gloves lodged by the Crown as productions before the trial began, but the same principles apply both prior to, and during, trial. The court has to weigh the potential prejudice to the accused in the preparation and presentation of his case against the public interest in the effective prosecution of crime. See also *MacNeil v. H.M. Advocate*, 1986 S.C.C.R. 288, where productions listed in the indictment had not been lodged it was held that objection should have been taken before the jury was sworn and the appropriate remedy in the event of prejudice was an adjournment. It is notable that in *H.M. Advocate v. Sorrie*, 1996 G.W.D. 30–1795 (discussed at Notes to s.65(1)(2) and (3) above), the Court of Appeal held that there had been no want of compliance with s.68(2) on the basis that the productions had been lost or destroyed. The absence of an opportunity to examine the missing banknotes was a matter for comment and appropriate direction (the Crown having already undertaken a fingerprint examination of the bank bags which contained the notes initially and averring no likelihood of prejudice in the whole circumstances). This is surely an extreme interpretation and one wonders what approach could have been taken had a written challenge (subs. (3)(b)) been taken.

The procedures regulating the access of jurors to productions are discussed in the notes to s.99 below.

Lodging of productions and their introduction as evidence is only necessary where they are best evidence bearing distinguishing or peculiar features; otherwise there will be no demonstrable prejudice to the accused and no requirement for the items to be produced to the court. See *Maciver v. Mackenzie*, 1942 S.L.T. 144, followed most recently in *Friel v. Leonard*, 1997 G.W.D. 12–494. Such prejudice to the accused must be of a substantial degree (see *Anderson v. Laverock*, 1976 S.L.T. 62 followed in *Allan v. Napier*, 1999 G.W.D. 29–1364).

See also *McQuade v. Vannet*, 2000 S.C.C.R. 18 where a plea in bar of trial based upon the unavailability of a CCTV video tape which had been viewed by a police officer, found to contain nothing significant, returned to its owner and re-used, was repelled. The video tape had never been considered as a production in the summary trial. The Appeal Court noted that if it transpired in the course of the trial the missing production became significant, and its absence then became gravely prejudicial, it would then be appropriate for the court to desert the diet: see *McFadyen v. Annan*, 1992 S.L.T. 163; 1992 S.C.C.R. 186.

Notice of previous convictions

69.—(1) No mention shall be made in the indictment of previous convictions, nor shall extracts of previous convictions be included in the list of productions annexed to the indictment.

(2) If the prosecutor intends to place before the court any previous conviction, he shall cause to be served on the accused along with the indictment a notice in the form set out in an Act of Adjournal or as nearly as may be in such form, and any conviction specified in the notice shall be held to apply to the accused unless he gives, in accordance with subsection (3) below, written intimation objecting to such conviction on the ground that it does not apply to him or is otherwise inadmissible.

(3) Intimation objecting to a conviction under subsection (2) above shall be given—

(a) where the accused is cited to the High Court for the trial diet, to the Crown Agent; or

(b) where the accused is cited to the sheriff court for the trial diet, to the procurator fiscal,

at least five clear days before the first day of the sitting in which the trial diet is to be held.

(4) Where notice is given by the accused under section 76 of this Act of his intention to plead guilty and the prosecutor intends to place before the court any previous conviction, he shall cause to be served on the accused along with the indictment a notice in the form set out in an Act of Adjournal or as nearly as may be in such form.

(5) Where the accused pleads guilty at any diet, no objection to any conviction of which notice has been served on him under this section shall be entertained unless he has, at least two clear days before the diet, given intimation to the procurator fiscal of the district to the court of which the accused is cited for the diet.

DEFINITIONS
"extract of previous conviction": s.307(1).
"indictment": s.307(1).
"prosecutor": s.307(1).

GENERAL NOTE
The Notice of Previous Convictions which the Crown may place before the court in the event of conviction of the accused should conform to Form 8.3 in the 1996 Act of Adjournal.

Broadly these provisions repeat those found in s.68 of the 1975 Act, but subs. (5) now appears as a distinct (and clearer) requirement than heretofore. At any diet at which the accused pleads guilty, apart from the trial diet itself where subs. (3) demands five clear days' notice of any disputed conviction, the accused must give not less than two clear days' notice of any conviction libelled which he disputes: accordingly subs. (5) is relevant to the circumstances of accelerated pleas tendered under s.76 (the successor to s.76 of the 1975 Act), and to pleas tendered at any first diet or preliminary diet (see ss.71 and 72 of the 1995 Act).

Previous convictions which are under appeal should not be libelled (*McCall v. Mitchell* (1911) 6 Adam 303) and no previous conviction omitted from the Notice should be taken into account by the court considering sentence, unless it is disclosed in a social enquiry or other report before the court (*Sharp v. Stevenson* 1948 S.L.T. (Notes) 79).

Although the provisions of subs. (1) appear to be absolute, they must be read in conjunction with s.101(2) of the 1995 Act which permits the leading of evidence of an accused's previous convictions where it is a necessary element of proof of the substantive charge.

The anomalous position of previous convictions libelled against bodies corporate and any named officer in the indictment against that body is discussed in the notes to s.70 below.

Criminal Procedure (Scotland) Act 1995

Proceedings against bodies corporate

70.—(1) This section applies to proceedings on indictment against a body corporate.

(2) The indictment may be served by delivery of a copy of the indictment together with notice to appear at the registered office or, if there is no registered office or the registered office is not in the United Kingdom, at the principal place of business in the United Kingdom of the body corporate.

(3) Where a letter containing a copy of the indictment has been sent by registered post or by the recorded delivery service to the registered office or principal place of business of the body corporate, an acknowledgement or certificate of the delivery of the letter issued by the Post Office shall be sufficient evidence of the delivery of the letter at the registered office or place of business on the day specified in such acknowledgement or certificate.

(4) A body corporate may, for the purpose of—

(a) stating objections to the competency or relevancy of the indictment or proceedings; or

(b) tendering a plea of guilty or not guilty; or

(c) making a statement in mitigation of sentence,

appear by a representative of the body corporate.

(5) Where at the trial diet the body corporate does not appear as mentioned in subsection (4) above, or by counsel or a solicitor, the court shall, on the motion of the prosecutor, if it is satisfied that subsection (2) above has been complied with, proceed to hear and dispose of the case in the absence of the body corporate.

(6) Where a body corporate is sentenced to a fine, the fine may be recovered in like manner in all respects as if a copy of the sentence certified by the clerk of the court were an extract decree of the Court of Session for the payment of the amount of the fine by the body corporate to the Queen's and Lord Treasurer's Remembrancer.

(7) Nothing in section 77 of this Act shall require a plea tendered by or on behalf of a body corporate to be signed.

(8) In this section, "representative", in relation to a body corporate, means an officer or employee of the body corporate duly appointed by it for the purpose of the proceedings; and a statement in writing purporting to be signed by the managing director of, or by any person having or being one of the persons having the management of the affairs of the body corporate, to the effect that the person named in the statement has been appointed the representative of the body corporate for the purpose of any proceedings to which this section applies shall be sufficient evidence of such appointment.

DEFINITIONS

"diet": s.307(1).
"fine": s.307(1).
"indictment": s.307(1).
"prosecutor": s.307(1).
"representative": s.70(8).

GENERAL NOTE

Provisions in s.70 refer to prosecution on indictment. Section 143 of the Act deals with summary prosecutions of partnerships, trustees in their corporate capacity and companies. A number of statutory provisions, namely the Insurance Companies Act 1982 (c. 50), s.92(4), the Companies Act, 1985 (c. 6), s.734(4), the Financial Services Act 1986 (c. 60), s.203(4), the Banking Act 1987 (c. 22), s.98(4) and the Companies Act 1989 (c. 40), ss.44(4) and 91(4) extended the terms of s.74 of the 1975 Act to unincorporated bodies. In the absence of contrary provisions, s.70 of the 1995 Act is similarly extended.

Once the court is satisfied that an indictment has been lawfully served upon a limited company or incorporation, it is entitled, on the motion of the prosecutor, to proceed to consider the evidence at a trial diet and dispose of the case at that time even if the body is unrepresented

(it seems implicit from the reference to "the trial diet" in subs. (5) that a failure to appear at any earlier diet has to be treated as a plea of not guilty). If the body prosecuted does elect to make an appearance at any diet, this can be made on its behalf by an authorised representative and need not be by a solicitor or counsel.

The prosecutor may opt to prosecute the corporate body alone, proceed against a responsible officer of the company, or both. In the absence of specific statutory provision in regard to the previous convictions of bodies corporate, the general rules expressed in ss.69 and 101(7) would appear to apply. However if proceedings are taken solely against an officer of the company as its responsible representative, it would surely be inequitable to libel against him previous convictions incurred by the company.

Subsection (6) enacts that fines imposed upon bodies corporate are recoverable by civil diligence.

The growing importance of criminal sanctions in cases of environmental pollution and health and safety offences has made prosecutions on indictment of limited companies more commonplace. See for example *H.M. Advocate v. Kettle Produce Ltd*, 1996 G.W.D. 3–159 (unauthorised connection between sewage outflow pipe and the public water supply causing widescale illness in the vicinity; fine £60,000) and *Balmoral Group Ltd v. H.M. Advocate*, 1996 G.W.D. 10–576 (death of employee struck by crane chain and death of a second employee in a second, unrelated incident; fines of £35,000 and £10,000 respectively).

Pre-trial proceedings

First diet

71.—(1) At a first diet the court shall, so far as is reasonably practicable, ascertain whether the case is likely to proceed to trial on the date assigned as the trial diet and, in particular—

(a) the state of preparation of the prosecutor and of the accused with respect to their cases; and

(b) the extent to which the prosecutor and the accused have complied with the duty under section 257(1) of this Act.

(2) In addition to the matters mentioned in subsection (1) above the court shall, at a first diet, consider any matter mentioned in any of paragraphs (a) to (d) of section 72(1) of this Act of which a party has, not less than two clear days before the first diet, given notice to the court and to the other parties.

(3) At a first diet the court may ask the prosecutor and the accused any question in connection with any matter which it is required to ascertain or consider under subsection (1) or (2) above.

(4) The accused shall attend a first diet of which he has been given notice and the court may, if he fails to do so, grant a warrant to apprehend him.

(5) A first diet may proceed notwithstanding the absence of the accused.

(6) The accused shall, at the first diet, be required to state how he pleads to the indictment, and section 77 of this Act shall apply where he tenders a plea of guilty.

(7) Where at a first diet the court concludes that the case is unlikely to proceed to trial on the date assigned for the trial diet, the court—

(a) shall, unless having regard to previous proceedings in the case it considers it inappropriate to do so, postpone the trial diet; and

(b) may fix a further first diet.

(8) Subject to subsection (7) above, the court may, if it considers it appropriate to do so, adjourn a first diet.

(9) In this section "the court" means the sheriff court.

DEFINITIONS
   "court": subs. (9).
   "diet": s.307(1).
   "prosecutor": s.307(1).

GENERAL NOTE
   Mandatory first diets for sheriff and jury cases were introduced by s.13 of the Criminal Justice (Scotland) Act 1995 (c. 20). Separate provision is made for preliminary diets as an optional procedure in High Court cases.

Mandatory first diets require to be held not less than 15 clear days after service of the indictment upon the accused, and not less than 10 clear days before trial (s.66(6)(a)) at which time the court is obliged to ascertain the state of readiness of all parties for the pending trial and the extent of evidence capable of being agreed by them. Section 71 has a dual purpose; first to reduce the incidence of unforeseen adjournments or cancellations of trial (a reform aided by the right of the Crown to seek a warrant under subs. (4) if the accused is absent without authority); secondly, to restrict the length and expense of trials, and inconvenience to witnesses, by focusing the parties' attention at an early stage upon the duty to seek agreement of uncontentious evidence. Note that s.78(3)(b) anticipates that notices of incrimination and special defences will be lodged at or prior to the first diet. In *H.M. Advocate v. Shepherd*, 1997 S.C.C.R. 246 the High Court deprecated the use of first diets as a means of resolving points of admissibility, which were likely to arise in the course of any trial; the issue in that case is discussed at p. 43 above. It may at times be difficult to distinguish issues of this sort from matters of relevancy in the indictment itself; see *H.M. Advocate v. Carson*, 1997 G.W.D. 12–498.

The powers and duties of the sheriff in conducting a first diet are identical to those given to the High Court for the optional preliminary diets introduced in s.72 of the Act.

It will be noted that the court has a discretion to grant a warrant for the accused's arrest should he fail to appear, but subs. (5) also permits the diet to proceed in his absence. Obviously a first diet can continue against an accused notwithstanding the absence of co-accused, but matters become more problematical when the provisions of subs. (6) are considered. Is it intended that all accused are to tender pleas at the conclusion of the hearing or that pleas only be recorded from the accused who are present in court? The only clue may be offered by the references in subs. (6) to s.77 which enacts that an accused, other than a body corporate, shall tender a guilty plea by subscribing its terms in the record, and the use of the word "states" in the subsection both which tend to suggest that in the absence of an accused the court has two options; either to issue a warrant or continue the case in terms of subs. (7) to a further first diet against the absent accused or all accused.

In this context it is perhaps curious that the provisions against delay found in s.65 restate the familiar requirement that the calculation of the statutory time-bars is solely by reference to the commencement of the trial (s.65(9)), and takes no account of the timing of a first, or a preliminary, diet. No doubt delay occasioned by the need to continue the diet to a late date (which still constitutes a first diet in view of the statutory definition of "diet" found at s.307(1) below) could be a factor the court might address if it became necessary to consider extensions of statutory time-bars.

Failure to record the accused's plea at a first, or preliminary, diet is not fatal to the proceedings; in *Hogg v. H.M. Advocate*, 1999 S.L.T. 371, the Appeal Court took a purposive approach noting that the function of such a diet is to facilitate the administration of court business. See *Cannon v. H.M. Advocate*, 1999 S.L.T. 358 where it was held to be competent, albeit undesirable, for the sheriff presiding at the first diet to pass consideration of preliminary points to another sheriff who heard the pleas *de novo*.

Subs. (7)

While it is clear that the first diet must occur not less than 15 clear days after service of the indictment and more than 10 clear days before any trial (see s.66(6)(a) above), once that strict timescale has been met the diet can be continued up to any date before the trial diet itself (see *O'Connell v. H.M. Advocate*, 1996 S.C.C.R. 614). However while the Act stipulates in s.78(4)(a)(i) that, in sheriff solemn cases, the list of defence witnesses and productions must be lodged at or prior to the first diet, it is notable that any special defences or notices of incrimination must be intimated not less than 10 clear days before the trial diet (s.78(1)(ii)) and thereafter can only be accepted on cause shown.

At the first diet it is open to the court to postpone the trial diet (separate procedures are available in s.80 below to adjourn or postpone a trial at the time of calling the indictment for trial); care must be taken to ensure that the diet fixed complies with the statutory time-bars set out in s.65 or that an appropriate extension of time is granted by the court in bail cases, or application made for extension to the High Court in custody cases (see s.65(3) and (5)). If it is decided that the trial diet is to be postponed three points are noteworthy; first, it will not be necessary to re-indict the case since the original indictment will remain valid; secondly, any additional witnesses or productions will require to be added by way of s.67 notice; thirdly, if the court fixes a further first diet (see s.71(7)(b)) the date of that diet will have to be fixed at the time of postponement, intimated to the accused at that time and, it is submitted, comply with the time constraints imposed under s.66(6)(a) discussed earlier.

Given the potential for error it may be of some comfort to the Crown that following the *ratio* in *H.M. Advocate v. Dow* and in *Smith v. H.M. Advocate* cited at p. 112 above it would be competent to raise a fresh indictment instead: it will be seen that s.72(4) in allowing the postponement of trial diets after a preliminary diet in High Court cases, enacts that any resultant delay in proceedings shall not count towards any "time limit".

Stewart v. H.M. Advocate, 1997 G.W.D. 23–1145 suggests that, where a case is re-indicted for trial, earlier unsuccessful pleas in bar of trial (in *Stewart* a plea in bar of insanity which had been repelled at first instance and on appeal and is reported as *Stewart v. H.M. Advocate* (No. 1) 1997 S.C.C.R. 330) may competently be restated, the court having the option in terms of s.73(5) and s.80 of the Act to postpone trial to enable further inquiry. It is of course the case that an accused's fitnes for trial can alter between indictments and could thus require to be reconsidered; issues of competency or relevancy, it is submitted, could not be resurrected in the same way.

It will be observed that, adopting the provisions of s.72(1), means that notices specifying any one of the preliminary objections (*i.e.* competency or relevancy of the libel, objections to the validity of any citation, any plea in bar of trial, motions for separation or conjunction of charges or trials, challenges to any special capacity libelled, including the currency of bail orders, and any objection to the admission of the judicial examination transcript or transcript of an accused's declaration) must be notified not less than two days before the first diet or its continuation.

Less familiar grounds for a hearing are now contained in s.72(1)(c) and (d): any party can call for the court at the first diet to review documentary evidence whose contents are felt to be capable of agreement (subs. 72(1)(c)), or raise a general matter which should be resolved before trial (subs. 72(1)(d)). This latter provision could conceivably be deployed to deal with matters which traditionally had to be considered in "a trial within a trial"; there is no authority on the point.

Once a notice has been served and a hearing fixed, it will be seen that further matters can be raised on a day's notice (subs. 72(3)).

After consideration of any preliminary pleas or other matters raised before the court it is essential that pleas be tendered and recorded to any charges left on the libel.

Notwithstanding this proposition it is of note that in *Roselli v. Vannet*, 1997 S.C.C.R. 655, a summary complaint, advocation of proceedings was held to be competent to review events at an intermediate diet.

Act of Adjournal

Chapter 9 of the Act of Adjournal (Criminal Procedure Rules) 1996 regulates procedures in both first diets and preliminary diets. Form 9.1 is the style for any minute of notice; Form 9.9 is the notice of abandonment of matters which were to have been raised at such a diet.

Mandatory first diets (then called pleading diets) were abolished by s.12 of the Criminal Justice (Scotland) Act 1980 (c.62) when it was perceived that they had been reduced to mere formal appearances. The new first diets are essential elements in retaining public confidence in the courts and it is to be hoped that the Bench exercises its powers in subs. (1) to (3) vigorously. Note however that the court can apply no *compulsitor* upon parties who do not enter into the spirit of s.258(1) and that that provision does not apply to accused who are unrepresented. It is debatable how far the court can venture in its enquiries under s.71 or s.72 where an accused is not legally represented.

Appeal procedures

Appeals arising from decisions of the court at first diets or preliminary diets are considered by the High Court under s.74 of the Act: in the event of an appeal, part, or all of the postponement period can be discounted by the High Court from any time bar calculation and, by implication, this can be done with retrospective effect. Appeals must be raised within two days upon Form 9.12 given in the Act of Adjournal and, if need be, abandoned by Form 9.17. Note that decisions to adjourn the first, or preliminary, diet or to postpone the trial diet cannot be appealed under s.74 (see subs. (2)(a)) but that such decisions can be challenged by an accused in an appeal against conviction or sentence (s.106) and by the Lord Advocate in an appeal against an unduly lenient sentence (s.108).

Preliminary diet: notice

72.—(1) Subject to subsections (4) and (5) below, where a party to a case which is to be tried in the High Court within the appropriate period gives written notice to the court and to the other parties—

    (a) that he intends to raise—

> (i) a matter relating to the competency or relevancy of the indictment; or
> (ii) an objection to the validity of the citation against him, on the ground of any discrepancy between the record copy of the indictment and the copy served on him, or on account of any error or deficiency in such service copy or in the notice of citation;

(b) that he intends—
> (i) to submit a plea in bar of trial;
> (ii) to apply for separation or conjunction of charges or trials;
> (iii) to raise a preliminary objection under section 255 of this Act; or
> (iv) to make an application under section 278(2) of this Act;

(c) that there are documents the truth of the contents of which ought to be admitted, or that there is any other matter which in his view ought to be agreed;

(d) that there is some point, as regards any matter not mentioned in paragraph (a) to (c) above, which could in his opinion be resolved with advantage before the trial and that he therefore applies for a diet to be held before the trial diet,

the court shall in a case to which paragraph (a) above applies, and in any other case may, order that there be a diet before the trial diet, and a diet ordered under this subsection is in this Act referred to as a "preliminary diet".

(2) A party giving notice under subsection (1) above shall specify in the notice the matter or, as the case may be, the grounds of submission or the point to which the notice relates.

(3) The fact that a preliminary diet has been ordered on a particular notice under subsection (1) above shall not preclude the court's consideration at that diet of any other such notice as is mentioned in that subsection, which has been intimated to the court and to the other parties at least 24 hours before that diet.

(4) Subject to subsection (5) below, the court may on ordering a preliminary diet postpone the trial diet for a period not exceeding 21 days; and any such postponement (including postponement for a period which by virtue of the said subsection (5) exceeds 21 days) shall not count towards any time limit applying in respect of the case.

(5) Any period mentioned in subsection (4) above may be extended by the High Court in respect of the case.

(6) In subsection (1) above, "appropriate period" means as regards notice—

(a) under paragraph (a) of that subsection, the period of 15 clear days after service of the indictment;

(b) under paragraph (b) of that subsection, the period from service of the indictment to 10 clear days before the trial diet; and

(c) under paragraph (c) or (d) of that subsection, the period from service of the indictment to the trial diet.

DEFINITIONS
"High Court": s.307(1).
"indictment": s.307(1).

GENERAL NOTE
It will be observed that most of the procedural features are common to both first diets (s.71) and preliminary diets (s.72) and, accordingly reference should be made to the General Note to s.71. However unlike first diets which are compulsory in sheriff and jury cases, preliminary diets which now apply in High Court cases are not mandatory but are initiated by service of notice in accordance with Chap. 9 of the Act of Adjournal (Criminal Procedure Rules) 1996 and Form 9.1 therein. Subsection (6) provides for several different timescales to be met, all under reference to the interval from service of the indictment to the days leading to trial. Yet the

reasons for these different time-limits are unclear particularly when it is seen that subs. (3) allows any other form of notice thereafter to be considered on 24 hours' notice to other parties. All preliminary diets are considered in the High Court of Justiciary sitting in Edinburgh. At the conclusion of any preliminary diet the accused, if present, must be called upon to plead to the charges. It is submitted that where attendance has been waived by the court (s.73(2)) it is axiomatic that pleas should be tendered in absence and recorded.

Note that unlike the Sheriff court procedure, where a preliminary diet is fixed the court can, at that diet, both order postponement of the trial diet up to 21 days (beyond the date when the indictment should otherwise call), and deduct that period from computation of any statutory time-limit. Subsection (5) suggests that the same court as distinct from the Court of Appeal can further extend the period of postponement as necessary.

Subsection (1)(a) stipulates that a preliminary diet must be held to consider any issue of competency or relevancy or want of proper citation, but that any other written motion for such a diet to consider matters arising from subs. (1)(b), (c) or (d) is at the discretion of the court. Section 74 of the Act regulates appeal procedures both from first diets in the sheriff court and preliminary diets in the High Court. It is not clear however whether a decision by a High Court judge *not* to order a preliminary diet can be appealed by this route. Section 74(1) refers to appeal against "a decision at a first diet or a preliminary diet", but if there has been a decision by the court not to hold a preliminary diet then it would seem that appeal would be to the *nobile officium* (refer also to the notes "Appeal Procedures" in s.71 above).

Subsection (1)(b)(iv) refers to the striking out of parts of a judicial transcript. Plainly there will be matters under this head which are only capable of a decision on fairness and admissibility when set in the context of evidence at a trial in which situation s.278 of the Act applies (see too the discussion in notes to s.36 above): however it would be open to the court conducting a preliminary diet to consider what relationship or similarity there was between the charges libelled in the petition and the indictment charges and, accordingly the propriety of excluding all, or part of the judicial examination transcript from the indictment.

Potentially the right of parties to identify to the court under subs. (1)(c) documents which it is felt should be agreed, or evidence of formal facts which are not in dispute, could help diminish the length of trials and, perhaps, focus the issues before the court more effectively. Of course the court is not obliged to fix a diet in these circumstances and there is no duty upon other parties to agree such evidence at all. Preliminary diets were not made mandatory in the High Court largely because of the logistical problems involved in processing and administering them in the limited time before trial.

Section 73 below enacts that at the conclusion of a preliminary diet an accused is called upon to plead; this assumes that objections to competency or relevancy have been repelled. Where a plea in bar of insanity had been unsuccessful at an earlier preliminary diet, and the case was re-indicted, the Appeal Court held that the same plea in bar could be tendered in answer to a subsequent indictment (*Stewart v. H.M. Advocate, (No. 2)*, 1997 S.L.T. 1056). It is submitted that this decision depends heavily upon the nature of the plea in bar trial: the extent of pre-trial publicity and the appropriateness of a trial in a particular jurisdiction (as in *McLeod v. H.M. Advocate*, 1998 S.L.T. 60) could well merit reconsideration but it is doubtful that it could be applied in relation to a plea of tholed assize.

In the event of postponement, s.82 provides that the original warrant of committal shall remain in force.

European Convention on Human Rights

Although the Act of Adjournal (Devolution Issues Rules) 1999 (S.I. 1999 No. 1346) sets out specific rules, including time-scales, for intimation of devolution issues with which the accused had not complied in *H.M. Advocate v. Montgomery*, 1999 G.W.D. 32–1523, the Appeal Court upheld the trial judge's decision to permit further devolution points to be added late (in fact some six weeks after the expiry of the one week *induciae* calculated from the time an indictment was served—see Rule 40.2(1)) to those intimated originally. It was held that while a devolution issue had been raised late on a reading of the Rules, the new issue was a plea of oppression and thus could always be taken as a preliminary plea in terms of s.72(3).

It is of note that the Rules do not set out the procedures to be followed in dealing with devolution issues, and in the absence of such, existing preliminary and trial diets provide the only means for considering devolution issues. S.I. 1999 No. 1346 is reprinted in full in 1999 S.L.T. Issue 21 as well as being incorporated into the Act of Adjournal (Criminal Procedure Rules) 1996 in Division B.

Act of Adjournal
    See A4.165 above.

Preliminary diet: procedure

73.—(1) Where a preliminary diet is ordered, subject to subsection (2) below, the accused shall attend it, and he shall be required at the conclusion of the diet to state how he pleads to the indictment.

(2) The court may permit the diet to proceed notwithstanding the absence of an accused.

(3) At a preliminary diet the court shall, in addition to disposing of any matter specified in a notice given under subsection (1) of section 72 of this Act or referred to in subsection (3) of that section, ascertain, so far as is reasonably practicable, whether the case is likely to proceed to trial on the date assigned as the trial diet and, in particular—

    (a) the state of preparation of the prosecutor and of the accused with respect to their cases; and

    (b) the extent to which the prosecutor and the accused have complied with the duty under section 257(1) of this Act.

(4) At a preliminary diet the court may ask the prosecutor and the accused any question in connection with any matter specified in a notice under subsection (1) of the said section 72 or referred to in subsection (3) of that section or which it is required to ascertain under subsection (3) above.

(5) Where at a preliminary diet the court concludes that the case is unlikely to proceed to trial on the date assigned for the trial diet, the court—

    (a) shall, unless having regard to previous proceedings in the case it considers it inappropriate to do so, postpone the trial diet; and

    (b) may fix a further preliminary diet.

(6) Subject to subsection (5) above, the court may, if it considers it appropriate to do so, adjourn a preliminary diet.

(7) Where an objection is taken to the relevancy of the indictment under subsection (1)(a)(i) of the said section 72, the clerk of court shall minute whether the objection is sustained or repelled and sign the minute.

(8) In subsection (1) above, the reference to the accused shall, without prejudice to section 6(c) of the Interpretation Act 1978, in any case where there is more than one accused include a reference to all of them.

DEFINITIONS
    "indictment": s.307(1).
    "prosecutor": s.307(1).

GENERAL NOTE
    This section sets out the options available to the court in dealing with preliminary diets. As has been noted, subs. (1) proceeds on the basis that pleas to competency or relevancy have been repelled and that the diet has not simply been adjourned. In dealing with a matter raised as a preliminary diet the court then has the same powers as a sheriff exercises under s.71; the court has then to ascertain the readiness of the parties and the extent of evidence which the parties feel to be capable of agreement.
    Subsection (2) permits preliminary diets to proceed in the absence of an accused, but as was noted in the discussion of s.71 it is not clear whether this provision is to enable a diet to proceed to its trial diet despite the absence of one, or all, accused (in which case pleas in accordance with subs. (1) would have to be tendered in absence) or simply to enable a diet to proceed in respect of those accused present at the time. It seems to be that in the case of High Court proceedings the first interpretation is to be preferred; the diets are not compulsory (unlike sheriff solemn first diets), they can be called on relatively short notice making intimation on an accused personally a problem, and may have to be heard in the High Court in Edinburgh rather than within the sheriffdom where the assize is due to convene for the trial diet. Certainly it was recognised that scheduling preliminary diets in all High Court cases would pose logistical difficulties of a much greater sort than arise in sheriff solemn cases. In any event if the court deemed it necessary that all accused should be present at the preliminary diet, subs. (b) would allow the fixing of a further diet for that purpose, or simply an adjournment, procedures which cannot be appealed under s.74(2).

It is important to note that in contrast to the similar sheriff court procedures, s.72(4) entitles the High Court to postpone a trial diet when ordering that a preliminary diet be fixed and discount all, or part, of the time thereafter from time-bar calculations.

The reference in subs. (3) to fulfilling the demands of s.258(1) of the Act (duty to seek agreement of evidence) does not apply to accused who are unrepresented (see s.258(2)).

Incidental procedural matters are regulated by Rule 9.10 in the 1996 Act of Adjournal and the whole proceedings must be recorded or noted in shorthand in accordance with s.93 of the Act.

In *H.M. Advocate. v. Montgomery,* 1999 S.C.C.R. 959, where fuller grounds were argued before the court than had been identified in the accuseds' notices, leave to appeal was granted without all matters raised in the hearing having been resolved. The Appeal Court disapproved this approach generally while acknowledging that the novelty and complexity of issues raised (particularly the interplay between the rules governing devolution issues and existing procedures for preliminary diets) justified the judge's actions in the instant case.

Appeals in connection with preliminary diets

74.—(1) Without prejudice to—

(a) any right of appeal under section 106 or 108 of this Act; and

(b) section 131 of this Act,

and subject to subsection (2) below, a party may with the leave of the court of first instance (granted either on the motion of the party or *ex proprio motu*) in accordance with such procedure as may be prescribed by Act of Adjournal, appeal to the High Court against a decision at a first diet or a preliminary diet.

(2) An appeal under subsection (1) above—

(a) may not be taken against a decision to adjourn the first or, as the case may be, preliminary diet or to postpone the trial diet;

(b) must be taken not later than 2 days after the decision.

(3) Where an appeal is taken under subsection (1) above, the High Court may postpone the trial diet for such period as appears to it to be appropriate and may, if it thinks fit, direct that such period (or some part of it) shall not count towards any time limit applying in respect of the case.

(4) In disposing of an appeal under subsection (1) above the High Court—

[1](a) may affirm the decision of the court of first instance or may remit the case to it with such directions in the matter as it thinks fit;

(b) where the court of first instance has dismissed the indictment or any part of it, may reverse that decision and direct that the court of first instance fix a trial diet, if it has not already fixed one as regards so much of the indictment as it has not dismissed; and

[2](c) may on cause shown extend the period mentioned in section 65(1) of this Act.

DEFINITIONS

"first diet": s.71(1).

"High Court": s.307(1).

"preliminary diet": s.72(1).

NOTES

[1]Words deleted by the Crime and Punishment (Scotland) Act 1997 (c. 48), s.62(1) Sched. 1, para. 21(10)(a) with effect from August 1, 1997 as provided by the Crime and Punishment (Scotland) Act 1997 (Commencement and Transitional Provisions) Order 1997 (S.I. 1997 No. 1712) Art. 3 and Sched. 1.

[2]Inserted by para. 21(10)(b) of the above-mentioned Act with effect from August 1, 1997 in terms of the above Order.

GENERAL NOTE

Refer to the discussion *"Appeal procedures"* in the notes to s.71 above. Parties can competently appeal decisions at a first diet or preliminary diet *ex proprio motu*, or with leave of the court. Subsection (4)(b) refers to the appellate court's power to fix a trial diet if this has not been done; this provision would appear to deal with situations where an indictment has been dismissed on grounds of competency or relevancy and, accordingly, no trial diet fixed.

While subs. (2)(b) stipulates that appeals from a first, or a preliminary, diet must be taken within two days, in *H.M. Advocate v. Sorrie*, 1996 G.W.D. 30–1795 (which is also discussed at p. 117 above) the Crown, having failed to appeal a decision upholding S's plea in bar timeously, proceeded by bill of advocation, and were successful in securing an extension of the statutory time-bar on proceedings.

Computation of certain periods

75. Where the last day of any period mentioned in section 66(6), 67(3), 72 or 74 of this Act falls on a Saturday, Sunday or court holiday, such period shall extend to and include the next day which is not a Saturday, Sunday or court holiday.

GENERAL NOTE
The timescales specified in s.66(6) refer both to the dates within which a first diet must occur in the Sheriff court and the time lapse from service of an indictment until trial; in either event the due date is extended to the next working day. A similar provision covers the time-limit for service of a notice objecting to the description of witnesses in that indictment. The section's reference to s.72 is understandable in that subs. (6) defines "the appropriate period" for notice of the matters to be raised at a preliminary diet. It will be appreciated that s.75's terms do not interfere in any way with the provisions in s.65 against delay.

Plea of guilty

Procedure where accused desires to plead guilty

76.—(1) Where an accused intimates in writing to the Crown Agent that he intends to plead guilty and desires to have his case disposed of at once, the accused may be served with an indictment (unless one has already been served) and a notice to appear at a diet of the appropriate court not less than four clear days after the date of the notice; and it shall not be necessary to lodge or give notice of any list of witnesses or productions.

(2) In subsection (1) above, "appropriate court" means—

(a) in a case where at the time of the intimation mentioned in that subsection an indictment had not been served, either the High Court or the sheriff court; and

(b) in any other case, the court specified in the notice served under section 66(6) of this Act on the accused.

(3) If at any such diet the accused pleads not guilty to the charge or pleads guilty only to a part of the charge, and the prosecutor declines to accept such restricted plea, the diet shall be deserted *pro loco et tempore* and thereafter the cause may proceed in accordance with the other provisions of this Part of this Act; except that in a case mentioned in paragraph (b) of subsection (2) above the court may postpone the trial diet and the period of such postponement shall not count towards any time limit applying in respect of the case.

DEFINITIONS
"High Court": s.307(1).
"indictment": s.307(1).
"witnesses": s.307(1).

GENERAL NOTE
Section 76 re-enacts the familiar accelerated plea provisions of s.102 of the 1975 Act. Although the statute requires written intimation of a proposed plea by the accused to the Crown Agent, it is customary for the letter intimating the terms of the plea to be sent to the procurator fiscal at whose instance the petition charges were raised. It is of course competent to serve an indictment without any prior petition but in that event it will be difficult to negotiate a satisfactory plea practically.

On receipt of a letter, the procurator fiscal is under a duty to comply with the Procurator Fiscal Service's Book of Regulations and deliver the letter along with a report outlining his views on its merits, or otherwise, to the Crown Agent. While the section stipulates that the letter be sent to the Crown Agent, the Crown as a matter of course indicate the date of its receipt by the procurator fiscal to the court when the plea of guilt is recorded, since this may have a bearing upon any sentence; this is particularly pertinent now given the terms of s.196 of the Act which allows courts a discretion to consider as a sentencing parameter, the point in proceedings at which a plea was tendered.

It will be observed that a plea tendered prior to service of any indictment leaves the issue open as to whether the plea should be heard before a sheriff or in the High Court (subs. (2)(a)) and the choice of forum may be a material factor in the plea tendered; by contrast, once an indictment has been served, subs. (2)(b) enacts that a s.76 letter will only have the effect of accelerating the hearing before that court. Rule 10.1–(2) of the 1996 Act of Adjournal provides that cases set down for trial in the High Court, and by necessary inference, charges in which the High Court has exclusive jurisdiction—treason, murder and rape, can be called for disposal in the High Court sitting in Edinburgh instead of at the sitting originally scheduled elsewhere in Scotland.

If the plea offered by the accused is acceptable to the Crown, a notice conforming to the style of Form 10.1–A where no indictment has yet been served, or Form 10.1–B, when an indictment has still to be served, will accompany the indictment now served upon the accused. Cases in which a s.76 plea is offered prior to service of an indictment (see subs. (2)(a)) will ordinarily proceed upon an edited indictment which does not include lists of productions and witnesses; this is not an absolute requirement, but obviously economises on Crown resources. Cases which have simply been brought forward after service of the indictment competently proceed on the full indictment previously served on the accused.

The practice of obtaining the accused's written instructions detailing the precise terms of the plea to be tendered is expedient. Refer to p. 129 for a general discussion of the issue.

Subsection (3) works to the benefit of the Crown; if, at the accelerated diet the accused reneges on his plea, the court can postpone the trial diet and discount the period of the postponement in any calculation of statutory time-bars. This concession only applies to cases proceeding under subs. (2)(b), *i.e.* where an accelerated plea has been offered after service of the indictment. Note however that Rule 10.1–(3) of the 1996 Act of Adjournal only permits such a postponement when all of the accused have tendered s.76 notices and all are present at the accelerated diet and the court grants the postponement in response to a motion made at that time. It is difficult to envisage practical instances in which these circumstances would apply: it may arise where one (or more) accused recants on a "package" deal involving a number of the accused, thus rendering the totality unacceptable to the Crown. Ordinarily the Crown would probably accept pleas from other accused and elect to proceed to trial later against the recalcitrant accused and a subs. (3) motion for postponement could then be made quite properly.

The Induciae

This section proceeds upon an *induciae* between service of the edited form of indictment, and its calling, of four clear days. The *induciae* can be waived by the accused but in *McKnight v. H.M. Advocate*, 1991 S.C.C.R. 751 where the accused pleaded to an indictment served upon him 10 minutes beforehand, the Court of Appeal doubted the wisdom of proceeding in such a summary fashion and indicated that the Crown should be hesitant to accept pleas tendered in such circumstances. It may be said too that with the current re-evaluation by the Appeal Court of the relationship between criminal practitioners and clients (see, for example, *Anderson v. H.M. Advocate*, 1996 S.L.T. 155), it could be regarded as imprudent to advise clients to waive the four day *induciae*.

Withdrawal of the Plea

A plea tendered at the accelerated diet can be withdrawn competently at a later diet, but the court would have to be satisfied that the accused had substantially misunderstood his position and had been prejudiced by that misunderstanding. See *Healy v. H.M. Advocate*, 1990 S.C.C.R. 110, where the indictment had been read over to the accused by the sheriff at the first diet and accepted by the accused who sought to withdraw her plea before a different sheriff at the diet of deferred sentence; and *Paul v. H.M. Advocate* (1914) 7 Adam 343 where the accused sought to change his plea following upon a remit to the High Court for sentence. In *Weightman v. H.M. Advocate*, 1997 G.W.D. 3–85 the court looked to the absence of any dissent by the accused, during narration of the facts and mitigation, in rejecting his later claims that he had been bullied or pressured to plead during his trial.

So far as the Crown is concerned, any mitigation tendered which is felt to be inconsistent with a guilty plea, or, it is suggested, any defence explanation of the factual circumstances which is disputed, must be made known to the court of first instance. Otherwise the Crown will likely be held to have acquiesced and will be barred from raising the matter in any appeal (*Bennett v. H.M. Advocate*, 1996 S.C.C.R. 331 and see also s.118(8) below). In the event of such an unsatisfactory plea the court is obliged to invoke the provisions of subs. (3) (refer to A4.174 above). Guidance on the procedures open to the court where disagreement on the terms of the plea surfaces is given in *McCartney v. H.M. Advocate*, 1997 S.C.C.R. 644.

Plea of guilty

77.—(1) Where at any diet the accused tenders a plea of guilty to the indictment or any part thereof he shall do so in open court and, subject to section 70(7) of this Act, shall, if he is able to do so, sign a written copy of the plea; and the judge shall countersign such copy.

(2) Where the plea is to part only of the charge and the prosecutor does not accept the plea, such non-acceptance shall be recorded.

(3) Where an accused charged on indictment with any offence tenders a plea of guilty to any other offence of which he could competently be found guilty on the trial of the indictment, and that plea is accepted by the prosecutor, it shall be competent to convict the accused of the offence to which he has so pled guilty and to sentence him accordingly.

DEFINITIONS
"diet": s.307(1).
"indictment": s.307(1).
"prosecutor": s.307(1).

GENERAL NOTE
This section substantially re-enacts the provisions of s.103 of the 1975 Act. Obviously if for some reason the accused is unable to subscribe his plea, the court is under an additional responsibility to ensure that the plea as recorded reflects his intention. Thereafter the judge is required to countersign the plea on the same papers; failure to do so constitutes a nullity (see *H.M. Advocate v. MacDonald* (1896) 3 S.L.T. 317). The prosecutor must ensure that any mitigation offered by the accused whose terms are not accepted by the Crown is objected to at the first diet, failing which the Crown will be taken as having acquiesced in the matter (see p. 128).

Prosecutor's refusal of pleas
There is no obligation upon the prosecutor to accept a plea of guilt to the libel (indeed, historically, in capital crimes the Crown always elected to prove its case when a guilty plea was offered).

The rules for such eventualities were stated in *Strathern v. Sloan*, 1937 J.C. 76 at 80 but had little practical impact once the 1980 Act abolished mandatory pleading diets. The re-introduction of mandatory first diets, and preliminary diets, in ss.71 and 72 of the 1995 Act may render that judgment more topical. If a guilty plea is tendered at the earlier diet but refused by the Crown, the minute should record that the plea was tendered and rejected; it should not record the plea as one of not guilty. At the trial diet the accused should not be called upon to plead *de novo*, in the interim, unless the prosecutor has decided to accept the plea previously tendered (it will be appreciated that the terms of s.196, which have already been discussed in the notes to s.76 above, may well make it advantageous to tender partial pleas at a first diet even if, at that juncture, they are not acceptable to the Crown). If the trial proceeds, and the plea previously tendered becomes acceptable to the Crown, the accused should then be called upon to state his plea publicly. No reference in the course of a trial should be made by the Crown to the fact that such a plea has been proferred.

Prosecutor's acceptance of pleas
Following upon *Anderson v. H.M. Advocate*, 1996 S.C.C.R. 487 it is submitted to be a prudent practice to secure a client's written instructions before tendering a guilty plea to the court; this view accords with The Faculty of Advocates' Code of Professional Conduct. In *Crossan v. H.M. Advocate*, 1996 S.C.C.R. 279, C appealed his conviction following a guilty plea to a murder charge (his co-accused having pled guilty to assault), and sought to withdraw his plea the following day, a procedure which was not competent to the court. In terms of s.252(d) of the 1975 Act (now s.104 of the 1995 Act) the Court of Appeal remitted the matter to a single judge for a report on the circumstances surrounding the appeal. It will be noted that the evidence to

that judge was not given on oath and was heard in chambers outwith the presence of the accused, it being a matter within the sole discretion of the appointed judge to determine procedures necessary for the preparation of his report.

Act of Adjournal
    Refer to Chap. 10 of the 1996 Act of Adjournal.

Notice by accused

Special defences, incrimination and notice of witnesses, etc.

78.—(1) It shall not be competent for an accused to state a special defence or to lead evidence calculated to exculpate the accused by incriminating a co-accused unless—
    (a) a plea of special defence or, as the case may be, notice of intention to lead such evidence has been lodged and intimated in writing in accordance with subsection (3) below—
        (i) where the accused is cited to the High Court for the trial diet, to the Crown Agent; and
        (ii) where he is cited to the sheriff court for the trial diet, to the procurator fiscal,
    and to any co-accused not less than 10 clear days before the trial diet; or
    (b) the court, on cause shown, otherwise directs.
(2) Subsection (1) above shall apply to a defence of automatism or coercion as if it were a special defence.
(3) A plea or notice is lodged and intimated in accordance with this subsection—
    (a) where the accused is cited to the High Court for the trial diet, by lodging the plea or notice with the Clerk of Justiciary and by intimating the plea or notice to the Crown Agent and to any co-accused not less than 10 clear days before the trial diet;
    (b) where the accused is cited to the sheriff court for the trial diet, by lodging the plea or notice with the sheriff clerk and by intimating it to the procurator fiscal and to any co-accused at or before the first diet.
(4) It shall not be competent for the accused to examine any witnesses or to put in evidence any productions not included in the lists lodged by the prosecutor unless—
    (a) written notice of the names and addresses of such witnesses and of such productions has been given—
        (i) where the case is to be tried in the sheriff court, to the procurator fiscal of the district of the trial diet at or before the first diet; and
        (ii) where the case is to be tried in the High Court, to the Crown Agent at least ten clear days before the day on which the jury is sworn; or
    (b) the court, on cause shown, otherwise directs.
(5) A copy of every written notice required by subsection (4) above shall be lodged by the accused with the sheriff clerk of the district in which the trial diet is to be held, or in any case the trial diet of which is to be held in the High Court in Edinburgh with the Clerk of Justiciary, at or before the trial diet, for the use of the court.

DEFINITIONS
    "Clerk of Justiciary": s.307(1).
    "High Court": s.307(1).
    "procurator fiscal": s.307(1).

GENERAL NOTE
    Section 78 stipulates the periods of notice to be given by the accused to the prosecutor, and any co-accused of any defence, special defence, list of witnesses or productions. Note that

different periods of notice apply in sheriff and jury and High Court cases and that these procedures have to be seen in the context of the preliminary diets and first diets introduced by ss.71 and 72 of the 1995 Act.

Service of Lists and Notices in Sheriff Solemn cases

Section 71 now stipulates that a first diet has to occur not less than 15 clear days after service of an indictment and not more than 10 days before the trial diet. Section 78(4) enacts that any lists of witnesses or productions (other than those included in the indictment by the prosecutor) must be served upon the Crown, and a copy lodged with the court, no later than at the first diet. Note that there is no obligation to serve these lists upon any co-accused. Failure to lodge the lists timeously renders the examination of either productions or witnesses incompetent unless, in terms of subs. (4)(b), the accused can show cause for this failure. This timescale demands earlier action on the part of the accused than heretofore; s.82(2) of the 1975 Act only stipulated three clear days' notice of witnesses and productions to the prosecutor in any solemn case, calculated by reference to the date on which the jury was sworn.

It will be recalled that at the first diet the sheriff is obliged to enquire as to the state of preparation of the parties for trial (s.71(1)(a)). Accordingly it may be expected that later lodging of lists will entail a considerable burden in persuading the court that these should still be received. The same can be said for notices of special defences (extended to include defences of coercion and automatism): these have to be served upon the prosecutor and any co-accused at or before the first diet though, again, a discretion is open to the court to permit late lodging on cause shown.

A special defence is a fact which if established must lead to the acquittal of the accused upon the libel (*Adam v. McNeill*, 1971 S.L.T. (Notes) 80). The effect of such a defence, if successful, is to divorce the accused from all blame or culpability in the charge libelled and secure his acquittal. Thus in *McQuade v. H.M. Advocate*, 1996 S.C.C.R. 347 where only one of three accused gave evidence, admitted shooting the deceased during a robbery and implicated his co-accused, it was held on appeal that a notice of incrimination had not been necessary since that evidence could not have secured his acquittal. See also *McShane v. H.M. Advocate*, 1989 S.C.C.R. 687 and *Collins v. H.M. Advocate*, 1991 S.C.C.R. 898: unlike other special defences a notice of incrimination does not require to be read to the jury or be referred to in the course of the judge's charge.

A notice of alibi is not required when it is to be asserted that the accused was at the *locus* for an innocent purpose (*Balsillie v. H.M. Advocate*, 1993 S.C.C.R. 760). In relation to special defences of self defence *O'Connell v. H.M. Advocate*, 1996 S.C.C.R. 614 is authority for the proposition that the particulars of the defence must be properly specified to be received by the court; at an adjourned first diet the special defence had been inspecifically stated causing the sheriff to adjourn the matter further. The defence of coercion or necessity was recognised in *Moss v. Howdle*, 1997 S.L.T. 782 following *Thomson v. H.M. Advocate*, 1983 S.L.T. 682; 1983 S.C.C.R. 368. See also the discussion in "Necessity and Coercion in Criminal Law" by P.W. Ferguson, 1997 S.L.T. 127. (The issue of withdrawal of a special defence from a jury where only the thinnest evidence is available is ruled on in *Whyte v. H.M. Advocate*, 1996 G.W.D. 25–1411.)

It is doubtful that a notice of defence, not in proper form, can be treated as complying with the time-limit for notice imposed in subs. (1)(a), but it might serve to indicate a lack of readiness for trial (see s.71(1)(a)) if produced at a first, or preliminary, diet as occurred in *O'Connell*.

Note that in terms of Chap. 11 of the 1996 Act of Adjournal notices under s.78(1) and lists of witnesses and productions under s.78(4) can be served on the solicitor acting for a co-accused rather than upon the co-accused personally. Despite their effect upon any trial, pleas of diminished responsibility or provocation, which may focus strongly upon technical or medical evidence and necessitate further investigation by the Crown, need not be intimated before trial.

It remains open to the prosecutor to waive timeous notice, and to the court to consider the broad interests of justice when assessing whether due cause has been shown for notices to be received late, but such an assessment must surely now take account of any potential prejudice to co-accused since they too are entitled to timeous notification. In *Lowson v. H.M. Advocate*, 1943 J.C. 141, where a list of defence witnesses had not been lodged due to a change of trial venue, the trial judge disallowed the evidence on the view (shared by the procurator fiscal who had objected), that there was no discretion to permit examination of unintimated witnesses; the Lord Justice-General (at 145) while noting that the provisions existed to prevent the introduction of evidence which the prosecutor has no means of meeting, stated:

> "But I am clear that rules, being conceived in the interests of the prosecution, may competently, and should, be waived where the interests of justice are better served by waiving them than by insisting on them."

Despite the apparent mandatory nature of many of the 1995 Act's provisions this broad principle should still hold good.

Service of Lists and Notices in the High Court
   The absence of mandatory first diets in the High Court has meant that a simple time-limit is imposed in these cases; any list of witnesses or productions and any notice must be served not less than 10 clear days before the trial diet. As with sheriff solemn cases, the accused is obliged to serve notices upon any co-accused, but need not intimate lists of witnesses or productions to them (see Chap. 11 of the 1996 Act of Adjournal). Section 72(6) specifies the "appropriate period" applicable to the variety of circumstances which can give rise to a preliminary diet but it has to be borne in mind that the need to lodge lists or notices proceeds entirely without reference to the timetable of any preliminary diet.

Act of Adjournal
   Refer to Chap. 11 of the 1996 Act of Adjournal and especially note the alteration to r.11.2 effected by the Act of Adjournal (Criminal Procedure Rules Amendment) (Miscellaneous) 1996; this permits service of notices under s.78(4) on the accused's solicitor.

Preliminary pleas

   79.—(1) Except by leave of the court on cause shown, no application, matter or point mentioned in subsection (1) of section 72 of this Act or that subsection as applied by section 71 of this Act shall be made, raised or submitted by an accused unless his intention to do so has been stated in a notice under the said subsection (1) or, as the case may be, under subsection (2) of the said section 71.
   (2) No discrepancy, error or deficiency such as is mentioned in paragraph (a)(ii) of subsection (1) of the said section 72 or that subsection as applied by the said section 71 shall entitle the accused to object to plead to the indictment unless the court is satisfied that the discrepancy, error or deficiency tended substantially to mislead and prejudice the accused.

DEFINITION
   "indictment": s.307(1).

GENERAL NOTE
   No objection to competency or relevancy of an indictment, claim of want of lawful citation, application for separation of charges or trials, or objection to a special capacity libelled shall be entertained once the first diet has passed in sheriff solemn cases, or after lapse of the "appropriate period" specified in s.72(6). The intention of the section is to ensure that all preliminary matters are resolved before any case calls for trial; see generally ss.71(2) and 72(1) which apply the provisions of the latter section to sheriff and jury proceedings.
   After the time for preliminary pleas to be stated has passed, the court will only exceptionally permit such pleas to be stated later if it is clear that the accused was not afforded an earlier opportunity (see *McAllister v. H.M. Advocate*, 1985 S.C.C.R. 36 where there had been a total failure to serve the indictment on the accused and hence no notice of preliminary plea could be stated) or substantial prejudice would otherwise result; for example, a tholed assize or other fundamental nullity, or failure by the Crown to lodge the judicial examination as a production (refer to *H.M. Advocate v. Cafferty*, 1984 S.C.C.R. 444 discussed in the notes to s.68).

Alteration, etc, of diet

Alteration and postponement of trial diet

   80.—(1) Where an indictment is not brought to trial at the trial diet and a warrant for a subsequent sitting of the court on a day within two months after the date of the trial diet has been issued under section 66(1) of this Act by the clerk of court, the court may adjourn the trial diet to the subsequent sitting, and the warrant shall have effect as if the trial diet had originally been fixed for the date of the subsequent sitting.
   (2) At any time before the trial diet, a party may apply to the court before which the trial is to take place for postponement of the trial diet.

(3) Subject to subsection (4) below, after hearing all the parties the court may discharge the trial diet and either fix a new trial diet or give leave to the prosecutor to serve a notice fixing a new trial diet.

(4) Where all the parties join in an application to postpone the trial diet, the court may proceed under subsection (3) above without hearing the parties.

(5) Where there is a hearing under this section the accused shall attend it, unless the court permits the hearing to proceed notwithstanding the absence of the accused.

(6) In subsection (5) above, the reference to the accused shall, without prejudice to section 6(c) of the Interpretation Act 1978, in any case where there is more than one accused include a reference to all of them.

DEFINITIONS
"indictment": s.307(1).
"prosecutor": s.307(1).

GENERAL NOTE
This section now consolidates the amendment made to the 1975 Act by the Criminal Justice (Scotland) Act 1995, Sched. 6, para. 24, the primary effect of which is to permit an adjournment of up to two months in any solemn case (previously s.77 of the 1975 Act granted such a length of adjournment only in High Court cases; sheriff solemn cases could be adjourned only for one month).

The purpose of s.80 is to postpone the trial of a case while keeping the existing indictment alive. This avoids the expense of preparing and serving a fresh indictment and, with the arrival of first and preliminary diets introduced by ss.71(1) and 72(1) of the 1995 Act, will obviate the need for repetition of those diets. Although adjournments have customarily been obtained in the past by calling the indictment during the sitting (rather than by way of a preliminary diet), it has to be said that the provisions of s.80(1) are a second-best expedient to deal with the sorts of unforeseen events the occurrence of which seems to be one of the few certainties in any solemn sitting. If it can be anticipated that a trial cannot proceed, and the Crown wish to preserve the indictment, it is probably better to have the case postponed by way of s.71(7) in the sheriff court, or s.72(4) in the High Court. It is statutorily provided by s.72(4) that the period of postponement, in the High Court only, may be discounted from any time-bar calculation (see notes to s.65 above) but it could well be that when either a postponement or adjournment of trial is sought, the parties may seek an extension of the relevant time-bar provision; indeed, agreement to an adjournment might well depend upon an assent to an extension of the time-bar.

An element of duplication occurs when the terms of ss.71 and 72 are compared against subs. (2) since all refer to postponement of the trial but the grounds for postponement under the former sections are identified by the court as a result of enquiry at the preliminary diet, whereas in a s.80, any of the parties can initiate an application for such postponement. From a technical stance, a s.80 adjournment could only be granted when a later sitting had already been warranted in accordance with the terms of s.66(1) of the Act and in the absence of such a sitting would simply not be competent; ss.71 and 72 proceed without reference to future sittings of the court though no doubt in practice the dates of future sittings would be taken into account.

Chapter 12 of the 1996 Act of Adjournal specifies the procedures to be followed. Where an application for postponement is to be moved it should be in the style of Form 12.2.–A; joint applications proceed on Form 12.2.–B. It is possible for hearings under s.80 to proceed without the presence of the accused being required but, in that event, it falls to the prosecutor to intimate the new diet to the accused (Rule 12.1.–(4)): see *H.M. Advocate v. Carruthers*, 1994 S.L.T. 900, a case where the Crown failed to intimate properly but, notwithstanding, all accused duly appeared for trial and took objection to further procedure.

The aims of the section can be seen in r.12.5(1) of that Act of Adjournal which enables the court, on being satisfied that there are no other cases set for the sitting postponed in terms of subss. (3) and (4), to carry over the citation of jurors called to the sitting to the new trial diet.

It is not merely semantic to stress that s.80 provides for adjournment to a *sitting* within the coming two-month period. The adjournment can only be granted under s.80 when a warrant has already been granted for a subsequent sitting. While it is equally competent to adjourn to a specific date within a sitting, this commits the Crown to calling the indictment on that date come what may, failing which the instance will fall. The prudent course is to adjourn to the relevant sitting which commences on a given date. In *H.M. Advocate v. Smith*, 1993 S.C.C.R. 987 a diet was adjourned in error to a *dies non*, the sitting commencing the day after. The Crown sought a Bill of Advocation to alter the date but also prepared and served a fresh, identical, indictment.

The Appeal Court held that the instance fell once the adjournment was allowed, but upheld the Crown's decision to re-indict, noting the absence of any prejudice to the accused's case (see also *H.M. Advocate v. Dow*, 1992 S.L.T. 577, a further example of the use of "dual indictments"). By contrast in *H.M. Advocate v. Willoughby*, 2000 S.C.C.R. 73 the Crown moved to adjourn a trial to a non—existent sitting (there being no warrant live to constitute the sitting) and, on realising the error sought a warrant for a special sitting *ex post facto,* a device which could not preserve the indictment which was held to have fallen after the original incompetent motion. Unsurprisingly a motion for extension of the year time-bar was both opposed, and refused.

Any warrant for committal will remain in force when a diet is postponed under subs. 80(1): see s.82 below and Rule 12.1.–(6).

Act of Adjournal
Refer to Chap. 12 of the 1996 Act of Adjournal for procedural guidance and see Form 12.1 (Intimation by prosecutor of new trial diet fixed in terms of s.80(1)) which relates only to trials fixed in absence of the accused, Forms 12.2–A (minute for postponement), 12.2–B (joint minute for postponement), and 12.6 (intimation by prosecutor of a new diet fixed by way of either s.80(3) or (4) of the Act.

Procedure where trial does not take place

81.—(1) Where at the trial diet—
(a) the diet has been deserted *pro loco et tempore* for any cause; or
(b) an indictment is for any cause not brought to trial and no order has been given by the court postponing such trial or appointing it to be held at a subsequent date at some other sitting of the court,
it shall be lawful at any time within nine clear days after the last day of the sitting in which the trial diet was to be held to give notice to the accused on another copy of the indictment to appear to answer the indictment at a further diet either in the High Court or in the sheriff court when the charge is one that can be lawfully tried in that court, notwithstanding that the original citation to a trial diet was to a different court.

(2) Without prejudice to subsection (1) above, where a trial diet has been deserted *pro loco et tempore* and the court has appointed a further trial diet to be held on a subsequent date at the same sitting the accused shall require to appear and answer the indictment at that further diet.

(3) The prosecutor shall not raise a fresh libel in a case where the court has deserted the trial *simpliciter* and its decision in that regard has not been reversed on appeal.

(4) The notice referred to in subsection (1) above shall be in the form prescribed by Act of Adjournal or as nearly as may be in such form.

(5) The further diet specified in the notice referred to in subsection (1) above shall be not earlier than nine clear days from the giving of the notice.

[1,2](6) On or before the day on which notice referred to in subsection (1) above is given, a list of jurors shall be prepared, ... and kept by the sheriff clerk of the district to which the notice applies in the manner provided in section 85(2) of this Act.

(7) The warrant issued under section 66(1) of this Act shall be sufficient warrant for the citation of accused and witnesses to the further diet.

DEFINITIONS
"High Court": s.307(1).
"indictment": s.307(1).
"prosecutor": s.307(1).
"witness": s.307(1).

NOTES
[1]Deleted by the Crime and Punishment (Scotland) Act 1997 (c. 48), s.62(1) and Sched. 1, para. 21(11) with effect from August 1, 1997 in terms of the Crime and Punishment (Scotland) Act 1997 (Commencement and Transitional Provisions) Order 1997 (S.I. 1997 No. 1712) para. 3.
[2]Inserted by the above Act and Schedule and commenced as above.

GENERAL NOTE

The terms of s.127 of the 1975 Act have been extended in this section of the 1995 Act. Where an indictment has been deserted *pro loco et tempore* or has not called for trial, it is open to the Crown to preserve the terms of the indictment already served upon the accused and serve a notice along with a copy of the indictment fixing a new trial diet on a shortened *induciae*. Like the provisions for adjournment of trial contained in s.80 above, this procedure has the advantage of avoiding preparation of a new indictment.

Section 127 of the 1975 Act demanded that service of a notice under the section had to be effected within nine clear days after the abortive trial diet; the equivalent provision in the 1995 Act stipulates that such notice should be served within nine clear days after the final day of the sitting in which the case had been due to proceed. Thereafter an *induciae*, of a further nine clear days is necessary before the case can proceed to trial. While the terms of the original indictment remain extant, this has to be confirmed to the accused by serving a copy of it on him along with the notice intimating the new diet. It is essential that any s.67(5) notices, which add witnesses or productions to the original indictment, are served anew; obviously this can be done most economically by effecting service along with the notice and copy indictment.

The form of the original indictment will remain unaltered (except in so far as added to by s.67 notices) but note that s.81(1) permits the calling of the indictment in a different forum; so irrespective of where the indictment was to be called originally, the accused can be called to trial in either a sheriff and jury court or in the High Court, the only limitation being that the charges must be ones which can be competently heard before that court. It is a necessary condition of proceedings under s.81 that the sheriff clerk, in compliance with subs. (6), has prepared and makes available a list of jurors by the time the s.81 notice is served on the accused.

Act of Adjournal

The notice specified in subs. (1) follows the style of Form 8.2–B set out in the 1996 Act of Adjournal.

Desertion or postponement where accused in custody

82. Where—
  (a) a diet is deserted *pro loco et tempore*;
  (b) a diet is postponed or adjourned; or
  (c) an order is issued for the trial to take place at a different place from that first given notice of,
the warrant of committal on which the accused is at the time in custody till liberated in due course of law shall continue in force.

GENERAL NOTE

This section keeps the original committal warrant extant in circumstances where the indictment served has not proceeded to trial or a plea.

Circumstances giving rise to the need to keep the original warrant alive occur in cases of postponement under ss.71(7) and 72(4), s.74(3), adjournment of a trial diet by s.80(1) and desertion *pro loco et tempore* in terms of s.81(1)(a); s.82(c) relates both to situations in which the prosecutor alters the forum of trial (s.81(1)), or the court, before trial, in accordance with s.83 below, grants the prosecutor's motion to transfer the trial to another sheriff court in the sheriffdom.

Transfer of sheriff court solemn proceedings

83.—[1](1) Where an accused person has been cited to attend a sitting of the sheriff court the prosecutor may, at any time before the commencement of his trial, apply to the sheriff to adjourn the trial and transfer it to a sitting of a sheriff court, appointed as mentioned in section 66(1) of this Act, in any other district in that sheriffdom.
  [2](2) On an application under subsection (1) above the sheriff may—
  (a) after giving the accused or his counsel or solicitor an opportunity to be heard; or
  (b) on the joint application of the parties,
adjourn the trial and make an order for the transfer of the trial as mentioned in subsection (1) above.
  [3](3) Where a warrant to cite any person to attend a sitting of the sheriff

court has been issued by the sheriff clerk under section 66(1) of this Act and the trial has been adjourned and transferred by an order under subsection (2) above, the warrant shall have effect as if the trial diet had originally been fixed for the court, and the date of the sitting of that court, to which the trial is so transferred.

DEFINITION
"prosecutor": s.307(1).

NOTES
[1]Substituted by the Crime and Punishment (Scotland) Act 1997 (c. 48), s.62(1) and Sched. 1, para. 21(12)(a) with effect from August 1, 1997 in terms of the Crime and Punishment (Scotland) Act 1997 (Commencement and Transitional Provisions) Order 1997 (S.I. 1997 No. 1712) para. 3.
[2]Inserted by s.62(1) and Sched. 1, para. 21(12)(b) of the above Act with effect from August 1, 1997 by means of the above Order.
[3]Inserted by s.62(1) and Sched. 1, para. 21(12)(c) of the above Act with effect from August 1, 1997 in terms of the above Order.

GENERAL NOTE
This provision was introduced into the 1975 Act by Sched. 6, para. 41 of the Criminal Justice (Scotland) Act 1995 and is untested. The most obvious use of this section is to permit the transfer of a case to a court equipped to take the evidence of a child via a live television link (see s.271(9) and (10) below), but the section is widely drafted and could, for example, be used to enable the transfer of a sitting to another sheriff court in the sheriffdom if a previous sitting had badly overrun. The amendments introduced by the 1997 Act are of a technical nature, but serve to ensure that the original warrant to cite the accused and witnesses holds good despite any change of venue. Note however that s.83 makes no provision for extension of any time bar; reference still has to be had to the general provisions of s.65 above.

Jurors for sittings

Juries: returns of jurors and preparation of lists

84.—(1) For the purposes of a trial, the sheriff principal shall return such number of jurors as he thinks fit or, in relation to a trial in the High Court, such other number as the Lord Justice Clerk or any Lord Commissioner of Justiciary may direct.

(2) The Lord Justice General, whom failing the Lord Justice Clerk, may give directions as to the areas from which and the proportions in which jurors are to be summoned for trials to be held in the High Court, and for any such trial the sheriff principal of the sheriffdom in which the trial is to take place shall requisition the required number of jurors from the areas and in the proportions so specified.

(3) Where a sitting of the High Court is to be held at a town in which the High Court does not usually sit, the jury summoned to try any case in such a sitting shall be summoned from the list of potential jurors of the sheriff court district in which the town is situated.

(4) For the purpose of a trial in the sheriff court, the clerk of court shall be furnished with a list of names from lists of potential jurors of the sheriff court district in which the court is held containing the number of persons required.

(5) The sheriff principal, in any return of jurors made by him to a court, shall take the names in regular order, beginning at the top of the list of potential jurors in each of the sheriff court districts, as required; and as often as a juror is returned to him, he shall mark or cause to be marked, in the list of potential jurors of the respective sheriff court districts the date when any such juror was returned to serve; and in any such return he shall commence with the name immediately after the last in the preceding return, without regard to the court to which the return was last made, and taking the subsequent names in the order in which they are entered, as directed by this subsection, and so to the end of the lists respectively.

(6) Where a person whose name has been entered in the lists of potential jurors dies, or ceases to be qualified to serve as a juror, the sheriff principal, in making returns of jurors in accordance with the Jurors (Scotland) Act 1825, shall pass over the name of that person, but the date at which his name has been so passed over, and the reason therefor, shall be entered at the time in the lists of potential jurors.

(7) Only the lists returned in accordance with this section by the sheriffs principal to the clerks of court shall be used for the trials for which they were required.

(8) The persons to serve as jurors at sittings of the High Court shall be listed and their names and addresses shall be inserted in one roll to be signed by the judge, and the list made up under this section shall be known as the "list of assize".

(9) When more than one case is set down for trial at a sitting of the High Court, it shall not be necessary to prepare more than one list of assize, and such list shall be authenticated by the signature of a judge of the Court, and shall be the list of assize for the trial of all parties cited to that particular sitting; and the persons included in such list shall be summoned to serve generally for the trials of all the accused cited to the sitting, and only one general execution of citation shall be returned against them; and a copy of the list of assize, certified by one of the clerks of court, shall have the like effect, for all purposes for which the list may be required, as the principal list of assize authenticated as aforesaid.

(10) No irregularity in—
(a) making up the lists in accordance with the provisions of this Act;
(b) transmitting the lists;
(c) the warrant of citation;
(d) summoning jurors; or
(e) in returning any execution of citation,
shall constitute an objection to jurors whose names are included in the jury list, subject to the ruling of the court in relation to the effect of an objection as to any criminal act by which jurors may be returned to serve in any case contrary to this Act or the Jurors (Scotland) Act 1825.

DEFINITIONS
"High Court": s.307(1).
"Lord Commissioner of Justiciary": s.307(1).
"Lord Justice Clerk": s.307(1).
"Lord Justice General": s.1(1).

GENERAL NOTE
This section lays out the administrative procedures to be followed in drawing up and maintaining a list of assize. Particularly note that subs. (9) makes it competent for those who have served on a jury during the sitting to be balloted for later trials in the sitting.

Rule 13.1 of the 1996 Act of Adjournal requires the clerk of court to pay heed to the postponement or adjournment of trials under s.74(5), the postponement of trial following upon the withdrawal of an accelerated plea of guilty (s.76(3)) and the alteration and postponement of a trial during a sitting, when drawing up lists of jurors.

Act of Adjournal
Refer to Chap. 13 of the 1996 Act of Adjournal.

Juries: citation and attendance of jurors

85.—[1](1) It shall not be necessary to serve any list of jurors upon the accused ...
[1](2) A list of jurors shall—
(a) contain not less than 30 names;
(b) be prepared under the directions of the clerk of the court before which the trial is to take place;

(c) be kept at the office of the sheriff clerk of the district in which the court of the trial diet is situated; and

(d) be headed "List of Assize for the sitting of the High Court of Justiciary (or the sheriff court of. at.) on the. of.".

(2A) The clerk of the court before which the trial is to take place shall, on an application made to him by or on behalf of an accused, supply the accused, free of charge on the day on which the trial diet is called, and before the oath has been administered to the jurors for the trial of the accused, with a copy of a list of jurors prepared under subsection (2) above.

(2B) Where an accused has been supplied under subsection (2A) above with a list of jurors—

(a) neither he nor any person acting on his behalf shall make a copy of that list, or any part thereof; and

(b) he or his representatives shall return the list to the clerk of the court after the oath has been administered to the jurors for his trial.

(2C) A person who fails to comply with subsection (2B) above shall be guilty of an offence and shall be liable on summary conviction to a fine not exceeding level 1 on the standard scale.

(3) It shall not be necessary to summon all the jurors contained in any list of jurors under this Act, but it shall be competent to summon such jurors only, commencing from the top of the list, as may be necessary to ensure a sufficient number for the trial of the cases which remain for trial at the date of the citation of the jurors, and such number shall be fixed by the clerk of the court in which the trial diet is to be called, or in any case in the High Court by the Clerk of Justiciary, and the jurors who are not so summoned shall be placed upon the next list issued, until they have attended to serve.

(4) The sheriff clerk of the sheriffdom in which a sitting of the High Court is to be held or the sheriff clerk of the sheriff court district in which any juror is to be cited where the citation is for a trial before a sheriff, shall fill up and sign a proper citation addressed to each such juror, and shall cause the same to be transmitted to him by letter, sent to him at his place of residence as stated in the lists of potential jurors by registered post or recorded delivery or to be served on him by an officer of law; and a certificate under the hand of such sheriff clerk of the citation of any jurors or juror in the manner provided in this subsection shall be a legal citation.

(5) The sheriff clerk of the sheriffdom in which a sitting of the High Court is to be held shall issue citations to the whole jurors required for the sitting, whether the jurors reside in that or in any other sheriffdom.

(6) Persons cited to attend as jurors may, unless they have been excused in respect thereof under section 1 of the Law Reform (Miscellaneous Provisions) (Scotland) Act 1980, be fined up to level 3 on the standard scale if they fail to attend in compliance with the citation.

(7) A fine imposed under subsection (6) above may, on application, be remitted—

(a) by a Lord Commissioner of Justiciary where imposed in the High Court;

(b) by the sheriff court where imposed in the sheriff court,

and no court fees or expenses shall be exigible in respect of any such application.

(8) A person shall not be exempted by sex or marriage from the liability to serve as a juror.

DEFINITIONS
"Clerk of Justiciary": s.307(1).
"High Court": s.307(1).
"indictment": s.307(1).

"Lord Commissioner of Justiciary": s.307(1).
"sheriff clerk": s.307(1).

NOTE
[1]As amended by the Crime and Punishment (Scotland) Act 1997 (c. 48), s.58 with effect from August 1, 1997 (Commencement and Transitional Provisions) Order 1997, (S.I. 1997 No. 1712) para. 3.

GENERAL NOTE
This section, amended by the 1997 Act, removes the accused's right to receive a copy of the List of Assize once his indictment has been served upon him; from August 1, 1997 the right is limited to sight of the Assize List on the day the case is called for trial.

The modified provision is directed against intimidation of jurors and was introduced into the 1997 Act at a late stage (January 20, 1997) without opposition. "Jury nobbling" has become a recognised phenomenon in other jurisdictions and the potential for abuse which advance access to jurors' particulars could present is obvious. Concern was heightened by the discovery of a current High Court Assize List circulating amongst prisoners.

Both the accused and his agent are only entitled to sight of the Assize List on the day the indictment calls for trial and may neither retain, nor copy, the List which must be returned to the Clerk once the jury is empannelled. It will be noted that subs. (2B) creates a criminal offence for any breach of that provision.

Jurors: excusal and objections

86.—(1) Where, before a juror is sworn to serve, the parties jointly apply for him to be excused the court shall, notwithstanding that no reason is given in the application, excuse that juror from service.

(2) Nothing in subsection (1) above shall affect the right of the accused or the prosecutor to object to any juror on cause shown.

(3) If any objection is taken to a juror on cause shown and such objection is founded on the want of sufficient qualification as provided by section 1(1) of the Law Reform (Miscellaneous Provisions) (Scotland) Act 1980, such objection shall be proved only by the oath of the juror objected to.

(4) No objection to a juror shall be competent after he has been sworn to serve.

DEFINITION
"prosecutor": s.307(1).

GENERAL NOTE
The right of peremptory challenge to a number of jurors without showing cause was abolished by s.8 of the Criminal Justice (Scotland) Act 1995 and subs. (1) was substituted; where parties concur, jurors can still be excused without cause being shown, a measure largely intended to enable patently unsuitable or unfit jurors to be relieved of possible selection without open challenge. Although the obvious time for such an agreement to be reached is when the assize presents itself for ballot, the section does not rule out an earlier agreement between parties after the list of assize has been inspected. The court has no power to intervene in the matter.

Subsection (2) preserves the traditional right of challenge on cause shown to a juror selected in the ballot. "Cause shown" has to relate to the juror personally and to his inability to try the case impartially or without importing personal knowledge of the circumstances of the alleged offence or of the parties listed in the indictment. So in *H.M. Advocate v. Devine* (1962) 78 S.C. Rep. 173, objection on the basis that a juror had already served on a jury in the same assize dealing with a similar incident to that now libelled at the same *locus*, and might thus be against the accused, was repelled.

In *McCadden v. H.M. Advocate*, 1985 S.C.C.R. 282 the court disfavoured any suggestion that vetting of a jury was permissible. Objections to jurors must be stated as subs. (4) provides, before the jury is sworn; thereafter they cannot be entertained (also see *McArthur v. H.M. Advocate*, 1902 S.L.T. 310).

The Law Reform (Miscellaneous Provisions) (Scotland) Act 1980 (c.55), s.1(1) broadly enacts that persons aged between 18 and 65 years, ordinarily resident in the United Kingdom and registered as an elector are qualified for jury service; those persons exempted, barred or disqualified from jury service are detailed in Sched. I to that Act.

Non-availability of judge

Non-availability of judge

87.—(1) Where the court is unable to proceed owing to the death, illness or absence of the presiding judge, the clerk of court may convene the court (if necessary) and—
>   (a) in a case where no evidence has been led, adjourn the diet and any other diet appointed for that sitting to—
>> (i) a time later the same day, or a date not more than seven days later, when he believes a judge will be available; or
>> (ii) a later sitting not more than two months after the date of the adjournment; or
>   (b) in a case where evidence has been led—
>> (i) adjourn the diet and any other diet appointed for that sitting to a time later the same day, or a date not more than seven days later, when he believes a judge will be available; or
>> (ii) with the consent of the parties, desert the diet *pro loco et tempore.*

(2) Where a diet has been adjourned under sub-paragraph (i) of either paragraph (a) or paragraph (b) of subsection (1) above the clerk of court may, where the conditions of that subsection continue to be satisfied, further adjourn the diet under that sub-paragraph; but the total period of such adjournments shall not exceed seven days.

(3) Where a diet has been adjourned under subsection (1)(b)(i) above the court may, at the adjourned diet—
>   (a) further adjourn the diet; or
>   (b) desert the diet *pro loco et tempore.*

(4) Where a diet is deserted in pursuance of subsection (1)(b)(ii) or (3)(b) above, the Lord Advocate may raise and insist in a new indictment, and—
>   (a) where the accused is in custody it shall not be necessary to grant a new warrant for his incarceration, and the warrant or commitment on which he is at the time in custody till liberation in due course of law shall continue in force; and
>   (b) where the accused is at liberty on bail, his bail shall continue in force.

DEFINITIONS
   "bail": s.307(1).
   "indictment ": s.307(1).

GENERAL NOTE
   This section provides powers to the clerk of court, in the event of illness or death of the presiding judge, to convene the court and defer the business of the sitting to a later date or dates.
   Two different situations are envisaged: first where no evidence has been led (subs. (1)(a)), the clerk may in the absence of an available judge adjourn any such case for a maximum of seven days on the assumption that the presiding judge can within that time return to business, or alternatively, *ex proprio motu* adjourn the sitting for up to two months. Subsection (2) discussed below, limits the scale of these adjournments to a total of seven days.
   On the other hand, where evidence has already been led (subs. (1)(b)) the options are to adjourn cases in the sitting up to seven days, or with consent of the parties, desert the diet *pro loco et tempore.* If any of the parties will not agree to desertion, then resort has to be had to an adjournment up to seven days of the trial; in terms of subs. (3) it only becomes competent (in the absence of the parties' concurrence) for the clerk to desert the diet after the first adjournment under subs. (1)(b)(i) has elapsed. To complicate matters further, subs. (2) limits the use of an administrative adjournment by the clerk to a total period of seven days.
   Once a diet has been adjourned in these circumstances, or indeed, another judge has deserted the case due to the continued unavailability of the trial judge, subs. (4) entitles the Lord Advocate to re-raise the proceedings. Any bail order or warrant of committal remains in force.

Circumstances of the sort described in s.67 would surely entitle the Crown to seek an extension of the time-limits prescribed by s.65 above, since no fault for the delay could be ascribed to the Crown.

Jury for trial

Plea of not guilty, balloting and swearing of jury, etc.

88.—(1) Where the accused pleads not guilty, the clerk of court shall record that fact and proceed to ballot the jury.

(2) The jurors for the trial shall be chosen in open court by ballot from the list of persons summoned in such manner as shall be prescribed by Act of Adjournal, and the persons so chosen shall be the jury to try the accused, and their names shall be recorded in the minutes of the proceedings.

(3) It shall not be competent for the accused or the prosecutor to object to a juror on the ground that the juror has not been duly cited to attend.

(4) Notwithstanding subsection (1) above, the jurors chosen for any particular trial may, when that trial is disposed of, without a new ballot serve on the trials of other accused, provided that—

  (a) the accused and the prosecutor consent;

  (b) the names of the jurors are contained in the list of jurors; and

  (c) the jurors are duly sworn to serve on each successive trial.

(5) When the jury has been balloted, the clerk of court shall inform the jury of the charge against the accused—

  (a) by reading the words of the indictment (with the substitution of the third person for the second); or

  (b) if the presiding judge, because of the length or complexity of the indictment, so directs, by reading to the jury a summary of the charge approved by the judge,

and copies of the indictment shall be provided for each member of the jury without lists of witnesses or productions.

(6) After reading the charge as mentioned in subsection (5) above and any special defence as mentioned in section 89(1) of this Act, the clerk of court shall administer the oath in common form.

(7) The court may excuse a juror from serving on a trial where the juror has stated the ground for being excused in open court.

(8) Where a trial which is proceeding is adjourned from one day to another, the jury shall not be secluded during the adjournment, unless, on the motion of the prosecutor or the accused or *ex proprio motu* the court sees fit to order that the jury be kept secluded.

DEFINITION
  "prosecutor": s.307(1).

GENERAL NOTE
This section deals with the selection of a trial jury from the list of assize prepared beforehand. Chapter 14 of the Act of Adjournal 1996 regulates the mechanics of the ballot and Forms 14.3.–A and 14.3.–B respectively stipulate the oath or affirmation to be administered to all jurors. While parties can concur to excuse jurors without showing cause (see the notes to s.86 above), in any other case objection to a juror serving on the jury must be on cause shown: the right to peremptory challenge of jurors has been abolished. It remains the case that a juror who is not exempted or disqualified from service by the provisions of the Law Reform (Miscellaneous Provisions) (Scotland) Act 1980, s.1 must serve on the jury unless he can give reason in terms of subs. (7) why he should be excused. Ordinarily personal knowledge of the circumstances of the case, or of the accused or witnesses would be telling factors but ultimately the determining factor has to be whether the court can be assured that the juror can try the accused according to the evidence, without importing outside knowledge or prejudice; if there is any doubt, fairness dictates that the juror should not be called upon to serve. In *Hay v. H.M. Advocate*, 1995 S.C.C.R. 639 an appeal was taken founding on the fact that two of the jurors had knowledge of the accused (a fact made known to the clerk and the sheriff by five of the assize) while a third juror had had dealings with an associate of the accused; no challenge had been

given to the selection of the jury. The Appeal Court noted that the sheriff followed the guidance given in *Pullar v. H.M. Advocate*, 1993 S.C.C.R. 514 and emphasised (at 643C) that the issues raised in the appeal should properly have been aired prior to the trial; the appeal against conviction was dismissed.

Before the jury is empanelled, the clerk of court is required to have made the assembled assize aware of the particulars of the accused and of any witness named in the charges on the indictment and to have advised them to inform him of any prior knowledge of these parties which they have (*Pullar v. H.M. Advocate*).

The presiding judge should also make enquiry of the jurors once the indictment has been read to them and before evidence is led, if they know of any reason why they should not serve (*Spink v. H.M. Advocate*, 1989 S.C.C.R. 413 and also *Russell v. H.M. Advocate*, 1992 S.L.T. 25).

Subsection (4) re-enacts the rarely-used provision of s.132 of the 1975 Act: a jury which has just concluded a trial can be selected to sit in the following case in the sitting without the necessity of a ballot. However, this abbreviated procedure can only be used where; (i) the accused and the Crown consent and thus have no challenge on cause shown and; (ii) the jurors themselves pronounce no personal knowledge of the case, the accused or witnesses. Furthermore it is implicit that the whole of that prior jury must serve in the new case and subs. (4)(c) stipulates that the jury must be put on oath anew. A consent to the use of this shortened procedure can be withdrawn by an objection from the accused which is stated before the jury has been sworn (*Daniel or Donald Stuart, Re* (1829) Bell's Notes 237). Chapter 14 of the Act of Adjournal provides a short form of minute, recording the particulars of the jury by reference to the record of proceedings of the previous trial.

While subs. (5)(b) allows for a summary form of the indictment charges approved by the judge to be read to the jury, it is interesting to note that this is not a matter which has to be addressed expressly at either a first, or preliminary diet (the same observation could equally be made in relation to the provision in s.89(2) which allows for a condensed version of any special defence to be read to the jury instead of the notice intimated to the court).

Unempanelled jurors are not released until evidence is begun and the trial is lawfully under way.

Subsection (8) is broadly drafted. The statutory authority for the overnight accommodation of jurors who are deliberating upon their verdict is contained in s.99(4) below. Hence subs. (8) would appear to be intended for use at earlier points in the trial, while evidence is still being led.

Jury to be informed of special defence

89.—(1) Subject to subsection (2) below, where the accused has lodged a plea of special defence, the clerk of court shall, after informing the jury, in accordance with section 88(5) of this Act, of the charge against the accused, and before administering the oath, read to the jury the plea of special defence.

(2) Where the presiding judge on cause shown so directs, the plea of special defence shall not be read over to the jury in accordance with subsection (1) above; and in any such case the judge shall inform the jury of the lodging of the plea and of the general nature of the special defence.

(3) Copies of a plea of special defence shall be provided for each member of the jury.

DEFINITION
"judge": s.307(1).

GENERAL NOTE
Special defences require to be notified to the court and other parties in accordance with s.78 of the Act; in sheriff solemn cases, intimation has to be given at or before the first diet (s.78(3)(b)) while in High Court cases, where preliminary diets are not mandatory, such intimation has to be made not less than 10 clear days before trial. The 1995 Act in s.78(2) adds defences of coercion and automatism to the existing categories of special defence which require advance notice (examples of defences of automatism are found in *Sorley v. H.M. Advocate*, 1992 S.L.T. 867 and *Ross v. H.M. Advocate*, 1991 S.L.T. 564).

Once the indictment is read to the jury by the clerk of court, the next procedure is to read the terms of any special defence over to the jury. Failure to read over the special defence will not necessarily amount to a miscarriage of justice; see *Moar v. H.M. Advocate*, 1949 J.C. 31. Indeed it is often asserted that the only purpose of a notice of special defence is to give notice to the Crown of a possible line of defence evidence and, accordingly, the reading over of the terms of a notice which may not ultimately form a part of the defence case is both unnecessary and likely to confuse. Refer to *Mullen v. H.M. Advocate*, 1978 S.L.T. (Notes) 33. Nonetheless the provisions of s.89 are unequivocal: the terms of the notice must be made known to the jury before the trial begins. Subsection (2) allows the judge following a motion by one or other of the parties to withhold the full terms of the notice from the jury and to substitute a condensed account of the notice's meaning. In this context it has to be assumed that the terms of subs. (3), which instructs the distribution of copies of the notice of special defence, would not be adhered to, since that would appear to defeat the purpose of editing the original notice as lodged.

A plea of insanity must always be made known to the jury since the accused's state of mind at the time of the commission of the crime is a fundamental issue. It is not proper to read over a notice of incrimination of a co-accused; see *Collins v. H.M. Advocate*, 1991 S.C.C.R. 898.

Death or illness of jurors

90.—(1) Where in the course of a trial—
(a) a juror dies; or
(b) the court is satisfied that it is for any reason inappropriate for any juror to continue to serve as a juror,
the court may in its discretion, on an application made by the prosecutor or an accused, direct that the trial shall proceed before the remaining jurors (if they are not less than twelve in number), and where such direction is given the remaining jurors shall be deemed in all respects to be a properly constituted jury for the purpose of the trial and shall have power to return a verdict accordingly whether unanimous or, subject to subsection (2) below, by majority.

(2) The remaining jurors shall not be entitled to return a verdict of guilty by majority unless at least eight of their number are in favour of such verdict and if, in any such case, the remaining jurors inform the court that—
(a) fewer than eight of their number are in favour of a verdict of guilty; and
(b) there is not a majority in favour of any other verdict,
they shall be deemed to have returned a verdict of not guilty.

GENERAL NOTE
This section regulates the composition of the jury which, of course, must comprise of 15 people at the outset of the trial, and stipulates that a majority verdict in any case requires eight of the jury at least to favour a guilty verdict. Once the trial has begun, the size of the jury can be reduced by reason of death, illness or other suitable cause (including misconduct by a juror himself) but in no case can the trial proceed with a jury numbering less than 12 persons. Recent experience in long-running trials might have suggested that the preservation of jurors' numbers is no small feat; see for example the sheriff's note in *MacDonald v. H.M. Advocate*, 1995 S.C.C.R. 663 which lends an insight into the major logistical problems experienced in lengthy trials.

The subsection does not of course require that the trial must proceed with a reduced number of jurors though that is the normal procedure; it would be open to the court to consider motions to desert the trial diet and to exercise such powers as were competent to the court under s.65 of the Act to extend statutory time-bars. However in *H.M. Advocate v. Khan*, 1997 S.C.C.R. 100 where a juror was certified unfit in the course of a trial, leaving less than 12 jurors to continue, and the sheriff refused a Crown motion to adjourn the trial for a period to permit the juror to return to health, instead deserting the trial *pro loco et tempore*, Crown advocation of that sentence was upheld, the Appeal Court having regard to both the length of proceedings and possible prejudice to the accused in a retrial.

The procedure to be followed when the jury seeks guidance on the calculation of their verdict is described in *Kerr v. H.M. Advocate*, 1992 S.C.C.R. 281; 1992 S.L.T. 1031, where the trial judge was handed a slip of paper from the jury showing a split verdict, eight for acquittal, seven (the arithmetical majority) for guilt and after further direction a conviction resulted; quashed on appeal.

Trial

Trial to be continuous

91. Every trial shall proceed from day to day until it is concluded unless the court sees cause to adjourn over a day or days.

Although it is generally the case that trials will continue from day to day until concluded, this section affords the presiding judge an element of discretion in allowing for variations from that norm when appropriate. See *MacDonald v. H.M. Advocate*, 1995 S.C.C.R. 663 for an insight into the conduct of longer trials.

Section 102 below permits the interruption of proceedings to receive the verdict in another case. See also rr. 14.8 and 14.9 of the 1996 Act of Adjournal.

Trial in presence of accused

92.—(1) Without prejudice to section 54 of this Act, and subject to subsection (2) below, no part of a trial shall take place outwith the presence of the accused.

(2) If during the course of his trial an accused so misconducts himself that in the view of the court a proper trial cannot take place unless he is removed, the court may order—

    (a) that he is removed from the court for so long as his conduct makes it necessary; and

    (b) that the trial proceeds in his absence,

but if he is not legally represented the court shall appoint counsel or a solicitor to represent his interests during such absence.

(3) From the commencement of the leading of evidence in a trial for rape or the like the judge may, if he thinks fit, cause all persons other than the accused and counsel and solicitors to be removed from the court-room.

DEFINITION
"judge": s.307(1).

GENERAL NOTE
The hearing of evidence in all cases should occur in the presence of the accused unless he so misconducts himself as to necessitate his removal from the court. In *Aitken v. Wood*, 1921 J.C. 84 magistrates examined alleged injuries on the complainer's arm in private. The conviction was quashed. See also *Livingston v. H.M. Advocate*, 1991 S.C.C.R. 350; 1992 S.L.T. 481, where the removal of productions from the court for expert examination during the trial was held not to breach the general prohibition then contained in s.145 of the 1975 Act. In *McColl v. H.M. Advocate*, 1989 S.C.C.R. 229; 1989 S.L.T. 691 the clerk of court was called to the jury room and was asked for guidance upon the judge's directions which he gave; the conviction was quashed. See also *Kerr v. H.M. Advocate*, 1992 S.C.C.R. 281; 1992 S.L.T. 1031 discussed in the notes to s.90 above.

While the courts are generally public courts, subs. (3) permits the presiding judge in cases involving a charge of rape or other charges of a sexual nature, to close the court to the public from the outset of proceedings. Further provisions in regard to the line of questioning permissible in sexual offences are to be found at s.274 below. Specifically in relation to the evidence of children it will also be recalled that s.50(3) enables the court to be cleared of all but the immediately interested parties during the hearing of that evidence. The general principle need not extend to any proceedings deemed necessary in connection with an appeal: see *Crossan v. H.M. Advocate*, 1996 S.C.C.R. 279 discussed at A4.179/1 above.

The distinction between matters of an administrative character (which can be dealt with outwith the presence of the accused) and matters intrinsic to the trial itself (where the accused's presence is a prerequisite except in the circumstances set out in s.54 or in s.92(2) above) was discussed in *Thomson v. H.M. Advocate*, 1998 S.L.T. 364.

Act of Adjournal
See Form 14.7 in the 1996 Act of Adjournal.

Record of trial

93.—(1) The proceedings at the trial of any person who, if convicted, is entitled to appeal under Part VIII of this Act, shall be recorded by means of shorthand notes or by mechanical means.

(2) A shorthand writer shall—
(a) sign the shorthand notes taken by him of such proceedings and certify them as being complete and correct; and
(b) retain the notes.
(3) A person recording such proceedings by mechanical means shall—
(a) certify that the record is true and complete;
(b) specify in the certificate the proceedings or, as the case may be, the part of the proceedings to which the record relates; and
(c) retain the record.
(4) The cost of making a record under subsection (1) above shall be defrayed, in accordance with scales of payment fixed for the time being by Treasury, out of money provided by Parliament.
(5) In subsection (1) above "proceedings at the trial" means the whole proceedings including, without prejudice to that generality—
(a) discussions—
(i) on any objection to the relevancy of the indictment;
(ii) with respect to any challenge of jurors; and
(iii) on all questions arising in the course of the trial;
(b) the decision of the court on any matter referred to in paragraph (a) above;
(c) the evidence led at the trial;
(d) any statement made by or on behalf of the accused whether before or after the verdict;
(e) the judge's charge to the jury;
(f) the speeches of counsel or agent;
(g) the verdict of the jury;
(h) the sentence by the judge.

DEFINITION
"judge": s.307(1).

GENERAL NOTE
A shorthand or recorded record of the entire proceedings in all solemn cases must be maintained and preserved lest a call is made (in terms of s.94) for them to be produced. Additionally Chap. 14 of the Act of Adjournal 1996 enacts that the trial judge is obliged to preserve and authenticate his own notes of evidence and produce them (or a certified copy) to the High Court when requested. The same rules stipulate that where reliance is placed on a recording of the proceedings instead of shorthand notes, the clerk of court must record the fact in his minutes of proceedings.

On appeal in *Kyle v. H.M. Advocate*, 1987 S.C.C.R. 116, weight was placed by the appellant upon the apparent inconsistency of a part of the judge's charge, the shorthand notes having been certified as accurate. In fact the terms of the notes suggested that the shorthand writer had some doubts about the accuracy of that section of the transcription; the High Court held that while the notes had to be so certified, the court was not bound to accept them as such and that, in any event, no miscarriage of justice had occurred.

However the absence of a shorthand record altogether has been held to have left the Appeal Court in doubt as to additional directions given to the jury, the sheriff having re-convened the court in the absence of the shorthand writer in breach of the provisions of s.274(1) of the 1975 Act. The aggravated element of the conviction which had been the reason for further directions was quashed and a lesser conviction substituted (see *McLaughlan v. H.M. Advocate*, 1995 G.W.D. 38–1935).

Comparison of this decision with that in *Carroll v. H.M. Advocate*, 1999 S.L.T. 1185; 1999 S.C.C.R. 617 is instructive; on one reading the sheriff had wilfully proceeded with his directions to the jury in the knowledge that no record of the proceedings was being made in *McLaughlan* whereas in *Carroll* none of the parties was aware of a defect in the recording equipment, and this only became an issue when an appeal on entirely unrelated grounds was taken and the defect discovered. The Appeal Court declined to quash the conviction simply on account of the absence of a record of trial, looked to the judge's report and ruled that the appellant would have to point to an irregularity or misdirection to maintain an appeal. The Court declined to regard the absence of a record as fatal to any conviction.

Transcripts of record and documentary productions

94.—(1) The Clerk of Justiciary may direct that a transcript of a record made under section 93(1) of this Act, or any part thereof, be made and delivered to him for the use of any judge.

(2) Subject to subsection (3) below, the Clerk of Justiciary shall, if requested to do so by—

    (a) the Secretary of State; or

    (b) any other person on payment of such charges as may be fixed for the time being by Treasury,

direct that such a transcript be made and sent to the person who requested it.

(3) The Secretary of State may, after consultation with the Lord Justice General, by order made by statutory instrument provide that in any class of proceedings specified in the order the Clerk of Justiciary shall only make a direction under subsection (2)(b) above if satisfied that the person requesting the transcript is of a class of person so specified and, if purposes for which the transcript may be used are so specified, intends to use it only for such a purpose; and different purposes may be so specified for different classes of proceedings or classes of person.

(4) Where subsection (3) above applies as respects a direction, the person to whom the transcript is sent shall, if purposes for which that transcript may be used are specified by virtue of that subsection, use it only for such a purpose.

(5) A statutory instrument containing an order under subsection (3) above shall be subject to annulment in pursuance of a resolution of either House of Parliament.

(6) A direction under subsection (1) or (2) above may require that the transcript be made by the person who made the record or by such competent person as may be specified in the direction; and that person shall comply with the direction.

(7) A transcript made in compliance with a direction under subsection (1) or (2) above—

    (a) shall be in legible form; and

    (b) shall be certified by the person making it as being a correct and complete transcript of the whole or, as the case may be, the part of the record purporting to have been made and certified, and in the case of shorthand notes signed, by the person who made the record.

(8) The cost of making a transcript in compliance with a direction under subsection (1) or (2)(a) above shall be defrayed, in accordance with scales of payment fixed for the time being by the Treasury, out of money provided by Parliament.

(9) The Clerk of Justiciary shall, on payment of such charges as may be fixed for the time being by the Treasury, provide a copy of any documentary production lodged in connection with an appeal under this Part of this Act to such of the following persons as may request it—

    (a) the prosecutor;

    (b) any person convicted in the proceedings;

    (c) any other person named in, or immediately affected by, any order made in the proceedings; and

    (d) any person authorised to act on behalf of any of the persons mentioned in paragraphs (a) to (c) above.

DEFINITIONS

    "Clerk of Justiciary": s.307(1).

    "judge": s.307(1).

    "Lord Justice General": s.307(1).

GENERAL NOTE

The effect of certification of a transcript of evidence as correct was raised in *Kyle v. H.M. Advocate*, 1987 S.C.C.R. 116. See the discussion in the notes to s.93 above.

In *H.M.Advocate, v. Nulty,* 2000 S.L.T. 528; 2000 S.C.C.R. 431, a retrial in which the Crown gave notice of its intention to utilise the hearsay provisions found in s.259 of the Act, to lodge the testimony of a principal witness from the abortive trial, she now being unfit to testify, it is of note that use was made of the original tapes of evidence rather than a transcript of evidence. (It could be argued that the tape was now the best evidence.)

Verdict by judge alone

95.—(1) Where, at any time after the jury has been sworn to serve in a trial, the prosecutor intimates to the court that he does not intend to proceed in respect of an offence charged in the indictment, the judge shall acquit the accused of that offence and the trial shall proceed only in respect of any other offence charged in the indictment.

(2) Where, at any time after the jury has been sworn to serve in a trial, the accused intimates to the court that he is prepared to tender a plea of guilty as libelled, or such other plea as the Crown is prepared to accept, in respect of any offence charged in the indictment, the judge shall accept the plea tendered and shall convict the accused accordingly.

(3) Where an accused is convicted under subsection (2) above of an offence—

  (a) the trial shall proceed only in respect of any other offence charged in the indictment; and

  (b) without prejudice to any other power of the court to adjourn the case or to defer sentence, the judge shall not sentence him or make any other order competent following conviction until a verdict has been returned in respect of every other offence mentioned in paragraph (a) above.

DEFINITIONS

  "indictment": s.307(1).
  "judge": s.307(1).
  "offence": s.307(1).
  "prosecutor": s.307(1).

GENERAL NOTE

Section 95 deals with situations in the course of a trial in which the jury is not called upon to reach a verdict upon the evidence, either because the Crown has withdrawn a charge (subs. (1)) or acceptable pleas have been tendered (subs. (2)). In the latter case, it is implicit that acceptance of pleas tendered is signified by the prosecutor subscribing his minute of acceptance following the signatures of the accused and the presiding judge. Subsection (2) also deals with the tendering of a partial plea in circumstances where other charges remain outstanding against the accused. In that situation, where the prosecutor is maintaining the other charges on the libel, care must be taken to ensure that the prosecutor's endorsement is restricted solely to the charges in relation to which the plea was tendered.

It will be noted that the onus of assenting to the pleas tendered strictly lies with the trial judge, not with the jury. No sentence can competently be pronounced until a verdict is reached on all the charges on the indictment.

In determining sentence, the court may take account of the point in the proceedings at which a plea or pleas were tendered (see s.196 below).

Particlarly in solemn proceedings the court will not readily consent to the withdrawal of a guilty plea; see *Weightman v. H.M. Advocate*, 1997 G.W.D. 3–85 and the discussion at pp. 128–129 above.

Amendment of indictment

96.—(1) No trial shall fail or the ends of justice be allowed to be defeated by reason of any discrepancy or variance between the indictment and the evidence.

(2) It shall be competent at any time prior to the determination of the case,

unless the court see just cause to the contrary, to amend the indictment by deletion, alteration or addition, so as to—

(a) cure any error or defect in it;

(b) meet any objection to it; or

(c) cure any discrepancy or variance between the indictment and the evidence.

(3) Nothing in this section shall authorise an amendment which changes the character of the offence charged, and, if it appears to the court that the accused may in any way be prejudiced in his defence on the merits of the case by any amendment made under this section, the court shall grant such remedy to the accused by adjournment or otherwise as appears to the court to be just.

(4) An amendment made under this section shall be sufficiently authenticated by the initials of the clerk of the court.

DEFINITION

"indictment": s.307(1).

GENERAL NOTE

Schedule 3 of the Act states the general rules concerning latitudes in time and place, implied terms and implied alternatives. Section 96 re-enacts the provisions contained in s.123 of the 1975 Act relating to the power of amendment of an indictment in the course of a trial. The Crown may seek leave to amend the terms of the libel at a first, or preliminary, diet to meet any preliminary objection, but s.96 deals with such motions in the course of trial. While wide powers of amendment are available to the Crown this is qualified by the provisos that; (i) they cannot be used to introduce an essential requisite into a criminal charge—a fundamentally defective libel cannot be cured (*Stevenson v. McLevy*, (1879) 4 Couper 196 and *Thomson, Petr*, 1997 S.L.T. 322 where the libel lacked a *locus delicti*) and (ii) they must not change the character of the charge to such a degree as to prejudice the accused's defence on the merits (see subs. (3)). Any amendment has to be justified to the court, and while amendment of either the libel or the description of a witness can be craved, amendment of the description of a production in the indictment is not competent (see *H.M. Advocate v. Swift*, 1983 S.C.C.R. 204 discussed in the notes to s.67(5)). *Thomson , Petr*, cited above also indicates that there can be no question of a tholed assize where the libel itself was a fundamental nullity.

Amendment of an indictment which omitted the accused's name in one of the three charges (the murder charge), when he had been correctly described in the instance, has been allowed (*Keane v. H.M. Advocate*, 1986 S.C.C.R. 491); the decision might have been quite different if there had been other accused on the indictment.

In the event that amendment is allowed by the court, the remedy for the accused is ordinarily adjournment. The presiding judge's decision on the issue will only be overturned on appeal if the Appeal Court is satisfied that the public interest or the interest of the accused has been adversely affected (see *Cumming v. Frame*, (1909) 6 Adam 57).

Customarily, deletions from the libel are made to bring it into line with the extent of corroborated evidence heard by the jury. See however *Clarke v. Ruxton*, 1997 G.W.D. 10–408 in relation, at least, to sexual offences discussed at p. 252 below.

No case to answer

97.—(1) Immediately after the close of the evidence for the prosecution, the accused may intimate to the court his desire to make a submission that he has no case to answer both—

(a) on an offence charged in the indictment; and

(b) on any other offence of which he could be convicted under the indictment.

(2) If, after hearing both parties, the judge is satisfied that the evidence led by the prosecution is insufficient in law to justify the accused being convicted of the offence charged in respect of which the submission has been made or of such other offence as is mentioned, in relation to that offence, in paragraph (b) of subsection (1) above, he shall acquit him of the offence charged in respect of which the submission has been made and the trial shall proceed only in respect of any other offence charged in the indictment.

(3) If, after hearing both parties, the judge is not satisfied as is mentioned in subsection (2) above, he shall reject the submission and the trial shall proceed, with the accused entitled to give evidence and call witnesses, as if such submission had not been made.

(4) A submission under subsection (1) above shall be heard by the judge in the absence of the jury.

DEFINITIONS
"indictment": s.307(1).
"judge": s.307(1).
"offence": s.307(1).

GENERAL NOTE
The no case to answer submission was introduced into Scots criminal law by the Criminal Justice (Scotland) Act 1980, s.19 and the terms of that section are repeated in s.97 above. A common law submission could always be made at the conclusion of evidence, before the judge's charge but a s.97 submission, unlike the common law type, is concerned only with the sufficiency of evidence, not its quality. The submission is made outwith the presence of the jury and can relate to any, or all, of the charges on the indictment. Note that s.97 refers to "an offence" not "a charge" on the indictment; so where a number of offences are libelled as part of one charge a submission can competently be made upon each offence: the Crown cannot, by creative draftsmanship, withhold the right of an accused to make a s.97 motion (see *Cordiner v. H.M. Advocate*, 1991 S.C.C.R. 652).

It will be observed that a submission can be made in regard to the charge libelled or any other offence which is implied by the libel but, in practical terms, the starting point will be the sufficiency, or otherwise, of the charge libelled before proceeding to a consideration of any alternative charge. Any challenge to the competency or admissibility of evidence must be raised at, or prior to, the point in proceedings at which that evidence is being received by the court; it is too late to air such issues at the point of a no case to answer submission when no prior objection has been taken (*McGee v. McNaughtan*, 1996 G.W.D. 17–977).

If in terms of subs. (3) the accused's submissions are rejected, he has to decide whether or not to lead evidence, a dilemma heightened by the introduction of the prosecutor's right to comment upon the failure of the accused to lead evidence (see s.32 of the Criminal Justice (Scotland) Act 1995). It remains to be seen what use will be made of this provision and to what effect. What is the position if the judge incorrectly rejects a submission of no case to answer and the accused then leads evidence which confirms the Crown case? The problem was recognised but not addressed in *Little v. H.M. Advocate*, 1983 S.C.C.R. 56. The same problems occurred in *Mackie v. H.M. Advocate*, 1994 S.C.C.R. 277 and there the judge read the elements of the charge as a unity in what was, by any standard, a complex libel.

It is permissible for the Crown to submit to the jury at the conclusion of evidence that the withdrawal of charges at the submission stage does not necessarily reflect adversely upon prosecution witnesses; it is however one step too far to suggest that the accused might still have committed the offences of which he had been acquitted earlier (see *Dudgeon v. H.M. Advocate*, 1988 S.C.C.R. 147). In that case the improper remarks of the prosecutor were held to have been cured by the directions of the trial judge and no miscarriage to have resulted.

Defence to speak last

98. In any trial the accused or, where he is legally represented, his counsel or solicitor shall have the right to speak last.

Seclusion of jury to consider verdict

99.—(1) When the jury retire to consider their verdict, the clerk of court shall enclose the jury in a room by themselves and, except in so far as provided for, or is made necessary, by an instruction under subsection (4) below, neither he nor any other person shall be present with the jury after they are enclosed.

(2) Except in so far as is provided for, or is made necessary, by an instruction under subsection (4) below, until the jury intimate that they are ready to return their verdict—

    (a) subject to subsection (3) below, no person shall visit the jury or communicate with them; and

(b) no juror shall come out of the jury room other than to receive or seek a direction from the judge or to make a request—
  (i) for an instruction under subsection (4)(a), (c) or (d) below; or
  (ii) regarding any matter in the cause.
(3) Nothing in paragraph (a) of subsection (2) above shall prohibit the judge, or any person authorised by him for the purpose, communicating with the jury for the purposes—
  (a) of giving a direction, whether or not sought under paragraph (b) of that subsection; or
  (b) responding to a request made under that paragraph.
(4) The judge may give such instructions as he considers appropriate as regards—
  (a) the provision of meals and refreshments for the jury;
  (b) the making of arrangements for overnight accommodation for the jury and for their continued seclusion if such accommodation is provided;
  (c) the communication of a personal or business message, unconnected with any matter in the cause, from a juror to another person (or vice versa); or
  (d) the provision of medical treatment, or other assistance, immediately required by a juror.
(5) If the prosecutor or any other person contravenes the provisions of this section, the accused shall be acquitted of the crime with which he is charged.
(6) During the period in which the jury are retired to consider their verdict, the judge may sit in any other proceedings; and the trial shall not fail by reason only of his so doing.

DEFINITIONS
"judge": s.307(1).
"prosecutor": s.307(1).

GENERAL NOTE
Until the point at which the jury is directed to retire to consider its verdict, all proceedings in a trial must take place in the presence of the accused (see s.92). Once the jury withdraws to the jury room, s.99 stipulates that no contact should be made with its members unless the jury requests directions or has need to seek assistance from the court. The provisions of s.99 are mandatory and conduct constituting a breach (subs. (5)) is fatal to any conviction.
Points of appeal have arisen from allegations of inappropriate communication between the jury and court officials; the Appeal Court may remit the case for enquiry and report under s.104(d) below (see for example *Squire v. H.M. Advocate*, 1998 G.W.D. 28–1410) but has emphasised that such enquiry should confine itself to establishing the factual background and must not concern itself with the jury's deliberations.
In *Swankie v. H.M. Advocate*, 1999 S.C.C.R. 1, an appeal against conviction rested on the alleged conduct during jury deliberations of a juror in making known a previous conviction of the accused, an incident which was stated to have been disclosed by another juror to an acquaintance of S. (Such a disclosure would have been in breach of s.8 of the Contempt of Court Act 1981). The appeal proceeded by way of an affidavit from the acquaintance. Leaving aside the hearsay nature of the affidavit, the Appeal Court itself examined the quality of the evidence before the jury and the apparent extent of its deliberations, cast doubt on the veracity of the affidavit and declined to initiate a s.104 enquiry.

Subss. (2) and (3)
Unfortunately the cases arising from s.153 (the statutory predecessor to s.99) tend to suggest that in their zeal to provide for the seclusion of the jury, officers of the court have on occasion overlooked the obligations (now) created by s.92 and trespassed into matters which should have been dealt with in open court.
It is the jury's right to examine productions referred to in the evidence but subject to any directions given by the court. The procedure to be followed is laid out in *Hamilton v. H.M. Advocate*, 1980 J.C. 66; the Lord Justice Clerk (at 69) stated:
  "If the jury make a request to see a production, this request should be communicated to the clerk of court who should inform counsel on both sides and then refer the matter to the trial judge for his decision."

A practice has developed, in part to delay the jury's deliberations as little as possible and to avoid the need to reconvene the court repeatedly, of trial judges clarifying with the parties which productions can, and which cannot, be given to the jury on request. This is done in open court immediately after the jury retires and has the merit of focusing this issue even before the need arises and commits parties' views to the shorthand notes. There is no statutory authority for this procedure but, it is submitted, it complies with the directions in *Hamilton*. Support for this reading can be found in *Bertram v. H.M. Advocate*, 1990 S.C.C.R. 394, where the judge in his charge permitted access to all productions admitted in evidence during the trial. See also *Martin v. H.M. Advocate*, 1989 S.C.C.R. 546 where the sheriff gave directions which were inspecific and were acted upon by the clerk of court without reference to the parties and *Boyle v. H.M. Advocate*, 1990 S.C.C.R. 480 where productions not spoken of in evidence were given to the jurors in error. Once the error was appreciated, the sheriff gave further directions to the jury to ignore the content of these productions; the conviction was upheld in the circumstances.

It is clear that the question of access to productions is one upon which parties should be heard; it is not an administrative matter to be resolved between the clerk of court and the presiding judge. The complex issues which can surface are amply illustrated by *Collins v. H.M. Advocate*, 1991 S.C.C.R. 898 where the trial judge withheld statements by various of the accused on the grounds that they could be misapplied and wrongly used as evidence against other accused. Similar problems arose, but were dealt with quite differently (the judge allowing transcripts of police interviews given by all accused to be made available following a request by the jury, but giving additional directions on the inadmissibility against others of statements made outwith their presence) in *Munro v. H.M.Advocate*, 2000 S.L.T. 950. It is of note that the Appeal Court considered it might well be preferable in such circumstances to lead evidence by means of edited transcripts.

In the past, difficulty has also been caused by the interpretation of the provisions against contact being made with the jury room (subs. (2)). In *Brownlie v. H.M. Advocate* (1966) S.C.C.R. Supp. 14, the clerk of court on the judge's instructions went to the jury room door and asked if the jury had understood the judge's direction. This had followed earlier difficulty and further directions. The appeal, which had founded upon both the recall of the jury for further directions and the judge's actions in causing the clerk to communicate with the jury was refused. The right of the judge to recall the jury for further directions was upheld in *McBeth v. H.M. Advocate* (1976) S.C.C.R. Supp. 123.

In *Cunningham v. H.M. Advocate*, 1984 S.C.C.R. 40 written requests for directions were delivered to the judge in chambers in the presence of both counsel and dealt with by further written directions; these events occurred outwith the presence of the accused and were not recorded in the shorthand notes. While the conviction was quashed, the court held that the Crown was not at fault and gave authority for fresh proceedings, surely the only just solution in the circumstances. An appeal against conviction on grounds of miscarriage was refused where a jury's request for further directions could not be dealt with by the judge for over an hour, since another jury was being empanelled. In the interval the jury reached a verdict and it is of note that the Appeal Court took note of the discriminating nature of that verdict as evidence of a considered, and not a capricious, jury. (*Brown v. H.M. Advocate* 1997 S.C.C.R. 201). *McColl v. H.M. Advocate*, 1989 S.C.C.R. 229 is a rare example of communication of an order so extreme as to constitute a miscarriage, a decision the Court of Appeal reached after granting authority to parties to precognosce the clerk of court. The clerk had given formal directions to the jurors on the instructions of the presiding judge and the court did not reconvene; no record existed of the communings between the clerk and the jurors, all of which had occurred outwith the presence of the accused. It was by no means clear whether the circumstances had been brought to the attention of both counsel but the lack of a record of proceedings was critical and the verdict was overturned.

Difficulties have arisen when the court has been faced with a verdict at odds with the judge's directions: in *Whyte v. H.M. Advocate*, 1999 G.W.D. 16–745 the Crown case rested entirely on application of the *Moorov* doctrine, and the court was advised by the foreman that guidance was needed because the jury was coming to two dissimilar verdicts. Additional directions were given but, on appeal, *Whyte* contended that once such an impasse had been reached in a *Moorov* case he should have been acquitted. The Appeal Court noted that no settled verdict had been reached and, following *Took v. H.M. Advocate*, 1989 S.L.T. 425, indicated that where different verdicts would be mutually inconsistent, further directions would be appropriate. Broadly where the jury seeks to return a verdict patently at odds with the judge's directions, or returns a verdict which simply is not lawful, it is no part of the court's function to let a verdict based on confusion, error or inconsistency pass unchecked. The judge in such circumstances must consider issuing further directions to assist the jury to reach a clear and sustainable verdict (see *Cameron (J.P.) v. H.M. Advocate*, 1999 S.C.C.R. 476).

A novel problem (but one likely to concern courts in the future) arose in *Matthewson v. H.M. Advocate*, 1989 S.C.C.R. 101 when the jury asked to be shown parts of a video tape produced in evidence. The only operator available was the procurator fiscal depute who, in the presence of counsel for one of the accused and the clerk, showed a juror how to operate the video recorder, the jury having had to return to the court in order to view the tape. In *Gray v. H.M. Advocate*, 1999 S.L.T. 533; 1999 S.C.C.R. 24, an assault and robbery in which video evidence was central to identification of the accused by witnesses who had seen him earlier that day, the trial judge refused a jury request to view the video again. On appeal against conviction the Appeal Court distinguished between the jurors viewing the tape again for the purpose of testing the accuracy and reliability of the witnesses' evidence (which could be permitted in open court) and undertaking an investigation or assessment of the contents of the tape for themselves (which would be unacceptable). *Gray* holds that it is competent to grant such jury requests; however it has to be doubted that such subtle distinctions will be clear to the jury even after additional directions. The jury also sought assistance from the court in *Moir v. H.M. Advocate*, 1993 S.C.C.R. 1191 to "hear if possible ... all or part of the evidence given by [J]". Plainly at that stage in proceedings the witness could not be recalled and, in the absence of a transcript, the judge had declined to read over his own notes of evidence lest this influence the jury's own recall. The Appeal Court (at 1197) followed *Hamilton v. H.M. Advocate*, 1938 S.L.T. 333 at 337 and held that the notes could have been read if the judge so chose, but that the issue was one which fell to the judge's discretion in determining the best way to conduct the case and not subject to review by the Appeal Court.

Subs. (4)

At earlier stages in the proceedings, arrangements for accommodating jurors overnight during adjournments of trial can be made (s.88(8)) and it is presumed that the requirements of subs. (4) would then be applied to those situations. Once the jury has been charged there is no doubt that its deliberations should be interrupted only for the purposes of subs. (4). It is implicit that the jury should be unhindered in its deliberations and should in no way be pressured directly or indirectly to hasten to a verdict. See *McKenzie v. H.M. Advocate*, 1986 S.C.C.R. 94 and *Love v. H.M. Advocate*, 1995 S.C.C.R. 501. The distinction between eliciting a report on the jury's progress (necessary for the planning of accommodation) and pressing for a conclusion, can be a fine, but telling, one. Contrast *Robertson v. H.M. Advocate*, 1996 S.C.C.R. 243 and *Sinclair v. H.M. Advocate*, 1996 S.C.C.R. 221. It would seem to be good practice to remind jurors that they should reach a verdict in their own good time and should feel under no pressure to reach a verdict. An alternative, and perhaps less satisfactory, approach was used by the sheriff in *Eraker v. H.M. Advocate* 1997 G.W.D. 5–183 when the jury was asked if they were happy to consider "at least in the first instance trying to make a decision this evening"; presumably, since this left the jury to resolve whether to try to reach a verdict later that day (as they did) rather than directing them to do so, no element of pressure was evident.

The clearest breach of the s.99 provisions is found in *Thomson v. H.M. Advocate*, 1997 S.C.C.R 121; learning that the jury felt unable to reach a verdict that evening the judge instructed the jury to break from its deliberations, only to learn later, that no suitable overnight accommodation could be found. Treating the provisions of subs. (4) as discretionary, the judge allowed the jury to return home under directions not to discuss the case further. The Appeal Court ruled this to be a serious irregularity, quashed the conviction and granted authority for new proceedings. (The only option open to the trial judge would have been to seclude the jurors with suitable breaks for meals or refreshments until a verdict was achieved, a situation in which immense care would be needed to avoid any hint of pressuring the jury for a verdict. It may be recalled that until the passage of the Criminal Justice (Scotland) Act 1980, s.24, once a jury retired to consider its verdict, its members remained secluded without interruption until a verdict could be reached).

Subs. (6)

This provision was introduced by the Prisoners and Criminal Proceedings (Scotland) Act 1993 (c. 9), s.40(1) into the 1975 Act as s.155A. Section 91 enacts that trials shall proceed from day to day until concluded, while the marginal note stipulates "Trial to be continuous". Technical objections as to want of procedure of the sort raised in *Boyle v. H.M. Advocate* above should not occur. The logical corollary of subs. (6) is s.102 below which permits other proceedings to be interrupted for the taking of a verdict, deal with the requests of, or issue further directions to, the jury in a prior trial. Section 158 of the Act allows summary proceedings to be interrupted for the same purposes.

Verdict and conviction

Verdict of jury

100.—(1) The verdict of the jury, whether the jury are unanimous or not, shall be returned orally by the foreman of the jury unless the court directs a written verdict to be returned.

(2) Where the jury are not unanimous in their verdict, the foreman shall announce that fact so that the relative entry may be made in the record.

(3) The verdict of the jury may be given orally through the foreman of the jury after consultation in the jury box without the necessity for the jury to retire.

GENERAL NOTE

The jury's verdict can be returned competently in court immediately on conclusion of the judge's charge; it is not essential that they retire to the jury room (subs. (3)) or deliberate for any length of time (*Crowe v. H.M. Advocate*, 1989 S.C.C.R. 681).

The verdict should be delivered orally to the court, a written verdict being competent only when the court has previously directed that the verdict be given to the court in that form. In part this ensures that all proceedings occur within the view and hearing of the accused; see *Kerr v. H.M. Advocate*, 1992 S.L.T. 1031; 1992 S.C.C.R. 281 discussed in the notes to s.90. It has been held in *Neil v. H.M. Advocate*, 1948 J.C. 12 that the judge is not obliged to explain the meaning of the not proven verdict on the grounds that it is well understood in Scotland, but this is surely debatable.

On rare occasions the nature of evidence can be such as to require the withdrawal of the not proven verdict from the jury; see *Reid v. H.M. Advocate*, 1947 S.L.T. 156. The presiding judge is obliged to explain the meaning of a majority verdict to the jury and it must be made clear that at least eight of the jury are minded to convict: the jury will only be asked whether the verdict is unanimous or by a majority and no further enquiry should be made into the arithmetic involved (*Pullar v. H.M. Advocate*, 1993 S.C.C.R. 514). The manner of calculating a majority has to be well understood by jurors particularly because of the availability (usually) of three verdicts and because the size of the jury can be reduced in certain circumstances to consist of as few as 12 jurors (s.90(1)). Refer to *Affleck v. H.M. Advocate*, 1987 S.C.C.R. 150. In *Docherty v. H.M. Advocate*, 1997 S.C.C.R. 345 confusion arose in a murder trial where the jury had voted by a majority for a guilty verdict, but were divided as to whether to convict for murder or culpable homicide. The Appeal Court held that those who had voted for an acquittal should not thereafter vote upon which of the alternative verdicts of guilt should be pronounced. Of consent, a conviction of culpable homicide was substituted by the Appeal Court. In the light of *Docherty* it would seem that modification of the standard directions given to juries would be appropriate in cases were alternative charges are libelled.

Once the verdict has been recorded by the clerk of court, read back to them and assented as correct, it cannot be subject to further consideration by the trial court, the verdict being finally pronounced (see *McGarry v. H.M. Advocate*, 1959 J.C. 30). It has been held however that failure to read back a verdict to the jury is not itself fatal to the conviction (*Torri v. H.M. Advocate*, 1923 J.C. 52).

Previous convictions: solemn proceedings

101.—(1) Previous convictions against the accused shall not be laid before the jury, nor shall reference be made to them in presence of the jury before the verdict is returned.

(2) Nothing in subsection (1) above shall prevent the prosecutor—

(a) asking the accused questions tending to show that he has been convicted of an offence other than that with which he is charged, where he is entitled to do so under section 266 of this Act; or

(b) leading evidence of previous convictions where it is competent to do so under section 270 of this Act, and nothing in this section or in section 69 of this Act shall prevent evidence of previous convictions being led in any case where such evidence is competent in support of a substantive charge.

(3) Previous convictions shall not be laid before the presiding judge until the prosecutor moves for sentence, and in that event the prosecutor shall lay before the judge a copy of the notice referred to in subsection (2) or (4) of section 69 of this Act.

(4) On the conviction of the accused it shall be competent for the court, subject to subsection (5) below, to amend a notice of previous convictions so laid by deletion or alteration for the purpose of curing any error or defect.

[1](5) ...

(6) Any conviction which is admitted in evidence by the court shall be entered in the record of the trial.

(7) Where a person is convicted of an offence, the court may have regard to any previous conviction in respect of that person in deciding on the disposal of the case.

(8) Where any such intimation as is mentioned in section 69 of this Act is given by the accused, it shall be competent to prove any previous conviction included in a notice under that section in the manner specified in section 285 of this Act, and the provisions of the said section shall apply accordingly.

DEFINITIONS
"judge": s.307(1).
"previous conviction": s.307(5).
"prosecutor": s.307(1).

NOTE
[1]As amended by the Crime and Punishment (Scotland) Act 1997 (c. 48) s.31 with effect from August 1, 1997 (Commencement and Transitional Provisions) Order 1997 (S.I. 1997 No. 1712) para. 3.

GENERAL NOTE

Previous convictions in the course of trial
The previous convictions of the accused should not normally be made known to the court until a conviction is recorded and the prosecutor moves for sentence. There are two accepted exceptions to this general rule: first where proof of the conviction is an essential to proof of the substantive charge (for example, driving while disqualified, or contravening the provisions of the Firearms Act 1968 (c. 27), s.21, or prison-breaking—see *Russell v. H.M. Advocate*, 1991 S.C.C.R. 785; *Varey v. H.M. Advocate*, 1986 S.L.T. 321 and *Harkin v. H.M. Advocate*, 1996 S.C.C.R. 5); secondly when the accused has represented himself to be of good character or impugned the character of prosecution witnesses, the complainer or the prosecutor (see ss.266(4) and 270(1)). The prosecutor is also under a duty not to question the accused in a fashion calculated to show that he has been involved in other criminal charges which are not before the court.

The consequences of revealing previous convictions, even when this is done by the prosecutor, are not necessarily fatal; much depends on the circumstances in which the section's provisions were breached, whether the information was wilfully elicited or was imparted unexpectedly, what objection, if any, was offered to the evidence and who sought the evidence in the first place. The approach adopted by the Court of Appeal is to consider whether a miscarriage of justice has occurred (having regard, *inter alia*, to any steps taken by the trial judge to address the issue, or consciously avoid it, in his charge) and then to consider whether the breach constituted a sufficiently substantial miscarriage to merit the quashing of the conviction or amendment of the verdict. So in *McCuaig v. H.M. Advocate*, 1982 S.C.C.R. 125 where a police officer in response to a question from the trial judge read over the full terms of a charge preferred to him, making reference to the accused's previous convictions, it was held that no substantial miscarriage had occurred. Similarly in *Binks v. H.M. Advocate*, 1984 S.C.C.R. 335; 1985 S.L.T. 59 where in reading a statement given by the accused, a Customs officer during his examination-in-chief read the phrase "I don't want to go back to jail again", the court took the view that the mere disclosure of a previous conviction might be of little or no significance in the circumstances of the case. See generally *Kepple v. H.M. Advocate*, 1936 J.C. 76 and *H.M. Advocate v. McIlwain* 1965 S.L.T. 311.

By contrast a very similar reply to caution and charge elicited by the prosecutor in *Graham v. H.M. Advocate*, 1984 S.L.T. 67 was held to be deliberate and fatal to conviction. Compare *McAvoy v. H.M. Advocate*, 1991 S.C.C.R. 123 in which the prosecutor asked a police officer about "known associates" of the accused a question, which though criticised by the Appeal

Court, was held not to have breached the provisions. The central issue in studying the conduct of the prosecutor is whether the disclosure came about as a result of calculation or unacceptable want of care on his part, or whether it occurred unexpectedly or as part of a wilful ploy by a witness or co-accused. See *Deeney v. H.M. Advocate*, 1986 S.C.C.R. 393 where a witness mentioned that the accused was on licence at the time of offences, an answer not anticipated from the Crown's question and which was held not to have breached the section's provisions. More recently in *Robertson v. H.M. Advocate*, 1995 S.C.C.R. 497 where a Crown witness repeatedly referred to the accused being provided accommodation by SACRO (Scottish Association for Care and Resettlement of Offenders), using only the acronym and without divulging the objects of the organisation, the disclosure was held to be accidental and to have been dealt with sensitively in the judge's charge to the jury. In *Campbell v. H.M. Advocate*, 1999 S.L.T. 399 (driving while disqualified) the prosecutor's brief questioning of C. about his previous conviction notwithstanding that C. had stated no preliminary objection to the special capacity, was upheld. The court took the view that the Crown could still elect to prove the terms of the qualifying conviction; see the discussion at pp. 342–343 below.

It will be noted that the section bars any reference to an accused's previous convictions (unless the provisions of subs. (2) apply) but this cannot guard against wilful conduct on the part of co-accused or defence witnesses; in such circumstances this is almost certain to be prejudicial but the court will not rush to hold that a miscarriage has occurred. See *Slane v. H.M. Advocate*, 1984 S.L.T. 293. In the first instance the judge presiding at the trial has to decide whether to mention such inadmissible evidence in order to direct that it be disregarded or whether, in the whole circumstances, it is more discreet, and effective, to say nothing at all and in so doing avoid resurrecting the objectionable evidence (see *Fyfe v. H.M. Advocate*, 1989 S.C.C.R. 429; 1990 S.L.T. 50 and *Gallagher v. H.M. Advocate*, 1992 G.W.D. 6–355).

The deletion of subs. (5) introduced by the 1997 Act means that it is now competent to amend the schedule of previous convictions to correct errors. This concession would have had a considerable impact if the Government had commenced the scheme of automatic sentences set out in Part I of the 1997 Act; in that scheme the precise terms of a prior conviction would have dictated whether a re-offending accused was subject to an automatic sentence on indictment.

Previous convictions and the sentencing process

When moving for sentence the Crown is entitled to place a schedule detailing previous convictions before the court as material relevant to sentence. The question now is what in the way of more detailed information about the nature and circumstances of prior background, including convictions, should be disclosed to the court, and considered by it. Until now the directions laid down in *Connel v. Mitchell*, 1909 S.C.(J.) 13 (broadly that the court could not look behind previous convictions) had been applied, albeit previous convictions not libelled by the Crown but revealed in social enquiry reports could be taken into account once the accused had been given the opprtunity to challenge them or comment (*Sillars v. Copeland*, 1966 J.C. 8). Otherwise the court would seek no more information as to the factual circumstances of previous offences.

In *Riley v. H.M. Advocate*, 1999 S.C.C.R. 644, the Appeal Court has signalled a broader approach and has approved a practice of the Crown serving extracts of convictions whose factual detail is being founded upon in any narration. Nonetheless it was emphasised that a sentencing court would not wish to become embroiled in disputes over the fine detail of convictions, and would limit scrutiny to the terms of charges, and only then in exceptional cases.

The purpose of schedules of previous convictions and social enquiry reports is to enable the sentencing judge to pass an appropriate disposal having regard to all the known circumstances: thus in *Penman v. H.M. Advocate*, 1999 S.C.C.R. 740 where no previous convictions were put before the court but a report referred to convictions for offences committed subsequent to the sexual misconduct libelled, the Appeal Court approved the use of this information provided that the record was not treated as an aggravating feature. *Penman*'s recent pattern of offending justified the view that he was a danger to the public.

European Convention on Human Rights

In *Andrew v. H.M. Advocate*, 1999 G.W.D. 32–1517 the Appeal Court rejected the contention that disclosure of an accused's previous conviction in the course of trial necessarily amounted to a breach of art. 6(1) or (2). It is of note that the disclosure arose through no fault of the Crown.

Interruption of trial for other proceedings

102.—(1) When the jury have retired to consider their verdict, and the diet in another criminal cause has been called, then, subject to subsection (3) below, if it appears to the judge presiding at the trial to be appropriate, he may interrupt the proceedings in such other cause—

(a) in order to receive the verdict of the jury in the preceding trial, and thereafter to dispose of the case;

(b) to give a direction to the jury in the preceding trial upon any matter upon which the jury may wish a direction from the judge or to hear any request from the jury regarding any matter in the cause.

(2) Where in any case the diet of which has not been called, the accused intimates to the clerk of court that he is prepared to tender a plea of guilty as libelled or such qualified plea as the Crown is prepared to accept, or where a case is remitted to the High Court for sentence, then, subject to subsection (3) below, any trial then proceeding may be interrupted for the purpose of receiving such plea or dealing with the remitted case and pronouncing sentence or otherwise disposing of any such case.

(3) In no case shall any proceedings in the preceding trial take place in the presence of the jury in the interrupted trial, but in every case that jury shall be directed to retire by the presiding judge.

(4) On the interrupted trial being resumed the diet shall be called *de novo*.

(5) In any case an interruption under this section shall not be deemed an irregularity, nor entitle the accused to take any objection to the proceedings.

DEFINITIONS
  "High Court": s.307(1).
  "judge": s.307(1).

GENERAL NOTE
    This section and, in some circumstances, s.99(6) fall to be read in conjunction. While s.91 of the Act requires that the trial shall proceed from day to day, procedural difficulties can develop when it is necessary to interpose other solemn business. See for example *Boyle v. H.M. Advocate*, 1990 S.C.C.R. 480. These problems became yet more acute when a jury trial had spilled over from a previous sitting; then the disposal of business called to the later (delayed) sitting often demanded dexterity of a high order. Section 102 admits a degree of flexibility into the administration of court business but it will be noted that when a jury trial is interrupted to deal with other business before the court, that jury is to be excluded until the fresh business is concluded.

    The section also enables a jury in a later trial to be empanelled while an earlier jury deliberates, a provision which may assist on occasion to utilise court time more effectively.

    Rule 14.8. of the 1996 Act of Adjournal enacts that a minute of continuation shall be entered in the minutes of the interrupted trial; Rule 14.9.–(1) permits other matters, which have been deferred for sentence to await the outcome of the jury trial, to be called once a verdict has been reached in that trial without the need to adjourn.

    It will be observed that it is still necessary to call the diet anew after any such interruption (subs. (4)).

PART VIII

APPEALS FROM SOLEMN PROCEEDINGS

Appeal sittings

    103.—(1) The High Court shall hold both during session and during vacation such sittings as are necessary for the disposal of appeals and other proceedings under this Part of this Act.

    (2) Subject to subsection (3) below, for the purpose of hearing and determining any appeal or other proceeding under this Part of this Act three of the Lords Commissioners of Justiciary shall be a quorum of the High Court, and the determination of any question under this Part of this Act by the court shall be according to the votes of the majority of the members of the court sitting, including the presiding judge, and each judge so sitting shall be entitled to pronounce a separate opinion.

    [1](3) For the purpose of hearing and determining any appeal under section

156

106(1)(b) to (e) of this Act, or any proceeding connected therewith, two of the Lords Commissioners of Justiciary shall be a quorum of the High Court, and each judge shall be entitled to pronounce a separate opinion; but where the two Lords Commissioners of Justiciary are unable to reach agreement on the disposal of the appeal, or where they consider it appropriate, the appeal shall be heard and determined in accordance with subsection (2) above.

[1](4) Subsections (1) to (3) above shall apply to cases certified to the High Court by a single judge of the said court and to appeals by way of advocation in like manner as they apply to appeals under this Part of this Act.

(5) The powers of the High Court under this Part of this Act—
(a) to extend the time within which intimation of intention to appeal and note of appeal may be given;
(b) to allow the appellant to be present at any proceedings in cases where he is not entitled to be present without leave; and
(c) to admit an appellant to bail,
may be exercised by any judge of the High Court, sitting and acting wherever convenient, in the same manner as they may be exercised by the High Court, and subject to the same provisions.

(6) Where a judge acting under subsection (5) above refuses an application by an appellant to exercise under that subsection any power in his favour, the appellant shall be entitled to have the application determined by the High Court.

[1](7) Subject to subsections (5) and (6) above and without prejudice to it, preliminary and interlocutory proceedings incidental to any appeal or application may be disposed of by a single judge.

(8) In all proceedings before a judge under section (5) above, and in all preliminary and interlocutory proceedings and applications except such as are heard before the full court, the parties may be represented and appear by a solicitor alone.

DEFINITIONS
"appellant": s.132.
"bail": s.307(1).
"High Court" s.307(1).
"judge": s.307(1).
"Lords Commissioners of Justiciary": s.307(1).
"sentence": s.132.

NOTE
[1]As amended by the Crime and Punishment (Scotland) Act 1997 (c. 48), s.62(1) and Sched. 1, para. 21(13) with effect from August 1, 1997 in terms of the Crime and Punishment (Scotland) Act 1997 (Commencement and Transitional Provisions) Order 1997 (S.I. 1997 No. 1712) para. 3.

GENERAL NOTE
The structure of the 1975 Act in regard to solemn appeals was to deal with the right of appeal (ss.228 *et seq.*) and then to consider procedure at the hearing (ss.245 *et seq.*). The 1995 Act considers the sitting of the High Court of Justiciary to deal with appeals and then the law of appeals in general.

One of the most potent changes for practitioners in the appeal court is the quorum of the High Court of Justiciary. By s.245 of the 1975 Act the quorum for "any appeal" was three and the simple logic was that in the event of division there would be a majority. Commendable as this approach is, there was for nearly all appeals no possibility of division because of judicial uniformity in approach, especially to sentencing.

The fundamental split between appeals against conviction and appeals against sentence is now reflected in the necessary quorum. For any appeal under Pt. VIII of the 1995 Act the quorum is three judges except that for appeals against sentence alone the quorum is two judges. This includes appeals against decision not to exercise the power contained in section 205B(3) and a decision to remit to the Principal Reporter in terms of section 49(1)(a).

The effect of this change, especially when taken with the requirement to obtain leave to appeal, is likely to reduce dramatically the extent of appellate business in the High Court of

Justiciary and to reduce the time waiting for appeals to appear on the roll. In cases not covered by the 1995 Act it is for the court to determine the appropriate quorum—*Express Newspapers PLC Petr.*, 1999 S.C.C.R. 262.

If one of the judges in a court is subsequently held not to be impartial then proceedings are treated as if he had not been present. If there are insufficient judges remaining to form a quorum then there is no validly constituted court and hence no valid interlocutor in terms of s.124—*Hoekstra v. H.M. Advocate* (No.2), 2000 S.C.C.R. 368.

Subsection (4)—certification is a procedure whereby a judge on circuit can refer a point of law for decision by the High Court: see *H.M. Advocate v. Cunningham*, 1963 J.C. 80 and *H.M. Advocate v. Burns*, 1967 J.C. 15.

Subsection (5)—The quorum is one judge in relation to the matters of extending the time within which intimation of intention to appeal and note of appeal may be given, of allowing the appellant to be present at any proceedings in cases where leave is necessary and to admit the appellant to bail. Only a quorum of 3 judges can entertain an application for bail by a person accused or convicted of murder—see *H.M. Advocate v. Renicks*, 1998 S.C.C.R. 417.

Prior to the incorporation of the ECHR into domestic law submissions regarding delays in the hearing of appeals received short shrift in the Appeal Court—*Ucak v. H.M. Advocate*, 1998 S.C.C.R. 518. Article 6 and the right to a fair trial within a reasonable time covers appeal proceedings and has already arisen in *H.M. Advocate v. McGlinchey*, 2000 S.C.C.R. 593 and *Lawrie v. H.M. Advocate*, 2000 G.W.D. 28–1081.

An argument by the Crown in *Clark v. Kelly*, 2000 S.C.C.R. 821 that in cases involving minor charges where alleged breaches of article 6 occurred the opportunity to challenge any conviction by appeal cured the breach was dismissed by the Appeal Court.

The failure to take objection timeously that temporary sheriffs did not amount to an independent and impartial tribunal in terms of article 6 was held to amount to a tacit waiver of the entitlement to do so thereby precluding the matter being raised post conviction / sentence on appeal—*Millar v. Dickson*, 2000 S.C.C.R. 793.

Power of High Court in appeals

104.—(1) Without prejudice to any existing power of the High Court, it may for the purposes of an appeal under section 106(1) or 108 of this Act—
  (a) order the production of any document or other thing connected with the proceedings;
  (b) hear any evidence relevant to any alleged miscarriage of justice or order such evidence to be heard by a judge of the High Court or by such other person as it may appoint for that purpose;
  (c) take account of any circumstances relevant to the case which were not before the trial judge;
  (d) remit to any fit person to enquire and report in regard to any matter or circumstance affecting the appeal;
  (e) appoint a person with expert knowledge to act as assessor to the High Court in any case where it appears to the court that such expert knowledge is required for the proper determination of the case.

(2) The evidence of any witnesses ordered to be examined before the High Court or before any judge of the High Court or other person appointed by the High Court shall be taken in accordance with the existing law and practice as to the taking of evidence in criminal trials in Scotland.

(3) The appellant or applicant and the respondent or counsel on their behalf shall be entitled to be present at and take part in any examination of any witness to which this section relates.

DEFINITIONS
  "appellant": s.132.
  "High Court": s.307(1).
  "judge": s.307(1).

GENERAL NOTE
  The central question in appeals against conviction is whether there has been a miscarriage of justice: s.106(3). The essence of s.104 is to allow the High Court of Justiciary, in addition to any

existing powers, statutory powers relating to the investigation of an allegation of a miscarriage of justice. The substance of s.104(1) is essentially that of s.252 of the 1975 Act although it is an indication of how allegations have developed that s.104(2) and (3) clarifies doubts, if there were any, about the manner of taking evidence in the presence of the appellant and his lawyer.

Subsection (1)(a): In *Hoekstra v. H.M. Advocate (No.1)*, 2000 S.C.C.R. 263 "disclosure minutes" were prepared by the appellants seeking recovery of new material not available at the trial. It was held that "in general terms the court should not order the Crown to disclose new material in the course of an appeal unless the court was satisfied that the material was likely to be of value for the purpose of evaluating the grounds of appeal and determining whether or not there had been a miscarriage of justice, but the court might be prepared to consider ordering the production of new material which was shown to be of potential importance even if it was not material which was, on a strict reading, relevant to an existing ground of appeal, provided that the material sought could provide the basis for a new or amended ground of appeal which the appellant should, at a late stage be allowed to advance". The court declined in that case to order disclosure. In *Porter & Smith Petrs*, 2000 G.W.D. 2–46 a petition for commission and diligence was sought and granted in respect of material evidence not heard at the trial, the existence of which did not become known until later confiscation proceedings. Subsection (1)(b) has been amended by the Crime and Punishment (Scotland) Act 1997 Sched. 1, para. 21(14). The word "additional" has been removed in light of the new ground of appeal in section 106(3). For cases where evidence was heard by the Appeal Court see *Morland v. H.M. Advocate* 1985 S.C.C.R. 316; *Kinnon v. H.M. Advocate*, 1997 S.C.C.R. 552; *O'Neill v. H.M. Advocate*, 1996 G.W.D. 29–1728 and *Daly v. H.M. Advocate*, 1997 G.W.D. 22–1067; *Jackson v. H.M. Advocate*, 1998 S.C.C.R. 539; Subsection (1)(c), see *Rubin v. H.M. Advocate*, 1984 S.C.C.R. 96; *Carrington v. H.M. Advocate*, 1994 S.C.C.R. 567 and *Tarbett v. H.M. Advocate*, 1994 S.C.C.R. 867; Subsection (1)(d), see *McCadden v. H.M. Advocate*, 1985 S.C.C.R. 282; *Robertson v. H.M. Advocate*, 1996 S.C.C.R. 243; *Crossan v. H.M. Advocate*, 1996 S.C.C.R. 279; *Squire v. H.M. Advocate*, 1998 G.W.D. 28–1410; *Feely v. H.M. Advocate*, 2000 G.W.D. 12–422 and *Kerr v. H.M. Advocate*, 1999 S.C.C.R. 763. As Sheriff Gordon points out in his commentary the remit to a single judge required to be specific in its terms so as not to conflict with s.8 of the Contempt of Court Act 1981.

The form an investigation should take is set out in *Squire v. H.M. Advocate*, 1998 G.W.D. 28–1410, a case concerning alleged communications between the jury and the clerk of court. In considering the question of an alleged miscarriage of justice, in *Clark v. H.M. Advocate*, 2000 S.C.C.R. 767 the tape of part of the judge's charge was played to the Appeal Court.

Appeal against refusal of application

105.—(1) When an application or applications have been dealt with by a judge of the High Court, under section 103(5) of this Act, the Clerk of Justiciary shall—

(a) notify to the applicant the decision in the form prescribed by Act of Adjournal or as nearly as may be in such form; and

(b) where all or any of such applications have been refused, forward to the applicant the prescribed form for completion and return forthwith if he desires to have the application or applications determined by the High Court as fully constituted for the hearing of appeals under this Part of this Act.

(2) Where the applicant does not desire a determination as mentioned in subsection (1)(b) above, or does not return within five days to the Clerk the form duly completed by him, the refusal of his application or applications by the judge shall be final.

(3) Where an applicant who desires a determination by the High Court as mentioned in subsection (1)(b) above—

(a) is not legally represented, he may be present at the hearing and determination by the High Court of the application;

(b) is legally represented, he shall not be entitled to be present without leave of the court.

(4) When an applicant duly completes and returns to the Clerk of Justiciary within the prescribed time the form expressing a desire to be present at the hearing and determination by the court of the applications mentioned in this section, the form shall be deemed to be an application by the applicant for leave to be so present, and the Clerk of Justiciary, on

receiving the form, shall take the necessary steps for placing the application before the court.

(5) If the application to be present is refused by the court, the Clerk of Justiciary shall notify the applicant; and if the application is granted, he shall notify the applicant and the Governor of the prison where the applicant is in custody and the Secretary of State.

(6) For the purpose of constituting a Court of Appeal, the judge who has refused any application may sit as a member of the court, and take part in determining the application.

DEFINITIONS
"clerk of justiciary": s.307(1).
"High Court": s.307(1).
"judge": s.307(1).

GENERAL NOTE
Under s.103(5) the quorum is one judge in relation to the matters of extending the time within which intimation of intention to appeal and note of appeal may be given, of allowing the appellant to be present at any proceedings in cases where leave is necessary and to admit the appellant to bail.

Section 105 prescribes the procedure to appeal against a refusal of an application under s.103(5). Such an appeal (not being an appeal against sentence) requires to be heard by three judges. It is strange to see that for the purposes of constituting a Court of Appeal, the judge who has refused any application may sit as a member of the court, and take part in determining the application: s.105(6).

Right of appeal

106.—(1) Any person convicted on indictment may, with leave granted in accordance with section 107 of this Act, appeal in accordance with this Part of this Act, to the High Court—

(a) against such conviction;
(b) subject to subsection (2) below, against the sentence passed on such conviction;
²(bb) against any decision not to exercise the power conferred by section 205A(3) or 205B(3) of this Act;
(c) against his absolute discharge or admonition;
(d) against any probation order or any community service order;
³(da) against any decision to remit made under section 49(1)(a) of this Act;
(e) against any order deferring sentence; or
(f) against both such conviction and, subject to subsection (2) below, such sentence or disposal or order.

(2) There shall be no appeal against any sentence fixed by law.

¹(3) By an appeal under subsection (1) above a person may bring under review of the High Court any alleged miscarriage of justice, which may include such a miscarriage based on—

(a) subject to subsections (3A) to (3D) below, the existence and significance of evidence which was not heard at the original proceedings; and
(b) the jury's having returned a verdict which no reasonable jury, properly directed, could have returned.

(3A) Evidence such as is mentioned in subsection (3)(a) above may found an appeal only where there is a reasonable explanation of why it was not so heard.

(3B) Where the explanation referred to in subsection (3A) above or, as the case may be, (3C) below is that the evidence was not admissible at the time of the original proceedings, but is admissible at the time of the appeal, the court may admit that evidence if it appears to the court that it would be in the interests of justice to do so.

(3C) Without prejudice to subsection (3A) above, where evidence such as is mentioned in paragraph (a) of subsection (3) above is evidence—

(a) which is—
   (i) from a person; or
   (ii) of a statement (within the meaning of section 259(1) of this Act) by a person,
  who gave evidence at the original proceedings; and

(b) which is different from, or additional to, the evidence so given,

it may not found an appeal unless there is a reasonable explanation as to why the evidence now sought to be adduced was not given by that person at those proceedings, which explanation is itself supported by independent evidence.

(3D) For the purposes of subsection (3C) above, "independent evidence" means evidence which—

(a) was not heard at the original proceedings;

(b) is from a source independent of the person referred to in subsection (3C) above; and

(c) is accepted by the court as being credible and reliable.

(4) Any document, production or other thing lodged in connection with the proceedings on the trial of any person who, if convicted, is entitled or may be authorised to appeal under this Part of this Act, shall, in accordance with subsections (5) to (9) below, be kept in the custody of the court in which the conviction took place.

(5) All documents and other productions produced at the trial of a convicted person shall be kept in the custody of the court of trial in such manner as it may direct until any period allowed under or by virtue of this Part of this Act for lodging intimation of intention to appeal has elapsed.

(6) Where no direction is given as mentioned in subsection (5) above, such custody shall be in the hands of the sheriff clerk of the district of the court of the second diet to whom the clerk of court shall hand them over at the close of the trial, unless otherwise ordered by the High Court on an intimation of intention to appeal being lodged, and if within such period there has been such lodgement under this Part of this Act, they shall be so kept until the appeal, if it is proceeded with, is determined.

(7) Notwithstanding subsections (5) and (6) above, the judge of the court in which the conviction took place may, on cause shown, grant an order authorising any of such documents or productions to be released on such conditions as to custody and return as he may deem it proper to prescribe.

(8) All such documents or other productions so retained in custody or released and returned shall, under supervision of the custodian thereof, be made available for inspection and for the purpose of making copies of documents or productions to a person who has lodged an intimation of intention to appeal or as the case may be, to the convicted person's counsel or agent, and to the Crown Agent and the procurator fiscal or his deputes.

(9) Where no intimation of intention to appeal is lodged within the period mentioned in subsection (6) above, all such documents and productions shall be dealt with as they are dealt with according to the existing law and practice at the conclusion of a trial; and they shall be so dealt with if, there having been such intimation, the appeal is not proceeded with.

DEFINITIONS
   "community service order": s.238.
   "High Court": s.307(1).
   "indictment": s.307(1).
   "judge": s.307(1).
   "probation order": s.228.
   "procurator fiscal": s.307(1).
   "sentence": s.307(1).

"sheriff court": s.307(1).

NOTES

[1] As amended by the Crime and Punishment (Scotland) Act 1997 (c. 48), s.17 with effect from August 1, 1997 in terms of the Crime and Punishment (Scotland) Act 1997 (Commencement and Transitional Provisions) Order 1997 (S.I. 1997 No. 1712) para. 3.

[2] Inserted by the Crime and Punishment (Scotland) Act 1997 (c. 48), s.18 with effect from October 20, 1997 in terms of the Crime and Punishment (Scotland) Act 1997 (Commencement No. 2 and Transitional Provisions) Order 1997 (S.I. 1997 No. 2323) Art. 3, Sched. 1; amended by the Crime and Disorder Act 1998 (c. 37), Sched. 8, para. 119 (effective September 30, 1998: S.I. 1998 No. 2327).

[3] Inserted by the Crime and Punishment (Scotland) Act 1997 (c. 48), s.23 with effect from August 1, 1997 in terms of the Crime and Punishment (Scotland) Act 1997 (Commencement and Transitional Provisions) Order 1997 (S.I. 1997 No. 1712) para. 3.

GENERAL NOTE

The Crime and Punishment Act 1997 radically altered this section and in particular subsection (3) containing the single ground of appeal. The changes followed a report by the Sutherland Committee who were appointed to examine the criteria for consideration of appeals by the Appeal Court and to consider any changes that may be required (Cmnd 3245).

An appeal under s.106 must be "with leave granted in accordance with s.107 of this Act". Reference may be made to that section and the General Note to it for a full understanding of this hurdle to be cleared.

Assuming that leave has been granted, an appeal against conviction alone is possible under s.106(1)(a) and against both conviction and sentence disposal or other order under s.106(1)(f). The hearing of these appeals will be by three judges: s.103(2). Further assuming that leave has been granted, an appeal against sentence and other similar disposals is possible under s.106(1)(b) to (e) inclusive. The hearing of these appeals will be by two judges: s.103(2).

Subs. (1)

From October 20, 1997, a convicted person can also appeal against a decision to impose a minimum sentence for drug trafficking. From August 1, 1997 a convicted person can appeal against any decision by the court to remit to the Principal Reporter in terms of section 49(1)(a) to arrange for disposal by a Children's Hearing.

Subs. (2)

There is no appeal against any sentence fixed by law. The clearest example of this is the sentence of imprisonment for life for murder: s.205(1). A minimum recomendation can be appealed: see s.205(6).

Subs. (3)

The provision implementing the new subs. 3 took effect on August 1, 1997. It applies to all appeals in existence at that date and all appeals raised thereafter. The single ground of appeal remains on the basis of a miscarriage of justice but gone is the one example of the existence and significance of additional evidence. This has been replaced with two examples namely (a) the existence and significance of evidence which was not heard at the original proceedings and (b) a verdict returned by a jury which no reasonable jury properly directed could have returned. The retention of "miscarriage of justice" was recommended by the Sutherland Committee on the basis that the phrase was adaptable to changing circumstances citing the case of *Anderson v. H.M. Advocate*, 1996 S.C.C.R. 114 as an example of this. The miscarriage need no longer occur "in the proceedings". The Sutherland Committee considered that this created room for uncertainty and argument as a miscarriage of justice could arise as a result of an event prior to the trial or evidence emerging post conviction.

The first appeal case to consider the new subsections (3) and (3A) to (3D) was *Campbell and Steele v. H.M. Advocate*, 1998 S.C.C.R. 214.

Subs. 3(a)

The evidence no longer requires to be "additional" as outlined in e.g. *Mitchell v. H.M. Advocate*, 1989 S.C.C.R. 502 and *McCormack v. H.M. Advocate*, 1993 S.C.C.R. 581. Therefore subject to subs. 3A (see below) recovery of memory could now qualify and so too could change of story by a witness, subject to subs. 3C.

It was held in *Kidd v. H.M. Advocate*, 2000 S.C.C.R. 513 that the governing question in any appeal based on fresh evidence is whether the fact that it was not heard at the trial represents a miscarriage of justice. It is not a question of whether the additional evidence is significant but whether it is of such significance as to lead to the conclusion that a verdict returned in ignorance of it must be regarded as a miscarriage of justice. The sole test is miscarriage of justice. The significance of the evidence includes considerations regarding relevance, materiality and importance and quality in the point of credibility and reliability. None of these factors is determinative. It is the overall impression which is created. The court pointed out that the Appeal Court is different in function from the trial court and does not enjoy the advantages of hearing and seeing the original witnesses and that there are inherent limitations in an appeal court determining what the trial court would have made of the additional evidence when considered in the context of the original evidence. It is sufficient that the Appeal Court be satisfied that the evidence is capable of being regarded by a reasonable jury as both credible and reliable but that the importance of its quality must be emphasised and that its cogency is of critical importance.

A discrepancy previously was thought to exist between the criterion set out in *Cameron v. H.M. Advocate*, 1987 S.C.C.R. 608 and *Church v. H.M. Advocate*, 1996 S.C.C.R. 29. In *Kidd supra* the Appeal Court considered that there was no essential difference between the approach in *Cameron* and *Church*. McCluskey and McBride on "Criminal Appeals" appear to disagree as does Sheriff Gordon in his commentary to *McLay v. H.M. Advocate*, 2000 S.C.C.R. 579. See also *Fraser v. H.M. Advocate*, 2000 S.C.C.R. 755 on the applicable test.

Subs. 3(b)

Section 2(1) of the Criminal Appeal (Scotland) Act 1926 (c. 15) provided *inter alia* that a verdict of a jury could be set aside on the grounds that it was unreasonable or could not be supported by the evidence, but the proviso to the section required a "substantial miscarriage of justice" before an appeal would be allowed (see *Webb v. H.M. Advocate*, 1927 J.C. 92). The test of unreasonableness was as set out in the current provision namely a verdict which no reasonable jury properly directed could have returned (see *Slater v. H.M. Advocate*, 1928 J.C. 94). In *McMillan v. H.M. Advocate*, 1927 J.C. 62 and *Webb supra* the court stated that the Appeal Court was not a court of review and it could not upset a verdict because it disagreed with a jury's view of evidence or credibility of witnesses. There had to be circumstances of a special character before the court would set aside a jury's verdict.

Post 1980 legislation did not contain provision for review of unreasonable verdicts provoking concern about verdicts considered to be unsafe.

The Sutherland Committee recognised that the test to be applied in the current legislation is very similar to the test applied by the Appeal Court under the 1926 legislation. They envisaged that an appeal based on this subsection would succeed only in exceptional cases. They expected however "a broader recognition of the potential for such cases" than with the 1926 Act. Subsection 3(b) was considered by the Appeal Court in *King v. H.M. Advocate*, 1999 S.C.C.R. 330. It was held that the Appeal Court could quash the verdict of a jury only if satisfied that, on the evidence led at the trial, no reasonable jury could have been satisfied beyond a reasonable doubt that the accused was guilty. (The court observed that this formulation was not dissimilar to that in Webb but gave no indication whether in future cases it would be as strictly interpreted.) The test is an objective one. The Appeal Court will not simply substitute their view of the evidence for the jury's view. There will not be a miscarriage of justice simply because the Appeal Court might have entertained a reasonable doubt on the evidence. In determining such cases the Appeal Court will have regard to the fact that the jury had the advantage of seeing and hearing the evidence. In King four witnesses led by the Crown contradicted the Crown case in that they claimed to have seen the deceased alive and well some three hours after the murder allegedly occurred. The Appeal Court held that the jury would have been entitled to accept or reject the evidence of the four witnesses and it could not be said that no reasonable jury could have been satisfied beyond a reasonable doubt that the Appellant was guilty and appeal refused; see also *McAllan v. H.M. Advocate*, 1999 G.W.D. 18–826.

A verdict cannot be attacked under this provision on the basis of "fresh evidence" as the attack must be based on evidence actually before the jury: see *Campbell and Steele v. H.M. Advocate, supra*. Otherwise an appellant would be able to circumvent subss. (3A) to (3D).

Subs. (3A)

Additional evidence required to be evidence which was not available and could not have reasonably been made available at the trial. The test was an exacting one and had to be fully satisfied see *Carr v. Lees*, 1993 S.C.C.R. 316 and *Tolmie v. H.M. Advocate*, 1997 G.W.D. 26–1312. The reasonable availability test has now gone and all that is required is that a "reasonable explanation" be provided as to why the evidence was not heard at the original proceedings see subs. 3A.

"Reasonable explanation". The Sutherland Committee recommended no attempt be made to qualify or interpret the term and that it be a matter for the court to decide. They did consider that the comments of Lord Justice-Clerk Thomson in *Gallacher v. H.M. Advocate*, 1951 J.C. 38 regarding an adequate explanation for a failure to produce fresh evidence at a trial were relevant. His Lordship stated:

"No general rule can possibly be laid down and the explanation in any particular case must be viewed, not in the light of any technicality or rule of practice or procedure but solely in the light of the dominating consideration that we may order new evidence if we think it necessary or expedient in the interests of justice."

The Appeal Court in *Campbell and Steele v. H.M. Advocate, supra*, considered that although the words "necessary or expedient in the interests of justice", which were used by the Lord Justice-Clerk in reference to section 6 of the 1926 Act, were not included in subsection 3A in determining whether the terms of that subsection were satisfied the court should have regard to the interests of justice according to the circumstances of the particular case. As the Lord Justice-Clerk states "the underlying intention of the new legislation is that the court should take a broad and flexible approach in taking account of the circumstances of the particular case".

A "reasonable explanation" Lord Sutherland defined as an "explanation which, in the circumstances of the particular case is one which the court is persuaded to regard as some justification for the failure to lead the evidence bearing in mind the context that what is being enquired into is an alleged miscarriage of justice which in turn involves the concept of the interests of justice as a whole".

Lord McCluskey considered that "where an appellant is able to tender an explanation which cannot be shown without enquiry to be untrue and which is one that the court can objectively regard as plausible, sufficient and not unreasonable" the Appeal Court would then ask if it was necessary or expedient in the interests of justice to hear the evidence. The L.J.C. stated that the explanation must be adequate to account for the fact that a witness evidence was not heard.

It is for the appellant to satisfy the test of reasonable explanation in sub. 3A and reasonable explanation will be interpreted in an objective way. The Court must be persuaded to treat the explanation as genuine rather than as true as the latter would require what Lord McCluskey describes as "preliminary proof as to the truth or otherwise of the explanation" and hence "depart dramatically from the relatively simple approach which the Sutherland Committee recommended, the Government expressly accepted and which Parliament approved and enacted".

The L.J.C. and Lord Sutherland agreed with the English Court of Appeal in *R. v. Shields and Patrick* [1977] Crim.L.R. 281 that a decision not to call a witness whose evidence was viewed as dangerous would seldom be a reasonable explanation. Their Lordships considered that a tactical decision not to call a witness could not provide a reasonable explanation nor could an appellant being unaware of the existence of a witness or if aware, not aware he was able or willing to give evidence of any significance. The Lord Justice-Clerk did however go on to state that if the appellant could show that at the time of the trial he had no good reason for thinking that the witness existed or as the case might be that he would give the evidence in question then this might amount to a reasonable explanation. It "might depend on the steps which the appellant could reasonably be expected to have taken in the light of what was known at the time." Failure by defence solicitors to precognosce a witness on the Crown list could not, according to Lord Sutherland, amount to a reasonable explanation.

In the English case of *R. v. Beresford* (1971) 56 Cr.App.R. 143 the court confirmed that in order to satisfy the reasonable explanation requirement "the court has in general to be satisfied that the evidence could not with reasonable diligence have been obtained for use at the trial".

In *Hall v. H.M. Advocate* 1998 S.C.C.R. 525 the Appeal Court accepted that a reasonable explanation existed in respect of a witness who had not been on the Crown list of witnesses, who had given 2 statements to the police making no mention of the evidence he was now giving and who at the time he was interviewed by the police was anxious to conceal his presence near to the locus. The appellant argued that given the witness' position at the time of the trial the defence could not, in the exercise of reasonable diligence, have been aware of the significance of the witness. The Appeal Court also agreed to hear the evidence of a witness who was on the list of Crown witnesses but who was not called at the trial diet. Her evidence had become significant in the light of the first witness whose evidence was to be heard. Her significance, it was argued, could not have been discovered by the defence at the time. The Appeal Court stressed that even if there is a reasonable explanation provided the evidence will only be heard if it is "significant evidence" in the light of the test set out in *Cameron v. H.M. Advocate*, 1987 S.C.C.R. 608 at 619.

The Appeal Court in *Hall v. H.M. Advocate, supra* observed that adequate specification should be given in the grounds of appeal of what is proposed to be adduced as additional evidence and what is merely a change in the evidence.

In *Hall v. H.M. Advocate (No. 2)*, 1999 S.C.C.R. 130, in quashing the conviction, it was held that the terms of ss.3A suggest that the reasonable explanation question should be looked at from the point of view of those who represented the appellant at the time of the trial, which includes the period when the defence was being prepared and that if it was shown that despite reasonable steps having been taken to investigate the case, it did not appear that a person would provide information which would be of assistance, whether by way of challenging the Crown case or advancing the case for the defence, there could be a reasonable explanation of why the witness was not adduced at the trial. In attempting to satisfy the ss.3A requirements it is important that the appellant should be able to point to information as to what was known to those who represented the appellant at the time and what steps they took to investigate the defence. Information should also be provided regarding any reason or reasons for thinking no further enquiries were necessary, if appropriate—*Barr v. H.M. Advocate*, 1999 S.C.C.R. 13.

In *Mills v. H.M. Advocate*, 1999 S.C.C.R. 202 it was held that the decision not to call an incriminee as a witness at a trial precluded his evidence and evidence of alleged confessions made by him being led in terms of s.106(3) at the stage of an appeal as the test in ss.3A had not been satisfied. The Crown conceded in that case that the fact that a co-accused did not give evidence and could not be compelled to give evidence amounted to a reasonable explanation. The court, however reserved their opinion regarding this concession. They did suggest that in such circumstances a motion for separation of trials would have been appropriate. As Sheriff Gordon notes in his commentary on this case if such a motion was refused it could be argued that the test in ss.3A had been satisfied.

In *Karling v. H.M. Advocate*, 1999 S.C.C.R. 359 the Appeal Court observed that a reasonable explanation why evidence was not led from one witness does not necessarily apply to another witness. If a reasonable explanation is advanced regarding part of a witness' evidence it does not necessarily apply to the whole of their evidence. In that case a reasonable explanation for not seeking further expert opinion was held to have been made out where a defence expert provided advice to the appellant's solicitors confirming the Crown evidence as to one possible cause of death. The Court rejected this explanation regarding another possible cause of death which had been raised at the trial. If the existence of a witness is not known this may amount to a reasonable explanation *Fraser v. H.M. Advocate*, 2000 S.C.C.R. 755.

Subs. 3B

In *Conway v. H.M. Advocate*, 1996 S.C.C.R. 570 the accused was unable to benefit from a change in the hearsay provisions where his trial had been concluded prior to a change in the rules, the court holding that the evidence must have been admissible at the original trial. Under the new provision the law current at the date of the hearing of the appeal would apply.

Subs. 3C

Mitchell v. H.M. Advocate, 1989 S.C.C.R. 502 and *Brodie v. H.M. Advocate*, 1993 S.C.C.R. 371 established that the Appeal Court will not entertain an appeal on the basis that a witness who has given evidence at the trial wishes to change his story. The Sutherland Committee recommended that this be changed but added the proviso that the reason for the change of testimony be supported by additional credible and reliable evidence. The Government originally rejected this proposal but at the committee stage in the House of Lords introduced the present provision. The section relates not only to oral evidence from a person but also a statement under the exceptions to the hearsay provisions in terms of s.259. The evidence sought to be adduced can be different or additional. A reasonable explanation must be provided as to why the evidence sought to be led was not given by that person at the trial. The section also provides for a check in the form of "independent evidence" which is defined in subs. 3D to support the reasonable explanation.

The main ground of appeal in *Campbell and Steele v. H.M.Advocate, supra*, was the changing of the evidence of a material witness. The Lord Justice-Clerk and Lord Sutherland considered that in such appeals the words "without prejudice to ss.3A" meant that the first hurdle to be overcome was that a reasonable explanation had to be provided by the appellant as to why the evidence was not heard and thereafter a reasonable explanation would be required from the witness as to why the evidence was not given.

Lord McCluskey in his opinion however dissented from the two reasonable explanations requirement. As His Lordship points out there are cases where a witness cannot or will not provide an explanation hence the reference to the hearsay provisions in s.259. Parliament's intention was not to so prejudice an appellant.

Reasonable explanation in this subsection is as defined for subs. 3A.

In *Hall v. H.M. Advocate, supra* the appellant sought to argue that a transcript of a police interview (post conviction) with a witness who gave evidence at the trial was a statement that fell within s.106(3C)(a)(ii), namely evidence different or additional to that given at the trial. As the requirements of s.259(2) had not been satisfied the attempt to rely on subs. (3C)(a)(ii) foundered. The appellant then sought to rely on subs. (3C)(a)(i) namely that it was evidence from a person different or additional to the evidence given at the trial. The reasonable explanation for not giving this evidence at the trial was said to be that the witness was a fantasist or untruthful. Independent evidence was said to come from other false allegations made. The Appeal Court held that the reasonable explanation test was not satisfied. No explanation had been provided by the witness. The Appeal Court considered it unnecessary to express a concluded view on whether the reasonable explanation should come from the witness himself. The Court also held that there was no independent evidence to support the explanation. See also *McLay v. H.M. Advocate*, 2000 S.C.C.R. 579.

Subs. 3D

The independent evidence must satisfy three requirements. In respect of part (a) it is the evidence which requires not to have been heard, not the witness and therefore if a witness is called to give evidence at a trial diet but not asked about a particular matter then the provision would be satisfied—or as in the case of *Cameron v. H.M. Advocate*, 1994 S.C.C.R. 502 a witness could state that they were not prepared to give evidence to that effect at the trial. The Sutherland Committee considered that the additional supporting evidence could be evidence which was heard at the trial but clearly given the terms of part (a) this could not be the case.

Part (b) provides that the evidence must be independent of the person who is changing his story. This was discussed in some detail at the committee stage in the House of Lords (see *Hansard*, H.L. March 10, 1997 cols 37 to 39). The Lord Advocate explained that independent evidence could derive from a relative or colleague, more importantly however, the independent evidence should relate to the reason why the new evidence was not given at the earlier trial and should not relate to the particulars of the new account. This would cover the situation in *McCormack supra* where an accused was suffering from amnesia (see the comments of L.J. Hope and the Lord Advocate in *Hansard*, H.L. March 10, 1997 col. 39) and the independent evidence could be from a doctor that the accused was suffering from this condition. If however the reasonable explanation is that the witness had been pressurised into withholding evidence it may be difficult to find independent evidence to support this.

In *Campbell and Steele v. H.M. Advocate, supra*, the appellants sought to employ, as independent evidence *inter alia* the evidence of police officers of what Love said during interview post conviction of the two accused. The Appeal Court held that this could not be independent evidence as the evidence was of statements from the same source, *i.e.* Love.

Part (c) provides that the evidence must be credible and reliable.

It is for the Appeal Court to decide whether or not the evidence is credible and reliable.

Subss. (4) to (9)

The remaining subsections of s.106 are concerned with the custody of trial documents, productions and related matters. The emphasis in Scotland on real evidence means that there are or can be a substantial quantity of material to be kept safe for the possible consideration of the appellate judges or until such time as it seems reasonable to consider that there is not to be an appeal. In *Strock, Petr.*, 1996 S.C.C.R. 432 the court indicated that the proviso in s.270(2) of the 1975 Act now s.106(7) can operate even though an appeal against conviction was pending. If the outstanding appeal relates to the person seeking release of productions conditions might have to be imposed as to custody and return of productions.

Sentence

The foregoing note is directed principally to any alleged miscarriage of justice in relation to conviction but it is competent to bring under review of the High Court of Justiciary any alleged miscarriage of justice, including one which arises in relation to sentence on the basis of evidence not *heard at the original proceedings*: see *Renton and Brown* (5th ed.) para. 11–47, at p. 208. At any rate in appeals against sentence the test is no longer (as before 1980) whether the sentence was harsh and oppressive but whether it was excessive: *Addison v. Mackinnon*, 1983 S.C.C.R. 52; *Donaldson v. H.M. Advocate*, 1983 S.C.C.R. 216. A bold statement that a sentence is excessive might reasonably be said to be lacking in specification. There must be an indication of the circumstances to be relied on. One important reason for that is to allow the trial judge or the sheriff to report fully upon them for the appellate judges, see Practice Note "Appeals in Solemn Procedure and Appeals against Sentence in Summary Procedure", March 29, 1985. For an example of an appeal against sentence on the basis of fresh evidence see *Baikie v. H.M. Advocate*, 2000 S.C.C.R. 119. Medical reports obtained post sentence disclosed the appellant was suffering from an undiagnosed mental condition at the time of sentence. A hospital order was substituted.

Appeal against automatic sentences where earlier conviction quashed

[1]**106A.**[2][(1) This subsection applies where—
  (a) a person has been sentenced under section 205A(2) of this Act;

(b) he had, at the time at which the offence for which he was so sentenced was committed, only one previous conviction for a qualifying offence or a relevant offence within the meaning of that section; and

(c) after he has been so sentenced, the conviction mentioned in paragraph (b) above has been quashed.]

(2) This subsection applies where—

(a) a person has been sentenced under section 205B(2) of this Act;

(b) he had, at the time at which the offence for which he was so sentenced was committed, only two previous convictions for class A drug trafficking offences within the meaning of that section; and

(c) after he has been so sentenced, one of the convictions mentioned in paragraph (b) above has been quashed.

³(3) Where subsection (1) or (2) above applies, the person may appeal under section 106(1)(b) of this Act against the sentence imposed on him under [section 205A(2) or, as the case may be], 205B(2) of this Act.

(4) An appeal under section 106(1)(b) of this Act by virtue of subsection (3) above—

(a) may be made notwithstanding that the person has previously appealed under that section; and

(b) shall be lodged within two weeks of the quashing of the conviction as mentioned in subsection (1)(c) or, as the case may be, (2)(c) above.

(5) Where an appeal is made under section 106(1)(b) by virtue of this section, the following provisions of this Act shall not apply in relation to such an appeal, namely—

(a) section 121; and

(b) section 126.

NOTES

¹Inserted by the Crime and Punishment (Scotland) Act 1997 (c. 48) s.19 with effect from October 20, 1997 in terms of the Crime and Punishment (Scotland) Act 1997 (Commencement No. 2 and Transitional Provisions) Order 1997 (S.I. 1997 No. 2323) Art. 3, Sched. 1.

²Prospective insertion by the above.

³Inserted by the above and effective except in so far as it refers to section 205(A)(2) of the 1995 Act.

GENERAL NOTE

From the October 20, 1997 where an earlier conviction which qualified an accused of a minimum sentence for drug trafficking is quashed by the Appeal Court, an accused who has received the minimum sentence may appeal. The appeal is in terms of s.106(1)(b) and must be made within two weeks of the conviction being quashed. A previous appeal against sentence does not preclude an appeal under this section.

Subs. (5) provides that suspension of disqualification etc and the provisions relating to extract convictions shall not apply where there is an appeal under this section.

Leave to appeal

107.—(1) The decision whether to grant leave to appeal for the purposes of section 106(1) of this Act shall be made by a judge of the High Court who shall—

(a) if he considers that the documents mentioned in subsection (2) below disclose arguable grounds of appeal, grant leave to appeal and make such comments in writing as he considers appropriate; and

(b) in any other case—

(i) refuse leave to appeal and give reasons in writing for the refusal; and

(ii) where the appellant is on bail and the sentence imposed on his conviction is one of imprisonment, grant a warrant to apprehend and imprison him.

(2) The documents referred to in subsection (1) above are—

(a) the note of appeal lodged under section 110(1)(a) of this Act;

(b) in the case of an appeal against conviction or sentence in a sheriff court, the certified copy or, as the case may be, the record of the proceedings at the trial;

(c) where the judge who presided at the trial furnishes a report under section 113 of this Act, that report; and

(d) where, by virtue of section 94(1) of this Act, a transcript of the charge to the jury of the judge who presided at the trial is delivered to the Clerk of Justiciary, that transcript.

(3) A warrant granted under subsection (1)(b)(ii) above shall not take effect until the expiry of the period of 14 days mentioned in subsection (4) below without an application to the High Court for leave to appeal having been lodged by the appellant under that subsection.

(4) Where leave to appeal is refused under subsection (1) above the appellant may, within 14 days of intimation under subsection (10) below, apply to the High Court for leave to appeal.

(5) In deciding an application under subsection (4) above the High Court shall—

(a) if, after considering the documents mentioned in subsection (2) above and the reasons for the refusal, the court is of the opinion that there are arguable grounds of appeal, grant leave to appeal and make such comments in writing as the court considers appropriate; and

(b) in any other case—

(i) refuse leave to appeal and give reasons in writing for the refusal; and

(ii) where the appellant is on bail and the sentence imposed on his conviction is one of imprisonment, grant a warrant to apprehend and imprison him.

(6) Consideration whether to grant leave to appeal under subsection (1) or (5) above shall take place in chambers without the parties being present.

(7) Comments in writing made under subsection (1)(a) or (5)(a) above may, without prejudice to the generality of that provision, specify the arguable grounds of appeal (whether or not they are contained in the note of appeal) on the basis of which leave to appeal is granted.

(8) Where the arguable grounds of appeal are specified by virtue of subsection (7) above it shall not, except by leave of the High Court on cause shown, be competent for the appellant to found any aspect of his appeal on any ground of appeal contained in the note of appeal but not so specified.

(9) Any application by the appellant for the leave of the High Court under subsection (8) above—

(a) shall be made not less than seven days before the date fixed for the hearing of the appeal; and

(b) shall, not less that seven days before that date, be intimated by the appellant to the Crown Agent.

(10) The Clerk of Justiciary shall forthwith intimate—

(a) a decision under subsection (1) or (5) above; and

(b) in the case of a refusal of leave to appeal, the reasons for the decision, to the appellant or his solicitor and to the Crown Agent.

DEFINITIONS
"bail": s.307(1).
"High Court": s.307(1).
"judge": s.307(1).

NOTE
[1]Inserted by the Crime and Punishment (Scotland) Act 1997 (c. 48) Sched. 1, para. 21(15) with effect from August 1, 1997 in terms of the Crime and Punishment (Scotland) Act 1997 (Commencement and Transitional Provisions) Order 1997 (S.I. 1997 No. 1712) para. 3.

GENERAL NOTE

It is probably more convenient in seeking to understand the full import of this section to consider the law under the headings of, on the one hand, leave to appeal and, on the other, application for leave to appeal. Separate consideration of the hearing must be made.

Leave to appeal

The procedure of seeking leave to appeal existed prior to this change of the law to the extent that leave to appeal was required for an appeal arising out of a preliminary diet: s.76A(1) of the 1975 Act. However, under the previous law leave to appeal was not required for any appeal after conviction and now that such leave is required there can be said to have been a major change in the law.

Section 106 allows a right of appeal to any person convicted on indictment and such appeal may be against conviction or sentence or both. The right of appeal is conditional on a ground of leave to appeal by a judge of the High Court of Justiciary in terms of s.107. Before the judge can decide the grant he must have documents before him and these are specified as the note of appeal, the certified copy or actual record of proceedings for a sheriff court trial, a judge's report and a transcript of the charge to the jury by the judge, as necessary: subs. (2). Having considered these documents the judge must decide whether they disclose arguable grounds of appeal: subs. (1)(a). The action that follows such a decision depends on which way the decision goes. Before considering the alternatives the turning point requires analysis: what are "arguable grounds of appeal"?

To answer that question one might start with "High Court of Justiciary Practice Note" dated March 29, 1985 (*Renton and Brown* (6th ed.) Appendix E, at p. 726). There, judicial criticism is directed predominantly at grounds of appeal which are found in notes of appeal to be "wholly unspecific". The examples given in the Note are, first, an allegation of "misdirection" without any specification whatever. Secondly, "insufficient evidence" without any specification of the particular point, if any, which is to be taken. Examples are also given in relation to appeals against sentence where the ground of appeal is "more often than not equally uninformative" with a bare allegation of a sentence being excessive or severe.

The Practice Note indicated in terms that it was intended to remind practitioners that grounds of appeal must be stated with sufficient specification to identify the particular criticism of the conviction or sentence which the appellant hopes to present at the hearing.

It can readily be seen that appellate judges require detail in the grounds of appeal such as allows some insight as to the appellant's complaint. Detail alone may not take matters far: although the allegation of a miscarriage of justice is the only ground of appeal, there are various particular grounds of appeal, which are commonly advanced as a basis for the conclusion that there has been a miscarriage of justice.

Lord McCluskey in *Criminal Appeals* (1992) at pp. 177–189 discusses some of the possible types or categories of appeal: it may be that there is alleged to have been a misdirection by the presiding judge (by omission, with an error of law, or regarding corroboration), that the conduct of the trial judge, the prosecutor or the defence advocate was improper, that the proceedings were incompetent or that there were some other irregularities. There are ample precedents for all these allegations. In short, "arguable grounds of appeal" are such to indicate, in Lord McCluskey's words, *ibid.* at p. 177, "clarity, accuracy, brevity and comprehensiveness" and which invite a conclusion that there has been in law a miscarriage of justice.

The judge of the High Court of Justiciary who will consider the documents to decide whether they disclose arguable grounds of appeal does so in chambers without the parties being present: s.107(6). If the judge considers that the documents do disclose arguable grounds of appeal he then grants leave to appeal and he makes such comments in writing as he considers appropriate: s.107(1)(a). If the judge considers that the documents do not disclose arguable grounds of appeal he then refuses leave to appeal and he gives reasons in writing for the refusal: subs. (1)(b)(i).

The appellant, who is at this stage on bail and who had a sentence of imprisonment imposed on conviction, will then be the subject of a warrant to apprehend granted by the judge and on implementation the appellant will be imprisoned: subs. (1)(b)(ii).

The warrant to apprehend and imprison under subs. (1)(b)(ii) shall not take effect until the expiry of the period of 14 days during which period the appellant may, in effect, appeal by making an application to the High Court of Justiciary: subs. (4). If no such application is to be made then the appellant's solicitor has the time available to arrange for the client to surrender to the warrant.

Application for leave to appeal

There can be no doubt that this change in law will end any practice, if there is one, of lodging broad and vague grounds of appeal against conviction or sentence to be supplemented with speculative advocacy before the appellate judges. A clear ground will require to be formulated at a far earlier point in the procedure.

There are no statutory grounds for the reason for, in effect, appealing the decision of the single judge in chambers. The provision merely states that if leave to appeal is refused under subs. (1) then the appellant may within 14 days of intimation apply to the High Court of Justiciary for leave to appeal against the original conviction or sentence or both: subs. (4).

Who decides the application in terms of subs. (4) depends on what is at issue, namely, on appeal against conviction, sentence or conviction and sentence. By s.103(2) "for the purpose of hearing and determining any appeal or other proceeding under this Part of this Act" the quorum is three judges, except that by s.103(3) for appeals against sentence alone the quorum is two judges.

The various judges of the High Court of Justiciary who must consider the documents to decide whether they disclose arguable grounds of appeal do so in chambers without the parties being present: subs. (6).

In deciding the application the judges must consider the documents that had been before the single judge in chambers and also consider the reasons for the earlier refusal but thereafter, if the court is of the opinion that there are arguable grounds of appeal, then the court should grant leave to appeal and make such comments in writing as the court considers appropriate: subs. (5)(a). In any other case, leave to appeal will be refused with reasons in writing and a warrant to apprehend and imprison is to be granted if appropriate: subs. (5)(b).

In *Connolly Petr.*, 1997 S.C.C.R. 205 it was held that it was incompetent to invoke the *nobile officium* where an application in terms of s.107(4) was not lodged timeously.

Hearing of appeal

Regard must be paid to the comments in writing made either by the single judge in chambers by subs. (1)(a) or by a greater number of judges in chambers by subs. (5)(a). The importance of the comments in writing lies in the possibility that they "may specify the arguable grounds of appeal (whether or not they are contained in the note of appeal) on the basis of which leave to appeal is granted": subs. (7).

It is very easy to imagine on the wording of subs. (1)(a) a single judge in chambers granting leave to appeal, not on the original grounds in the note of appeal, but on the basis of comments in writing which amend, alter or distil the original grounds in the note of appeal. The new grounds of appeal, having been specified, in effect dictate the ground of appeal to be argued at the hearing: subs. (8).

The appellant who wishes to found any aspect of his appeal on any ground of appeal contained in the note of appeal but not so specified in the comments in writing provided under subs. (1)(a) or subs. (5)(a) may seek leave of the High Court of Justiciary to do so: subs. (8). Application for such leave under subs. (8) must be made not less than seven days before the date fixed for the hearing of the appeal: subs. (9). It is not immediately clear from a reading of the statute as to whom an application under subs. (8) will be directed. As it is not so much an appeal as a request to broaden an approach to an appeal it may simply be returned to those who made the comments in writing under subss. (1)(a) or (5)(a).

In *Milne v. H.M. Adocate*, 1998 G.W.D. 17–848, the Appeal Court held that in determining the appeal it was irrelevant that the sifting judge considered the matter arguable.

Lord Advocate's right of appeal against disposal

[1]**108.**—(1) Where a person has been convicted on indictment, the Lord Advocate may, in accordance with subsection (2) below, appeal against any of the following disposals, namely—

  (a) a sentence passed on conviction;
  (b) a decision under section 209(1)(b) of this Act not to make a supervised release order;
  (c) a decision under section 234A(2) of this Act not to make a non-harassment order;
  (d) a probation order;
  (e) a community service order;
  (f) a decision to remit to the Principal Reporter made under section 49(1)(a) of this Act;
  (g) an order deferring sentence;
  (h) an admonition; or
  (i) an absolute discharge.

(2) An appeal under subsection (1) above may be made—

(a) on a point of law;
(b) where it appears to the Lord Advocate, in relation to an appeal under—
- (i) paragraph (a), (h) or (i) of that subsection, that the disposal was unduly lenient;
- (ii) paragraph (b) or (c) of that subsection, that the decision not to make the order in question was inappropriate;
- (iii) paragraph (d) or (e) of that subsection, that the making of the order concerned was unduly lenient or was on unduly lenient terms;
- (iv) under paragraph (f) of that subsection, that the decision to remit was inappropriate;
- (v) under paragraph (g) of that subsection, that the deferment of sentence was inappropriate or was on unduly lenient conditions.

NOTE
[1]Substituted by the Crime and Punishment (Scotland) Act 1997 (c. 48), s.21 with effect from August 1, 1997 in terms of the Crime and Punishment (Scotland) Act 1997 (Commencement and Transitional Provisions) Order 1997 (S.I. 1997 No. 1712) para. 3.

DEFINITIONS
"community service order": s.238.
"indictment": s.307(1).
"probation order": s.228.

GENERAL NOTE
As there was no tariff for sentences in the criminal courts of Scotland the selection of the appropriate sentence was clearly a matter for the individual discretion of the sentencer: *Strawhorn v. Mcleod*, 1987 S.C.C.R. 413. The present Act invites the High Court of Justiciary, in appropriate circumstances, to pronounce an opinion on the sentence or other disposal or order which is appropriate in any similar case: ss.118(7) and 189(7). The Crown can appeal on a point of law (*e.g. H.M. Advocate v. Foley*, 1999 G.W.D. 17–788) or on the ground that the sentence or other disposal is either unduly lenient or inappropriate as provided in subsection (2).

The Crown right of appeal against an unduly lenient sentence can only proceed in circumstances where "it appears" that a sentence is unduly lenient: s.228A of the 1975 Act as amended, and now s.108 of the present Act. A new reorganised s.108 was introduced by section 21(1) of the Crime and Punishment (Scotland) Act 1997 with effect from August 1, 1997. It introduces a right of appeal by the Lord Advocate against decisions by a court not to make a supervised release order; non harassment order and decision to remit to the principal Reporter. The right to bring an appeal under this section entitles the Crown to take an interest in sentencing which they did not have before—*H.M. Advocate v. McKinlay*, 1998 S.C.C.R. 201.

The first appeal taken by the Crown was successful: see *H.M. Advocate v. McPhee*, 1994 S.C.C.R. 830. There have been a number of appeals since then and the Appeal Court has indicated that a high standard of care and accuracy is expected of the Crown who do not require leave to appeal: see *H.M. Advocate v. Mackay*, 1996 S.C.C.R. 410; *H.M. Advocate v. Ross*, 1996 S.C.C.R. 107 and *H.M. Advocate v. Wallace*, 1999 S.C.C.R. 309. The grounds of appeal must be specific although the Appeal Court have allowed amendments to same: see *H.M. Advocate v. Lee*, 1996 S.C.C.R. 205. In *Mackay, supra*, the court deplored the Crown's seeking to abandon the appeal at the hearing.

Furthermore the Crown must ensure that if they challenge a sentence as being unduly lenient the basis for the challenge has properly been laid in the trial court: see *H.M. Advocate v. Bennett*, 1996 S.C.C.R. 331. If the Crown seek to maintain a sentence was unduly lenient because due consideration had not been given to a particular factor by a trial judge then the Crown have to show that the factor was fully drawn to the trial judge's attention: see *H.M. Advocate v. Donaldson*, 1997 S.C.C.R. 738. Relevant factors to be taken into account in the determination of such appeals are the forum in which the Crown choose to proceed—see *H.M. Advocate v. Robertson*, 1997 G.W.D. 5–187; the nature of any pleas accepted by the Crown: see *H.M. Advocate v. Campbell*, 1997 S.L.T. 354 and if a non custodial option was imposed whether or not it was complied with—*H.M. Advocate v. Jamieson*, 1996 S.C.C.R. 836; *H.M. Advocate v. Carnall*, 1999 G.W.D. 31–1485; *H.M. Advocate v. Paterson*, 2000 S.C.C.R. 309; *H.M. Advocate v. Drain*, 2000 S.C.C.R. 256 but *cf. H.M. Advocate v. McKinlay*, 1998 S.C.C.R. 201. The Crown are not specifically entitled to ask for a deterrent sentence—*H.M. Advocate v. McKinlay, supra*.

Before the Appeal Court will interfere with a sentence it must be unduly lenient or inappropriate as provided by the section. Unduly lenient was defined in *H.M. Advocate v. Bell*, 1995 S.C.C.R. 244 and *H.M. Advocate v. O'Donnell*, 1995 S.C.C.R. 745 namely "The sentence must be seen to be unduly lenient. That means that it must fall outside the range of sentences which the judge at first instance, applying his mind to all the relevant factors, could reasonably have considered appropriate". It was held in *H.M. Advocate v. Carnall*, 1999 G.W.D. 31–1485 even if the Appeal Court considered that an order was unduly lenient the court still has a discretion in terms of s.118(4) as to the course to adopt in determining disposal of the appeal. Due weight will be given by the Appeal Court to the views of the trial judge especially where he has had the advantage of seeing and hearing all the evidence—*H.M. Advocate v. Wheldon*, 1998 S.C.C.R. 710. Lord Johnstone in that case described the task facing the Crown in such appeals as "formidable".

In *H.M. Advocate v. Lee supra* the court observed that although it was not the practice of the Appeal Court to lay down sentencing guidelines decisions of the Appeal Court in appeals against sentence especially unduly lenient sentence appeals do from time to time provide guidelines as to what is or is not appropriate and that a judge who fails to take account of that guidance cannot be said to have acted within the proper limits of his discretion as a sentencer: see *H.M. Advocate v. Lee, supra*. Section 197 of this Act now provides that a court in passing sentence shall have regard to any relevant opinion pronounced in terms of sections 118(7) or 189(7). The question of setting down minimum sentences was rejected in *H.M. Advocate v. Mackay, supra*.

Guidelines can be found in *H.M. Advocate v. Brough*, 1996 S.C.C.R. 377 (lewd and libidinous practices; teacher; custodial sentence well nigh inevitable); *H.M. Advocate v. McPhee*, 1994 S.C.C.R. 830 (supply of Class A drug to teenage girls; custodial sentences must be imposed); *H.M. Advocate v. Fallan*, 1996 S.C.C.R. 80 (unprovoked sexual attack on stranger in street at night; custodial sentence should normally be imposed); *H.M. Advocate v. Lee*, 1996 S.C.C.R. 205 (being concerned in the supply of a Class A drug; substantial custodial sentence will be inevitable) and *H.M. Advocate v. Carnall, supra; H.M. Advocate v. Jamieson*, 1996 S.C.C.R. 836 (assault to severe injury and danger of life; only in an unusual case should the court refrain from imposing custodial sentence) see also *H.M. Advocate v. Smith*, 1998 S.C.C.R. 637; *H.M. Advocate v. Spiers*, 1997 G.W.D. 23–1157 (a custodial sentence was the only appropriate disposal where an assault occurred by stabbing with a broken bottle). The Appeal Court declined to set down a minimum sentence for culpable homicide where death was caused by kicking—*H.M. Advocate v. Wheldon, supra*. The Appeal Court has also provided guidelines in appeals under this section as to factors that a judge is entitled to take into account in determining sentence. The fact that an accused pled guilty to a reduced charge is a mitigatory factor which a judge can take into account—*H.M. Advocate v. Brand*, 1998 S.C.C.R. 71. A judge is not obliged to take account of an early plea of guilty but is entitled to give it the weight appropriate in the circumstances—*H.M. Advocate v. Forrest*, 1998 S.C.C.R. 153. In cases involving kicking and punching it is appropriate for a sentencing judge to have regard to the nature of the conduct in determining whether an attack is violent and savage rather than the resulting injuries—*H.M. Advocate v. Allan*, 2000 S.C.C.R. 219. For other Crown appeals see *H.M. Advocate v. Gordon and Foy*, 1996 S.C.C.R. 274; *H.M. Advocate v. McColl*, 1996 S.C.C.R. 523; *H.M. Advocate v. Callaghan*, 1996 S.C.C.R. 709; *H.M. Advocate v. McPherson*, 1996 S.C.C.R. 802; *H.M. Advocate v. Campbell*, 1997 S.L.T. 354; *H.M. Advocate v. McC.*, 1996 S.C.C.R. 842; *H.M. Advocate v. McK.*, 1996 S.C.C.R. 866; *H.M. Advocate v. M.*, 1997 S.L.T. 359; *H.M. Advocate v. Scottish Hydro Electric plc*, 1997 S.L.T. 359 and *H.M. Advocate v. Speirs* 1997 S.C.C.R. 479; *H.M. Advocate v. Hodgson*, 1998 S.C.C.R. 320; *H.M. Advocate v. Heron*, 1998 S.C.C.R. 449 and *H.M. Advocate v. Carpenter*, 1998 S.C.C.R. 706; *H.M. Advocate v. Duff*, 1999 S.C.C.R. 193; *H.M. Advocate v. Davidson*, 1999 S.C.C.R. 729; *H.M. Advocate v. Millard*, 2000 G.W.D. 25–939 and *H.M. Advocate v. Briody*, 2000 G.W.D. 29–1138.

The Crown has a right under s.121A to seek suspension of a probation order, community service order, supervised attendance order and restriction of liberty order pending determination of the appeal. Failure to exercise this right is a factor which the Appeal Court will take into account in determining appeals against sentence by the Crown—*H.M. Advocate v. Carnall, supra*.

Lord Advocate's appeal against decision not to impose automatic sentence in certain cases

[1]**108A.** Where the court has exercised the power conferred by section 205A(3) or 205B(3) of this Act, the Lord Advocate may appeal against that decision.

NOTE
[1]Inserted by the Crime and Punishment (Scotland) Act 1997 (c. 48), s.18(2) with effect from October 20, 1997 in terms of the Crime and Punishment (Scotland) Act 1997 (Commencement No. 2 and Transitional Provisions) Order 1997 (S.I. 1997 No. 2323) Art. 3, Sched. 1; as amended by the Crime and Disorder Act 1998 (c. 37), Sched. 8, para. 120 (effective September 30, 1998: S.I. 1998 No. 2327).

GENERAL NOTE
Some account of the origins of this involved section has to be attempted; it involves a provision on the statute book not brought into force, a provision now live and a third which has been repealed without ever coming into force.

Section 108A was introduced into the 1995 Act by the Crime and Punishment (Scotland) Act 1997 (c. 48), s.18(2) to afford the Lord Advocate a specific right of appeal against the court's decision not to impose: (i) an automatic life sentence on conviction of a qualifying offence (s.205A of the 1995 Act as prospectively inserted by the 1997 Act s.1); (ii) an automatic minimum sentence on a third solemn conviction for drug trafficking (s.205B of the 1995 Act as now in force); or (iii) a supervised release order on conviction of a qualifying offence (s.209 of the 1995 Act as prospectively substituted by s.4 of the 1997 Act).

To date only the second provision, s.205B has been brought into force but it remains open for the regime of automatic life sentences to be activated should this be desired. The 1998 amendment to s.108A takes account of the fact that s.4 of the 1997 Act has been repealed; see Sched. 10 of the 1998 Act.

Intimation of intention to appeal

109.—(1) Subject to section 111(2) of this Act and to section 10 of the Proceeds of Crime (Scotland) Act 1995 (postponed confiscation orders), where a person desires to appeal under section 106(1)(a) or (f) of this Act, he shall within two weeks of the final determination of the proceedings, lodge with the Clerk of Justiciary written intimation of intention to appeal which shall identify the proceedings and be in as nearly as may be the form prescribed by Act of Adjournal.

(2) A copy of intimation given under subsection (1) above shall be sent to the Crown Agent.

(3) On intimation under subsection (1) above being lodged by a person in custody, the Clerk of Justiciary shall give notice of the intimation to the Secretary of State.

(4) Subject to subsection (5) below, for the purposes of subsection (1) above and section 106(5) to (7) of this Act, proceedings shall be deemed finally determined on the day on which sentence is passed in open court.

(5) Where in relation to an appeal under section 106(1)(a) of this Act sentence is deferred under section 202 of this Act, the proceedings shall be deemed finally determined on the day on which sentence is first so deferred in open court.

(6) Without prejudice to section 10 of the said Act of 1995, the reference in subsection (4) above to "the day on which sentence is passed in open court" shall, in relation to any case in which, under subsection (1) of that section, a decision has been postponed for a period, be construed as a reference to the day on which that decision is made, whether or not a confiscation order is then made or any other sentence is then passed.

DEFINITIONS
"Clerk of Justiciary": s.307(1).
"sentence": s.307(1).

GENERAL NOTE
It is crucial to recall that the right of appeal under s.106(1) relates to all convictions on indictment. It is as important to know that all appeals following conviction on indictment are initiated in the justiciary office and not in the sheriff court. The intimation of an intention to appeal required under this section is important for it gives an office in Edinburgh notice of an appeal from a trial that may have occurred in any one of the sheriff courts of Scotland or one of the towns where the High Court has been on circuit. Those who may be required to produce

notes or reports can thus be put on notice. Where there are several accused on one indictment the trial of all of them must be brought to a finality before any one of them can exercise the right of appeal: see *Evans, Petr.*, 1991 S.C.C.R. 160.

Once an intimation to appeal against conviction is lodged a transcript of the charge to the jury will be ordered to enable the grounds of appeal to be prepared. The unavailabilty of the transcript will not necessarily result in the appeal being allowed. Prejudice must be shown—*Carroll v. H.M. Advocate*, 1999 S.C.C.R. 616.

Note of appeal

110.—(1) Subject to section 111(2) of this Act—

[1](a) within six weeks of lodging intimation of intention to appeal or, in the case of an appeal under section 106(1)(b) to (e) of this Act, within two weeks of the appropriate date (being, and the case may be, the date on which sentence was passed, the order disposing of the case was made, sentence was deferred or the previous conviction was quashed as mentioned in section 106A(1)(c) or (2)(c) of this Act) (or, as the case may be, of the making of the order disposing of the case or deferring sentence) in open court, the convicted person may lodge a written note of appeal with the Clerk of Justiciary who shall send a copy to the judge who presided at the trial and to the Crown Agent; or, as the case may be,

(b) within four weeks of the passing of the sentence in open court, the Lord Advocate may lodge such a note with the Clerk of Justiciary, who shall send a copy to the said judge and to the convicted person or that person's solicitor.

(2) The period of six weeks mentioned in paragraph (a) of subsection (1) above may be extended, before it expires, by the Clerk of Justiciary.

(3) A note of appeal shall—

(a) identify the proceedings;

(b) contain a full statement of all the grounds of appeal; and

(c) be in as nearly as may be the form prescribed by Act of Adjournal.

(4) Except by leave of the High Court on cause shown, it shall not be competent for an appellant to found any aspect of his appeal on a ground not contained in the note of appeal.

(5) Subsection (4) above shall not apply as respects any ground of appeal specified as an arguable ground of appeal by virtue of subsection (7) of section 107 of this Act.

(6) On a note of appeal under section 106(1)(b) to (e) of this Act being lodged by an appellant in custody the Clerk of Justiciary shall give notice of that fact to the Secretary of State.

DEFINITIONS
"Clerk of Justiciary": s.307(1).
"judge": s.307(1).

NOTE
[1]As amended by the Crime and Punishment (Scotland) Act 1997 (c. 48), s.19(2) with effect from October 20, 1997 in terms of the Crime and Punishment (Scotland) Act 1997 (Commencement No. 2 and Transitional Provisions) Order 1997 (S.I. 1997 No. 2323) Art. 3, Sched. 1.

GENERAL NOTE
Three periods of time are envisaged by this section. First, for all solemn appeals against conviction or conviction and sentence written intimation of intention to appeal should be lodged within two weeks of the final determination with the Clerk of Justiciary by s.109(1). Thereafter a convicted person has six weeks to lodge a written note of appeal. Alternatively, and secondly, if the appeal is only against sentence then the period is two weeks from the date sentence was passed, or order disposing of the case was made, or sentence deferred etc.: subs. (1)(a). It is clear that if conviction is accepted fewer papers are required and less preparatory work is necessary. Thirdly, if the Crown wishes to appeal (against, for example, what appears to be an unduly lenient sentence) a note of appeal must be lodged within four weeks: subs. (1)(b).

Those lodging notes of appeal must have regard to two important points. The note of appeal must contain a full statement of all the grounds of appeal: subs. (3)(b). There are a number of reported cases that emphasise the importance of specification; see, for example, *Mitchell v. H.M. Advocate*, 1991 S.C.C.R. 216. *Smith v. H.M. Advocate*, 1983 S.C.C.R. 30: *Lindsay v. H.M. Advocate*, 1993 S.C.C.R. 868, and *McGregor v. H.M. Advocate*, 1996 G.W.D. 9–471. If the grounds of appeal are deficient the presiding judge may be unable to fully comment on the appeal—*MacLeay v. H.M. Advocate*, 2000 G.W.D. 8–278. In *H.M. Advocate v. Bagan*, 1996 G.W.D. 29–1734 the court observed that there was a professional responsibility to ensure that grounds of appeal were formulated which had a sound basis in fact. The importance is accentuated by the new requirement to disclose arguable grounds of appeal in the note of appeal for the consideration of a single judge in chambers to obtain leave to appeal: s.107(1)(a) and (2)(a).

Further, it is not competent, except by leave of the High Court of Justiciary on cause shown, for an appellant to found any aspect of his appeal on a ground not contained in the note of appeal: subs. (4). The narrow approach is also emphasised earlier in the Act: s.107(8). If a ground of appeal is abandoned it cannot be resurrected at a later stage—*McGinty v. H.M. Advocate*, 2000 S.C.C.R. 394.

Subsection (1) has been amended by section 19(2) of the Crime and Punishment (Scotland) Act 1997 with effect from October 20, 1997 to take account of the provisions in section 106A that an accused can appeal against sentence where he no longer qualifies for an automatic sentence. He has two weeks from the sentence being quashed to appeal.

Provisions supplementary to sections 109 and 110

111.—(1) Where the last day of any period mentioned in sections 109(1) and 110(1) of this Act falls on a day on which the office of the Clerk of Justiciary is closed, such period shall extend to and include the next day on which such office is open.

(2) Any period mentioned in section 109(1) or 110(1)(a) of this Act may be extended at any time by the High Court in respect of any convicted person; and an application for such extension may be made under this subsection and shall be in as nearly as may be the form prescribed by Act of Adjournal.

DEFINITIONS
"Clerk of Justiciary": s.307(1).
"High Court": s.307(1).

GENERAL NOTE
For examples of extensions considered, see *Spence v. H.M. Advocate*, 1945 J.C. 65 and *Birrell v. H.M. Advocate*, 1993 S.C.C.R. 812. See *Grant v. H.M. Advocate*, 1996 G.W.D. 19–1077—an appeal against refusal to extend the time.

Admission of appellant to bail

112.—(1) Subject to subsection (2) below, the High Court may, if it thinks fit, on the application of a convicted person, admit him to bail pending the determination of—
  (a) his appeal; or
  [1](b) any relevant appeal by the Lord Advocate under section 108 or 108A of this Act.
(2) The High Court shall not admit a convicted person to bail under subsection (1) above unless—
  (a) where he is the appellant and has not lodged a note of appeal in accordance with section 110(1)(a) of this Act, the application for bail states reasons why it should be granted and sets out the proposed grounds of appeal; or
  (b) where the Lord Advocate is the appellant, the application for bail states reasons why it should be granted,
and, in either case, the High Court considers there to be exceptional circumstances justifying admitting the convicted person to bail.
(3) A person who is admitted to bail under subsection (1) above shall,

unless the High Court otherwise directs, appear personally in court on the day or days fixed for the hearing of the appeal.

(4) Where an appellant fails to appear personally in court as mentioned in subsection (3) above, the court may—

    (a) if he is the appellant—

        (i) decline to consider the appeal; and

        (ii) dismiss it summarily; or

    (b) whether or not he is the appellant—

        (i) consider and determine the appeal; or

        (ii) without prejudice to section 27 of this Act, make such other order as the court thinks fit.

(5) For the purposes of subsections (1), (3) and (4) above, "appellant" includes not only a person who has lodged a note of appeal but also one who has lodged an intimation of intention to appeal.

[2](6) Subject to subsection (7) below, the High Court may, if it thinks fit, on the application of a convicted person, admit him to bail pending the determination of any appeal under paragraph 13(a) of Schedule 6 to the Scotland Act 1998 and the disposal of the proceedings by the High Court thereafter.

[2](7) The High Court shall not admit a convicted person to bail under subsection (6) above unless the application for bail states reasons why it should be granted and the High Court considers there to be exceptional circumstances justifying admitting the convicted person to bail.

[2](8) A person who is admitted to bail under subsection (6) above shall, unless the High Court otherwise directs, appear personally in the High Court at any subsequent hearing in the High Court in relation to the proceedings; and if he fails to do so the court may, without prejudice to section 27 of this Act, make such order as it thinks fit.

DEFINITIONS

    "appellant": s.112(5).

    "bail": s.307(1).

    "High Court": s.307(1).

NOTES

[1]As amended by the Crime and Punishment (Scotland) Act 1997 (c. 48), s.18(3) with effect from October 20, 1997 in terms of the Crime and Punishment (Scotland) Act 1997 (Commencement No. 2 and Transitional Provisions) Order 1997 (S.I. 1997 No. 2323) Art. 3, Sched. 1.

[2]Inserted by the Scotland Act 1998 (Consequential Modifications) (No.1) Order 1999 (S.I. 1999 No.1042) art.3, Sched.1, para.13 (effective May 6, 1999).

GENERAL NOTE

This section follows earlier authorities that allowed the High Court of Justiciary, if it thought fit, to admit an appellant to bail pending determination of the appeal. It is, however, for the appellant to show cause why he should be admitted to bail: *Young v. H.M. Advocate*, 1946 J.C. 5. The Appeal Court in *Ogilvie Petr.*, 1998 S.C.C.R. 187, held that there was no rule that bail could only be granted under this section in exceptional circumstances, thereby clarifying any doubts arising from *Young, supra*. The mere fact, however, that a person has been given leave to appeal is not in itself sufficient to show cause why bail should be granted. It is just another factor to be taken into account, *e.g.* the prospects of success of the appeal.

With effect from October 20, 1997 section 112(1)(b) has been extended to allow a convicted person to be admitted to bail pending appeal by the Lord Advocate against a decision to appeal against the failure to impose a minimum sentence in terms of s.205B.

Judge's report

113.—(1) As soon as is reasonably practicable after receiving the copy note of appeal sent to him under section 110(1) of this Act, the judge who presided at the trial shall furnish the Clerk of Justiciary with a written report giving the judge's opinion on the case generally and on the grounds contained in the note of appeal.

(2) The Clerk of Justiciary shall send a copy of the judge's report—

(a) to the convicted person or his solicitor;

(b) to the Crown Agent; and

[1](c) in a case referred under Part XA of this Act, to the Commission.

(3) Where the judge's report is not furnished as mentioned in subsection (1) above, the High Court may call for the report to be furnished within such period as it may specify or, if it thinks fit, hear and determine the appeal without the report.

(4) Subject to subsection (2) above, the report of the judge shall be available only to the High Court, the parties and, on such conditions as may be prescribed by Act of Adjournal, such other persons or classes of persons as may be so prescribed.

DEFINITIONS

"Clerk of Justiciary": s.307(1).
"High Court": s.307(1).
"judge": s.307(1).

NOTE

[1]As amended by the Crime and Punishment (Scotland) Act 1997, Sched. 1, para. 21(16) (effective April 1, 1999: S.I. 1999 No. 652).

GENERAL NOTE

In *McLaren v. H.M. Advocate*, 1994 S.C.C.R. 855 the Appeal Court observed that where more than one accused has appealed against conviction or sentence the trial judge should prepare separate reports and it is desirable these be self-contained and set out points the judge considers appropriate in response to the grounds of appeal.

Where the ground of appeal is based on the wrongful rejection of a no case to answer submission the form of the judge's report should be as set out in *Horne v. H.M. Advocate*, 1991 S.C.C.R. 248 and *Vetters v. H.M. Advocate*, 1994 S.C.C.R. 305. It was observed in *McPhelim v. H.M. Advocate*, 1996 S.C.C.R. 647 that judges should comment on all grounds of appeal and not just those raising questions of fact. Delay by a trial judge in producing a report for the Appeal Court was only one factor to be considered in assessing the issue of reasonable time in terms of article 6—*H.M. Advocate v. McGlinchey*, 2000 S.C.C.R. 593.

Applications made orally or in writing

114. Subject to any provision of this Part of this Act to the contrary, any application to the High Court may be made by the appellant or respondent as the case may be or by counsel on his behalf, orally or in writing.

DEFINITIONS

"appellant": s.132.
"High Court": s.307(1).

Presentation of appeal in writing

115.—(1) If an appellant, other than the Lord Advocate, desires to present his case and his argument in writing instead of orally he shall, at least four days before the diet fixed for the hearing of the appeal—

(a) intimate this desire to the Clerk of Justiciary;

(b) lodge with the Clerk of Justiciary three copies of his case and argument; and

(c) send a copy of the intimation, case and argument to the Crown Agent.

(2) Any case or argument presented as mentioned in subsection (1) above shall be considered by the High Court.

(3) Unless the High Court otherwise directs, the respondent shall not

make a written reply to a case and argument presented as mentioned in subsection (1) above, but shall reply orally at the diet fixed for the hearing of the appeal.

(4) Unless the High Court otherwise allows, an appellant who has presented his case and argument in writing shall not be entitled to submit in addition an oral argument to the court in support of the appeal.

DEFINITIONS
"appellant": s.132.
"Clerk of Justiciary": s.307(1).
"High Court": s.307(1).

GENERAL NOTE
It is interesting to note the willingness of the Appeal Court in certain cases to entertain written submissions both from appellants and the Lord Advocate: see *Anderson v. H.M. Advocate*, 1996 S.C.C.R. 114. In *Campbell v. H.M. Advocate*, 1998 S.C.C.R. 214, the court ordered the Crown to lodge a written history of the case.

Abandonment of appeal

116.—(1) An appellant may abandon his appeal by lodging with the Clerk of Justiciary a notice of abandonment in as nearly as may be the form prescribed by Act of Adjournal; and on such notice being lodged the appeal shall be deemed to have been dismissed by the court.

[1](2) A person who has appealed against both conviction and sentence (or, as the case may be, against both conviction and a decision such as is mentioned in section 106(1)(bb) or both conviction and disposal or order) may abandon the appeal in so far as it is against conviction and may proceed with it against sentence (or, as the case may be, decision, disposal or order) alone.

DEFINITIONS
"appellant": s.132.
"Clerk of Justiciary": s.307(1).
"sentence": s.132.

NOTE
[1]As amended by the Crime and Punishment (Scotland) Act 1997 (c. 48), s.18(4) with effect from October 20, 1997 in terms of the Crime and Punishment (Scotland) Act 1997 (Commencement No. 2 and Transitional Provisions) Order 1997 (S.I. 1997 No. 2323) Art. 3, Sched. 1.

GENERAL NOTE
In *Ferguson, Petr.*, 1980 S.L.T. 21 the petitioner made a motion to abandon the appeal at the calling of the case before the Appeal Court. The court refused the motion and increased the sentence. At the hearing of a subsequent petition to the nobile officium the court indicated that formal abandonment under the then s.244 of the Criminal Procedure (Scotland) Act 1975 could be made at any time prior to the calling of the case by the Appeal Court, but if not done any oral motion to abandon is subject to the discretion of the court. See also *West v. H.M. Advocate*, 1955 S.L.T. 425.
Where a Notice of Abandonment has been lodged the competent mode of reinstating the appeal is by petition to the nobile officium: see *Young, Petr.*, 1994 S.L.T. 269 and *McIntosh, Petr.*, 1995 S.C.C.R. 327.
The Crown seeking to abandon an appeal against an unduly lenient sentence at the hearing was deplored in the case of *H.M. Advocate v. Mackay*: see s.108, *supra*.
An appellant who has appealed against conviction and the imposition of a minimum sentence may abandon the appeal against conviction and proceed only with the appeal against sentence—s.18(4) of the Crime and Punishment (Scotland) Act 1997.

Presence of appellant or applicant at hearing

117.—(1) Where an appellant or applicant is in custody the Clerk of Justiciary shall notify—

(a) the appellant or applicant;

(b) the Governor of the prison in which the appellant or applicant then is; and

(c) the Secretary of State,

of the probable day on which the appeal or application will be heard.

(2) The Secretary of State shall take steps to transfer the appellant or applicant to a prison convenient for his appearance before the High Court at such reasonable time before the hearing as shall enable him to consult his legal adviser, if any.

(3) A convicted appellant, notwithstanding that he is in custody, shall be entitled to be present if he desires it, at the hearing of his appeal.

(4) When an appellant or applicant is to be present at any diet—

(a) before the High Court or any judge of that court; or

(b) for the taking of additional evidence before a person appointed for that purpose under section 104(1)(b) of this Act, or

(c) for an examination or investigation by a special commissioner in terms of section 104(1)(d) of this Act,

the Clerk of Justiciary shall give timeous notice to the Secretary of State, in the form prescribed by Act of Adjournal or as nearly as may be in such form.

(5) A notice under subsection (4) above shall be sufficient warrant to the Secretary of State for transmitting the appellant or applicant in custody from prison to the place where the diet mentioned in that subsection or any subsequent diet is to be held and for reconveying him to prison at the conclusion of such diet.

(6) The appellant or applicant shall appear at any diet mentioned in subsection (4) above in ordinary civilian clothes.

(7) Where the Lord Advocate is the appellant, subsections (1) to (6) above shall apply in respect of the convicted person, if in custody, as they apply to an appellant or applicant in custody.

(8) The Secretary of State shall, on notice under subsection (4) above from the Clerk of Justiciary, ensure that sufficient male and female prison officers attend each sitting of the court, having regard to the list of appeals for the sitting.

(9) When the High Court fixes the date for the hearing of an appeal or of an application under section 111(2) of this Act, the Clerk of Justiciary shall give notice to the Crown Agent and to the solicitor of the convicted person, or to the convicted person himself if he has no known solicitor.

DEFINITIONS

"appellant": s.132.
"Clerk of Justiciary": s.307(1).
"diet": s.307(1).
"governor": s.307(1).
"High Court": s.307(1).
"judge": s.307(1).

GENERAL NOTE

An appellant who is in custody need not be present at his appeal hearing: see *Manuel v. H.M. Advocate*, 1958 J.C. 41 where the accused accepted counsel's advice that it was not in his best interest to be there. However if an appellant does wish to be present subsection (3) entitles him to be there.

Disposal of appeals

118.—(1) The High Court may, subject to subsection (4) below, dispose of an appeal against conviction by—

(a) affirming the verdict of the trial court;
(b) setting aside the verdict of the trial court and either quashing the conviction or, subject to subsection (2) below, substituting therefor an amended verdict of guilty; or
(c) setting aside the verdict of the trial court and quashing the conviction and granting authority to bring a new prosecution in accordance with section 119 of this Act.

(2) An amended verdict of guilty substituted under subsection (1) above must be one which could have been returned on the indictment before the trial court.

(3) In setting aside, under subsection (1) above, a verdict the High Court may quash any sentence imposed on the appellant (or, as the case may be, any disposal or order made) as respects the indictment, and—

(a) in a case where it substitutes an amended verdict of guilty, whether or not the sentence (or disposal or order) related to the verdict set aside; or
(b) in any other case, where the sentence (or disposal or order) did not so relate,

may pass another (but not more severe) sentence or make another (but not more severe) disposal or order in substitution for the sentence, disposal or order so quashed.

(4) The High Court may, subject to subsection (5) below, dispose of an appeal against sentence by—

(a) affirming such sentence; or
¹(b) if the Court thinks that, having regard to all the circumstances, including any evidence such as is mentioned in section 106(3) of this Act, a different sentence should have been passed, quashing the sentence and passing another sentence whether more or less severe in substitution therefor,

and, in this subsection, "appeal against sentence" shall, without prejudice to the generality of the expression, be construed as including an appeal under section 106(1)(bb) to (e), and any appeal under section 108, of this Act; and other references to sentence shall be construed accordingly.

²(4A) On an appeal under section 108A of this Act, the High Court may dispose of the appeal—

(a) by affirming the decision and any sentence or order passed;
(b) where it is of the opinion mentioned in section 205A(3) or, as the case may be, 205B(3) of this Act but it considers that a different sentence or order should have been passed, by affirming the decision but quashing any sentence or order passed and passing another sentence or order whether more or less severe in substitution therefor; or
(c) in any other case, by setting aside the decision appealed against and any sentence or order passed by the trial court and where the decision appealed against was taken under—
(i) subsection (3) of section 205A of this Act, by passing the sentence mentioned in subsection (2) of that section;
(ii) subsection (3) of section 205B of this Act, by passing a sentence of imprisonment of at least the length mentioned in subsection (2) of that section; or
(iii) [*Repealed by the 1998 Act, Sched. 8, para. 121.*]

(5) In relation to any appeal under section 106(1) of this Act, the High Court shall, where it appears to it that the appellant committed the act charged against him but that he was insane when he did so, dispose of the appeal by—

(a) setting aside the verdict of the trial court and substituting therefor a verdict of acquittal on the ground of insanity; and
(b) quashing any sentence imposed on the appellant (or disposal or order made) as respects the indictment and—

(i) making, in respect of the appellant, any order mentioned in section 57(2)(a) to (d) of this Act; or

(ii) making no order.

(6) Subsections (3) and (4) of section 57 of this Act shall apply to an order made under subsection (5)(b)(i) above as they apply to an order made under subsection (2) of that section.

(7) In disposing of an appeal under section 106(1)(b) to (f) or 108 of this Act the High Court may, without prejudice to any other power in that regard, pronounce an opinion on the sentence or other disposal or order which is appropriate in any similar case.

(8) No conviction, sentence, judgment, order of court or other proceeding whatsoever in or for the purposes of solemn proceedings under this Act—

(a) shall be quashed for want of form; or

(b) where the accused had legal assistance in his defence, shall be suspended or set aside in respect of any objections to—

(i) the relevancy of the indictment, or the want of specification therein; or

(ii) the competency or admission or rejection of evidence at the trial in the inferior court,

unless such objections were timeously stated.

[3](9) The High Court may give its reasons for the disposal of any appeal in writing without giving those reasons orally.

DEFINITIONS
"appeal against sentence": s.118(4).
"High Court": s.307(1).
"sentence": s.307(1).

NOTES
[1]As amended by the Crime and Punishment (Scotland) Act 1997 (c. 48), Sched. 1, para. 21(17) with effect from August 1, 1997 in terms of the Crime and Punishment (Scotland) Act 1997 (Commencement and Transitional Provisions) Order 1997 (S.I. 1997 No. 1712) para. 3. As amended by the Crime and Punishment (Scotland) Act 1997 (c. 48), s.18(5) with effect from October 20, 1997 in terms of the Crime and Punishment (Scotland) Act 1997 (Commencement No. 2 and Transitional Provisions) Order 1997 (S.I. 1997 No. 2323) Art. 3, Sched. 1.

[2]Inserted by the Crime and Punishment (Scotland) Act 1997 (c. 48), s.18(5) with effect from October 20, 1997 in terms of the Crime and Punishment (Scotland) Act 1997 (Commencement No. 2 and Transitional Provisions) Order 1997 (S.I. 1997 No. 2323) Art. 3, Sched. 1.

[3]Inserted by the Crime and Punishment (Scotland) Act 1997 (c. 48), Sched. 1, para. 21(17) with effect from August 1, 1997 in terms of the Crime and Punishment (Scotland) Act 1997 (Commencement and Transitional Provisions) Order 1997 (S.I. 1997 No. 1712) para. 3.

GENERAL NOTE

Appeal against conviction
Subsection (1) is concerned with appeals against conviction following solemn proceedings. The High Court of Justiciary may dispose of an appeal by affirming the verdict of the trial court: subs. (1)(a). Alternatively, the High Court of Justiciary may dispose of an appeal by setting aside the verdict of the trial court: subs. (1)(b) and (c). What follows after setting aside the verdict depends on what has gone wrong and how that is to be corrected. The Appeal Court is not obliged to give effect to a concession by the Crown at the appeal. It is for the court to determine if there has been a miscarriage of justice—*Duffy v. H.M. Advocate*, 1999 G.W.D. 37–1791. In *Santini v. H.M. Advocate*, 2000 S.C.C.R. 726 the Appeal Court declined to accept a Crown concession to restrict the libel to 2 days on the basis that there was no justification in law for this.

The High Court of Justiciary may set aside the verdict and quash the conviction and that may be done where the irregularity was substantial: *e.g. Gardiner v. H.M. Advocate*, 1978 S.L.T. 118. Alternatively, the High Court of Justiciary may set aside the verdict and substitute therefor an amended verdict of guilty: *e.g. Salmond v. H.M. Advocate*, 1991 S.C.C.R. 43 in which it was clear that the jury held some criminal behaviour proved but returned an incorrect verdict owing to a misunderstanding of the law. See *White v. H.M. Advocate*, 1989 S.C.C.R. 553 and *Ainsworth v. H.M. Advocate*, 1996 S.C.C.R. 631.

The High Court of Justiciary may set aside the verdict of the trial court and quash the conviction and grant, on statutory grounds, authority to bring a new prosecution: *e.g. Mackenzie v. H.M. Advocate*, 1982 S.C.C.R. 499 through many cases to *McDade v. H.M. Advocate*, 1994 S.C.C.R. 627. See *Sinclair v. H.M. Advocate*, 1996 S.C.C.R. 221; *O'Neill v. H.M. Advocate*, 1996 G.W.D. 4–183; *Hutton v. H.M. Advocate*, 1996 G.W.D. 31–1907; *Hobbins v. H.M. Advocate*, 1996 S.C.C.R. 637, *McPhelim v. H.M. Advocate*, 1996 S.C.C.R. 647 and *Hoy v. H.M. Advocate*, 1997 S.L.T. 26.

The setting aside of the verdict of the trial court and the quashing of the conviction in the context of a misdirection to the jury does not necessarily lead to the grant of authority to bring a new prosecution. In *Farooq v. H.M. Advocate*, 1993 S.L.T. 1271 the ages of child witnesses and the generally unsatisfactory nature of the evidence resulted in such authority being refused. In *Jones v. H.M. Advocate*, 1991 S.C.C.R. 290 the appellants were convicted of murder. They then gave evidence for the Crown at the trial of another on the same charge having been called as socii. The appellants' convictions were set aside on appeal. Authority to bring prosecution was refused as the setting aside of the conviction operated retroactively and as the appellants had given evidence for the Crown as socii they were immune from prosecution. See also *Kerr v. H.M. Advocate*, 1992 S.C.C.R. 281. In *Hoy v. H.M. Advocate*, 1998 S.C.C.R. 8, authority for a second retrial was refused on the basis that there had been insufficient evidence before the jury to convict of murder. Repeated indictments do not necessarily preclude authority being granted for a new prosecution—*Callan v. H.M. Advocate*, 1999 S.C.C.R. 57 (murder charge and no fault on the part of the Crown) but see *Cameron v. H.M. Advocate*, 1999 S.C.C.R. 11 (appellant previously undergone two trials and long delay in proceedings—authority refused). See also *Muirhead v. H.M. Advocate*, 1999 G.W.D. 4–176 and *Cathcart v. H.M. Advocate*, 1999 G.W.D. 5–241. The power in subs. (1) to set aside the verdict of the court necessarily requires a comparable power to deal with the question of sentence. Subsection (3) allows variation of sentence but whenever a sentence is varied a substituted sentence may only be the same or less than the original sentence. An appeal against conviction alone does not allow a variation of sentence for the imposition of a more severe sentence: *cf.* the earlier position, *e.g.* in *O'Neil v. H.M. Advocate*, 1976 S.L.T.(Notes) 7.

Appeals against sentence

Subsection (4) is concerned with appeals against sentence following solemn proceedings. The High Court of Justiciary may dispose of an appeal by affirming the sentence complained of: subs. (4)(a). Alternatively, the High Court of Justiciary may dispose of an appeal by quashing the sentence complained of and passing another sentence "whether more or less severe" in substitution. In doing the latter, the High Court of Justiciary may have regard to additional evidence such as that mentioned in s.106(3) of this Act.

An example of a more severe sentence being substituted is to be found in *Donnelly v. H.M. Advocate*, 1988 S.C.C.R. 386 where 18 months' detention was quashed and two years' detention substituted for a youth who had a CS gas canister at a football match. In contrast, a less serious sentence was substituted in *McIntyre v. H.M. Advocate*, 1994 G.W.D. 28–1687 where 20 years' imprisonment was quashed and was substituted with 14 years' imprisonment for culpable homicide for throwing or pouring acid on another. See also *Donnell v. H.M. Advocate*, 1997 G.W.D. 17–762 where the Appeal Court declined to exercise their power under subsection (4). The new subsection 4A was added by section 18(5) of the Crime and Punishment Act 1997 with effect from October 20, 1997. This provides that on appeal by the Prosecutor in terms of s.108A the court can (1) affirm the original decision; or (2) whilst agreeing that the minimum sentence should not be imposed for the reasons set out in s.205B(3) alter the sentence or (3) impose the appropriate sentence prescribed by the Act.

Supplementary provisions

In relation to any appeal under s.106(1) of this Act, the High Court of Justiciary is required to set aside the verdict of the trial court and quash the sentence and make an order where it appears that the appellant committed the act charged against him but that he was insane when he did so: subss. (5) and (6).

When disposing of appeals against sentence generally, the High Court of Justiciary may pronounce an opinion on the sentence or other disposal or order which is appropriate in any similar case: subs. (7). In *O'Neill v. H.M. Advocate*, 1998 S.C.C.R. 644 the Appeal Court set out guidelines for dealing with confidential material in mitigation. In *H.M. Advocate v. Carnall*, 1999 G.W.D. 31–1485 the Appeal Court observed that although reference in the course of an appeal hearing to disposals in previous, similar appeals against sentence may indicate to some extent the appropriate level of sentence for an offence they could not provide guidance to the whole range of sentences appropriate. See also *H.M. Advocate v. Wheldon*, 1999 J.C. 5.

Two other matters may have important consequences for appeals. First, no conviction, sentence, judgment, order of court or other proceedings whatsoever in or for the purposes of solemn proceedings shall be quashed for want of form: subs. (8)(A).

Secondly, and similarly, no conviction, sentence, judgment, order of court or other proceeding whatsoever in or for the purposes of solemn proceedings, where the accused had legal assistance in his defence, shall be suspended or set aside in respect of any objection to, either, the relevancy of the indictment, or the want of specification, or, the competency or admission or rejection of evidence at trial in the lower court, unless such objections were timeously stated: subs. (8)(b)(i) and (ii).

The concept of timeous objection was to be found in s.454 of the 1975 Act in relation to summary trials and it was said to be "special to summary trials": Renton and Brown (5th ed.) para. 14–61 at p. 300. For a recent case of how the section worked, see *McPherson v. McNaughton*, 1992 S.L.T. 600. See notes at s.192.

Subsection (9) was introduced by para. 21(17) of Sched. 1 of the Crime and Punishment Act with effect from August 1, 1997. This provides that the High Court may give written reasons without giving these reasons orally. This does away with the necessity of having advisings.

The deletion of s.118(4A)(c)(iii) occurs as a consequence of the repeal of s.4 of the 1997 Act wrought by the 1998 Act, Sched. 10.

Provision where High Court authorises new prosecution

119.—(1) Subject to subsection (2) below, where authority is granted under section 118(1)(c) of this Act, a new prosecution may be brought charging the accused with the same or any similar offence arising out of the same facts; and the proceedings out of which the appeal arose shall not be a bar to such new prosecution.

(2) In a new prosecution under this section the accused shall not be charged with an offence more serious than that of which he was convicted in the earlier proceedings.

(3) No sentence may be passed on conviction under the new prosecution which could not have been passed on conviction under the earlier proceedings.

(4) A new prosecution may be brought under this section, notwithstanding that any time limit, other than the time limit mentioned in subsection (5) below, for the commencement of such proceedings has elapsed.

(5) Proceedings in a prosecution under this section shall be commenced within two months of the date on which authority to bring the prosecution was granted.

(6) In proceedings in a new prosecution under this section it shall, subject to subsection (7) below, be competent for either party to lead any evidence which it was competent for him to lead in the earlier proceedings.

(7) The indictment in a new prosecution under this section shall identify any matters as respects which the prosecutor intends to lead evidence by virtue of subsection (6) above which would not have been competent but for that subsection.

(8) For the purposes of subsection (5) above, proceedings shall be deemed to be commenced—

(a) in a case where a warrant to apprehend or to cite the accused is executed without unreasonable delay, on the date on which the warrant is granted; and

(b) in any other case, on the date on which the warrant is executed.

(9) Where the two months mentioned in subsection (5) above elapse and no new prosecution has been brought under this section, the order under section 118(1)(c) of this Act setting aside the verdict shall have the effect, for all purposes, of an acquittal.

(10) On granting authority under section 118(1)(c) of this Act to bring a new prosecution, the High Court shall, after giving the parties an opportunity of being heard, order the detention of the accused person in custody or admit him to bail.

(11) Subsections (4)(b) and (7) to (9) of section 65 of this Act (prevention of delay in trials) shall apply to an accused person who is detained under

subsection (10) above as they apply to an accused person detained by virtue of being committed until liberated in due course of law.

DEFINITIONS
   "High Court": s.307(1).
   "offence": s.307(1).
   "prosecutor": s.307(1).
   "sentence": s.307(1).

GENERAL NOTE
Subs. (1)
   There have been a considerable number of new prosecutions on statutory authority in its earlier form: see, *e.g. Mackenzie v. H.M. Advocate*, 1982 S.C.C.R. 499, *King v. H.M. Advocate*, 1985 S.C.C.R. 322, *McGhee v. H.M. Advocate*, 1991 S.C.C.R. 510, and *Allison v. H.M. Advocate*, 1994 S.C.C.R. 464. The grant of such authority does not mean that the Crown is bound to initiate new proceedings: see *e.g. Sinclair v. H.M. Advocate*, 1990 S.C.C.R. 412.

Subs. (2)
   In a new prosecution under s.119 the accused is not to be *charged* with an offence more serious than that of which he was convicted in the earlier proceedings. The clearest example of this restriction is the case of Daniel Boyle. He had been charged with murder and after trial in the High Court of Justiciary at Glasgow he was convicted of culpable homicide in November 1991. He was sentenced to 10 years' detention. He appealed against conviction and that verdict was set aside in July 1992: *Boyle v. H.M. Advocate*, 1993 S.L.T. 577. The High Court of Justiciary, in setting aside that verdict, granted authority to the Crown to bring a new prosecution in accordance with s.254(1)(c) of the 1975 Act.
   A new indictment with a charge of murder was served on Boyle on July 30, 1992 for trial on August 31, 1992 but the trial diet was overtaken by an appeal by the Crown against a decision at a preliminary diet: see s.76A of the 1975 Act. The Crown appeal arose in this way: at the preliminary diet the accused argued that the jury, having returned a verdict of culpable homicide, had barred the Crown from indicting Boyle for the more serious crime of murder. The Crown argued otherwise.
   At the preliminary diet the judge held that the action of the Crown was competent in law but unfair in the circumstances and dismissed the indictment. The Crown appeal from the preliminary diet was allowed, it being for the Crown not the court to decide any charges brought, and the indictment for murder was remitted to the trial court to proceed: *H.M. Advocate v. Boyle*, 1992 S.C.C.R. 939.
   Thereafter, Boyle petitioned the *nobile officium* of the High Court of Justiciary to complain that that court had exceeded its own authority in the original appeal in setting aside certain charges on the indictment which Boyle had been convicted of but had not appealed. The petition was refused: *Boyle, Petr*, 1992 S.L.T. 1085.
   For the sake of completeness it should be added that at the adjourned trial diet in November 1992 the trial was again adjourned to January 1993 because of difficulties that the Crown had with citing witnesses. Boyle had been in custody since August 1991 and he again petitioned the *nobile officium* of the High Court of Justiciary, this time for bail. That was granted (unusually for those on a murder charge) in terms of s.35 of the 1975 Act: *Boyle, Petr*, 1993 S.C.C.R. 251. Daniel Boyle was acquitted at his second murder trial.

Subs. (3)
   This provision ensures that at a second trial in the event of conviction a sentence cannot competently be passed if it could not have been passed on conviction under the earlier proceedings.

Subs. (4)
   This provision permits a new prosecution notwithstanding any existing time-limits except for that in subs. (5).

Subs. (5)
   Proceedings in a prosecution under s.119 must be commenced within two months of the date on which authority to bring the prosecution was granted. Authority for a new prosecution was

granted in *Maillie v. H.M. Advocate*, 1993 S.C.C.R. 535. Delay in implementing a subsequent petition warrant results in that petition being dismissed: *Friel v. Mailley*, 1993 S.C.C.R. 928.

Subss. (6) to (7)
   The requirements of s.119(7) apply to cases where evidence could be led only in terms of s.119(6). If the evidence is admissible in terms of *e.g. Nelson v. H.M. Advocate*, 1994 S.C.C.R. 192 and *Cairns v. H.M. Advocate*, 1967 J.C. 37 then subs. (7) does not apply—*Diamond v. H.M. Advocate*, 1999 S.C.C.R. 411.

Subss. (8) to (11)
   In *McPhelim v. H.M. Advocate*, 1997 S.C.C.R. 87 the Crown raised an indictment within the statutory two months but the indictment was thereafter deserted *pro loco et tempore*. A fresh indictment was raised outwith the two month period. This was held to be competent as proceedings had been commenced timeously.
   The competency by subs. (10) of bail for the accused reflects the position that Boyle found himself in and that resulted in his petition to the *nobile officium*: see *Boyle, Petr*, 1993, above.

Appeals: supplementary provisions

   120.—(1) Where—
   (a) intimation of the diet appointed for the hearing of the appeal has been made to the appellant;
   (b) no appearance is made by or on behalf of an appellant at the diet; and
   (c) no case or argument in writing has been timeously lodged,
the High Court shall dispose of the appeal as if it had been abandoned.
   (2) The power of the High Court to pass any sentence under this Part of this Act may be exercised notwithstanding that the appellant (or, where the Lord Advocate is the appellant, the convicted person) is for any reason not present.
   (3) When the High Court has heard and dealt with any application under this Part of this Act, the Clerk of Justiciary shall (unless it appears to him unnecessary so to do) give to the applicant if he is in custody and has not been present at the hearing of such application notice of the decision of the court in relation to the said application.
   (4) On the final determination of any appeal under this Part of this Act or of any matter under section 103(5) of this Act, the Clerk of Justiciary shall give notice of such determination—
   (a) to the appellant or applicant if he is in custody and has not been present at such final determination;
   (b) to the clerk of the court in which the conviction took place; and
   (c) to the Secretary of State.

DEFINITIONS
   "appellant": s.132.
   "diet": s.307(1).
   "High Court": s.307(1).

GENERAL NOTE
   These supplementary provisions in practice are important because a not inconsiderable number of appeals are refused for want of insistence. The appellant cannot, however, fail to meet any obligation placed on him and expect to have the court overlook it. In *Manson, Petr*, 1991 S.L.T. 96 the petitioner sought to have heard an appeal against sentence which had been dismissed for want of insistence. Manson claimed not to have been notified of the date of appeal but he had failed to notify the court of a change of address as required by s.2(2) of the 1980 Act and the petition was refused.
   In *Boyle, Petr*, 1992 S.C.C.R. 949 the Appeal Court held that intimation under the then s.261 of the Criminal Procedure (Scotland) Act 1975 was not an interlocutor and is open to correction by the court, the opinion of the court being the best evidence of what was decided by the court.

Suspension of disqualification, forfeiture, etc.

   121.—(1) Any disqualification, forfeiture or disability which attaches to a person by reason of a conviction shall not attach—

(a) for the period of four weeks from the date of the verdict against him; or

¹(b) where an intimation of intention to appeal or, in the case of an appeal under section 106(1)(b) to (e), 108 or 108A of this Act, a note of appeal is lodged, until the appeal, if it is proceeded with, is determined.

(2) The destruction or forfeiture or any order for the destruction or forfeiture of any property, matter or thing which is the subject of or connected with any prosecution following upon a conviction shall be suspended—

(a) for the period of four weeks after the date of the verdict in the trial; or

¹(b) where an intimation of intention to appeal or, in the case of an appeal under section 106(1)(b) to (e), 108 or 108A of this Act, a note of appeal is lodged, until the appeal, if it is proceeded with, is determined.

(3) This section does not apply in the case of any disqualification, destruction or forfeiture or order for destruction or forfeiture under or by virtue of any enactment which makes express provision for the suspension of the disqualification, destruction or forfeiture or order for destruction or forfeiture pending the determination of an appeal against conviction or sentence.

¹(4) Where, upon conviction, a fine has been imposed on a person or a compensation order has been made against him under section 249 of this Act, then, for a period of four weeks from the date of the verdict against such person or, in the event of an intimation of intention to appeal (or in the case of an appeal under section 106(1)(b) to (e), 108 or 108A of this Act a note of appeal) being lodged under this Part of this Act, until such appeal, if it is proceeded with, is determined—

(a) the fine or compensation order shall not be enforced against that person and he shall not be liable to make any payment in respect of the fine or compensation order; and

(b) any money paid by that person under the compensation order shall not be paid by the clerk of court to the person entitled to it under subsection (9) of the said section 249.

²(5) In this section—

(a) "appeal" includes an appeal under paragraph 13(a) of Schedule 6 to the Scotland Act 1998; and

(b) in relation to such an appeal, references to an appeal being determined are to be read as references to the disposal of the proceedings by the High Court following determination of the appeal.

DEFINITION
"fine": s.307(1).

NOTES
¹As amended by the Crime and Punishment (Scotland) Act 1997 (c. 48) s.18(6) with effect from October 20, 1997 in terms of the Crime and Punishment (Scotland) Act 1997 (Commencement No. 2 and Transitional Provisions) Order 1997 S.I. 2323, Art. 3, Sched. 1.
²Inserted by the Scotland Act 1998 (Consequential Modifications) (No.1) Order 1999 (S.I. 1999 No.1042) art.3, Sched.1, para.13(3) (effective May 6, 1999).

Suspension of certain sentences pending determination of appeal

¹**121A.**—(1) Where an intimation of intention to appeal or, in the case of an appeal under section 106(1)(b) to (e), 108 or 108A of this Act, a note of appeal is lodged, the court may on the application of the appellant direct that the whole, or any remaining part, of a relevant sentence shall be suspended until the appeal, if it is proceeded with, is determined.

(2) Where the court has directed the suspension of the whole or any remaining part of a person's relevant sentence, the person shall, unless the

High Court otherwise directs, appear personally in court on the day or days fixed for the hearing of the appeal.

(3) Where a person fails to appear personally in court as mentioned in subsection (2) above, the court may—

(a) if he is the appellant—
 (i) decline to consider the appeal; and
 (ii) dismiss it summarily; or
(b) whether or not he is the appellant—
 (i) consider and determine the appeal; or
 (ii) make such other order as the court thinks fit.

(4) In this section "relevant sentence" means any one or more of the following—

(a) a probation order;
(b) a supervised attendance order made under section 236(6) of this Act;
(c) a community service order;
[2](d) a restriction of liberty order.

[3](5) Subsections (1), (2) and (4) above apply to an appeal under paragraph 13(a) of Schedule 6 to the Scotland Act 1998 and, in relation to such an appeal—

(a) references to an appeal being determined are to be read as references to the disposal of the proceedings by the High Court following determination of the appeal; and
(b) the reference in subsection (2) to the hearing of the appeal is to be read as a reference to any subsequent hearing in the High Court in relation to the proceedings.

[3](6) Where a person fails to appear personally in court as mentioned in subsection (2) as read with subsection (5) above, the court may make such order as it thinks fit.

NOTES

[1]Inserted by the Crime and Punishment (Scotland) Act 1997 (c. 48), s.24 with effect from August 1, 1997 in terms of the Crime and Punishment (Scotland) Act 1997 (Commencement and Transitional Provisions) Order 1997 (S.I. 1997 No. 1712) para. 3.

[2]Inserted by the Crime and Punishment (Scotland) Act 1997 (c. 48), s.24 (effective July 1, 1998: S.I. 1998 No. 2323).

[3]Inserted by the Scotland Act 1998 (Consequential Modifications) (No.1) Order 1999 (S.I. 1999 No.1042) art.3, Sched.1, para.13(4) (effective May 6, 1999).

GENERAL NOTE

With effect from August 1, 1997 sentences detailed in subs. (4) are to be suspended pending the determination of an appeal. This should prevent the situation as arose in *H.M. Advocate v. Jamieson*, 1996 S.C.C.R. 836 where an accused had completed the majority of a community service order and paid most of a compensation order prior to the hearing of an appeal. The Crown appeal against sentence was refused. In *H.M. Advocate v. McKinlay*, 1998 S.C.C.R. 201, however, the Appeal Court upheld a Crown appeal against sentence despite completion of community service. Partial completion of probation and community service will be taken into account in any subsequent unduly lenient sentence appeal *H.M. Advocate v. Paterson*, 2000 S.C.C.R. 309 and *H.M. Advocate v. Drain*, 2000 S.C.C.R. 256. The fact that the Crown failed to exercise its right under s.121A is a relevant factor in determining unduly lenient sentence appeals—*H.M. Advocate v. Carnall*, 1999 G.W.D. 31–1485.

Fines and caution

122.—(1) Where a person has on conviction been sentenced to payment of a fine and in default of payment to imprisonment, the person lawfully authorised to receive the fine shall, on receiving it, retain it until the determination of any appeal in relation to the conviction or sentence.

(2) If a person sentenced to payment of a fine remains in custody in default of payment of the fine he shall be deemed, for the purposes of this Part of this Act, to be a person sentenced to imprisonment.

(3) An appellant who has been sentenced to the payment of a fine, and has

paid it in accordance with the sentence, shall, in the event of his appeal being successful, be entitled, subject to any order of the High Court, to the return of the sum paid or any part of it.

[1](4) A convicted person who has been sentenced to the payment of a fine and has duly paid it shall, if an appeal against sentence by the Lord Advocate or any appeal by the Lord Advocate or the Advocate General for Scotland under paragraph 13(a) of Schedule 6 to the Scotland Act 1998 results in the sentence being quashed and no fine, or a lesser fine than that paid, being imposed, be entitled, subject to any order of the High Court, to the return of the sum paid or as the case may be to the return of the amount by which that sum exceeds the amount of the lesser fine.

[2](5) In subsections (1) and (3) above, "appeal" includes an appeal under paragraph 13(a) of Schedule 6 to the Scotland Act 1998.

DEFINITIONS
 "appellant": s.132.
 "fine": s.307(1).
 "High Court": s.307(1).

NOTES
 [1]As amended by the Scotland Act 1998 (Consequential Modifications) (No.1) Order 1999 (S.I. 1999 No.1042) art.3, Sched.1, para.13(5)(a) (effective May 6, 1999).
 [2]Inserted by the Scotland Act 1998 (Consequential Modifications) (No.1) Order 1999 (S.I. 1999 No.1042) art.3, Sched.1, para.13(5)(b) (effective May 6, 1999).

Lord Advocate's reference

123.—(1) Where a person tried on indictment is acquitted or convicted of a charge, the Lord Advocate may refer a point of law which has arisen in relation to that charge to the High Court for their opinion; and the Clerk of Justiciary shall send to the person and to any solicitor who acted for the person at the trial, a copy of the reference and intimation of the date fixed by the Court for a hearing.

(2) The person may, not later than seven days before the date so fixed, intimate in writing to the Clerk of Justiciary and to the Lord Advocate either—

 (a) that he elects to appear personally at the hearing; or
 (b) that he elects to be represented thereat by counsel,

but, except by leave of the Court on cause shown, and without prejudice to his right to attend, he shall not appear or be represented at the hearing other than by and in conformity with an election under this subsection.

(3) Where there is no intimation under subsection (2)(b) above, the High Court shall appoint counsel to act at the hearing as *amicus curiae*.

(4) The costs of representation elected under subsection (2)(b) above or of an appointment under subsection (3) above shall, after being taxed by the Auditor of the Court of Session, be paid by the Lord Advocate.

(5) The opinion on the point referred under subsection (1) above shall not affect the acquittal or, as the case may be, conviction in the trial.

DEFINITIONS
 "Clerk of Justiciary": s.307(1).
 "High Court": s.307(1).
 "indictment": s.307(1).

GENERAL NOTE
 There is no appeal against acquittal in solemn proceedings: see the terms of s.106(1) of this Act. It is incompetent in such proceedings to advocate either a verdict of acquittal by a jury, or an acquittal by a judge on a submission of no case to answer. However, should there then be a doubt about the law to be applied then the Lord Advocate may invoke the reference procedure provided by s.123.
 A few such references have been taken on a diverse range of points of law: see *Lord*

Advocate's Reference No. 1 of 1983, 1984 S.C.C.R. 62 (taped interviews); *Lord Advocate's Reference No. 1 of 1985*, 1987 S.L.T. 187 (perjury); *Lord Advocate's Reference No. 1 of 1992*, 1992 S.L.T. 1010 (building societies); *Lord Advocate's Reference No. 2 of 1992*, 1992 S.C.C.R. 960 (joke as motive); *Lord Advocate's Reference No. 1 of 1994*, 1995 S.L.T. 248 (supply of a controlled drug), and *Lord Advocate's Reference No. 1 of 1996*, 1996 S.C.C.R. 516 (bankers' books).

The costs of representation elected under s.123(2)(b) are, after being taxed by the Auditor of the Court of Session, paid by the Lord Advocate: s.123(4).

Finality of proceedings and Secretary of State's reference

124.—[1](1) Nothing in this Part or Part XA of this Act shall affect the prerogative of mercy.

[1,2](2) Subject to Part XA of this Act and paragraph 13(a) of Schedule 6 to the Scotland Act 1998, every interlocutor and sentence pronounced by the High Court under this Part of this Act shall be final and conclusive and not subject to review by any court whatsoever and, except for the purposes of an appeal under paragraph 13(a) of that Schedule, it shall be incompetent to stay or suspend any execution or diligence issuing from the High Court under this Part of this Act.

(3)–(5) [*Repealed by the Crime and Punishment (Scotland) Act 1997, Sched. 1, para. 21(18) and Sched. 3 (effective April 1, 1999: S.I. 1999 No. 652).*]

DEFINITIONS
"High Court": s.307(1).
"sentence": s.132.

NOTES
[1]As amended by the Crime and Punishment (Scotland) Act 1997, Sched. 1, para. 21(18).
[2]As amended by the Scotland Act 1998 (Consequential Modifications) (No.1) Order 1999 (S.I. 1999 No.1042) art.3, Sched.1, para.13(6) (effective May 6, 1999).

GENERAL NOTE
Subs. (1)
The prerogative of mercy remains unaffected by the provisions in Pt. VIII of the 1995 Act. Precisely what this subsection means, in the context of subs. (3), is a matter of some interest. Some assistance may be found in *H.M. Advocate v. Waddell*, 1976 S.L.T. (Notes) 61 and C. Gane *The Effect of a Pardon in Scots Law* 1980 J.R. 18.

Subs. (2)
This limitation applies to interlocutors and sentences pronounced by the High Court in appeals from solemn proceedings—*Express Newspapers PLC Petrs*, 1999 S.C.C.R. 262. Subsection (2) has been amended to permit appeals to the Judicial Committee of the Privy Council in terms of the Scotland Act 1998.

The *nobile officium* cannot be invoked to review the merits of decisions of the court exercising its appellate jurisdiction but it can be used to alter or correct an order pronounced by the Appeal Court where the court has exceeded its powers. See *Perrie Petr*, 1991 S.C.C.R. 475; *Beattie Petr*, 1997 S.C.C.R. 949 and *Windsor Petr*, 1994 S.C.C.R. 59. In *Express Newspapers PLC Petrs, supra*, a petition to the *nobile officium* was used to appeal fines imposed for contempt of court.

A valid interlocutor cannot be pronounced if a quorum of the Appeal Court is not constituted—*Hoekstra v. H.M. Advocate (No.2)*, 2000 S.C.C.R. 368.

Reckoning of time spent pending appeal

125.—(1) Subject to subsection (2) below, where a convicted person is admitted to bail under section 112 of this Act, the period beginning with the date of his admission to bail and ending on the date of his readmission to prison in consequence of the determination or abandonment of—

(a) his appeal; or, as the case may be,
[1](b) any relevant appeal by the Lord Advocate under section 108 or 108A of this Act,

shall not be reckoned as part of any term of imprisonment under his sentence.

[1](2) The time, including any period consequent on the recall of bail during which an appellant is in custody pending the determination of his appeal or, as the case may be, of any relevant appeal by the Lord Advocate under section 108 or 108A of this Act shall, subject to any direction which the High Court may give to the contrary, be reckoned as part of any term of imprisonment under his sentence.

(3) Subject to any direction which the High Court may give to the contrary, imprisonment of an appellant or, where the appellant is the Lord Advocate, of a convicted person—

(a) who is in custody in consequence of the conviction or sentence appealed against, shall be deemed to run as from the date on which the sentence was passed;

(b) who is in custody other than in consequence of such conviction or sentence, shall be deemed to run or to be resumed as from the date on which his appeal was determined or abandoned;

(c) who is not in custody, shall be deemed to run or to be resumed as from the date on which he is received into prison under the sentence.

(4) In this section references to a prison and imprisonment shall include respectively references to a young offenders institution or place of safety or, as respects a child sentenced to be detained under section 208 of this Act, the place directed by the Secretary of State and to detention in such institution, centre or place of safety, or, as respects such a child, place directed by the Secretary of State and any reference to a sentence shall be construed as a reference to a sentence passed by the court imposing sentence or by the High Court on appeal as the case may require.

DEFINITIONS
"bail": s.307(1).
"prison": s.307(1).
"sentence": s.132.
"young offender's institution": s.307(1).

NOTE
[1]As amended by the Crime and Punishment (Scotland) Act 1997 (c. 48), s.18(7) with effect from October 20, 1997 in terms of the Crime and Punishment (Scotland) Act 1997 (Commencement and Transitional Provisions) Order 1997 (S.I. 1997 No. 2323) Art. 3, Sched. 1.

GENERAL NOTE
Subsections 1 and 2 have been amended with effect from October 20, 1997 to provide that where an appellant is released on bail pending an appeal under s.108A by the Lord Advocate this shall not be reckoned towards the calculation of the period of imprisonment.

Subsection (2)—see *Scott v. H.M. Advocate*, 1946 J.C. 68 where an accused made a frivolous application for extension of time. The court refused to direct that the time he was treated as an appellant should count as part of his sentence.

Extract convictions

126. No extract conviction shall be issued—

(a) during the period of four weeks after the day on which the conviction took place, except in so far as it is required as a warrant for the detention of the person convicted under any sentence which has been pronounced against him; nor

[1](b) where an intimation of intention to appeal or, in the case of an appeal under section 106(1)(b) to (e), 108 or 108A of this Act, a note of appeal is lodged, until the appeal, if it is proceeded with, is determined.

DEFINITIONS
"extract conviction": s.307(1).

"sentence": s.132.

NOTE
[1] As amended by the Crime and Punishment (Scotland) Act 1997 (c. 48), s.18(8) with effect from October 20, 1997 in terms of the Crime and Punishment (Scotland) Act 1997 (Commencement and Transitional Provisions) Order 1997 S.I. 2323, Art. 3, Sched. 1.

GENERAL NOTE
This has been amended with effect from October 20, 1997 to include appeals under s.108A.

Forms in relation to appeals

127.—(1) The Clerk of Justiciary shall furnish the necessary forms and, instructions in relation to intimations of intention to appeal, notes of appeal or notices of application under this Part of this Act to—
(a) any person who demands them; and
(b) to officers of courts, governors of prisons, and such other officers or persons as he thinks fit.

(2) The governor of a prison shall cause the forms and instructions mentioned in subsection (1) above to be placed at the disposal of prisoners desiring to appeal or to make any application under this Part of this Act.

(3) The governor of a prison shall, if requested to do so by a prisoner, forwarded on the prisoner's behalf to the Clerk of Justiciary any intimation, note or notice mentioned in subsection (1) above given by the prisoner.

DEFINITIONS
"Clerk of Justiciary": s.307(1).
"governor": s.307(1).
"prison": s.307(1).

Fees and expenses

128. Except as otherwise provided in this Part of this Act, no court fees, or other fees or expenses shall be exigible from or awarded against an appellant or applicant in respect of an appeal or application under this Part of this Act.

Non-compliance with certain provisions may be waived

129.—(1) Non-compliance with—
(a) the provisions of this Act set out in subsection (3) below; or
(b) any rule of practice for the time being in force under this Part of this Act relating to appeals,
shall not prevent the further prosecution of an appeal if the High Court or a judge thereof considers it just and proper that the non-compliance is waived or, in the manner directed by the High Court or judge, remedied by amendment or otherwise.

(2) Where the High Court or a judge thereof directs that the non-compliance is to be remedied, and the remedy is carried out, the appeal shall proceed.

(3) The provisions of this Act referred to in subsection (1) above are:—
section 94
section 103(1), (4), (6) and (7)
section 104(2) and (3)
section 105 — *Two subs*
section 106(4)
section 111 — *Three subs*
section 114
section 115 —
section 116
section 117
section 120(1), (3) and (4) —

section 121
section 122
section 126
section 128.

(4) This section does not apply to any rule of practice relating to appeals under section 60 of this Act.

DEFINITIONS
   "High Court": s.307(1).
   "judge": s.307(1).

GENERAL NOTE
   This general saving power permits an appeal against conviction or sentence to proceed notwithstanding non-compliance with the rules specified in s.129(3) if it appears just and proper to proceed or if a consequential problem can be remedied.

Bill of suspension not competent

130. It shall not be competent to appeal to the High Court by bill of suspension against any conviction, sentence, judgement or order pronounced in any proceedings on indictment in the sheriff court.

DEFINITIONS
   "indictment": s.307(1).
   "sentence": s.132.

GENERAL NOTE
   The origins of this section lie in the Criminal Appeal (Scotland) Act 1926 which, by s.13, abolished appeal by suspension, but appeal by advocation from the sheriff in solemn procedure remained competent. A bill of suspension for an appeal by a witness found in contempt in the course of solemn proceedings in the sheriff court was held competent in *Butterworth v. Herron*, 1975 S.L.T. (Notes) 56. This was later over-ruled when five judges held in *George Outram & Co. v. Lees*, 1992 S.L.T. 32 that the correct mode of appeal was a petition to the *nobile officium*. In *Mellors v. Normand (No. 1)*, 1996 S.C.C.R. 500 the Appeal Court held it was appropriate to use a bill of suspension to suspend a committal warrant.

Prosecution appeal by bill of advocation

131.—(1) Without prejudice to section 74 of this Act, the prosecutor's right to bring a decision under review of the High Court by way of bill of advocation in accordance with existing law and practice shall extend to the review of a decision of any court of solemn jurisdiction.

(2) Where a decision to which a bill of advocation relates is reversed on the review of the decision the prosecutor may, whether or not there has already been a trial diet at which evidence has been led, proceed against the accused by serving him with an indictment containing, subject to subsection (3) below, the charge or charges which were affected by the decision.

(3) The wording of the charge or charges referred to in subsection (2) above shall be as it was immediately before the decision appealed against.

DEFINITIONS
   "High Court": s.307(1).
   "prosecutor": s.307(1).

GENERAL NOTE
   An example of the use of this power is found in *H.M. Advocate v. Sinclair*, 1987 S.L.T. 161 where a shrieval decision to desert an indictment *pro loco et tempore* was successfully challenged by the Crown. The competency of the use of advocation by the Crown to review a sheriff's decision during the currency, rather than at the conclusion, of proceedings, and before final judgment was upheld in *H.M. Advocate v. Khan*, 1997 S.C.C.R. 100 and in *H.M. Advocate v. Shepherd*, 1997 S.C.C.R. 246 (see p. 143 and p. 43 above). In *H.M. Advocate v. Sorrie*, 1996 S.C.C.R. 778 the Appeal Court indicated that if the Crown seek to use a bill of advocation rather than an appeal in terms of s.74 of the Act the accused should be alerted to the fact. In *H.M.*

Advocate v. Khan, 1997 S.C.C.R. 100 the Crown successfully brought a Bill of Advocation against a sheriff's refusal to adjourn a diet and to grant a defence motion to discharge a juror.

Interpretation of Part VIII

132. In this Part of this Act, unless the context otherwise requires—
"appellant" includes a person who has been convicted and desires to appeal under this Part of the Act;
"sentence" includes any order of the High Court made on conviction with reference to the person convicted or his wife or children, and any recommendation of the High Court as to the making of a deportation order in the case of a person convicted and the power of the High Court to pass a sentence includes a power to make any such order of the court or recommendation, and a recommendation so made by the High Court shall have the same effect for the purposes of Articles 20 and 21 of the Aliens Order 1953 as the certificate and recommendation of the convicting court.

PART IX

SUMMARY PROCEEDINGS

General

Application of Part IX of Act

133.—(1) This Part of this Act applies to summary proceedings in respect of any offence which might prior to the passing of this Act, or which may under the provisions of this or any Act, whether passed before or after the passing of this Act, be tried summarily.

(2) Without prejudice to subsection (1) above, this Part of this Act also applies to procedure in all courts of summary jurisdiction in so far as they have jurisdiction in respect of—
(a) any offence or the recovery of a penalty under any enactment or rule of law which does not exclude summary procedure as well as, in accordance with section 211(3) and (4) of this Act, to the enforcement of a fine imposed in solemn proceedings; and
(b) any order *ad factum praestandum*, or other order of court or warrant competent to a court of summary jurisdiction.

(3) Where any statute provides for summary proceedings to be taken under any public general or local enactment, such proceedings shall be taken under this Part of this Act.

(4) Nothing in this Part of this Act shall—
(a) extend to any complaint or other proceeding under or by virtue of any statutory provision for the recovery of any rate, tax, or impost whatsoever; or
(b) affect any right to raise any civil proceedings.

(5) Except where any enactment otherwise expressly provides, all prosecutions under this Part of this Act shall be brought at the instance of the procurator fiscal.

DEFINITIONS
"court of summary jurisdiction": s.5(1) and (2) and s.307(1).
"offence": s.307(1).
"statute": s.307(1).
"summarily": s.5(1) and (2) and s.7(5) and (6).

GENERAL NOTE
Part IX of the Act regulates the procedure in all summary cases including proceedings raised under local enactments as well as statutory provisions which apply generally. Revenue offences

involving the Inland Revenue and H.M. Customs and Excise only adopt the procedures in Pt IX of the Act insofar as expressly stipulated within their relevant statutes.

It will be seen that subs. (2)(a) provides that summary provisions also apply to the enforcement of monetary fines imposed following solemn convictions and to the enforcement of fines imposed by other courts in Scotland, England and Wales unless such a jurisdiction is specifically excluded.

Incidental applications

134.—(1) This section applies to any application to a court for any warrant or order of court—

(a) as incidental to proceedings by complaint; or

(b) where a court has power to grant any warrant or order of court, although no subsequent proceedings by complaint may follow thereon.

(2) An application to which this section applies may be made by petition at the instance of the prosecutor in the form prescribed by Act of Adjournal.

(3) Where it is necessary for the execution of a warrant or order granted under this section, warrant to break open shut and lockfast places shall be implied.

DEFINITION
"complaint": s.307(1).

GENERAL NOTE
This section determines that the form specified in the 1996 Act of Adjournal (Form 16.4.–A) shall be used for applications to the court by the prosecutor or the accused when summary proceedings have begun (subs. (1)(a)) or when the prosecutor, in carrying out his investigative role, seeks a search warrant, or other warrant, from a sheriff or magistrate even before any person has been charged with an offence (subs. (1)(b)); this latter provision will doubtless remain the most common use of this section. Examples of the range of warrants sought, can be found in *Carmichael, Complainer*, 1993 S.L.T. 305 (to precognosce a complainer on oath); *Frame v. Houston*, 1992 S.L.T. 205 (warrant for hair samples of accused sought after indictment served); *Normand, Complainer*, 1992 S.L.T. 478 (warrant at common law to inspect bankers' books before proceedings have begun). Applications made under s.31 of the Criminal Law (Consolidation) (Scotland) Act 1995 by the prosecutor for an "inspection order" or a "production order" are made by such an incidental application.

Summary warrants to apprehend which are used to commence proceedings and empower the arrest of a known accused are granted under s.139(1)(c) below.

In addition to the statutory power of apprehension and search enacted in s.135 below, a multiplicity of statutes contain their own express powers of search, detention and arrest, notably the Misuse of Drugs Act 1971, the Road Traffic Act 1988 and the Firearms Act 1968: these express provisions override the general powers contained in s.134.

In *Douglas v. Procurator Fiscal, Kirkcaldy* (High Court, November 1991) the procurator fiscal resorted to incidental application procedure to have citations as defence witnesses for himself and the Law Officers rescinded on the grounds that they had no evidence to offer pertinent to the case; the accused, on appeal, stated that citations had been served because he had a separate grievance against the procurator fiscal. His appeal by advocation was refused.

Note that where one of the parties has declined to make a joint application to the court to alter a diet as enabled by s.137 below, s.137(4) permits the use of an incidental application to put the matter before the court for consideration.

Reduction of incidental applications is by way of a bill of suspension. See, for example, *McIntyre v. Munro*, 1999 G.W.D. 9–419 where an inept apprehension warrant was quashed.

Warrants of apprehension and search

135.—(1) A warrant of apprehension or search may be in the form prescribed by Act of Adjournal or as nearly as may be in such form, and any warrant of apprehension or search shall, where it is necessary for its execution, imply warrant to officers of law to break open shut and lockfast places.

(2) A warrant of apprehension of an accused in the form mentioned in

subsection (1) above shall imply warrant to officers of law to search for and to apprehend the accused, and to bring him before the court issuing the warrant, or before any other court competent to deal with the case, to answer to the charge on which such warrant is granted, and, in the meantime, until he can be so brought, to detain him in a police station, police cell, or other convenient place.

(3) A person apprehended under a warrant or by virtue of power under any enactment or rule of law shall wherever practicable be brought before a court competent to deal with the case not later than in the course of the first day after he is taken into custody.

(4) The reference in subsection (3) above to the first day after he is taken into custody shall not include a Saturday, a Sunday or a court holiday prescribed for that court under section 8 of this Act; but nothing in this subsection shall prevent a person being brought before the court on a Saturday, a Sunday or such a court holiday where the court is, in pursuance of the said section 8, sitting on such day for the disposal of criminal business.

(5) A warrant of apprehension or other warrant shall not be required for the purpose of bringing before the court an accused who has been apprehended without a written warrant or who attends without apprehension in answer to any charge made against him.

DEFINITION
"officers of law": s.307(1).

GENERAL NOTE
As subs. (5) makes clear, the provisions of this section are intended to initiate proceedings against an accused whose identity is known to the prosecutor but who, for one reason or another, has not been apprehended and brought before the court to answer the charge against him. Rule 16.5.–(1) of the 1996 Act of Adjournal stipulates that such warrants are to follow the styles shown as Forms 16.5–A and B (Warrants to apprehend following a failure to appear at a diet are granted under s.150 of the Act).

While the power granted by warrant under subs. (2) is to arrest the accused, it is competent for the prosecutor instead to exercise a discretion to invite the accused to appear at a specified court or police station on a given date and thus avoid the pains of arrest; see *Spowart v. Burr* (1895) 1 Adam 539. It was held in *Young v. Smith*, 1981 S.L.T.(Notes) 101; 1981 S.C.C.R. 85 that where an accused attended voluntarily in response to such an invitation the warrant had not been executed. Similarly failure to respond to such an invitation with the result that a warrant is executed, cannot work to the benefit of the accused (*Young v. McLeod*, 1993 S.C.C.R. 479 where pleas of undue delay were repelled).

The wording of subss. (3) and (4) paraphrases the terms of s.321(3) of the 1975 Act and, following *Robertson v. MacDonald*, 1993 S.L.T. 1337; 1992 S.C.C.R. 916 would appear to be directory rather than mandatory in its effect. In *Robertson*, the accused had been arrested upon a petition warrant, granted at Wick Sheriff Court, in Glasgow. He was conveyed to Wick and made his appearance on summary complaint four days later when he took objection to the competency of proceedings. Albeit a breach of the subsection had occurred, the court upheld Crown submissions that itself did not vitiate proceedings.

Time limit for certain offences

136.—(1) Proceedings under this Part of this Act in respect of any offence to which this section applies shall be commenced—
  (a) within six months after the contravention occurred;
  (b) in the case of a continuous contravention, within six months after the
       last date of such contravention,
and it shall be competent in a prosecution of a contravention mentioned in paragraph (b) above to include the entire period during which the contravention occurred.

(2) This section applies to any offence triable only summarily and consisting of the contravention of any enactment, unless the enactment fixes a different time limit.

(3) For the purposes of this section proceedings shall be deemed to be

commenced on the date on which a warrant to apprehend or to cite the accused is granted, if the warrant is executed without undue delay.

DEFINITION
   "offence": s.307(1).

GENERAL NOTE
   The peremptory nature of these provisions in the 1975 Act inevitably produced a substantial volume of case law. Section 136 appears to re-enact the terms of s.331 of the 1975 Act which applied a six-month time bar to the raising of summary prosecutions of statutory offences; however subs. (2) now restricts the operation of the provisions to cases which are triable summarily only, and to statutory enactments which contain their own express time bar provisions. See for example *Gilday v. Ritchie*, 1999 G.W.D. 32–1528, a prosecution under the Misuse of Drugs 1971 on summary complaint, where it was held that the statute's specific time bar was not set aside by the terms of s.136 above.
   Note that this time-bar provision, which now applies to a more limited number of statutory offences than were affected by s.331 of the 1975 Act, does not apply to the libelling of common law offences. While pleas to the competency of proceedings on the grounds of time-bar should now be less commonplace, it may be noted that a delay on the part of the Crown in initiating proceedings could well justify a plea of *mora*. (For *mora* see generally *Tudhope v. McCarthy*, 1985 J.C. 48; 1985 S.L.T. 395; *McFarlane v. Jessop*, 1988 S.L.T. 596; 1988 S.C.C.R. 186; *Connachan v. Douglas*, 1990 S.L.T. 563; 1990 S.C.C.R. 101).
   Proceedings will normally be commenced by the postal service of a citation and service copy complaint upon the accused, but can also be started by an initiating warrant or by obtaining an assigned diet within the six-month period for a diet outwith that period; the question of whether the prosecutor has complied with the statutory timebar provisions has to be approached differently in each of these situations. Service by post of a complaint timeously to call at a diet within the six-month date offers no difficulty; the proceedings commence on the date of posting of the complaint. The same rule applies to the service of a complaint to call at a diet after the expiry of six-months; in that event the proceedings are still competent, provided that the complaint is sent and received within the six-month date and calls at the cited diet (see *Keily v. Tudhope*, 1986 S.C.C.R. 351; 1987 S.L.T. 99; *Orr v. Lowdon*, 1987 S.C.C.R. 515): it is desirable that the prosecutor is able to produce an execution of service of the complaint in that latter situation.
   Different considerations apply when the prosecutor elects to proceed instead by way of either an initiating warrant or by a warrant to cite the accused to an assigned diet. The grant of either form of warrant signals the commencement of the proceedings and to preserve those proceedings the warrant must in either case be executed without undue delay. It must be emphasised however that while an initiating warrant may well be a valid basis for proceedings months later (if the prosecutor can show that there was no undue delay on his part, a matter discussed later), in the case of a warrant to cite the complaint will either stand or fall on the date of the assigned diet (*Tudhope v. Buckner*, 1985 S.C.C.R. 352).
   If service has not been effected upon the accused prior to the diet then the complaint necessarily falls. The only option available to the prosecutor should he learn of difficulty in effecting service of a warrant to cite, is to withdraw the warrant and reraise by means of an initiating warrant if this can be done before the expiry of the timebar.
   Once an initiating warrant or a warrant to cite has been obtained, any undue delay in its execution must not be attributable to the actions (or inactions) of the prosecutor. Generally, reported cases have focused upon what constitutes "undue delay" and it has to be stressed that even where a warrant to cite an accused to a diet outwith the six-month period is granted timeously, the prosecutor must still effect service of the complaint swiftly. The onus of proof of "no undue delay" rests with the Crown and if facts are in dispute, the court should hear evidence of the steps taken to execute the warrant (*McCartney v. Tudhope*, 1985 S.C.C.R. 373; 1986 S.L.T. 159). An incorrect address in the instance of the complaint and frustrated efforts to serve at the correct address by post and personally were held not to constitute "undue delay"; see *McKay v. Normand*, 1995 G.W.D. 39–1995.

Statutory Exceptions
   It is well understood that where a statute provides specific time limits for procedures or proceedings, then those time limits apply and are not affected by the generality of s.136; see for example *Gilday v. Ritchie*, 2000 S.C.C.R. 53, a Misuse of Drugs Act 1971 prosecution which was time-barred.

Computation of Time

The six-month period is calculated *de die in diem* and not *de momento in momentum* (see *Tudhope v. Lawson*, 1983 S.C.C.R. 435; *Lees v. Lovell*, 1992 S.L.T. 967; 1992 S.C.C.R. 557 following *Keenan v. Carmichael*, 1991 S.C.C.R. 680), *i.e.* excluding the date of offence.

In the exceptional circumstances produced by the death, illness or absence of the judge, which has interrupted a part-heard trial, s.151(2) permits a new prosecution of a statutory complaint raised within two months of its desertion, notwithstanding the usual timebar on statutory proceedings.

Undue Delay

Warrants are sought for arrest or for the assignment of a diet for a date usually outwith the normal prescriptive period. Undue delay where established is fatal to proceedings on that complaint and the result of such a finding is to preclude any further proceedings on a statutory (but not a common law) charge. The delay has to be attributable to the prosecutor alone and will be assessed according to the facts of each case. The presiding judge has a broad discretion in deciding the issue. Execution of the warrant extends to any action taken by the prosecutor to effect citation whether by post or other means (*Lockhart v. Bradley*, 1977 S.L.T. 5); "undue delay" was defined in *Smith v. Peter Walker and Son (Edinburgh)*, 1978 J.C. 44.

Examples of undue delay are found in *Carmichael v. Sardar and Sons*, 1983 S.C.C.R. 433 (unexplained period of six days), *Harvey v. Lockhart*, 1991 S.C.C.R. 83; 1992 S.L.T. 68 (14 days but the sheriff had erred in reaching a decision without hearing explanations for the delay), *Robertson v. Carmichael*, 1993 S.C.C.R. 841 (four days unexplained and not investigated).

Undue delay was not established in *Stagecoach v. MacPhail*, 1986 S.C.C.R. 184 (seven days between warrant to cite and service), *Anderson v. Lowe*, 1991 S.C.C.R. 712 (warrant mislaid in Sheriff Clerk's office for three days), *Buchan v. McNaughtan*, 1990 S.C.C.R. 688; 1991 S.L.T. 410 (delay attributed to conduct of accused), *Young v. MacPhail*, 1991 S.C.C.R. 630; 1992 S.L.T. 98 (a warrant granted for accused then serving a prison sentence in England not being executed until his date of release), or in *Melville v. Normand*, 1996 G.W.D. 10–542 (a combination of public holidays, the warrant being sent to the wrong police office and execution being delayed by the police until the conclusion of the accused's High Court trial on other charges, this last practice being viewed as a sound one), *Alexander v. Normand*, 1997 S.L.T. 370 (a delay of 13 days before issuing the warrant to the police where the time-bar was still two months away followed by three abortive attempts to execute the warrant), *McGlennan v. Singh*, 1993 S.C.C.R. 341 (16 days lapsed from grant of warrant till its execution, but the sheriff had moved too summarily in finding against the Crown).

The period to be taken into account in assessing delay is from the date of granting of the warrant until its execution, not the time from the expiry of the prescriptive period until the execution of the warrant (see *MacNeill v. Cowie*, 1984 S.C.C.R. 449; *McNellie v. Walkingshaw*, 1990 S.C.C.R. 428; 1991 S.L.T. 892) but it must be emphasised that the issue of delay will only arise where service is effected outwith the six-month time-bar period. Hence in *Chow v. Lees*, 1997 S.C.C.R. 253, where the prosecutor was granted an apprehension warrant shortly before expiry of the time-bar and elected to invite the accused to appear voluntarily on a date after that expiry, the Appeal Court directed the sheriff (who had repelled a plea to the competency) to consider the issue of undue delay; it had taken Crown over a week to instruct an invitation to be sent to the accused and a further week to intimate to him a date for his appearance.

Reduction of Proceedings to Summary Complaint

The anticipated impact of the decision in *Gardner v. Lees* 1996 S.C.C.R. 168, which required that any petition proceedings later reduced to a summary complaint had to be concluded within a year of the original appearance on petition, has been blunted by the express provisions of the Criminal Procedure and Investigations Act 1996 (c. 25), s.73(3). This statutory provision, which amended s.65(1) of the 1995 Act, has the effect of removing any time-bar on such summary proceedings while restating the time-bar applicable to solemn proceedings (carried over from s.101 of the 1975 Act, *i.e.* one year from petition appearance to the date of commencement of indictment proceedings).

While *Gardner v. Lees* may assist in understanding the constitutional origins of the statutory time-bar, the jurisprudential justification for applying those principles equally to non-custodial summary proceedings was, to say the least, doubtful; the leap of logic which required summary trial proceedings to be concluded within a year (rather than commenced as s.101 demanded of solemn proceedings) was more questionable still. Effectively the statutory amendment to s.65 brings the law back to that stated in *MacDougall v. Russell*, 1985 S.C.C.R. 441 and *Whitelaw v.*

Dickinson, 1993 S.C.C.R. 164. See p. 107 in relation to the computation of the time of such proceedings and *Duke v. Lees*, 1997 G.W.D. 15–659.

Alteration of diets

137.—(1) Where a diet has been fixed in a summary prosecution, it shall be competent for the court, on a joint application in writing by the parties or their solicitors, to discharge the diet and fix an earlier diet in lieu.

(2) Where the prosecutor and the accused make joint application to the court (orally or in writing) for postponement of a diet which has been fixed, the court shall discharge the diet and fix a later diet in lieu unless the court considers that it should not do so because there has been unnecessary delay on the part of one of more of the parties.

(3) Where all the parties join in an application under subsection (2) above, the court may proceed under that subsection without hearing the parties.

(4) Where the prosecutor has intimated to the accused that he desires to postpone or accelerate a diet which has been fixed, and the accused refuses, or any of the accused refuse, to make a joint application to the court for that purpose, the prosecutor may make an incidental application for that purpose under section 134 of this Act; and after giving the parties an opportunity to be heard, the court may discharge the diet and fix a later diet or, as the case may be, an earlier diet in lieu.

(5) Where an accused had intimated to the prosecutor and to all the other accused that he desires such postponement or acceleration and the prosecutor refuses, or any of the other accused refuse, to make a joint application to the court for that purpose, the accused who has so intimated may apply to the court for that purpose; and, after giving the parties an opportunity to be heard, the court may discharge the diet and fix a later diet or, as the case may be, an earlier diet in lieu.

DEFINITIONS
"diet": s.307(1).
"prosecutor": s.307(1).

GENERAL NOTE
This section provides procedures for applications to the court for alteration of summary diets on joint motion, and for such applications to be made by a party in the absence of agreement of all parties. Subsection (1) permits acceleration of a diet by means of a joint written application; subs. (2) relates to joint applications to postpone a summary diet and gives expression to the right of the court to refuse such an application which, unlike a motion for acceleration, can be made either orally or in writing. Where all parties concur in making a written application timeously, the court can dispose of it administratively. Note however that the court's power to refuse an application for postponement on grounds of unnecessary delay by one of the parties suggests that a hearing would be required before the motion could be decided by the court.

Subsections (4) and (5) respectively provide for the prosecutor and the accused to make application individually to the court for variation of the diet in situations where other parties will not concur. The prosecutor should make application by way of an incidental application (see s.134 above) while the accused, although it is not stipulated in subs. (5), can petition using Form 16.7 provided in the 1996 Act of Adjournal.

In *White v. Ruxton*, 1996 S.C.C.R. 427 it was held in the absence of a court minute recording a new diet of trial fixed by Joint Minute of Acceleration that the minute itself, whose terms were not in dispute, was sufficient for the purpose. Objections to the competency of the proceedings were rejected.

Complaints

Complaints

138.—(1) All proceedings under this Part of this Act for the trial of offences or recovery of penalties shall be instituted by complaint signed by the prosecutor or by a solicitor on behalf of a prosecutor other than the procurator fiscal.

(2) The complaint shall be in the form—
(a) set out in Schedule 5 to this Act; or
(b) prescribed by Act of Adjournal,
or as nearly as may be in such form.

(3) A solicitor may appear for and conduct any prosecution on behalf of a prosecutor other than the procurator fiscal.

(4) Schedule 3 to this Act shall have effect as regards complaints under this Act.

DEFINITIONS
"complaint": s.307(1).
"judge": s.307(1).
"procurator fiscal": s.307(1).
"prosecutor": s.307(1).

GENERAL NOTE
The complaint will ordinarily proceed at the instance of the procurator fiscal having jurisdiction over a locus where it is alleged an offence was committed. Section 138 also permits other authorised prosecutors (for example the local education authority) to initiate proceedings by a complaint and to prosecute such cases.

The form of complaint should correspond to Form 16.1.–A in the 1996 Act of Adjournal, a style identical to the format used under the 1975 Act. The citation form now shown in Form 16.1.–B is similarly familiar. Examples of statutory charges are given in Sched. 5 to the Act which in turn adopts the somewhat esoteric charges listed as indictment styles in Sched. 2; Sched. 5 may lack some of the colour of the earlier schedule but at least has the merit of being of some practical (if limited) use. More importantly, the provisions of Sched. 3 in relation to implied terms and alternative verdicts, which were previously contained in s.312 of the 1975 Act are applied to all summary complaints. See for example *MacQueen v. Hingston*, 1997 S.C.C.R. 561, a Skye Bridge case in which, on appeal, it was held that the Crown was not obliged to lead proof of the currency of an Order where no preliminary plea to relevancy had been taken. No *nomen juris* need be stipulated in a complaint (see *Lippe v. Wilson*, 1997 G.W.D. 17–766 and pp. 104–105 above).

Essential Elements of a Complaint
The principal complaint has to be signed by the prosecutor but only the citation form to the accused need be signed (1996 Act of Adjournal Rule 16.2.–(1)). Rule 16.2.–(2) suggests that signature of any part of the papers sent to an accused as a service copy complaint would be sufficient to render proceedings competent. Failure by the prosecutor to sign the principal complaint creates a nullity (*Lowe v. Bee*, 1989 S.C.C.R. 476): loss of the principal complaint has till now been held to be fatal to proceedings and could not be remedied by seeking to substitute a certified copy (*McSeveney v. Annan*, 1990 S.C.C.R. 573; *Wilson v. Carmichael*, 1992 S.L.T. 54; 1991 S.C.C.R. 587; *Scott v. MacKay*, 1983 S.C.C.R. 210). However, s.157 of the Act now permits the substitution of a certified copy of the complaint in the event of such loss.

A discrepancy between the libel in the principal complaint and the service copy is no more than a technical defect unless it can be shown that the variation has caused substantial prejudice (*Fletcher v. Webster*, 1991 S.L.T. 256; 1991 S.C.C.R. 379 following *Dunsmore v. Threshie* (1896) 2 Adam 202).

Rule 16.1. above directs that the copy complaint should include a reply form and a means form, which again are familiar in appearance; failure to include these two forms will not vitiate proceedings on that complaint (Rule 16.3.).

It will be noted that this section does not require a complaint to include notices of penalty; such notices were previously essential to any sentence upon conviction of a statutory offence on summary complaint. The complaint should include any previous convictions to be founded upon by the prosecutor in the event of a conviction of the accused; previous convictions are discussed in notes to s.166 below.

Although it is statutorily enacted that any proceedings must be initiated by the procurator fiscal or an authorised prosecutor, the cases of *Thomson v. Scott*; *Walker v. Emslie* (1899) 3 Adam 102 and *Hill v. Finlayson* (1883) 5 Couper 284 support the view that the court itself has an inherent power to appoint a prosecutor *pro hac vice* to conduct those proceedings in the event of the death, illness or unavoidable absence of the prosecutor.

Complaints: orders and warrants

139.—(1) On any complaint under this Part of this Act being laid before a judge of the court in which the complaint is brought, he shall have power on the motion of the prosecutor—

    (a) to pronounce an order assigning a diet for the disposal of the case to which the accused may be cited as mentioned in section 141 of this Act;

    (b) to grant warrant to apprehend the accused where this appears to the judge expedient;

    (c) to grant warrant to search the person, dwelling-house and repositories of the accused and any place where he may be found for any documents, articles, or property likely to afford evidence of his guilt of, or guilty participation in, any offence charged in the complaint, and to take possession of such documents, articles or property;

    (d) to grant any other order or warrant of court or warrant which may be competent in the circumstances.

(2) The power of a judge under subsection (1) above—

    (a) to pronounce an order assigning a diet for the disposal of the case may be exercised on his behalf by the clerk of court;

    (b) to grant a warrant to apprehend the accused shall be exercisable notwithstanding that there is power whether at common law or under any Act to apprehend him without a warrant.

DEFINITIONS

    "complaint": s.307(1).
    "judge": s.307(1).
    "prosecutor": s.307(1).

GENERAL NOTE

    As subs. (2)(a) provides, cited diets are normally assigned administratively by the clerk of court, the judge initially needing only to be involved in considering the grant of an expediency or initiating warrant (subs. (1)(b)) or search warrants (subs. (1)(c)). It is the responsibility of the prosecutor to indicate to the clerk whether a specific date for the complaint to be called is needed; the complaint itself will show whether an assigned diet is craved and it then falls to the prosecutor to ensure that service is effected timeously (see notes to s.136 above).

    When the prosecutor decides to begin proceedings by means of an initiating warrant the practice is for the complaint to be considered by the judge in chambers without hearing the prosecutor; it is unusual, but perfectly competent for the judge to require the prosecutor to specify the grounds which lie behind the application for a warrant. Commonly an initiating warrant will be necessary in order to obtain the accused's fingerprints or other samples in an admissible fashion or to place him before an identification parade.

    As its name suggests, an expediency warrant is granted at the discretion of the court where a complaint is already current before the court and serves to keep the proceedings on it alive, provided that there are then reasonable grounds for believing that the complaint has been validly served: such a warrant cannot be used to validate a defect in the service of a complaint or as a means of overcoming a statutory timebar which would otherwise nullify the proceedings. In *Heywood v. McLennan*, 1994 S.C.C.R. 1 where a complaint had been continued without plea, and later was established not to have been served, the depute moved to desert the case *pro loco et tempore* and sought an initiating warrant on that complaint. In such circumstances the proper course should have been to raise a fresh complaint craving an initiating warrant, the first complaint having fallen. See also *Lees v. Malcolm*, 1992 S.C.C.R. 589.

    The extent of the procurator fiscal's common law power to apply for a search warrant as part of his investigative role, before proceedings are initiated, was discussed in *MacNeill, Complainer*, 1983 S.C.C.R. 450.

Citation

140.—[1](1) This Act shall be a sufficient warrant for

[1](a) the citation of witnesses for precognition by the prosecutor, whether or not any person has been charged with the offence in relation to which the precognition is taken; and

(b) the citation of the accused and witnesses in a summary prosecution to any ordinary sitting of the court or to any special diet fixed by the court or any adjournment thereof.

(2) Such citation shall be in the form prescribed by Act of Adjournal or as nearly as may be in such form and shall, in the case of the accused, proceed on an induciae of at least 48 hours unless in the special circumstances of the case the court fixes a shorter induciae.

[2](3) ...

DEFINITIONS

"diet": s.307(1).

"judge": s.307(1).

"prosecutor": s.307(1).

NOTES

[1]Inserted by the Crime and Punishment (Scotland) Act 1997 (c. 48) s.57(2) with effect from August 1, 1997 in terms of the Crime and Punishment (Scotland) Act 1997 (Commencement and Transitional Provisions) Order 1997 (S.I. 1997 No. 1712) para. 3.

[2]Deleted by s.57(2)(b) of the Act above in terms of the above Order.

GENERAL NOTE

Chapter 16 of the 1996 Act of Adjournal provides that the citation of an accused shall be by Form 16.1–B while witnesses should be cited by post using Form 16.6–A and, personally, by Form 16.6–C. Omission of the date of the diet from the accused's citation creates a nullity (*Beattie v. MacKinnon*, 1977 J.C. 64).

As with solemn witness citations, the Act of Adjournal envisages that any witness cited postally to attend, will acknowledge receipt of the citation by returning a pre-paid envelope with a further form (Form 16.6–B) within 14 days of citation. The objective of this reform, particularly now that intermediate diets are to be mandatory in summary cases (see s.148 below), is to enable parties to be in a position to advise the court confidently about their readiness for trial; however well-intended this provision may be, serious doubts must remain as to its practical worth. No citation of a witness or an accused is valid until the principal complaint has been signed (*Stewart v. Lang* (1894) 1 Adam 493).

Subsection (2) prescribes an *induciae* in the case of service of a citation upon an accused of at least 48 hours. This period, in the case of postal citation, is reckoned from 24 hours after the time of posting (see s.141(6) below). The *induciae* can of course be waived by the accused or, exceptionally, be reduced by the court itself on cause shown, but must not be so shortened as to prejudice the accused in the conduct of his defence. No such time scale is applied to the citation of witnesses but Rule 16.6 in the Act of Adjournal plainly envisages a greater period of notice being given to witnesses.

As well as providing for the citation of accused and witnesses in summary prosecutions, subs. (1) as now amended provides a mechanism for the prosecutor to obtain a warrant to cite witnesses for precognition even before any proceedings are active before the court. See also s.67A of Act dealing with the failure of a witness to attend for precognition by the prosecutor. Both petition and summary warrants as a matter of course give power to the prosecutor to cite for precognition but subs. (1) enables the Crown to make preliminary investigations even before proceedings are initiated; it is usual to petition the court by way of an incidental application in circumstances where it is believed that witnesses will not attend for precognition voluntarily. This procedure is rarely used.

Manner of citation

141.—(1) The citation of the accused and witnesses in a summary prosecution to any ordinary sitting of the court or to any special diet fixed by the court or to any adjourned sitting or diet shall be effected by delivering the citation to him personally or leaving it for him at his dwelling-house or place of business with a resident or, as the case may be, employee at that place or, where he has no known dwelling-house or place of business, at any other place in which he may be resident at the time.

(2) Notwithstanding subsection (1) above, citation may also be effected—

(a) where the accused or witness is the master of, or a seaman or person employed in a vessel, if the citation is left with a person on board the vessel and connected with it;

(b) where the accused is a partnership, association or body corporate—

(i) if the citation is left at its ordinary place of business with a partner, director, secretary or other official; or

(ii) if it is cited in the same manner as if the proceedings were in a civil court; or

(c) where the accused is a body of trustees, if the citation is left with any one of them who is resident in Scotland or with their known solicitor in Scotland.

[1](3) Subject to subsection (4) below, the citation of the accused or a witness to a sitting or diet or adjourned sitting or diet as mentioned in subsection (1) above shall be effective if it is — ...

[2](a) in the case of the accused signed by the prosecutor and sent by post in a registered envelope or through the recorded delivery service; and

[2](b) in the case of a witness, sent by or on behalf of the prosecutor by ordinary post,

to the dwelling-house or place of business of the accused or witness or, if he has no known dwelling-house or place of business, to any other place in which he may be resident at the time.

(4) Where the accused fails to appear at a diet or sitting or adjourned diet or sitting to which he has been cited in the manner provided by this section, subsections (3) and (5) to (7) of section 150 of this Act shall not apply unless it is proved to the court that he received the citation or that its contents came to his knowledge.

(5) The production in court of any letter or other communication purporting to be written by or on behalf of an accused who has been cited as mentioned in subsection (3) above in such terms as to infer that the contents of such citation came to his knowledge, shall be admissible as evidence of that fact for the purposes of subsection (4) above.

[2](5A) The citation of a witness to a sitting or diet or adjourned sitting or diet as mentioned in subsection (1) above shall be effective if it is sent by the accused's solicitor by ordinary post to the dwelling house or place of business of the witness or if he has no known dwelling house or place of business, to any other place in which he may be resident at the time.

(6) When the citation of any person is effected by post in terms of this section or any other provision of this Act to which this section is applied, the induciae shall be reckoned from 24 hours after the time of posting.

(7) It shall be sufficient evidence that a citation has been sent by post in terms of this section or any other provision of this Act mentioned in subsection (6) above, if there is produced in court a written execution, signed by the person who signed the citation in the form prescribed by Act of Adjournal, or as nearly as may be in such form, together with the post office receipt for the relative registered or recorded delivery letter.

DEFINITIONS
"diet": s.307(1).
"prosecutor": s.307(1).

NOTES
[1]Deleted by the Crime and Punishment (Scotland) Act 1997 (c. 48) s.62(1) and Sched. 1, para. 21(19)(a) with effect from August 1, 1997 in terms of the Crime and Punishment (Scotland) Act 1997 (Commencement and Transitional Provisions) Order 1997 (S.I. 1997 No. 1712) para. 3.

[2]Inserted by the 1997 Act s.62(1) and Sched. 1, para. 21(19)(a) with effect from August 1, 1997 in terms of the above Order.

[3]Inserted by the 1997 Act s.62(1) and Sched. 1, para. 21(19)(b) with effect from August 1, 1997 in terms of the above Order.

GENERAL NOTE

This section deals with the methods of citation of both accused and any witnesses to court in criminal proceedings. Minor changes introduced by the 1997 Act have brought a measure of clarity, and economy, to this procedure; subs. (3) relates to citations to be served by the Crown, while subs. (5A) makes distinct provisions for citation of defence witnesses and makes postal service an acceptable form of citation. The section does not preclude personal service by either police or sheriff officers, but indicates that postal service should normally be sufficient.

The date of postal citation is the date of posting, not receipt, of a citation (*Lockhart v. Bradley*, 1977 S.L.T. 5) and no warrant for citation exists until the principal citation has been signed (see the discussion "Essential Elements of a Complaint" at p. 199 and *Stewart v. Lang* (1894) 1 A. 493).

Section 150 entitles the court to grant a warrant to arrest an accused following failure to appear at a diet to which he has been cited or notified to appear. The prosecutor must satisfy the court that service has been validly effected in accordance with this section and may found upon the recorded delivery execution of service of the complaint or any letter sent by, or on behalf of the accused which indicates the accused's awareness of the diet (see *Aitchison v. Wringe*, 1985 S.L.T. 449; 1985 S.C.C.R. 134; *Orr v. Lowdon*, 1987 S.C.C.R. 515 while in *Normand v. Harkins*, 1996 S.C.C.R. 355 service was upheld where the complaint was left in the hands of a person bearing to be a flatmate of the accused and accepted service, the process server having acted in good faith. Compare *Normand v. Buchanan*, 1996 S.C.C.R. 363 where service was not effected at the accused's address, the complaint being left elsewhere in the hands of relatives (also accused) to pass to the accused, which they duly did; in that case the prosecutor failed to prove valid service of a complaint and penalty notices). In certain statutory enactments it may be competent to proceed to trial in the absence of the accused (s.150(5)) but again this is contingent upon the court being satisfied that the accused knew of the diet.

In the case of limited companies, partnerships or other bodies, citation can be effected at the home of a responsible officer of that entity at his home address as well as at the place of business (*Kirkcudbright Scallop Gear Ltd v. Walkingshaw*, 1994 S.C.C.R. 372).

Kelly v. Rae, 1917 J.C. 12 is still authority for the view that neither the accused apprehended *in flagrante delicto*, or his agent, need receive a copy complaint at least when the accused has been brought before the first available custody court; the case is mentioned tentatively since no previous convictions could be put before the court, and, it has to be said, that any conviction would be liable to be quashed if it was shown that the defence had suffered substantial prejudice as a result of this omission.

Children

Summary proceedings against children

142.—(1) Where summary proceedings are brought in respect of an offence alleged to have been committed by a child, the sheriff shall sit either in a different building or room from that in which he usually sits or on different days from those on which other courts in the building are engaged in criminal proceedings: and no person shall be present at any sitting for the purposes of such proceedings except—

    (a) members and officers of the court;

    (b) parties to the case before the court, their solicitors and counsel, and witnesses and other persons directly concerned in that case;

    (c) *bona fide* representatives of news gathering or reporting organisations present for the purpose of the preparation of contemporaneous reports of the proceedings;

    (d) such other persons as the court may specially authorise to be present.

    (2) A sheriff sitting summarily for the purpose of hearing a charge against, or an application relating to, a person who is believed to be a child may, if he thinks fit to do so, proceed with the hearing and determination of the charge or application, notwithstanding that it is discovered that the person in question is not a child.

    (3) When a sheriff sitting summarily has remanded a child for information

to be obtained with respect to him, any sheriff sitting summarily in the same place—

(a) may in his absence extend the period for which he is remanded provided that he appears before a sheriff or a justice at least once every 21 days;

(b) when the required information has been obtained, may deal with him finally,

and where the sheriff by whom he was originally remanded has recorded a finding that he is guilty of an offence charged against him it shall not be necessary for any court which subsequently deals with him under this subsection to hear evidence as to the commission of that offence, except in so far as it may consider that such evidence will assist the court in determining the manner in which he should be dealt with.

(4) Any direction in any enactment that a charge shall be brought before a juvenile court shall be construed as a direction that he shall be brought before the sheriff sitting as a court of summary jurisdiction, and no such direction shall be construed as restricting the powers of any justice or justices to entertain an application for bail or for a remand, and to hear such evidence as may be necessary for that purpose.

(5) This section does not apply to summary proceedings before the sheriff in respect of an offence where a child has been charged jointly with a person who is not a child.

DEFINITIONS
"justice": s.307(1).
"offence": s.307(1).
"sheriff": s.5(1).

GENERAL NOTE
Section 42 stipulates that where criminal offences alleged to have been committed by children are prosecuted by the criminal courts, rather than being referred to the Principal Reporter, such offences must be prosecuted in the sheriff court or a higher court (see generally the discussion in the notes to s.42 above). This stipulation does not extend to cases in which a co-accused is over 16 years old; in that event the proceedings can be taken in any court if it is felt that referring the child to the children's panel is inappropriate and proceedings must be taken against both parties.

The district court will not have jurisdiction over complaints against juvenile offenders but subs. (4) provides that this is without prejudice to any right of a justice (as defined in s.307(1) this includes sheriffs, stipendiary magistrates and justices of the peace) to determine applications for bail or remand.

The object of subs. (1) is to ensure that the juvenile criminal proceedings brought against children are conducted in court facilities distinct from those used in the course of summary proceedings against young persons and adults. This is intended to prevent the child coming into contact with older offenders and means that a separate juvenile court should convene to hear any custody, diet or trial business whose accused are solely children. The provision is directory in character and non-observance of it is not fatal to a finding of guilt (*Heywood v. B.*, 1994 S.C.C.R. 554).

Chapter 6 of the 1996 Act of Adjournal also provides that efforts be made to prevent the mixing of children attending any juvenile court hearing.

In addition to requiring separate courts for juvenile hearings, s.142 enacts that those proceedings will not be held in open court; access is restricted to the parties specified by subs. (1)(a) to (c) and is otherwise at the discretion of the court.

Subsection (2) preserves the validity of any finding made by a court which has proceeded on the mistaken belief that the accused, or one of the accused, is a child.

Subsection (3) provides for an administrative continuation of a juvenile's case by another sheriff in the absence of the sheriff who made the original remand for information and, in situations where the latter sheriff is unavailable at the time of receipt of that information, his colleague may dispose of the case. A period of remand of a juvenile can exceed 21 days provided that the child is brought before a justice at least once every 21 days.

Companies

Prosecution of companies, etc.

143.—(1) Without prejudice to any other or wider powers conferred by statute, this section shall apply in relation to the prosecution by summary procedure of a partnership, association, body corporate or body of trustees.

(2) Proceedings may be taken against the partnership, association body corporate or body of trustees in their corporate capacity, and in that event any penalty imposed shall be recovered by civil diligence in accordance with section 221 of this Act.

(3) Proceedings may be taken against an individual representative of a partnership, association or body corporate as follows:—

(a) in the case of a partnership or firm, any one of the partners, or the manager or the person in charge or locally in charge of its affairs;

(b) in the case of an association or body corporate, the managing director or the secretary or other person in charge, or locally in charge, of its affairs,

may be dealt with as if he was the person offending, and the offence shall be deemed to be the offence of the partnership, association or body corporate.

DEFINITION
"offence": s.307(1).

GENERAL NOTE
See generally the notes to s.70 above.

An unincorporated company may be charged in the name of the company or the partners' names or both (*City and Suburban Dairies v. Mackenna*, 1918 J.C. 105). The same approach can be followed against partnerships.

Proceedings against a registered club can be taken against its office bearers (*Burnette v. Mackenna*, 1917 J.C. 20).

It is competent to proceed against directors of a limited company or against a manager or employee locally responsible for its affairs (*Bean v. Sinclair*, 1930 J.C. 31) but previous convictions libelled against the company cannot be used against that individual (*Campbell v. MacPherson* (1910) 6 Adam 394). A manager can competently represent the company at any diet (*McAlpine v. Ronaldson* (1901) 3 Adam 405). Only convictions libelled against the accused company can be founded upon by the Crown, but where such convictions exist and have not been libelled against the company, it is not open to the defence to make claims at odds with the terms of those convictions; *Massily Packaging (U.K.) Ltd v. MacDonald*, 1997 G.W.D. 3–87.

Amendment of the complaint where the company is incorrectly named is problematical; see *Hoyers (U.K.) v. Houston*, 1991 S.L.T. 934; 1991 S.C.C.R. 919 where the description of the accused was amended at the trial diet, by which time a new complaint would have been timebarred. In *Ralston v. Carmichael*, 1995 G.W.D. 38–1933 a complaint against "Henry Ralston Ltd" was amended to "Henry Ralston" when it was discovered that the limited company did not exist; an appearance and correspondence had already passed before the amendment was sought and it could not be contended that prejudice was caused by the amendment. The issues are whether the error in the name or designation is trivial and if an appearance is made in answer to the complaint (*Poli v. Thomson* (1910) 5 Adam 261); in that event amendment is competent.

Even on summary complaint the level of penalties which can be imposed on limited companies, notably in the environmental field or for health and safety breaches, can be severe; examples are found in *Howdle v. Castelli Girola UK Ltd (No. 2)*, a fine of £15,000 under the Control of Pollution Act 1974 for a second offence; *AMEC Construction (Scotland) Ltd v. Lees*, 1996 G.W.D. 3–161 statutory maximum (currently £20,000) imposed on first offender for failure to provide a guardrail on a ledge from which an employee fell and sustained injury.

For service of citations against bodies corporate, see s.141 above.

First diet

Procedure at first diet

144.—(1) Where the accused is present at the first calling of the case in a summary prosecution and—

    (a) the complaint has been served on him, or
    (b) the complaint or the substance thereof has been read to him, or
    (c) he has legal assistance in his defence,
he shall, unless the court adjourns the case under the section 145 of this Act and subject to subsection (4) below, be asked to plead to the charge.

    (2) Where the accused is not present at a calling of the case in a summary prosecution and either—

    (a) the prosecutor produces to the court written intimation that the accused pleads not guilty or pleads guilty and the court is satisfied that the intimation has been made or authorised by the accused; or

    (b) counsel or a solicitor, or a person not being counsel or a solicitor who satisfies the court that he is authorised by the accused, appears on behalf of the accused and tenders a plea of not guilty or a plea of guilty,

subsection (3) below shall apply.

    (3) Where this subsection applies—

    (a) in the case of a plea of not guilty, this Part of this Act except section 146(2) shall apply in like manner as if the accused had appeared and tendered the plea; and

    (b) in the case of a plea of guilty, the court may, if the prosecutor accepts the plea, proceed to hear and dispose of the case in the absence of the accused in like manner as if he had appeared and pled guilty, or may, if it thinks fit, continue the case to another diet and require the attendance of the accused with a view to pronouncing sentence in his presence.

    (4) Any objection to the competency or relevancy of a summary complaint or the proceedings thereon, or any denial that the accused is the person charged by the police with the offence shall be stated before the accused pleads to the charge or any plea is tendered on his behalf.

    (5) No objection or denial such as is mentioned in subsection (4) above shall be allowed to be stated or issued at any future diet in the case except with the leave of the court, which may be granted only on cause shown.

    (6) Where in pursuance of subsection (3)(b) above the court proceeds to hear and dispose of a case in the absence of the accused, it shall not pronounce a sentence of imprisonment or of detention in a young offenders institution, remand centre or other establishment.

    (7) In this section a reference to a plea of guilty shall include a reference to a plea of guilty to only part of the charge, but where a plea of guilty to only part of a charge is not accepted by the prosecutor it shall be deemed to be a plea of not guilty.

    (8) It shall not be competent for any person appearing to answer a complaint, or for counsel or a solicitor appearing for the accused in his absence, to plead want of due citation or informality therein or in the execution thereof.

    (9) In this section, a reference to the first calling of a case includes a reference to any adjourned diet fixed by virtue of section 145 of this Act.

DEFINITIONS
    "complaint": s.307(1).
    "diet": s.307(1).
    "imprisonment": s.308.
    "prosecutor": s.307(1).
    "sentence": s.307(1).
    "young offenders institution": s.307(1).

GENERAL NOTE
    Appearance at a first diet cures any deficiency in citation (subs. (8)); the accused can make an appearance in person, by way of attendance at court by a solicitor or other authorised representative or by letter. Want of form, which is curable by appearance, should not be

confused with a nullity; an unsigned complaint (*Lowe v. Bee*, 1989 S.C.C.R. 476), a complaint which failed to specify a date or locus or in which the court had no jurisdiction (*McMillan v. Grant*, 1924 J.C. 13; *Duffy v. Ingram*, 1987 S.C.C.R. 286) or a missing principal complaint (*McSeveney v. Annan*, 1990 S.C.C.R. 573) are all fundamental procedural defects which cannot be remedied. Note in the last instance, the terms of s.157 which appear to permit the use of a certified copy complaint to preserve proceedings.

Before any plea is tendered any plea in bar, plea to the competency or relevancy (including any allegation of undue delay in executing any warrant to apprehend or cite), notice that the accused disputes having been cautioned and charged with the offences libelled should be stated (subs. (4)), as should any objection to the libelling of a special capacity (s.255).

Mental Disorder

Section 52 expressly, and s.145 impliedly, require both the prosecutor and the court to ensure that the accused is not suffering any mental disorder and the diet should be adjourned without plea for the purpose of investigation (in the former section the prosecutor should place medical evidence before the court; in the latter the court itself may adjourn without plea, to enable the prosecutor to obtain a medical report). Until the issue is resolved, any continuation is to be treated as a first diet (subs. (9)). See generally the notes at 4.122 above, *Sloan v. Crowe*, 1996 S.C.C.R. 200 and *MacDonald v. Munro*, 1996 S.C.C.R. 595 for discussion of the Crown's obligations under this section.

Pleas to Competency and Relevancy and Special Capacity

Subsection (5) stipulates that any such pleas must normally be stated at the first diet, though subs. (9) has the effect of permitting a continuation without plea under s.145, to permit proper formulation of any such objections. After the first diet, any objection can only be heard on cause shown; in *H.M. Advocate v. Bell* (1892) 3 White 313, the court at a second diet was held to be entitled to consider such objections not previously stated where otherwise a gross injustice would result. See also *McLeay v. Hingston*, 1994 S.L.T. 720; 1994 S.C.C.R. 116 where objection to a complaint devoid of a locus was stated only part way through a trial, the Appeal Court noting that the case could have been adjourned pending resolution of an appeal, the sheriff having repelled objections and granted leave to appeal. The introduction of mandatory intermediate diets in all summary cases (see s.148 below) may serve to limit the late introduction of any such motion.

The Appeal Court has indicated that it is primarily a matter for the discretion of the trial judge whether or not to entertain late pleas to competency, relevancy or capacity (which of course necessarily involve the withdrawal of any pleas previously tendered in regard to the charges) and that that discretion will only be reviewed in light of fundamental objections (*Henderson v. Ingram*, 1982 S.C.C.R. 135). See also *Scott v. Annan*, 1981 S.C.C.R. 172; 1982 S.L.T. 90; *Wimpey Homes Holdings v. Lees*, 1993 S.L.T. 564.

The principal ground for consideration of a plea to relevancy of a complaint is whether the libel is sufficiently specific to give the defence fair notice of the offences (*Clydesdale Group v. Normand*, 1994 S.L.T. 1302).

If a preliminary plea is wholly sustained, then the complaint falls. In the event that the complaint is upheld in whole or part, ordinarily the accused should then be called upon to plead to the charges (a continuation without plea, for example to obtain further instructions, would be competent in terms of s.145). It is important to note that even if the defence move for, or are granted, leave to appeal against the decision relating to the preliminary plea (by way of s.174 below), a plea of guilty or not guilty should be tendered and recorded and a trial diet assigned as necessary (see *Lafferty v. Jessop*, 1989 S.L.T. 846; 1989 S.C.C.R. 451 and *Jessop v. First National Securities*, 1988 S.C.C.R. 1). Note that in the latter case having decided the issue of relevancy, the sheriff, no doubt conscious that his decision was likely to be appealed, canvassed the views of parties and decided to issue a written note of his judgment. Procedurally the proper course would have been to give no decision and continue the case to a later diet for the judgment or, alternatively, give his decision and defer any written comment for his Report, should an appeal be taken against the judgment and the call upon the accused to plead.

Although the court may continue a case for the personal appearance of the accused for sentence (subs. (3)(b)), it does not follow that sentence is contingent upon such an appearance (see *Taylor v. Lees*, 1993 S.C.C.R. 947). The only stricture upon sentence in absence is stated in subs. (6); a sentence of imprisonment or detention can only be imposed when an accused is personally present.

The prosecutor is never obliged to accept a plea of guilty either to the whole or part of a complaint: (*Kirkwood v. Coalburn District Cooperative Society*, 1930 J.C. 38). However where a plea of guilt is tendered, it has been held that appeal by way of bill of suspension will rarely be appropriate; see *Aitken v. Reith*, 1996 G.W.D. 2–79 where following a letter plea of guilty and a personal appearance for sentence, the accused subsequently claimed to have been unaware that he had been charged with dangerous, rather than careless, driving and had been too timid to withdraw his plea at the deferred diet.

The court would require to be satisfied that the accused had substantially misunderstood his position and been prejudiced, or had been unreasonably pressured by his solicitor into pleading and had been prejudiced as a result (see *McGuire v. Normand*, 1997 G.W.D. 3–86; *Simpson v. McKay*, 1997 G.W.D. 14–588 where the Crown's narration went unchallenged; *Kerr v. Friel*, 1997 S.C.C.R. 317 a "plea of convenience" case; and *Bieniwoski v. Ruxton*, 1997 G.W.D. 23–1143 a plea to dangerous driving by speeding, allegedly tendered in ignorance of the penalties, the conviction was not suspended, the Appeal Court noting the service of a penalty notice on the accused).

Where the accused is present in court, the terms of his plea should be confirmed directly from him, even if he is represented; failure to follow the procedure set out in the Act of Adjournal (Criminal Procedure Rules) 1996, r.18.1(1) creates a nullity (*McGowan v. Ritchie*, 1997 S.C.C.R. 332 where authority for fresh proceedings on the original charges libelled was granted).

In *Ettinger v. McFadyen*, 2000 G.W.D. 22–851 the Appeal Court held it to be a breach of natural justice for the sheriff, having found an unexplained period of delay on the part of the Crown in initiating proceedings, to permit an adjournment for the Crown to produce further evidence after parties had concluded submissions. See also *McAnea v. H.M.Advocate*, 2001 S.L.T. 12; 2000 S.C.C.R. 779 where the trial judge, having ruled upon defence objections to a line of evidence, was held to have wrongly permitted further Crown submissions on the point thereafter.

Adjournment for inquiry at first calling

145.—(1) Without prejudice to section 150(1) to (7) of this Act, at the first calling of a case in a summary prosecution the court may, in order to allow time for inquiry into the case or for any other cause which it considers reasonable, adjourn the case under this section, for such period as it considers appropriate, without calling on the accused to plead to any charge against him but remanding him in custody or on bail or ordaining him to appear at the diet thus fixed; and, subject to subsections (2) and (3) below, the court may from time to time so adjourn the case.

(2) Where the accused is remanded in custody, the total period for which he is so remanded under this section shall not exceed 21 days and no one period of adjournment shall, except on special cause shown, exceed 7 days.

(3) Where the accused is remanded on bail or ordained to appear, no one period of adjournment shall exceed 28 days.

DEFINITIONS
"bail": s.307(1).
"diet": s.307(1).
"remand": s.307(1).

GENERAL NOTE
The court's power to continue a case without plea on the motion of a party or *ex proprio motu* is preserved. However where an accused is remanded in custody in relation to the complaint before the court, no continuation should exceed seven days save on cause shown, and the total period of continuations cannot exceed 21 days (subs. (2)). It will be remembered that the period involved in any such continuation has to be included in the calculation of time spent in custody awaiting summary trial since the bringing of the complaint (see s.147 below).

The maximum period of adjournment allowed at any one time in cases where the accused is bailed or ordained to appear is 28 days (subs. (3)). A continuation without plea for debate would appear not to be subject to the time limit imposed by subs. (3) following the *ratio* in *Pearson v. Crowe*, 1994 S.L.T. 378, but is obviously affected by the strictures imposed in custody cases by subs. (2).

Plea of not guilty

146.—(1) This section applies where the accused in a summary prosecution—

(a) pleads not guilty to the charge; or
(b) pleads guilty to only part of the charge and the prosecutor does not accept the partial plea.
(2) The court may proceed to trial at once unless either party moves for an adjournment and the court considers it expedient to grant it.
(3) The court may adjourn the case for trial to as early a diet as is consistent with the just interest of both parties, and the prosecutor shall, if requested by the accused, furnish him with a copy of the complaint if he does not already have one.
(4) Where the accused is brought before the court from custody the court shall inform the accused of his right to an adjournment of the case for not less than 48 hours and if he requests such adjournment before the prosecutor has commenced his proof, subject to subsection (5) below, the adjournment shall be granted.
(5) Where the court considers that it is necessary to secure the examination of witnesses who otherwise would not be available, the case may proceed to trial at once or on a shorter adjournment than 48 hours.
(6) Where the accused is in custody, he may be committed to prison or to legalised police cells or to any other place to which he may lawfully be committed pending trial—
(a) if he is neither granted bail nor ordained to appear; or
(b) if he is granted bail on a condition imposed under section 24(6) of this Act that a sum of money is deposited in court, until the accused or a cautioner on his behalf has so deposited that sum.
(7) The court may from time to time at any stage of the case on the motion of either party or *ex proprio motu* grant such adjournment as may be necessary for the proper conduct of the case, and where from any cause a diet has to be continued from day to day it shall not be necessary to intimate the continuation to the accused.
(8) It shall not be necessary for the prosecutor to establish a charge or part of a charge to which the accused pleads guilty.
(9) The court may, in any case where it considers it expedient, permit any witness for the defence to be examined prior to evidence for the prosecution having been led or concluded, but in any such case the accused shall be entitled to lead additional evidence after the case for the prosecution is closed.

DEFINITIONS
"bail": s.307(1).
"diet": s.307(1).
"legalised police cells": s.307(1).
"prison": s.307(1).
"prosecutor": s.307(1).

GENERAL NOTE
Provided that any preliminary pleas have been repelled, the accused should then be called upon to plead to the charges still current on the complaint. The prosecutor may, but is not obliged to, accept any partial pleas tendered. Subject to the exceptional provisions of subs. (5), in custody cases the accused is entitled to an *induciae* of 48 hours before his trial occurs, an *induciae* which he may waive, but his right to which the court must make known to him; failure to do so will almost certainly vitiate any conviction (see *Ferguson v. Brown*, 1942 J.C. 113). The refusal of an adjournment which is needed, in order to enable the accused to lead evidence in support of his alibi defence once trial has begun, may constitute oppression; *McKellar v. Dickson* (1898) 2 Adam 504.
In accordance with subs. (2), the court can proceed to trial immediately unless any of the parties moves for an adjournment. In practice, such a peremptory diet of trial is rare though subs. (5) allows for such a trial then or within 48 hours, where this is essential to secure witnesses' evidence even in custody cases. It is perfectly competent to adjourn the trial once such evidence has been heard or at any point in any summary trial (subs. (7)).
Subsection (6) permits a remand in custody in cases where bail is either not granted or not

sought, or more unusually, where a sum of money bail is required to be deposited with the court as an additional bail condition in terms of s.24(6).

Guidance on the courses which the court may follow where there is disagreement between the parties in the factual narration is given in *McCartney v. H.M. Advocate*, 1997 S.C.C.R. 644.

Subsection (9) echoes the little-used terms of s.337(h) of the 1975 Act and permits the calling of defence evidence prior to, or during, Crown evidence. It is suggested that this provision envisages the leading of defence evidence, a preferable alternative to the Crown, as an expedient means of assisting the defence—calling defence witnesses during the Crown case formally, then leaving the defence to lead the witness' evidence in cross-examination.

Pre-trial procedure

Prevention of delay in trials

147.—(1) Subject to subsections (2) and (3) below, a person charged with an offence in summary proceedings shall not be detained in that respect for a total of more than 40 days after the bringing of the complaint in court unless his trial is commenced within that period, failing which he shall be liberated forthwith and thereafter he shall be for ever free from all question or process for that offence.

(2) The sheriff may, on application made to him for the purpose, extend the period mentioned in subsection (1) above and order the accused to be detained awaiting trial for such period as he thinks fit where he is satisfied that delay in the commencement of the trial is due to—

(a) the illness of the accused or of a judge;

(b) the absence or illness of any necessary witness; or

(c) any other sufficient cause which is not attributable to any fault on the part of the prosecutor.

(3) The grant or refusal of any application to extend the period mentioned in subsection (1) above may be appealed against by note of appeal presented to the High Court; and that Court may affirm, reverse or amend the determination made on such application.

(4) For the purposes of this section, a trial shall be taken to commence when the first witness is sworn.

DEFINITIONS

"complaint": s.307(1).
"High Court": s.307(1).
"judge": s.307(1).
"offence": s.307(1).
"prosecutor": s.307(1).
"sheriff": s.5(1).
"witness": s.307(1).

GENERAL NOTE

This section preserves the provisions introduced into the 1975 Act by s.14(2) of the Criminal Justice (Scotland) Act 1980 to limit the period of remand affecting persons awaiting summary trial. A person remanded in custody in terms of s.146(6) may only be held in custody pending trial for 40 days in relation to that complaint.

Note that the period only begins from "the bringing of the complaint" so a period on remand following an appearance on petition would not, it is submitted, be included in calculation of the 40 days, notwithstanding the recent decision in *Gardner v. Lees*, 1996 S.C.C.R. 186 (itself since superseded by the terms of s.65(1) as now amended) which dealt with a non-custodial reduction of petition proceedings to summary proceedings.

Similarly, the period spent in custody must be attributable wholly to matters awaiting trial; a person serving a sentence, or a person remanded for trial but who then becomes a serving prisoner thus effectively interrupting the remand period, cannot benefit from the protection of the provisions against delay in trial. However in *Lockhart v. Robb*, 1988 S.C.C.R. 381 it was held by the sheriff that a remand for pre-sentencing reports on another complaint did not interrupt the running of 40 days in a custody complaint.

Two extensions were permitted where the accused's plea in bar on grounds of insanity had to be investigated by the Crown, and through no fault on the Crown's part one of the reports was not available to the court; the accused was remanded awaiting trial for 70 days (*Sweeney v. Douglas*, 1997 G.W.D. 28—1408).

In calculating the 40 day period, the whole of the day on which the remand order is made is discounted, while the whole of the final day is included: see *Hazlett v. McGlennan*, 1992 S.C.C.R. 799; 1993 S.L.T. 74 and the discussion "Computation of Time" in notes to s.136 above. As subs. (4) enacts, the period expires when the trial begins. In *Grugen v. Jessop*, 1988 S.C.C.R. 182 the accused took a Bill of Advocation founding upon the actions of the prosecutor who commenced his trial on the fortieth day, in the knowledge that the trial would have to be adjourned only part-heard due to the known unavailability of Crown witnesses. The Appeal Court refused the Bill and declined to hold these procedures to be an abuse of process.

The court on application can extend the 40 day period on the grounds specified in subs. (2); considerations similar to those applying to s.65(4) in solemn procedure are relevant. Appeal to the High Court against such extension proceeds on Form 17.1 while Rule 17.1.–(2) of the 1996 Act of Adjournal stipulates service of copies of the Form upon the prosecutor and the clerk of court. Appeals against extensions of the 40 day period are marked using Form 17.1 in the Act of Adjournal.

Subsection (4) was interpreted in *Mitchell v. Vannet*, 1999 G.W.D. 20–928.

See pp. 215–216.

Intermediate diet

148.—(1) The court may, when adjourning a case for trial in terms of section 146(3) of this Act, and may also, at any time thereafter, whether before, on or after any date assigned as a trial diet, fix a diet (to be known as an intermediate diet) for the purpose of ascertaining, so far as is reasonably practicable, whether the case is likely to proceed to trial on any date assigned as a trial diet and, in particular—

(a) the state of preparation of the prosecutor and of the accused with respect to their cases;

(b) whether the accused intends to adhere to the plea of not guilty; and

(c) the extent to which the prosecutor and the accused have complied with the duty under section 257(1) of this Act.

(2) Where at an intermediate diet the court concludes that the case is unlikely to proceed to trial on the date assigned for the trial diet, the court—

(a) shall, unless having regard to previous proceedings in the case it considers it inappropriate to do so, postpone the trial diet; and

(b) may fix a further intermediate diet.

(3) Subject to subsection (2) above, the court may, if it considers it appropriate to do so, adjourn an intermediate diet.

(4) At an intermediate diet, the court may ask the prosecutor and the accused any question for the purposes mentioned in subsection (1) above.

(5) The accused shall attend an intermediate diet of which he has received intimation or to which he has been cited unless—

(a) he is legally represented; and

(b) the court considers that there are exceptional circumstances justifying him not attending.

(6) A plea of guilty may be tendered at the intermediate diet.

(7) The foregoing provisions of this section shall have effect as respects any court prescribed by the Secretary of State by order, in relation to proceedings commenced after such date as may be so prescribed, with the following modifications—

[1](a) in subsection (1), for the word "may" where it first appears there shall be substituted "shall, subject to subsection (1A) below,"; and

(b) after subsection (1) there shall be inserted the following subsections—

"(1A) If, on a joint application by the prosecutor and the accused made at any time before the commencement of the intermediate diet, the court considers it inappropriate to have such a diet, the duty under subsection (1) above shall not apply and the court shall discharge any such diet already fixed.

(1B) The court may consider an application under subsection (1A) above without hearing the parties.".

(8) An order under subsection (7) above shall be made by statutory instrument, which shall be subject to annulment in pursuance of a resolution of either House of Parliament.

DEFINITIONS
"diet": s.307(1).
"prosecutor": s.307(1).

NOTE
[1]As amended by the Criminal Procedure (Intermediate Diets) (Scotland) Act 1998 (c. 10) s.1 (effective April 8, 1998).

GENERAL NOTE
The Criminal Procedure (Intermediate Diets) (Scotland) Act 1998 (c. 10) received Royal Assent on April 9, 1998 and was a legislative response to the High Court's decisions in *Mackay v. Ruxton*, 1998 S.C.C.R. 790 and *Kerr v. Carnegie*, 1998 S.C.C.R. 168, both of which explored the consequences of failure to fix an intermediate diet, and *Vannet v. Milligan*, 1998 S.C.C.R. 305, dealing with a purported alteration of a trial diet at an incompetent intermediate diet. (The practice had developed in summary courts of assigning an intermediate diet prior to the trial diet as s.148(1) dictates and further such diets, ostensibly under s.148(1), where the trial did not proceed and had to be adjourned to a later trial diet.)

It is some measure of the uncertainty which these decisions engendered and the far-reaching implications for a large volume of summary trial business that the new Act was treated by Parliament as emergency legislation and, most unusually, came into force with retrospective effect. The new provisions require summary courts to fix an intermediate diet when a trial diet is first assigned and give those courts a discretion to fix further intermediate diets, as necessary, during the currency of any criminal complaint which is proceeding to trial. Generally however there is likely to be little practical benefit in assigning a further intermediate diet once a trial diet has been adjourned unless there has been a tangible change in circumstances; joint minute procedures arguably provide a more flexible tool for the purpose, at least where parties agree the need for the court to consider afresh (see s.137 above).

Intermediate diets were introduced in 1980 in a drive to avoid the waste of court resources, the expense and the needless inconvenience to the public caused by the large numbers of cases which, for one reason or another, did not proceed at trial diets.

Section 14 of the Criminal Justice (Scotland) Act 1995 (c. 20) extended the scope of intermediate diets and envisaged a more pro-active role on the part of the Bench in ascertaining the state of preparation of parties for the impending trial. It will be remembered that s.196 of the Criminal Procedure (Scotland) Act 1995 allowed the courts to take account of the point in proceedings at which the accused tendered a guilty plea: a formal diet calling prior to the trial, but after the parties had concluded their preparation, could materially assist both in speeding the flow of court business and disposing of pleas.

Subsections (2) and (3) enable the courts to ascertain whether a trial will proceed or not and, if not, to postpone the trial diet (with or without a further intermediate diet being fixed) or adjourn the intermediate diet while preserving the trial diet.

The Appeal Court has held that the purpose of intermediate (or first) diets is an administrative one rather than being a fundamental, and necessary, process any procedural lapse in which would vitiate proceedings (*Hogg v. H.M. Advocate*, 1999 S.L.T. 371 applying *Kerr v. Carnegie*, 1998 S.C.C.R. 168). In *Kerr*, a custody trial, no intermediate diet was fixed, an omission which the Appeal Court declined to view as an irremediable defect. Indeed the Court went on to point to the fact that it was s.148(7) of the Act which required mandatory, rather than discretionary, intermediate diets and that that only took effect at the behest of the Secretary of State by order—clearly the exercise of an administrative function. It may also be significant in this context that s.146(2) of the Act entitles a summary court to proceed immediately to trial as soon as a plea of not guilty is tendered, a long-standing provision wholly at odds with *Kerr* contentions, but one which underlines the incidental rather than fundamental nature of intermediate diets. See too *Reith v. Bates*, 1998 S.C.C.R. 426; 1999 S.L.T. 380, a case in which at a second intermediate diet the court was minuted as having adjourned the imminent trial diet; the Appeal Court looked to the intention of the prosecutor and the sheriff to postpone the trial and thus repelled the accused's objection to the competency of the proceedings which was founded on inaccurate minutes.

The essentially administrative character of intermediate diets is underlined by *Brown v. Vannet*, 1999 G.W.D. 19–873 in which an unsuccessful appeal founded upon the availability of an interpreter at the intermediate diet for a deaf-mute accused. Compare the position at trial; see *Mikhailitchenko v. Normand*, 1993 S.L.T. 1138.

Alibi

149. It shall not be competent for the accused in a summary prosecution to found on a plea of alibi unless he gives, at any time before the first witness is sworn, notice to the prosecutor of the plea with particulars as to time and place and of the witnesses by whom it is proposed to prove it; and, on such notice being given, the prosecutor shall be entitled, if he so desires, to an adjournment of the case.

DEFINITIONS
"prosecutor": s.307(1).
"witness": s.307(1).

GENERAL NOTE
Schedule 6, para. 121 of the Criminal Justice (Scotland) Act 1995 introduced only one small clarifying amendment to s.339 of the 1975 Act, which carried over into s.149 of the current Act. An alibi has now to be intimated before the first witness is sworn, whereas in the 1975 Act intimation had to be made "prior to the examination of the first witness".

Failure of accused to appear

Failure of accused to appear

150.—(1) This section applies where the accused in a summary prosecution fails to appear at any diet of which he has received intimation, or to which he has been cited other than a diet which, by virtue of section 148(5) of this Act, he is not required to attend.

(2) The court may adjourn the proceedings to another diet, and order the accused to attend at such diet, and appoint intimation of the diet to be made to him.

(3) The court may grant warrant to apprehend the accused.

(4) Intimation under subsection (2) above shall be sufficiently given by an officer of law, or by letter signed by the clerk of court or prosecutor and sent to the accused at his last known address by registered post or by the recorded delivery service, and the production in court of the written execution of such officer or of an acknowledgement or certificate of the delivery of the letter issued by the Post Office shall be sufficient evidence of such intimation having been duly given.

(5) Where the accused is charged with a statutory offence for which a sentence of imprisonment cannot be imposed in the first instance, or where the statute founded on or conferring jurisdiction authorises procedure in the absence of the accused, the court, on the motion of the prosecutor and upon being satisfied that the accused has been duly cited, or has received due intimation of the diet where such intimation has been ordered, may subject to subsections (6) and (7) below, proceed to hear and dispose of the case in the absence of the accused.

(6) Unless the statute founded on authorises conviction in default of appearance, proof of the complaint must be led to the satisfaction of the court.

(7) In a case to which subsection (5) above applies, the court may, if it considers it expedient, allow counsel or a solicitor who satisfies the court that he has authority from the accused so to do, to appear and plead for and defend him.

(8) An accused who without reasonable excuse fails to attend any diet of which he has been given due notice, shall be guilty of an offence and liable on summary conviction—

(a) to a fine not exceeding level 3 on the standard scale; and
(b) to a period of imprisonment not exceeding—
        (i) in the district court, 60 days; or
        (ii) in the sheriff court, 3 months.

(9) The penalties provided for in subsection (8) above may be imposed in addition to any other penalty which it is competent for the court to impose, notwithstanding that the total of penalties imposed may exceed the maximum penalty which it is competent to impose in respect of the original offence.

(10) An accused may be dealt with for an offence under subsection (8) above either at his diet of trial for the original offence or at a separate trial.

DEFINITIONS
   "complaint": s.307(1).
   "diet": s.307(1).
   "imprisonment": s.307(6).
   "offence": s.307(1).
   "officer of law": s.307(1).
   "prosecutor": s.307(1).

GENERAL NOTE
   Section 141, which specifies the methods of citation of accused, and this section which deals with the consequences of a failure by an accused to appear at a summary diet need to be considered together. Intimation of any diet can be made by notice sent by registered or recorded post, by personal service of such a notice by an officer of law, or by the fixing of the diet in the accused's presence. While s.141 relates to the way in which proceedings are launched, s.150 has general application once a complaint has been placed before the court until the proceedings are concluded.
   The failure by an accused to attend a diet of which he has been given notice lawfully, entitles the prosecutor to seek an apprehension warrant in terms of s.150 and to libel a further complaint founding upon failure to appear. The penalties disclosed in subs. (8) are in addition to any penalty the court may impose on the original complaint and, cumulatively, the penalties exacted on the original and second complaint can competently exceed the statutory ceilings fixed in summary proceedings; these are defined in s.5(2) and (3) for the sheriff court, and in s.7(6) and (7) in relation to the district court.
   On proof of citation or notice of a diet being produced to the court, the prosecutor may seek a warrant to apprehend the accused. The court may grant a warrant or continue the diet to a later diet and order intimation of the diet on the accused as provided by subs. (2). This underlines the importance of the Crown being able to exhibit evidence of service of the complaint or of intimation of the diet when required by the court. See *Beattie v. Mackinnon*, 1977 J.C. 64 where no date of citation had been placed on the accused's citation and service copy complaint, a fact unknown to the court when a warrant to apprehend was granted following an apparent failure to appear.
   The court is not obliged to issue a warrant following failure to appear by the accused (subs. (2) permits adjournment of proceedings) but must pronounce some order and cannot simply refrain from action; see *Skeen v. Sullivan*, 1980 S.L.T.(Notes) 11. Equally the prosecutor can only proceed under this section to take a warrant, when he is satisfied that service of the complaint has been effected and, hence, that it is validly before the court for further procedure; see *Lees v. Malcolm*, 1992 S.L.T. 1137; 1992 S.C.C.R. 589 where a fresh complaint was raised to maintain proceedings, and *Heywood v. McLennan*, 1994 S.C.C.R. 1 where efforts were made to "convert" an unserved complaint into an initiating warrant, despite the complaint having fallen.
   Subsections (5), (6) and (7) provide for trial proceedings in the absence of the accused only once the court is satisfied that the accused has either been cited or received an intimation of the diet deemed necessary by the court.

Non-availability of judge

Death, illness or absence of judge

151.—(1) Where the court is unable to proceed owing to the death, illness or absence of the presiding judge, it shall be lawful for the clerk of court—
   (a) where the diet has not been called, to convene the court and adjourn the diet;

(b) where the diet has been called but no evidence has been led, to adjourn the diet; and

(c) where the diet has been called and evidence has been led—

      (i) with the agreement of the parties, to desert the diet *pro loco et tempore*; or

      (ii) to adjourn the diet.

(2) Where, under subsection (1)(c)(i) above, a diet has been deserted *pro loco et tempore*, any new prosecution charging the accused with the same or any similar offence arising out of the same facts shall be brought within two months of the date on which the diet was deserted notwithstanding that any other time limit for the commencement of such prosecution has elapsed.

(3) For the purposes of subsection (2) above, a new prosecution shall be deemed to commence on the date on which a warrant to apprehend or to cite the accused is granted, if such warrant is executed without undue delay.

DEFINITIONS

    "judge": s.307(1).

    "offence": s.307(1).

GENERAL NOTE

The purpose of this section is to provide for the adjournment, or desertion *pro loco et tempore*, of summary proceedings where the court cannot proceed due to the death, illness or absence of the "presiding judge", a phrase equally applicable to sheriff or district court proceedings. Similar provisions, taking due account of differences in procedure, apply to solemn proceedings by s.87 above.

In summary proceedings the court has a common law authority to fix a new diet when a judge is taken ill during a trial and therefore the possibility of postponement of a trial, for that same reason, was acknowledged in s.331A(2)(a) of the 1975 Act. However until the passage of s.30 of the Criminal Justice (Scotland) Act 1995, no statutory provision existed in summary cases to regulate proceedings in the event of the death of a judge.

Desertion of the diet necessarily means that the instance in the complaint falls. To preserve the public interest, particularly in cases which would otherwise be time-barred in accordance with s.136 above, subs. (2) permits the re-raising of any proceedings deserted in terms of s.151. In that event proceedings can be initiated anew, but must be effected upon the accused without undue delay (for "undue delay" see generally the notes to s.136 above).

A separate provision dealing with the illness or death of a judge in the course of preparation of an appeal by stated case is found at s.176(4).

Trial diet

Desertion of diet

152.—(1) It shall be competent at the diet of trial, at any time before the first witness is sworn, for the court, on the application of the prosecutor, to desert the diet *pro loco et tempore*.

(2) If, at a diet of trial, the court refuses an application by the prosecutor to adjourn the trial or to desert the diet *pro loco et tempore*, and the prosecutor is unable or unwilling to proceed with the trial, the court shall desert the diet *simpliciter*.

(3) Where the court has deserted a diet *simpliciter* under subsection (2) above (and the court's decision in that regard has not been reversed on appeal), it shall not be competent for the prosecutor to raise a fresh libel.

DEFINITIONS

    "diet": s.307(1).

    "prosecutor": s.307(1).

    "trial": s.307(1).

    "witness": s.307(1).

GENERAL NOTE

The terms of s.338A of the 1975 Act are preserved. Section 147(4) of this Act enacts that a trial begins when the first witness is sworn; until that time it is open to the prosecutor to move the court to desert the diet *pro loco et tempore*, or to move to adjourn the trial. Once either of these motions has been made however, the court can refuse the motion and, instead, desert the trial *simpliciter*, a step which brings proceedings to an end. In some instances the Crown might better achieve its purpose simply by not calling the case for trial at all, since, although the instance in the current complaint would fall, the right to proceed might still be retained. It remains the case, as subs. (3) states, that the unreasonable refusal by the judge of a Crown motion to adjourn or desert *pro loco et tempore* can still be appealed.

In *Tudhope v. Gough*, 1982 S.C.C.R. 157 it was held competent for the Crown to move to desert *pro loco* even after the refusal of a motion to adjourn and see *Fay v. Vannet*, 1998 S.L.T. 1099, where desertion of a complaint of police assault by the prosecutor following the sheriff's refusal of adjournment was competently followed by a fresh complaint of common law assault, a step which was held not to be oppressive. In *Fay v. Vannet*, 1998 S.L.T. 1099 it was affirmed that desertion *simpliciter* could only be exercised by the court in terms of s.152(2) after refusal of both of the prosecutor's motions to adjourn and to desert *pro loco et tempore*. A more novel, but inappropriate, use of desertion *simpliciter* is found in *MacLeod v. Williamson*, 1993 S.L.T. 144 where the sheriff did so *ex proprio motu* having overheard witnesses during an adjournment and having drawn the nature of the eavesdropping to the attention of the prosecutor.

The Appeal Court indicated that if the sheriff had come to the view that he could no longer preside over the trial, he should have discharged the trial diet and fixed a new diet to go before another sheriff; desertion *simpliciter* was invalid. In a similar vein, see *Carmichael v. Monaghan*, 1986 S.C.C.R. 598.

In *McMahon v. Hamilton*, 1992 S.C.C.R. 351, the prosecutor deserted one of two charges on a complaint *simpliciter*, a plea of not guilty being recorded for the second charge. Issue was thereafter taken with the competency of proceeding on the latter charge. The plea to competency was repelled but the Appeal Court, rather than express any view on the competency of deserting a charge (as distinct from a complaint) *simpliciter* elected to treat both charges as live and to treat the minuting of the pleas as *pro non scripto*: it remains unresolved whether such a motion is competent or not, though the simplest solution is surely to accept a plea of not guilty to the charge in normal circumstances.

See *Normand v. West*, 1992 S.C.C.R. 76 as an example of an unreasonable refusal by the court to permit an adjournment in the absence of essential witnesses. Desertion *simpliciter* by the court and the premature ending of a prosecution is a step which, in *Tudhope v. Laurie*, 1979 S.L.T.(Notes) 13 at 14, "must be exercised only after the most careful consideration on weighty grounds and with due and accurate regard to the interests which will be affected or prejudiced by that exercise".

See also *Normand v. Milne*, 1996 G.W.D. 19–1078, where the Crown succeeded on appeal by advocation against the sheriff's refusal to permit a desertion *pro loco*.

Ruxton v. Borland, 2000 S.L.T. 612; 2000 S.C.C.R. 484 re-introduces a measure of familiarity, and clarity, to summary proceedings after the uncertainties produced by the Appeal Court in *Mitchell v. Vannet*, 1999 S.L.T 934 , which bore to follow *Handley v. Pirie*, 1977 S.L.T. 30 , both of which *Ruxton v. Borland,* a five judge decision, has overruled. Following this decision and its three judge precursor (found at 2000 G.W.D. 9–326) it can be said that after the tendering of a plea of not guilty on a summary complaint, it is only necessary thereafter to ascertain whether the plea previously tendered is adhered to, and that unless there is evident prejudice to the accused, there is no necessity for the same judge to deal with the case at all times once it has been put down for trial.

Trial in presence of accused

153.—(1) Without prejudice to section 150 of this Act, and subject to subsection (2) below, no part of a trial shall take place outwith the presence of the accused.

(2) If during the course of his trial an accused so misconducts himself that in the view of the court a proper trial cannot take place unless he is removed, the court may order—

    (a) that he is removed from the court for so long as his conduct makes it necessary; and

    (b) that the trial proceeds in his absence,

but if he is not legally represented the court shall appoint counsel or a solicitor to represent his interests during such absence.

Definition
  "trial": s.307(1).

GENERAL NOTE

Subject to the statutory enactments which permit trial in the absence of the accused (see s.150(5)), it is generally the case that any trial can only competently proceed in the accused's presence (see *Aitken v. Wood*, 1921 J.C. 84) for justice to be seen to be done. Section 153 introduces a further exception to the generality in circumstances where the accused so misconducts himself as to preclude proper conduct of the case. In that event the accused can be removed from the court and trial continue with the accused represented by his solicitor or counsel, or if he has not been legally represented, by an agent appointed by the court to act on his behalf, during the period of absence. This provision does not, of course, resolve what action the court may take at the conclusion of the trial to deal with any contempt.

The general principle that justice must not only be done, but be seen to be done, underpins this provision. Thus, the obligation of the court to ensure the fairness of proceedings persists even after a verdict has been reached on the evidence. In *Doherty v. McGlennan*, 1996 G.W.D. 27–1580 a conviction was quashed where the sheriff, having convicted the accused, then deferred sentence and invited the complainer (a local Member of Parliament) to meet in chambers. *Harper v. Heywood*, 1998 G.W.D. 3–110, is perhaps an extreme example of unjudicial conduct which resulted in the quashing of the conviction and authority being granted for a new prosecution. However expressions of sympathy towards a victim during sentence of an accused, which caused an accused to aver that his conviction had resulted from the sheriff's sympathy, were held not to be improper, the court having moved from weighing the evidence to sentence (*Bagan v. Normand*, 1997 G.W.D. 14–596). In *Lowe v. Brown*, 1997 S.C.C.R. 340, the Appeal Court observed that judges should question witnesses with restraint and avoid any indication of disbelieving a witness' account during examination. In *Clark v. H.M. Advocate,* 2000 S.L.T. 1107; 2000 S.C.C.R. 767 the Appeal Court listened to the tape of the sheriff's charge to the jury and quashed the accused's conviction on the ground that the tone used in posing a series of rhetorical questions was such as to intrude into the jury's role as masters of fact.

Section 153(1)'s principles need not apply however in relation to enquiries conducted in connection with appeals where further evidence is heard; see *Crossan v. H.M. Advocate*, 1996 S.C.C.R. 279 and the discussion at p. 129 above. It is noted that the accused's counsel and solicitor were present in chambers during the appointed judge's examination of evidence.

The equivalent provision in solemn proceedings is found at s.92(2) above.

Proof of official documents

154.—[*Repealed by the Crime and Punishment (Scotland) Act s.28*]

GENERAL NOTE

This section was deleted by s.28(1) of the Crime and Punishment (Scotland) Act 1997 and its provisions are now to be found in s.279A of the Act which extends the provisions in relation to official documents to all criminal proceedings. Section 154, which only applied to summary proceedings, ceased to have effect from August 1, 1997 in terms of S.I. 1997 No. 1712.

Punishment of witness for contempt

155.—(1) If a witness in a summary prosecution—

(a) wilfully fails to attend after being duly cited; or
(b) unlawfully refuses to be sworn; or
(c) after the oath has been administered to him refuses to answer any question which the court may allow; or
(d) prevaricates in his evidence,

he shall be deemed guilty of contempt of court and be liable to be summarily punished forthwith for such contempt by a fine not exceeding level 3 on the standard scale or by imprisonment for any period not exceeding 21 days.

(2) Where punishment is summarily imposed as mentioned in subsection (1) above, the clerk of court shall enter in the record of the proceedings the acts constituting the contempt or the statements forming the prevarication.

(3) Subsections (1) and (2) above are without prejudice to the right of the prosecutor to proceed by way of formal complaint for any such contempt where a summary punishment, as mentioned in the said subsection (1), is not imposed.

(4) Any witness who, having been duly cited in accordance with section 140 of this Act—

(a) fails without reasonable excuse, after receiving at least 48 hours' notice, to attend for precognition by a prosecutor at the time and place mentioned in the citation served on him; or

(b) refuses when so cited to give information within his knowledge regarding any matter relative to the commission of the offence in relation to which such precognition is taken,

shall be liable to the like punishment as is provided in subsection (1) above.

DEFINITIONS
"prosecutor": s.307(1).
"witness": s.307(1).

GENERAL NOTE
A finding of contempt will only be justified where there has been wilful or deliberate conduct or an affront or challenge to the court's authority (*Johnston v. Normand*, 1997 G.W.D. 3–81, *McTavish v. Hamilton*, 1997 G.W.D. 11–451 and, generally, *McMillan v. Carmichael*, 1993 S.C.C.R. 943; 1994 S.L.T. 510). A solicitor can be held in contempt, in the course of proceedings applying the same test, should he refuse to comply with the clear ruling of the court (*Blair-Wilson, Petr.*, 1997 S.L.T. 621).

The court must indicate that consideration is being given to making a finding of contempt and afford the party an opportunity to explain the circumstances and submit why such a finding should not be made (*Johnston v. Normand* above, *Harkness v. Westwater*, 1997 G.W.D. 15–650 and *Dickson v. Reith*, 1997 G.W.D. 23–1139). The broad lesson from all these cases is that the court has to proceed with cool deliberation, specify the nature of the misconduct, give the offending party ample opportunity to explain himself and, possibly, purge any contempt, rather than leaping too swiftly to an untenable conclusion which will not be supported.

In minuting the act which constituted the contempt, care must be taken to specify in detail the nature of the misconduct; see *Strang v. Annan*, 1991 S.L.T. 676; *Sze v. Wilson*, 1992 S.L.T. 569; 1992 S.C.C.R. 54. In *Riaviz v. Howdle*, 1996 S.C.C.R. 22 the Appeal Court proceeded to deal with a bill of suspension (following a finding of prevarication) despite the absence of minutes recording the witness' misconduct; the court founded upon the contents of the sheriff's report and applied a purposive, rather than literal, reading of this section. Since s.155(1) refers to punishment "forthwith", there is no necessity to obtain social enquiry reports and the punishment imposed is not a "sentence" (see *Forrest v. Wilson*, 1994 S.L.T. 490; 1993 S.C.C.R. 631 and the statutory definition of "sentence" at s.307(1)). Although subs. (4) refers back to the provisions of subs. (1), it would appear that the same comments would apply. As subs. (1) states the maximum penalty following a finding of contempt or prevarication is a sentence of twenty one days imprisonment; see *Logan v. McGlennan*, 1999 G.W.D. 22–1041.

The factors justifying precognition on oath are set out in *Carmichael, Complainer*, 1992 S.C.C.R. 553, where a Bill of Advocation followed refusal of an application to precognosce on oath. Precognition on oath applications by the defence proceed by way of s.291 below.

Apprehension of witness

156.—(1) Where a witness, having been duly cited, fails to appear at the diet fixed for his attendance and no just excuse is offered by him or on his behalf, the court may, if it is satisfied that he received the citation or that its contents came to his knowledge, issue a warrant for his apprehension.

(2) Where the court is satisfied by evidence on oath that a witness is not likely to attend to give evidence without being compelled so to do, it may issue a warrant for his apprehension.

(3) A warrant of apprehension of a witness in the form mentioned in section 135(1) of this Act shall imply warrant to officers of law to search for and apprehend the witness, and to detain him in a police station, police cell, or other convenient place, until—

(a) the date fixed for the hearing of the case; or
(b) the date when security to the amount fixed under subsection (4) below is found,

whichever is the earlier.

(4) A witness apprehended under a warrant under subsection (1) or (2) above shall, wherever practicable, be brought immediately by the officer of law who executed that warrant before a justice, who shall fix such sum as he

considers appropriate as security for the appearance of the witness at all diets.

Record of proceedings

157.—(1) Proceedings in a summary prosecution shall be conducted summarily *viva voce* and, except where otherwise provided and subject to subsection (2) below, no record need be kept of the proceedings other than the complaint, or a copy of the complaint certified as a true copy by the procurator fiscal, the plea, a note of any documentary evidence produced, and the conviction and sentence or other finding of the court.

(2) Any objection taken to the competency or relevancy of the complaint or proceedings, or to the competency or admissibility of evidence, shall, if either party desires it, be entered in the record of the proceedings.

Interruption of summary proceedings for verdict in earlier trial

158. Where the sheriff is sitting in summary proceedings during the period in which the jury in a criminal trial in which he has presided are retired to consider their verdict, it shall be lawful, if he considers it appropriate to do so, to interrupt those proceedings—
  (a) in order to receive the verdict of the jury and dispose of the cause to which it relates;
  (b) to give a direction to the jury on any matter on which they may wish one from him, or to hear a request from them regarding any matter,
and the interruption shall not affect the validity of the proceedings nor cause the instance to fall in respect of any person accused in the proceedings.

Amendment of complaint

159.—(1) It shall be competent at any time prior to the determination of the case, unless the court see just cause to the contrary, to amend the complaint or any notice of previous conviction relative thereto by deletion, alteration or addition, so as to—
  (a) cure any error or defect in it;
  (b) meet any objection to it; or
  (c) cure any discrepancy or variance between the complaint or notice and the evidence.

(2) Nothing in this section shall authorise an amendment which changes the character of the offence charged, and, if it appears to the court that the accused may in any way be prejudiced in his defence on the merits of the case by any amendment made under this section, the court shall grant such remedy to the accused by adjournment or otherwise as appears to the court to be just.

(3) An amendment made under this section shall be sufficiently authenticated by the initials of the clerk of the court.

DEFINITIONS
  "complaint": s.138 and Sched. 5.
  "offence": s.307(1).
  "previous conviction": s.307(5).

GENERAL NOTE
The Act permits wide powers of amendment to a summary complaint but subject to the proviso that the amendment proposed must not alter the character of the offence charged, and cannot be used to validate a complaint which is radically defective in its essentials (*Stevenson v. McLevy* (1879) 4 Couper 196; *Lowe v. Bee*, 1989 S.C.C.R. 476). Note that no one can be competently convicted upon a complaint which is a fundamental nullity and, accordingly, there has been no tholed assize (*Thomson, Petr.*, 1997 S.L.T. 322).

The court cannot amend the complaint *ex proprio motu* in the absence of such a motion from the prosecutor (*Grant v. Lockhart*, Crown Office Circular A3/91). The refusal or grant of a proposed amendment rests in the discretion of the trial judge and will not readily be interfered with by the Appeal Court (*Cumming v. Frame* (1909) 6 Adam 57). Such a motion can be made at any point in the case prior to the determination of proceedings (see *Cochrane v. The West Calder Cooperative Society*, 1978 S.L.T. (Notes) 22 and *Matheson v. Ross* (1885) 5 Couper 582, where the date libelled was found to be incorrect after the close of the Crown case, the accused not being prejudiced and declining an adjournment). The point in the proceedings at which amendment is moved can itself be significant; in *MacArthur v. MacNeill*, 1986 S.C.C.R. 552; 1987 S.L.T. 299 the Crown sought to amend a road traffic complaint, substituting failure to supply a blood specimen in a libel which originally averred failure to provide breath specimens at the close of evidence, a manoeuvre which the Appeal Court held to have changed the character of the offence (compare with *Fenwick v. Valentine*, 1994 S.L.T. 485; 1993 S.C.C.R. 892).

Amendment of the Preamble and Instance
Adding a heading to the complaint to read "Under the Summary Jurisdiction (Scotland) Acts 1864 and 1881, and the Criminal Procedure (Scotland) Act 1887 "by amendment, was allowed in *Finlayson v. Bunbury* (1898) 2 Adam 478; correction of the heading on a complaint which referred to a District Court jurisdiction when the accused had been cited to, and the case called in, the relevant sheriff court was upheld on appeal (*Doonin Plant v. Lees*, 1994 S.L.T. 313; 1993 S.C.C.R. 511).

Altering the name of the accused even after the statutory time bar has expired was allowed in *Hoyers (U.K.) v. Houston*, 1991 S.L.T. 934; 1991 S.C.C.R. 919 and see also *Ralston v. Carmichael*, 1995 G.W.D. 38–1933 discussed in Notes to s.143 above. More curiously in *Montgomery Transport v. Walkingshaw*, 1992 S.C.C.R. 17 the complainers brought a Bill of Suspension following a guilty plea to a complaint which, it was later discovered, had libelled the wrong section of the statute albeit the narrative accurately set out the offence: they argued the complaint to be a nullity, but the High Court treated it as merely irrelevant and capable of amendment noting that the complainers had not taken objection before the sheriff.

However in *Lockhart v. British School of Motoring*, 1982 S.C.C.R. 118, amendment to the libel was refused on the grounds that, if allowed, it would deprive co-accused of a statutory defence. Amendment to change the identity of the accused was refused in *Valentine v. Thistle Leisure*, 1983 S.C.C.R. 515; by contrast, amendment of a nature which altered the capacity of the accused was allowed on appeal in *Tudhope v. Chung*, 1985 S.C.C.R. 139.

Amendment of Offence Dates

See *Matheson v. Ross* cited above. In *Duffy v. Ingram* (also cited above), where the offence date was omitted in the first charge and adopted in the second charge and detailed as "said 30 November 1985" in the last charge on the complaint, an objection to relevancy was repelled by the sheriff who allowed amendments to cure the defects in the libel.

Amendment of Locus

It is generally competent to amend the locus stated in a summary charge so as to bring the libel into accord with the evidence, and amendment should be permitted unless it alters the nature of the charge. Amendment is permissible even if it involves including a locus outwith the court's jurisdiction (see *Craig v. Keane*, 1982 S.L.T. 198; 1981 S.C.C.R. 166 and, more generally, *Belcher v. MacKinnon*, 1987 S.L.T. 298).

In *Herron v. Gemmell*, 1975 S.L.T.(Notes) 93 the sheriff refused an amendment to add "Glasgow" to the specification "on the road on the Glasgow Inner Ring Road, at a part thereof near Charing Cross underpass" a decision which was overturned on appeal.

A more radical amendment in *Brown v. McLeod*, 1986 S.C.C.R. 615 had the effect of extending the locus to include driving between two towns. In response, the sheriff offered the defence the opportunity of an adjournment to lead additional evidence in light of the amendment but this was declined. His decision was upheld on appeal. Similarly in *Tudhope v. Fulton*, 1986 S.C.C.R. 567 amendment of the *locus delicti*, where the offence was failure to provide breath specimens at an incorrectly specified police office, was allowed on appeal; this follows reasoning similar to that employed in *Belcher v. MacKinnon* cited above.

Where the *locus* is inspecific, as above, the acid test is whether the details specified in the libel are sufficient to enable the court to ascertain whether it has jurisdiction or not; see *Yarrow Shipbuilders Ltd v. Normand*, 1995 S.L.T. 1215; 1995 S.C.C.R. 224 and *Caven v. Cumming*, 1998 S.L.T. 768.

Amendment and Statutory Offences

Amendment may be used to alter an incorrectly specified contravention of statute or regulations, but must not change the nature of the offence libelled. In *MacKenzie v. Brougham*, 1985 S.L.T. 276; 1984 S.C.C.R. 434, the charge narrated the statute and regulations contravened but omitted reference to the precise regulation which created a criminal offence and was poorly specified; it was held that the complaint was not a nullity and could be cured by amendment. Amendment of a complaint to reflect the terms of the current statutory legislation is competent even where this renders an accused liable, on conviction, to an increased penalty (*Wadbister Offshore Ltd. v. Adam*, 1998 S.L.T. 33 following *Cook v. Jessop* cited below). The broad test to be applied is whether the charge as specified affords the defence fair notice of what the Crown was seeking to prove; see *Blair v. Keane*, 1981 S.L.T.(Notes) 4; *Clydesdale Group v. Normand*, 1994 S.L.T. 1302; 1993 S.C.C.R. 958; *Gullett v. Hamilton*, 1997 G.W.D. 14–592.

In *Sterling-Winthrop Group v. Allan*, 1987 S.C.C.R. 25, a prosecution under the Health and Safety at Work etc. Act 1974 (c. 37), objections to the relevancy of charges were repelled by the sheriff. Before the Appeal Court the Crown sought, and were permitted, to amend the charges to meet the objections previously stated. Even where a repealed statute has been libelled, amendment of the charge to make reference to the correct statutory provision is permissible, despite the greater penalties which can be imposed. See *Cook v. Jessop*, 1990 S.C.C.R. 211, where a charge of harbouring an escaper from an approved school was made, contrary to the Children and Young Persons (Scotland) Act 1937, a statute which had been repealed and replaced by the Social Work (Scotland) Act 1968: it will be noted however that the libel gave clear warning of the character of the offence and there could be little cause to argue prejudice or lack of specification of the *species facti* (see also *High-Clad Roofing v. Carmichael*, "The Scotsman" Law Reports February 24, 1989, where the wrong regulation under the Factories Act 1961 (c. 34) had been libelled).

Schedule 3 of the Act contains the provisions relating to latitudes in time and place and alternative verdicts which previously appeared in s.312 of the 1975 Act. Particularly, the terms of paras 11 to 14 are of significance in relation to the libelling of statutory offences.

The Nomen Juris

It is well accepted that the charge in an indictment need not specify the *nomen juris* of the alleged crime, it being sufficient that the facts described in the libel are relevant and set forth a crime known to the law of Scotland (*Cameron v. H.M. Advocate*, 1971 S.L.T. 333 (piracy)). By the same token, since it is the *species facti* which indicate the nature of the crime complained of, and not the *nomen juris* attached (*Lippe v. Wilson*, 1997 G.W.D. 17–766), it follows that amendment of the *nomen juris* is competent (see *Dyce v. Aitchison*, 1985 S.C.C.R. 184 (contempt of court libelled)).

No case to answer

160.—(1) Immediately after the close of the evidence for the prosecution, the accused may intimate to the court his desire to make a submission that he has no case to answer both—
(a) on an offence charged in the complaint; and
(b) on any other offence of which he could be convicted under the complaint were the offence charged the only offence so charged.

(2) If, after hearing both parties, the judge is satisfied that the evidence led by the prosecution is insufficient in law to justify the accused being convicted of the offence charged in respect of which the submission has been made or of such other offence as is mentioned, in relation to that offence, in paragraph (b) of subsection (1) above, he shall acquit him of the offence charged in respect of which the submission has been made and the trial shall proceed only in respect of any other offence charged in the complaint.

(3) If, after hearing both parties, the judge is not satisfied as is mentioned in subsection (2) above, he shall reject the submission and the trial shall proceed, with the accused entitled to give evidence and call witnesses, as if such submission had not been made.

DEFINITIONS
"complaint": s.307(1).
"judge": s.307(1).
"offence": s.307(1).

GENERAL NOTE
The sufficiency in law of evidence presented by the prosecution falls to be considered at the close of the Crown case. The criteria for acceptance or rejection of a no case to answer submission were set out in *Williamson v. Wither*, 1981 S.C.C.R. 214, but the court must also assess the admissibility at that stage of evidence led in support of the prosecution case (see *Jessop v. Kerr*, 1989 S.C.C.R. 417) and make known the result of this assessment.

The court must give both parties the opportunity to make submissions before reaching a decision on sufficiency, and cannot consider the issue in the absence of a motion from the accused (*Stewart v. Lowe*, 1991 S.C.C.R. 317—a case in which the sheriff had rejected a submission without having heard the prosecutor, and convicted the accused without first hearing from the defence agent; see also *Taylor v. Douglas*, 1984 S.L.T. 69). Where a number of submissions are advanced, the court is obliged to determine upon them all, rather than dismissing the case upon a consideration of only one. Consideration of all submissions avoids needless duplication of appeal procedures in the event of the Crown successfully appealing the court's original decision on sufficiency (*Lockhart v. Milne*, 1992 S.C.C.R. 864). In *Duffin v. Normand*, 1993 S.C.C.R. 864, the court having rejected a submission under the section, and there being no defence submission, proceeded to convict without hearing further from the parties: the court is obliged to hear submissions at the close of evidence upon the quality of evidence, an issue which cannot be considered at the time of a s.160 submission. The conviction was quashed.

The form of questions to be posed in stated cases challenging decisions on submissions of no case to answer are discussed in the commentary to *Cassidy v. Normand*, 1994 S.C.C.R. 325, while guidance on the form of the stated case itself is given in *Keane v. Bathgate*, 1983 S.L.T. 651, since at that stage in the case the court cannot state findings-in-fact.

It will be noted that in *Tudhope v. Stewart*, 1986 S.L.T. 659; 1986 S.C.C.R. 384 it was held that use of a no case to answer submission, founding upon the inadmissibility of evidence which had earlier been led without objection, was inappropriate (see also *Skeen v. Murphy*, 1978 S.L.T.(Notes) 2 and *McGee v. McNaughton*, 1996 G.W.D. 17–977 ; as a general rule objections to the admissibility of evidence should be taken at the time when that evidence is tendered).

In *Walls v. Heywood*, 2000 S.L.T. 841; 2000 S.C.C.R. 21 where the lay magistrate returned a

Criminal Procedure (Scotland) Act 1995

guilty verdict at the s.160 stage, and had to be corrected by the assessor, it was held on appeal, following *Lorimar v. Normand*, 1997 S.L.T.1277; 1997 S.C.C.R. 582 that the necessity for an intervention by the assessor might lead an impartial observer to conclude that the judge had reached a verdict prematurely.

Defence to speak last

161. In any trial the accused or, where he is legally represented, his counsel or solicitor shall have the right to speak last.

GENERAL NOTE
"There is no doubt that the panel is entitled to the last word in criminal trials" *Watson v. Stuart* (1878) 4 Couper 67. See also *Duffin v. Normand* discussed in the notes to s.160 above. Similarly, following conviction the defence must be offered the opportunity to plead in mitigation, before sentence is considered (*Meikle v. Lees*, 1997 G.W.D. 3–88).

Verdict and conviction

Judges equally divided

162. In a summary prosecution in a court consisting of more than one judge, if the judges are equally divided in opinion as to the guilt of the accused, the accused shall be found not guilty of the charge or part thereof on which such division of opinion exists.

DEFINITION
"judge": s.307(1).

GENERAL NOTE
Where two judges sit and reach different verdicts, no conviction can follow (*Dorward v. Mackay* (1870) 1 Couper 392).

Conviction: miscellaneous provisions

163.—(1) Where imprisonment is authorised by the sentence of a court of summary jurisdiction, an extract of the finding and sentence in the form prescribed by Act of Adjournal shall be a sufficient warrant for the apprehension and commitment of the accused, and no such extract shall be void or liable to be set aside on account of any error or defect in point of form.

(2) In any proceedings in a court of summary jurisdiction consisting of more than one judge, the signature of one judge shall be sufficient in all warrants or other proceedings prior or subsequent to conviction, and it shall not be necessary that the judge so signing shall be one of the judges trying or dealing with the case otherwise.

DEFINITIONS
"court of summary jurisdiction": s.307(1).
"imprisonment": s.307(1).
"judge": s.307(1).

Conviction of part of charge

164. A conviction of a part or parts only of the charge or charges libelled in a complaint shall imply dismissal of the rest of the complaint.

DEFINITION
"complaint": s.307(1).

"Conviction" and "sentence" not to be used for children

165. The words "conviction" and "sentence" shall not be used in relation to children dealt with summarily and any reference in any enactment,

223

whether passed before or after the commencement of this Act, to a person convicted, a conviction or a sentence shall in the case of a child be construed as including a reference to a person found guilty of an offence, a finding of guilt or an order made upon such a finding as the case may be.

Definitions
    "child": s.307(1) and the Children (Scotland) Act 1995 s.93(2)(b).
    "enactment": s.307(1).
    "finding of guilt": s.307(8).
    "sentence": s.307(1).

Previous convictions: summary proceedings

166.—(1) This section shall apply where the accused in a summary prosecution has been previously convicted of any offence and the prosecutor has decided to lay a previous conviction before the court.

(2) A notice in the form prescribed by Act of Adjournal or as nearly as may be in such form specifying the previous conviction shall be served on the accused with the complaint where he is cited to a diet, and where he is in custody the complaint and such a notice shall be served on him before he is asked to plead.

(3) The previous conviction shall not be laid before the judge until he is satisfied that the charge is proved.

(4) If a plea of guilty is tendered or if, after a plea of not guilty, the accused is convicted the prosecutor shall lay the notice referred to in subsection (2) above before the judge, and—

(a) in a case where the plea of guilty is tendered in writing the accused shall be deemed to admit any previous conviction set forth in the notice, unless he expressly denies it in the writing by which the plea is tendered;

(b) in any other case the judge or the clerk of court shall ask the accused whether he admits the previous conviction,

and if such admission is made or deemed to be made it shall be entered in the record of the proceedings; and it shall not be necessary for the prosecutor to produce extracts of any previous convictions so admitted.

(5) Where the accused does not admit any previous conviction, the prosecutor unless he withdraws the conviction shall adduce evidence in proof thereof either then or at any other diet.

(6) A copy of any notice served on the accused under this section shall be entered in the record of the proceedings.

(7) Where a person is convicted of an offence, the court may have regard to any previous conviction in respect of that person in deciding on the disposal of the case.

(8) Nothing in this section shall prevent the prosecutor—

(a) asking the accused questions tending to show that the accused has been convicted of an offence other than that with which he is charged, where he is entitled to do so under section 266 of this Act; or

(b) leading evidence of previous convictions where it is competent to do so—

(i) as evidence in support of a substantive charge; or
(ii) under section 270 of this Act.

Definitions
    "complaint": s.307(1).
    "diet": s.307(1).
    "judge": s.307(1).
    "offence": s.307(1).

"previous conviction": s.307(1).
"prosecutor": s.307(1).

GENERAL NOTE

The general principles of placing previous convictions before the court are discussed in the notes to s.101 above. Unless adducing a previous conviction is necessary to prove the substantive charge, or the accused has either attacked the character of Crown witnesses or misrepresented his own character, no reference can be made to the accused's criminal record until he has been convicted.

Any previous convictions to be founded upon by the Crown for the purposes of sentence must accompany the citation and service copy complaint (see Rule 16.1.–(4) and Form 16.1–E in the 1996 Act of Adjournal) and have to be laid before the court by the prosecutor; see *Clark v. Connell*, 1952 J.C. 119; 1952 S.L.T. 421; convictions which have not been libelled cannot be considered by the court (*Adair v. Hill*, 1943 J.C. 9 and *Massily Packaging (U.K.) Ltd. v. MacDonald*, 1997 G.W.D. 3–87 discussed at A4.309 above) except where they are referred to in a social enquiry report prepared for the purpose of sentence (*Sharp v. Stevenson*, 1948 S.L.T. (Notes) 79; *Sillars v. Copeland*, 1966 C.L.R. 686); in such circumstances the accused should be afforded the opportunity of admitting or denying such additional convictions. The growth of European Union legislation raises previously unconsidered issues. In *Redman v. Sehmel*, 1997 G.W.D. 9–370, the accused plead guilty to contravening Articles of the Sea Fishing (Enforcement of Community Control Measures) Order 1994, by failing to record his vessel's true catch and admitted a prior conviction for the same offence only weeks earlier imposed by an Irish court. While not a conviction imposed by a U.K. court, it is submitted that the earlier conviction was competently libelled in the circumstances; the question remains how far this precedent can properly extend for other contraventions of European Union regulations.

It will be noted that subs. (4)(a) continues the presumption that any convictions not expressly disputed by the accused when tendering a letter plea are held to be admitted. Difficulty can arise where the plea contained in a letter is rejected by the prosecutor; care then has to be taken to ensure that any schedule of convictions is not retained with the complaint at any subsequent diet, though this has been held not to amount to laying of convictions before the court by the prosecutor (see *O'Neill v. Tudhope*, 1984 S.L.T. 424; 1984 S.C.C.R. 276). See also *McKee v. Brown*, 2000 G.W.D. 34–1302 where, after a change of plea, the accused's schedule of convictions remained with the complaint and was seen and troubled the trial judge, the conviction was quashed. It would have been preferable for the proceedings to be deserted but parties may have felt compelled to proceed with the trial because the case (which centred on Road Traffic Act offences) would otherwise be timebarred.

The use of extract convictions as evidence in support of a substantive charge, for example the Road Traffic Act 1988 (c. 52) s.103 (driving while disqualified) has generated a considerable volume of case law. The cardinal rule is that so far as practicable, the extract used must disclose only the minimum necessary to prove the currency of a disqualification and nothing more (see *Mitchell v. Dean*, 1979 S.L.T. (Notes) 12; *Boustead v. McLeod*, 1979 S.L.T. (Notes) 48) but note also *Moffat v. Robertson*, 1983 S.C.C.R. 392 in which a defence appeal against conviction, founding upon the use of an extract conviction which libelled both driving without a licence and without insurance, was held *not* to be prejudicial.

The general principles applicable to the disclosure either wilfully or inadvertently by the prosecutor are discussed in the notes to s.101; see also *Kerr v. Jessop*, 1991 S.C.C.R. 27, an instance of questioning too far and thus breaching the provision and *Carmichael v. Monaghan*, 1987 S.L.T. 338; 1986 S.C.C.R. 598, where the sheriff's decision that there had been a breach by the unanticipated revelation that the accused had been apprehended in relation to a means warrant, was overruled. *Kerr v. Jessop* was followed in *MacLean v. Buchanan*, 1997 S.L.T. 91, the sheriff holding that the adducing of a reply in breach of this provision (but which had been led without objection) was the result of inexperience or lack of preparation, a careless incident which had not been pressed further.

Refer to s.285 in relation to proof of previous convictions by means of a certificate completed on behalf of the Chief Constable and s.286, which provides means by which the service of extract convictions upon the accused can be treated as sufficient evidence.

Forms of finding and sentence

167.—(1) Every sentence imposed by a court of summary jurisdiction shall unless otherwise provided be pronounced in open court in the presence of the accused, but need not be written out or signed in his presence.

(2) The finding and sentence and any order of a court of summary jurisdiction, as regards both offences at common law and offences under any enactment, shall be entered in the record of the proceedings in the form, as nearly as may be, prescribed by Act of Adjournal.

(3) The record of the proceedings shall be sufficient warrant for all execution on a finding, sentence or order and for the clerk of court to issue extracts containing such executive clauses as may be necessary for implement thereof.

(4) When imprisonment forms part of any sentence or other judgement, warrant for the apprehension and interim detention of the accused pending his being committed to prison shall, where necessary, be implied.

(5) Where a fine imposed by a court of summary jurisdiction is paid at the bar it shall not be necessary for the court to refer to the period of imprisonment applicable to the non-payment thereof.

(6) Where several charges at common law or under any enactment are embraced in one complaint, a cumulo penalty may be imposed in respect of all or any of such charges of which the accused is convicted.

[1](7) Subject to section 204A of this Act, a court of summary jurisdiction may frame—

(a) a sentence following on conviction; or
(b) an order for committal in default of payment of any sum of money or for contempt of court,

so as to take effect on the expiry of any previous sentence or order which, at the date of the later conviction or order, the accused is undergoing.

(8) It shall be competent at any time before imprisonment has followed on a sentence for the court to alter or modify it; but no higher sentence than that originally pronounced shall be competent, and—

(a) the signature of the judge or clerk of court to any sentence shall be sufficient also to authenticate the findings on which such sentence proceeds; and
(b) the power conferred by this subsection to alter or modify a sentence may be exercised without requiring the attendance of the accused.

DEFINITIONS
"complaint": s.307(1).
"court of summary jurisdiction": s.307(1).
"enactment": s.307(1).
"fine": s.307(1).
"imprisonment": s.307(6).
"judge": s.307(1).
"offences": s.307(1).
"prison": s.307(1).
"sentence": s.307(1).

NOTE
[1]Inserted by the Crime and Disorder Act 1998 (c. 37), Sched. 8, para. 122 (effective September 30, 1998: S.I. 1998 No. 2327).

GENERAL NOTE
While sentence is normally pronounced in the accused's presence this does not apply to the circumstances covered by s.150(5) or, arguably, where the accused misconducts himself in the course of his trial (s.153(2)) provided he is legally represented. Section 144(6) of the Act provides that sentences of imprisonment or detention cannot be imposed in the absence of the accused.

Subsection (6) enacts that *cumulo* sentences can be imposed in relation to all the charges libelled on a complaint; conversely if the Crown elects to place on separate complaints, matters which could properly have been incorporated in one complaint, then consecutive sentences should not be imposed; *Kesson v. Heatly*, 1964 J.C. 40. See also *Noble v. Guild*, 1987 S.C.C.R. 518 where a delay in imposing a sentence of imprisonment rendered it incompetent to apply imprisonment consecutive to a term which by then was already being served. However, where an accused was sentenced on indictment to 18-months' detention and had outstanding fines, the

Appeal Court upheld the imposition of the alternative periods of detention in lieu of the fines, these being effective consecutive to each other, and to the 18-months' sentence (*Cartledge v. McLeod*, 1988 S.L.T. 389; 1988 S.C.C.R. 129). The fact that an earlier sentence is the subject of appeal, and thus is not being "undergone", does not debar a court sentencing in respect of other matters from imposing a consecutive sentence to begin at such time as the matter under appeal is resolved (*Thorne v. Stott*, 1999 G.W.D. 28–1332).

The appropriateness and effect upon eligibility for licence of consecutive terms of detention were discussed in *Clayton, Petr.*, 1992 S.L.T. 404.

Section 218(2) sets out the table of fines and alternative periods of imprisonment applicable to proceedings under the Act. The minimum period of imprisonment which can be imposed summarily is five days (see s.205).

Caution

168.—(1) This section applies with regard to the finding, forfeiture, and recovery of caution in any proceedings under this Part of this Act.

(2) Caution may be found by consignation of the amount with the clerk of court, or by bond of caution signed by the cautioner.

(3) Where caution becomes liable to forfeiture, forfeiture may be granted by the court on the motion of the prosecutor, and, where necessary, warrant granted for the recovery of the caution.

(4) Where a cautioner fails to pay the amount due under his bond within six days after he has received a charge to that effect, the court may—

(a) order him to be imprisoned for the maximum period applicable in pursuance of section 219 of this Act to that amount or until payment is made; or

(b) if it considers it expedient, on the application of the cautioner grant time for payment; or

(c) instead of ordering imprisonment, order recovery by civil diligence in accordance with section 221 of this Act.

DEFINITIONS
"imprisonment": s.306(7).
"prosecutor": s.307(1).

Detention in precincts of court

169.—(1) Where a court of summary jurisdiction has power to impose imprisonment or detention on an offender it may, in lieu of so doing and subject to subsection (2) below, order that the offender be detained within the precincts of the court or at any police station, till such hour, not later than eight in the evening on the day on which he is convicted, as the court may direct.

(2) Before making an order under this section a court shall take into consideration the distance between the proposed place of detention and the offender's residence (if known to, or ascertainable by, the court), and shall not make any such order under this section as would deprive the offender of a reasonable opportunity of returning to his residence on the day on which the order is made.

DEFINITIONS
"court of summary jurisdiction": s.307(1).
"impose imprisonment or detention": s.307(1).
"imprisonment": s.307(6).

GENERAL NOTE
This is a rarely-used sentencing provision and would appear to escape the restrictions placed upon the imposition of sentences of imprisonment or detention contained in s.203(1) and (2)

below. The style of the order of detention is contained in Form 18.6 of the 1996 Act of Adjournal.

Miscellaneous

Damages in respect of summary proceedings

170.—(1) No judge, clerk of court or prosecutor in the public interest shall be found liable by any court in damages for or in respect of any proceedings taken, act done, or judgment, decree or sentence pronounced in any summary proceedings under this Act, unless—

(a) the person suing has suffered imprisonment in consequence thereof; and

(b) such proceedings, act, judgment, decree or sentence has been quashed; and

(c) the person suing specifically avers and proves that such proceeding, act, judgment, decree or sentence was taken, done or pronounced maliciously and without probable cause.

(2) No such liability as aforesaid shall be incurred or found where such judge, clerk of court or prosecutor establishes that the person suing was guilty of the offence in respect whereof he had been convicted, or on account of which he had been apprehended or had otherwise suffered, and that he had undergone no greater punishment than was assigned by law to such offence.

(3) No action to enforce such liability as aforesaid shall lie unless it is commenced within two months after the proceeding, act, judgment decree or sentence founded on, or in the case where the Act under which the action is brought fixes a shorter period, within that shorter period.

(4) In this section "judge" shall not include "sheriff", and the provisions of this section shall be without prejudice to the privileges and immunities possessed by sheriffs.

DEFINITIONS
  "imprisonment": s.307(6).
  "judge": ss.170(6) and 307(1).
  "prosecutor": s.307(1).
  "sentence": s.307(1).

GENERAL NOTE

In the conduct of proceedings on indictment the Lord Advocate, and subordinates appointed by him to prepare and conduct such proceedings, enjoy absolute privilege and thus immunity from actions for damages (see *Hester v. MacDonald*, 1961 S.C. 370; 1961 S.L.T. 414). This immunity extends to procurators fiscal in solemn proceedings but is restricted in summary proceedings by the operation of s.170: the right to seek damages from the criminal authorities in relation to any summary proceedings is available to an accused person who can satisfy all the requirements of subs. (1); see *Graham v. Strathern*, 1924 S.C. 699. Any proceedings must be commenced within two months of the conduct complained of or any shorter period specifically stated. Subsection (2) provides immunity from civil liability for court officials only while they are proceeding under the Act (*Graham v. Strathern* at 724; *Ferguson v. MacDonald* (1885) 12 Rettie 1083). The practical effect of subs. (4) is to afford a sheriff sitting in summary proceedings a greater degree of immunity at common law, than was conferred on other judges in summary proceedings. See the extensive discussion of the issue in *Russell v. Dickson*, 1997 G.W.D. 22–1058.

See *Bell v. McGlennan*, 1992 S.L.T. 237, where proceedings were held to have been competently raised against the prosecutor as vicariously liable over the retention of property as evidence in a case which did not proceed, due to the intervention of the statutory time bar.

Recovery of penalties

171.—(1) All penalties, for the recovery of which no special provision has been made by any enactment may be recovered by the public prosecutor in any court having jurisdiction.

(2) Where a court has power to take cognisance of an offence the penalty attached to which is not defined, the punishment therefore shall be regulated by that applicable to common law offences in that court.

DEFINITIONS
"offence": s.307(1).
"prosecutor": s.307(1).

GENERAL NOTE
Unless it is expressly stipulated to the contrary by statute, the public prosecutor holds a general title to prosecute for the recovery of penalties (subs. (1)). In the absence of any express provision, the competent punishment in summary proceedings shall be dictated by reference to the penalties applicable to common law offences (see s.21).

Forms of procedure

172.—(1) The forms of procedure for the purposes of summary proceedings under this Act and appeals therefrom shall be in such forms as are prescribed by Act of Adjournal or as nearly as may be in such forms.

(2) All warrants (other than warrants of apprehension or search), orders of court, and sentences may be signed either by the judge or by the clerk of court, and execution upon any warrant, order of court, or sentence may proceed either upon such warrant, order of court, or sentence itself or upon an extract thereof issued and signed by the clerk of court.

(3) Where, preliminary to any procedure, a statement on oath is required, the statement may be given before any judge, whether the subsequent procedure is in his court or another court.

DEFINITIONS
"judge": s.307(1).
"sentence": s.307(1).

GENERAL NOTE
The 1996 Act of Adjournal substantially revises the format of many forms to be utilised in criminal proceedings.
Although subs. (2) provides that all warrants (except those for apprehension or search) may be subscribed by the judge or the clerk of court, and that extracts thereof shall be equally valid, this presupposes that the order or warrant must first have been granted by a judge (see *Skeen v. Ives Cladding*, 1976 S.L.T. (Notes) 31). Failure to complete proper minutes of proceedings and thus maintain a proper record of the proceedings is a fundamental defect (*Heywood v. Stewart* C.O. Circ. A54/91).

PART X

APPEALS FROM SUMMARY PROCEEDINGS

General

Quorum of High Court in relation to appeals

173.—(1) For the purpose of hearing and determining any appeal under this Part of this Act, or any proceeding connected therewith, three of the Lords Commissioners of Justiciary shall be a quorum of the High Court, and the determination of any question under this Part of this Act by the court shall be according to the votes of the majority of the members of the court sitting, including the presiding judge, and each judge so sitting shall be entitled to pronounce a separate opinion.

(2) For the purpose of hearing and determining appeals under section 175(2)(b) or (c) of this Act, or any proceeding connected therewith, two of the Lords Commissioners of Justiciary shall be a quorum of the High Court, and each judge shall be entitled to pronounce a separate opinion; but where

the two Lords Commissioners of Justiciary are unable to reach agreement on the disposal of the appeal, or where they consider it appropriate, the appeal shall be heard and determined in accordance with subsection (1) above.

DEFINITIONS
"High Court": s.307(1).
"judge": s.307(1).
"Lords Commissioners of Justiciary": s.307(1).

GENERAL NOTE
Part X of this Act is concerned with appeals from summary proceedings. For the purpose of hearing and determining any appeal under this Part of this Act the quorum of judges is three: s.173(1). However, for the purpose of hearing and determining appeals against sentence or against absolute discharge or admonition or any probation order or any community service order or any order deferring sentence the quorum of judges is two: s.173(2). If the two judges cannot agree or consider it appropriate for another reason, *e.g.* consideration of a point of law by a larger court they can remit to three judges, *e.g. Bain v. Wilson*, 1998 S.C.C.R. 454. This provision, particularly the latter, is likely to reduce the considerable burden that has been placed on appellate judges because of the enormous increase in appeals, and especially appeals against summary sentences.

Appeals relating to preliminary pleas

174.—(1) Without prejudice to any right of appeal under section 175(1) to (6) or 191 of this Act, a party may, with the leave of the court (granted either on the motion of the party or *ex proprio motu*) and in accordance with such procedure as may be prescribed by Act of Adjournal, appeal to the High Court against a decision of the court of first instance (other than a decision not to grant leave under this subsection) which relates to such objection or denial as is mentioned in section 144(4) of this Act; but such appeal must be taken not later than two days after such decision.

(2) Where an appeal is taken under subsection (1) above, the High Court may postpone the trial diet (if one has been fixed) for such period as appears to it to be appropriate and may, if it thinks fit, direct that such period (or some part of it) shall not count towards any time limit applying in respect of the case.

(3) If leave to appeal under subsection (1) above is granted by the court it shall not proceed to trial at once under subsection (2) of section 146 of this Act; and subsection (3) of that section shall be construed as requiring sufficient time to be allowed for the appeal to be taken.

(4) In disposing of an appeal under subsection (1) above the High Court may affirm the decision of the court of first instance or may remit the case to it with such directions in the matter as it thinks fit; and where the court of first instance had dismissed the complaint, or any part of it, may reverse that decision and direct that the court of first instance fix a trial diet (if it has not already fixed one as regards so much of the complaint as it has not dismissed.)

DEFINITIONS
"diet": s.307(1).
"High Court": s.307(1).

GENERAL NOTE
Section 184(4) of this Act follows on the provision in s.334(2A) of the 1975 Act. These subsections require any objection to the competency, relevancy of a summary complaint or the proceedings thereon, or any denial that the accused is the person charged by the police with the offence shall be stated before the accused pleads to the charge or any plea is tendered on his behalf.
Section 174(1) allows "a party" with leave of the court to appeal to the High Court of Justiciary against a decision of the court of first instance which relates to such objection or denial as is mentioned in s.144(4). This appeal must be taken within two days after that decision. Refusal of leave to appeal is not applicable.

Practitioners should remember that there are two hurdles in relation to appeals relating to preliminary pleas. First, appeal must be made with the leave of the court although such leave may be either on the motion of the party or *ex proprio motu*. Secondly, a note of appeal is required to be lodged with the sheriff clerk. For the procedure under the 1975 Act, see Act of Adjournal (Consolidation) 1988 rr. 34 and 35. Form 17 of Sched. 1 sets out the angle for the note of appeal.

For examples of the substantive and procedural complexities that can arise in this regard see *Johnston v. MacGillivray*, 1993 S.L.T. 120 and *McLeay v. Hingston*, 1994 S.L.T. 720. The Crown is a party and has a right of appeal: see *Walkingshaw v. Robison & Davidson Ltd*, 1989 S.C.C.R. 359. In *H.M. Advocate v. Sorrie*, 1996 G.W.D. 30–1795 the Appeal Court indicated that if the Crown seek to use a Bill of Advocation rather than an appeal under the section the accused should be alerted to the fact. An accused person need not appeal a preliminary matter immediately but can appeal post-conviction by Stated Case or Bill of Suspension: see *Harvey v. Lockhart*, 1991 S.C.C.R. 83.

Subsections (2), (3) and (4) make consequential provision for postponing the trial diet, allowing time for the appeal and setting out the powers of the High Court of Justiciary in relation to affirming the decision at first instance or remitting the case with directions. The Appeal Court in *MacNeill v. Sutherland*, 1998 S.C.C.R. 474 observed that a sheriff should reach conclusions on all submissions made to him as part of a preliminary plea.

Right of appeal

175.—(1) This section is without prejudice to any right of appeal under section 191 of this Act.

(2) Any person convicted, or found to have committed an offence, in summary proceedings may, with leave granted in accordance with section 180 or, as the case may be, 187 of this Act, appeal under this section to the High Court—

   (a) against such conviction, or finding;

   (b) against the sentence passed on such conviction;

   (c) against his absolute discharge or admonition or any probation order or any community service order or any order deferring sentence; or

[1](ca) against any decision to remit made under section 49(1)(a) or (7)(b) of this Act;

   (d) against both such conviction and such sentence or disposal or order.

(3) The prosecutor in summary proceedings may appeal under this section to the High Court on a point of law—

   (a) against an acquittal in such proceedings; or

   (b) against a sentence passed on conviction in such proceedings.

[2](4) The prosecutor in summary proceedings, in any class of case specified by order made by the Secretary of State, may, in accordance with subsection (4A) below, appeal to the High Court against any of the following disposals, namely—

   (a) a sentence passed on conviction;

   (b) a decision under section 209(1)(b) of this Act not to make a supervised release order;

   (c) a decision under section 234A(2) of this Act not to make a non-harassment order;

   (d) a probation order;

   (e) a community service order;

   (f) a decision to remit to the Principal Reporter made under section 49(1)(a) or (7)(b) of this Act;

   (g) an order deferring sentence;

   (h) an admonition; or

   (i) an absolute discharge.

(4A) An appeal under subsection (4) above may be made—

   (a) on a point of law;

   (b) where it appears to the Lord Advocate, in relation to an appeal under—

      (i) paragraph (a), (h) or (i) of that subsection, that the disposal was unduly lenient;

(ii) paragraph (b) or (c) of that subsection, that the decision not to make the order in question was inappropriate;

(iii) paragraph (d) or (e) of that subsection, that the making of the order concerned was unduly lenient or was on unduly lenient terms;

(iv) under paragraph (f) of that subsection, that the decision to remit was inappropriate;

(v) under paragraph (g) of that subsection, that the deferment of sentence was inappropriate or was on unduly lenient conditions.

[3](5) By an appeal under subsection (2) above, an appellant may bring under review of the High Court any alleged miscarriage of justice which may include such a miscarriage based, subject to subsections (5A) to (5D) below, on the existence and significance of evidence which was not heard at the original proceedings.

(5A) Evidence which was not heard at the original proceedings may found an appeal only where there is a reasonable explanation of why it was not so heard.

(5B) Where the explanation referred to in subsection (5A) above or, as the case may be, (5C) below is that the evidence was not admissible at the time of the original proceedings, but is admissible at the time of the appeal, the court may admit that evidence if it appears to the court that it would be in the interests of justice to do so.

[4](5C) Without prejudice to subsection (5A) above, where evidence such as is mentioned subsection (5) above is evidence—

(a) which is—

(i) from a person; or

(ii) of a statement (within the meaning of section 259(1) of this Act) by a person,

who gave evidence at the original proceedings; and

(b) which is different from, or additional to, the evidence so given,

it may not found an appeal unless there is a reasonable explanation as to why the evidence now sought to be adduced was not given by that person at those proceedings, which explanation is itself supported by independent evidence.

(5D) For the purposes of subsection (5C) above, "independent evidence" means evidence which—

(a) was not heard at the original proceedings;

(b) is from a source independent of the person referred to in subsection (5C) above; and

(c) is accepted by the court as being credible and reliable.

(5E) By an appeal against acquittal under subsection (3) above a prosecutor may bring under review of the High Court any alleged miscarriage of justice.

(6) The power of the Secretary of State to make an order under subsection (4) above shall be exercisable by statutory instrument; and any order so made shall be subject to annulment in pursuance of a resolution of either House of Parliament.

(7) Where a person desires to appeal under subsection (2)(a) or (d) or (3) above, he shall pursue such appeal in accordance with sections 176 to 179, 181 to 185, 188, 190 and 192(1) and (2) of this Act.

(8) A person who has appealed against both conviction and sentence, may abandon the appeal in so far as it is against conviction and may proceed with it against sentence alone, subject to such procedure as may be prescribed by Act of Adjournal.

(9) Where a convicted person or as the case may be a person found to have committed an offence desires to appeal under subsection (2)(b) or (c) above, or the prosecutor desires so to appeal by virtue of subsection (4) above, he shall pursue such appeal in accordance with sections 186, 189(1) to (6), 190 and 192(1) and (2) of this Act; but nothing in this section shall prejudice any

right to proceed by bill of suspension, or as the case may be advocation, against an alleged fundamental irregularity relating to the imposition of sentence.

(10) Where any statute provides for an appeal from summary proceedings to be taken under any public general or local enactment, such appeal shall be taken under this Part of this Act.

DEFINITIONS

"community service order": s.238.
"offence": s.307(1).
"probation order": s.228.
"prosecutor": s.307(1).
"sentence": s.307(1).

NOTES

[1]Inserted by the Crime and Punishment (Scotland) Act 1997 (c. 48), s.23 with effect from August 1, 1997 in terms of the Crime and Punishment (Scotland) Act 1997 (Commencement and Transitional Provisions) Order 1997 (S.I. 1997 No. 1712) para. 3.

[2]Inserted by the Crime and Punishment (Scotland) Act 1997 (c. 48), s.21 with effect from August 1, 1997 in terms of the Crime and Punishment (Scotland) Act 1997 (Commencement and Transitional Provisions) Order 1997 (S.I. 1997 No. 1712) para. 3.

[3]Inserted by the Crime and Punishment (Scotland) Act 1997 (c. 48), s.17(2) with effect from August 1, 1997 in terms of the Crime and Punishment (Scotland) Act 1997 (Commencement and Transitional Provisions) Order 1997 (S.I. 1997 No. 1712) para. 3.

[4]As amended by the Crime and Disorder Act 1998 (c. 37), Sched. 8, para. 123 (effective September 30, 1998: S.I. 1998 No. 2327).

GENERAL NOTE

Subs. (1)

The right of appeal from summary proceedings to the High Court of Justiciary may be exercised without prejudice to an appeal by suspension or advocation on the ground of miscarriage of justice: see s.191.

Subs. (2)

Section 175 relies heavily on the terms of s.442 of the 1975 Act but with several crucial differences. The most important in law and in practice is undoubtedly the qualification that an appeal under s.175 must be "with leave granted in accordance with s.180 or, as the case may be, s.187 of this Act". Reference should be made to these two sections and the General Notes to them.

Assuming that leave has been granted, an appeal against conviction alone is possible under s.175(1)(a) and against sentence under s.175(1)(b) and against orders by way of sentence under s.175(1)(c) or against both conviction and sentence or orders under s.175(1)(d).

Appeals in terms of s.175(1)(a) and s.175(1)(d) will be heard by three judges: s.173(1). Appeals in terms of s.175(1)(b) and s.175(1)(c) will be heard by two judges: s.173(2). Paragraph (ca)—with effect from August 1, 1997 a right of appeal is introduced against a decision to remit under s.49(1)(a) or (7)(b) of the Act. A supervised attendance order is not a sentence passed on conviction and cannot be appealed under this section—*McGregor Petr*, 1999 S.C.C.R. 225.

Subs. (3)

This provision allows for a Crown appeal against acquittal on a point of law or against a sentence passed on conviction, again on a point of law. The second head appears to be designed to catch incompetent sentences.

Subss. (4) and (4A)

These subsections equate with the Lord Advocate's appeal against sentence under s.108 of this Act, but there is a crucial distinction. A sentence passed after conviction on indictment or summary complaint must appear to the Lord Advocate to be unduly lenient or inappropriate depending on the nature of the sentence imposed. A sentence passed after conviction on summary complaint must also be "in any class of case specified by order made by the Secretary of State". This last restriction is likely to curb the enthusiasm of prosecutors by being limited to a very narrow range of classes, if any. The prosecutor's right of appeal against unduly lenient sentences in summary proceedings came into force on November 1, 1996. Classes of cases where the prosecutor can appeal against sentence or other disposal were specified by the Secretary of

State in The Prosecutors Right of Appeal in Summary Proceedings (Scotland) Order 1996 (S.I. 1996 No 2548) namely—where a sentence is passed or a probation order, community service order or order made deferring sentence or admonition or absolute discharge is made.

Subsection 4 was reorganised by s.21 of the Crime and Punishment (Scotland) Act 1997 with effect from August 1, 1997 introducing the new s.4A. A right of appeal by the Lord Advocate against a decision by a court not to make a supervised release order; non-harassment order and decision to remit to the Principal Reporter has been introduced. In *MacGlennan v. McKinnon*, 1998 S.C.C.R. 285, the Crown unsuccessfully appealed the failure by the sheriff to make a non-harassment order.

Subs. (5)

As with s.106(3) the Crime and Punishment (Scotland) Act 1997 has radically altered this subsection. With effect from August 1997 the single ground of appeal in summary proceedings remains on the basis of a miscarriage of justice. The one example previously given of additional evidence has been amended to the existence and significance of evidence which was not heard at the original proceedings. The test to be applied is one of reasonable explanation and as with solemn appeals change of testimony by a witness can now form the basis for such an appeal: See subsections (5A) to (5E). For further comment on this see s.106. In *Ward v. Crowe*, 1999 S.C.C.R. 219 it was held that an averment in an initial writ in a subsequent civil action did not constitute "evidence" in terms of s.175(5). The error in subs. (5C) referred to by the court in their opinion was rectified by Sched. 8 of the Crime and Disorder Act 1998.

Subs. (5c)

The deletion introduced by the 1998 Act serves only to remedy an error in draftsmanship.

Stated case

Stated case: manner and time of appeal

176.—(1) An appeal under section 175(2)(a) or (d) or (3) of this Act shall be by application for a stated case, which application shall—
   (a) be made within one week of the final determination of the proceedings;
   (b) contain a full statement of all the matters which the appellant desires to bring under review and, where the appeal is also against sentence or disposal or order, the ground of appeal against that sentence or disposal or order; and
   (c) be signed by the appellant or his solicitor and lodged with the clerk of court,
and a copy of the application shall, within the period mentioned in paragraph (a) above, be sent by the appellant to the respondent or the respondent's solicitor.

(2) The clerk of court shall enter in the record of the proceedings the date when an application under subsection (1) above was lodged.

(3) The appellant may, at any time within the period of three weeks mentioned in subsection (1) of section 179 of this Act, or within any further period afforded him by virtue of section 181 (1) of this Act, amend any matter stated in his application or add a new matter; and he shall intimate any such amendment, or addition, to the respondent or the respondent's solicitor.

(4) Where such an application has been made by the person convicted, and the judge by whom he was convicted dies before signing the case or is precluded by illness or other cause from doing so, it shall be competent for the convicted person to present a bill of suspension to the High Court and to bring under the review of that court any matter which might have been brought under review by stated case.

(5) The record of the procedure in the inferior court in an appeal mentioned in subsection (1) above shall be as nearly as may be in the form prescribed by Act of Adjournal.

Subs. (1)

An application for stated case is not competent until the cause has been finally determined and sentence pronounced: see *Lee v. Lasswade Local Authority* (1893) 5 Couper 329 and *Torrance v. Miller* (1892) 3 White 254.

A case is finally determined when particulars of conviction and sentence are entered in the record of proceedings: see *Tudhope v. Colbert*, 1978 S.L.T.(Notes) 57 and *Tudhope v. Campbell*, 1979 J.C. 24. Where sentence is deferred in terms of s.202 then the final determination for summary proceedings is the date on which sentence is first deferred.

An application for a stated case is an application for a document that sets forth "the particulars of any matters competent for review which the appellant desires to bring under the review of the High Court, and of the facts, if any, proved in the case, and any point of law decided, and the grounds of the decision": subs. (2).

The nature and content of a stated case is emphasised because of the requirement in subs. (1)(b) that the application for a stated case contain "a full statement of all the matters which the appellant desires to bring under review". If the application does not have a comprehensive and accurate description of the point at issue the stated case will in the fullness of time reflect that.

Superficial applications can be held not to have met the requirements of the section: hence "insufficient evidence for conviction" did not lead to a stated case being issued: *Galloway v. Hillary*, 1983 S.C.C.R. 119. An allegation of insufficient evidence must proceed to highlight the part of the evidence said to be insufficient: *Durant v. Lockhart*, 1986 S.L.T. 312 and *Anderson v. McClory*, 1991 S.C.C.R. 571. See also *McDougall, Petr.*, 1986 S.C.C.R., 128; *McTaggart, Petr.*, 1987 S.C.C.R. 638; *McQuarry v. Carmichael*, 1989 S.C.C.R. 371, and *Anderson v. McClory* 1991 S.C.C.R. 571.

It may be that notwithstanding the brevity of an application a sheriff can state a case although not obliged to do so. The High Court of Justiciary would then proceed to hear an appeal: *Dickson v. Valentine*, 1988 S.C.C.R. 325. See also *McTaggart, Petr.*, 1987 S.C.C.R. 638, *Crowe, Petr.*, 1994 S.C.C.R. 784 and *Leonard, Petr.*, 1995 S.C.C.R. 39. *H.M. Advocate Petr*, 1996 G.W.D. 20–1155 and *Reid Petr.*, 1996 G.W.D. 33–1965.

A further concern arising from applications for stated cases that do not contain full statements relates to the hearing of the appeal. An application for a stated case, and in turn the stated case itself, that does not properly focus the real issue can unduly hamper those presenting the appeal: *Cameron v. Normand*, 1997 G.W.D. 9–367. In *Walton v. Crowe*, 1993 S.C.C.R. 885 an attempt by the appellant to raise an issue which had not been mentioned in the application was refused. That restriction can also apply to the Crown: *Normand v. Walker*, 1994 S.C.C.R. 875.

The main practical problem is the failure to meet the requirements of subs. (1)(b) about a full statement. Making an application within one week of the final determination is less of a general problem: see subs. (1)(a) which must be read with s.194(3) for the meaning of "final determination".

Subs. (3)

The draft stated case that follows from a proper application may on authority be amended or added to and if that is done there must be intimation to the other side.

Subs. (4)

An appeal cannot proceed on the basis of a draft stated case. Either there is a signed stated case to found the appeal or there is not. If there is no stated case in the terms set out in this subsection then the correct mode is a bill of suspension: see *Brady v. Barbour*, 1994 S.C.C.R. 890 and *Clark v. Ruxton*, 1997 G.W.D. 10–408.

Procedure where appellant in custody

177.—(1) If an appellant making an application under section 176 of this Act is in custody, the court of first instance may—

(a) grant bail;

(b) grant a sist of execution;

(c) make any other interim order.

(2) An application for bail shall be disposed of by the court within 24 hours after such application has been made.

(3) If bail is refused or the appellant is dissatisfied with the conditions imposed, he may, within 24 hours after the judgment of the court, appeal against it by a note of appeal written on the complaint and signed by himself

or his solicitor, and the complaint and proceedings shall thereupon be transmitted to the Clerk of Justiciary, and the High Court or any judge thereof, either in court or in chambers, shall, after hearing parties, have power to review the decision of the inferior court and to grant bail on such conditions as the Court or judge may think fit, or to refuse bail.

(4) No clerks' fees, court fees or other fees or expenses shall be exigible from or awarded against an appellant in custody in respect of an appeal to the High Court against the conditions imposed or on account of refusal of bail by a court of summary jurisdiction.

(5) If an appellant who has been granted bail does not thereafter proceed with his appeal, the inferior court shall have power to grant warrant to apprehend and imprison him for such period of his sentence as at the date of his bail remained unexpired and, subject to subsection (6) below, such period shall run from the date of his imprisonment under the warrant or, on the application of the appellant, such earlier date as the court thinks fit, not being a date later than the date of expiry of any term or terms of imprisonment imposed subsequently to the conviction appealed against.

(6) Where an appellant who has been granted bail does not thereafter proceed with his appeal, the court from which the appeal was taken shall have power, where at the time of the abandonment of the appeal the person is in custody or serving a term or terms of imprisonment imposed subsequently to the conviction appealed against, to order that the sentence or, as the case may be, the unexpired portion of that sentence relating to that conviction should run from such date as the court may think fit, not being a date later than the date on which any term or terms of imprisonment subsequently imposed expired.

(7) The court shall not make an order under subsection (6) above to the effect that the sentence or, as the case may be, unexpired portion of the sentence shall run other than concurrently with the subsequently imposed term of imprisonment without first notifying the appellant of its intention to do so and considering any representations made by him or on his behalf.

[1](8) Subsections (6) and (7) of section 112 of this Act (bail pending determination of appeals under paragraph 13(a) of Schedule 6 to the Scotland Act 1998) shall apply to appeals arising in summary proceedings as they do to appeals arising in solemn proceedings.

DEFINITIONS
   "bail": s.307(1).
   "Clerk of Justiciary": s.307(1).
   "High Court": s.307(1).
   "order": s.307(1).

NOTE
[1]Inserted by the Scotland Act 1998 (Consequential Modifications) (No.1) Order 1999 (S.I. 1999 No.1042) art.3, Sched.1, para.13(7) (effective May 6, 1999).

GENERAL NOTE
   This section sets out the immediate procedure if the appellant makes an application for a stated case and is in custody. If bail is sought an application would be disposed of within 24 hours of such an application or, if refused, a note of appeal may be lodged to review the decision to refuse: subss. (2) and (3).
   Appeals are frequently not pursued despite the initial enthusiasm. Where the appellant is at liberty when he abandons his appeal the warrant to imprison him in accordance with his sentence shall run from the date of his imprisonment under the warrant or, on application, such earlier date as the court thinks fit, not being a date later than the date of expiry of any term of imprisonment imposed subsequently to the conviction appealed against: subs. (5).
   This may be contrasted with the circumstances where the appellant is in custody when he abandons his appeal, then the unexpired portion of that sentence should run from such date as the court thinks fit, not being a date later than the date on which any term of imprisonment subsequently imposed expired: subs. (6).

Subsection (7) gives statutory effect to *Proudfoot v. Wither*, 1990 S.L.T. 742 and requires sentences under subs. (6) to be served concurrently but if the court is minded to do otherwise then the appellant must be notified and the court must consider any representations he wishes to make.

Stated case: preparation of draft

178.—(1) Within three weeks of the final determination of proceedings in respect of which an application for a stated case is made under section 176 of this Act—

(a) where the appeal is taken from the district court and the trial was presided over by a justice of the peace or justices of the peace, the Clerk of Court; or

(b) in any other case the judge who presided at the trial,

shall prepare a draft stated case, and the clerk of the court concerned shall forthwith issue the draft to the appellant or his solicitor and a duplicate thereof to the respondent or his solicitor.

(2) A stated case shall be, as nearly as may be, in the form prescribed by Act of Adjournal, and shall set forth the particulars of any matters competent for review which the appellant desires to bring under the review of the High Court, and of the facts, if any, proved in the case, and any point of law decided, and the grounds of the decision.

DEFINITION
"judge": s.307(1).

GENERAL NOTE
In the district court the draft stated case is prepared by the clerk of court: see *Mackinnon v. McGarry*, 1987 S.C.C.R. 522. If the justice fails to comply with the statutory provisions the conviction will be quashed: see *Mitchell v. Smith*, Crown Office circular A2/81. In *Clarke v. Ruxton*, 1997 G.W.D. 10–408 the accused had to proceed by way of a bill of suspension following the death of the sheriff before a stated case could be prepared.

Subs. (2)
The form of the draft stated case has been considered a number of times and the following guidelines have been given: (1) it is not necessary to narrate the charges; (2) the facts proved should be fully set out: see *Gordon v. Hansen* (1914) 7 Adam 441; *Waddell v. Kinnaird*, 1922 J.C. 40; *Gordon v. Allan*, 1987 S.L.T. 400; *Duncan v. MacLeod*, 1997 G.W.D. 13–550; (3) it should set out objections taken to admissibility or rejection of evidence and the reasons for upholding or repelling same should be explained: see *Falconer v. Brown* (1893) 1 Adam 96; (4) any findings in fact made should be based on the whole evidence: see *Jordan v. Allan*, 1989 S.C.C.R. 202 and *Bowman v. Jessop*, 1989 S.C.C.R. 597; (5) where a no case to answer submission is made then the form of the stated case should be as set out in *Wingate v. MacGlennan*, 1991 S.C.C.R. 133. See also *MacDonald v. Normand*, 1994 S.C.C.R. 121; *Cassidy v. Normand*, 1994 S.C.C.R. 325, and *Thomson v. Barber*, 1994 S.C.C.R. 485; (6) the reasons for the final decision should be set out: see *Lyon v. Don Brothers, Buist & Co*, 1944 J.C. 1 including the reasons the evidence was believed or disbelieved. See *Petrovich v. Jessop*, 1990 S.C.C.R. 1; *Roberton v. McGlennan*, 1994 S.C.C.R. 394, and *Leask v. Vannet*, 1996 G.W.D. 36–1960; (7) questions should be stated for the opinion of the court: see *Needes v. MacLeod*, November 7 1984, unreported. Notwithstanding that questions are not properly framed the court may proceed: see *Robertson v. Aitchison*, 1981 S.C.C.R. 149; *Marshall v. Smith*, 1983 S.C.C.R. 156, and *Waddell v. MacPhail*, 1986 S.C.C.R. 593. In *Jackson v. Vannet*, 1997 G.W.D. 23–1146 the stated case was sent back for restatement where the justice did not summarise the entire evidence of a number of essential witnesses.

Stated case: adjustment and signature

179.—(1) Subject to section 181(1) of this Act, within three weeks of the issue of the draft stated case under section 178 of this Act, each party shall cause to be transmitted to the court and to the other parties or their solicitors a note of any adjustments he proposes be made to the draft case or shall intimate that he has no such proposal.

[1](2) The adjustments mentioned in subsection (1) above shall relate to

evidence heard or purported to have been heard at the trial and not to such evidence as is mentioned in section 175(5) of this Act.

(3) Subject to section 181(1) of this Act, if the period mentioned in subsection (1) above has expired and the appellant has not lodged adjustments and has failed to intimate that he has no adjustments to propose, he shall be deemed to have abandoned his appeal; and subsection (5) of section 177 of this Act shall apply accordingly.

(4) If adjustments are proposed under subsection (1) above or if the judge desires to make any alterations to the draft case there shall, within one week of the expiry of the period mentioned in that subsection or as the case may be of any further period afforded under section 181(1) of this Act, be a hearing (unless the appellant has, or has been deemed to have, abandoned his appeal) for the purpose of considering such adjustments or alterations.

(5) Where a party neither attends nor secures that he is represented at a hearing under subsection (4) above, the hearing shall nevertheless proceed.

(6) Where at a hearing under subsection (4) above—
   (a) any adjustment proposed under subsection (1) above by a party (and not withdrawn) is rejected by the judge; or
   (b) any alteration proposed by the judge is not accepted by all the parties,
that fact shall be recorded in the minute of the proceedings of the hearing.

(7) Within two weeks of the date of the hearing under subsection (4) above or, where there is no hearing, within two weeks of the expiry of the period mentioned in subsection (1) above, the judge shall (unless the appellant has been deemed to have abandoned the appeal) state and sign the case and shall append to the case—
   (a) any adjustment, proposed under subsection (1) above, which is rejected by him, a note of any evidence rejected by him which is alleged to support that adjustment and the reasons for his rejection of that adjustment and evidence; and
   (b) a note of the evidence upon which he bases any finding of fact challenged, on the basis that it is unsupported by the evidence, by a party at the hearing under subsection (4) above.

(8) As soon as the case is signed under subsection (7) above the clerk of court—
   (a) shall send the case to the appellant or his solicitor and a duplicate thereof to the respondent or his solicitor; and
   (b) shall transmit the complaint, productions and any other proceedings in the cause to the Clerk of Justiciary.

(9) Subject to section 181(1) of this Act, within one week of receiving the case the appellant or his solicitor, as the case may be, shall cause it to be lodged with the Clerk of Justiciary.

(10) Subject to section 181(1) of this Act, if the appellant or his solicitor fails to comply with subsection (9) above the appellant shall be deemed to have abandoned the appeal; and subsection (5) of section 177 of this Act shall apply accordingly.

DEFINITIONS
   "Clerk of Justiciary": s.307(1).
   "judge": s.307(1).

NOTE
   [1]As amended by the Crime and Punishment (Scotland) Act 1997 (c. 48) Schedule. 1, para. 21(20) with effect from August 1, 1997 in terms of the Crime and Punishment (Scotland) Act 1997 (Commencement and Transitional Provisions) Order 1997 (S.I. 1997 No. 1712) para. 3.

GENERAL NOTE
   Section 179 consolidates s.448 of the 1975 Act which had been much amended. There are only two practical points which need to be emphasised. First, many appeals are deemed to be abandoned because adjustments are not lodged or because the appellant does not intimate that he has no adjustments to propose. This requirement still exists in subs. (3). Similarly, within one

week of receiving the stated case itself it should be lodged with the Clerk of Justiciary: subs. (9). Failure to comply with that requirement also results in an appeal being deemed to be abandoned: subs. (10).

Secondly, adjustments must relate to the evidence heard or purported to have been heard at trial not to any fresh evidence: subs. (2). Adjustments can be proposed to: (1) findings in fact: see *Wilson v. Carmichael*, 1982 S.C.C.R. 528; (2) the trial judge's note: see *Ballantyne v. McKinnon*, 1983 S.C.C.R. 97, and *MacDonald v. Scott*, 1993 S.C.C.R. 78; and (3) questions of law: see *O'Hara v. Tudhope*, 1984 S.C.C.R. 283. However, if any adjustments are rejected by the judge then reasons for that rejection must be given: subs. (7)(a). The court can take account of material rejected by the sheriff: see *Wilson v. Carmichael, supra*, and s.182 below.

Where reasons are not given the case may be remitted for the purpose of having reasons given. That was done in *Owens v. Crowe*, 1994 S.C.C.R. 310 and on reporting the sheriff gave sound reasons.

Leave to appeal against conviction etc.

180.—(1) The decision whether to grant leave to appeal for the purposes of section 175(2)(a) or (d) of this Act shall be made by a judge of the High Court who shall—
   (a) if he considers that the documents mentioned in subsection (2) below disclose arguable grounds of appeal, grant leave to appeal and make such comments in writing as he considers appropriate; and
   (b) in any other case—
      (i) refuse leave to appeal and give reasons in writing for the refusal; and
      (ii) where the appellant is on bail and the sentence imposed on his conviction is one of imprisonment, grant a warrant to apprehend and imprison him.
(2) The documents referred to in subsection (1) above are—
   (a) the stated case lodged under subsection (9) of section 179 of this Act; and
   (b) the documents transmitted to the Clerk of Justiciary under subsection (8)(b) of that section.
(3) A warrant granted under subsection (1)(b)(ii) above shall not take effect until the expiry of the period of 14 days mentioned in subsection (4) below without an application to the High Court for leave to appeal having been lodged by the appellant under that subsection.
(4) Where leave to appeal is refused under subsection (1) above the appellant may, within 14 days of intimation under subsection (10) below, apply to the High Court for leave to appeal.
(5) In deciding an application under subsection (4) above the High Court shall—
   (a) if, after considering the documents mentioned in subsection (2) above and the reasons for the refusal, the court is of the opinion that there are arguable grounds of appeal, grant leave to appeal and make such comments in writing as the court considers appropriate; and
   (b) in any other case—
      (i) refuse leave to appeal and give reasons in writing for the refusal; and
      (ii) where the appellant is on bail and the sentence imposed on his conviction is one of imprisonment, grant a warrant to apprehend and imprison him.
(6) The question whether to grant leave to appeal under subsection (1) or (5) above shall be considered and determined in chambers without the parties being present.
(7) Comments in writing made under subsection (1)(a) or (5)(a) above may, without prejudice to the generality of that provision, specify the arguable grounds of appeal (whether or not they are contained in the stated case) on the basis of which leave to appeal is granted.
(8) Where the arguable grounds of appeal are specified by virtue of

subsection (7) above it shall not, except by leave of the High Court on cause shown, be competent for the appellant to found any aspect of his appeal on any ground of appeal contained in the stated case but not so specified.

(9) Any application by the appellant for the leave of the High Court under subsection (8) above—

(a) shall be made not less than seven days before the date fixed for the hearing of the appeal; and

(b) shall, not less that seven days before that date, be intimated by the appellant to the Crown Agent.

(10) The Clerk of Justiciary shall forthwith intimate—

(a) a decision under subsection (1) or (5) above; and

(b) in the case of a refusal of leave to appeal, the reasons for the decision,

to the appellant or his solicitor and to the Crown Agent.

DEFINITIONS

"bail": s.307(1).

"High Court": s.307(1).

"judge": s.307(1).

GENERAL NOTE

This section mirrors so far as possible the provisions for solemn appeals which are to be found in s.107. Reference therefore might conveniently be made to the general note to that section.

Leave to appeal

The requirement to obtain a grant of appeal is likely to reduce substantially the number of summary appeals against conviction and, separately, appeals against conviction and sentence actually heard in court. For many years a considerable volume of these sorts of cases have got to a hearing more in hope than expectation of a setting aside of the conviction.

Section 175(2)(a) and (d) has provided for a right of appeal against conviction and, separately, appeal against conviction and sentence. The right of appeal is conditional on a grant of leave to appeal by a judge of the High Court of Justiciary in terms of s.180. Before the judge can decide the grant he must have documents before him and these are specified as the stated case, the complaint, the productions and any other proceedings: subs. (2). Having considered these documents the judge must decide whether they disclose arguable grounds of appeal: subs. (1)(a). The action that follows such a decision depends on which way the decision goes.

In the General Note to s.107 some thought was given to what is meant by "arguable grounds of appeal". On the principle that the greater (solemn procedure) includes the lesser (summary procedure) the considerations in relation to s.107 also apply to s.180. There are two procedural differences that may affect the meaning of "arguable grounds of appeal". First, in solemn procedure the presence of a jury means that there are aspects, *e.g.* the judge's charge to the jury, that do not apply to summary appeals: Renton and Brown (5th ed.) para. 11–38 at p. 199–200 sets out the law on the point.

Secondly, the pivotal role of the stated case in summary appeals is emphasised repeatedly in the case law, and the scrutiny applied to its terms gives rise to different issues: *e.g.* the nature of irregularity will be different: Renton and Brown (5th ed.) para. 16–28 at p. 337.

To return to the appeal, the judge of the High Court of Justiciary who must consider the documents to decide whether they disclose arguable grounds of appeal does so in chambers without the parties being present: subs. (6). If the judge considers that the documents do disclose arguable grounds of appeal he then grants leave to appeal and he makes such comments in writing as he considers appropriate: subs. (1)(a). If the judge considers that the documents do not disclose arguable grounds of appeal he then refuses leave to appeal and he gives reasons in writing for the refusal: subs. (1)(b)(i), *e.g. MacNeill v. Skelly*, 1997 G.W.D. 6—230. The appellant, who is at this stage on bail and the sentence imposed on his conviction was one of imprisonment, will then be the subject of a warrant to apprehend granted by the judge and on implementation the appellant will be imprisoned: subs. (1)(b)(ii).

The warrant to apprehend and imprison under subs. (1)(b)(ii) shall not take effect until the expiry of the period of 14 days during which period the appellant may, in effect, appeal by making an application to the High Court of Justiciary: subs. (4). If no such application is to be made then the appellant's solicitor has the time available to arrange for the client to surrender to the warrant.

Application for leave to appeal

The refusal of leave to appeal by a single judge in chambers may therefore be followed by an application to the High Court of Justiciary for leave to appeal: subs. (4). This is in effect an appeal in itself. Who decides the application depends on what is at issue, namely an appeal against conviction, sentence or both.

By s.173(1) "for the purpose of hearing and determining any appeal under this Part of this Act or any proceeding connected therewith" the quorum is three judges, except that by s.173(2) for appeals against sentence alone the quorum is two judges. Accordingly, an application in terms of subs. (4) will generally be decided by three judges unless the appeal concerns sentence alone, in which event the quorum is two.

The various judges of the High Court of Justiciary who must consider the documents to decide whether they disclose arguable grounds of appeal do so in chambers without the parties being present: subs. (6). In deciding the application the judges must consider the documents that had been before the single judge in chambers and also consider the reasons for the earlier refusal but, thereafter, if the court is of the opinion that there are arguable grounds of appeal then the court should grant leave to appeal and make such comments in writing as the court considers appropriate: subs. (5)(a).

In any other case, leave to appeal will be refused with reasons in writing, and a warrant to apprehend and imprison is to be granted if appropriate: subs. (5)(b).

Hearing of appeal

Regard must be paid to the comments in writing made either by the single judge in chambers by subs. (1)(a) or by a greater number of judges in chambers by subs. (5)(a). The importance of the comments in writing lies in the possibility that they "may specify the arguable grounds of appeal (whether or not they are contained in the note of appeal) on the basis of which leave to appeal is granted": subs. (7).

It is very easy to imagine on the wording of subs. (1)(a) a single judge in chambers granting leave to appeal, not on the original ground in the note of appeal, but on the basis of comments in writing which amend, alter or distil the original grounds in the note of appeal. The new grounds of appeal, having been specified, in effect dictate the ground of appeal to be argued at the hearing: subs. (8).

The appellant who wishes to found any aspect of his appeal on any ground of appeal contained in the stated case but not so specified in the comments in writing provided under subs. (1)(a) or subs. (5)(a) may seek leave to do so: subs. (8). Application for such leave under subs. (8) must be made not less than seven days before the date fixed for the hearing of the appeal: subs. (9). It is not immediately clear from a reading of the statute as to whom an application under subs. (8) will be directed. As it is not so much an appeal as a request to broaden an approach to an appeal, it may simply be returned to those who made the comments in writing under subs. (1)(a) or subs. (5)(a).

Stated case: directions by High Court

181.—(1) Without prejudice to any other power of relief which the High Court may have, where it appears to that court on application made in accordance with subsection (2) below, that the applicant has failed to comply with any of the requirements of—

(a) subsection (1) of section 176 of this Act; or

(b) subsection (1) or (9) of section 179 of this Act,

the High Court may direct that such further period of time as it may think proper be afforded to the applicant to comply with any requirement of the aforesaid provisions.

(2) Any application for a direction under subsection (1) above shall be made in writing to the Clerk of Justiciary and shall state the ground for the application, and, in the case of an application for the purposes of paragraph (a) of subsection (1) above, notification of the application shall be made by the appellant or his solicitor to the clerk of the court from which the appeal is to be taken, and the clerk shall thereupon transmit the complaint, documentary productions and any other proceedings in the cause to the Clerk of Justiciary.

(3) The High Court shall dispose of any application under subsection (1) above in like manner as an application to review the decision of an inferior court on a grant of bail, but shall have power—
    (a) to dispense with a hearing; and
    (b) to make such enquiry in relation to the application as the court may think fit,
and when the High Court has disposed of the application the Clerk of Justiciary shall inform the clerk of the inferior court of the result.

DEFINITIONS
    "Clerk of Justiciary": s.307(1).
    "High Court": s.307(1).

GENERAL NOTE
    The complex arrangements for applying for a stated case and thereafter attending to adjustments and hearings will all be done within a short time frame: see s.176(1) and s.179(1) to (9). A pragmatic power is granted to the High Court of Justiciary to afford an appropriate further time to comply with these arrangements: s.181(1). An application for a grant is made in writing: subs. 181(2). A hearing is not necessary and the High Court may make enquiry: subs. (5).

Stated case: hearing of appeal

182.—(1) A stated case under this Part of this Act shall be heard by the High Court on such date as it may fix.
    (2) For the avoidance of doubt, where an appellant, in his application under section 176(1) of this Act (or in a duly made amendment or addition to that application), refers to an alleged miscarriage of justice, but in stating a case under section 179(7) of this Act the inferior court is unable to take the allegation into account, the High Court may nevertheless have regard to the allegation at a hearing under subsection (1) above.
    (3) Except by leave of the High Court on cause shown, it shall not be competent for an appellant to found any aspect of his appeal on a matter not contained in his application under section 176(1) of this Act (or in a duly made amendment or addition to that application).
    (4) Subsection (3) above shall not apply as respects any ground of appeal specified as an arguable ground of appeal by virtue of subsection (7) of section 180 of this Act.
    (5) Without prejudice to any existing power of the High Court, that court may in hearing a stated case—
    (a) order the production of any document or other thing connected with the proceedings;
    [1](b) hear any evidence relevant to any alleged miscarriage of justice or order such evidence to be heard by a judge at the High Court or by such other person as it may appoint for that purpose;
    (c) take account of any circumstances relevant to the case which were not before the trial judge;
    (d) remit to any fit person to enquire and report in regard to any matter or circumstance affecting the appeal;
    (e) appoint a person with expert knowledge to act as assessor to the High Court in any case where it appears to the court that such expert knowledge is required for the proper determination of the case;
    (f) take account of any matter proposed in any adjustment rejected by the trial judge and of the reasons for such rejection;
    (g) take account of any evidence contained in a note of evidence such as is mentioned in section 179(7) of this Act.
    (6) The High Court may at the hearing remit the stated case back to the inferior court to be amended and returned.

DEFINITIONS
    "judge": s.307(1).
    "single court": s.307(1).

NOTE
    [1]As amended by the Crime and Punishment (Scotland) Act 1997 (c. 48) Sched. 1, para. 21(21) with effect from August 1, 1997 in terms of the Crime and Punishment (Scotland) Act 1997 (Commencement and Transitional Provisions) Order 1997 (S.I. 1997 No. 1712) para. 3.

GENERAL NOTE
    The court in *Egan v. Normand*, 1997 S.C.C.R. 211 observed that it was unacceptable for an appellant at the hearing of an appeal to seek a postponement to allow enquiries to be made into a possible ground of appeal based on *Anderson v. H.M. Advocate*. It remains the position (notwithstanding earlier strictures) that if in an application for a stated case a miscarriage of justice is alleged but for some reason has not been dealt with in the stated case itself, the High Court of Justiciary at a hearing of the appeal may still have regard to the earlier allegation: subs. (2). An appellant cannot himself found on a matter not contained in the application for a stated case without the leave of the court: subs. (3). See *West v. McNaughton*, 1990 S.C.C.R. 439; *Stein v. Lowe*, 1991 S.C.C.R. 692; *Fulton v. Lees*, 1992 S.C.C.R. 923; *Normand v. Walker*, 1994 S.C.C.R. 875, and *Campbell v. McClory*, 1996 G.W.D. 28–1659. However, if the appellant wishes to extend his position beyond any ground of appeal specified as an arguable ground of appeal then he may not do so: subs. (4).
    Prior to disposing of the appeal the High Court of Justiciary has a wide range of powers to assist in attaining justice: subs. (5). Re paragraph (b) see *MacLeod v. Lowe*, 1993 S.L.T. 475 and *Marshall v. MacDougall*, 1987 S.L.T. 123. Re para. (c) see *Hogg v. Heattle*, 1961 S.L.T. 38. Re para. (d) *Marshall v. MacDougall, supra*, but see also *Faroux v. Brown*, 1996 S.C.C.R. 891. Paragraph (f) see *Wilson v. Carmichael*, 1982 S.C.C.R. 528; *Paterson v. Lees*, 1992 S.C.C.R. 300; *Ballantyne v. McKinnon*, 1983 S.C.C.R. 97 and *MacDonald v. Scott*, 1993 S.C.C.R. 78. Subsection 6—See *Jackson v. Vannet*, 1997 G.W.D. 23–1146.

Stated case: disposal of appeal

183.—(1) The High Court may, subject to subsection (3) below and to section 190(1) of this Act, dispose of a stated case by—
   (a) remitting the cause to the inferior court with its opinion and any direction thereon;
   (b) affirming the verdict of the inferior court;
   (c) setting aside the verdict of the inferior court and either quashing the conviction or, subject to subsection (2) below, substituting therefor an amended verdict of guilty; or
   (d) setting aside the verdict of the inferior court and granting authority to bring a new prosecution in accordance with section 185 of this Act.
   (2) An amended verdict of guilty substituted under subsection (1)(c) above must be one which could have been returned on the complaint before the inferior court.
   (3) The High Court shall, in an appeal—
   (a) against both conviction and sentence, subject to section 190(1) of this Act, dispose of the appeal against sentence; or
   (b) by the prosecutor, against sentence, dispose of the appeal,
by exercise of the power mentioned in section 189(1) of this Act.
   (4) In setting aside, under subsection (1) above, a verdict the High Court may quash any sentence imposed on the appellant as respects the complaint, and—
   (a) in a case where it substitutes an amended verdict of guilty, whether or not the sentence related to the verdict set aside; or
   (b) in any other case, where the sentence did not so relate,
may pass another (but not more severe) sentence in substitution for the sentence so quashed.

(5) For the purposes of subsections (3) and (4) above, "sentence" shall be construed as including disposal or order.

(6) Where an appeal against acquittal is sustained, the High Court may—

(a) convict and, subject to subsection (7) below, sentence the respondent;

(b) remit the case to the inferior court with instructions to convict and sentence the respondent, who shall be bound to attend any diet fixed by the court for such purpose; or

(c) remit the case to the inferior court with their opinion thereon.

(7) Where the High Court sentences the respondent under subsection (6)(a) above it shall not in any case impose a sentence beyond the maximum sentence which could have been passed by the inferior court.

(8) Any reference in subsection (6) above to convicting and sentencing shall be construed as including a reference to—

(a) convicting and making some other disposal; or

(b) convicting and deferring sentence.

(9) The High Court shall have power in an appeal under this Part of this Act to award such expenses both in the High Court and in the inferior court as it may think fit.

(10) Where, following an appeal, other than an appeal under section 175(2)(b) or (3) of this Act, the appellant remains liable to imprisonment or detention under the sentence of the inferior court, or is so liable under a sentence passed in the appeal proceedings the High Court shall have the power where at the time of disposal of the appeal the appellant—

(a) was at liberty on bail, to grant warrant to apprehend and imprison or detain the appellant for a term, to run from the date of such apprehension, not longer than that part of the term or terms of imprisonment or detention specified in the sentence brought under review which remained unexpired at the date of liberation;

(b) is serving a term or terms of imprisonment or detention imposed in relation to a conviction subsequent to the conviction appealed against, to exercise the like powers in regard to him as may be exercised, in relation to an appeal which has been abandoned, by a court of summary jurisdiction in pursuance of section 177(6) of this Act.

DEFINITIONS

"High Court": s.307(1).
"sentence": s.183(5).

GENERAL NOTE

The general approach to disposing of appeals by way of stated case in s.183 is very similar to the general approach to disposing of solemn appeals in s.118. Reference may be made to the General Note to that section.

It should be emphasised that the different nature of the procedure means that the cause under this section may be remitted to the lower court with any necessary direction: subs. (1)(a). This includes an instruction to convict where an appeal against acquittal has been successful: subs. (6)(b). For examples under sub. (1): Para. (c) see *Robertson v. Scott*, 1993 S.C.C.R. 450 and *McCusker v. Whitelaw*, 1993 S.C.C.R. 198; Para. (d) see *Miller v. Lees*, 1991 S.C.C.R. 799; *Stewart v. Normand*, 1991 S.C.C.R. 940; *McSorley v. Normand*, 1991 S.C.C.R. 949, and *Brims v. MacDonald*, 1993 S.C.C.R. 1061. But see also *Kelly v. Docherty*, 1991 S.C.C.R. 312 and *O'Brien v. Ruxton*, 1999 S.C.C.R. 216. For a case under subs. (4)(b) see *Robertson v. Scott*, 1993 S.C.C.R. 450. Subsection (6) see *Aitchison v. Rizza*, 1985 S.C.C.R. 299 and *Heywood v. Ross* 1993 S.C.C.R. 101.

Abandonment of appeal

184.—(1) An appellant in an appeal such as is mentioned in section 176(1) of this Act may at any time prior to lodging the case with the Clerk of Justiciary abandon his appeal by minute signed by himself or his solicitor, written on the complaint or lodged with the clerk of the inferior court, and

intimated to the respondent or the respondent's solicitor, but such abandonment shall be without prejudice to any other competent mode of appeal,
review, advocation or suspension.

(2) Subject to section 191 of this Act, on the case being lodged with the
Clerk of Justiciary, the appellant shall be held to have abandoned any other
mode of appeal which might otherwise have been open to him.

DEFINITION
"Clerk of Justiciary": s.307(1).

New prosecution

Authorisation of new prosecution

185.—(1) Subject to subsection (2) below, where authority is granted
under section 183(1)(d) of this Act, a new prosecution may be brought
charging the accused with the same or any similar offence arising out of the
same facts; and the proceedings out of which the stated case arose shall not
be a bar to such prosecution.

(2) In a new prosecution under this section the accused shall not be
charged with an offence more serious than that of which he was convicted in
the earlier proceedings.

(3) No sentence may be passed on conviction under the new prosecution
which could not have been passed on conviction under the earlier
proceedings.

(4) A new prosecution may be brought under this section, notwithstanding that any time limit (other than the time limit mentioned in subsection (5)
below) for the commencement of such proceedings has elapsed.

(5) Proceedings in a prosecution under this section shall be commenced
within two months of the date on which authority to bring the prosecution
was granted.

(6) In proceedings in a new prosecution under this section it shall, subject
to subsection (7) below, be competent for either party to lead any evidence
which it was competent for him to lead in the earlier proceedings.

(7) The complaint in a new prosecution under this section shall identify
any matters as respects which the prosecutor intends to lead evidence by
virtue of subsection (6) above which would not have been competent but for
that subsection.

(8) For the purposes of subsection (5) above, proceedings shall be deemed
to be commenced—

(a) in a case where such warrant is executed without unreasonable delay,
on the date on which a warrant to apprehend or to cite the accused is
granted; and

(b) in any other case, on the date on which the warrant is executed.

(9) Where the two months mentioned in subsection (5) above elapse and
no new prosecution has been brought under this section, the order under
section 183(1)(d) of this Act setting aside the verdict shall have the effect, for
all purposes, of an acquittal.

(10) On granting authority under section 183(1)(d) of this Act to bring a
new prosecution, the High Court may, after giving the parties an opportunity
of being heard, order the detention of the accused person in custody; but an
accused person may not be detained by virtue of this subsection for a period
of more than 40 days.

GENERAL NOTE
See notes to s.183, para. (d) above, for examples. In *Heywood Petr.*, 1998 S.C.C.R. 335, the
Crown brought a petition to the nobile officium to amend the record of the interlocutor
pronounced by the court which did not reflect the fact that the Crown had been granted leave to
raise a fresh prosecution in respect of all charges. In granting the petition the court held that as

the order granting authority had been pronounced in open court the Crown needed no further authority to bring a fresh prosecution.

Appeals against sentence

Appeals against sentence only

186.—(1) An appeal under section 175(2)(b) or (c), or by virtue of section 175(4), of this Act shall be by note of appeal, which shall state the ground of appeal.

(2) The note of appeal shall, where the appeal is—

(a) under section 175(2)(b) or (c) be lodged, within one week of—

(i) the passing of the sentence; or

(ii) the making of the order disposing of the case or deferring sentence,

with the clerk of the court from which the appeal is to be taken; or

(b) by virtue of section 175(4) be so lodged within four weeks of such passing or making.

(3) The clerk of court on receipt of the note of appeal shall—

(a) send a copy of the note to the respondent or his solicitor; and

(b) obtain a report from the judge who sentenced the convicted person or, as the case may be, who disposed of the case or deferred sentence.

(4) Subject to subsection (5) below, the clerk of court shall within two weeks of the passing of the sentence or within two weeks of the disposal or order against which the appeal is taken—

(a) send to the Clerk of Justiciary the note of appeal, together with the report mentioned in subsection (3)(b) above, a certified copy of the complaint, the minute of proceedings and any other relevant documents; and

(b) send copies of that report to the appellant and respondent or their solicitors.

¹(5) Where a judge—

(a) is temporarily absent from duty for any cause;

(b) is a part-time sheriff; or

(c) is a justice of the peace,

the sheriff principal of the sheriffdom in which the judgment was pronounced may extend the period of two weeks specified in subsection (4) above for such period as he considers reasonable.

(6) Subject to subsection (4) above, the report mentioned in subsection (3)(b) above shall be available only to the High Court, the parties and, on such conditions as may be prescribed by Act of Adjournal, such other persons or classes of persons as may be so prescribed.

(7) Where the judge's report is not furnished within the period mentioned in subsection (4) above or such period as extended under subsection (5) above, the High Court may extend such period, or, if it thinks fit, hear and determine the appeal without the report.

(8) Section 181 of this Act shall apply where an appellant fails to comply with the requirement of subsection (2)(a) above as they apply where an applicant fails to comply with any of the requirements of section 176(1) of this Act.

(9) An appellant under section 175(2)(b) or (c), or by virtue of section 175(4), of this Act may at any time prior to the hearing of the appeal abandon his appeal by minute, signed by himself or his solicitor, lodged—

(a) in a case where the note of appeal has not yet been sent under subsection (4)(a) above to the Clerk of Justiciary, with the clerk of court;

(b) in any other case, with the Clerk of Justiciary,

and intimated to the respondent.

(10) Sections 176(5), 177 and 182(5)(a) to (e) of this Act shall apply to

appeals under section 175(2)(b) or (c), or by virtue of section 175(4), of this Act as they apply to appeals under section 175(2)(a) or (d) of this Act, except that, for the purposes of such application to any appeal by virtue of section 175(4), references in subsections (1) to (4) of section 177 to the appellant shall be construed as references to the convicted person and subsections (6) and (7) of that section shall be disregarded.

DEFINITIONS
"High Court": s.307(1).
"judge": s.307(1).
"sentence": s.307(1).

NOTE
[1]As amended by the Bail, Judicial Appointments etc. (Scotland) Act (asp 9), s.12 and Sched., para. 7(4).

GENERAL NOTE
A brief glance at the vast number of criminal cases reported in Green's Weekly Digest will reveal that in all probability the single biggest category of cases is appeals against summary sentences. Whether this remains the position is open to doubt with the new procedure.

A note of appeal stating the ground of appeal commences the action: subs. (1). Merely to complain of an excessive sentence will not suffice and the High Court of Justiciary is very likely to support sheriffs who complain of minimal specification: *Campbell v. MacDougall*, 1991 S.C.C.R. 218. The sheriff's report is required to set out the circumstances of the offence and of the appellants. See *Henry v. Docherty*, 1989 S.C.C.R. 426. In *Mullins v. Walkingshaw*, 1996 G.W.D. 27–159 it was observed that each of the three justices did not have to prepare a report. Confusion as to the facts of a case in a Sheriff's report was a factor taken into account by the Appeal Court in allowing an appeal against sentence—*Scott v. Fraser*, 1998 G.W.D. 11–533.

Leave to appeal against sentence

187.—(1) The decision whether to grant leave to appeal for the purposes of section 175(2)(b) or (c) of this Act shall be made by a judge of the High Court who shall—
   (a) if he considers that the note of appeal and other documents sent to the Clerk of Justiciary under section 186(4)(a) of this Act disclose arguable grounds of appeal, grant leave to appeal and make such comments in writing as he considers appropriate; and
   (b) in any other case—
      (i) refuse leave to appeal and give reasons in writing for the refusal; and
      (ii) where the appellant is on bail and the sentence imposed on his conviction is one of imprisonment, grant a warrant to apprehend and imprison him.

(2) A warrant granted under subsection (1)(b)(ii) above shall not take effect until the expiry of the period of 14 days mentioned in subsection (3) below without an application to the High Court for leave to appeal having been lodged by the appellant under that subsection.

(3) Where leave to appeal is refused under subsection (1) above the appellant may, within 14 days of intimation under subsection (9) below, apply to the High Court for leave to appeal.

(4) In deciding an application under subsection (3) above the High Court shall—
   (a) if, after considering the note of appeal and other documents mentioned in subsection (1) above and the reasons for the refusal, it is of the opinion that there are arguable grounds of appeal, grant leave to appeal and make such comments in writing as he considers appropriate; and
   (b) in any other case—
      (i) refuse leave to appeal and give reasons in writing for the refusal; and

(ii) where the appellant is on bail and the sentence imposed on his conviction is one of imprisonment, grant a warrant to apprehend and imprison him.

(5) The question whether to grant leave to appeal under subsection (1) or (4) above shall be considered and determined in chambers without the parties being present.

(6) Comments in writing made under subsection (1)(a) or (4)(a) above may, without prejudice to the generality of that provision, specify the arguable grounds of appeal (whether or not they are contained in the note of appeal) on the basis of which leave to appeal is granted.

(7) Where the arguable grounds of appeal are specified by virtue of subsection (6) above it shall not, except by leave of the High Court on cause shown, be competent for the appellant to found any aspect of his appeal on any ground of appeal contained in the note of appeal but not so specified.

(8) Any application by the appellant for the leave of the High Court under subsection (7) above—
(a) shall be made not less than seven days before the date fixed for the hearing of the appeal; and
(b) shall, not less that seven days before that date, be intimated by the appellant to the Crown Agent.

(9) The Clerk of Justiciary shall forthwith intimate—
(a) a decision under subsection (1) or (4) above; and
(b) in the case of a refusal of leave to appeal, the reasons for the decision, to the appellant or his solicitor and to the Crown Agent.

DEFINITIONS
"bail": s.307(1).
"High Court": s.307(1).
"judge": s.307(1).
"sentence": s.307(1).

GENERAL NOTE
The procedure to be followed in regard to appeals against summary sentences necessarily requires leave to appeal. The note of appeal containing the ground of appeal is placed before a single judge in chambers along with, principally, the trial judge's report: subs. (1)(a). There is consideration and determination without the parties being present: subs. (5). As there is no longer the opportunity to explain or expand upon the grounds of appeal by advocacy the written note of appeal assumes far greater significance: such a note no longer merely initiates an appeal, it is now the substance of the leave to appeal. When leave to appeal is refused further application can be made: subs. (3) which follows identical procedure under, *e.g.* s.180(3).

Disposal of appeals

Setting aside conviction or sentence: prosecutor's consent or application

188.—(1) Without prejudice to section 175(3) or (4) of this Act, where—
(a) an appeal has been taken under section 175(2) of this Act or by suspension or otherwise and the prosecutor is not prepared to maintain the judgment appealed against he may, by a relevant minute, consent to the conviction or sentence or, as the case may be, conviction and sentence ("sentence" being construed in this section as including disposal or order) being set aside either in whole or in part; or
(b) no such appeal has been taken but the prosecutor is, at any time, not prepared to maintain the judgment on which a conviction is founded or the sentence imposed following such conviction he may, by a relevant minute, apply for the conviction or sentence or, as the case may be, conviction and sentence to be set aside.

(2) For the purposes of subsection (1) above, a "relevant minute" is a minute, signed by the prosecutor—
  (a) setting forth the grounds on which he is of the opinion that the judgment cannot be maintained; and
  (b) written on the complaint or lodged with the clerk of court.

(3) A copy of any minute under subsection (1) above shall be sent by the prosecutor to the convicted person or his solicitor and the clerk of court shall—
  (a) thereupon ascertain and note on the record, whether that person or solicitor desires to be heard by the High Court before the appeal, or as the case may be application, is disposed of; and
  (b) thereafter transmit the complaint and relative proceedings to the Clerk of Justiciary.

(4) The Clerk of Justiciary, on receipt of a complaint and relative proceedings transmitted under subsection (3) above, shall lay them before any judge of the High Court either in court or in chambers who, after hearing parties if they desire to be heard, may—
  (a) set aside the conviction or the sentence, or both, either in whole or in part and—
        (i) award such expenses to the convicted person, both in the High Court and in the inferior court, as the judge may think fit;
        (ii) where the conviction is set aside in part, pass another (but not more severe) sentence in substitution for the sentence imposed in respect of that conviction; and
        (iii) where the sentence is set aside, pass another (but not more severe) sentence; or
  (b) refuse to set aside the conviction or sentence or, as the case may be, conviction and sentence, in which case the complaint and proceedings shall be returned to the clerk of the inferior court.

(5) Where an appeal has been taken and the complaint and proceedings in respect of that appeal returned under subsection (4)(b) above, the appellant shall be entitled to proceed with the appeal as if it had been marked on the date of their being received by the clerk of the inferior court on such return.

(6) Where an appeal has been taken and a copy minute in respect of that appeal sent under subsection (3) above, the preparation of the draft stated case shall be delayed pending the decision of the High Court.

(7) The period from an application being made under subsection (1)(b) above until its disposal under subsection (4) above (including the day of application and the day of disposal) shall, in relation to the conviction to which the application relates, be disregarded in any computation of time specified in any provision of this Part of this Act.

DEFINITIONS
  "complaint": s.307(1).
  "High Court": s.307(1).
  "prosecutor": s.307(1).
  "relevant minute": s.188(2).
  "sentence": s.188(1)(a).

GENERAL NOTE
  A set of procedural or other circumstances may have arisen resulting in a clear and unequivocal miscarriage of justice having occurred so that the Crown would not wish to maintain a judgment. This section provides for a conviction being set aside with the prosecutor's consent or on the prosecutor's application depending on the circumstances.
  Subsection (2)(a)—in *MacRae v. Hingston*, 1992 S.C.C.R. 911 the Appeal Court made it clear that where the procedure under this section is to be used any minute should be accompanied by sufficient material to satisfy the single judge that grounds of law exist to set aside the conviction.

Subsection (4)(b)—see *O'Brien v. Adair*, 1947 J.C. 180 where the court refused to set aside a conviction.

Disposal of appeal against sentence

189.—(1) An appeal against sentence by note of appeal shall be heard by the High Court on such date as it may fix, and the High Court may, subject to section 190(1) of this Act, dispose of such appeal by—

(a) affirming the sentence; or

[1](b) if the Court thinks that, having regard to all the circumstances, including any evidence such as is mentioned in section 175(5) of this Act, a different sentence should have been passed, quashing the sentence and, subject to subsection (2) below, passing another sentence, whether more or less severe, in substitution therefor.

(2) In passing another sentence under subsection (1)(b) above, the Court shall not in any case increase the sentence beyond the maximum sentence which could have been passed by the inferior court.

(3) The High Court shall have power in an appeal by note of appeal to award such expenses both in the High Court and in the inferior court as it may think fit.

(4) Where, following an appeal under section 175(2)(b) or (c), or by virtue of section 175(4), of this Act, the convicted person remains liable to imprisonment or detention under the sentence of the inferior court or is so liable under a sentence passed in the appeal proceedings, the High Court shall have power where at the time of disposal of the appeal the convicted person—

(a) was at liberty on bail, to grant warrant to apprehend and imprison or detain the appellant for a term, to run from the date of such apprehension, not longer than that part of the term or terms of imprisonment or detention specified in the sentence brought under review which remained unexpired at the date of liberation; or

(b) is serving a term or terms of imprisonment or detention imposed in relation to a conviction subsequent to the conviction in respect of which the sentence appealed against was imposed, to exercise the like powers in regard to him as may be exercised, in relation to an appeal which has been abandoned, by a court of summary jurisdiction in pursuance of section 177(6) of this Act.

(5) In subsection (1) above, "appeal against sentence" shall, without prejudice to the generality of the expression, be construed as including an appeal under section 175(2)(c), and any appeal by virtue of section 175(4), of this Act; and without prejudice to subsection (6) below, other references to sentence in that subsection and in subsection (4) above shall be construed accordingly.

(6) In disposing of any appeal in a case where the accused has not been convicted, the High Court may proceed to convict him; and where it does, the reference in subsection (4) above to the conviction in respect of which the sentence appealed against was imposed shall be construed as a reference to the disposal or order appealed against.

(7) In disposing of an appeal under section 175(2)(b) to (d), (3)(b) or (4) of this Act the High Court may, without prejudice to any other power in that regard, pronounce an opinion on the sentence or other disposal or order which is appropriate in any similar case.

DEFINITIONS
  "appeal against sentence": s.189(5).
  "High Court": s.307(1).
  "sentence": s.307(1).

Criminal Procedure (Scotland) Act 1995

NOTE

[1] As amended by the Crime and Punishment (Scotland) Act 1997 (c. 48) Sched. 1 para. 21(22) with effect from August 1, 1997 in terms of the Crime and Punishment (Scotland) Act 1997 (Commencement and Transitional Provisions) Order 1997 (S.I. 1997 No. 1712) para. 3.

GENERAL NOTE

Subs. (1)

The sole test for appeals is whether there has been a miscarriage of justice and the question in relation to sentence is whether the sentence complained of is excessive: *Addison v. Mackinnon*, 1983 S.C.C.R. 52; *Donaldson v. H.M. Advocate*, 1983 S.C.C.R. 216. The High Court of Justiciary may affirm the sentence or quash it and impose another of greater or lesser severity. The latter option is not often used to increase a summary sentence although it has been done: *Briggs v. Guild*, 1987 S.C.C.R. 141. The Court of Appeal is not authorised to alter a sentence on a charge which has not been appealed: see *Allan, Petr.*, 1993 S.C.C.R. 686. In *Kelly v. Vannet*, 2000 S.L.T. 75 in an appeal against sentence it was held that the appellant had pled to a non offence and an absolute discharge was substituted.

Disposal of appeal where appellant insane

190.—(1) In relation to any appeal under section 175(2) of this Act, the High Court shall, where it appears to it that the appellant committed the act charged against him but that he was insane when he did so, dispose of the appeal by—

(a) setting aside the verdict of the inferior court and substituting therefor a verdict of acquittal on the ground of insanity; and

(b) quashing any sentence imposed on the appellant as respects the complaint and—

(i) making, in respect of the appellant, any order mentioned in section 57(2)(a) to (d) of this Act; or

(ii) making no order.

(2) Subsection (4) of section 57 of this Act shall apply to an order made under subsection (1)(b)(i) above as it applies to an order made under subsection (2) of that section.

Miscellaneous

Appeal by suspension or advocation on ground of miscarriage of justice

191.—(1) Notwithstanding section 184(2) of this Act, a party to a summary prosecution may, where an appeal under section 175 of this Act would be incompetent or would in the circumstances be inappropriate, appeal to the High Court, by bill of suspension against a conviction or, as the case may be, by advocation against an acquittal on the ground of an alleged miscarriage of justice in the proceedings.

(2) Where the alleged miscarriage of justice is referred to in an application under section 176(1) of this Act, for a stated case as regards the proceedings (or in a duly made amendment or addition to that application), an appeal under subsection (1) above shall not proceed without the leave of the High Court until the appeal to which the application relates has been finally disposed of or abandoned.

(3) Sections 182(5)(a) to (e), 183(1)(d) and (4) and 185 of this Act shall apply to appeals under this section as they apply to appeals such as are mentioned in section 176(1) of this Act.

(4) This section is without prejudice to any rule of law relating to bills of suspension or advocation in so far as such rule of law is not inconsistent with this section.

251

Criminal Procedure (Scotland) Act 1995

GENERAL NOTE

For examples see *Pettigrew v. Ingram*, 1982 S.L.T. 435; *MacKinnon v. Craig*, 1983 S.L.T. 475 and *Durant v. Lockhart*, 1985 S.C.C.R. 72. In *Clarke v. Ruxton* 1997 G.W.D. 10–408 the accused proceeded by bill of suspension following the death of the sheriff before a stated case could be prepared. This last case is of broader evidential interest, since C's partial admissions of sexual misconduct with a child were held to corroborate evidence of the full libel given by the child.

Appeals: miscellaneous provisions

192.—(1) Where an appellant has been granted bail, whether his appeal is under this Part of this Act or otherwise, he shall appear personally in court at the diet appointed for the hearing of the appeal.

(2) Where an appellant who has been granted bail does not appear at such a diet, the High Court shall either—

(a) dispose of the appeal as if it had been abandoned (in which case subsection (5) of section 177 of this Act shall apply accordingly); or

(b) on cause shown permit the appeal to be heard in his absence.

(3) No conviction, sentence, judgement, order of court or other proceeding whatsoever in or for the purposes of summary proceedings under this Act—

(a) shall be quashed for want of form; or

(b) where the accused had legal assistance in his defence, shall be suspended or set aside in respect of any objections to—

(i) the relevancy of the complaint, or to the want of specification therein; or

(ii) the competency or admission or rejection of evidence at the trial in the inferior court,

unless such objections were timeously stated.

(4) The provisions regulating appeals shall, subject to the provisions of this Part of this Act, be without prejudice to any other mode of appeal competent.

(5) Any officer of law may serve any bill of suspension or other writ relating to an appeal.

DEFINITIONS

"bail": s.307(1).
"High Court": s.307(1).
"officer of law": s.307(1).
"sentence": s.307(1).

GENERAL NOTE

Subsection (3)(a)—see *Paterson v. MacLennan* (1914) 7 Adam 128 where the accused was found guilty but not as libelled. The appeal was refused. See also *Ogilvie v. Mitchell* (1903) 4 Adam 273; *Miller v. Brown*, 1941 J.C. 2, and *Gilmour v. Gray*, 1951 J.C. 70.

Subsection (2)—in *Gemmell v. MacDougall*, 1993 S.C.C.R. 238 the appeal by stated case was continued on a number of occasions because the appellant was medically unfit to attend. On the motion of the Crown and in the presence of counsel for the appellant the appeal was heard in the absence of the appellant, the view being taken that as the appeal was on a question of law the appellant would not be prejudiced by his absence.

In *Pratt v. Normand*, 1995 S.C.C.R. 881 the appellant failed to appear at the hearing of his appeal. The case was continued to give him an opportunity to appear. At the continued hearing he appeared and gave an explanation with which the Appeal Court were not satisfied. They refused the appeal for want of insistence: see also *Flynn v. Vannet*, 1997 G.W.D. 31–1555.

First, highly pedantic points cannot be taken on procedural or other matters as no conviction, sentence, judgment, order of court or other proceedings in or for the purposes of summary proceedings can be quashed for want of form: subs. (3)(a).

Secondly, the failure to object timeously to the relevancy of the complaint or to the want of specification or to the competency or admission or rejection of evidence prevents later suspension of a conviction or sentence if the accused had legal assistance: subs. (3)(b). See *e.g. Jardine v. Howdle*, 1997 S.C.C.R. 294 where an appeal against conviction, founding on the sheriff's placing a 13-year-old child on oath without ascertaining the age of a child witness or

252

satisfying himself that the child understood the nature of the oath, was refused, no objection having been taken at the time.

If however the objection amounts to a fundamental nullity then this can be challenged at any time: see *Czajkowski v. Lewis*, 1956 J.C. 8; *Coventry v. Douglas*, 1944 J.C. 13; *Rendle v. Muir*, 1952 J.C. 115; *Aitkenhead v. Cuthbert*, 1961 J.C. 12, and *Shaw v. Smith*, Crown Office circular A43/78.

Suspension of disqualification, forfeiture etc.

193.—(1) Where upon conviction of any person—
(a) any disqualification, forfeiture or disability attaches to him by reason of such conviction; or
(b) any property, matters or things which are the subject of the prosecution or connected therewith are to be or may be ordered to be destroyed or forfeited,

if the court before which he was convicted thinks fit, the disqualification, forfeiture or disability or, as the case may be, destruction or forfeiture or order for destruction or forfeiture shall be suspended pending the determination of any appeal against conviction or sentence (or disposal or order).

(2) Subsection (1) above does not apply in respect of any disqualification, forfeiture or, as the case may be, destruction or forfeiture or order for destruction or forfeiture under or by virtue of any enactment which contains express provision for the suspension of such disqualification, forfeiture or, as the case may be, destruction or forfeiture or order for destruction or forfeiture pending the determination of any appeal against conviction or sentence (or disposal or order).

(3) Where, upon conviction, a fine has been imposed upon a person or a compensation order has been made against him under section 249 of this Act—
(a) the fine or compensation order shall not be enforced against him and he shall not be liable to make any payment in respect of the fine or compensation order; and
(b) any money paid under the compensation order shall not be paid by the clerk of court to the entitled person under subsection (9) of that section,

pending the determination of any appeal against conviction or sentence (or disposal or order).

Suspension of certain sentences pending determination of appeal

[1]**193A.**—(1) Where a convicted person or the prosecutor appeals to the High Court under section 175 of this Act, the court may on the application of the appellant direct that the whole, or any remaining part, of a relevant sentence shall be suspended until the appeal, if it is proceeded with, is determined.

(2) Where the court has directed the suspension of the whole or any remaining part of a person's relevant sentence, the person shall, unless the High Court otherwise directs, appear personally in court on the day or days fixed for the hearing of the appeal.

(3) Where a person fails to appear personally in court as mentioned in subsection (2) above, the court may—
(a) if he is the appellant—
(i) decline to consider the appeal; and
(ii) dismiss it summarily; or
(b) whether or not he is the appellant—
(i) consider and determine the appeal; or
(ii) make such other order as the court thinks fit.

(4) In this section "relevant sentence" means any one or more of the following—

(a) a probation order;
(b) a supervised attendance order made under section 236(6) of this Act;
(c) a community service order;
²(d) a restriction of liberty order.

NOTES
¹Inserted by the Crime and Punishment (Scotland) Act 1997 (c. 48) s.24(2) with effect from August 1, 1997 in terms of the Crime and Punishment (Scotland) Act 1997 (Commencement and Transitional Provisions) Order 1997 (S.I. 1997 No. 1712) para. 3.
²Inserted by the Crime and Punishment (Scotland) Act 1997 (c. 48) s.24(2) (effective July 1, 1998: S.I. 1998 No. 2323).

GENERAL NOTE
With effect from August 1, 1997 certain sentences as detailed in subs. 4 can be suspended pending the determination of an appeal. Prevents a situation as arose in *H.M. Advocate v. Jamieson*, 1996 S.C.C.R. 836.

Computation of time

194.—(1) If any period of time specified in any provision of this Part of this Act relating to appeals expires on a Saturday, Sunday or court holiday prescribed for the relevant court, the period shall be extended to expire on the next day which is not a Saturday, Sunday or such court holiday.
¹(2) Where a judge against whose judgment an appeal is taken—
(a) is temporarily absent from duty for any cause;
(b) is a part-time sheriff; or
(c) is a justice of the peace,
the sheriff principal of the sheriffdom in which the court at which the judgment was pronounced is situated may extend any period specified in sections 178(1) and 179(4) and (7) of this Act for such period as he considers reasonable.
(3) For the purposes of sections 176(1)(a) and 178(1) of this Act, summary proceedings shall be deemed to be finally determined on the day on which sentence is passed in open court; except that, where in relation to an appeal—
(a) under section 175(2)(a) or (3)(a); or
(b) in so far as it is against conviction, under section 175(2)(d),
of this Act sentence is deferred under section 202 of this Act, they shall be deemed finally determined on the day on which sentence is first so deferred in open court.

NOTE
¹As amended by Bail, Judicial Appointments etc. (Scotland) Act (asp 9), s.12 and Sched., para. 7(5).

PART XA

SCOTTISH CRIMINAL CASES REVIEW COMMISSION

The Scottish Criminal Cases Review Commission

Scottish Criminal Cases Review Commission

¹**194A.**—(1) There shall be established a body corporate to be known as the Scottish Criminal Cases Review Commission (in this Act referred to as "the Commission").
(2) The Commission shall not be regarded as the servant or agent of the Crown or as enjoying any status, immunity or privilege of the Crown; and the Commission's property shall not be regarded as property of, or held on behalf of, the Crown.

(3) The Commission shall consist of not fewer than three members.

(4) The members of the Commission shall be appointed by Her Majesty on the recommendation of the Secretary of State.

(5) At least one third of the members of the Commission shall be persons who are legally qualified; and for this purpose a person is legally qualified if he is an advocate or solicitor of at least ten years' standing.

(6) At least two thirds of the members of the Commission shall be persons who appear to the Secretary of State to have knowledge or experience of any aspect of the criminal justice system; and for the purposes of this subsection the criminal justice system includes, in particular, the investigation of offences and the treatment of offenders.

(7) Schedule 9A to this Act, which makes further provision as to the Commission, shall have effect.

NOTE
[1]Inserted by s.25 of the Crime and Punishment (Scotland) Act 1997 with effect from April 1, 1999 as provided by the Crime and Punishment (Scotland) Act 1997 (Commencement No. 5 and Transitional Provisions and Savings) Order 1999 (S.I. 1999 No. 652).

GENERAL NOTE
This part of the Act provides for a Scottish Criminal Cases Review Commission. The Sutherland Commission recommended the setting up of a new body to consider alleged miscarriages of justice and to refer deserving cases to the Court of Appeal. The Secretary of State would be removed from this process. The Committee was of the view that the Secretary of State's role was incompatible with the constitutional separation of powers between the executive and the courts. An independent body would be seen to be impartial. The Committee recognised that the Secretary of State was however accountable to Parliament whilst the Commission would be subject to judicial review.

The Sutherland Committee reported there was a strong body of opinion that there was no need for change, and defects in the system would be remedied by the amended ground of appeal. The Government latched onto this and made no provision for the Commission in the Bill. Despite the best efforts of Lord McClusky at the committee stage in the House of Lords, the Government resisted amendments to remedy the omission (see Hansard, HL, March 10, 1997, cols. 56 to 62). The legislative timetable however resulted in a Government concession (see Hansard, HL, March 10, 1997, cols. 945 to 952). The provisions on the whole follow the Sutherland Committee's recommendations.

Further provisions for the workings of the Commission can be found in Schedule 9A.

s.194A
Provision is made for at least three members of the Commission and the Sutherland Committee envisaged that these will be part-time appointments. At least one-third of the members requires to be legally qualified and at least two-thirds need knowledge or experience of the investigation of offences and treatment of offenders. There are currently seven commissioners.

References to High Court

Cases dealt with on indictment

[1]**194B.**—[2](1) The Commission on the consideration of any conviction of a person or of the sentence (other than sentence of death) passed on a person who has been convicted on indictment or complaint may, if they think fit, at any time, and whether or not an appeal against such conviction or sentence has previously been heard and determined by the High Court, refer the whole case to the High Court and the case shall be heard and determined, subject to any directions the High Court may make, as if it were an appeal under Part VIII or, as the case may be, Part X of this Act.

(2) The power of the Commission under this section to refer to the High Court the case of a person convicted shall be exercisable whether or not that person has petitioned for the exercise of Her Majesty's prerogative of mercy.

(3) This section shall apply in relation to a finding under section 55(2) and

an order under section 57(2) of this Act as it applies, respectively, in relation to a conviction and a sentence.

(4) For the purposes of this section "person" includes a person who is deceased.

NOTES

[1]Inserted by s.25 of the Crime and Punishment (Scotland) Act 1997 with effect from April 1, 1999 as provided by the Crime and Punishment (Scotland) Act 1997 (Commencement No. 5 and Transitional Provisions and Savings) Order 1999 (S.I. 1999 No. 652).

[2]As amended by S.I. 1999 No. 1181, para. 3 (effective April 1, 1999).

GENERAL NOTE

s.194B

Subs. (1)

A reference can be made at any time (in *Preece v. H.M. Advocate* [1981] Crim.L.R. 783, the reference by the Secretary of State was made seven years after conviction) **post conviction**, whether or not the case has been previously heard by the Appeal Court. The appeal is then treated as an ordinary appeal. The Commission may, as could the Secretary of State, refer the whole case or part thereof to the Appeal Court (see *e.g. Slater v. H.M. Advocate*, 1928 J.C. 94; *Gallacher v. H.M. Advocate*, 1951 J.C. 38 and *Beattie v. H.M. Advocate*, 1995 S.C.C.R. 93). The first reference by the SCCRC was *Bonca–Tomaszewski v. H.M. Advocate*, 2000 S.C.C.R. 657. It was held that the Appeal Court in considering the reference would proceed on the basis of current understanding of common law and present day standards although that could result in the court criticising their predecessors by reference to different criterion than was applicable then.

Subs. (2)

The prerogative of mercy is still exercisable by the Secretary of State but the Commission may refer a case even if a petition for the Royal Prerogative has previously been made.

Subs. (3)

A reference can be made in respect of a finding that an accused committed an act where he is insane in bar of trial and also in respect of disposals where an accused is insane at the time of the offence.

Subs. (4)

A reference can be made in respect of a deceased.

Grounds for reference

[1]**194C.** The grounds upon which the Commission may refer a case to the High Court are that they believe—
    (a) that a miscarriage of justice may have occurred; and
    (b) that it is in the interests of justice that a reference should be made.

NOTE

[1]Inserted by s.25 of the Crime and Punishment (Scotland) Act 1997 with effect from April 1, 1999 as provided by the Crime and Punishment (Scotland) Act 1997 (Commencement No. 5 and Transitional Provisions and Savings) Order 1999 (S.I. 1999 No. 652).

GENERAL NOTE

s.194C

The administrative criteria by which the Secretary of State assessed cases involving a miscarriage of justice was considered by the Sutherland Committee. The criteria were whether there was relevant material to suggest a miscarriage of justice and further, would the Appeal Court as a matter of law entertain the case on a reference.

The Committee considered that the criteria for references by the commission should reflect the "broad and flexible miscarriage of justice" ground of appeal. It appears that part (a) incorporates the previous criteria used by the Secretary of State, there being no point in referring an alleged miscarriage of justice which the appeal court as a matter of law would not entertain.

The Committee also recommended that the normal appeal procedures should have been exhausted but this has not been incorporated in the current provisions.

Further provision as to references

[1]**194D.**—(1) A reference of a conviction, sentence or finding may be made under section 194B of this Act whether or not an application has been made by or on behalf of the person to whom it relates.

(2) In considering whether to make a reference the Commission shall have regard to—

(a) any application or representations made to the Commission by or on behalf of the person to whom it relates;

(b) any other representations made to the Commission in relation to it; and

(c) any other matters which appear to the Commission to be relevant.

(3) In considering whether to make a reference the Commission may at any time refer to the High Court for the Court's opinion any point on which they desire the Court's assistance; and on a reference under this subsection the High Court shall consider the point referred and furnish the Commission with their opinion on the point.

(4) Where the Commission make a reference to the High Court under section 194B of this Act they shall—

(a) give to the Court a statement of their reasons for making the reference; and

(b) send a copy of the statement to every person who appears to them to be likely to be a party to any proceedings on the appeal arising from the reference.

(5) In every case in which—

(a) an application has been made to the Commission by or on behalf of any person for the reference by them of any conviction, sentence or finding; but

(b) the Commission decide not to make a reference of the conviction, sentence or finding,

they shall give a statement of the reasons for their decision to the person who made the application.

NOTE
[1]Inserted by s.25 of the Crime and Punishment (Scotland) Act 1997 with effect from April 1, 1999 as provided by the Crime and Punishment (Scotland) Act 1997 (Commencement No. 5 and Transitional Provisions and Savings) Order 1999 (S.I. 1999 No. 652).

GENERAL NOTE
s.194D
Subs. (1)
   This allows an application to be made to the Commission on someone's behalf, e.g. someone who is mentally ill or deceased. Although the Sutherland Committee recommended that this should be allowed only if there was a good reason, this requirement has not been incorporated.

Subs. (2)
   In *R v. Secretary of State for Home Department, ex p. Hickey (No.2)* [1995] 1 All E.R. 490, it was held that prior to the Secretary of State's decision regarding a referral, a petitioner should be given the opportunity to make representations upon whatever material had been revealed by the Secretary of State's enquiries and that sufficient disclosure should be given to enable the petitioner to present his case.
   It may well be that the Commission will have to disclose relevant material to enable the applicant to make full representations.

Subs. (3)
   This is not limited to a point of law. Hopefully this may be used to clarify points such as mentioned above.

Subs. (4)
   A statement of reasons for making the reference must be sent to every person the Commission considers likely to be a party to any proceedings. In most cases this will just be the

Crown and the accused but there is also the possibility of a co-accused. The principal statement of reasons is given to the court.

In *Bonca–Tomaszewski v. H.M. Advocate, supra* after the reference was lodged by the SCCRC the appellant lodged fresh grounds of appeal. Following a procedural hearing the court suggested that the grounds of appeal be amended to include the original grounds of appeal and ordered written submissions.

Subs. (5)

If a decision is taken not to make a reference, a statement of reasons must be given to the applicant. The decision will no doubt be subject to judicial review.

Extension of Commission's remit to summary cases

[1]**194E.**—(1) The Secretary of State may by order provide for this Part of this Act to apply in relation to convictions, sentences and findings made in summary proceedings as they apply in relation to convictions, sentences and findings made in solemn proceedings, and may for that purpose make in such an order such amendments to the provisions of this Part as appear to him to be necessary or expedient.

(2) An order under this section shall be made by statutory instrument, and shall not have effect unless a draft of it has been laid before and approved by a resolution of each House of Parliament.

NOTE

[1]Inserted by s.25 of the Crime and Punishment (Scotland) Act 1997 with effect from April 1, 1999 as provided by the Crime and Punishment (Scotland) Act 1997 (Commencement No. 5 and Transitional Provisions and Savings) Order 1999 (S.I. 1999 No. 652).

GENERAL NOTE

s.194E

The Sutherland Committee considered that the Commission should also be able to consider summary cases but that to ensure that priority was given to solemn cases and to ensure that the Commission was not overwhelmed, then the Secretary of State could extend the Commission's remit at a later stage to summary cases. The Committee envisaged that the Commission would rarely have to consider summary cases as the existing appeal procedures for summary cases were well established. The Commission remit was extended to summary cases by means of the Scottish Criminal Cases Review Commission (Application to Summary Proceedings) Order 1999 (S.I. 1999 No. 1181).

Further powers

[1]**194F.** The Commission may take any steps which they consider appropriate for assisting them in the exercise of any of their functions and may, in particular—

(a) themselves undertake inquiries and obtain statements, opinions or reports; or

(b) request the Lord Advocate or any other person to undertake such inquiries or obtain such statements, opinions and reports.

NOTE

[1]Inserted by s.25 of the Crime and Punishment (Scotland) Act 1997 with effect from April 1, 1999 as provided by the Crime and Punishment (Scotland) Act 1997 (Commencement No. 5 and Transitional Provisions and Savings) Order 1999 (S.I. 1999 No. 652).

GENERAL NOTE

s.194F

The Commission has power to undertake enquiries, obtain statements, opinions or reports or request the Lord Advocate or others to do so. As the emphasis is on independence and justice being seen to be done the Commission undertakes the majority of enquiries themselves employing a number of case workers. Previously, investigations were dealt with through Crown Office, the Procurator Fiscal or the police—including the precognition of witnesses, obtaining forensic reports, etc. One of the major criticisms of the old procedure was that those bodies responsible for prosecuting a person thereafter were involved in investigating any alleged miscarriage of justice.

Supplementary provision

[1]**194G.**—(1) The Secretary of State may by order make such incidental, consequential, transitional or supplementary provisions as may appear to him to be necessary or expedient for the purpose of bringing this Part of this Act into operation, and, without prejudice to the generality of the foregoing, of dealing with any cases being considered by him under section 124 of this Act at the time when this Part comes into force, and an order under this section may make different provision in relation to different cases or classes of case.

(2) An order under this section shall be made by statutory instrument subject to annulment in pursuance of a resolution of either House of Parliament.

NOTE
[1]Inserted by s.25 of the Crime and Punishment (Scotland) Act 1997 with effect from April 1, 1999 as provided by the Crime and Punishment (Scotland) Act 1997 (Commencement No. 5 and Transitional Provisions and Savings) Order 1999 (S.I. 1999 No. 652).

Powers of investigation of Commission

Power to request precognition on oath

[1]**194H.**—(1) Where it appears to the Commission that a person may have information which they require for the purposes of carrying out their functions, and the person refuses to make any statement to them, they may apply to the sheriff under this section.

(2) On an application made by the Commission under this section, the sheriff may, if he is satisfied that it is reasonable in the circumstances, grant warrant to cite the person concerned to appear before the sheriff in chambers at such time or place as shall be specified in the citation, for precognition on oath by a member of the Commission or a person appointed by them to act in that regard.

(3) Any person who, having been duly cited to attend for precognition under subsection (2) above and having been given at least 48 hours notice, fails without reasonable excuse to attend shall be guilty of an offence and liable on summary conviction to a fine not exceeding level 3 on the standard scale or to imprisonment for a period not exceeding 21 days; and the court may issue a warrant for the apprehension of the person concerned ordering him to be brought before a sheriff for precognition on oath.

(4) Any person who, having been duly cited to attend for precognition under subsection (2) above, attends but—

(a) refuses to give information within his knowledge or to produce evidence in his possession; or

(b) prevaricates in his evidence,

shall be guilty of an offence and shall be liable to be summarily subjected to a fine not exceeding level 3 on the standard scale or to imprisonment for a period not exceeding 21 days.

NOTE
[1]Inserted by s.25 of the Crime and Punishment (Scotland) Act 1997 with effect from April 1, 1999 as provided by the Crime and Punishment (Scotland) Act 1997 (Commencement No. 5 and Transitional Provisions and Savings) Order 1999 (S.I. 1999 No. 652).

GENERAL NOTE
New s.194H
This allows for precognition on oath. Other parties would not be entitled to be present (see Hume Vol. ii. 82).

Power to obtain documents etc.

[1]**194I.**—(1) Where the Commission believe that a person or a public body has possession or control of a document or other material which may assist them in the exercise of any of their functions, they may apply to the High Court for an order requiring that person or body—

    (a) to produce the document or other material to the Commission or to give the Commission access to it; and

    (b) to allow the Commission to take away the document or other material or to make and take away a copy of it in such form as they think appropriate,

and such an order may direct that the document or other material must not be destroyed, damaged or altered before the direction is withdrawn by the Court.

(2) The duty to comply with an order under this section is not affected by any obligation of secrecy or other limitation on disclosure (including any such obligation or limitation imposed by or by virtue of any enactment) which would otherwise prevent the production of the document or other material to the Commission or the giving of access to it to the Commission.

(3) The documents and other material covered by this section include, in particular, any document or other material obtained or created during any investigation or proceedings relating to—

    (a) the case in relation to which the Commission's function is being or may be exercised; or

    (b) any other case which may be in any way connected with that case (whether or not any function of the Commission could be exercised in relation to that other case).

(4) In this section—

"Minister" means a Minister of the Crown as defined by section 8 of the Ministers of the Crown Act 1975;

"police force" means any police force maintained for a local government area under section 1(1) of the Police (Scotland) Act 1967 and references to a chief constable are references to the chief constable of such a force within the meaning of that Act; and

"public body" means

    (a) any police force;

    (b) any government department, local authority or other body constituted for the purposes of the public service, local government or the administration of justice; or

    [2](c) any other body whose members are appointed by Her Majesty, any Minister, the Scottish Minister or any government department or whose revenues consist wholly or mainly of money provided by Parliament.

NOTE

[1]Inserted by s.25 of the Crime and Punishment (Scotland) Act 1997 with effect from April 1, 1999 as provided by the Crime and Punishment (Scotland) Act 1997 (Commencement No.5 and Transitional Provisions and Savings) Order 1999 (S.I.1999 No.652).

[2]As amended by the Scotland Act 1998 (Consequential Modifications) (No.2) Order 1999 (S.I.1999 No.1820) art.4 and Sched.2, para.122(2) (effective July 1, 1999).

GENERAL NOTE

The Commission's broad rights to recover and examine documents were upheld in *Scottish Criminal Cases Review Commission v. H.M.Advocate*, 2000 S.C.C.R. 842; 2000 G.W.D 28–1080, where the Crown had opposed access to its papers. The Appeal Court held that SCCRC were not precluded from recovering *e.g.* departmental documents, the nature and circumstance of the creation of the document not being sufficient objection to recovery. While the court accepted that there might be certain classes of documents which would warrant denial of access to the Commission, the Crown still had to justify refusal of a request for materials by the Commission. On the other hand it would be difficult for the Commission to make out a case for access to documents whose contents were entirely unknown to it. The court held that averments setting out the history of the case satisfied the requirements of s.194I. It was recognised that it was only when the SCCRC saw the documents they would be able to ascertain if they were material.

Disclosure of information

Offence of disclosure

[1]**194J.**—(1) A person who is or has been a member or employee of the Commission shall not disclose any information obtained by the Commission in the exercise of any of their functions unless the disclosure of the information is excepted from this section by section 194K of this Act.

(2) A member of the Commission shall not authorise the disclosure by an employee of the Commission of any information obtained by the Commission in the exercise of any of their functions unless the authorisation of the disclosure of the information is excepted from this section by section 194K of this Act.

(3) A person who contravenes this section is guilty of an offence and liable on summary conviction to a fine of an amount not exceeding level 5 on the standard scale.

Note
[1]Inserted by s.25 of the Crime and Punishment (Scotland) Act 1997 with effect from April 1, 1999 as provided by the Crime and Punishment (Scotland) Act 1997 (Commencement No. 5 and Transitional Provisions and Savings) Order 1999 (S.I. 1999 No. 652).

Exceptions from obligations of non-disclosure

[1]**194K.**—(1) The disclosure of information, or the authorisation of the disclosure of information, is excepted from section 194J of this Act by this section if the information is disclosed, or is authorised to be disclosed—
  (a) for the purposes of any criminal, disciplinary or civil proceedings;
  (b) in order to assist in dealing with an application made to the Secretary of State for compensation for a miscarriage of justice;
  (c) by a person who is a member or an employee of the Commission to another person who is a member or an employee of the Commission;
  (d) in any statement or report required by this Act;
  (e) in or in connection with the exercise of any function under this Act; or
  (f) in any circumstances in which the disclosure of information is permitted by an order made by the Secretary of State.

(2) The disclosure of information is also excepted from section 194J of this Act by this section if the information is disclosed by an employee of the Commission who is authorised to disclose the information by a member of the Commission.

(3) The disclosure of information, or the authorisation of the disclosure of information, is also excepted from section 194J of this Act by this section if the information is disclosed, or is authorised to be disclosed, for the purposes of—
  (a) the investigation of an offence; or
  (b) deciding whether to prosecute a person for an offence,
unless the disclosure is or would be prevented by an obligation or other limitation on disclosure (including any such obligation or limitation imposed by, under or by virtue of any enactment) arising otherwise than under that section.

(4) Where the disclosure of information is excepted from section 194J of this Act by subsection (1) or (2) above, the disclosure of the information is not prevented by any obligation of secrecy or other limitation on disclosure (including any such obligation or limitation imposed by, under or by virtue of any enactment) arising otherwise than under that section.

(5) The power to make an order under subsection (1)(f) above is exercisable by statutory instrument which shall be subject to annulment in pursuance of a resolution of either House of Parliament.

NOTE
[1]Inserted by s.25 of the Crime and Punishment (Scotland) Act 1997 with effect from April 1, 1999 as provided by the Crime and Punishment (Scotland) Act 1997 (Commencement No. 5 and Transitional Provisions and Savings) Order 1999 (S.I. 1999 No. 652).

Consent of disclosure

[1]**194L.**—(1) Where a person or body is required by an order under section 194I of this Act to produce or allow access to a document or other material to the Commission and notifies them that any information contained in the document or other material to which the order relates is not to be disclosed by the Commission without his or its prior consent, the Commission shall not disclose the information without such consent.

(2) Such consent may not be withheld unless—

(a) (apart from section 194I of this Act) the person would have been prevented by any obligation of secrecy or other limitation on disclosure from disclosing the information without such consent; and

(b) it is reasonable for the person to withhold his consent to disclosure of the information by the Commission.

(3) An obligation of secrecy or other limitation on disclosure which applies to a person only where disclosure is not authorised by another person shall not be taken for the purposes of subsection (2)(a) above to prevent the disclosure by the person of information to the Commission unless—

(a) reasonable steps have been taken to obtain the authorisation of the other person; or

(b) such authorisation could not reasonably be expected to be obtained.".

NOTE
[1]Inserted by s.25 of the Crime and Punishment (Scotland) Act 1997 with effect from April 1, 1999 as provided by the Crime and Punishment (Scotland) Act 1997 (Commencement No. 5 and Transitional Provisions and Savings) Order 1999 (S.I. 1999 No. 652).

PART XI

SENTENCING

General

Remit to High Court for sentence

195.—(1) Where at any diet in proceedings on indictment in the sheriff court, sentence falls to be imposed but the sheriff holds that any competent sentence which he can impose is inadequate so that the question of sentence is appropriate for the High Court, he shall—

(a) endorse upon the record copy of the indictment a certificate of the plea or the verdict, as the case may be;

(b) by interlocutor written on the record copy remit the convicted person to the High Court for sentence; and

(c) append to the interlocutor a note of his reasons for the remit,

and a remit under this section shall be sufficient warrant to bring the accused before the High Court for sentence and shall remain in force until the person is sentenced.

(2) Where under any enactment an offence is punishable on conviction on indictment by imprisonment for a term exceeding three years but the enactment either expressly or impliedly restricts the power of the sheriff to impose a sentence of imprisonment for a term exceeding three years, it shall

be competent for the sheriff to remit the accused to the High Court for sentence under subsection (1) above; and it shall be competent for the High Court to pass any sentence which it could have passed if the person had been convicted before it.

(3) When the Clerk of Justiciary receives the record copy of the indictment he shall send a copy of the note of reasons to the convicted person or his solicitor and to the Crown Agent.

(4) Subject to subsection (3) above, the note of reasons shall be available only to the High Court and the parties.

DEFINITIONS
    "Clerk of Justiciary": s.307(1).
    "diet": s.307(1).
    "enactment": s.307(1).
    "High Court": s.307(1).
    "indictment": s.307(1).
    "sentence": s.307(1).

GENERAL NOTE

Subs. (1)
    This subsection reproduces the terms of s.104(1) of the 1975 Act in requiring a remit where "the sheriff holds that any competent sentence which he can impose is inadequate so that the question of sentence is appropriate for the High Court". This contrasts with the original position in s.31 of the Criminal Procedure (Scotland) Act 1887 (c. 35) which required a remit if the sheriff held that if the case was "of so grave a nature" that the question of punishment should be disposed of by the High Court of Justiciary. Care must be taken that the plea and remit are properly authenticated: *H.M. Advocate v. Galloway*, (1894) 1 Adam 375 and *H.M. Advocate v. McDonald*, (1896) 3 S.L.T. 317. The sheriff who remits the accused merely means the sheriff who has the duty to sentence: *Borland v. H.M. Advocate*, 1976 S.L.T.(Notes) 12.

Subs. (2)
    This subsection reproduces the terms of s.104(1A) of the 1975 Act as amended. The maximum competent sentence must be considered by the sheriff before remit, and where there are two or more indictments, each indictment must be considered separately. Where the maximum sentence which could be imposed on an indictment was within the competence of the sheriff then he must deal with that indictment: *H.M. Advocate v. Anderson*, 1946 J.C. 81. Each of several indictments must be considered separately: *H.M. Advocate v. Stern*, 1974 S.L.T. 2.

Sentence following guilty plea

196.—(1) In determining what sentence to pass on, or what other disposal or order to make in relation to, an offender who has pled guilty to an offence, a court may take into account—

    (a) the stage in the proceedings for the offence at which the offender indicated his intention to plead guilty, and

    (b) the circumstances in which that indication was given.

(2) Where the court is passing sentence on an offender under section 205B(2) of this Act and that offender has pled guilty to the offence for which he is being so sentenced, the court may, after taking into account the matters mentioned in paragraphs (a) and (b) of subsection (1) above, pass a sentence of less than seven years imprisonment or, as the case may be, detention but any such sentence shall not be of a term of imprisonment or period of detention of less than five years, two hundred and nineteen days.

DEFINITION
    "sentence": s.307(1).

NOTE
    [1]Inserted by the Crime and Punishment (Scotland) Act 1997 (c. 48) s.2(2) with effect from October 20, 1997 in terms of the Crime and Punishment (Scotland) Act 1997 (Commencement No. 2 and Transitional Provisions) Order 1997 (S.I. 1997 No. 2323) Art. 3 and Sched. 1.

GENERAL NOTE

This section emphasises the need for subtlety at the sentencing stage of criminal procedure. It is certain that, notwithstanding a long criminal record, any accused is entitled to go to trial and that is not to be held against the accused at the sentencing stage: *Young v. H.M. Advocate*, 1995 S.C.C.R. 418. While the court must note the point in proceedings when a guilty plea has been tendered there is no absolute right to receive a discount in sentence (*Docherty v. McGlennan*, 1998 G.W.D. 4–176). Balancing the broad pubic interest, given the nature and circumstances of the offences, against an accused's timeous guilty plea can properly result in no reduction in sentence (see *Gardiner v. H.M. Advocate*, 1999 G.W.D. 16–763). Similarly a guilty plea contingent upon acceptance of a co-accused's plea of not guilty being accepted by the prosecutor, may entitle the court to disregard the provisions of s.196 (*Robertson v. Gallagher*, 1999 G.W.D. 27–1280).

However, it has been said that it is generally irrelevant for sentencing purposes whether an accused pleads guilty or not guilty: D. Kelly *Criminal Sentences* (1993) at p. 6. In particular, it has been held that to operate a policy of discounting on sentences for guilty pleas would fetter judicial discretion to consider each case on its own merits: *Strawhorn v. Mcleod*, 1987 S.C.C.R. 413. That view can be contrasted directly with the English practice of giving a percentage reduction: *R. v. Williams* [1983] Crim.L.R. 693.

The reality of court business is that a guilty plea does amount to a saving of court and judicial time and may well result in a substantial saving of public funds. It is doubtful whether one can infer full remorse merely from a guilty plea but the results of such a plea very properly can be acknowledged and this section permits a court to take such a plea into account in determining a sentence. The court may do so in either or both of two sets of circumstances.

An early plea of guilty does not automatically infer that a discount on sentence must follow (*Tennie v. Munro*, 1999 S.C.C.R. 70).

Subs. (a)

The court may take into account the stage in the proceedings for the offence at which the offender indicated his intention to plead guilty. There are various stages from arrest to a letter of intention to plead guilty to an instruction to a solicitor at which the intention may be stated: see *Backdating Sentences and Imprisonment* (1995) 40 J.L.S. 383 and especially at p. 384 for a discussion of these stages and various authorities.

Subs. (b)

The court may take into account the circumstances in which the indication was given. Context is important because a guilty plea may save children from giving evidence: *Khaliq v. H.M. Advocate*, 1984 S.C.C.R. 483. Similar considerations must apply to other vulnerable witnesses but there can be little thought for an accused who puts such witnesses to the test and then pleads guilty at the end of the Crown case without having diminished the Crown case in any way.

In *Johnston v. Wilson*, 1996 G.W.D. 17–986 the Appeal Court further backdated a sentence from the date upon which the accused had plead guilty to the date of his incarceration on remand, J. having faced 40 charges originally and pleas having been accepted to only 13 of those charges.

Subs. (2)

It was only after the Committee stage of the Crime and Punishment Bill that the Government moved the amendments, now found in subs. (2), to enable the High Court to mitigate the automatic minimum sentences introduced as s.205B of the 1995 Act in cases where a timeous guilty plea has been tendered. The mandatory sentence of seven years may in such circumstances be reduced to a period of not less than 5 years 219 days, a 20% discount. Clarification of the interplay between subs. (2) above and s.205B(3) which relates to the extent of judicial discretion in sentencing after trial is found in s.199(3)(c) below. Section 199 serves to limit the range of sentencing options available at the judge's discretion in the circumstances set out in s.205B; accordingly, it is submitted that the sentencing options specified in s.199(2) of the Act do not apply to a third conviction before the High Court for a class A drug trafficking offence—an offender has to be incarcerated for a term of imprisonment, or detention, of at least 5 years 219 days in any such case.

Sentencing guidelines

197. Without prejudice to any rule of law, a court in passing sentence shall have regard to any relevant opinion pronounced under section 118(7) or section 189(7) of this Act.

GENERAL NOTE

Sections 254 and 455 of the 1975 Act (and now ss.118 and 189 of this Act) provided powers for the disposal of appeals by the High Court of Justiciary. These powers were concerned only with the individual appeal then before the court. On one view, for the court to give an exposition of sentencing policy in generality for similar cases would be *ultra vires*. However, by ss.118(7) and 189(7) of this Act the High Court of Justiciary may pronounce an opinion in relation to similar cases. By s.197, in sentencing a court must have regard to any such opinion.

Form of sentence

198.—(1) In any case the sentence to be pronounced shall be announced by the judge in open court and shall be entered in the record in the form prescribed by Act of Adjournal.

(2) In recording a sentence of imprisonment, it shall be sufficient to minute the term of imprisonment to which the court sentenced the accused, without specifying the prison in which the sentence is to be carried out; and an entry of sentence, signed by the clerk of court, shall be full warrant and authority for any subsequent execution of the sentence and for the clerk to issue extracts for the purposes of execution or otherwise.

(3) In extracting a sentence of imprisonment, the extract may be in the form set out in an Act of Adjournal or as nearly as may be in such form.

DEFINITION

"sentence": s.307(1).

GENERAL NOTE

O'Neill v. H.M. Advocate, 1999 S.C.C.R. 364 establishes that all information which an accused seeks to place before a sentencing court as mitigation must be produced in open court. (In *O'Neill's* case information showing his previous co-operation with the police was produced to the trial judge who declined to consider the papers on the basis that the contents could not be discussed publicly.)

Power to mitigate penalties

199.—(1) Subject to subsection (3) below, where a person is convicted of the contravention of an enactment and the penalty which may be imposed involves—

(a) imprisonment;

(b) the imposition of a fine;

(c) the finding of caution for good behaviour or otherwise whether or not imposed in addition to imprisonment or a fine,

subsection (2) below shall apply.

(2) Where this subsection applies, the court, in addition to any other power conferred by statute, shall have power—

(a) to reduce the period of imprisonment;

(b) to substitute for imprisonment a fine (either with or without the finding of caution for good behaviour);

(c) to substitute for imprisonment or a fine the finding of caution;

(d) to reduce the amount of the fine;

(e) to dispense with the finding of caution.

(3) Subsection (2) above shall not apply—

(a) in relation to an enactment which carries into effect a treaty, convention, or agreement with a foreign state which stipulates for a fine of a minimum amount;

(b) to proceedings taken under any Act relating to any of Her Majesty's regular or auxiliary forces; or

[1] (c) to any proceedings in which the court on conviction is under a duty to impose a sentence under section 205A(2) or 205B(2) of this Act.

(4) Where, in summary proceedings, a fine is imposed in substitution for imprisonment, the fine—

Criminal Procedure (Scotland) Act 1995

(a) in the case of an offence which is triable either summarily or on indictment, shall not exceed the prescribed sum; and

(b) in the case of an offence triable only summarily, shall not exceed level 4 on the standard scale.

(5) Where the finding of caution is imposed under this section—

(a) in respect of an offence which is triable only summarily, the amount shall not exceed level 4 on the standard scale and the period shall not exceed that which the court may impose under this Act; and

(b) in any other case, the amount shall not exceed the prescribed sum and the period shall not exceed 12 months.

DEFINITIONS
"fine": s.307(1).
"indictment": s.307(1).
"level 4": s.225(2). [*i.e.* £2,500].
"prescribed sum": s.225(8).
"standard scale": s.225(1).

NOTE
[1]Inserted by the Crime and Punishment (Scotland) Act 1997 with effect from October 20, 1997 as provided by the Crime and Punishment (Scotland) Act 1997 (Commencement No. 2) and Transitional and Consequential Provisions) Order 1997 (S.I. 1997 No. 2323).

Pre-sentencing procedure

Remand for inquiry into physical or mental condition

200.—(1) Without prejudice to any powers exercisable by a court under section 201 of this Act, where—

(a) the court finds that an accused has committed an offence punishable with imprisonment; and

(b) it appears to the court that before the method of dealing with him is determined an inquiry ought to be made into his physical or mental condition,

subsection (2) below shall apply.

(2) Where this subsection applies the court shall—

(a) for the purpose of inquiry solely into his physical condition, remand him in custody or on bail;

(b) for the purpose of inquiry into his mental condition (whether or not in addition to his physical condition), remand him in custody or on bail or, where the court is satisfied—

(i) on the written or oral evidence of a medical practitioner, that the person appears to be suffering from a mental disorder; and

(ii) that a hospital is available for his admission and suitable for his detention,

make an order committing him to that hospital,

for such period or periods, no single period exceeding three weeks, as the court thinks necessary to enable a medical examination and report to be made.

(3) where the court is of the opinion that a person ought to continue to be committed to hospital for the purpose of inquiry into his mental condition following the expiry of the period specified in an order for committal to hospital under paragraph (b) of subsection (2) above, the court may—

(a) if the condition in sub-paragraph (i) of that paragraph continues to be satisfied and a suitable hospital is available for his continued detention, renew the order for such further period not exceeding three weeks as the court thinks necessary to enable a medical examination and report to be made; and

(b) in any other case, remand the person in custody or on bail in accordance with subsection (2) above.

(4) An order under subsection (3)(a) above may, unless objection is made by or on behalf of the person to whom it relates, be made in his absence.

(5) Where, before the expiry of the period specified in an order for committal to hospital under subsection (2)(b) above, the court considers, on an application made to it, that committal to hospital is no longer required in relation to the person, the court shall revoke the order and may make such other order, under subsection (2)(a) above or any other provision of this Part of this Act, as the court considers appropriate.

(6) Where an accused is remanded on bail under this section, it shall be a condition of the order granting bail that he shall—

    (a) undergo a medical examination by a duly qualified registered medical practitioner or, where the inquiry is into his mental condition, and the order granting bail so specifies, two such practitioners; and

    (b) for the purpose of such examination, attend at an institution or place, or on any such practitioner specified in the order granting bail and, where the inquiry is into his mental condition, comply with any directions which may be given to him for the said purpose by any person so specified or by a person of any class so specified,

and, if arrangements have been made for his reception, it may be a condition of the order granting bail that the person shall, for the purpose of the examination, reside in an institution or place specified as aforesaid, not being an institution or place to which he could have been remanded in custody, until the expiry of such period as may be so specified or until he is discharged therefrom, whichever first occurs.

(7) On exercising the powers conferred by this section to remand in custody or on bail the court shall—

    (a) where the person is remanded in custody, send to the institution or place in which he is detained; and

    (b) where the person is released on bail, send to the institution or place at which or the person by whom he is to be examined,

a statement of the reasons for which it appears to the court that an inquiry ought to be made into his physical or mental condition, and of any information before the court about his physical or mental condition.

(8) On making an order of committal to hospital under subsection (2)(b) above the court shall send to the hospital specified in the order a statement of the reasons for which the court is of the opinion that an inquiry ought to be made into the mental condition of the person to whom it relates, and of any information before the court about his mental condition.

(9) A person remanded under this section may appeal against the refusal of bail or against the conditions imposed and a person committed to hospital under this section may appeal against the order of committal within 24 hours of his remand or, as the case may be, committal, by note of appeal presented to the High Court, and the High Court, either in court or in chambers, may after hearing parties—

    (a) review the order and grant bail on such conditions as it thinks fit; or

    (b) confirm the order; or

    (c) in the case of an appeal against an order of committal to hospital, revoke the order and remand the person in custody.

(10) The court may, on cause shown, vary an order for committal to hospital under subsection (2)(b) above by substituting another hospital for the hospital specified in the order.

(11) Subsection (2)(b) above shall apply to the variation of an order under subsection (10) above as it applies to the making of an order for committal to hospital.

DEFINITIONS

    "bail": s.307(1).

    "hospital": s.307(1).

    "registered medical practitioner": s.2 of the Medical Act 1983 (c. 54).

Power of court to adjourn case before sentence

201.—(1) Where an accused has been convicted or the court has found that he committed the offence and before he has been sentenced or otherwise dealt with, subject to subsection (3) below, the court may adjourn the case for the purpose of enabling inquiries to be made or of determining the most suitable method of dealing with his case.

(2) Where the court adjourns a case solely for the purpose mentioned in subsection (1) above, it shall remand the accused in custody or on bail or ordain him to appear at the adjourned diet.

(3) A court shall not adjourn the hearing of a case as mentioned in subsection (1) above for any single period exceeding—

(a) where the accused is remanded in custody, three weeks; and

(b) where he is remanded on bail or ordained to appear, four weeks or, on cause shown, eight weeks.

(4) An accused who is remanded under this section may appeal against the refusal of bail or against the conditions imposed within 24 hours of his remand, by note of appeal presented to the High Court, and the High Court, either in court or in chambers, may, after hearing parties—

(a) review the order appealed against and either grant bail on such conditions as it thinks fit or ordain the accused to appear at the adjourned diet; or

(b) confirm the order.

DEFINITIONS
"bail": s.307(1).
"diet": s.307(1).
"remand": s.307(1).

GENERAL NOTE

The antecedent provisions conjoined for this section have produced a considerable number of authorities, those provisions being ss.179 and 380 of the 1975 Act as amended. The principal point to note is that it is of paramount importance for courts at first instance to have in mind the clear statutory distinction between adjourning a case before sentence and deferring sentence. In *H.M. Advocate v. Clegg*, 1991 S.L.T. 192 it was held that to obtain various reports for sentencing the correct approach is to adjourn the case and not to defer sentence, a distinction that was emphasised in *McRobbie v. H.M. Advocate*, 1990 S.C.C.R 767. Refer also to *Airlie v. Heywood*, 1996 S.C.C.R. 562 where sentence had been deferred for good behaviour, social inquiry reports and to ascertain the effect of conviction upon the accused's taxi licence; it was held that the adjournment had been at common law and was not a statutory one limited to eight weeks.

At the very least when adjourning a case for sentence in excess of four weeks, it must be recorded in the minutes that the adjournment was on cause shown otherwise the Appeal Court can have no inkling of its purpose (*Dingwall v. Vannet*, 1997 S.C.C.R. 515). Although there is no requirement that the reason for such a length of adjournment be stated either in court or in the minutes themselves, it would seem sensible (if only as a means of answering any points taken on appeal) that such steps be taken.

The necessity of abiding by the statutory time-limits was shown in *Wilson v. Donald*, 1993 S.L.T. 31 because, while the continuation was recorded as a deferred sentence, the obtaining of a DVLA printout during a period greater than three weeks was an adjournment to which the time-limits applied. This point was applied in *Holburn v Lees*, 1993 S.C.C.R. 426 and *Burns v. Wilson*, 1993 S.C.C.R. 418 although it was held that convictions were unaffected by these appeals on procedural points although the sentences were suspended: see also *McCulloch v. Scott*, 1993 S.L.T. 901.

A further distinction became apparent in *Douglas v. Jamieson*, 1993 S.L.T. 816 and *Douglas v. Peddie*, 1993 S.C.C.R. 717 where it was held that with a combination of guilty and not guilty pleas leading to an adjourned trial diet the court was exercising its power at common law to adjourn at any stage when it seemed appropriate to do so. See also *Mcleod v. Hutton* (Sh.Ct.), 1993 S.C.C.R. 747.

The statutory distinction was also held not to apply in *Johnstone v. Lees*, 1994 S.L.T. 551 where an adjournment of eight weeks to await the outcome of other cases was deemed competent at common law. A continuation for a proof of a previous conviction is a matter at common law: *Burns v. Lees*, 1994 S.C.C.R. 780. "Cause shown" (subs. (3)(9b)) was held to extend to an extension of the four week period of deferment at Christmas where a social worker had requested additional time to obtain additional material for the accused's report (*Porteous v. Hamilton*, 1996 G.W.D. 21–1199).

In the authorities cited, objection to the competency of the various proceedings was taken timeously and to delay without explanation a complaint about competency may amount to acquiescence especially with a long passage of time and a payment of fines as ordered: *Storie v. Friel*, 1993 S.C.C.R. 955.

Finally, in *Long v. H.M. Advocate*, 1984 S.C.C.R. 161 it was held that review of the court's decision on bail (s.30 of the 1975 Act and this Act) had no application to bail in relation to the power of the court to adjourn a case before sentence.

Deferred sentence

202.—(1) It shall be competent for a court to defer sentence after conviction for a period and on such conditions as the court may determine.

(2) If it appears to the court which deferred sentence on an accused under subsection (1) above that he has been convicted during the period of deferment, by a court in any part of Great Britain of an offence committed during that period and has been dealt with for that offence, the court which deferred sentence may—

(a) issue a warrant for the arrest of the accused; or

(b) instead of issuing such a warrant in the first instance, issue a citation requiring him to appear before it at such time as may be specified in the citation,

and on his appearance or on his being brought before the court it may deal with him in any manner in which it would be competent for it to deal with him on the expiry of the period of deferment.

(3) Where a court which has deferred sentence on an accused under subsection (1) above convicts him of another offence during the period of deferment, it may deal with him for the original offence in any manner in which it would be competent for it to deal with him on the expiry of the period of deferment, as well as for the offence committed during the said period.

DEFINITION
"sentence": s.307(1).

GENERAL NOTE
It is of paramount importance for courts at first instance to have in mind the clear statutory distinction between adjourning a case before sentence and deferring sentence. Regard might be had to the cases in the General Note to s.201 of this Act for the authorities arising from this distinction. The note by A.D. Smith on *Deferred Sentences in Scotland*, 1968 S.L.T.(Notes) 153 is still of interest.

In *Valentine v. Parker*, 1992 S.C.C.R. 695 an appeal was taken during a deferred sentence but in the absence of the court papers the sheriff held the calling of the case on the appropriate date for consideration was incompetent. A Crown Bill of Advocation was passed and it was held by the High Court of Justiciary that the deferred sentence had been superceded by the appeal proceedings and the case was remitted to the sheriff for sentence.

In *Maitland v. McNaughtan*, 1996 G.W.D. 22–1261 sentence had been deferred for good behaviour. The Appeal Court held that the sheriff erred in holding M. to be in breach, when a conviction, for an offence which predated the deferment, and a pending trial, for an offence alleged to have occurred during the period of deferment, were disclosed: the correct approach would have been to defer to await the outcome of the trial.

In *Fletcher v. Walkingshaw*, 1997 G.W.D. 8–327 where sentences of imprisonment were imposed upon the accused, after an initial deferment for restitution had not been complied with, the Appeal Court took account of a non-analogous record and the social enquiry report obtained before deferral, which had concluded that a custodial sentence was inappropriate; a probation order allied to community service (as proposed in the report) was substituted.

When deferring sentence it is probably unwise for the judge either to predict or promise a particular disposal. Any such statement would not be binding on the judge himself or any other judge called upon to dispose of the case (*Laing v. Heywood*, 1998 S.L.T. 458). When deferring sentence for good behaviour the conditions imposed should not be unduly restrictive—the aim is to confirm that the accused is capable of behaving "in ordinary life in an acceptable way"; see *Islam v. Heywood*, 1999 S.C.C.R. 68.

Reports

203.—(1) Where a person specified in section 27(1)(b)(i) to (vi) of the Social Work (Scotland) Act 1968 commits an offence, the court shall not dispose of the case without obtaining from the local authority in whose area the person resides a report as to—
(a) the circumstances of the offence; and
(b) the character of the offender, including his behaviour while under the supervision, or as the case may be subject to the order, so specified in relation to him.
(2) In subsection (1) above, "the court" does not include a district court.
(3) Where, in any case, a report by an officer of a local authority is made to the court with a view to assisting the court in determining the most suitable method of dealing with any person in respect of an offence, a copy of the report shall be given by the clerk of the court to the offender or his solicitor.

DEFINITIONS
"local authority": s.307(1).
"offence": s.307(1).

GENERAL NOTE
This section requires the court to obtain a report targeted on new offences by an offender who is subject to statutory supervision. So in *Hendry v. H.M. Advocate*, 1999 G.W.D. 21–1004, a sentence of imprisonment was suspended on appeal where the sheriff had failed to obtain a local authority report on *H.* who was on probation at the time of the offence. The provisions of the section only apply when the person committing the offences libelled is already subject to the provisions of s.27(1)(b) of the Social Work (Scotland) Act 1968 (see *Townsley v. McGlennan*, 1998 S.L.T. 104). The circumstances of the new offences are an aspect distinct from the offender's behaviour on supervision.

Imprisonment, etc.

Restrictions on passing sentence of imprisonment or detention

204.—(1) A court shall not pass a sentence of imprisonment or of detention in respect of any offence, nor impose imprisonment, or detention, under section 214(2) of this Act in respect of failure to pay a fine, on an accused who is not legally represented in that court and has not been previously sentenced to imprisonment or detention by a court in any part of the United Kingdom, unless the accused either—
(a) applied for legal aid and the application was refused on the ground that he was not financially eligible; or
(b) having been informed of his right to apply for legal aid, and having had the opportunity, failed to do so.
[1](2) A court shall not pass a sentence of imprisonment on a person of or over twenty-one years of age who has not been previously sentenced to imprisonment or detention by a court in any part of the United Kingdom unless the court considers that no other method of dealing with him is appropriate ...
[2](2A) For the purpose of determining under subsection (2) above whether any other method of dealing with such a person is appropriate, the court shall take into account—
(a) such information as it has been able to obtain from an officer of a local authority or otherwise about his circumstances;
(b) any information before it concerning his character and mental and physical condition;
(c) its power to make a hospital direction in addition to imposing a sentence of imprisonment.

(3) Where a court of summary jurisdiction passes a sentence of imprisonment on any such person as is mentioned in subsection (2) above, the court shall state the reason for its opinion that no other method of dealing with him is appropriate, and shall have that reason entered in the record of the proceedings.

(4) The court shall, for the purpose of determining whether a person has been previously sentenced to imprisonment or detention by a court in any part of the United Kingdom—

    (a) disregard a previous sentence of imprisonment which, having been suspended, has not taken effect under section 23 of the Powers of Criminal Courts Act 1973 or under section 19 of the Treatment of Offenders Act (Northern Ireland) 1968;

    (b) construe detention as meaning—

        (i) in relation to Scotland, detention in a young offenders institution or detention centre;

(3) Where a court of summary jurisdiction passes a sentence of imprisonment on any such person as is mentioned in subsection (2) above, the court shall state the reason for its opinion that no other method of dealing with him is appropriate, and shall have that reason entered in the record of the proceedings.

(4) The court shall, for the purpose of determining whether a person has been previously sentenced to imprisonment or detention by a court in any part of the United Kingdom—

    (a) disregard a previous sentence of imprisonment which, having been suspended, has not taken effect under section 23 of the Powers of Criminal Courts Act 1973 or under section 19 of the Treatment of Offenders Act (Northern Ireland) 1968;

    (b) construe detention as meaning—

        (i) in relation to Scotland, detention in a young offenders institution or detention centre;

        (ii) in relation to England and Wales a sentence of youth custody, borstal training or detention in a young offender institution or detention centre; and

        (iii) in relation to Northern Ireland, detention in a young offenders centre.

        (5) This section does not affect the power of a court to pass sentence on any person for an offence the sentence for which is fixed by law.

        (6) In this section—

"legal aid" means legal aid for the purposes of any part of the proceedings before the court;

"legally represented" means represented by counsel or a solicitor at some stage after the accused is found guilty and before he is dealt with as referred to in subsection (1) above.

DEFINITIONS
"court of summary jurisdiction": s.307(1).
"fine": s.307(1).
"impose imprisonment": s.307(1).
"legal aid": s.204(6).
"legally represented": s.204(6).
"offence": s.307(1).
"sentence": s.307(1).

NOTES
[1]Words deleted by s.6(3) of the Crime and Punishment (Scotland) Act 1997 with effect from January 1, 1998 as provided by the Crime and Punishment (Scotland) Act 1997 (Commencement No. 2 and Transitional and Consequential Provisions) Order 1997 (S.I. 1997 No. 2323) Art. 4 and Sched. 2.

[2]Inserted by s.6(3) of the above Act and commenced on January 1, 1998 in terms of the above Order.

GENERAL NOTE
This section conjoins the provisions in ss.41 and 42 of the 1980 Act. Imprisonment as a sentence or as a penalty for fine default can only be imposed once the accused has been legally represented in the proceedings (subs. (1)). In addition the court can now impose a hospital direction (discussed at ss.59 and 60 above) as part of such sentence or penalty. In all cases there is a general obligation to have regard to any information about the accused's character, physical and mental condition.
Two authorities are worth considering here. First, the duty (in subs. (2)) to obtain information from a local authority "or otherwise" is not fulfilled by obtaining information from the prosecution or the defence: *Auld v. Herron*, 1969 J.C. 4. It should be noted that the duty is qualified by the phrase "such information as it can" although that is not defined. Secondly, the imprisonment or detention relates only to the U.K. and that necessarily excludes the Republic of Ireland: *Mawhinney v. H.M. Advocate*, 1950 S.L.T. 135. It is difficult to see why imprisonment or detention elsewhere is excluded in this way but it may be information bearing on the accused's character. While it is not necessary for the sentencing judge to enumerate the other disposals considered before arriving at a custodial sentence, for the purposes of compliance with the requirements of subs.(2), and particularly in preparing a report for any appeal, a judge should indicate that the sentencing options have been fully considered (*Keogh v. Watt*, 2000 S.C.C.R. 443).

Restriction on consecutive sentences for released prisoners

[1]**204A.** A court sentencing a person to imprisonment or other detention shall not order or direct that the term of imprisonment or detention shall commence on the expiration of any other such sentence from which he has been released at any time under the existing or new provisions within the meaning of Schedule 6 to the Prisoners and Criminal Proceedings (Scotland) Act 1993.

DEFINITIONS
"imprisonment": s.307(1) of the 1995 Act.
"detention": s.307(1) of the 1995 Act.
"sentence": s.307(1) of the 1995 Act.

NOTE
[1]Inserted by the Crime and Disorder Act 1998 (c. 37) s.112 (effective September 30, 1998: S.I. 1998 No. 2327).

GENERAL NOTE
In keeping with the provisions in s.111(1) of the 1998 Act, which added s.1A to the Prisoners and Criminal Proceedings (Scotland) Act 1993 (c. 9), this section stipulates that prisoners released on licence who are sentenced, in relation to other offences, to another term of imprisonment should not receive a sentence running consecutive to the expiry of that imprisonment term. Only by imposing an immediate and concurrent sentence of further imprisonment (which may of course result in incarceration beyond the end of the earlier sentence) can the release provisions set down in the 1993 Act, as amended, function effectively.
This provision came into force on September 30, 1998 in terms of S.I. 1998 No. 2327.
See for example, *H.M. Advocate v. Graham*, 1999 G.W.D. 26–1235 and *Thomson, Petr*, 2000 G.W.D. 8–289.

Punishment for murder

205.—(1) Subject to subsections (2) and (3) below, a person convicted of murder shall be sentenced to imprisonment for life.
(2) Where a person convicted of murder is under the age of 18 years he shall not be sentenced to imprisonment for life but to be detained without limit of time and shall be liable to be detained in such place, and under such conditions, as the Secretary of State may direct.
(3) Where a person convicted of murder has attained the age of 18 years

but is under the age of 21 years he shall not be sentenced to imprisonment for life but to be detained in a young offenders institution and shall be liable to be detained for life.

(4) On sentencing any person convicted of murder a judge may make a recommendation as to the minimum period which should elapse before, under section 1(4) of the Prisoners and Criminal Proceedings (Scotland) Act 1993, the Secretary of State releases that person on licence.

(5) When making a recommendation under subsection (4) above, the judge shall state his reasons for so recommending.

(6) Notwithstanding subsection (2) of section 106 of this Act it shall be competent to appeal under paragraph (b) or (f) of subsection (1) of that section against a recommendation made under subsection (4) above; and for the purposes of such appeal (including the High Court's power of disposal under section 118(4)(b) of this Act) the recommendation shall be deemed part of the sentence passed on conviction.

DEFINITIONS
    "judge": s.307(1).
    "sentence": s.307(1).

GENERAL NOTE
    The recommendation permitted by subs. (4) appears to be fairly common now. A good example is *Birrell v. H.M. Advocate*, 1993 S.C.C.R. 812 where previous convictions were held not to be a factor of significance in this case. The important factors had been the method used to commit the crime, the degree of planning and premeditation and the ruthlessness exhibited in the acts which had been perpetrated. A recommendation of a minimum of 15 years was held to be correctly decided. This approach was followed in *Greenfield v. H.M. Advocate*, 1996 G.W.D. 20–1162 it being noted that the trial judge had given weight to the fact that the accused had lain in wait for his victim, a factor not libelled in the murder charge and expressly deliberated upon by the jury but consistent with the evidence. A similar period was imposed on appeal in *Casey v. H.M. Advocate*, 1994 S.L.T. 54 where it was observed by the Appeal Court that it would not expect a recommendation to be made for a period of less than 12 years.

Minimum sentence for third conviction of certain offences relating to drug trafficking

[1]**205B.**—(1) This section applies where—
(a) a person is convicted on indictment in the High Court of a class A drug trafficking offence committed after the commencement of section 2 of the Crime and Punishment (Scotland) Act 1997;
(b) at the time when that offence was committed, he had attained the age of at least 18 years and had been convicted in any part of the United Kingdom of two other class A drug trafficking offences, irrespective of—
    (i) whether either of those offences was committed before or after the commencement of section 2 of the Crime and Punishment (Scotland) Act 1997;
    (ii) the court in which any such conviction was obtained; and
    (iii) his age at the time of the commission of either of those offences; and
(c) one of the offences mentioned in paragraph (b) above was committed after he had been convicted of the other.

(2) Subject to subsection (3) below, where this section applies the court shall sentence the person—
(a) where he has attained the age of 21 years, to a term of imprisonment of at least seven years; and
(b) where he has attained the age of 18 years but is under the age of 21 years, to detention in a young offenders institution for a period of at least seven years.

(3) The court shall not impose the sentence otherwise required by

subsection (2) above where it is of the opinion that there are specific circumstances which—
    (a) relate to any of the offences or to the offender; and
    (b) would make that sentence unjust.
    (4) For the purposes of section 106(2) of this Act a sentence passed under subsection (2) above in respect of a conviction for a class A drug trafficking offence shall not be regarded as a sentence fixed by law for that offence.
    (5) In this section "class A drug trafficking offence" means a drug trafficking offence committed in respect of a class A drug; and for this purpose—
        "class A drug" has the same meaning as in the Misuse of Drugs Act 1971;
        "drug trafficking offence" means a drug trafficking offence within the meaning of—
            (i) the Drug Trafficking Act 1994;
            (ii) the Proceeds of Crime (Scotland) Act 1995; or
            (iii) the Proceeds of Crime (Northern Ireland) Order 1996.

DEFINITIONS
    "indictment": s.307(1) of the 1995 Act.
    "High Court": s.307(1) of the Act.
    "class A drug": s.2(1) and Schedule 2, Part I of the Misuse of Drugs Act 1971 (c. 38).
    "drug trafficking offence": s.49(5) of the Proceeds of Crime (Scotland) Act 1995 (c. 43); s.1(3) of the Drug Trafficking Act 1994 (c. 37); Proceeds of Crime (Northern Ireland) Order 1996.
    "offence": s.307(1) of the 1995 Act.
    "United Kingdom": Schedule 1 of the Interpretation Act 1978 (c. 30).
    "conviction": s.3 of the 1997 Act.
    "young offenders institutution": s.307(1) of the 1995 Act.
    "sentence": s.307(1) of the 1995 Act.

NOTE
[1]Inserted by the Crime and Punishment (Scotland) Act 1997 (c. 48), s.2 with effect from January 20, 1998 as provided by the Crime and Punishment (Scotland) Act 1997 (Commencement No. 2 and Transitional and Consequential Provisions) Order 1997 (S.I. 1997 No. 2323) Art. 3, Sched. 1.

GENERAL NOTE
    This section was introduced into the 1995 Act by s.2 of the Crime and Punishment (Scotland) Act with effect from October 20, 1997 as provided by the Crime and Punishment (Scotland) Act 1997 (Commencement No. 2 and Transitional and Consequential Provisions) 1997 S.I. 2323.
    Section 205B provides that, where a person convicted of a drug trafficking offence before the High Court in relation to a class A drug, has two distinct prior convictions for trafficking in class A drugs (a number of incidents conjoined in one conviction would not suffice), he shall be sentenced to a minimum period of imprisonment or detention of seven years. Reference to the legislation mentioned in subs. (5) shows that "drug trafficking offence" has a much wider meaning than merely dealing in, or being concerned in, the supply of controlled drugs. It is important to note that the two prior convictions can have been imposed by any United Kingdom court at any time—these provisions can operate retrospectively. Subsection (1)(b) stipulates that such a minimum sentence can only be imposed upon an offender who had reached 18 years of age at the time of committing the third offence.
    Reservations have to be expressed however as to whether information currently available in previous convictions will highlight that the prior convictions related specificaly to class A drugs. This problem may lead the Crown to lodge certified copies of the complaints or indictments, and related Minutes of Procedure, and perhaps a s.285 certificate (now a Secretary of State's rather than a Chief Constable's certificate, following s.59 of the 1997 Act) to lay out the provenance of previous convictions.
    It will be appreciated that the broad intention of s.205B is to limit the sentencing discretion available to judges when dealing with recidivist drug trafficking offenders but the wording of s.205B(3) is not free of difficulty, particularly when read along with s.196(2) of the 1995 Act. While the Government adhered to the familiar notion that a sentencing court would have to look to the circumstances of the current offence before it, and to any previous convictions, the Lord Advocate did concede that "the procedure for laying details of the circumstances of the

first qualifying offence before the court will have to be addressed" (*Hansard*, March 4, 1997, col. 1821). It is submitted that it would be quite proper for the court to have regard to the sentences imposed in relation to the earlier convictions, and that in something of a departure from current sentencing practices, subs. (3) suggest that some investigation of the factual background to those convictions could be undertaken by the court. This is a marked departure from the principles set out in *Connell v. Mitchell* (1908) 5 A. 641 and *Baker v. McFadyean*, 1952 S.L.T. (Notes) 69 which disapproved of "looking behind convictions". See however the discussion at pp. 154–155 above.

Interestingly it was only after the Committee stage of the Crime and Punishment (Scotland) Bill that the Government moved an amendment to s.196 of the 1995 Act to permit the sentencing court to pass a lower sentence where a guilty plea had been tendered. Accordingly the mandatory minimum sentence can be reduced to one of 5 years 219 days, a discount of 20 per cent of sentence, to reflect a timeous guilty plea. It would appear that the judicial discretion to reduce the mandatory seven year sentence (subs. (3)) operates separately from, and not as an addition to, any discount in sentence awarded under s.196: in other words, that discretion cannot be invoked to reduce the sentence following a guilty plea below the statutory minimum of 5 years 219 days. Reference should be made to s.199(3)(c) which, it is submitted, has the effect of ensuring that the penalty for any contravention of s.205B has to be a term of imprisonment of at least 5 years 219 days: see the discussion at p. 264 above.

Section 205B(4) preserves the right of appeal against sentence since s.205B provides for an automatic, not a mandatory sentence; by definition the latter form of sentence cannot be appealed.

Meaning of "conviction"

Reference to s.205C below reveals that the automatic sentence for a third relevant drug trafficking offence will apply even if one, or both, of the earlier convictions was disposed of by way of admonition or a probation order. Such a disposal would, in the event of conviction after trial for a third drug trafficking offence, still fall to be considered under subs. (3) above as a ground for refraining from imposing the seven year minimum sentence.

Meaning of "conviction" for purposes of sections 205A and 205B

[1]**205C.**—(1) For the purposes of paragraph (b) of subsection (1) of each sections 205A and 205B of this Act "conviction" includes—

    (a) a finding of guilt in respect of which the offender was admonished under section 181 of the Criminal Procedure (Scotland) Act 1975 (admonition); and

    (b) a conviction for which an order is made placing the offender on probation,

and related expressions shall be construed accordingly.

DEFINITIONS

"admonished": s.246 of the Criminal Procedure (Scotland) Act 1995.
"probation": s.247 of said Act.
"offence": s.307(1) of said Act.
"Class A drug": s.2(1) and Schedule 2, Part I of the Misuse of Drugs Act 1971.
"drug trafficking offence": s.49(5) of the Proceeds of Crime (Scotland) Act 1995, s.1(3) of the Drug Trafficking Act 1994 and s.1(3) of the Proceeds of Crime (Northern Ireland) Order 1996.

NOTE

[1]Inserted by the Crime and Punishment (Scotland) Act 1997 (c. 48), s.3 (in part) with effect from October 20, 1997 as provided by the Crime and Punishment (Scotland) Act 1997 (Commencement No. 2 and Transitional and Consequential Provisions) Order 1997 (S.I. 1997 No. 2323) Art. 3, Sched. 1.

GENERAL NOTE

This section defines the meaning of "conviction", a concept central to the operation of Part I of the 1997 Act. It will be recalled that the 1997 Act introduced two "automatic" sentences, requiring the High Court to impose life sentences in a range of serious offences and minimum sentences for class A drug trafficking offences. The incoming Government has not commenced the regime of automatic life sentences specified in s.1 of the 1997 Act, and has commenced only part of s.205B (the full text of the section appears as s.3 of the 1997 Act) with effect from 20 October 1997.

The ethos of the 1997 Act, which sought to impose more severe penalties upon offenders by removing large elements of sentencing discretion from judges, is still to be found in s.205B: it will be noted that the imposition of a probation order, an order which as s.247(1) of the 1995 Act provides, is not deemed to be a conviction, is nonetheless a disposal for the purposes of s.205B, counting as a conviction. (As originally drafted even absolute and conditional discharges were included also as "convictions" but this was withdrawn late in the life of the Bill).

Although the mechanism is in place to permit drug trafficking convictions imposed by military courts martial to count as prior convictions for the purposes of s.205B (see subs. (2) of s.205B as it appears in the 1997 Act) no steps have been taken to activate that provision as yet.

Minimum periods of imprisonment

206.—(1) No person shall be sentenced to imprisonment by a court of summary jurisdiction for a period of less than five days.

(2) Where a court of summary jurisdiction has power to impose imprisonment on an offender, it may, if any suitable place provided and certified as mentioned in subsection (4) below is available for the purpose, sentence the offender to be detained therein, for such period not exceeding four days as the court thinks fit, and an extract of the finding and sentence shall be delivered with the offender to the person in charge of the place where the offender is to be detained and shall be a sufficient authority for his detention in that place in accordance with the sentence.

(3) The expenses of the maintenance of offenders detained under this section shall be defrayed in like manner as the expenses of the maintenance of prisoners under the Prisons (Scotland) Act 1989.

(4) The Secretary of State may, on the application of any police authority, certify any police cells or other similar places provided by the authority to be suitable places for the detention of persons sentenced to detention under this section, and may by statutory instrument make regulations for the inspection of places so provided, the treatment of persons detained therein and generally for carrying this section into effect.

(5) No place certified under this section shall be used for the detention of females unless provision is made for their supervision by female officers.

(6) In this section the expression "police authority" has the same meaning as in the Police (Scotland) Act 1967.

DEFINITIONS
"court of summary jurisdiction": s.307(1).
"imprisonment": s.307(1).
"police authority": s.206(6).

Act of Adjournal
The style of the extract for detention in police custody is set out in Form 20.2 in the 1996 Act of Adjournal.

Detention of young offenders

207.—(1) It shall not be competent to impose imprisonment on a person under 21 years of age.

[1](2) Subject to section 205(2) and (3), 205A(2)(b) and 205B(2)(b) of this Act and to subsections (3) and (4) below, a court may impose detention (whether by way of sentence or otherwise) on a person, who is not less than 16 but under 21 years of age, where but for subsection (1) above the court would have power to impose a period of imprisonment; and a period of detention imposed under this section on any person shall not exceed the maximum period of imprisonment which might otherwise have been imposed.

(3) The court shall not under subsection (2) above impose detention on an offender unless it is of the opinion that no other method of dealing with him is appropriate; and the court shall state its reasons for that opinion, and, except in the case of the High Court, those reasons shall be entered in the record of proceedings.

(4) To enable the court to form an opinion under subsection (3) above, it shall obtain from an officer of a local authority or otherwise such information as it can about the offender's circumstances; and it shall also take into account any information before it concerning the offender's character and physical and mental condition.

²(4A) In forming an opinion under subsection (3) above the court shall take into account its power to make a hospital direction in addition to imposing a period of detention.

(5) A sentence of detention imposed under this section shall be a sentence of detention in a young offenders institution.

DEFINITIONS
"imprisonment": s.307(1).
"hospital direction": s.9A of the 1997 Act.
"local authority": s.307(1).
"young offender's institution": s.307(1).

NOTES
¹Inserted by the Crime and Punishment (Scotland) Act 1997 (c. 48), Sched. 1, para. 21(25) with effect from October 20, 1997 by the Crime and Punishment (Scotland) Act 1997 (Commencement No. 2 and Transitional and Consequential Provisions) Order 1997 (S.I. 1997 No. 2323) Art. 3, Sched. 1.
²Inserted by the Crime and Punishment (Scotland) Act 1997 s.6(4) with effect from January 1, 1998 in terms of the Crime and Punishment (Scotland) Act 1997 (Commencement No. 2 and Transitional and Consequential Provisions) Order 1997 (S.I. 1997 No. 2323) Art. 4 and Sched. 2.

GENERAL NOTE
The correct approach for the court in deciding the issue of detention for a young offender is to ask, in terms of subs. (3), what methods of dealing with the accused are appropriate. If the court is of the opinion that no method other than detention is appropriate then detention should be imposed: see *Milligan v. Jessop*, 1988 S.C.C.R. 137; *Dunsmore v. Allan*, 1991 S.C.C.R. 946 and *Divers v. Friel*, 1994 S.L.T. 247 in which the approaches were flawed. Having formed the opinion that no other method of dealing with the accused is appropriate, the court is required to state its reasons for that opinion and those reasons shall be entered in the record of proceedings. For the effect of failure to obtemper an earlier version of this subsection, see *Binnie v. Farrell*, 1972 S.L.T. 212. The common reasons so stated are "character, gravity or nature of the offence" and "previous record of the accused", variations of which were used in *Dunsmore v. Allan*, above. Some support for these are to be found in s.214(4) of this Act.

It is not sufficient for the purposes of subs. (3) for the sentencing judge to recall the terms of earlier reports upon the accused. The Appeal Court did approve the use of an up to date report prepared in regard to other proceedings provided that a copy of that report is placed before the court; see *Bain v. McNaughtan*, 1999 S.L.T. 410.

The court may now incorporate a hospital direction into any sentence of detention imposed upon a young offender. See generally s.59A above.

Detention of children convicted on indictment

208. Subject to section 205 of this Act, where a child is convicted on indictment and the court is of the opinion that no other method of dealing with him is appropriate, it may sentence him to be detained for a period which it shall specify in the sentence; and the child shall during that period be liable to be detained in such place and on such conditions as the Secretary of State may direct.

DEFINITIONS
"child": s.307(1).
"indictment": s.307(1).
"sentence": s.307(1).

GENERAL NOTE
The correct approach for the court in deciding the issue of detention for a child convicted on indictment is the same as that for young offenders, namely to ask what methods of dealing with the child are appropriate. If the court is of the opinion that no method other than detention is

appropriate then the child shall be detained for a specified period. See for example *Sneddon v. H.M. Advocate*, 1998 G.W.D. 22–1131.

In *R.J.K. v. H.M. Advocate*, 1993 S.L.T. 237 it was held that (in relation to s.206 of the 1975 Act from which this section is derived) the sentence of detention "without limit of time" is a specified sentence and the absence of those words from the section did not impose any restriction on a court to pass such a sentence. Such a sentence, however, is in effect a life sentence: *R.F. v. H.M. Advocate*, 1994 S.C.C.R. 71.

Supervised release orders

[1]**209.**—(1) Where a person is convicted on indictment of an offence other than a sexual offence within the meaning of section 210A of this Act and is sentenced to imprisonment for a term of less than four years, the court on passing sentence may, if it considers that it is necessary to do so to protect the public from serious harm from the offender on his release, make such order as is mentioned in subsection (3) below.

(2) A court shall, before making an order under subsection (1) above, consider a report by a relevant officer of a local authority about the offender and his circumstances and, if the court thinks it necessary, hear that officer.

(3) The order referred to in subsection (1) above (to be known as a "supervised release order") is that the person, during a relevant period—

(a) be under the supervision either of a relevant officer of a local authority or of a probation officer appointed for or assigned to a petty sessions area (such local authority or the justices for such area to be designated under section 14(4) or 15(1) of the Prisoners and Criminal Proceedings (Scotland) Act 1993);

(b) comply with;

(i) such requirements as may be imposed by the court in the order; and

(ii) such requirements as that officer may reasonably specify,

for the purpose of securing the good conduct of the person or preventing, or lessening the possibility of, his committing a further offence (whether or not an offence of the kind for which he was sentenced); and

(c) comply with the standard requirements imposed by virtue of subsection (4)(a)(i) below.

(4) A supervised release order—

(a) shall—

(i) without prejudice to subsection (3)(b) above, contain such requirements (in this section referred to as the "standard requirements"); and

(ii) be as nearly as possible in such form,

as may be prescribed by Act of Adjournal;

(b) for the purposes of any appeal or review constitutes part of the sentence of the person in respect of whom the order is made; and

(c) shall have no effect during any period in which the person is subject to a licence under Part I of the said Act of 1993.

(5) Before making a supervised release order as respects a person the court shall explain to him, in as straightforward a way as is practicable, the effect of the order and the possible consequences for him of any breach of it.

(6) The clerk of the court by which a supervised release order is made in respect of a person shall—

(a) forthwith send a copy of the order to the person and to the Secretary of State; and

(b) within seven days after the date on which the order is made, send to the Secretary of State such documents and information relating to the case and to the person as are likely to be of assistance to a supervising officer.

(7) In this section—

"relevant officer" has the same meaning as in Part I of the Prisoners and Criminal Proceedings (Scotland) Act 1993;

"relevant period" means such period as may be specified in the supervised release order, being a period—

(a) not exceeding twelve months after the date of the person's release; and

(b) no part of which is later than the date by which the entire term of imprisonment specified in his sentence has elapsed; and

"supervising officer" means, where an authority has or justices have been designated as is mentioned in subsection (3)(a) above for the purposes of the order, any relevant officer or, as the case may be, probation officer who is for the time being supervising for those purposes the person released.

[2](7A) Where a person—

(a) is serving a sentence of imprisonment and on his release from that sentence will be subject to a supervised release order; and

(b) is sentenced to a further term of imprisonment, whether that term is to run consecutively or concurrently with the sentence mentioned in paragraph (a) above,

the relevant period for any supervised release order made in relation to him shall begin on the date when he is released from those terms of imprisonment; and where there is more than one such order he shall on his release be subject to whichever of them is for the longer or, as the case may be, the longest period.

(8) This section applies to a person sentenced under section 207 of this Act as it applies to a person sentenced to a period of imprisonment.

DEFINITIONS

"local authority": s.307(1).
"relevant officer": s.209(7).
"relevant period": s.209(7).
"supervised release order": s.209(3).
"supervising officer": s.209(7).

NOTES

[1]As amended by the Crime and Disorder Act 1998 (c. 37), s.86(2) (effective September 30, 1998: S.I. 1998 No. 2327).

[2]Inserted by the Crime and Punishment (Scotland) Act 1997, Sched. 1, para. 21(26) (effective April 1, 1999: S.I. 1999 No. 652).

GENERAL NOTE

These minor amendments to s.209 of the 1995 Act serve two purposes: firstly, supervised release orders are not available to solemn courts when sentencing offenders for any sexual offence now specified in s.210A(8) of the 1995 Act (see the General Notes to s.210); in *Craig v. H.M.Advocate*, 2000 G.W.D. 34–1313 the Appeal Court accepted Crown submissions that, having been convicted of sexual offences, the accused should have been made subject of an extended sentence order in terms of s.210A of the Act, not a supervised release order. Note however that the court declined to impose an extended sentence on appeal on the grounds that the social enquiry report prepared originally had not addressed the risk to the public posed by the accused; secondly, it is s.209 that empowers solemn courts to make such orders in relation to offenders sentenced to imprisonment for a period of less than four years. Separate provisions, introducing extended sentences for sexual offenders, and for violent offenders sentenced to more than four years imprisonment, are to be found in s.210A. These provisions came into force on September 30, 1998 in terms of the Crime and Disorder Act 1998 (Commencement No. 2 and Transitional Provisions) Order 1998 (S.I. 1998 No. 2327); the provisions do not apply to sex offences committed before September 30, 1998—supervised release orders could still be imposed in such circumstances.

Act of Adjournal

The style of supervised release order is set out in Form 20.3 in the 1996 Act of Adjournal as amended by the Act of Adjournal (Criminal Procedure Rules Amendment) (Miscellaneous)

2000 (S.S.I. 2000 No. 65) which came into force on April 7, 2000; whose text is found in 2000 S.L.T. 121.

Consideration of time spent in custody

210.—(1) A court, in passing a sentence of imprisonment or detention on a person for an offence, shall—

[1](a) in determining the period of imprisonment or detention, have regard to any period of time spent in custody by the person on remand awaiting trial or sentence, or spent in custody awaiting extradition to the United Kingdom, or spent in hospital awaiting trial or sentence by virtue of an order made under section 52, 53 or 200 of this Act;

(b) specify the date of commencement of the sentence; and

(c) if the person—

    (i) has spent a period of time in custody on remand awaiting trial or sentence; or

    (ii) is an extradited prisoner for the purposes of this section, or

    [1](iii) has spent a period of time in hospital awaiting trial or sentence by virtue of an order under section 52, 53 or 200 of this Act,

and the date specified under paragraph (b) above is not earlier than the date on which sentence was passed, state its reasons for not specifying an earlier date.

(2) A prisoner is an extradited prisoner for the purposes of this section if—

(a) he was tried for the offence in respect of which his sentence of imprisonment was imposed—

    (i) after having been extradited to the United Kingdom; and

    (ii) without having first been restored to the state from which he was extradited or having had an opportunity of leaving the United Kingdom; and

(b) he was for any period in custody while awaiting such extradition.

(3) In this section "extradited to the United Kingdom" means returned to the United Kingdom—

(a) in pursuance of extradition arrangements (as defined in section 3 of the Extradition Act 1989);

(b) under any law which corresponds to that Act and is a law of a designated Commonwealth country (as defined in section 5(1) of that Act);

(c) under that Act as extended to a colony or under any corresponding law of a colony;

(d) in pursuance of arrangements with a foreign state in respect of which an Order in Council under section 2 of the Extradition Act 1870 is in force; or

(e) in pursuance of a warrant of arrest endorsed in the Republic of Ireland under the law of that country corresponding to the Backing of Warrants (Republic of Ireland) Act 1965.

DEFINITION
"sentence": s.307(1).

NOTE
[1]Inserted by the Crime and Punishment (Scotland) Act 1997 (c. 48), s.12 and commenced on August 1, 1997 by the Crime and Punishment (Scotland) Act 1997 (Commencement and Transitional Provisions) Order 1997 (S.I. 1997 No. 1712) para. 3.

GENERAL NOTE
The obligation placed on a court by this section is to "have regard to any period of time spent in custody by the person awaiting trial or sentence, or spent in custody awaiting extradition to the United Kingdom". The 1997 Act extended this obligation to any prisoner spending time on remand in hospital prior to plea or trial to ascertain his mental state (s.52 of the 1995 Act), prior to sentence when an interim hospital order had been made (s.53 of that Act as amended) or when remanded to hospital during a deferment of sentence (s.200 of the 1995 Act). This

obligation normally exists even when the conviction is one of murder which, of course, carries a mandatory life sentence; while subs. (1)(a) has no application in such a case the remaining provisions do, and can affect the date upon which a prisoner might first be eligible for parole (*Elliott v. H.M. Advocate*, 1997 G.W.D. 1–15).

In effect, it is submitted, the court should have such a period in mind when selecting a sentence: it does not follow that such a period should be deducted automatically or that the sentence passed should be backdated to a commencement date that in effect deducts the period in mind. In practice, however, many sentences are backdated to a suitable commencement date: for a survey of the very considerable number of authorities on this point see *Backdating Sentences of Imprisonment* (1995) 40 J.L.S. 383.

While the extent and seriousness of the accused's previous convictions and the gravity of the offences before the court are factors which would justify not backdating a term of imprisonment (see for example *Robertson v. H.M. Advocate*, 1996 G.W.D. 14–836; *Wilson v. Lees*, 1996 G.W.D. 8–441, and *Grant v. H.M. Advocate*, 1996 G.W.D. 25–1421), due attention has to be paid to the extent of the charges where the accused has been convicted when set against those libelled originally: see *Johnston v. Wilson*, 1996 G.W.D. 17–986; *Craig v. H.M. Advocate*, 1997 G.W.D. 8–306 and *Blacklock v. H.M. Advocate*, 1998 G.W.D. 7–328 and *Pugh v. Hingston*, 1999 G.W.D. 13–605.

Time spent on remand resulting from an accused's own failure to appear for trial is unlikely to merit backdating (*Galbraith v. Vannet*, 1998 G.W.D. 5–215 following *Wojciechowski v. McLeod*, 1992 S.C.C.R. 563) but backdating only to the date of intimation of an acceptable plea, rather than to the date of being taken into custody, will only be upheld if reasons for so doing are stated (*Taylor v. H.M. Advocate*, 1998 G.W.D. 28–1415). However contrast *McAuley v. McLeod*, 1998 G.W.D. 37–1918 where a breach of bail and an appalling record of shoplifting offences was held to justify a refusal to backdate sentence.

Even following a conviction for murder, the mandatory sentence of life imprisonment should be backdated unless there are sound reasons stated to the contrary (*Elliott v. H.M. Advocate (No. 2)* 1997 S.L.T. 1229).

Ordinarily the reasons for refraining from backdating have to be noted when sentence is imposed (subs. (1)(c)) as in *Young v. H.M. Advocate*, 1996 G.W.D. 15–667 and *McGhee v. H.M. Advocate*, 1997 G.W.D. 17–772, cases in which regard was had to offending while on bail or very soon after the commission of other offences; failure to state them generally results in sentence being backdated on appeal (*Egan v. McGlennan*, 1996 G.W.D. 17–985 and *Dailly v. H.M. Advocate*, 1996 S.C.C.R. 580). In the latter case matters were further complicated by the need to take account of s.16 of the Prisoners and Criminal Proceedings (Scotland) 1993 which makes no provision for backdating; such sentences either must be served before any additional sentence imposed by the court or concurrently with such additional sentence. See also *McLaughlin v. H.M. Advocate*, 1996 G.W.D. 23–1315 in which the sheriff refrained from backdating on the basis that, had he done so, he would have remitted the accused to the High Court for sentence. The Court of Appeal paid the same regard to the accused's record, albeit that had not been expressly referred to in the sentencing minutes.

Sexual or violent offenders

Extended sentences for sex and violent offenders

[1]**210A.**—(1) Where a person is convicted on indictment of a sexual or violent offence, the court may, if it—

   (a) intends, in relation to—

      (i) a sexual offence, to pass a determinate sentence of imprisonment; or

      (ii) a violent offence, to pass such a sentence for a term of four years or more; and

   (b) considers that the period (if any) for which the offender would, apart from this section, be subject to a licence would not be adequate for the purpose of protecting the public from serious harm from the offender,

pass an extended sentence on the offender.

   (2) An extended sentence is a sentence of imprisonment which is the aggregate of—

   (a) the term of imprisonment ("the custodial term") which the court would have passed on the offender otherwise than by virtue of this section; and

(b) a further period ("the extension period") for which the offender is to be subject to a licence and which is, subject to the provisions of this section, of such length as the court considers necessary for the purpose mentioned in subsection (1)(b) above.

(3) The extension period shall not exceed, in the case of—

(a) a sexual offence, ten years; and

(b) a violent offence, five years.

(4) A court shall, before passing an extended sentence, consider a report by a relevant officer of a local authority about the offender and his circumstances and, if the court thinks it necessary, hear that officer.

(5) The term of an extended sentence passed for a statutory offence shall not exceed the maximum term of imprisonment provided for in the statute in respect of that offence.

(6) Subject to subsection (5) above, a sheriff may pass an extended sentence which is the aggregate of a custodial term not exceeding the maximum term of imprisonment which he may impose and an extension period not exceeding three years.

(7) The Secretary of State may by order—

(a) amend paragraph (b) of subsection (3) above by substituting a different period, not exceeding ten years, for the period for the time being specified in that paragraph; and

(b) make such transitional provision as appears to him to be necessary or expedient in connection with the amendment.

(8) The power to make an order under subsection (7) above shall be exercisable by statutory instrument; but no such order shall be made unless a draft of the order has been laid before, and approved by a resolution of, each House of Parliament.

(9) An extended sentence shall not be imposed where the sexual or violent offence was committed before the commencement of section 86 of the Crime and Disorder Act 1998.

(10) For the purposes of this section—

"licence" and "relevant officer" have the same meaning as in Part I of the Prisoners and Criminal Proceedings (Scotland) Act 1993;

"sexual offence" means—

(i) rape;

(ii) clandestine injury to women;

(iii) abduction of a woman or girl with intent to rape or ravish;

(iv) assault with intent to rape or ravish;

(v) indecent assault;

(vi) lewd, indecent or libidinous behaviour or practices;

(vii) shameless indecency;

(viii) sodomy;

(ix) an offence under section 170 of the Customs and Excise Management Act 1979 in relation to goods prohibited to be imported under section 42 of the Customs Consolidation Act 1876, but only where the prohibited goods include indecent photographs of persons;

(x) an offence under section 52 of the Civic Government (Scotland) Act 1982 (taking and distribution of indecent images of children);

(xi) an offence under section 52A of that Act (possession of indecent images of children);

(xii) an offence under section 1 of the Criminal Law (Consolidation) (Scotland) Act 1995 (incest);

(xiii) an offence under section 2 of that Act (intercourse with a stepchild);

(xiv) an offence under section 3 of that Act (intercourse with child under 16 by person in position of trust);

(xv) an offence under section 5 of that Act (unlawful intercourse with girl under 16);

(xvi) an offence under section 6 of that Act (indecent behaviour towards girl between 12 and 16);

(xvii) an offence under section 8 of that Act (abduction of girl under 18 for purposes of unlawful intercourse);

(xviii) an offence under section 10 of that Act (person having parental responsibilities causing or encouraging sexual activity in relation to a girl under 16); and

(xix) an offence under subsection (5) of section 13 of that Act (homosexual offences);

"imprisonment" includes—

(i) detention under section 207 of this Act; and

(ii) detention under section 208 of this Act; and

"violent offence" means any offence (other than an offence which is a sexual offence within the meaning of this section) inferring personal violence.

(11) Any reference in subsection (10) above to a sexual offence includes—

(a) a reference to any attempt, conspiracy or incitement to commit that offence; and

(b) except in the case of an offence in paragraphs (i) to (viii) of the definition of "sexual offence" in that subsection, a reference to aiding and abetting, counselling or procuring the commission of that offence.

DEFINITIONS
"indictment": s.307(1) of the 1995 Act.
"sexual offence": s.210A(8) of the 1995 Act as inserted by s.86(1) of the 1998 Act.
"violent offence": as last above.
"imprisonment": s.307(1) of the 1995 Act and s.210A(8) of that Act as inserted by s.86(1) of the 1998 Act.

NOTE
[1]Inserted by the Crime and Disorder Act 1998 (c. 37), s.86 (effective September 30, 1998: S.I. 1998 No. 2327).

GENERAL NOTE
These provisions came into force on September 30, 1998 in terms of the Crime and Disorder Act 1998 (Commencement No. 2 and Transitional Provisions) Order 1998 (S.I. 1998 No. 2327).

This section inserted into the 1995 Act as s.210A has to be read in conjunction with s.26A of the Prisoners and Criminal Proceedings (Scotland) Act 1993 (c. 9) which, confusingly, inserts "extended sentence" provisions into that latter Act.

Solemn courts imposing imprisonment for serious sexual offences or violent crimes attracting a term of imprisonment of four years or more now have a discretion to place the offender on licence, and thus subject to recall, when it is considered that the offender may pose a serious threat to public safety after his release.

(Section 87 of the 1998 Act is inserted into Pt I of the Prisoners and Criminal Proceedings (Scotland) Act 1993 and ss.12 and 17 of the 1993 Act set out the meaning of "licence"; however Scheds. 1 and 3 of the Crime and Punishment (Scotland) Act 1997 (c. 48) contain prospective changes to these sections.)

Henceforth courts opting to place an offender on licence for a qualifying offence will impose an extended sentence comprising the period of imprisonment or detention (dubbed "the custodial term") and a period of licence ("the extension term"). Subsection (10) by defining "imprisonment" under reference to ss.207 and 208 of the 1995 Act stipulates that these discretionary sentencing powers can be applied to children and young offenders as well as to adult offenders. The provisions can only apply to determinate sentences—those serving indeterminate sentences, *i.e.* life imprisonment, are dealt with separately.

It has to be emphasised that extended sentences are discretionary and, necessarily, only operate in circumstances where a term of imprisonment has been imposed on indictment and it is felt that the offender will constitute a threat to public safety on release and, then, subject to several qualifications. A common law "sexual offence" as defined by s.210A(10) can involve a period of licence of up to 10 years, while the extended sentence for a statutory "sexual offence" is to be not more than the maximum period of imprisonment statutorily provided for that offence, or the 10 year ceiling already mentioned, whichever is lower. It will be recalled that some statutory sexual offences, notably contraventions of ss.1 to 3 of the Criminal Law (Consolidation) (Scotland) Act 1995 (c. 39) can attract life imprisonment. It is submitted that s.210A(3) and (4) have to be read in conjunction.

The new provisions in s.210A in regard to violent offences only apply to sentences of over four years imprisonment, the point at which prisoners are regarded as long-term prisoners (see s.27 of the 1993 Act) and in such cases the "extension period" cannot exceed five years. If the violent offence has been a statutory crime then, again, the extension period will be the lower of either the maximum period of imprisonment available under statute, or five years, due to the interaction of s.210A(3) and (4). It is worth noting that subs. (6) empowers the Secretary of State to increase "the extension period" in relation to violent offences (but not sexual offences) from the five years set out in subs. (3)(b) up to 10 years, by order.

For those convicted of a violent offence and sentenced to less than four years' imprisonment the option open to the court is to impose a supervised release order; see s.209 above. Until the increased shrieval powers provided for, but never yet brought into force in s.13 of the 1997 Act are invoked, the practical effect of s.210A will be that only the High Court will be able to impose extended sentences in cases involving violence (see s.210A(1)(a)(ii)).

Fines

Fines

211.—(1) Where an accused who is convicted on indictment of any offence (whether triable only on indictment or triable either on indictment or summarily other than by virtue of section 292(6) of this Act) would apart from this subsection be liable to a fine of or not exceeding a specified amount, he shall by virtue of this subsection be liable to a fine of any amount.

(2) Where any Act confers a power by subordinate instrument to make a person liable on conviction on indictment of any offence mentioned in subsection (1) above to a fine or a maximum fine of a specified amount, or which shall not exceed a specified amount, the fine which may be imposed in the exercise of that power shall by virtue of this subsection be a fine of an unlimited amount.

(3) Any sentence or decree for any fine or expenses pronounced by a sheriff court or district court may be enforced against the person or effects of any party against whom the sentence or decree was awarded—

    (a) in the district where the sentence or decree was pronounced; or

    (b) in any other such district.

(4) A fine imposed by the High Court shall be remitted for enforcement to, and shall be enforceable as if it had been imposed by—

    (a) where the person upon whom the fine was imposed resides in Scotland, the sheriff for the district where that person resides; and

    (b) where that person resides outwith Scotland, the sheriff before whom he was brought for examination in relation to the offence for which the fine was imposed.

(5) Any fine imposed in the High Court on the accused, and on a juror for non-attendance, and any forfeiture for non-appearance of a party, witness or juror in the High Court shall be payable to and recoverable by the Treasury, except where the High Court orders that the whole or any part of the fine shall be otherwise disposed of.

(6) All fines and expenses imposed in summary proceedings under this Act shall be paid to the clerk of court to be accounted for by him to the person entitled to such fines and expenses, and it shall not be necessary to specify in any sentence the person entitled to payment of such fines or expenses unless it is necessary to provide for the division of the penalty.

(7) A court in determining the amount of any fine to be imposed on an offender shall take into consideration, amongst other things, the means of the offender so far as known to the court.

"fine": s.307(1).
"High Court": s.307(1).
"indictment": s.307(1).
"sentence": s.307(1).
"witness": s.307(1).

GENERAL NOTE
This section presumes as a generality the proposition that fines following conviction on indictment are unlimited subject to statutory maxima for certain offences. It is of some interest that the only item which is specified as being required to be taken into consideration in imposing a fine is "the means of the offender so far as known to the court": subs. (7).

Fines in summary proceedings

212.—(1) Where a court of summary jurisdiction imposes a fine on an offender, the court may order him to be searched, and any money found on him on apprehension or when so searched or when taken to prison or to a young offenders institution in default of payment of the fine, may, unless the court otherwise directs and subject to subsection (2) below, be applied towards payment of the fine, and the surplus if any shall be returned to him.

(2) Money shall not be applied as mentioned in subsection (1) above if the court is satisfied that it does not belong to the person on whom it was found or that the loss of the money will be more injurious to his family than his imprisonment or detention.

(3) When a court of summary jurisdiction, which has adjudged that a sum of money shall be paid by an offender, considers that any money found on the offender on apprehension, or after he has been searched by order of the court, should not be applied towards payment of such sum, the court, shall make a direction in writing to that effect which shall be written on the extract of the sentence which imposes the fine before it is issued by the clerk of the court.

(4) An accused may make an application to such a court either orally or in writing, through the governor of the prison in whose custody he may be at that time, that any sum of money which has been found on his person should not be applied in payment of the fine adjudged to be paid by him.

(5) A person who alleges that any money found on the person of an offender is not the property of the offender, but belongs to that person, may apply to such court either orally or in writing for a direction that the money should not be applied in payment of the fine adjudged to be paid, and the court after enquiry may so direct.

(6) A court of summary jurisdiction, which has adjudged that a sum of money shall be paid by an offender, may order the attendance in court of the offender, if he is in prison, for the purpose of ascertaining the ownership of money which has been found on his person.

(7) A notice in the form prescribed by Act of Adjournal, or as nearly as may be in such form, addressed to the governor of the prison in whose custody an offender may be at the time, signed by the judge of a court of summary jurisdiction shall be a sufficient warrant to the governor of such prison for conveying the offender to the court.

"court of summary jurisdiction": s.307(1).
"fine": s.307(1).

Act of Adjournal
The procedure set out in subs. (1) uses Form 20.4–A in the 1996 Act of Adjournal. The notice described in subs. (7) follows the style of Form 20.4–B in that Act of Adjournal.

Remission of fines

213.—(1) A fine may at any time be remitted in whole or in part by—

(a) in a case where a transfer of fine order under section 222 of this Act is effective and the court by which payment is enforceable is, in terms of the order, a court of summary jurisdiction in Scotland, that court; or

(b) in any other case, the court which imposed the fine or, where that court was the High Court, by which payment was first enforceable.

(2) Where the court remits the whole or part of a fine after imprisonment has been imposed under section 214(2) or (4) of this Act, it shall also remit the whole period of imprisonment or, as the case may be, reduce the period by an amount which bears the same proportion to the whole period as the amount remitted bears to the whole fine.

(3) The power conferred by subsection (1) above shall be exercisable without requiring the attendance of the accused.

DEFINITIONS
"court of summary jurisdiction": s.307(1).
"fine": s.307(1).
"High Court": s.307(1).

GENERAL NOTE
In *Tudhope v. Furphy*, 1982 S.C.C.R. 575 a sheriff held *inter alia* that he has power to reduce or extinguish a compensation order in circumstances where it had subsequently been discovered that the payee had died before the order was made.

Fines: time for payment and payment by instalments

214.—(1) Where a court has imposed a fine on an offender or ordered him to find caution the court shall, subject to subsection (2) below, allow him at least seven days to pay the fine or the first instalment thereof or, as the case may be, to find caution; and any reference in this section and section 216 of this Act to a failure to pay a fine or other like expression shall include a reference to a failure to find caution.

(2) If on the occasion of the imposition of a fine—

(a) the offender appears to the court to possess sufficient means to enable him to pay the fine forthwith; or

(b) on being asked by the court whether he wishes to have time for payment, he does not ask for time; or

(c) he fails to satisfy the court that he has a fixed abode; or

(d) the court is satisfied for any other special reason that no time should be allowed for payment,

the court may refuse him time to pay the fine and, if the offender fails to pay, may exercise its power to impose imprisonment and, if it does so, shall state the special reason for its decision.

(3) In all cases where time is not allowed by a court for payment of a fine, the reasons of the court for not so allowing time shall be stated in the extract of the finding and sentence as well as in the finding and sentence itself.

(4) Where time is allowed for payment of a fine or payment by instalments is ordered, the court shall not, on the occasion of the imposition of a fine, impose imprisonment in the event of a future default in paying the fine or an instalment thereof unless the offender is before it and the court determines that, having regard to the gravity of the offence or to the character of the offender, or to other special reason, it is expedient that he should be imprisoned without further inquiry in default of payment; and where a court so determines, it shall state the special reason for its decision.

(5) Where a court has imposed imprisonment in accordance with subsection (4) above, then, if at any time the offender asks the court to commit him to prison, the court may do so notwithstanding subsection (1) of this section.

(6) Nothing in the foregoing provisions of this section shall affect any power of the court to order a fine to be recovered by civil diligence.

(7) Where time has been allowed for payment of a fine imposed by the court, it may, on an application by or on behalf of the offender, and after giving the prosecutor an opportunity of being heard, allow further time for payment.

(8) Without prejudice to subsection (2) above, where a court has imposed a fine on an offender, the court may, of its own accord or on the application of the offender, order payment of that fine by instalments of such amounts and at such time as it may think fit.

(9) Where the court has ordered payment of a fine by instalments it may—
(a) allow further time for payment of any instalment thereof;
(b) order payment thereof by instalments of lesser amounts, or at longer intervals, than those originally fixed,

and the powers conferred by this subsection shall be exercisable without requiring the attendance of the accused.

DEFINITIONS
"caution": s.227.
"fine": s.307(1).

GENERAL NOTE
Subs. (1)
Although the references are to both fines and cautions in practice it is rare for cautions to be imposed. It is incompetent to offer the accused the alternative of making a donation to charity in lieu of a monetary fine (*Wilson v. Transorganics*, 1996 G.W.D. 10–560). The guidelines applicable to the length of time over which a fine may be paid do not apply when compensation orders are imposed (*Ely v. Donnelly*, 1996 S.C.C.R. 537).

Subs. (2)(a) and (d)
In *Barbour v. Robertson* and *Ram v. Robertson*, 1943 J.C. 46 it was observed that in applying these provisions the nature of the offence can never be a relevant consideration when determining whether time should be allowed for payment where a substantial monetary penalty is imposed; the only relevant matters are the means of the offender and similar considerations. Where the nature of the offence is such as to warrant a sentence of imprisonment, the proper course to adopt is to impose such a sentence either without the option of a fine or with a fine in addition, and not to impose merely a pecuniary penalty of such an amount that when no time is allowed for payment the imposition of the fine is equivalent to a sentence of imprisonment without the option of a fine. Accordingly, where a fine is felt to be appropriate it should be imposed even if the accused, rather than seeking no time to pay, states his intention not to pay (*Sheridan v. MacDonald*, 1996 G.W.D. 9–481).

Subs. (2)(b)
A court of summary jurisdiction, when imposing a fine, has a discretion to allow or refuse time to pay and may allow time for payment where that has not been requested by the accused: *Fraser v. Herron*, 1968 S.L.T. 149.

Subs. (2)(d)
For an example of special reasons being recorded in the minutes see *Sullivan v. Mcleod*, 1980 S.L.T. (Notes) 99.

Subs. (4)
The relevant cases may be considered under the different parts of the subsection.
"*Unless the offender is before it*". The decision in *Campbell v. Jessop*, 1988 S.L.T. 160 made it clear that the accused had to be present when a sentence of imprisonment was imposed. Not least of the reasons is that the absence of the accused meant that there was no opportunity for representations to be made by or for the accused.
"*Having regard to the offence*". In *Finnie v. Mcleod*, 1983 S.C.C.R. 387 "barefaced shoplifting" justified an immediate alternative of imprisonment in default of payment of the fine by instalments but in *Dunlop v. Allan*, 1984 S.C.C.R. 329 careless driving did not allow such action nor did drunk driving in *Buchanan v. Hamilton*, 1988 S.C.C.R. 379.

"*The character of the offender*". *Paterson v. McGlennan*, 1991 S.L.T. 832 illustrates the error of proceeding under this head with only one minor road traffic previous conviction.
"*Other special reason*". Merely to have time still to serve in prison and to be unable to pay fines are not to be regarded as "special reasons"; *Robertson v. Jessop*, 1989 S.L.T. 843.

Act of Adjournal
   Form 20.5 in the 1996 Act of Adjournal is used for the purposes of subs. (7) above and for s.215(3) below. See r. 20.5.

Application for further time to pay fine

   215.—(1) An application by an offender for further time in which to pay a fine imposed on him by a court, or of instalments thereof, shall be made, subject to subsection (2) below, to that court.
   (2) Where a transfer of fine order has been made under section 222 of this Act, section 90 of the Magistrates' Courts Act 1980 or Article 95 of the Magistrates' Courts (Northern Ireland) Order 1981, an application under subsection (1) above shall be made to the court specified in the transfer order, or to the court specified in the last transfer order where there is more than one transfer.
   (3) A court to which an application is made under this section shall allow further time for payment of the fine or of instalments thereof, unless it is satisfied that the failure of the offender to make payment has been wilful or that the offender has no reasonable prospect of being able to pay if further time is allowed.
   (4) An application made under this section may be made orally or in writing.

DEFINITION
   "fine": s.307(1).

Act of Adjournal
   Orders under subs. (3) follow the style set out in Form 20.5 to the 1996 Act of Adjournal. See r. 20.5.

Fines: restriction on imprisonment for default

   216.—(1) Where a court has imposed a fine or ordered the finding of caution without imposing imprisonment in default of payment, subject to subsection (2) below, it shall not impose imprisonment on an offender for failing to make payment of the fine or, as the case may be, to find caution, unless on an occasion subsequent to that sentence the court has enquired into in his presence the reason why the fine has not been paid or, as the case may be, caution has not been found.
   (2) Subsection (1) above shall not apply where the offender is in prison.
   (3) A court may, for the purpose of enabling enquiry to be made under this section—
      (a) issue a citation requiring the offender to appear before the court at a time and place appointed in the citation; or
      (b) issue a warrant of apprehension.
   (4) On the failure of the offender to appear before the court in response to a citation under this section, the court may issue a warrant of apprehension.
   (5) The citation of an offender to appear before a court in terms of subsection (3)(a) above shall be effected in like manner, *mutatis mutandis*, as the citation of an accused to a sitting or diet of the court under section 141 of this Act, and—
      (a) the citation shall be signed by the clerk of the court before which the offender is required to appear, instead of by the prosecutor; and

(b) the forms relating to the citation of an accused shall not apply to such citation.

(6) The following matters shall be, or as nearly as may be, in such form as is prescribed by Act of Adjournal—

(a) the citation of an offender under this section;

(b) if the citation of the offender is effected by an officer of law, the written execution, if any, of that officer of law;

(c) a warrant of apprehension issued by a court under subsection (4) above; and

(d) the minute of procedure in relation to an enquiry into the means of an offender under this section.

(7) Where a child would, if he were an adult, be liable to be imprisoned in default of payment of any fine the court may, if it considers that none of the other methods by which the case may legally be dealt with is suitable, order that the child be detained for such period, not exceeding one month, as may be specified in the order in a place chosen by the local authority in whose area the court is situated.

DEFINITIONS
"caution": s.227.
"fine": s.307(1).
"officer of law": s.307(1).
"prosecutor": s.307(1).

GENERAL NOTE
The power to imprison under this authority may be constrained by statute: see *Fraser v. Herron*, 1968 S.L.T. 149. The imposition of consecutive custodial sentences in default of payment has been doubted: *Stevenson v. McGlennan*, 1990 S.L.T. 842 and *Robertson v. Jessop*, 1989 S.L.T. 843. Imprisonment under this authority must be immediate imprisonment: *Craig v. Smith*, 1990 S.C.C.R. 328.

Act of Adjournal
Refer to r. 20.6 and to Forms 20.6–A to 20.6–C.

Fines: supervision pending payment

217.—(1) Where an offender has been allowed time for payment of a fine, the court may, either on the occasion of the imposition of the fine or on a subsequent occasion, order that he be placed under the supervision of such person, in this section referred to as the "supervising officer", as the court may from time to time appoint for the purpose of assisting and advising the offender in regard to payment of the fine.

(2) An order made in pursuance of subsection (1) above shall remain in force so long as the offender to whom it relates remains liable to pay the fine or any part of it unless the order ceases to have effect or is discharged under subsection (3) below.

(3) An order under this section shall cease to have effect on the making of a transfer of fine order under section 222 of this Act in respect of the fine or may be discharged by the court that made it without prejudice, in either case, to the making of a new order.

(4) Where an offender under 21 years of age has been allowed time for payment of a fine, the court shall not order the form of detention appropriate to him in default of payment of the fine unless—

(a) he has been placed under supervision in respect of the fine; or

(b) the court is satisfied that it is impracticable to place him under supervision.

(5) Where a court, on being satisfied as mentioned in subsection (4)(b)

above, orders the detention of a person under 21 years of age without an order under this section having been made, the court shall state the grounds on which it is so satisfied.

(6) Where an order under this section is in force in respect of an offender, the court shall not impose imprisonment in default of the payment of the fine unless before doing so it has—

(a) taken such steps as may be reasonably practicable to obtain from the supervising officer a report, which may be oral, on the offender's conduct and means, and has considered any such report; and

(b) in a case where an enquiry is required by section 216 of this Act, considered such enquiry.

(7) When a court appoints a different supervising officer under subsection (1) above, a notice shall be sent by the clerk of the court to the offender in such form, as nearly as may be, as is prescribed by Act of Adjournal.

(8) The supervising officer shall communicate with the offender with a view to assisting and advising him in regard to payment of the fine, and unless the fine or any instalment thereof is paid to the clerk of the court within the time allowed by the court for payment, the supervising officer shall report to the court without delay after the expiry of such time, as to the conduct and means of the offender.

DEFINITION
"fine": s.307(1).

Act of Adjournal
The notice specified in subs. (7), in accordance with r. 20.7 in the 1996 Act of Adjournal, is in the style set out in Form 20.7.

Fines: supplementary provisions as to payment

218.—(1) Where under the provisions of section 214 or 217 of this Act a court is required to state a special reason for its decision or the grounds on which it is satisfied that it is undesirable or impracticable to place an offender under supervision, the reason or, as the case may be, the grounds shall be entered in the record of the proceedings along with the finding and sentence.

(2) Any reference in the said sections 214 and 217 to imprisonment shall be construed, in the case of an offender on whom by reason of his age imprisonment may not lawfully be imposed, as a reference to the lawful form of detention in default of payment of a fine appropriate to that person, and any reference to prison shall be construed accordingly.

(3) Where a warrant has been issued for the apprehension of an offender for non-payment of a fine, the offender may, notwithstanding section 211(6) of this Act, pay such fine in full to a constable; and the warrant shall not then be enforced and the constable shall remit the fine to the clerk of court.

DEFINITIONS
"fine": s.307(1).
"impose imprisonment": s.307(1).

Fines: periods of imprisonment for non-payment

219.—(1) Subject to sections 214 to 218 of this Act—

(a) a court may, when imposing a fine, impose a period of imprisonment in default of payment; or

(b) where no order has been made under paragraph (a) above and a person fails to pay a fine, or any part or instalment of a fine, by the time ordered by the court (or, where section 214(2) of this Act applies, immediately) the court may, subject to section 235(1) of this Act, impose a period of imprisonment for such failure either with immediate effect or to take effect in the event of the person failing to

290

pay the fine or any part or instalment of it by such further time as the
court may order,
whether or not the fine is imposed under an enactment which makes
provision for its enforcement or recovery.

(2) Subject to the following subsections of this section, the maximum
period of imprisonment which may be imposed under subsection (1) above
or for failure to find caution, shall be as follows—

Amount of Fine or Caution	Maximum Period of Imprisonment
Not exceeding £200	7 days
Exceeding £200 but not exceeding £500	14 days
Exceeding £500 but not exceeding £1,000	28 days
Exceeding £1,000 but not exceeding £2,500	45 days
Exceeding £2,500 but not exceeding £5,000	3 months
Exceeding £5,000 but not exceeding £10,000	6 months
Exceeding £10,000 but not exceeding £20,000	12 months
Exceeding £20,000 but not exceeding £50,000	18 months
Exceeding £50,000 but not exceeding £100,000	2 years
Exceeding £100,000 but not exceeding £250,000	3 years
Exceeding £250,000 but not exceeding £1 Million	5 years
Exceeding £1 Million	10 years

(3) Where an offender is fined on the same day before the same court for
offences charged in the same indictment or complaint or in separate
indictments or complaints, the amount of the fine shall, for the purposes of
this section, be taken to be the total of the fines imposed.

(4) Where a court has imposed a period of imprisonment in default of
payment of a fine, and—
(a) an instalment of the fine is not paid at the time ordered; or
(b) part only of the fine has been paid within the time allowed for
payment,
the offender shall be liable to imprisonment for a period which bears to the
period so imposed the same proportion, as nearly as may be, as the amount
outstanding at the time when warrant is issued for imprisonment of the
offender in default bears to the original fine.

(5) Where no period of imprisonment in default of payment of a fine has
been imposed and—
(a) an instalment of the fine is not paid at the time ordered; or
(b) part only of the fine has been paid within the time allowed for
payment,
the offender shall be liable to imprisonment for a maximum period which
bears, as nearly as may be, the same proportion to the maximum period of
imprisonment which could have been imposed by virtue of the Table in
subsection (2) above in default of payment of the original fine as the amount
outstanding at the time when he appears before the court bears to the
original fine.

(6) If in any sentence or extract sentence the period of imprisonment
inserted in default of payment of a fine or on failure to find caution is in
excess of that competent under this Part of this Act, such period of
imprisonment shall be reduced to the maximum period under this Part of
this Act applicable to such default or failure, and the judge who pronounced
the sentence shall have power to order the sentence or extract to be
corrected accordingly.

(7) The provisions of this section shall be without prejudice to the operation of section 220 of this Act.

(8) Where in any case—

(a) the sheriff considers that the imposition of imprisonment for the number of years for the time being specified in section 3(3) of this Act would be inadequate; and

(b) the maximum period of imprisonment which may be imposed under subsection (1) above (or under that subsection as read with either or both of sections 252(2) of this Act and section 14(2) of the Proceeds of Crime (Scotland) Act 1995) exceeds that number of years,

he shall remit the case to the High Court for sentence.

<small>DEFINITIONS</small>
　"caution": s.227.
　"fine": s.307(1).
　"impose imprisonment": s.307(1).
　"order": s.307(1).

<small>GENERAL NOTE</small>
　The imposition of an immediate alternative of imprisonment (subs. (1)) was criticised by the Appeal Court in *Stephen v. McKay*, 1997 G.W.D. 21–1024, since although the accused had a bad record, there was no indication of a history of failure to pay fines.
　Subsection (8) provides a power of remit from the sheriff court to the High Court of Justiciary in addition to that under s.195(1). The general directions on the imposition of concurrent and consecutive sentences arising from several complaints or indictments are found in *Nicholson v. Lees*, 1996 S.C.C.R. 551.

Fines: part payment by prisoners

220.—(1) Where a person committed to prison or otherwise detained for failure to pay a fine imposed by a court pays to the governor of the prison, under conditions prescribed by rules made under the Prisons (Scotland) Act 1989, any sum in part satisfaction of the fine, the term of imprisonment shall be reduced (or as the case may be further reduced) by a number of days bearing as nearly as possible the same proportion to such term as the sum so paid bears to the amount of the fine outstanding at the commencement of the imprisonment.

(2) The day on which any sum is paid as mentioned in subsection (1) above shall not be regarded as a day served by the prisoner as part of the said term of imprisonment.

(3) All sums paid under this section shall be handed over on receipt by the governor of the prison to the clerk of the court in which the conviction was obtained, and thereafter paid and applied *pro tanto* in the same manner and for the same purposes as sums adjudged to be paid by the conviction and sentence of the court, and paid and recovered in terms thereof, are lawfully paid and applied.

(4) In this section references to a prison and to the governor thereof shall include respectively references to any other place in which a person may be lawfully detained in default of payment of a fine, and to an officer in charge thereof.

<small>DEFINITIONS</small>
　"fine": s.307(1).
　"governor": s.307(1).
　"prison": s.307(1).

Fines: recovery by civil diligence

221.—(1) Where any fine falls to be recovered by civil diligence in pursuance of this Act or in any case in which a court may think it expedient to order a fine to be recovered by civil diligence, there shall be added to the finding of the court imposing the fine a warrant for civil diligence in a form prescribed by Act of Adjournal which shall have the effect of authorising—

 (a) the charging of the person who has been fined to pay the fine within the period specified in the charge and, in the event of failure to make such payment within that period, the execution of an earnings arrestment and the poinding of articles belonging to him and, if necessary for the purpose of executing the poinding, the opening of shut and lockfast places;

 (b) an arrestment other than an arrestment of earnings in the hands of his employer,

and such diligence, whatever the amount of the fine imposed, may be executed in the same manner as if the proceedings were on an extract decree of the sheriff in a summary cause.

(2) Subject to subsection (3) below, proceedings by civil diligence under this section may be taken at any time after the imposition of the fine to which they relate.

(3) No such proceedings shall be authorised after the offender has been imprisoned in consequence of his having defaulted in payment of the fine.

(4) Where proceedings by civil diligence for the recovery of a fine or caution are taken, imprisonment for non-payment of the fine or for failure to find such caution shall remain competent and such proceedings may be authorised after the court has imposed imprisonment for, or in the event of, the non-payment or the failure but before imprisonment has followed such imposition.

DEFINITION
 "fine": s.307(1).

GENERAL NOTE
 Prior to the 1995 Act the primary use of civil diligence as a criminal sanction was against bodies corporate. Note however that s.303(2)(a)(i) below now provides that in the event of default in payment of a fiscal fine, recovery of sums outstanding is enforced by civil diligence rather than by means courts.

Act of Adjournal
 Form 20.8 in the 1996 Act of Adjournal appears to be the style approved for the purposes of subs. (1) above.

Transfer of fine orders

222.—(1) Where a court has imposed a fine on a person convicted of an offence and it appears to the court that he is residing—

 (a) within the jurisdiction of another court in Scotland; or

 (b) in any petty sessions area in England and Wales; or

 (c) in any petty sessions district in Northern Ireland,

the court may order that payment of the fine shall be enforceable by that other court or in that petty sessions area or petty sessions district as the case may be.

(2) An order under this section (in this section referred to as a "transfer of fine order") shall specify the court by which or the petty sessions area or petty sessions district in which payment is to be enforceable and, where the court to be specified in a transfer of fine order is a court of summary jurisdiction, it shall, in any case where the order is made by the sheriff court, be a sheriff court.

(3) Subject to subsections (4) and (5) below, where a transfer of fine order is made with respect to any fine under this section, any functions under any enactment relating to that sum which, if no such order had been made, would have been exercisable by the court which made the order or by the clerk of that court shall cease to be so exercisable.

(4) Where—

(a) the court specified in a transfer of fine order is satisfied, after inquiry, that the offender is not residing within the jurisdiction of that court; and

(b) the clerk of that court, within 14 days of receiving the notice required by section 223(1) of this Act, sends to the clerk of the court which made the order notice to that effect,

the order shall cease to have effect.

(5) Where a transfer of fine order ceases to have effect by virtue of subsection (4) above, the functions referred to in subsection (3) above shall again be exercisable by the court which made the order or, as the case may be, by the clerk of that court.

(6) Where a transfer of fine order under this section, section 90 of the Magistrates' Courts Act 1980 or Article 95 of the Magistrates' Courts (Northern Ireland) Order 1981 specifies a court of summary jurisdiction in Scotland, that court and the clerk of that court shall have all the like functions under this Part of this Act in respect of the fine or the sum in respect of which that order was made (including the power to make any further order under this section) as if the fine or the sum were a fine imposed by that court and as if any order made under this section, the said Act of 1980 or the said Order of 1981 in respect of the fine or the sum before the making of the transfer of fine order had been made by that court.

(7) The functions of the court to which subsection (6) above relates shall be deemed to include the court's power to apply to the Secretary of State under any regulations made by him under section 24(1)(a) of the Criminal Justice Act 1991 (power to deduct fines etc. from income support).

(8) Where a transfer of fine order under section 90 of the Magistrates' Courts Act 1980, Article 95 of the Magistrates' Courts (Northern Ireland) Order 1981, or this section provides for the enforcement by a sheriff court in Scotland of a fine imposed by the Crown Court, the term of imprisonment which may be imposed under this Part of this Act shall be the term fixed in pursuance of section 31 of the Powers of Criminal Courts Act 1973 by the Crown Court or a term which bears the same proportion to the term so fixed as the amount of the fine remaining due bears to the amount of the fine imposed by that court, notwithstanding that the term exceeds the period applicable to the case under section 219 of this Act.

DEFINITIONS
"fine": s.307(1).
"order": s.222(2).
"transfer of fine order": s.307(1).

Act of Adjournal
See r. 20.9 and Forms 20.9–A to 20.9–C in the 1996 Act of Adjournal.

Transfer of fines: procedure for clerk of court

223.—(1) Where a court makes a transfer of fine order under section 222 of this Act, the clerk of the court shall send to the clerk of the court specified in the order—

(a) a notice in the form prescribed by Act of Adjournal, or as nearly as may be in such form;

(b) a statement of the offence of which the offender was convicted; and

(c) a statement of the steps, if any, taken to recover the fine,

and shall give him such further information, if any, as, in his opinion, is likely to assist the court specified in the order in recovering the fine.

(2) In the case of a further transfer of fine order, the clerk of the court which made the order shall send to the clerk of the court by which the fine was imposed a copy of the notice sent to the clerk of the court specified in the order.

(3) The clerk of the court specified in a transfer of fine order shall, as soon as may be after he has received the notice mentioned in subsection (1)(a) above, send an intimation to the offender in the form prescribed by Act of Adjournal or as nearly as may be in such form.

(4) The clerk of court specified in a transfer of fine order shall remit or otherwise account for any payment received in respect of the fine to the clerk of the court by which the fine was imposed, and if the sentence has been enforced otherwise than by payment of the fine, he shall inform the clerk of court how the sentence was enforced.

DEFINITIONS
"fine": s.307(1).
"order": s.307(1).
"transfer of fine order": s.222(2).

Act of Adjournal
See r. 20.9 and Forms 20.9–A for subs. (1) and Form 20.9–B for subs. (2).

Discharge from imprisonment to be specified

224. All warrants of imprisonment in default of payment of a fine, or on failure to find caution, shall specify a period at the expiry of which the person sentenced shall be discharged, notwithstanding the fine has not been paid, or caution found.

DEFINITIONS
"caution": s.307(1).
"fine": s.307(1).

Penalties: standard scale, prescribed sum and uprating

225.—(1) There shall be a standard scale of fines for offences triable only summarily, which shall be known as "the standard scale".
(2) The standard scale is shown below—

Level on the scale	Amount of Fine
1	£ 200
2	£ 500
3	£1,000
4	£2,500
5	£5,000

(3) Any reference in any enactment, whenever passed or made, to a specified level on the standard scale shall be construed as referring to the amount which corresponds to that level on the standard scale referred to in subsection (2) above.

(4) If it appears to the Secretary of State that there has been a change in the value of money since the relevant date, he may by order substitute for the sum or sums for the time being specified in the provisions mentioned in subsection (5) below such other sum or sums as appear to him justified by the change.

(5) The provisions referred to in subsection (4) above are—
(a) subsection (2) above;
(b) subsection (8) below;
(c) section 219(2) of this Act;
(d) column 5 or 6 of Schedule 4 to the Misuse of Drugs Act 1971 so far as the column in question relates to the offences under provisions of that Act specified in column 1 of that Schedule in respect of which the

maximum fines were increased by Part II of Schedule 8 to the Criminal Justice and Public Order Act 1994.

(6) In subsection (4) above "the relevant date" means—

(a) in relation to the first order made under that subsection, the date the last order was made under section 289D(1) of the Criminal Procedure (Scotland) Act 1975; and

(b) in relation to each subsequent order, the date of the previous order.

(7) An order under subsection (4) above—

(a) shall be made by statutory instrument subject to annulment in pursuance of a resolution of either House of Parliament and may be revoked by a subsequent order thereunder; and

(b) without prejudice to Schedule 14 to the Criminal Law Act 1977, shall not affect the punishment for an offence committed before that order comes into force.

(8) In this Act "the prescribed sum" means £5,000 or such sum as is for the time being substituted in this definition by an order in force under subsection (4) above.

DEFINITIONS
"fine": s.307(1).
"prescribed sum": s.225(8).
"relevant date": s.225(4).
"standard scale": s.225(1).

Penalties: exceptionally high maximum fines

226.—(1) The Secretary of State may by order amend an enactment specifying a sum to which this subsection applies so as to substitute for that sum such other sum as appears to him—

(a) to be justified by a change in the value of money appearing to him to have taken place since the last occasion on which the sum in question was fixed; or

(b) to be appropriate to take account of an order altering the standard scale which has been made or is proposed to be made.

(2) Subsection (1) above applies to any sum which—

(a) is higher than level 5 on the standard scale; and

(b) is specified as the fine or the maximum fine which may be imposed on conviction of an offence which is triable only summarily.

(3) The Secretary of State may by order amend an enactment specifying a sum to which this subsection applies so as to substitute for that sum such other sum as appears to him—

(a) to be justified by a change in the value of money appearing to him to have taken place since the last occasion on which the sum in question was fixed; or

(b) to be appropriate to take account of an order made or proposed to be made altering the statutory maximum.

(4) Subsection (3) above applies to any sum which—

(a) is higher than the statutory maximum; and

(b) is specified as the maximum fine which may be imposed on summary conviction of an offence triable either on indictment or summarily.

(5) An order under this section—

(a) shall be made by statutory instrument subject to annulment in pursuance of a resolution of either House of Parliament; and

(b) shall not affect the punishment for an offence committed before that order comes into force.

(6) In this section "enactment" includes an enactment contained in an Act

or subordinate instrument passed or made after the commencement of this Act.

DEFINITIONS
  "enactment": s.226(6) and s.307(1).
  "fine": s.307(1).
  "standard scale": s.225(1).

Caution

Caution

227. Where a person is convicted on indictment of an offence (other than an offence the sentence for which is fixed by law) the court may, instead of or in addition to imposing a fine or a period of imprisonment, ordain the accused to find caution for good behaviour for a period not exceeding 12 months and to such amount as the court considers appropriate.

DEFINITIONS
  "fine": s.307(1).
  "impose imprisonment": s.307(1).
  "indictment": s.307(1).
  "offence": s.307(1).

Probation

Probation orders

228.—(1) Subject to subsection (2) below, where an accused is convicted of an offence (other than an offence the sentence for which is fixed by law) the court if it is of the opinion that it is expedient to do so—
  (a) having regard to the circumstances, including the nature of the offence and the character of the offender; and
  (b) having obtained a report as to the circumstances and character of the offender,
may, instead of sentencing him, make an order requiring the offender to be under supervision for a period to be specified in the order of not less than six months nor more than three years; and such an order is, in this Act, referred to as a "probation order".

  (2) A court shall not make a probation order under subsection (1) above unless it is satisfied that suitable arrangements for the supervision of the offender can be made—
  (a) in a case other than that mentioned in paragraph (b) below, by the local authority in whose area he resides or is to reside; or
  (b) in a case where, by virtue of section 234(1) of this Act, subsections (3) and (4) below would not apply, by the probation committee for the area which contains the petty sessions area which would be named in the order.

  (3) A probation order shall be as nearly as may be in the form prescribed by Act of Adjournal, and shall—
  (a) name the local authority area in which the offender resides or is to reside; and
  (b) subject to subsection (4) below, make provision for the offender to be under the supervision of an officer of the local authority of that area.

  (4) Where the offender resides or is to reside in a local authority area in which the court which makes the order has no jurisdiction, the court shall name the appropriate court (being such a court as could have been named in

297

any amendment of the order in accordance with Schedule 6 to this Act) in the area of residence or intended residence, and the appropriate court shall require the local authority for that area to arrange for the offender to be under the supervision of an officer of that authority.

(5) Before making a probation order, the court shall explain to the offender in ordinary language—

(a) the effect of the order, including any additional requirements proposed to be inserted under section 229 or 230 of this Act; and

(b) that if he fails to comply with the order or commits another offence during the probation period he will be liable to be sentenced for the original offence,

and the court shall not make the order unless the offender expresses his willingness to comply with the requirements thereof.

(6) The clerk of the court by which a probation order is made or of the appropriate court, as the case may be, shall—

(a) cause copies of the probation order to be given to the officer of the local authority who is to supervise the probationer and to the person in charge of any institution or place in which the probationer is required to reside under the probation order; and

(b) cause a copy thereof to be given to the probationer or sent to him by registered post or by the recorded delivery service; and an acknowledgement or certificate of delivery of a letter containing such copy order issued by the Post Office shall be sufficient evidence of the delivery of the letter on the day specified in such acknowledgement or certificate.

DEFINITIONS

"local authority": s.307(1).
"offence": s.307(1).
"probation order": s.228(1).

GENERAL NOTE

In *Downie v. Irvine*, 1964 J.C. 52 it was held that a probation order and a sentence of imprisonment were wholly inconsistent and could not stand together. However in *Walker v. McGlennan*, 1997 G.W.D. 8–310, such a sentence was approved by the Appeal Court (albeit the term of imprisonment was reduced from six to three months) where the accused had been drunk and threatening when attending a social work office, in relation to the preparation of a report for earlier offences; the object was to provide a drying out period and early probation support.

Act of Adjournal

Refer to r. 20.10 of the 1996 Act of Adjournal. The form for a probation order is laid out in Form 20.10–A in the 1996 Act of Adjournal.

Probation orders: additional requirements

229.—(1) Subject to section 230 of this Act, a probation order may require the offender to comply during the whole or any part of the probation period with such requirements as the court, having regard to the circumstances of the case, considers—

(a) conducive to securing the good conduct of the offender or for preventing a repetition by him of the offence or the commission of other offences; or

(b) where the probation order is to include such a requirement as is mentioned in subsection (4) or (6) below, conducive to securing or, as the case may be, preventing the matters mentioned in paragraph (a) above.

(2) Without prejudice to the generality of subsection (1) above, a

probation order may, subject to subsection (3) below, include requirements relating to the residence of the offender.

(3) In relation to a probation order including a requirement such as is mentioned in subsection (2) above—

    (a) before making the order, the court shall consider the home surroundings of the offender; and

    (b) if the order requires the offender to reside in any institution or place, the name of the institution or place and the period for which he is so required to reside shall be specified in the order, and that period shall not extend beyond 12 months from the date of the requirement or beyond the date when the order expires.

(4) Without prejudice to the generality of subsection (1) above, where an offender has been convicted of an offence punishable by imprisonment and a court which is considering making a probation order—

    (a) is satisfied that the offender is of or over 16 years of age and that the conditions specified in paragraphs (a) and (c) of section 238(2) of this Act for the making of a community service order have been met;

    (b) has been notified by the Secretary of State that arrangements exist for persons who reside in the locality where the offender resides, or will be residing when the probation order comes into force, to perform unpaid work as a requirement of a probation order; and

    (c) is satisfied that provision can be made under the arrangements mentioned in paragraph (b) above for the offender to perform unpaid work under the probation order,

it may include in the probation order, in addition to any other requirement, a requirement that the offender shall perform unpaid work for such number of hours (being in total not less than 40 nor more than 240) as may be specified in the probation order.

(5) Sections 238 (except subsections (1), (2)(b) and (d) and (4)(b)), 239(1) to (3), and 240 of this Act shall apply, subject to any necessary modifications, to a probation order including a requirement such as is mentioned in subsection (4) above as they apply to a community service order, and in the application of subsection (5) of the said section 238 for the words "subsection (1) above" there shall be substituted the words "subsection (4) of section 229 of this Act".

(6) Without prejudice to the generality of subsection (1) above, where a court is considering making a probation order it may include in the probation order, in addition to any other requirement, a requirement that the offender shall pay compensation either in a lump sum or by instalments for any personal injury, loss or damage caused (whether directly or indirectly) by the acts which constituted the offence; and the following provisions of this Act shall apply to such a requirement as if any reference in them to a compensation order included a reference to a requirement to pay compensation under this subsection—

    section 249(3) to (5), (8) to (10);

    section 250(2);

    section 251(1) and (2)(b);

    section 253.

(7) Where the court imposes a requirement to pay compensation under subsection (6) above—

    (a) it shall be a condition of a probation order containing such a requirement that payment of the compensation shall be completed not more than 18 months after the making of the order or not later than two months before the end of the period of probation, whichever first occurs;

    (b) the court, on the application of the offender or the officer of the local authority responsible for supervising the offender, may vary the terms of the requirement, including the amount of any instalments, in consequence of any change which may have occurred in the circumstances of the offender; and

(c) in any proceedings for breach of a probation order where the breach consists only in the failure to comply with a requirement to pay compensation, a document purporting to be a certificate signed by the clerk of the court for the time being having jurisdiction in relation to the order that the compensation or, where payment by instalments has been allowed, any instalment has not been paid shall be sufficient evidence of such breach.

DEFINITIONS
"compensation": s.229(6).
"offence": s.307(1).
"probation order": s.228(1).

GENERAL NOTE
In *H.M. Advocate v. Jamieson*, 1997 S.L.T. 955, a conviction of assault to severe injury and danger of life, the Crown appealed as unduly lenient, a probation order for 12 months allied to 240 hours community service and a compensation order of £3,000 payable within 12 months. The Appeal Court upheld the Crown contention that s.229(7)(a) requried that the compensation order should have been ordered to be paid in full within 10 months, *i.e.* two months before the expiry of the probation order. While agreeing that the sentence imposed was indeed unduly lenient, the Court paid heed to the substantial number of hours of community service the accused had completed and the fact that £2,200 had not only been paid by him, but mistakenly had been paid to the victim by the Sheriff Clerk; the appeal was refused.

Probation orders: requirement of treatment for mental condition

[1]**230.**—(1) Where the court is satisfied, on the evidence of a registered medical practitioner approved for the purposes of section 20 or 39 of the Mental Health (Scotland) Act 1984, that the mental condition of an offender is such as requires and may be susceptible to treatment but is not such as to warrant his detention in pursuance of a hospital order under Part V of that Act, or under this Act, the court may, if it makes a probation order, include a requirement that the offender shall submit, for such period, not extending beyond 12 months from the date of the requirement, as may be specified in the order, to treatment by or under the direction of a registered medical practitioner or chartered psychologist with a view to the improvement of the offender's mental condition.

(2) The treatment required by virtue of subsection (1) above shall be such one of the following kinds of treatment as may be specified in the order, that is to say—

(a) treatment as a resident patient in a hospital within the meaning of the said Act of 1984, not being a State hospital within the meaning of the Act;

(b) treatment as a non-resident patient at such institution or place as may be specified in the order; or

(c) treatment by or under the direction of such registered medical practitioner or chartered psychologist as may be specified in the order,

but otherwise the nature of the treatment shall not be specified in the order.

(3) A court shall not make a probation order containing a requirement under subsection (1) above unless it is satisfied that arrangements have been made for the treatment intended to be specified in the order, and, if the offender is to be treated as a resident patient, for his reception.

(4) Where the registered medical practitioner or chartered psychologist by whom or under whose direction a probationer is receiving any of the

kinds of treatment to which he is required to submit in pursuance of a probation order is of the opinion—

(a) that the probationer requires, or that it would be more appropriate for him to receive, a different kind of treatment (whether in whole or in part) from that which he has been receiving, being treatment of a kind which subject to subsection (5) below could have been specified in the probation order; or

(b) that the treatment (whether in whole or in part) can be more appropriately given in or at a different institution or place from that where he has been receiving treatment in pursuance of the probation order,

he may, subject to subsection (6) below, make arrangements for the probationer to be treated accordingly.

(5) Arrangements made under subsection (4) above may provide for the probationer to receive his treatment (in whole or in part) as a resident patient in an institution or place notwithstanding that it is not one which could have been specified for that purpose in the probation order.

(6) Arrangements shall not be made under subsection (4) above unless—

(a) the probationer and any officer responsible for his supervision agree;

(b) the treatment will be given by or under the direction of a registered medical practitioner or chartered psychologist who has agreed to accept the probationer as his patient; and

(c) where such treatment entails the probationer's being a resident patient, he will be received as such.

(7) Where any such arrangements as are mentioned in subsection (4) above are made for the treatment of a probationer—

(a) any officer responsible for the probationer's supervision shall notify the appropriate court of the arrangements; and

(b) the treatment provided for by the arrangements shall be deemed to be treatment to which he is required to submit in pursuance of the probation order.

(8) Subsections (3) to (5) of section 61 of this Act shall apply for the purposes of this section as if for the reference in subsection (3) to section 58(1)(a) of this Act there were substituted a reference to subsection (1) above.

(9) Except as provided by this section, a court shall not make a probation order requiring a probationer to submit to treatment for his mental condition.

DEFINITIONS
"chartered psychologist": s.307(1).
"hospital": s.307(1).
"probation order": s.228(1).
"registered medical practitioner": s.2 of the Medicine Act 1968.
"State hospital": s.307(1).

NOTE
[1]Prospectively amended by the Adults with Incapacity (Scotland) Act (asp 4), s.88 and Sched. 6.

Probation orders: amendment and discharge

231.—(1) Schedule 6 to this Act shall have effect in relation to the discharge and amendment of probation orders.

(2) Where, under section 232 of this Act, a probationer is sentenced for the offence for which he was placed on probation, the probation order shall cease to have effect.

DEFINITION
"probation order": s.228(1).

Probation orders: failure to comply with requirement

232.—(1) If, on information from—

(a) the officer supervising the probationer;

(b) the chief social work officer of the local authority whose officer is supervising the probationer; or

(c) an officer appointed by the chief social work officer to act on his behalf for the purposes of this subsection,

it appears to the court which made the probation order or to the appropriate court that the probationer has failed to comply with any requirement of the order, that court may issue a warrant for the arrest of the probationer, or may, if it thinks fit, instead of issuing such a warrant in the first instance, issue a citation requiring the probationer to appear before the court at such time as may be specified in the citation.

(2) If it is proved to the satisfaction of the court before which a probationer appears or is brought in pursuance of subsection (1) above that he has failed to comply with a requirement of the probation order, the court may—

(a) except in the case of a failure to comply with a requirement to pay compensation and without prejudice to the continuance in force of the probation order, impose a fine not exceeding level 3 on the standard scale; or

(b) sentence the offender for the offence for which the order was made; or

(c) vary any of the requirements of the probation order, so however that any extension of the probation period shall terminate not later than three years from the date of the probation order; or

(d) without prejudice to the continuance in force of the probation order, in a case where the conditions required by sections 238 to 244 of this Act are satisfied, make a community service order, and those sections shall apply to such an order as if the failure to comply with the requirement of the probation order were the offence in respect of which the order had been made.

(3) For the purposes of subsection (2) above, evidence of one witness shall be sufficient evidence.

(4) A fine imposed under this section in respect of a failure to comply with the requirements of a probation order shall be deemed for the purposes of any enactment to be a sum adjudged to be paid by or in respect of a conviction or a penalty imposed on a person summarily convicted.

(5) A probationer who is required by a probation order to submit to treatment for his mental condition shall not be deemed for the purpose of this section to have failed to comply with that requirement on the ground only that he has refused to undergo any surgical, electrical or other treatment if, in the opinion of the court, his refusal was reasonable having regard to all the circumstances.

(6) Without prejudice to section 233 of this Act, a probationer who is convicted of an offence committed during the probation period shall not on that account be liable to be dealt with under this section for failing to comply with any requirement of the probation order.

(7) The citation of a probationer to appear before a court of summary jurisdiction in terms of subsection (1) above or section 233(1) of this Act shall be effected in like manner, *mutatis mutandis*, as the citation of an accused to a sitting or diet of the court under section 141 of this Act.

Definitions

"community service order": s.307(1).

"court of summary jurisdiction": s.307(1).

"fine": s.307(1).

"local authority": s.307(1).

"probation order": s.228(1).

"probationer": s.307(1).
"sentence": s.307(1).
"standard scale": s.225(1).

Act of Adjournal
Refer to r. 20.10 in the 1996 Act of Adjournal.
The form used for citing an offender for failure to comply with a probation order, or for further offending, is Form 20.10–B in the 1996 Act of Adjournal.
Note that r. 20.17 permits the use of certified copies of probation orders in any relevant proceedings before a court other than the court which imposed the order.

Probation orders: commission of further offence

233.—(1) If it appears to—
  (a) the court which made a probation order; or, as the case may be,
  (b) the appropriate court,
in this section referred to as "the court", that the probationer to whom the order relates has been convicted by a court in any part of Great Britain of an offence committed during the probation period and has been dealt with for that offence, the court may issue a warrant for the arrest of the probationer, or may, if it thinks fit, instead of issuing such a warrant in the first instance issue a citation requiring the probationer to appear before the court at such time as may be specified in the citation, and on his appearance or on his being brought before the court, the court may, if it thinks fit, deal with him under section 232(2)(b) of this Act.

(2) Where a probationer is convicted by the court of an offence committed during the probation period, the court may, if it thinks fit, deal with him under section 232(2)(b) of this Act for the offence for which the order was made as well as for the offence committed during the period of probation.

(3) Where—
  (a) a court has, under section 229(4) of this Act, included in a probation order a requirement that an offender shall perform unpaid work; and
  (b) the offender is convicted of an offence committed in the circumstances mentioned in subsection (4) below,
the court which sentences him for the offence shall, in determining the appropriate sentence for that offence, have regard to the fact that the offence was committed in those circumstances.

(4) The circumstances referred to in subsection (3) above are that the offence was committed—
  (a) during the period that the offender was subject to a requirement to perform unpaid work or within the period of three months following the expiry of that period; and
  (b) in any place where the unpaid work was being or had previously been performed.

(5) The court shall not, under subsection (3) above, have regard to the fact that the offence was committed in the circumstances mentioned in subsection (4) above unless that fact is libelled in the indictment or, as the case may be, specified in the complaint.

[1](6) The fact that the offence mentioned in subsection (3)(b) above was committed in the circumstances mentioned in subsection (4) above shall, unless challenged—
  (a) in the case of proceedings on indictment, by giving notice of a preliminary objection under paragraph (b) of section 72(1) of this Act or under that paragraph as applied by section 71(2) of this Act; or
  (b) in summary proceedings, by preliminary objection before his plea is recorded,
be held as admitted.

Criminal Procedure (Scotland) Act 1995

DEFINITIONS
"complaint": s.307(1).
"indictment": s.307(1).
"probation order": s.228(1).
"probationer": s.307(1).

NOTE
[1]Inserted by the Crime and Punishment (Scotland) Act 1997 (c. 48) s.26(1) and given effect from August 1, 1997 by the Crime and Punishment (Scotland) Act 1997 (Commencement and Transitional Provisions) Order 1997 (S.I. 1997 No. 1712) para. 3.

GENERAL NOTE
Subsection (2) above empowers a court before which the probationer appears for offending during the period of probation to sentence both the offences in respect of which the order had been made, and the fresh offences. Subsection (3), which originated in s.40 of the Criminal Justice (Scotland) Act 1995, creates a specific aggravating offence where a probationer on placement, during its currency or within three months of its expiry, commits an offence at that place. (A similar provision in relation to community service order placements is found in s.241(2), below); it is vital to note that the aggravation only arises if it is expressly libelled in the body of the complaint or indictment, failing which the court can have no regard to the aggravating factor. Two points spring to mind; first, it is submitted that like a disqualification from driving, the fact of being a probationer in terms of subs. (3) would fall to be regarded as a special capacity; secondly, that the commission of a relevant offence under subs. (3) would have to be libelled on a separate complaint or indictment from other charges much as is done with charges of disqualified driving. Neither point is yet settled but it is not difficult to envisage situations, for example where the Crown was relying upon the *Moorov* doctrine, in which the prosecutor might have to make a conscious decision to sacrifice the aggravating nature of the offence simply to achieve a conviction; it is doubtful that that was what the legislature had in mind.
The introduction of subs. (6) goes a little way towards easing the burden of proof by, in effect, treating the commission of an offence at a designated workplace within three months as a special capacity which, unless challenged need not be proved by the Crown. However the fact remains that the special capacity will have to be libelled in the body of the charge.

Act of Adjournal
See the note at A4.465 above.

Probation orders: persons residing in England and Wales

234.—(1) Where the court which made a probation order to which this subsection applies is satisfied that the offender has attained the age of 16 years and resides or will reside in England and Wales, subsections (3) and (4) of section 228 of this Act shall not apply to the order, but—
(a) the order shall contain a requirement that he be under the supervision of a probation officer appointed for or assigned to the petty sessions area in which the offender resides or will reside; and
(b) that area shall be named in the order,
and where the order includes a requirement that the probationer performs unpaid work for a number of hours, the number specified shall not exceed one hundred.
[2](2) Subsection (1) above applies to a probation order which is made under the said section 228 but does not include a requirement which would, if made, correspond to a requirement mentioned in paragraph 2 or 3 of Schedule 2 to the 2000 Act, but would, if included in a probation order made under that Act, fail to accord with a restriction as to days of presentation, participation or attendance mentioned in paragraph 2(4)(a) or (6)(a), or as the case may be 3(4)(a), of that Schedule.
(3) Where a probation order has been made under the said section 228 and the court in Scotland which made the order or the appropriate court is satisfied—
(a) that the probationer has attained the age of 16 years;
(b) that he proposes to reside, or is residing, in England and Wales; and

(c) that suitable arrangements for his supervision can be made by the probation committee for the area which contains the petty sessions area in which he resides or will reside,

the power of that court to amend the order under Schedule 6 to this Act shall include power to insert the provisions required by subsection (1) above or to vary any requirement for performance of unpaid work so that such hours as remain to be worked do not exceed one hundred, and the court may so amend the order without summoning the probationer and without his consent.

[3](4) A probation order made or amended by virtue of this section may, notwithstanding section 230(9) of this Act, include a requirement that the probationer shall submit to treatment for his mental condition, and—

(a) subsections (1), (3) and (8) of the said section 230 and paragraph 5(3) of Schedule 2 to the 2000 Act (all of which regulate the making of probation orders which include any such requirement) shall apply to the making of an order which includes any such requirement by virtue of this subsection as they apply to the making of an order which includes any such requirement by virtue of the said section 230 and paragraph 5 of the said Schedule 2 respectively; and

(b) sub-paragraphs (5) to (7) of the said paragraph 5 (functions of supervising officer and registered medical practitioner where such a requirement has been imposed) shall apply in relation to a probationer who is undergoing treatment in England and Wales in pursuance of a requirement imposed by virtue of this subsection as they apply in relation to a probationer undergoing such treatment in pursuance of a requirement imposed by virtue of that section.

[4](5) Sections 231(1) and 232(1) of this Act shall not apply to any order made or amended under this section; but subject to subsection (6) below, Schedule 3 to the 2000 Act shall apply to the order—

(a) except in the case mentioned in paragraph (b) below, as if that order were a probation order made under section 41 of that Act; and

(b) in the case of an order which contains a requirement such as is mentioned in section 229(4) of this Act, as if it were a combination order made under section 51 of that Act.

[5](6) Part III of Schedule 3 to the 2000 Act shall not apply as mentioned in subsection (5) above; and sub-paragraphs (4) and (5) of paragraph 4 of that Schedule shall so apply as if for the first reference in the said sub-paragraph (4) to the Crown Court there were substituted a reference to a court in Scotland and for other references in those sub-paragraphs to the Crown Court there were substituted references to the court in Scotland.

(7) If it appears on information to a justice acting for the petty sessions area named in a probation order made or amended under this section that the person to whom the order relates has been convicted by a court in any part of Great Britain of an offence committed during the period specified in the order he may issue—

(a) a summons requiring that person to appear, at the place and time specified in the summons, before the court in Scotland which made the probation order; or

(b) if the information is in writing and on oath, a warrant for his arrest, directing that person to be brought before the last-mentioned court.

(8) If a warrant for the arrest of a probationer issued under section 233 of this Act by a court is executed in England and Wales and the probationer cannot forthwith be brought before that court, the warrant shall have effect as if it directed him to be brought before a magistrates' court for the place where he is arrested; and the magistrates' court shall commit him to custody or release him on bail (with or without sureties) until he can be brought or appear before the court in Scotland.

[1](9) The court by which a probation order is made or amended in

accordance with the provisions of this section shall send three copies of the order to the clerk to the justices for the petty sessions area named in the order, together with such documents and information relating to the case as it considers likely to be of assistance to the court acting for that petty sessions area.

[6](10) Where a probation order which is amended under subsection (3) above is an order to which the provisions of this Act apply by virtue of paragraph 6 of Schedule 4 to the 2000 Act (which relates to probation orders under that Act relating to persons residing in Scotland) then, notwithstanding anything in that Schedule or this section, the order shall, as from the date of the amendment, have effect in all respects as if it were an order made under section 41 of that Act in the case of a person residing in England and Wales.

[7](11) In this section "the 2000 Act" means the Powers of Criminal Courts (Sentencing) Act 2000.

DEFINITIONS
"probation order": s.307(1).
"probationer": s.307(1).

NOTES
[1]Prospectively amended by the Access to Justice 1999 (c.22), s.90 and Sched. 13, para.175.
[2]As amended by the Powers of Criminal Courts (Sentencing) Act 2000 (c.6), s.165 and Sched. 9, para. 176(2)(a) and (b).
[3]As amended by the Powers of Criminal Courts (Sentencing) Act 2000 (c.6), s.165 and Sched. 9, para. 176(3)(a) and (b).
[4]As amended by the Powers of Criminal Courts (Sentencing) Act 2000 (c.6), s.165 and Sched. 9, para. 176(4)(a), (b) and (c).
[5]As amended by the Powers of Criminal Courts (Sentencing) Act 2000 (c.6), s.165 and Sched. 9, para. 176(5)(a), (b) and (c).
[6]As amended by the Powers of Criminal Courts (Sentencing) Act 2000 (c.6), s.165 and Sched. 9, para. 176(6)(a) and (b).
[7]As substituted by the Powers of Criminal Courts (Sentencing) Act 2000 (c.6), s.165 and Sched. 9, para. 176(7).

Non-harassment orders

[1]**234A.**—(1) Where a person is convicted of an offence involving harassment of a person ("the victim"), the prosecutor may apply to the court to make a non-harassment order against the offender requiring him to refrain from such conduct in relation to the victim as may be specified in the order for such period (which includes an indeterminate period) as may be so specified, in addition to any other disposal which may be made in relation to the offence.

(2) On an application under subsection (1) above the court may, if it is satisfied on a balance of probabilities that it is appropriate to do so in order to protect the victim from further harassment, make a non-harassment order.

(3) A non-harassment order made by a criminal court shall be taken to be a sentence for the purposes of any appeal and, for the purposes of this subsection "order" includes any variation or revocation of such an order made under subsection (6) below.

(4) Any person who is found to be in breach of a non-harassment order shall be guilty of an offence and liable—
  (a) on conviction on indictment, to imprisonment for a term not exceeding 5 years or to a fine, or to both such imprisonment and such fine; and
  (b) on summary conviction, to imprisonment for a period not exceeding 6 months or to a fine not exceeding the statutory maximum, or to both such imprisonment and such fine.

[2](5) ...

(6) The person against whom a non-harassment order is made, or the prosecutor at whose instance the order is made, may apply to the court which made the order for its revocation or variation and, in relation to any such application the court concerned may, if it is satisfied on a balance of probabilities that it is appropriate to do so, revoke the order or vary it in such manner as it thinks fit, but not so as to increase the period for which the order is to run.

(7) For the purposes of this section "harassment" shall be construed in accordance with section 8 of the Protection from Harassment Act 1997.

DEFINITIONS
"offence": s.307(1)
"harassment": s.8 of the Protection from Harassment Act 1997 (c. 40)
"prosecutor": s.307(1)
"sentence": s.307(1)
"indictment": s.307(1)
"imprisonment": s.307(1)
"fine": s.307(1)

NOTES
[1]Inserted by the Protection from Harassment Act 1997 (c. 40), s.11.
[2]Repealed by the Crime and Punishment (Scotland) Act 1997 (c. 48), s.62(1) and Sched. 1, para. 21(30) with effect from August 1, 1997 in terms of the Crime and Punishment (Scotland) Act 1997 (Commencement and Transitional Provisions) Order (S.I. 1997 No. 1712) para. 3.

GENERAL NOTE
The Protection from Harassment Act 1997 was directed at the prevention of stalking, anti-social behaviour by neighbours and racial harassment: *Tuppen v. Microsoft Corporation Ltd,* The Times Law Reports, November 15, 2000. This decision was based on a study of the relevant speeches in Hansard of the Government Ministers at the time the Bill was going through the Westminster Parliament.

This section, inserted by s.11 of the Protection from Harassment Act 1997, empowers both civil and criminal courts in Scotland to make a "non-harassment order" against an offending party. In the criminal courts, an order may only be granted on the motion of the prosecutor with the object of preventing any future misconduct, but can be made in addition to, or as, the disposal imposed in the proceedings. It is clear that an order can only be imposed when the conviction indicates misconduct on at least two occasions—the "course of conduct" specified in s.8(3) of the Protection from Harassment Act 1997; see *McGlennan v. McKinnon,* 1998 S.L.T. 494. It is notable that the Appeal Court rejected Crown attempts to found upon extract complaints and previous convictions as evidencing a course of conduct and that the Lord Justice General highlighted the need for carefully considered drafting of charges where a non-harassment order was likely to be sought. Given these limitations, in some instances it may well be more fruitful for a complainer to raise civil proceedings under the Protection from Harassment Act 1997.

A number of features are notable: firstly, the court has to be satisfied of the need for an order only on the balance of probabilities as a means of protecting an identified victim (subs. (2)); secondly, it is open to the prosecutor to appeal to the High Court against a court's refusal to impose an order, or it is submitted, to appeal the terms of the order itself—this based on a broad reading of "application" as defined in subs. (1); thirdly, either the prosecutor at whose initiative the order was imposed or the offender subject of the order (but not the victim specified in it) may apply to the court for variation or revocation of the order. It is not competent to extend the duration of an order by application, appeal in terms of subs. (5) being the only method by which this can be done.

A broad construction of subs. (1), and practice, would suggest that the Appeal Court can impose a non-harassment order as an element of sentence, even where the issue had not been raised in the court of first instance, provided that an appropriate motion is made by the prosecutor to the Appeal Court.

Breach of a non-harassment order, as subs. (4) provides, is a crime triable summarily or on indictment.

Robertson v. Vannet, 1999 S.L.T. 1081 underlines that an order can be imposed on criminal conviction even where the victim already holds an interdict or interim interdict against the accused. (By contrast, in the civil context s.8(5) of the Protection from Harrassment Act 1997 (c.40) precludes the currency, simultaneously, of both a non-harrassment order and an interdict (or interim interdict) arising from the same *species facti*). Interestingly, in *Robertson* too the Appeal Court construed reference to "the victim" as extending to the complainer's father who had not been expressly identified in the breach of the peace charges libelled, but had been alarmed by the accused's actions; it appears that the procurator fiscal when moving for the order had highlighted the effects on both the complainer and her father.

Although it has not been inserted into the 1995 Act, reference should also be made to s.12 of the Protection from Harassment Act and to the sweeping powers of certification vested in the Secretary of State. The section entitles the Secretary of State to certify conclusively that conduct which might otherwise constitute harassment of a person, on specific occasions by a specified person, related to national security, the economic well-being of the U.K. or the prevention or detection of serious crime. It would appear that the intention is to exempt legitimate surveillance operations from claims under the Act of harassment.

The Protection from Harassment Act 1997 received Royal Assent on March 19, 1997 and was commenced for Scottish proceedings by the Protection from Harassment Act 1997 (Commencement) (No. 1) Order 1997 S.I. 1418 on June 16, 1997. The Act of Adjournal (Criminal Procedure Rules Amendment No. 2) (Non-harassment order) 1997 S.I. 1526 inserts r. 20.10A and 20.10B into the 1996 Act of Adjournal. Forms 20.10A and 20.10B set out the forms of orders and applications for revocation. Civil proceedings are regulated by the Act of Sederunt (Rules of the Court of Session Amendment No. 6) (Actions of harassment) 1997 S.I. 1527.

In *Donaldson v. Gallacher*, 1999 G.W.D. 31–1460 a condition not to "approach" the complainer was held to include circumstances that amounted to following. There are several examples of non-harassment orders being made, *e.g. Robertson v. Vannet*, 1998 G.W.D. 36–1865 (5 years), *Lees v. Rys*, 1998 G.W.D. 28–1431 (10 years) and *Dickson v. Main*, 2001 G.W.D. 4–161 (2 years).

Drug treatment and testing order

[1]**234B.**—(1) This section applies where a person of 16 years of age or more is convicted of an offence, other than one for which the sentence is fixed by law, committed on or after the date on which section 89 of the Crime and Disorder Act 1998 comes into force.

(2) Subject to the provisions of this section, the court by or before which the offender is convicted may, if it is of the opinion that it is expedient to do so instead of sentencing him, make an order (a "drug treatment and testing order") which shall—

(a) have effect for a period specified in the order of not less than six months nor more than three years ("the treatment and testing period"); and

(b) include the requirements and provisions mentioned in section 234C of this Act.

(3) A court shall not make a drug treatment and testing order unless it—

(a) has been notified by the Secretary of State that arrangements for implementing such orders are available in the area of the local authority proposed to be specified in the order under section 234C(6) of this Act and the notice has not been withdrawn;

(b) has obtained a report by, and if necessary heard evidence from, an officer of the local authority in whose area the offender is resident about the offender and his circumstances; and

(c) is satisfied that—

(i) the offender is dependent on, or has a propensity to misuse, drugs;

(ii) his dependency or propensity is such as requires and is susceptible to treatment; and

(iii) he is a suitable person to be subject to such an order.

(4) For the purpose of determining for the purposes of subsection (3)(c) above whether the offender has any drug in his body, the court may by order require him to provide samples of such description as it may specify.

(5) A drug treatment and testing order or an order under subsection (4) above shall not be made unless the offender expresses his willingness to comply with its requirements.

(6) The Secretary of State may by order—

(a) amend paragraph (a) of subsection (2) above by substituting a different period for the minimum or the maximum period for the time being specified in that paragraph; and

(b) make such transitional provisions as appear to him necessary or expedient in connection with any such amendment.

(7) The power to make an order under subsection (6) above shall be exercisable by statutory instrument; but no such order shall be made unless a draft of the order has been laid before and approved by resolution of each House of Parliament.

(8) A drug treatment and testing order shall be as nearly as may be in the form prescribed by Act of Adjournal.

DEFINITIONS

"offence": s.307(1) of the 1995 Act.

"sentence": s.307(1) of the 1995 Act.

"drug treatment and testing order": ss.234B(2) and 234C(1) of the 1995 Act as inserted by ss.89 and 90 of the 1998 Act.

NOTE

[1]Inserted by the Crime and Disorder Act 1998 (c. 37), s.89 (effective September 30, 1998: S.I. 1998 No. 2327).

GENERAL NOTE

The provisions contained in ss.89 to 95 of the 1998 Act introduced a new form of court disposal for Scottish courts, the drug treatment and testing order (referred to henceforth as a DTTO), and echo the measures applied to England and Wales by ss.58 to 60 of that Act. The Scottish measures are all inserted in the 1995 Procedure Act as ss.234B to 234J and came into force on September 30, 1998 in terms of the Crime and Disorder Act 1998 (Commencement No. 2 and Transitional Provisions) Order 1998 (S.I. 1998 No. 2327.)

It will be observed that the provisions owe much to existing procedures used in relation to probation orders, a clear signal that the object of a DTTO is rehabilitation, rather than punishment, of the offender. A DTTO is an alternative to a criminal sentence, cannot be imposed following conviction of murder, and can be for a specified period of between six months and three years duration (subs. (2)) subject to several criteria being met. A DTTO can be imposed on its own or combined concurrently with either a probation order (see s.234J(1)) or a restriction of liberty order, or combined with both such orders (implied by s.234H(3)). The court must first receive a report indicating that the offender, who has to be aged 16 years or older, abuses drugs and that his condition is amenable to treatment (subs. (3)) aimed at reducing or ending his susceptibility to misuse drugs (s.234C(1)).

Secondly, the offender must express willingness to comply with the order which will be supervised by an officer nominated by the local authority and, particularly, must consent to attend an establishment for appropriate medical treatment (as an in-patient or out-patient or both), make himself available to the supervising officer as necessary and provide appropriate samples to enable his compliance with the order, and his progress, to be monitored (s.234C(2) and (3)).

The court can only impose a DTTO once the Secretary of State has given notice that suitable arrangements have been put in place in the locale (s.234B(3)) and once satisfied that appropriate medical care facilities are available there to provide the treatment proposed (s.234B(3)). In addition to the background report which must be furnished to it, the court is empowered to require the offender to provide samples for the purpose of confirming the presence of drugs in his body (s.234B(4)). This power is intended only for use at the investigative stage; once a DTTO has been imposed, samples for monitoring compliance are got using s.234C(2) and (3) of the Act.

Subsection (6) entitles the Secretary of State to alter the length of DTTOs, which can be imposed, by Statutory Instrument and gives a broad discretion to enact transitional arrangements.

Two points are worthy of note: it is not necessary that the offence giving rise to the DTTO was itself drug-related (though that will often be so)—what matters are the offender's circumstances; secondly, subs. (3)(b) stipulates that the duty of providing a report to the court rests with the local authority within whose area the offender resides—it does not follow that any element of the DTTO has to be provided in that area. However for practical purposes, like probation, a DTTO depends upon the offender having a regular abode, a qualification which may exclude rootless offenders with drug problems unless suitable in-patient or residential facilities are available.

Section 234G provides penalties for failure to comply with the requirements of a DTTO and entitles the court to issue either a citation or an apprehension warrant to bring an offender before it.

Reference should also be made to Sched. 6 to the 1998 Act which imports a number of amendments to enable DTTOs to be combined with both probation and restriction of liberty orders. Part II of the same Schedule contains provisions to deal with appeals arising from a sentence which includes a DTTO.

Requirements and provisions of drug treatment and testing orders

[1]**234C.**—(1) A drug treatment and testing order shall include a requirement ("the treatment requirement") that the offender shall submit, during the whole of the treatment and testing period, to treatment by or under the direction of a specified person having the necessary qualifications or experience ("the treatment provider") with a view to the reduction or elimination of the offender's dependency on or propensity to misuse drugs.

(2) The required treatment for any particular period shall be

(a) treatment as a resident in such institution or place as may be specified in the order; or

(b) treatment as a non-resident in or at such institution or place, and at such intervals, as may be so specified;

but the nature of the treatment shall not be specified in the order except as mentioned in paragraph (a) or (b) above.

(3) A court shall not make a drug treatment and testing order unless it is satisfied that arrangements have been made for the treatment intended to be specified in the order (including arrangements for the reception of the offender where he is required to submit to treatment as a resident).

(4) A drug treatment and testing order shall include a requirement ("the testing requirement") that, for the purpose of ascertaining whether he has any drug in his body during the treatment and testing period, the offender shall provide during that period, at such times and in such circumstances as may (subject to the provisions of the order) be determined by the treatment provider, samples of such description as may be so determined.

(5) The testing requirement shall specify for each month the minimum number of occasions on which samples are to be provided.

(6) A drug treatment and testing order shall specify the local authority in whose area the offender will reside when the order is in force and require that authority to appoint or assign an officer (a "supervising officer") for the purposes of subsections (7) and (8) below.

(7) A drug treatment and testing order shall—

(a) provide that, for the treatment and testing period, the offender shall be under the supervision of a supervising officer;

(b) require the offender to keep in touch with the supervising officer in accordance with such instructions as he may from time to time be given by that officer, and to notify him of any change of address; and

(c) provide that the results of the tests carried out on the samples provided by the offender in pursuance of the testing requirement shall be communicated to the supervising officer.

(8) Supervision by the supervising officer shall be carried out to such extent only as may be necessary for the purpose of enabling him—

(a) to report on the offender's progress to the appropriate court;

(b) to report to that court any failure by the offender to comply with the requirements of the order; and

(c) to determine whether the circumstances are such that he should apply to that court for the variation or revocation of the order.

DEFINITIONS

"drug treatment and testing order": ss.234B(2) and 234C(1) of the 1995 Act as inserted by ss.89 and 90 of the 1998 Act.

"offender": s.5 of the Crime and Punishment (Scotland) Act 1997 (c. 48).

"local authority": s.234K of the 1995 Act as inserted by s.95(1) of the 1998 Act.

NOTE
[1]Inserted by the Crime and Disorder Act 1998 (c. 37), s.90 (effective September 30, 1998: S.I. 1998 No. 2327).

GENERAL NOTE
This section indicates that the purpose of a drug treatment and testing order (hereafter referred to as a "DTTO") is to provide the offender with a programme to curb, or end, his propensity to misuse drugs. It came into force on September 30, 1998; see generally the Note to s.234B above.

Section 234C(2) enacts that appropriate treatment may be delivered by in-patient or out-patient treatment as directed, or varied, by the treatment provider specified in the order. The treatment provider is responsible for monitoring the medical aspects, including the regime of periodic sampling for drug testing purposes—a compulsory element in all DTTOs (subs. (4)), while a nominated member of the social work department is given the general duty to oversee the offender's conduct and to provide compulsory reports on the progress of the offender to the court (s.234F(1)).

In addition to the general requirements set out in s.234B(3) above, the court has to satisfy itself that satisfactory arrangements for the form of treatment identified as necessary in the report to combat the offender's misuse of drugs are in place (s.234C(3)); to stipulate the minimum number of testing samples to be provided monthly by the offender; to set the timescale (at least initially) for reviews of the order and require the supervising officer to provide a written progress report for consideration at each review (s.234F(1)). Each report must incorporate the results of drug tests and an assessment of the offender's progress by the treatment provider.

It may be appreciated that DTTOs will draw heavily upon medical and social work resources and demand similar commitment from the offenders involved. Failure to comply with the terms of a DTTO are to be reported to the court by the supervising officer who is also empowered to seek variation or revocation of the order (s.234C(8)). The offender himself can also apply to the court for variation or revocation of the order—see s.234E as inserted by s.92 of the 1998 Act.

Procedural matters relating to drug treatment and testing orders

[1]**234D.**—(1) Before making a drug treatment and testing order, a court shall explain to the offender in ordinary language—
  (a) the effect of the order and of the requirements proposed to be included in it;
  (b) the consequences which may follow under section 234G of this Act if he fails to comply with any of those requirements;
  (c) that the court has power under section 234E of this Act to vary or revoke the order on the application of either the offender or the supervising officer; and
  (d) that the order will be periodically reviewed at intervals provided for in the order.

(2) Upon making a drug treatment and testing order the court shall—
  (a) give, or send by registered post or the recorded delivery service, a copy of the order to the offender;
  (b) send a copy of the order to the treatment provider;
  (c) send a copy of the order to the chief social work officer of the local authority specified in the order in accordance with section 234C(6) of this Act; and
  (d) where it is not the appropriate court, send a copy of the order (together with such documents and information relating to the case as are considered useful) to the clerk of the appropriate court.

(3) Where a copy of a drug treatment and testing order has under subsection (2)(a) been sent by registered post or by the recorded delivery service, an acknowledgement or certificate of delivery of a letter containing a copy order issued by the Post Office shall be sufficient evidence of the

delivery of the letter on the day specified in such acknowledgement or certificate.

DEFINITIONS
    "drug treatment and testing order": ss.234B(2) and 234C(1) as inserted by ss.89 and 90 of the 1998 Act.
    "offender": s.5 of the Crime and Punishment (Scotland) Act 1998 (c. 48).
    "supervising officer": s.234C(6) of the 1995 Act as inserted by s.90 of the 1998 Act.

NOTE
    [1]Inserted by the Crime and Disorder Act 1998 (c. 37), s.91 (effective September 30, 1998: S.I. 1998 No. 2327).

GENERAL NOTE
    In addition to the provisions of s.234B(2) and s.234C which specify the nature of a drug treatment and testing order and the court's powers, this section sets out the obligation of the court to explain (as it would when imposing a probation order) the effects of the order and his obligations. Subs. (2) permits personal or postal intimation of the order upon the offender, and stipulates that notification has also to be given to the treatment provider (see s.234C(1)), to the local authority and, where necessary, to the sheriff clerk or clerk of court of the court within whose jurisdiction the offender will reside while subject to the drug treatment and testing order—a situation which will arise where the order has to be transferred from the court which dealt with the original offences.
    This section came into force on September 30, 1998 in terms of S.I. 1998 No. 2327; see the Notes to s.234B above.

Amendment of drug treatment and testing order

    [1]**234E.**—(1) Where a drug treatment and testing order is in force either the offender or the supervising officer may apply to the appropriate court for variation or revocation of the order.

    (2) Where an application is made under subsection (1) above by the supervising officer, the court shall issue a citation requiring the offender to appear before the court.

    (3) On an application made under subsection (1) above and after hearing both the offender and the supervising officer, the court may by order, if it appears to it in the interests of justice to do so—
    (a) vary the order by—
        (i) amending or deleting any of its requirements or provisions;
        (ii) inserting further requirements or provisions; or
        (iii) subject to subsection (4) below, increasing or decreasing the treatment and testing period; or
    (b) revoke the order.

    (4) The power conferred by subsection (3)(a)(iii) above shall not be exercised so as to increase the treatment and testing period above the maximum for the time being specified in section 234B(2)(a) of this Act, or to decrease it below the minimum so specified.

    (5) Where the court, on the application of the supervising officer, proposes to vary (otherwise than by deleting a requirement or provision) a drug treatment and testing order, sections 234B(5) and 234D(1) of this Act shall apply to the variation of such an order as they apply to the making of such an order.

    (6) If an offender fails to appear before the court after having been cited in accordance with subsection (2) above, the court may issue a warrant for his arrest.

DEFINITIONS
    "drug treatment and testing order": ss.234B(2) and 234C(1) of the 1995 Act as inserted by ss.89 and 90 of the 1998 Act.
    "offender": s.5 of the Crime and Punishment (Scotland) Act 1997 (c. 48).
    "supervising officer": s.234C(6) of the 1995 Act as inserted by s.90 of the 1998 Act.

"citation": s.141 of the 1995 Act.
"appropriate court": s.234K of the 1995 Act as inserted by s.95 of the 1998 Act.

NOTE
[1]Inserted by the Crime and Disorder Act 1998 (c. 37), s.92 (effective September 30, 1998: S.I. 1998 No. 2327).

GENERAL NOTE
On the application of either the offender, or his supervising officer, the court can be requested to vary the terms of a drug treatment and testing order (hereafter referred to as a "DTTO") or to revoke the order entirely. Note that while the court may continue, vary or revoke the order (or indeed specify additional requirements) after hearing parties, it must adhere to the terms of s.234B(2), *i.e.* it cannot alter the period of a DTTO which must be of not less than six months and not more than three years' duration.

On receipt of an application from the supervising officer for amendment or revocation of the DTTO, the court, if it considers there to be merit in the application, shall cite the offender to attend a hearing (subs. (4)). Note however that it is not mandatory to cite the offender to appear if the court intends only to delete a requirement or vary a provision of the order.

These procedures are in addition to, and distinct from, the mandatory programme of periodic reviews of all DTTOs set out in s.234F below; and came into force on September 30, 1998 in terms of S.I. 1998 No. 2327; see generally the Notes to s.234B above.

Periodic review of drug treatment and testing order

[1]**234F.**—(1) A drug treatment and testing order shall—
(a) provide for the order to be reviewed periodically at intervals of not less than one month;
(b) provide for each review of the order to be made, subject to subsection (5) below, at a hearing held for the purpose by the appropriate court (a "review hearing");
(c) require the offender to attend each review hearing;
(d) provide for the supervising officer to make to the court, before each review, a report in writing on the offender's progress under the order; and
(e) provide for each such report to include the test results communicated to the supervising officer under section 234C(7)(c) of this Act and the views of the treatment provider as to the treatment and testing of the offender.

(2) At a review hearing the court, after considering the supervising officer's report, may amend any requirement or provision of the order.
(3) The court—
(a) shall not amend the treatment or testing requirement unless the offender expresses his willingness to comply with the requirement as amended;
(b) shall not amend any provision of the order so as reduce the treatment and testing period below the minimum specified in section 234B(2)(a) of this Act or to increase it above the maximum so specified; and
(c) except with the consent of the offender, shall not amend any requirement or provision of the order while an appeal against the order is pending.

(4) If the offender fails to express his willingness to comply with the treatment or testing requirement as proposed to be amended by the court, the court may revoke the order.

(5) If at a review hearing the court, after considering the supervising officer's report, is of the opinion that the offender's progress under the order is satisfactory, the court may so amend the order as to provide for each subsequent review to be made without a hearing.

(6) A review without a hearing shall take place in chambers without the parties being present.

(7) If at a review without a hearing the court, after considering the

supervising officer's report, is of the opinion that the offender's progress is no longer satisfactory, the court may issue a warrant for the arrest of the offender or may, if it thinks fit, instead of issuing a warrant in the first instance, issue a citation requiring the offender to appear before that court as such time as may be specified in the citation.

(8) Where an offender fails to attend—

(a) a review hearing in accordance with a requirement contained in a drug treatment and testing order; or

(b) a court at the time specified in a citation under subsection (7) above,

the court may issue a warrant for his arrest.

(9) Where an offender attends the court at a time specified by a citation issued under subsection (7) above—

(a) the court may exercise the powers conferred by this section as if the court were conducting a review hearing; and

(b) so amend the order as to provide for each subsequent review to be made at a review hearing.

DEFINITIONS

"drug treatment and testing order": ss.234B(2) and 234C(1) of the 1998 Act as inserted by ss.89 and 90 of the 1998 Act.

"review hearing": s.234F(1)(b) of the 1998 Act.

"offender": s.5 of the Crime and Punishment (Scotland) Act 1997 (c. 48).

"the appropriate court": s.234K of the 1995 Act as inserted by s.95(1) of the 1998 Act.

NOTE

[1]Inserted by the Crime and Disorder Act 1998 (c. 37), s.92 (effective September 30, 1998: S.I. 1998 No. 2327).

GENERAL NOTE

This section sets out the mandatory procedures for review of an offender's performance of a drug treatment and testing order at a hearing. Each such order must specify the timescale for hearings, a process which operates separately from the right of either the offender, or the supervising officer, to apply to the court for variation or revocation of an order (see s.234E as inserted by s.92(1) of the 1998 Act).

Prior to the due review date the supervising officer is required to furnish a written report on the offender's progress to the court. Subsection (3) stipulates that the results of all "testing requirements" made by the "treatment officer" and any observations should be incorporated in each review report. Although the offender is required to attend all review hearings until that requirement is waived by the court in terms of subs. (5), nothing expressly stipulates that he be provided with a copy of the supervising officer's report.

The court is empowered to review, and amend, the terms of the existing order's treatment or testing requirements only with the offender's consent (subs. (3)(a)). Failing consent at this stage, the DTTO must proceed unaltered or be revoked but it should be noted that different considerations apply once the offender is held to have been in breach of his order; see s.234G(2) below.

As has been mentioned the offender's attendance at review hearings is mandatory until such time as the court itself resolves that his progress is sufficiently satisfactory to vary the DTTO, and dispense with such attendance. Future reviews would then be held in chambers and based solely on consideration of the supervising officer's report.

In the event of an adverse report being placed before the court in chambers, subs. (7) entitles the court either to cite the offender to appear at a specified time or, alternatively, to issue an arrest warrant. Failure to appear at a review as specified in the DTTO (subs. (1)(c)) or in answer to a citation issued by the court following receipt of an unsatisfactory report (subs. (7)) will entitle the court to issue an arrest warrant. A failure to appear on being given due notice can be treated as a breach of the order and attract the penalties set out in s.234G(2) of the 1995 Act (inserted by s.93 of the 1998 Act). Once a DTTO has been established to have been breached the court may elect to continue the order but strictly, in those circumstances, no longer needs the consent of the offender, albeit it would seem fairly fruitless to persist with treatment in the absence of consent.

These provisions came into force on September 30, 1998; see S.I. 1998 No. 2327.

Breach of drug treatment testing order

[1]**234G.**—(1) If at any time when a drug treatment and testing order is in force it appears to the appropriate court that the offender has failed to comply with any requirement of the order, the court may issue a citation requiring the offender to appear before the court at such time as may be specified in the citation or, if it appears to the court to be appropriate, it may issue a warrant for the arrest of the offender.

(2) If it is proved to the satisfaction of the appropriate court that the offender has failed without reasonable excuse to comply with any requirement of the order, the court may by order—

(a) without prejudice to the continuation in force of the order, impose a fine not exceeding level 3 on the standard scale;

(b) vary the order; or

(c) revoke the order.

(3) For the purposes of subsection (2) above, the evidence of one witness shall be sufficient evidence.

(4) A fine imposed under this section in respect of a failure to comply with the requirements of a drug treatment and testing order shall be deemed for the purposes of any enactment to be a sum adjudged to be paid by or in respect of a conviction or a penalty imposed on a person summarily convicted.

Definitions

"drug treatment and testing order": ss.234B(2) and 234C(1) of the 1995 Act as inserted by ss.89 and 90 of the 1998 Act.

"the appropriate court": s.234K of the 1998 Act as inserted by s.95(1) of the 1998 Act.

"offender": s.5 of the Crime and Punishment (Scotland) Act 1997 (c. 48).

"citation": s.141 of the 1995 Act.

"fine": s.307(1) of the 1995 Act.

"standard scale": s.225(1) of the 1995 Act.

"witness": s.307(1) of the 1995 Act.

Note

[1]Inserted by the Crime and Disorder Act 1998 (c. 37), s.93 (effective September 30, 1998: S.I. 1998 No. 2327).

General Note

Failure to comply with the requirements of a drug treatment and testing order (hereafter referred to as a "DTTO") which, it is submitted, can include a failure to appear at a review hearing as well as refusal to provide test samples or to co-operate with either the supervising or treatment officers, is an offence which can be proved on the evidence of one witness, *i.e.* without the necessity of corroborated evidence. Conviction attracts a monetary penalty up to Level 3 on the standard scale, and also entitles the court, as subs. (3) provides, to vary or revoke the order. In the latter case reference then has to be made to s.234H below which entitles the court to impose any other disposal competent at the time of the making of the DTTO.

Once the court has received information pointing to a breach of a DTTO it can either cite the offender to appear at a designated time or issue an arrest warrant. Plainly, when the offender subsequently appears before the court, he will be called upon to admit or deny breaching the order (a procedure already familiar in relation to alleged breaches of probation or community service orders) and, in the case of a denial, a proof will require to be fixed.

Subsection (4) provides that any fine imposed after a breach has been established shall fall subject to the fine provisions of the 1995 Act (see ss.211 to 223), and the offence itself may be libelled as a conviction.

It is submitted, with hesitation, that once a DTTO has been breached and the court decides to vary the terms of the order (rather than revoking it), and proceeds "by order" as subs. (2) allows, it is no longer necessary to secure the offender's willingness to comply with the revised terms of the order. Nonetheless, having regard to the resource implications of DTTOs, it would seem sensible to obtain an undertaking from the offender as to his future conduct, failing which to consider the range of alternative sentencing disposals.

These provisions came into force on September 30, 1998; see S.I. 1998 No. 2327.

Disposal on revocation of drugs treatment and testing order

[1]**234H.**—(1) Where the court revokes a drugs treatment and testing order under section 234E(3)(b), 234F(4) or 234G(2)(c) of this Act, it may dispose of the offender in any way which would have been competent at the time when the order was made.

(2) In disposing of an offender under subsection (1) above, the court shall have regard to the time for which the order has been in operation.

(3) Where the court revokes a drug treatment and testing order as mentioned in subsection (1) above and the offender is subject to—

(a) a probation order, by virtue of section 234J of this Act; or
(b) a restriction of liberty order, by virtue of section 245D of this Act; or
(c) a restriction of liberty order and a probation order, by virtue of the said section 245D,

the court shall, before disposing of the offender under subsection (1) above—

(i) where he is subject to a probation order, discharge that order;
(ii) where he is subject to a restriction of liberty order, revoke that order; and
(iii) where he is subject to both such orders, discharge the probation order and revoke the restriction of liberty order.

NOTE
[1]Inserted by the Crime and Disorder Act 1998 (c. 37), s.93 (effective September 30, 1998: S.I. 1998 No. 2327).

Concurrent drug treatment and testing and probation orders

[1]**234J.**—(1) Notwithstanding sections 228(1) and 234B(2) of this Act, where the court considers it expedient that the offender should be subject to a drug treatment and testing order and to a probation order, it may make both such orders in respect of the offender.

(2) In deciding whether it is expedient for it to exercise the power conferred by subsection (1) above, the court shall have regard to the circumstances, including the nature of the offence and the character of the offender and to the report submitted to it under section 234B(3)(b) of this Act.

(3) Where the court makes both a drug treatment and testing order and a probation order by virtue of subsection (1) above, the clerk of the court shall send a copy of each of the orders to the following—

(a) the treatment provider within the meaning of section 234C(1);
(b) the officer of the local authority who is appointed or assigned to be the supervising officer under section 234C(6) of this Act; and
(c) if he would not otherwise receive a copy of the order, the officer of the local authority who is to supervise the probationer.

(4) Where the offender by an act or omission fails to comply with a requirement of an order made by virtue of subsection (1) above—

(a) if the failure relates to a requirement contained in a probation order and is dealt with under section 232(2)(c) of this Act, the court may, in addition, exercise the power conferred by section 234G(2)(b) of this Act in relation to the drug treatment and testing order; and
(b) if the failure relates to a requirement contained in a drug treatment and testing order and is dealt with under section 234G(2)(b) of this Act, the court may, in addition, exercise the power conferred by section 232(2)(c) of this Act in relation to the probation order.

(5) Where an offender by an act or omission fails to comply with both a requirement contained in a drug treatment and testing order and in a probation order to which he is subject by virtue of subsection (1) above, he may, without prejudice to subsection (4) above, be dealt with as respects that

act or omission either under section 232(2) of this Act or under section 234G(2) of this Act but he shall not be liable to be otherwise dealt with in respect of that act or omission.

(2) Schedule 6 to this Act (Part I of which makes further provision in relation to the combination of drug treatment and testing orders with other orders and Part II of which makes provision in relation to appeals) shall have effect.

NOTE
[1]Inserted by the Crime and Disorder Act 1998 (c. 37), s.94 (effective September 30, 1998: S.I. 1998 No. 2327).

Drug treatment and testing orders: interpretation

[1]**234K.** In sections 234B to 234J of this Act—
"the appropriate court" means—
(a) where the drug treatment and testing order has been made by the High Court, that court;
(b) in any other case, the court having jurisdiction in the area of the local authority for the time being specified in the order under section 234C(6) of this Act, being a sheriff or district court according to whether the order had been made by a sheriff or district court, but in a case where an order has been made by a district court and there is no district court in that area, the sheriff court; and
"local authority" means a council constituted under section 2 of the Local Government etc. (Scotland) Act 1994 and any reference to the area of such an authority is a reference to the local government area within the meaning of that Act for which it is so constituted.

NOTE
[1]Inserted in terms of the Crime and Disorder Act 1998 (c. 37), s.95(1) (effective September 30, 1998: S.I. 1998 No. 2327).

GENERAL NOTE
It is evident that drug treatment and testing orders can be imposed by any Scottish criminal court, and that for the purposes of delivering the appropriate measures of treatment and supervision, it is competent for the offender to be supervised by a local authority other than that within whose area he offended. It should not be assumed that the local authority within whose area the offender resides (and which must furnish a background report—see s.234B(3) of the 1995 Act as inserted by s.89 of the 1998 Act) will necessarily be the authority named in the DTTO; much will depend upon the availability of suitable treatment facilities, residential or otherwise.

Supervised attendance

Supervised attendance orders

235.—(1) A court may make a supervised attendance order in the circumstances specified in subsection (3) below and shall, subject to paragraph 1 of Schedule 7 to this Act, make such an order where subsection (4) below applies.

(2) A supervised attendance order is an order made by a court in respect of an offender requiring him—
(a) to attend a place of supervision for such period, being a period of not less than 10 hours and not more than—
(i) where the amount of the fine, part or instalment which the offender has failed to pay does not exceed level 1 on the standard scale, 50 hours; and
(ii) in any other case, 100 hours, as is specified in the order; and

(b) during that period, to carry out such instructions as may be given to him by the supervising officer.

(3) The circumstances referred to in subsection (1) above are where—

(a) the offender is of or over 18 years of age; and

(b) having been convicted of an offence, he has had imposed on him a fine which (or any part or instalment of which) he has failed to pay and the court, but for this section, would also have imposed on him a period of imprisonment under subsection (1) of section 219 of this Act; and

(c) the court considers a supervised attendance order more appropriate than the serving of or, as the case may be, imposition of such a period of imprisonment.

(4) This subsection applies where—

(a) the court is a court prescribed for the purposes of this subsection by order made by the Secretary of State;

(b) the offender is of or over 18 years of age and is not serving a sentence of imprisonment;

(c) having been convicted of an offence, he has had imposed on him a fine which (or any part or instalment of which) he has failed to pay and the court, but for this section, would have imposed on him a period of imprisonment under section 219(1)(b) of this Act; and

(d) the fine, or as the case may be, the part or instalment, is of an amount not exceeding level 2 on the standard scale.

(5) An order under subsection (4)(a) above shall be made by statutory instrument, which shall be subject to annulment in pursuance of a resolution of either House of Parliament.

(6) The coming into force of a supervised attendance order shall have the effect of discharging the fine referred to in subsection (3)(b) or (4)(c) above or, as the case may be, section 236(3)(a) or 237(1) of this Act.

(7) Schedule 7 to this Act has effect for the purpose of making further and qualifying provision as to supervised attendance orders.

(8) In this section—

"imprisonment" includes detention;

"place of supervision" means such place as may be determined for the purposes of a supervised attendance order by the supervising officer; and

"supervising officer", in relation to a supervised attendance order, means a person appointed or assigned under Schedule 7 to this Act by the local authority whose area includes the locality in which the offender resides or will be residing when the order comes into force.

DEFINITIONS

"appropriate court": Sched. 7, para. 8.
"imprisonment": s.235(8).
"place of supervision": s.235(8).
"standard scale": s.225(1).
"supervised attendance order": s.235(2).
"supervising officer": s.235(8).

GENERAL NOTE

Section 62 of, and Sched. 6 to, the 1990 Act introduced supervised attendance orders ("SAOs") as an alternative to imprisonment for fine default. Under the provisions of the 1990 Act a court, with the consent of the offender, may impose an SAO where it would otherwise have imposed a term of imprisonment for fine default and where it has been notified by the Secretary of State that the appropriate arrangements exist in the area where the offender resides.

This provision extends the existing arrangements to provide that SAOs may be used as an alternative to, or replacement for, imprisonment for fine default. Under this section a court prescribed by the Secretary of State would be required to make an SAO for failure to pay a fine of less than the equivalent of level two on the standard scale (at present, £500: see s.225(2)) instead of imposing a period of imprisonment. The consent of the offender would no longer be required.

Act of Adjournal
The form of a supervised attendance order is shown in Form 20.11–A in the 1996 Act of Adjournal. A separate form (Form 20.11–B) is used in the case of orders imposed upon 16 and 17 year olds. Rule 20.17 permits the use of certified copies of such orders in relevant proceedings before a court other than the one which imposed the order.

Supervised attendance orders in place of fines for 16 and 17 year olds

236.—(1) This section applies where a person of 16 or 17 years of age is convicted of an offence by a court of summary jurisdiction and the court considers that, but for this section, the appropriate sentence is a fine.

(2) Where this section applies, the court shall determine the amount of the fine and shall consider whether the person is likely to pay a fine of that amount within 28 days.

(3) If the court considers that the person is likely to pay the fine as mentioned in subsection (2) above, it shall—

(a) impose the fine; and

(b) subject to paragraph 1 of Schedule 7 to this Act, make a supervised attendance order in default of payment of the fine within 28 days.

(4) A supervised attendance order made under subsection (3)(b) above—

(a) shall come into force on such date, not earlier than 28 days after the making of the order, as may be specified in the order, unless the person pays the fine within that period;

(b) shall, for the purposes of the said Schedule 7, be deemed to be made on the date when it comes into force.

(5) Where, before the coming into force of a supervised attendance order made under subsection (3)(b) above, the person pays part of the fine, the period specified in the order shall be reduced by the proportion which the part of the fine paid bears to the whole fine, the resulting figure being rounded up or down to the nearest 10 hours; but this subsection shall not operate to reduce the period to less than 10 hours.

(6) If the court considers that the person is not likely to pay the fine as mentioned in subsection (2) above, it shall, subject to paragraph 1 of Schedule 7 to this Act, make a supervised attendance order in respect of that person.

(7) Sections 211(3), 213, 214(1) to (7), 215, 216(1) to (6), 217 to 219, 222 and 223 of this Act shall not apply in respect of a person to whom this section applies.

(8) For the purposes of any appeal or review, a supervised attendance order made under this section is a sentence.

(9) In this section "supervised attendance order" means an order made in accordance with section 235(2), (7) and (8) of this Act.

DEFINITIONS
   "court of summary jurisdiction": s.307(1).
   "fine": s.307(1).
   "sentence": s.307(1).
   "supervised attendance order": s.235(2).

GENERAL NOTE
   This section extends the use of SAOs as respects 16 and 17 year olds as a replacement for a sentence of a fine. Refer to the General Note on p. 318.

Supervised attendance orders where court allows further time to pay fine

237.—(1) Where a court, on an application to it under section 215(1) of this Act, allows a person further time for payment of a fine or instalments thereof it may, in addition, subject to paragraph 1 of Schedule 7 to this Act, impose a supervised attendance order in default of payment of the fine or any instalment of it on the due date.

(2) A supervised attendance order made under subsection (1) above shall—

(a) if the person fails to pay the fine or any instalment of it on the due date, come into force on the day after the due date; and

(b) for the purposes of the said Schedule 7, be deemed to be made on the date when it comes into force.

(3) Where, before the coming into force of a supervised attendance order under subsection (1) above, the person pays part of the fine, the period specified in the order shall be reduced by the proportion which the part of the fine paid bears to the whole fine, the resulting figure being rounded up or down to the nearest 10 hours; but this subsection shall not operate to reduce the period to less than 10 hours.

(4) In this section "supervised attendance order" means an order made in accordance with section 235(2), (7) and (8) of this Act.

DEFINITIONS
 "fine": s.307(1).
 "offence": s.307(1).
 "sentence": s.307(1).
 "supervised attendance order": s.235(2).

Community service by offenders

Community service orders

238.—[1](1) Subject to the provisions of this Act, where a person of or over 16 years of age is convicted of an offence punishable by imprisonment, other than an offence the sentence for which is fixed by law, the court may, instead of imposing on him a sentence of, or including, imprisonment or any other form of detention, make an order (in this Act referred to as "a community service order") requiring him to perform unpaid work for such number of hours (being in total not less than 80 nor more than 300 on conviction on indictment, and not less than 80 nor more than 240 in any other case) as may be specified in the order.

(2) A court shall not make a community service order in respect of any offender unless—

(a) the offender consents;

(b) the court has been notified by the Secretary of State that arrangements exist for persons who reside in the locality in which the offender resides, or will be residing when the order comes into force, to perform work under such an order;

(c) the court is satisfied, after considering a report by an officer of a local authority about the offender and his circumstances, and, if the court thinks it necessary, hearing that officer, that the offender is a suitable person to perform work under such an order; and

(d) the court is satisfied that provision can be made under the arrangements mentioned in paragraph (b) above for the offender to perform work under such an order.

(3) A copy of the report mentioned in subsection (2)(c) above shall be supplied to the offender or his solicitor.

(4) Before making a community service order the court shall explain to the offender in ordinary language—

(a) the purpose and effect of the order and in particular the obligations on the offender as specified in subsections (1) to (3) of section 239 of this Act;

(b) the consequences which may follow under subsections (4) to (6) of that section if he fails to comply with any of those requirements; and

(c) that the court has under section 240 of this Act the power to review the order on the application either of the offender or of an officer of the local authority in whose area the offender for the time being resides.

(5) The Secretary of State may by order direct that subsection (1) above shall be amended by substituting, for the maximum or minimum number of hours specified in that subsection as originally enacted or as subsequently amended under this subsection, such number of hours as may be specified in the order; and an order under this subsection may specify a different maximum or minimum number of hours for different classes of case.

(6) An order under subsection (5) above shall be made by statutory instrument, but no such order shall be made unless a draft of it has been laid before, and approved by a resolution of, each House of Parliament; and any such order may be varied or revoked by a subsequent order under that subsection.

(7) Nothing in subsection (1) above shall be construed as preventing a court which makes a community service in respect of any offence from—

(a) imposing any disqualification on the offender;

(b) making an order for forfeiture in respect of the offence;

(c) ordering the offender to find caution for good behaviour.

(8) A community service order shall—

(a) specify the locality in which the offender resides or will be residing when the order comes into force;

(b) require the local authority in whose area the locality specified under paragraph (a) above is situated to appoint or assign an officer (referred to in this section and sections 239 to 245 of this Act as "the local authority officer") who will discharge the functions assigned to him by those sections; and

(c) state the number of hours of work which the offender is required to perform.

(9) Where, whether on the same occasion or on separate occasions, an offender is made subject to more than one community service order, or to both a community service order and a probation order which includes a requirement that that offender shall perform any unpaid work, the court may direct that the hours of work specified in any of those orders shall be concurrent with or additional to those specified in any other of those orders, but so that at no time shall the offender have an outstanding number of hours of work to perform in excess of the maximum provided for in subsection (1) above.

(10) Upon making a community service order the court shall—

(a) give, or send by registered post or the recorded delivery service, a copy of the order to the offender;

(b) send a copy of the order to the chief social work officer of the local authority in whose area the offender resides or will be residing where the order comes into force; and

(c) where it is not the appropriate court, send a copy of the order (together with such documents and information relating to the case as are considered useful) to the clerk of the appropriate court.

(11) Where a copy of a community service order has, under subsection (10)(a) above, been sent by registered post or by the recorded delivery service, an acknowledgement or certificate of delivery of a letter containing the copy order issued by the Post Office shall be sufficient evidence of the delivery of the letter on the day specified in such acknowledgement or certificate.

DEFINITIONS
"caution": s.227.
"local authority": s.307(1).
"local authority officer": s.238(8)(b).
"offence": s.307(1).
"sentence": s.307(1).

NOTE
[1] Substituted by the Community Service by Offenders (Hours of Work) (Scotland) Order 1996 (S.I. 1996 No. 1938), para. 3.

GENERAL NOTE
With effect from July 18, 1996, the Community Service by Offenders (Hours of Work) (Scotland) Order raised the minimum number of hours which could be imposed in a community service order from 40 to 80 in summary and solemn cases, and raised the maximum number of hours on indictment only from 240 to 300 hours. (The maximum length of an order imposed summarily remains at 240 hours.)

It is mandatory, following subs. (2) that a community service order cannot be imposed either alone, or in conjunction with another order, unless the court has first obtained a CSO report (see *Boyle v. McGlennan*, 1999 G.W.D. 28–1337).

Act of Adjournal
See Form 20.12–A for the style of community service orders. The citation for breach of such an order is set out in Form 20.12–B in the 1996 Act of Adjournal. Refer to r. 20.17 for use of certified copy documents in breach proceedings before any court other than the one which imposed the original order.

Community service orders: requirements

239.—(1) An offender in respect of whom a community service order is in force shall—

(a) report to the local authority officer and notify him without delay of any change of address or in the times, if any, at which he usually works; and

(b) perform for the number of hours specified in the order such work at such times as the local authority officer may instruct.

(2) Subject to section 240(1) of this Act, the work required to be performed under a community service order shall be performed during the period of 12 months beginning with the date of the order; but, unless revoked, the order shall remain in force until the offender has worked under it for the number of hours specified in it.

(3) The instructions given by the local authority officer under this section shall, so far as practicable, be such as to avoid any conflict with the offender's religious beliefs and any interference with the times, if any, at which he normally works or attends a school or other educational establishment.

(4) If at any time while a community service order is in force in respect of any offender it appears to the appropriate court, on information from the local authority officer, that that offender has failed to comply with any of the requirements of subsections (1) to (3) above (including any failure satisfactorily to perform the work which he has been instructed to do), that court may issue a warrant for the arrest of that offender, or may, if it thinks fit, instead of issuing a warrant in the first instance issue a citation requiring that offender to appear before that court at such time as may be specified in the citation.

(5) If it is proved to the satisfaction of the court before which an offender appears or is brought in pursuance of subsection (4) above that he has failed without reasonable excuse to comply with any of the requirements of the said subsections (1) to (3), that court may—

(a) without prejudice to the continuance in force of the order, impose on him a fine not exceeding level 3 on the standard scale;

(b) revoke the order and deal with that offender in any manner in which he could have been dealt with for the original offence by the court which made the order if the order had not been made; or

(c) subject to section 238(1) of this Act, vary the number of hours specified in the order.

(6) The evidence of one witness shall, for the purposes of subsection (5) above, be sufficient evidence.

DEFINITIONS
"community service order": s.238(1).
"local authority officer": s.238(8)(b).
"standard scale": s.225(2).

GENERAL NOTE
Failure to comply with a community service order invokes the procedures set out in subs. (5). In *Gilbert v. Buchanan*, 1998 S.L.T. 303, the sheriff revoked G's order and proceeded to sentence him to three months imprisonment in respect of the original offence and imposed a consecutive sentence of two months imprisonment for breach of the order. The latter sentence was held to be incompetent.

Community service orders: amendment and revocation etc.

240.—(1) Where a community service order is in force in respect of any offender and, on the application of that offender or of the local authority officer, it appears to the appropriate court that it would be in the interests of justice to do so having regard to circumstances which have arisen since the order was made, that court may—

(a) extend, in relation to the order, the period of 12 months specified in section 239(2) of this Act;

(b) subject to section 238(1) of this Act, vary the number of hours specified in the order;

(c) revoke the order; or

(d) revoke the order and deal with the offender for the original offence in any manner in which he could have been dealt with for that offence by the court which made the order if the order had not been made.

(2) If the appropriate court is satisfied that the offender proposes to change, or has changed, his residence from the locality for the time being specified under section 238(8)(a) of this Act to another locality and—

(a) that court has been notified by the Secretary of State that arrangements exist for persons who reside in that other locality to perform work under community service orders; and

(b) it appears to that court that provision can be made under those arrangements for him to perform work under the order,

that court may, and on the application of the local authority officer shall, amend the order by substituting that other locality for the locality for the time being specified in the order; and sections 238 to 245 of this Act shall apply to the order as amended.

(3) Where the court proposes to exercise its powers under subsection (1)(a), (b) or (d) above otherwise than on the application of the offender, it shall issue a citation requiring him to appear before the court and, if he fails to appear, may issue a warrant for his arrest.

DEFINITIONS
"community service order": s.238(1).
"local authority officer": s.228(8)(b).

Community service order: commission of offence while order in force

241.—(1) Where—
  (a) a court has made a community service order in respect of an offender; and
  (b) the offender is convicted of an offence committed in the circumstances mentioned in subsection (2) below,
  the court which sentences him for that offence shall, in determining the appropriate sentence for that offence, have regard to the fact that the offence was committed in those circumstances.

(2) The circumstances referred to in subsection (1) above are that the offence was committed—
  (a) during the period when the community service order was in force or within the period of three months following the expiry of that order; and
  (b) in any place where unpaid work under the order was being or had previously been performed.

(3) The court shall not, under subsection (1) above, have regard to the fact that the offence was committed in the circumstances mentioned in subsection (2) above unless that fact is libelled in the indictment or, as the case may be, specified in the complaint.

[1](4) The fact that the offence mentioned in subsection (1)(b) above was committed in the circumstances mentioned in subsection (2) above shall, unless challenged—
  (a) in the case of proceedings on indictment, by giving notice of a preliminary objection under paragraph (b) of section 72(1) of this Act or under that paragraph as applied by section 71(2) of this Act; or
  (b) in summary proceedings, by preliminary objection before his plea is recorded,
be held as admitted.

DEFINITIONS
"community service order": s.238(1).
"complaint": s.307(1).
"indictment": s.307(1).
"offence": s.307(1).

NOTE
[1]Inserted by the Crime and Punishment (Scotland) Act 1997 (c. 48) s.26(2) with effect from August 1, 1997 in terms of the Crime and Punishment (Scotland) Act 1997 (Commencement and Transitional Provisions) Order 1997 (S.I. 1997 No. 1712) para. 3.

GENERAL NOTE
  It seems a clear inference from the terms of this section that if an offence should be committed by an individual then performing unpaid work under a community service order at a relevant place, then that is an aggravation for the purposes of sentence. The court can only have regard to these facts if they have been libelled by the Crown: see subs. (3). However, reference to a community service order in the libel of a charge in itself implies previous convictions and may thus contravene ss.101(1) and 166(3) of this Act.
  The introduction of subs. (4), in effect creating a special capacity in these circumstances eases the evidential burden on the Crown but it seems unfortunate that the application of these provisions could not have been made known to the accused outwith the libel itself.
  It would seem that for a court to have regard to the accused's behaviour in relation to this statutory aggravation the Crown will require to be particularly circumspect in drafting the charge or place the single charge on a separate indictment or complaint if there are several charges. See also the discussion at p. 304 above.

Community service orders: persons residing in England and Wales

242.—(1) Where a court is considering the making of a community service order and it is satisfied that the offender has attained the age of 16 years and resides, or will be residing when the order comes into force, in England or Wales, then—

[1](a) section 238 of this Act shall have effect as if subsection (2) were amended as follows—

(i) paragraph (b) shall be omitted;

(ii) in paragraph (c) for the words "such an order" there shall be substituted the words "a community service order"; and

(iii) for paragraph (d) there shall be substituted the following paragraph—

"(d) it appears to that court that provision can be made for the offender to perform work under the order made under subsection (1) above under the arrangements which exist in the petty sessions area in which he resides or will be residing for persons to perform work under community service orders made under section 46 of the Powers of Criminal Courts (Sentencing) Act 2000;"; and

(b) the order shall specify that the unpaid work required to be performed by the order shall be performed under the arrangements mentioned in section 238(2)(d) of this Act as substituted by paragraph (a) above.

(2) Where a community service order has been made and—

(a) the appropriate court is satisfied that the offender has attained the age of 16 years and proposes to reside or is residing in England or Wales; and

[2](b) it appears to that court that provision can be made for the offender to perform work under the order made under the arrangements which exist in the petty sessions area in which he proposes to reside or is residing for persons to perform work under community service orders made under section 46 of the Powers of Criminal Courts (Sentencing) Act 2000,

it may amend the order by specifying that the unpaid work required to be performed by the order shall be performed under the arrangements mentioned in paragraph (b) of this subsection.

(3) A community service order made under section 238(1) as amended by or in accordance with this section shall—

(a) specify the petty sessions area in England or Wales in which the offender resides or will be residing when the order or the amendment comes into force; and

[3](b) require the probation committee for that area to appoint or assign a probation officer who will discharge in respect of the order the functions in respect of community service orders conferred on responsible officers by the Powers of Criminal Courts (Sentencing) Act 2000.

DEFINITION
"community service order": s.238(1).

GENERAL NOTE
[1]As amended by the Powers of Criminal Courts (Sentencing) Act 2000 (c.6), s.165 and Sched. 9, para. 177(2).
[2]As amended by the Powers of Criminal Courts (Sentencing) Act 2000 (c.6), s.165 and Sched. 9, para. 177(3).
[3]As amended by the Powers of Criminal Courts (Sentencing) Act 2000 (c.6), s.165 and Sched. 9, para. 177(4).

Community service orders: persons residing in Northern Ireland

243.—(1) Where a court is considering the making of a community service order and it is satisfied that the offender resides, or will be residing when the order comes into force, in Northern Ireland, then—

(a) section 238 of this Act shall have effect as if subsection (2) were amended as follows—
(i) paragraph (b) shall be omitted;
(ii) for paragraph (d) there shall be substituted the following paragraph—
"(d) it appears to the court that provision can be made by the Probation Board for Northern Ireland for him to perform work under such an order;";
(b) the order shall specify that the unpaid work required to be performed by the order shall be performed under the provision made by the Probation Board for Northern Ireland and referred to in section 238(2)(d) of this Act as substituted by paragraph (a) above.
(2) Where a community service order has been made and—
(a) the appropriate court is satisfied that the offender proposes to reside or is residing in Northern Ireland; and
(b) it appears to that court that provision can be made by the Probation Board for Northern Ireland for him to perform work under the order,
it may amend the order by specifying that the unpaid work required to be performed by the order shall be performed under the provision made by the Probation Board for Northern Ireland and referred to in paragraph (b) of this subsection.
(3) A community service order made under section 238(1) of this Act as amended by or in accordance with this section shall—
(a) specify the petty sessions district in Northern Ireland in which the offender resides or will be residing when the order or the amendment comes into force; and
(b) require the Probation Board for Northern Ireland to select an officer who will discharge in respect of the order the functions in respect of community service orders conferred on the relevant officer by the Treatment of Offenders (Northern Ireland) Order 1976.

DEFINITION
"community service order": s.238(1).

Community service orders: general provisions relating to persons living in England and Wales or Northern Ireland

244.—(1) Where a community service order is made or amended in the circumstances specified in section 242 or 243 of this Act, the court which makes or amends the order shall send three copies of it as made or amended to the home court, together with such documents and information relating to the case as it considers likely to be of assistance to that court.
(2) In this section—
"home court" means—
(a) if the offender resides in England or Wales, or will be residing in England or Wales at the relevant time, the magistrates' court acting for the petty sessions area in which he resides or proposes to reside; and
(b) if he resides in Northern Ireland, or will be residing in Northern Ireland, at the relevant time, the court of summary jurisdiction acting for the petty sessions district in which he resides or proposes to reside; and
"the relevant time" means the time when the order or the amendment to it comes into force.
(3) A community service order made or amended in the circumstances specified in section 242 or 243 of this Act shall be treated, subject to the following provisions of this section, as if it were a community service order made in the part of the United Kingdom in which the offender resides, or will be residing at the relevant time; and the legislation relating to community

service orders which has effect in that part of the United Kingdom shall apply accordingly.

(4) Before making or amending a community service order in those circumstances the court shall explain to the offender in ordinary language—

(a) the requirements of the legislation relating to community service orders which has effect in the part of the United Kingdom in which he resides or will be residing at the relevant time;

(b) the powers of the home court under that legislation, as modified by this section; and

(c) its own powers under this section,

and an explanation given in accordance with this section shall be sufficient without the addition of an explanation under section 238(4) of this Act.

(5) The home court may exercise in relation to the community service order any power which it could exercise in relation to a community service order made by a court in the part of the United Kingdom in which the home court exercises jurisdiction, by virtue of the legislation relating to such orders which has effect in that part of the United Kingdom, except—

(a) a power to vary the order by substituting for the number of hours' work specified in it any greater number than the court which made the order could have specified;

(b) a power to revoke the order; and

(c) a power to revoke the order and deal with the offender for the offence in respect of which it was made in any manner in which he could have been dealt with for that offence by the court which made the order if the order had not been made.

(6) If at any time while legislation relating to community service orders which has effect in one part of the United Kingdom applies by virtue of subsection (3) above to a community service order made in another part—

(a) it appears to the home court—

(i) if that court is in England or Wales, on information to a justice of the peace acting for the petty sessions area for the time being specified in the order; or

(ii) if it is in Northern Ireland, upon a complaint being made to a justice of the peace acting for the petty sessions district for the time being specified in the order,

that the offender has failed to comply with any of the requirements of the legislation applicable to the order; or

[1](b) it appears to the home court on the application of—

(i) the offender; or

(ii) if that court is in England and Wales, the responsible officers by the Powers of Criminal Courts (Sentencing) Act 2000; or

(iii) if that court is in Northern Ireland, the relevant officer under the Treatment of Offenders (Northern Ireland) Order 1976,

that it would be in the interests of justice to exercise a power mentioned in subsection (5)(b) or (c) above,

the home court may require the offender to appear before the court by which the order was made.

(7) Where an offender is required by virtue of subsection (6) above to appear before the court which made a community service order, that court—

(a) may issue a warrant for his arrest; and

(b) may exercise any power which it could exercise in respect of the community service order if the offender resided in the part of the United Kingdom where the court has jurisdiction,

and any enactment relating to the exercise of such powers shall have effect accordingly.

DEFINITIONS

"community service order": s.238(1).
"home court": s.244(2).
"relevant time": s.244(2).

[1]As amended by the Powers if Criminal Courts (Sentencing) Act 2000 (c.6) s.165 and Sched. 9, para. 178.

Community service orders: rules, annual report and interpretation

245.—(1) The Secretary of State may make rules for regulating the performance of work under community service orders or probation orders which include a requirement that the offender shall perform unpaid work.

(2) Without prejudice to the generality of subsection (1) above, rules under this section may—

  (a) limit the number of hours' work to be done by a person under such an order on any one day;
  (b) make provision as to the reckoning of time worked under such orders;
  (c) make provision for the payment of travelling and other expenses in connection with the performance of work under such orders;
  (d) provide for records to be kept of the work done by any person under such an order.

(3) Rules under this section shall be made by statutory instrument subject to annulment in pursuance of a resolution of either House of Parliament.

(4) The Secretary of State shall lay before Parliament each year, or incorporate in annual reports he already makes, a report of the working of community service orders.

(5) In sections 238 to 243 of this Act, "the appropriate court" means—

  (a) where the relevant community service order has been made by the High Court, the High Court;
  (b) in any other case, the court having jurisdiction in the locality for the time being specified in the order under section 238(8)(a) of this Act, being a sheriff or district court according to whether the order has been made by a sheriff or a district court, but in a case where the order has been made by a district court and there is no district court in that locality, the sheriff court.

DEFINITIONS
  "appropriate court": s.245(5).
  "community service orders": s.238(1).
  "probation orders": s.308(1).

Restriction of Liberty Orders

Restriction of liberty orders

[1]**245A.**—(1) Without prejudice to section 245D of this Act, where a person of 16 years of age or more is convicted of an offence (other than an offence the sentence for which is fixed by law) the court, if it is of opinion that it is the most appropriate method of disposal, may make an order under this section (in this Act referred to as a "restriction of liberty order") in respect of him; and in this section and sections 245B to 245I of this Act any reference to an "offender" is a reference to a person in respect of whom an order has been made under this subsection.

(2) A restriction of liberty order may restrict the offender's movements to such extent as the court thinks fit and, without prejudice to the generality of the foregoing, may include provision—

  (a) requiring the offender to be in such place as may be specified for such period or periods in each day or week as may be specified;
  (b) requiring the offender not to be in such place or places, or such class or classes of place or places, at such time or during such periods, as may be specified,

328

but the court may not, under paragraph (a) above, require the offender to be in any place or places for a period of periods totalling more than 12 hours in any one day.

(3) A restriction of liberty order may be made for any period up to 12 months.

(4) Before making a restriction of liberty order, the court shall explain to the offender in ordinary language—

(a) the effect of the order, including any requirements which are to be included in the order under section 245C of this Act;

(b) the consequences which may follow any failure by the offender to comply with the requirements of any order; and

(c) that the court has power under section 245E of this Act to review the order on the application either of the offender or of any person responsible for monitoring the order,

and the court shall not make the order unless the offender agrees to comply with its requirements.

(5) The clerk of the court by which a restriction of liberty order is made shall—

(a) cause a copy of the order to be sent to any person who is to be responsible for monitoring the offender's compliance with the order; and

(b) cause a copy of the order to be given to the offender or sent to him by registered post or by the recorded delivery service; and an acknowledgment or certificate of delivery of a letter containing such copy order issued by the Post Office shall be sufficient evidence of the delivery of the letter on the day specified in such acknowledgment or certificate.

(6) Before making a restriction of liberty order which will require the offender to remain in a specified place or places the court shall obtain and consider information about that place or those places, including information as to the attitude of persons likely to be affected by the enforced presence there of the offender.

(7) A restriction of liberty order shall be taken to be a sentence for the purposes of this Act and of any appeal.

[2](8) The Secretary of State may by regulations prescribe—

(a) which courts, or class or classes of courts, may make restriction of liberty orders;

(b) what method or methods of monitoring compliance with such orders may be specified in any such order by any such court; and

(c) the class or classes of offenders in respect of which restriction of liberty orders may be made,

and different provision may be made in relation to the matters mentioned in paragraphs (b) and (c) above in relation to different courts or classes of court.

[2](9) Without prejudice to the generality of subsection (8) above, in relation to district courts, regulations under that subsection may make provision as respects such courts by reference to whether the court is constituted by a stipendiary magistrate or by one or more justices.

[2](10) Regulations under subsection (8) above may make such transitional and consequential provisions, including provision in relation to the continuing effect of any restriction of liberty order in force when new regulations are made, as the Secretary of State considers appropriate.

[2](11) A court shall not make a restriction of liberty order which requires an offender to be in or, as the case may be, not to be in, a particular place or places unless it is satisfied that his compliance with that requirement can be monitored by the means of monitoring which it intends to specify in the order.

[2](12) The Secretary of State may by regulations substitute for the period of—

    (a) hours for the time being mentioned in subsection (2) above; or

    (b) months for the time being mentioned in subsection (3) above,

such period of hours or, as the case may be, months as may be prescribed in the regulations.

[2](13) Regulations under this section shall be made by statutory instrument.

[2](14) A statutory instrument containing regulations made under subsection (8) above shall be subject to annulment in pursuance of a resolution of either House of Parliament.

[2](15) No regulations shall be made under subsection (12) above unless a draft of the regulations has been laid before, and approved by a resolution of, each House of Parliament.

DEFINITIONS
    "restriction of liberty order": s.5 of the 1997 Act.
    "offender": s.5 of the 1997 Act.
    "stipendiary magistrate": s.5 of the District Courts (Scotland) Act 1975 and s.7(5) of the 1995 Act.
    "justice": ss.6 and 307(1) of the 1995 Act.
    "probation order": s.228 of the 1995 Act.
    "fine": s.307(1) of the 1995 Act.
    "standard scale": s.225(1) of the 1995 Act.

NOTES
[1]Inserted by the Crime and Punishment (Scotland) Act 1997 (c. 48), s.5 (in part) with (effective July 1, 1998: S.I. 1997 No. 2323).
[2]Inserted by the Crime and Punishment (Scotland) Act 1997 (c. 48), s.5 (in part) with effect from October 20, 1997 in terms of the Crime and Punishment (Scotland) Act 1997 (Commencement No. 2 and Transitional and Consequential Provisions) Order 1997 (S.I. 1997 No. 2323) Art. 3, Sched. 1.

GENERAL NOTE
    It is intended that the remainder of this section (whose full text can be found in s.5 of the 1997 Act) was brought into force on July 1, 1998. Previously, only subss. (8) to (14) of this section have been brought into effect, for the purpose of enabling the Secretary of State to make regulations, specify courts and enter electronic monitoring contracts, as a prelude to restriction of liberty orders. These subsections took effect on October 20, 1997 (see Sched. 1 to the Crime and Punishment (Scotland) Act 1997 (Commencement No. 2 and Transitional and Consequential Provisions) Order 1997 S.I. 2323.
    A fuller discussion about the form of restriction of liberty orders is to be found in the annotations to s.5 of the Crime and Punishment (Scotland) Act 1997 below.
    The forms for establishing and varying restriction of liberty orders are found in Act of Adjournal (Criminal Procedure Rules Amendment) (Restriction of Liberty Orders) 1998 (S.I. No. 1842).

Monitoring of restriction of liberty orders

[1]**245B.**—(1) Where the Secretary of State, in regulations made under section 245A(8) of this Act, empowers a court or a class of court to make restriction of liberty orders he shall notify the court or each of the courts concerned of the person or class or description of persons who may be designated by that court for the purpose of monitoring an offender's compliance with any such order.

(2) A court which makes a restriction of liberty order in respect of an offender shall include provision in the order for making a person notified by the Secretary of State under subsection (1) above, or a class or description of persons so notified, responsible for the monitoring of the offender's compliance with it.

(3) Where the Secretary of State changes the person or class or description

of persons notified by him under subsection (1) above, any court which has made a restriction of liberty order shall, if necessary, vary the order accordingly and shall notify the variation to the offender.

NOTE
[1]Inserted by the Crime and Punishment (Scotland) Act 1997 (c. 48), s.5 (effective July 1, 1998: S.I. 1997 No. 2323).

Remote monitoring

[1]**245C.**—(1) The Secretary of State may make such arrangements, including contractual arrangements, as he considers appropriate with such persons, whether legal or natural, as he thinks fit for the remote monitoring of the compliance of offenders with restriction of liberty orders, and different arrangements may be made in relation to different areas or different forms of remote monitoring.

(2) A court making a restriction of liberty order which is to be monitored remotely may include in the order a requirement that the offender shall, either continuously or for such periods as may be specified, wear or carry a device for the purpose of enabling the remote monitoring of his compliance with the order to be carried out.

(3) The Secretary of State shall by regulations specify devices which may be used for the purpose of remotely monitoring the compliance of an offender with the requirements of a restriction of liberty order.

(4) Regulations under this section shall be made by statutory instrument subject to annulment in pursuance of a resolution of either House of Parliament.

NOTE
[1]Inserted by the Crime and Punishment (Scotland) Act 1997 (c. 48), s.5 (effective July 1, 1998: S.I. 1997 No. 2323).

Concurrent probation and restriction of liberty orders

[1]**245D.**—(1) Notwithstanding sections 228(1) and 245A(1) of this Act, where the court—
  (a) intends to make a restriction of liberty order under section 245A(1); and
  (b) considers it expedient—
     (i) having regard to the circumstances, including the nature of the offence and the character of the offender; and
     (ii) having obtained a report as to the circumstances and character of the offender,
  that the offender should also be subject to a probation order made under section 228(1) of this Act,
it may make both such orders in respect of the offender.

(2) Where the court makes both a restriction of liberty order and a probation order by virtue of subsection (1) above, the clerk of the court shall send a copy of each order to both—
  (a) any person responsible for monitoring the offender's compliance with the restriction of liberty order; and
  (b) the officer of the local authority who is to supervise the probationer.

(3) Where the offender by an act or omission fails to comply with a requirement of an order made by virtue of subsection (1) above—
  (a) if the failure relates to a requirement contained in a probation order and is dealt with under section 232(2)(c) of this Act, the court may, in addition, exercise the power conferred by section 245F(2)(b) of this Act in relation to the restriction of liberty order; and
  (b) if the failure relates to a requirement contained in a restriction of liberty order and is dealt with under section 245F(2)(b) of this Act, the

court may, in addition, exercise the power conferred by section 232(2)(c) in relation to the probation order.

(4) Where the offender by an act or omission fails to comply with both a requirement contained in a probation order and a requirement contained in a restriction of liberty order to which he is subject by virtue of subsection (1) above, he may, without prejudice to subsection (3) above, be dealt with as respects that act or omission either under section 232(2) of this Act or under section 245F(2) of this Act but he shall not be liable to be otherwise dealt with in respect of that act or omission.

NOTE
[1]Inserted by the Crime and Punishment (Scotland) Act 1997 (c. 48), s.5 (effective July 1, 1998: S.I. 1997 No. 2323).

Variation of restriction of liberty order

245E.—(1) Where a restriction of liberty order is in force either the offender or any person responsible for monitoring his compliance with the order may apply to the court which made the order for a review of it.

(2) On an application made under subsection (1) above, and after hearing both the offender and any person responsible for monitoring his compliance with the order, the court may by order, if it appears to it to be in the interests of justice to do so—

(a) vary the order by—
(i) amending or deleting any of its requirements;
(ii) inserting further requirements; or
(iii) subject to subsection (3) of section 245A of this Act, increasing the period for which the order has to run; or
(b) revoke the order.

(3) Where the court, on the application of a person other than the offender, proposes to—

(a) exercise the power conferred by paragraph (a) of subsection (2) above to vary (otherwise than by deleting a requirement) a restriction of liberty order, it shall issue a citation requiring the offender to appear before the court and section 245A(4) shall apply to the variation of such an order as it applies to the making of an order; and
(b) exercise the power conferred by subsection (2)(b) above to revoke such an order and deal with the offender under section 245G of this Act, it shall issue a citation requiring him to appear before the court.

(4) If an offender fails to appear before the court after having been cited in accordance with subsection (3) above, the court may issue a warrant for his arrest.

NOTE
[1]Inserted by the Crime and Punishment (Scotland) Act 1997 (c. 48), s.5 (effective July 1, 1998: S.I. 1997 No. 2323).

Breach of restriction of liberty order

[1]**245F.**—(1) If at any time when a restriction of liberty order is in force it appears to the court which made the order that the offender has failed to comply with any of the requirements of the order the court may issue a citation requiring the offender to appear before the court at such time as may be specified in the citation or, if it appears to the court to be appropriate, it may issue a warrant for the arrest of the offender.

(2) If it is proved to the satisfaction of the court that the offender has failed without reasonable excuse to comply with any of the requirements of the order the court may by order—

(a) without prejudice to the continuance in force of the order, impose a fine not exceeding level 3 on the standard scale;

(b) vary the restriction of liberty order; or

(c) revoke that order.

A fine imposed under this section in respect of a failure to comply with the requirements of a restriction of liberty order shall be deemed for the purposes of any enactment to be a sum adjudged to be paid by or in respect of a conviction or a penalty imposed on a person summarily convicted.

(4) Where the court varies a restriction of liberty order under subsection (2) above it may do so in any of the ways mentioned in paragraph (a) of section 245E(2) of this Act.

NOTE
[1]Inserted by the Crime and Punishment (Scotland) Act 1997 (c. 48), s.5 (effective July 1, 1998: S.I. 1997 No. 2323).

Disposal on revocation of restriction of liberty order

[1]**245G.**—(1) Where the court revokes a restriction of liberty order under section 245E(2)(b) or 245F(2) of this Act, it may dispose of the offender in any way which would have been competent at the time when the order was made, but in so doing the court shall have regard to the time for which the order has been in operation.

(2) Where the court revokes a restriction of liberty order as mentioned in subsection (1) above, and the offender is, by virtue of section 245D(1) of this Act, subject to a probation order, it shall, before disposing of the offender under subsection (1) above, discharge the probatin order.

NOTE
[1]Inserted by the Crime and Punishment (Scotland) Act 1997 (c. 48), s.5 (effective July 1, 1998: S.I. 1997 No. 2323).

Documentary evidence in proceedings under section 245F

[1]**245H.**—(1) Evidence of the presence or absence of the offender at a particular place at a particular time may, subject to the provisions of this section, be given by the production of a document or documents bearing to be—

(a) a statement automatically produced by a device specified in regulations made under section 245C of this Act, by which the offender's whereabouts were remotely monitored; and

(b) a certificate signed by a person nominated for the purpose of this paragraph by the Secretary of State that the statement relates to the whereabouts of the person subject to the order at the dates and times shown in the statement.

(2) The statement and certificate mentioned in subsection (1) above shall, when produced at a hearing, be sufficient evidence of the facts set out in them.

(3) Neither the statement nor the certificate mentioned in subsection (1) above shall be admissible in evidence unless a copy of both has been served on the offender prior to the hearing and, without prejudice to the foregoing, where it appears to the court that the offender has had insufficient notice of the statement or certificate, it may adjourn a hearing or make any order which it thinks appropriate in the circumstances.

NOTE
[1]Inserted by the Crime and Punishment (Scotland) Act 1997 (c. 48), s.5 (effective July 1, 1998: S.I. 1997 No. 2323).

Procedure on variation or revocation of restriction of liberty order

[1]**245I.** Where a court exercises any power conferred by sections 232(3A), 245E(2) or 245F(2)(b) or (c) of this Act, the clerk of the court shall forthwith

give copies of the order varying or revoking the restriction of liberty order to any person responsible for monitoring the offender's compliance with that order and that person shall give a copy of the order to the offender.".

NOTE
    [1]Inserted by the Crime and Punishment (Scotland) Act 1997 (c. 48), s.5 (effective July 1, 1998: S.I. 1997 No. 2323).

Admonition and absolute discharge

Admonition and absolute discharge

246.—(1) A court may, if it appears to meet the justice of the case, dismiss with an admonition any person convicted by the court of any offence.

(2) Where a person is convicted on indictment of an offence (other than an offence the sentence for which is fixed by law), if it appears to the court, having regard to the circumstances including the nature of the offence and the character of the offender, that it is inexpedient to inflict punishment and that a probation order is not appropriate it may instead of sentencing him make an order discharging him absolutely.

(3) Where a person is charged before a court of summary jurisdiction with an offence (other than an offence the sentence for which is fixed by law) and the court is satisfied that he committed the offence, the court, if it is of the opinion, having regard to the circumstances including the nature of the offence and the character of the offender, that it is inexpedient to inflict punishment and that a probation order is not appropriate may without proceeding to conviction make an order discharging him absolutely.

DEFINITIONS
    "court of summary jurisdiction": s.307(1).
    "indictment": s.307(1).
    "offence": s.307(1).
    "probation order": s.307(1).

GENERAL NOTE
    The legal effect of an absolute discharge is stipulated in s.247, below. In *McLay v. Ruxton*, 1996 G.W.D. 23–1311 the Appeal Court granted an absolute discharge after allowing a motion to appeal against conviction to be made at the bar.

Effect of probation and absolute discharge

247.—(1) Subject to the following provisions of this section, a conviction of an offence for which an order is made placing the offender on probation or discharging him absolutely shall be deemed not to be a conviction for any purpose other than the purposes of the proceedings in which the order is made and of laying it before a court as a previous conviction in subsequent proceedings for another offence.

(2) Without prejudice to subsection (1) above, the conviction of an offender who is placed on probation or discharged absolutely as aforesaid shall in any event be disregarded for the purposes of any enactment which imposes any disqualification or disability upon convicted persons, or authorises or requires the imposition of any such disqualification or disability.

(3) Subsections (1) and (2) above shall not affect any right to appeal.

(4) Where a person charged with an offence has at any time previously been discharged absolutely in respect of the commission by him of an offence it shall be competent, in the proceedings for that offence, to lay before the court the order of absolute discharge in like manner as if the order were a conviction.

(5) Where an offender is discharged absolutely by a court of summary jurisdiction, he shall have the like right of appeal against the finding that he committed the offence as if that finding were a conviction.

(6) Where an offender, being not less than 16 years of age at the time of his conviction of an offence for which he is placed on probation as mentioned in subsection (1) above, is subsequently sentenced under this Act for that offence, the provisions of that subsection shall cease to apply to the conviction.

DEFINITIONS
"court of summary jurisdiction": s.307(1).
"offence": s.307(1).
"probation": s.307(1).

Disqualification

Disqualification where vehicle used to commit offence

248.—(1) Where a person is convicted of an offence (other than one triable only summarily) and the court which passes sentence is satisfied that a motor vehicle was used for the purposes of committing or facilitating the commission of that offence, the court may order him to be disqualified for such a period as the court thinks fit from holding or obtaining a licence to drive a motor vehicle granted under Part III of the Road Traffic Act 1988.

(2) A court which makes an order under this section disqualifying a person from holding or obtaining a licence shall require him to produce any such licence held by him and its counterpart.

(3) Any reference in this section to facilitating the commission of an offence shall include a reference to the taking of any steps after it has been committed for the purpose of disposing of any property to which it relates or of avoiding apprehension or detection.

(4) In relation to licences which came into force before 1st June 1990, the reference in subsection (2) above to the counterpart of a licence shall be disregarded.

DEFINITIONS
"offence": s.307(1).
"order": s.307(1).

General power to disqualify offenders

[1]**248A.**—(1) Subject to subsection (2) below, the court by or before which a person is convicted of an offence may, in addition to or instead of dealing with him in any other way, order him to be disqualified from holding or obtaining a licence to drive a motor vehicle granted under Part III of the Road Traffic Act 1988 for such period as it thinks fit.

(2) Where the person is convicted of an offence for which the sentence is fixed by law, subsection (1) above shall have effect as if the words "or instead of" were omitted.

(3) Subsections (2) and (4) of section 248 of this Act shall apply for the purposes of this section as they apply for the purposes of that section.

DEFINITIONS
"offence": s.307(1) of the 1995 Act.
"disqualified": s.98(1) of the Road Traffic Offenders Act 1988.
"motor vehicle": s.185(1) of the Road Traffic Act 1988.

NOTE
[1]Inserted by the Crime and Punishment (Scotland) Act 1997 (c. 48) s.15 with effect from January 1, 1998 in terms of the Crime and Punishment (Scotland) Act 1977 (Commencement

No. 2 and Transitional and Consequential Provisions) Order 1997 (S.I. 1997 No. 2323) Art. 3, Sched. 1.

GENERAL NOTE

This section, introduced at a late stage in the life of the Crime and Punishment (Scotland) Bill, gives courts or categories of courts selected by the Secretary of State, a general power of disqualification from driving as an element of sentence on conviction of any offence. This power is quite distinct from the specific provisions found in s.248 and may be used even where the offence leading to conviction was neither a road traffic contravention nor a crime involving the use of a motor vehicle in its commission. The section took effect on January 1, 1998 but only for offences committed after that date.

Section 248B of the Act, which took effect on the same date, provides for disqualification as a sentencing alternative to imprisonment in cases of fine default. It has to be said that these two provisions passed into law with little or no Parliamentary discussion.

A s.248A disqualification can be imposed as an element of any sentence including a sentence fixed by law (subs. (2)), and applies to an offender irrespective of whether or not he possesses a driving licence; subs. (3) serves to make it clear that any driving licence held by an accused will require to be produced to the court and it may now be necessary for agents to advise clients to ensure that driving licences are available at any court diet, and for agents to be ready to address the court on this aspect of sentence.

It is important to observe that this general power of disqualification may be imposed even where the original offence did not involve the use of a motor vehicle in the commission of the offence.

It remains to be seen how far, if at all, the sentencing principles, already established in relation to disqualification for Road Traffic offences, can properly apply to s.248A or s.248B disqualifications: notably where a conviction or sentence is under appeal, what mechanism, if any, exists for suspension of disqualification? It does not appear that the general provisions of ss.39 to 41 of the Road Traffic Offenders Act 1988 (c. 53) can be read into ss.248A and 248B. A fuller discussion is found in the annotations to s.15 of the Crime and Punishment (Scotland) Act 1997 below.

Power to disqualify fine defaulters

[1]**248B.**—(1) This section applies where the court has power to impose a period of imprisonment in default of payment of a fine, or any part or instalment of a fine.

(2) Where this section applies, the court may, instead of imposing such a period of imprisonment as is mentioned in subsection (1) above, order that where the offender is in default he shall be disqualfied from holding a licence to drive a motor vehicle granted under Part III of the Road Traffic Act 1988 for such period not exceeding twelve months as the court thinks fit.

(3) Where an order has been made under subsection (2) above in default of payment of any fine, or any part or instalment of a fine—

(a) on payment of the fine to any person authorised to receive it, the order shall cease to have effect; and

(b) on payment of any part of that fine to any such person, the period of disqualification to which the order relates shall be reduced (or, as the case may be, further reduced) by a number of days bearing as nearly as possible the same proportion to such period as the sum so paid bears to the amount of the fine outstanding at the commencement of that period.

(4) Subsections (2) and (4) of section 248 of this Act shall apply for the purposes of this section as they apply for the purposes of that section.

(5) Section 19 of the Road Traffic Offenders Act 1988 (proof of disqualification in Scottish proceedings) shall apply to an order under subsection (2) above as it applies to a conviction or extract conviction.

(6) The Secretary of State may by order made by statutory instrument vary the period specified in subsection (2) above; but not such order shall be made unless a draft of the order has been laid before, and approved by a resolution of, each House of Parliament.

DEFINITIONS
"imprisonment": s.307(1) of the 1995 Act.
"fine": s.307(1).
"extract conviction": s.307(1) above.

NOTE
[1]Inserted by the Crime and Punishment (Scotland) Act 1997 (c. 48) s.15 with effect from January 1, 1998 in terms of the Crime and Punishment (Scotland) Act 1997 (Commencement No. 2 and Transitional and Consequential Provisions) Order 1997 (S.I. 1997 No. 2323) Art. 3, Sched. 1.

Application of sections 248A and 248B

[1]**248C.**—(1) The Secretary of State may by order prescribe which courts, or class or classes of courts, may make orders under section 248A or 248B of this Act and, without prejudice to that generality, in relation to district courts an order under this subsection may make provision as respects such courts by reference to whether the court is constituted by a stipendiary magistrate or by one or more justices.

(2) An order made under subsection (1) above shall be made by statutory instrument and any such instrument shall be subject to annulment in pursuance of a resolution of either House of Parliament.

(3) Where an order has been made under subsection (1) above, section 248(1) of this Act shall not apply as respects any court, or class or classes of court prescribed by the order.

NOTE
[1]Inserted by the Crime and Punishment (Scotland) Act 1997 (c. 48) s.15 with effect from October 20, 1997 in terms of the Crime and Punishment (Scotland) Act 1997 (Commencement No. 2 and Transitional and Consequential Provisions) Order 1997 (S.I. 1997 No. 2323) Art. 3, Sched. 1.

GENERAL NOTE
Section 248C was brought into force on October 20, 1997 and empowers the Secretary of State to make orders to prescribe the particular courts, or categories of courts, which will ultimately have power to impose driving disqualification as a penalty on conviction of any offence (s.248A) or as an alternative to imprisonment following fine default (s.248B). The main provisions came into effect on January 1, 1998.

The purpose of this section, introduced at a late stage to the Bill, is to make disqualification from driving available as a punishment for a broad range of offences, including fine default. The majority of section 15 is inserted into the 1995 Procedure Act as ss.248A, 248B and 248C and to s.252, with only a small addition (subs. (3)) to the Proceeds of Crime (Scotland) Act 1995. Despite, or perhaps because of, the brevity of the draftsmanship, the mechanics of this new legislation are by no means clear and much depends upon the extent to which the provisions of the Road Traffic Offenders Act 1988 are held to apply to it.

Some concern was expressed during debate of this provision that the court should not impose a s.248 disqualification until suitability reports had first been considered; while social enquiry reports would usually have been sought before the court could consider imprisonment, such reports are not generally obtained in respect of fine defaulters who can now be disqualified under s.248B, as an alternative to imprisonment, for fine default. The Lord Advocate indicated that the new disqualification provisions would be tested by a number of pilot schemes in both urban and rural areas before consideration is given to their more widespread introduction. (*Hansard*, H.L., March 19, 1997, col. 942).

Compensation

Compensation order against convicted person

249.—(1) Subject to subsections (2) and (4) below, where a person is convicted of an offence the court, instead of or in addition to dealing with him in any other way, may make an order (in this Part of this Act referred to as "a compensation order") requiring him to pay compensation for any personal injury, loss or damage caused, whether directly or indirectly, by the acts which constituted the offence.

(2) It shall not be competent for a court to make a compensation order—

(a) where, under section 246(2) of this Act, it makes an order discharging him absolutely;

(b) where, under section 228 of this Act, it makes a probation order; or

(c) at the same time as, under section 202 of this Act, it defers sentence.

(3) Where, in the case of an offence involving dishonest appropriation, or the unlawful taking and using of property or a contravention of section 178(1) of the Road Traffic Act 1988 (taking motor vehicle without authority etc.) the property is recovered, but has been damaged while out of the owner's possession, that damage, however and by whomsoever it was in fact caused, shall be treated for the purposes of subsection (1) above as having been caused by the acts which constituted the offence.

(4) No compensation order shall be made in respect of—

(a) loss suffered in consequence of the death of any person; or

(b) injury, loss or damage due to an accident arising out of the presence of a motor vehicle on a road, except such damage as is treated, by virtue of subsection (3) above, as having been caused by the convicted person's acts.

(5) In determining whether to make a compensation order against any person, and in determining the amount to be paid by any person under such order, the court shall take into consideration his means so far as known to the court.

(6) For the purposes of subsection (5) above, in assessing the means of a person who is serving, or is to serve, a period of imprisonment or detention, no account shall be taken of earnings contingent upon his obtaining employment after release.

(7) In solemn proceedings there shall be no limit on the amount which may be awarded under a compensation order.

(8) In summary proceedings—

(a) a sheriff, or a stipendiary magistrate appointed under section 5 of the District Courts (Scotland) Act 1975, shall have power to make a compensation order awarding in respect of each offence an amount not exceeding the prescribed sum;

(b) a judge of a district court (other than such stipendiary magistrate) shall have power to make a compensation order awarding in respect of each offence an amount not exceeding level 4 on the standard scale.

(9) Payment of any amount under a compensation order shall be made to the clerk of the court who shall account for the amount to the person entitled thereto.

(10) Only the court shall have power to enforce a compensation order.

DEFINITIONS

"compensation order": s.249(1).
"offence": s.307(1).
"probation order": s.307(1).
"prescribed sum": s.225(8)
"standard scale": s.225(1).

GENERAL NOTE

Compensation orders have probably not been sought for as many offences as they might have but that may merely reflect the impecunious state of most convicted people in Scotland. Nevertheless the law to date has been clarified by several decisions: in *Stewart v. H.M. Advocate*, 1982 S.C.C.R. 203 it was held on appeal that an order made in respect of "inconvenience suffered" was not open to criticism.

In *Carmichael v. Siddique*, 1985 S.C.C.R. 145 a sheriff rejected an argument that a compensation order was competent and appropriate only where the legal position was clear and bereft of complexities and the damage was capable of precise valuation and was not great. Such an argument has not, apparently, been put forward again. In *Collins v. Lowe*, 1990 S.C.C.R. 605 it was held on appeal that it was competent to make a compensation order in addition to custodial sentences, an approach followed in *Moses v. MacDonald*, 1996 G.W.D. 1–62 where compensation was fixed to cover a vehicle insurance excess and other costs in addition to a maximum custodial sentence. In *Robertson v. Lees*, 1992 S.C.C.R. 545 the Appeal Court observed that the fact that the accused was a first offender was not a relevant factor when setting the amount of compensation: equally it has been held to be irrelevant that the complainer was insured (see *Ely v. Donnelly*, 1996 S.C.C.R. 537 which also holds that the guidelines relating to the period of time allowable for repayment of fines, have no bearing upon repayment of compensation orders).

In *Sullivan v. McLeod*, 1998 S.L.T. 552, the construction of "at the same time" in subs. (2)(c) was raised: S. had been convicted on a summary complaint containing two charges and a deferred sentence was imposed on one charge, a compensation order on the other. While observing that such a disposal would only rarely be appropriate, the Appeal Court held that all that subs. (2)(c) sought to prevent was the imposition of both a deferment of sentence and a compensation order for the same offence. Where a number of offences appeared on the same complaint, separate disposals could be considered in relation to each charge but *no cumulo* sentence could incorporate both a deferred sentence and a compensation order.

Compensation cannot be awarded simply for causing a complainer fear and alarm (see *Smillie v. Wilson*, 1990 S.C.C.R. 330, *Simpson v. Carmichael*, 1996 G.W.D. 32–1916 and *Armit v. Ruxton*, 1998 G.W.D. 23–1305), there must be loss, damage or injury. By the same token compensation cannot be awarded to a group or individual unconnected with the events prompting a compensation award; in *H.M. Advocate v. Nelson*, 1996 G.W.D. 26–1489 the Crown successfully appealed against a compensation award to Victim Support, where that organisation had no involvement in the incidents libelled, the award being quashed as incompetent. Imposition of a compensation order by the court may present practical difficulties should the Crown elect to appeal a sentence as unduly lenient; see *H.M. Advocate v. Jamieson*, 1997 S.L.T. 955, discussed at p. 300 above.

Finally, questions of causation must be examined closely, especially from the accused's point of view, for in *Nazir v. Normand*, 1994 S.C.C.R. 265 the appellant caused and permitted another to drive an uninsured car and the appellant's appeal against a consequential compensation order was refused.

Compensation orders: supplementary provisions

250.—(1) Where a court considers that in respect of an offence it would be appropriate to impose a fine and to make a compensation order but the convicted person has insufficient means to pay both an appropriate fine and an appropriate amount in compensation the court should prefer a compensation order.

(2) Where a convicted person has both been fined and had a compensation order made against him in respect of the same offence or different offences in the same proceedings, a payment by the convicted person shall first be applied in satisfaction of the compensation order.

(3) For the purposes of any appeal or review, a compensation order is a sentence.

(4) Where a compensation order has been made against a person, a payment made to the court in respect of the order shall be retained until the determination of any appeal in relation to the order.

DEFINITIONS
"compensation order": s.249(1).
"offence": s.307(1).

GENERAL NOTE
There are, having regard to subs. (3), several reported cases in which a compensation order has been appealed. For example, in *Brown v. Normand*, 1988 S.C.C.R. 229 a sentence of a fine and a compensation order was appealed on the ground that the sentence was excessive and it was allowed. Appeals were similarly allowed in *Smillie v. Wilson*, 1990 S.C.C.R. 133, *Hughes v.*

Brown, 1990 G.W.D. 13–670, *Crawford v. McGlennan*, 1990 G.W.D 21–1170, *McMahon v. Hamilton*, 1990 G.W.D. 37–2124, *Wilson v. Brown*, 1992 G.W.D. 6–288, *Currie v. Webster*, 1992 G.W.D. 13–722 and *Clark v. O'Brien*, 1995 G.W.D. 20–1130. Such appeals were refused in *McPhail v. Hamilton*, 1991 G.W.D. 24–1375 and *Barclay v. Douglas*, 1994 G.W.D. 1–37.

Review of compensation order

251.—(1) Without prejudice to the power contained in section 213 of this Act, (as applied by section 252 of this Act), at any time before a compensation order has been complied with or fully complied with, the court, on the application of the person against whom the compensation order was made, may discharge the compensation order or reduce the amount that remains to be paid if it appears to the court that—
   (a) the injury, loss or damage in respect of which the compensation order was made has been held in civil proceedings to be less than it was taken to be for the purposes of the compensation order; or
   (b) that property the loss of which is reflected in the compensation order has been recovered.
   (2) In subsection (1) above "the court" means—
   (a) in a case where, as respects the compensation order, a transfer of fine order under section 222 of this Act (as applied by the said section 252) is effective and the court by which the compensation order is enforceable is in terms of the transfer of fine order a court of summary jurisdiction in Scotland, that court; or
   (b) in any other case, the court which made the compensation order or, where that court was the High Court, by which the order was first enforceable.

DEFINITIONS
   "compensation order": s.249(1).
   "court": s.251(2).

Enforcement of compensation orders: application of provisions relating to fines

252.—(1) The provisions of this Act specified in subsection (2) below shall, subject to any necessary modifications and to the qualifications mentioned in that subsection, apply in relation to compensation orders as they apply in relation to fines; and section 91 of the Magistrates' Courts Act 1980 and article 96 of the Magistrates' Courts (Northern Ireland) Order 1981 shall be construed accordingly.
   (2) The provisions mentioned in subsection (1) above are—
   section 211(3), (4) and (7) to (9) (enforcement of fines);
   section 212 (fines in summary proceedings);
   section 213 (power to remit fines), with the omission of the words "or (4)" in subsection (2) of that section;
   section 214 (time for payment) with the omission of—
         (a) the words from "unless" to "its decision" in subsection (4); and
         (b) subsection (5);
   section 215 (further time for payment);
   section 216 (reasons for default);
   section 217 (supervision pending payment of fine);
   section 218 (supplementary provisions), except that subsection (1) of that section shall not apply in relation to compensation orders made in solemn proceedings;
   subject to subsection (3) below, section 219(1)(b), (2), (3), (5), (6) and (8) (maximum period of imprisonment for non-payment of fine);
   section 220 (payment of fine in part by prisoner);
   section 221 (recovery by civil diligence);

section 222 (transfer of fine orders);

section 223 (action of clerk of court on transfer of fine order);[1]

section 224 (discharge from imprisonment to be specified)[1]; and

[2]section 248B (driving disqualification for fine defaulters) so far as it relates to the power conferred by section 219(1)(b).

(3) In the application of the provisions of section 219 of this Act mentioned in subsection (2) above for the purposes of subsection (1) above—

(a) a court may impose imprisonment in respect of a fine and decline to impose imprisonment in respect of a compensation order but not vice versa; and

(b) where a court imposes imprisonment both in respect of a fine and of a compensation order the amounts in respect of which imprisonment is imposed shall, for the purposes of subsection (2) of the said section 219, be aggregated.

DEFINITION
   "fines": s.307(1).

NOTES
   [1]Amended by the Crime and Punishment (Scotland) Act 1997 (c. 48) s.15(2) with effect from January 1, 1998 in terms of the Crime and Punishment (Scotland) Act 1997 (Commencement No. 2 and Transitional and Consequential Provisions) Order 1997 (S.I. 1997 No. 2323) Art. 4 and Sched. 2.
   [2]Inserted by the above provisions.

Effect of compensation order on subsequent award of damages in civil proceedings

253.—(1) This section shall have effect where a compensation order or a service compensation order or award has been made in favour of any person in respect of any injury, loss or damage and a claim by him in civil proceedings for damages in respect thereof subsequently falls to be determined.

(2) The damages in the civil proceedings shall be assessed without regard to the order or award; but where the whole or part of the amount awarded by the order or award has been paid, the damages awarded in the civil proceedings shall be restricted to the amount (if any) by which, as so assessed, they exceed the amount paid under the order or award.

(3) Where the whole or part of the amount awarded by the order or award remains unpaid and damages are awarded in a judgment in the civil proceedings, then, unless the person against whom the order or award was made has ceased to be liable to pay the amount unpaid (whether in consequence of an appeal, or of his imprisonment for default or otherwise), the court shall direct that the judgment—

(a) if it is for an amount not exceeding the amount unpaid under the order or award, shall not be enforced; or

(b) if it is for an amount exceeding the amount unpaid under the order or award, shall not be enforced except to the extent that it exceeds the amount unpaid,

without the leave of the court.

(4) In this section a "service compensation order or award" means—

(a) an order requiring the payment of compensation under paragraph 11 of—

   (i) Schedule 5A to the Army Act 1955;

   (ii) Schedule 5A to the Air Force Act 1955; or

   (iii) Schedule 4A to the Naval Discipline Act 1957; or

(b) an award of stoppages payable by way of compensation under any of those Acts.

DEFINITIONS
    "compensation orders": s.249(1).
    "order": s.307(1).
    "service compensation order": s.253(4).

GENERAL NOTE
    Following *Goodhall v. Carmichael*, 1984 S.C.C.R. 247 it is clear that credible though uncorroborated evidence is sufficient to settle the value of the loss to be compensated, a practice that is now consistent with the civil law of evidence. The appeal by Goodhall was dismissed without Opinions being delivered. However, in an article following that appeal it was said that Lord Wheatley had commented during the appeal that "the whole point of compensation orders was to save victims the need to go to the civil courts": C.J. Docherty and G. Maher *Corroboration and Compensation Orders* 1984 S.L.T.(News) 125 at p. 126.

Forfeiture

Search warrant for forfeited articles

254. Where a court has made an order for the forfeiture of an article, the court or any justice may, if satisfied on information on oath—
    (a) that there is reasonable cause to believe that the article is to be found in any place or premises; and
    (b) that admission to the place or premises has been refused or that a refusal of such admission is apprehended,
issue a warrant of search which may be executed according to law.

PART XII

EVIDENCE

Special capacity

Special capacity

255. Where an offence is alleged to be committed in any special capacity, as by the holder of a licence, master of a vessel, occupier of a house, or the like, the fact that the accused possesses the qualification necessary to the commission of the offence shall, unless challenged—
    (a) in the case of proceedings on indictment, by giving notice of a preliminary objection under paragraph (b) of section 72(1) of this Act or under that paragraph as applied by section 71(2) of this Act; or
    (b) in summary proceedings, by preliminary objection before his plea is recorded,
be held as admitted.

DEFINITIONS
    "indictment": s.307(1).
    "offence": s.307(1).

GENERAL NOTE
    This section relates both to solemn and summary procedure. A special capacity is a capacity which is special to the accused and is necessary to the commission of the offence.
    In order to take advantage of this evidential concession, a prosecutor has to give notice in the libel of the capacity upon which he intends to found. Failure to do so will compel the prosecution to lead sufficient evidence to establish that the accused did possess the capacity essential to the commission of the offence. Furthermore if the Crown libels a special capacity and then proceeds to conduct its case by leading evidence of the fact, it risks being held to have waived the benefit of the presumption (*Wimpey Homes Holdings v. Lees*, 1991 S.C.C.R. 447; *Smith v. Ross*, 1937 J.C. 65). Note that production of an extract conviction in support of a charge of driving while disqualified does not constitute a waiver of the presumption by the Crown (*Paton v. Lees*, 1992 S.C.C.R. 212).
    A special capacity is not implied in any charge so while no express formula of words is

required, it must be patent that the accused was acting in that capacity at the time of the offence (*Ross v. Simpson*, 1994 S.C.C.R. 847).

Any denial of a special capacity must be stated at the first calling of a summary complaint (s.144(4)) and will only be permitted at future diets on cause shown (s.144(5)): in solemn proceedings s.72(1)(b)(iii) applies rather untidily to both sheriff and jury, the High Court, proceedings. (It will be remembered that first diets are mandatory in the case of sheriff and jury trials; while preliminary diets are normally optional in High Court cases—such a diet is essential to intimate a challenge under s.72(1)(b)(iii).)

Examples of special capacity are: being subject to bail conditions in terms of the Bail etc. (Scotland) Act 1980 and, now, in terms of s.27(4) of the 1996 Act as amended, being subject of bail conditions imposed after July 4, 1996; being a common prostitute (*Allan v. McGraw*, 1986 S.C.C.R. 257); being a known thief as defined in s.58 of the Civic Government (Scotland) Act 1982 (c. 45) (*Newlands v. MacPhail*, 1991 S.C.C.R. 88); being a disqualified driver (*Paton v. Lees*, cited above); ownership of a vessel (*Thomas W. Ward Ltd v. Waugh*, 1934 J.C. 13); and in certain circumstances, being the parent of a child (*Ross v. Simpson*, 1994 S.C.C.R. 847). It is submitted that ss.233 and 241 above which relate to offences committed at placements by those subject to probation or community service orders equally create categories of special capacity as well as being aggravated offences. See *McClory v. MacKinnon*, 1996 S.C.C.R. 367 in relation to the construction of "occupier".

Proof of age

[1]**255A.** Where the age of any person is specified in an indictment or complaint, it shall, unless challenged—

(a) in the case of proceedings on indictment by giving notice of a preliminary objection under paragraph (b) of section 72(1) of this Act or under that paragraph as applied by section 71(2) of this Act; or

(b) in summary proceedings—
    (i) by preliminary objection before the plea of the accused is recorded; or
    (ii) by objection at such later time as the court may in special circumstances allow,

be held as admitted.

DEFINITIONS
"complaint": s.307(1) of the 1995 Act.
"indictment": s.307(1) of the 1995 Act.

NOTE
[1]Inserted by the Crime and Punishment (Scotland) Act 1997 (c. 48) s.27 with effect from August 1, 1997 by the Crime and Punishment (Scotland) Act 1997 (Commencement and Transitional Provisions) Order 1997 (S.I. 1997 No. 1712) para. 3.

GENERAL NOTE
This provision was introduced into the 1997 Act at a relatively late stage and would apply to witness particulars in cases where the age of a witness is a necessary element of the offence, notably the broad range of sexual offences now contained in Part I of the Criminal Law (Consolidation) (Scotland) Act 1995, and in the Licensing (Scotland) Act 1976. This provision is sufficiently broadly drafted to apply to cirumstances where the libel indicates the age of the victim as an aggravating factor, for example in assaults or housebreakings, as well as where the age of the accused is a necessary element of the offence, as in the Firearms Act 1968 s.22 (acquisition and possession of firearms by minors).

It may be that specification of a witness's age in the list of witnesses on an indictment could create a rebuttable presumption. Any objection to specification of the age of a victim, witness or accused must be specified at a preliminary (or first) diet in solemn proceedings, or, in summary proceedings, by preliminary objection prior to tendering any plea (s.144(4) of the 1995 Act).

Agreed evidence

Agreements and admissions as to evidence

256.—(1) In any trial it shall not be necessary for the accused or for the prosecutor—

(a) to prove any fact which is admitted by the other; or
(b) to prove any document, the terms and application of which are not in dispute between them,

and, without prejudice to paragraph 1 of Schedule 8 to this Act, copies of any documents may, by agreement of the parties, be accepted as equivalent to the originals.

(2) For the purposes of subsection (1) above, any admission or agreement shall be made by lodging with the clerk of court a minute in that behalf signed—

(a) in the case of an admission, by the party making the admission or, if that party is the accused and he is legally represented, by his counsel or solicitor; and

(b) in the case of an agreement, by the prosecutor and the accused or, if he is legally represented, his counsel or solicitor.

(3) Where a minute has been signed and lodged as aforesaid, any facts and documents admitted or agreed thereby shall be deemed to have been duly proved.

DEFINITIONS
"prosecutor": s.307(1).
"trial": s.307(1).

GENERAL NOTE
This section applies to both solemn and summary procedure and provides for the lodging of Minutes of Agreement or Minutes of Admissions describing facts accepted as established in the proceedings. Documentary evidence or copies thereof can be admitted in this way; where such evidence is not formally agreed, or is not agreed with sufficient celerity, then recourse can be had to the provisions of s.258 which permits service of a statement of what is felt to be uncontroversial evidence upon other parties or, alternatively, the use of the procedures for setting up documentary evidence contained in Sched. 8 (this preserves the terms of Sched. 3 of the Prisoners and Criminal Proceedings (Scotland) Act 1993 (c. 9)).

It will be recalled that there is no timescale stipulated for agreement of evidence by Minutes of Agreement or Admission and, indeed, these can be prepared and lodged at any point in proceedings before evidence is closed; by contrast s.258 demands a response from the other party in seven days to any statement of facts served validly and is only available prior for use more than 14 days before trial.

Duty to seek agreement of evidence

257.—(1) Subject to subsection (2) below, the prosecutor and the accused (or each of the accused if more than one) shall each identify any facts which are facts—

(a) which he would, apart from this section, be seeking to prove;

(b) which he considers unlikely to be disputed by the other party (or by any of the other parties); and

(c) in proof of which he does not wish to lead oral evidence,

and shall, without prejudice to section 258 of this Act, take all reasonable steps to secure the agreement of the other party (or each of the other parties) to them; and the other party (or each of the other parties) shall take all reasonable steps to reach such agreement.

(2) Subsection (1) above shall not apply in relation to proceedings as respects which the accused (or any of the accused if more than one) is not legally represented.

(3) The duty under subsection (1) above applies—

(a) in relation to proceedings on indictment, from the date of service of the indictment until the swearing of the jury or, where intimation is given under section 76 of this Act, the date of that intimation; and

(b) in relation to summary proceedings, from the date on which the accused pleads not guilty until the swearing of the first witness or, where the accused tenders a plea of guilty at any time before the first witness is sworn, the date when he does so.

"indictment": s.307(1).
"prosecutor": s.307(1).

GENERAL NOTE

This section applies to both solemn and summary proceedings. The purpose of this, and the following section, is to identify evidence which is capable of being received without the need for its introduction by parole evidence and the need for witnesses to attend court. Prior to the introduction of these provisions there was no onus upon any party to identify, or agree, formal or uncontroversial evidence and while a duty is now placed on parties to consider such material, there is no sanction for failure to do so. The prosecutor and, only where he is legally represented the accused, are each required to identify factual evidence felt to be capable of agreement and to take all reasonable steps to agree these matters before trial.

Section 256 provides a mechanism for agreement of evidence, or for the admission of facts by one party; s.258 enacts a procedure for service of statements of fact upon other parties. Subsection (3) provides two different timescales during which the duties imposed on parties persist: in solemn proceedings this is the period from service of the indictment until the commencement of trial (see s.64(9)) or, in the case of accelerated pleas, until the accused gives notice in writing of a plea which is accepted by the Crown (see s.76(1)); in summary proceedings, the period from the date of the plea being recorded (s.146(1)) until trial begins (s.147(4)) or a plea of guilty is intimated.

Uncontroversial evidence

258.—(1) This section applies where, in any criminal proceedings, a party (in this section referred to as "the first party") considers that facts which that party would otherwise be seeking to prove are unlikely to be disputed by the other parties to the proceedings.

(2) Where this section applies, the first party may prepare and sign a statement—

(a) specifying the facts concerned; or

(b) referring to such facts as set out in a document annexed to the statement,

and shall, not less than 14 days before the trial diet, serve a copy of the statement and any such document on every other party.

(3) Unless any other party serves on the first party, not more than seven days after the date of service of the copy on him under subsection (2) above or by such later time as the court may in special circumstances allow, a notice that he challenges any fact specified or referred to in the statement, the facts so specified or referred to shall be deemed to have been conclusively proved.

(4) Where a notice is served under subsection (3) above, the facts specified or referred to in the statement shall be deemed to have been conclusively proved only in so far as unchallenged in the notice.

(5) Subsections (3) and (4) above shall not preclude a party from leading evidence of circumstances relevant to, or other evidence in explanation of, any fact specified or referred to in the statement.

(6) Notwithstanding subsections (3) and (4) above, the court—

(a) may, on the application of any party, where it is satisfied that there are special circumstances; and

(b) shall, on the joint application of all the parties,

direct that the presumptions in those subsections shall not apply in relation to such fact specified or referred to in the statement as is specified in the direction.

(7) An application under subsection (6) above may be made at any time after the commencement of the trial and before the commencement of the prosecutor's address to the court on the evidence.

(8) Where the court makes a direction under subsection (6) above it shall, unless all the parties otherwise agree, adjourn the trial and may, without

prejudice to section 268 of this Act, permit any party to lead evidence as to any such fact as is specified in the direction, notwithstanding that a witness or production concerned is not included in any list lodged by the parties and that the notice required by sections 67(5) and 78(4) of this Act has not been given.

(9) A copy of a statement or a notice required, under this section, to be served on any party shall be served in such manner as may be prescribed by Act of Adjournal; and a written execution purporting to be signed by the person who served such copy or notice together with, where appropriate, the relevant post office receipt shall be sufficient evidence of such service.

DEFINITIONS
"diet": s.307(1).
"prosecutor": s.307(1).

GENERAL NOTE
This section applies to solemn and summary proceedings. It introduces a new procedure for evidence, which a party regards as "unlikely to be disputed", to be held as admitted after a statement of facts has been served in conformity to subs. (2) and not challenged by its recipient as provided by subs. (3). At best this provision can be seen as a further means of securing agreement of evidence but, on a cautionary note, great vigilance will have to be exercised by parties to ensure that any evidence which would be disputed does not slip through without challenge. Subsection (3) does permit a notice of challenge to be tendered late but its acceptance by the court is far from automatic.

This procedure was introduced in the Criminal Justice (Scotland) Act 1995 (c. 20) and followed a recommendation by the Scottish Law Commission Report No. 137 "*Evidence: Report on Documentary Evidence and Proof of Undisputed Facts in Criminal Proceedings*" of such a procedure for use by the prosecution; it will be observed that s.258 is available for use by both prosecution and defence.

It will be noted that there seems to be no limit on the number of s.258 Notices which can be served more than 14 days prior to trial, and that subs. (5) still enables the leading of evidence in clarification or explanation of the statement of facts. Subsection (6) operates as a saving provision to enable the court, or the parties, during the trial to override the terms of a statement of facts which is not in accordance with the evidence, and where the court exercises these powers, to adjourn the trial to permit parties to lead evidence struck at by that operation (see subs. (7)). Note that such evidence can be received in solemn proceedings even when it has not been specified on Crown or defence lists of witnesses or productions.

Rules 21.1 and 21.2 in the 1996 Act of Adjournal specify that Forms 21.1–A and 21.2 are to be used to introduce a statement of fact or challenge same. Form 21.1–B provides a docquet for documents referred to in a statement of facts. The Act is silent as to how statements of fact, modified or unmodified by challenge, are to be introduced into the record of proceedings; they may be treated in the same way as a Minute of Agreement, being read to a jury by the clerk of court, or received by the judge in summary cases but this is not settled. It is apparent that parties serving statements of fact will need to preserve, and be able to produce to the court a copy notice and completed execution of service.

Hearsay

Exceptions to the rule that hearsay evidence is inadmissible

259.—(1) Subject to the following provisions of this section, evidence of a statement made by a person otherwise than while giving oral evidence in court in criminal proceedings shall be admissible in those proceedings as evidence of any matter contained in the statement where the judge is satisfied—

    (a) that the person who made the statement will not give evidence in the proceedings of such matter for any of the reasons mentioned in subsection (2) below;

    (b) that evidence of the matter would be admissible in the proceedings if that person gave direct oral evidence of it;

(c) that the person who made the statement would have been, at the time the statement was made, a competent witness in such proceedings; and

(d) that there is evidence which would entitle a jury properly directed, or in summary proceedings would entitle the judge, to find that the statement was made and that either—
　　　(i) it is contained in a document; or
　　　(ii) a person who gave oral evidence in the proceedings as to the statement has direct personal knowledge of the making of the statement.

(2) The reasons referred to in paragraph (a) of subsection (1) above are that the person who made the statement—

(a) is dead or is, by reason of his bodily or mental condition, unfit or unable to give evidence in any competent manner;

(b) is named and otherwise sufficiently identified, but is outwith the United Kingdom and it is not reasonably practicable to secure his attendance at the trial or to obtain his evidence in any other competent manner;

(c) is named and otherwise sufficiently identified, but cannot be found and all reasonable steps which, in the circumstances, could have been taken to find him have been so taken;

(d) having been authorised to do so by virtue of a ruling of the court in the proceedings that he is entitled to refuse to give evidence in connection with the subject matter of the statement on the grounds that such evidence might incriminate him, refuses to give such evidence; or

(e) is called as a witness and either—
　　　(i) refuses to take the oath or affirmation; or
　　　(ii) having been sworn as a witness and directed by the judge to give evidence in connection with the subject matter of the statement refuses to do so,
and in the application of this paragraph to a child, the reference to a witness refusing to take the oath or affirmation or, as the case may be, to having been sworn shall be construed as a reference to a child who has refused to accept an admonition to tell the truth or, having been so admonished, refuses to give evidence as mentioned above.

(3) Evidence of a statement shall not be admissible by virtue of subsection (1) above where the judge is satisfied that the occurrence of any of the circumstances mentioned in paragraphs (a) to (e) of subsection (2) above, by virtue of which the statement would otherwise be admissible, is caused by—

(a) the person in support of whose case the evidence would be given; or

(b) any other person acting on his behalf,
for the purpose of securing that the person who made the statement does not give evidence for the purposes of the proceedings either at all or in connection with the subject matter of the statement.

(4) Where in any proceedings evidence of a statement made by any person is admitted by reference to any of the reasons mentioned in paragraphs (a) to (c) and (e)(i) of subsection (2) above—

(a) any evidence which, if that person had given evidence in connection with the subject matter of the statement, would have been admissible as relevant to his credibility as a witness shall be admissible for that purpose in those proceedings;

(b) evidence may be given of any matter which, if that person had given evidence in connection with the subject matter of the statement, could have been put to him in cross-examination as relevant to his credibility as a witness but of which evidence could not have been adduced by the cross-examining party; and

(c) evidence tending to prove that that person, whether before or after making the statement, made in whatever manner some other statement which is inconsistent with it shall be admissible for the purpose of showing that he has contradicted himself.

(5) Subject to subsection (6) below, where a party intends to apply to have evidence of a statement admitted by virtue of subsection (1) above he shall, before the trial diet, give notice in writing of—

(a) that fact;

(b) the witnesses and productions to be adduced in connection with such evidence; and

(c) such other matters as may be prescribed by Act of Adjournal,

to every other party to the proceedings and, for the purposes of this subsection, such evidence may be led notwithstanding that a witness or production concerned is not included in any list lodged by the parties and that the notice required by sections 67(5) and 78(4) of this Act has not been given.

(6) A party shall not be required to give notice as mentioned in subsection (5) above where—

(a) the grounds for seeking to have evidence of a statement admitted are as mentioned in paragraph (d) or (e) of subsection (2) above; or

(b) he satisfies the judge that there was good reason for not giving such notice.

(7) If no other party to the proceedings objects to the admission of evidence of a statement by virtue of subsection (1) above, the evidence shall be admitted without the judge requiring to be satisfied as mentioned in that subsection.

(8) For the purposes of the determination of any matter upon which the judge is required to be satisfied under subsection (1) above—

(a) except to the extent that any other party to the proceedings challenges them and insists in such challenge, it shall be presumed that the circumstances are as stated by the party seeking to introduce evidence of the statement; and

(b) where such a challenge is insisted in, the judge shall determine the matter on the balance of probabilities, and he may draw any reasonable inference—

(i) from the circumstances in which the statement was made or otherwise came into being; or

(ii) from any other circumstances, including, where the statement is contained in a document, the form and contents of the document.

(9) Where evidence of a statement has been admitted by virtue of subsection (1) above on the application of one party to the proceedings, without prejudice to anything in any enactment or rule of law, the judge may permit any party to lead additional evidence of such description as the judge may specify, notwithstanding that a witness or production concerned is not included in any list lodged by the parties and that the notice required by sections 67(5) and 78(4) of this Act has not been given.

(10) Any reference in subsections (5), (6) and (9) above to evidence shall include a reference to evidence led in connection with any determination required to be made for the purposes of subsection (1) above.

DEFINITIONS

"child": s.307(1).

"criminal proceedings": s.262(3).

"document": s.262(3).

"judge": s.307(1).

"statement": s.262(1).

"witness": s.307(1).

GENERAL NOTE

This section statutorily extends the grounds for the admission of hearsay evidence in criminal proceedings and, in subs. (5) onwards, sets out the procedures necessary in most circumstances for such evidence to be received. It is important to note that while a "statement" is very widely defined in s.262(1), anything by nature of a precognition, save for a precognition on oath, is excluded from the ambit of s.259. It is stressed that the section's provisions operate in addition to, and do not replace, the categories of hearsay evidence which can be accepted by the courts at common law (see s.262(4), below); for that reason some mention is necessary of the pre-existing categories of hearsay evidence which were recognised as exceptions to the general bar on hearsay evidence.

Categories of hearsay admissible at common law

First, it is well-established that statements made by a deceased witness, while hearsay in character, are admissible; see *H.M. Advocate v. Irving*, 1978 J.C. 28, but it is unsettled whether this exception extends either as far as writings of a deceased, particularly if authorship is in dispute (the *Lauderdale Peerage* case (1885) 10 App. Cas. 692), or to a dying deposition. More tentatively, a statement made by a witness deemed permanently insane since its making could perhaps be adduced as evidence provided that it could be established that he had been lucid at the time when it was made (*H.M. Advocate v. Monson* (1893) 1 Adam 114). It is thought that a statement by a prisoner of war might be received as evidence.

It is well-established that statements forming part of the *res gestae* are admissible as are incriminating or mixed statements made by an accused, and that hearsay evidence can be admitted where it would be impossible to lead primary evidence, this on the basis that such hearsay now qualifies as best evidence. The making of prior inconsistent statements can be used as a means of discrediting a witness, but previous consistent statements cannot be used to bolster credibility; in neither case however is the prior statement admissible as evidence of its contents. In addition to statutory exceptions such as the Bankers' Book Evidence Act 1879 and the provisions now contained in Sched. 8 to the 1996 Act concerning categories of business documents, case law has also allowed evidence at second hand; of identification or description of an accused (*Muldoon v. Herron*, 1970 J.C. 30); of a vehicle (*Frew v. Jessop*, 1990 J.C. 15), and more recently, of a statement whose detail had been forgotten by a witness but assented to in evidence (*Jamieson v. H.M. Advocate (No. 2)*, 1994 S.C.C.R. 610).

While it might seem that the list of expected categories of hearsay evidence which can be adduced as evidence is endless, the fact remains that Scottish courts have exercised extreme caution before admitting such evidence largely on the grounds that it cannot be subjected to cross-examination and must be inherently less reliable than parole evidence. Yet the bar on admissible hearsay may cause unnecessary expense, probably smacks of pettifoggery and contrivance to lay witnesses whose flow of testimony is artificially constrained, and certainly can militate against the broader interests of justice: see especially the cases of *Perrie v. H.M. Advocate*, 1991 S.C.C.R. 255 and *McLay v. H.M. Advocate*, 1994 S.C.C.R. 397 in both of which it had been held inadmissible to lead evidence made to third parties by an incriminee.

The Scottish Law Commission's Report, *"Hearsay Evidence in Criminal Proceedings"* (No. 149), and to an extent, the experience of English courts in applying Pt. 2 of the Criminal Justice Act 1988 (c. 33) (which drew heavily upon the Roskill Report, *"Report of the Departmental Inquiry on Fraud Trials"*, Lord Chancellor's Department 1986), as well as the *Perrie* and *McLay* cases, have all influenced the shape of Pt. 12 of the 1995 Act. Section 259 broadens the categories of hearsay evidence which can be introduced into proceedings but provides a right to other parties to challenge such evidence—in which event the court will require to adjudicate prior to the commencement of a trial, and to lead counter-evidence in rebuttal.

Subs. (1)

Subsection (1) sets out several tests which any hearsay material has to meet before it can be founded upon, namely, the unavailability of the maker of the statement (for one of the reasons specified in subs. (2) below); the admissibility of the evidence had it been given in parole form (a ground which demands both that the evidence adduced is competent and does not contain hearsay, and that the maker of the statement would have qualified as a witness); and finally that the making of the statement can itself be proved by direct evidence. The witness' statement need not be in written form provided that other witnesses can speak to its contents but nor can it be by nature a precognition (a distinction itself often more apparent than real nowadays).

Subs. (2)

Following on from subs. (1)(a) the permissible grounds for the unavailability of a witness are defined. It is submitted that these statutory provisions are in addition to, and without prejudice to, the common law rules described above. In *H.M. Advocate v. Clancy* (High Court, Glasgow, February 9, 1997, unreported) the Crown sought to lead evidence in a murder trial of a statement from the victim without use of the statutory notice set out in subs. (5). Defence objections were upheld, but the indictment fell due to the illness of the judge, though it had been indicated that there was some sympathy for the Crown in the instant case for proceeding under common law and, in any event, there had been no prejudice to the accused. While this unreported case should spur parties to rely upon the statutory notice procedures, it will be noted that subs. (6)(b) does permit hearsay evidence to be adduced without prior notice where just cause can be shown: the deliberate disappearance, or the sudden death, of a witness in the course of a trial would surely justify such a motion. It is unclear whether dying depositions are to be considered competent for the purposes of s.259. Paragraph (b) enables the statement of a witness abroad to be received in evidence, but only if it can be shown, if required, that is is not reasonable to use other competent evidential devices, such as live television links, letters of request or commission.

Paragraph (c), in a fashion similar to the last paragraph, enables statements of identifiable witnesses who have disappeared to be admitted as evidence but only if it can be shown, if required, that all reasonable steps have been taken to trace the witness beforehand. Paragraph (d) deals with admissions of incriminees; it will now be possible to tender evidence of statements allegedly made by an incriminee who has been brought before the court but refuses to testify on grounds of self-incrimination.

Subtle differences exist between the last provision and the next, contained in para. (e)(i), which deals with a witness who simply misconducts himself and refuses to testify, or prevaricates. Paragraph (e) can apply to the evidence of a child "who has refused an admonition to tell the truth or, having been so admonished, refuses to give evidence"; this phrase would obviously apply to a recalcitrant child witness but would not apply to situations in which the child proved to be unable to give evidence or was tongue-tied. From *MacDonald v. H.M. Advocate*, 1999 S.L.T. 533; 1999 S.C.C.R. 146 it is clear that before subs. (2)(e)(ii) can operate in the case of a child, the judge must have directed the witness to answer and have been met with a refusal. It also seems that recourse to the s.259 provision would only be appropriate after some effort had been made to ascertain whether the child might adopt a prior admissible statement (see s.260 below). A further category of child witness has to be recognised—the child who does not understand the nature of the admonition; in such a case it is doubtful that an earlier statement could be taken in evidence at all, since the child was not a "competent witness" when the statement was made (subs. (1)(c)).

Several caveats have to be entered: first, subs. (3) precludes the application of s.259's provisions where the judge is satisfied the party tendering the evidence, or his followers, have colluded in bringing about the unavailability or recalcitrance of the witness identified. This provision would readily apply to assisting in, or engineering the disappearance of a witness (arguably an attempt to pervert the course of justice in many circumstances) but more complex issues might arise for example in child abuse cases where emotional pressures may be brought to bear on the child.

Secondly, subs. (5) stipulates that for hearsay evidence to be admitted in most circumstances notice of the intention to do so must be served on all other parties before the trial. (The form of notice is found in Form 21.3 in the 1996 Act of Adjournal.) Broadly notice has to be served where it is anticipable that a witness will be unavailable; subs. (6) exempts situations described in para. (2)(d) and (e) namely, failures to testify by incriminees or by witnesses who misconduct themselves, from the normal requirement of advance notice. Thirdly, a failure to challenge appropriate notice under subs. (5) means that the statement's contents can be lead in evidence without further ado (subs. (7)). Nonetheless it is submitted that some circumspection is necessary here: it cannot be right that the terms of subs. (7) would preclude a common law challenge during the proceedings if it is demonstrable that the evidence being adduced would ordinarily be incompetent or otherwise inadmissible.

Only in the event of a challenge does the presiding judge have to decide the issue before the trial commences (subs. (8)) and it will be noted that it is presumed that the terms of the Form 21.3 are correct, a presumption which is capable of rebuttal, and that the issue is determined on the balance of probabilities. The main benefit of subs. (8) is that a "trial within a trial" to resolve the admissibility of the statement can be avoided, thus saving time and inconvenience to all involved since the issue will be aired, possibly by leading evidence, before trial. Subsection (4) permits parties to lead evidence to support the credibility of the absent witness, challenge his credibility, or demonstrate prior inconsistent statements. (The only exceptions to this generality occur in the circumstances outlined in subs. (2)(d) and (e)(i) where, by definition, no evidence has been heard from the witness.) Reference to "any proceedings" suggests that such evidence could well be adduced before the judge determining the admissibility of a challenged notice.

Although it may be self-evident, the above hearsay provisions do not extend to statements made by an accused in his favour (see s.261(1) below). Less obviously, given the terms of s.261(2) of the Act, a statement by a co-accused B can be adduced as evidence by an accused A where B declines to give evidence: the statement can be used as evidence by A but not by B. Section 261(4) provides that this can only occur where A has given notice in terms of s.259(5) and, it is submitted, where it can be shown that no pressure was exerted by A to prevent B testifying, and the Crown itself has not lead B's statement. To say the least the interplay of ss.259 and 261 is likely to create situations of byzantine complexity, particularly in cases involving several accused; will all accused founding upon B's statement require to serve a s.259 notice as prudence might suggest?

Finally it will be noted that both s.259(5) and (9) permit the leading of witnesses or productions, not formally intimated, either for the purpose of setting up a hearsay statement or, with leave of the court, as additional evidence.

European Convention on Human Rights

The introduction of the Convention into Scots criminal law will undoubtedly lead to a re-appraisal of many well-accepted practices. For that reason the discussion which follows is necessarily of some length, albeit the basic issue—the need to achieve a proper balance between a fair trial for the accused and the need to detect and suppress serious crime (*Irving v. H.M. Advocate*, 1998 J.C. 28) remains unchanged.

Objection to the admission of hearsay evidence, founding upon an anticipated breach of the accused's article 6 Convention Rights, was taken by preliminary diet in *H.M. Advocate v. McKenna* (High Court of Justiciary, October 11, 1999, unreported). In this murder trial the Crown gave notice of its intention to lead the statements of an incriminee who had since died. The defence objected that this would deny the accused an opportunity to cross-examine the deceased who, it was asserted, was drug and alcohol addicted, was of bad character and had had every reason to seek to exculpate himself.

The Crown advanced seven broad principles in support of the admission of the hearsay evidence; in particular it was noted that the leading of hearsay evidence is not *per se* in conflict with Convention rights provided the accused has the opportunity to challenge the statement, and, more importantly, following *Kostovski v. The Netherlands* (1989) 12 E.H.R.R. 434 and *Asch v. Austria* (1992) 15 E.H.R.R. 597, that this evidence is not either the sole or main evidence. In his judgment Lord Caplan noted that the European Court does not lay down prescriptive rules (a difficult, if not impossible task given the variety of criminal systems) but proceeds by an overall assessment of the whole proceedings, not individual incidents.

The defence Minutes were repelled in *McKenna*.

In *McKenna v. H.M. Advocate*, 2000 S.L.T. 508; 2000 S.C.C.R. 159 the accused raised objection by preliminary diet to the Crown leading evidence of a statement from the third person present at the scene of a murder , and since identified as a suspect but who had since died, on grounds that not only could this evidence not be subject to cross-examination but that there was evidence that the witness would likely have given a partial and self-serving account. Particular emphasis was placed upon alleged oppression on the part of the Crown (in contravention of the European Convention) in seeking to lead evidence of this sort; the Crown responded by outlining seven general principles (which the Court approved) in relation to the leading of hearsay evidence from a deceased person foremost of which was the fact that this was neither the sole or principal, evidence against the accused. On appeal, the Appeal Court indicated that only on rare occasions could the issue of the potential for prejudice to the achievement of a fair trial be determined in advance of the trial itself (compare the approach in *Brown v. Stott*, 2000 S.C.C.R. 314 where the fundamental issue, as a matter of law, of a suspect's right not to be called upon to incriminate himself, notwithstanding the terms of the Road Traffic Act 1988 (c. 52), s.172, was so resolved).

In *Patterson v. H.M.Advocate*, 2000 S.L.T. 302 the Appeal Court ruled as competent evidence for the purposes of the section, the statement of a deceased witness who had intimated to the defence that she was an alcoholic and had given her police statement while under the influence of drink. It was held that the reliability of the witness was not a determining factor in assessing the competency of her statement. Note that the Court also held that it was not necessary for the Crown to meet an inspecific challenge to the witness' mental capacity by proving her sanity; the general evidential presumption (that witnesses are deemed to have the ordinary physical and mental faculties) applied.

In *H.M.Advocate v. Nulty*, 2000 S.L.T. 528 the Crown sought to lead evidence of a complainer in a rape trial by reference to her taped evidence from an earlier trial diet which had, unfortunately, been deserted for procedural reasons. Since giving her evidence and being cross-examined at the first trial, the complainer had become mentally unwell and was unfit to give evidence, causing the Crown to use the best evidence available, her prior testimony. Two points are of note; first, the court apparently had no difficulty in reconciling this approach with the terms of subs.(1) which excludes from the ambit of s.259 oral evidence given in the course of criminal proceedings no doubt on the basis that the evidence to be received had not been given in the instant proceedings; second, the trial judge was unwilling to hold that unfairness necessarily arose because the accused could not cross—examine the complainer. Following *Doorson v. Netherlands* (1996) 22 E.H.R.R. 330 fairness had to be assessed overall and had to take account of the balance between the defence's interests and those of the victims.

Admissibility of prior statements of witnesses

260.—(1) Subject to the following provisions of this section, where a witness gives evidence in criminal proceedings, any prior statement made by the witness shall be admissible as evidence of any matter stated in it of which direct oral evidence by him would be admissible if given in the course of those proceedings.

(2) A prior statement shall not be admissible under this section unless—
(a) the statement is contained in a document;
(b) the witness, in the course of giving evidence, indicates that the statement was made by him and that he adopts it as his evidence; and
(c) at the time the statement was made, the person who made it would have been a competent witness in the proceedings.

(3) For the purposes of this section, any reference to a prior statement is a reference to a prior statement which, but for the provisions of this section, would not be admissible as evidence of any matter stated in it.

(4) Subsections (2) and (3) above do not apply to a prior statement—
(a) contained in a precognition on oath; or
(b) made in other proceedings, whether criminal or civil and whether taking place in the United Kingdom or elsewhere,
and, for the purposes of this section, any such statement shall not be admissible unless it is sufficiently authenticated.

DEFINITIONS
"criminal proceedings": s.262(3).
"statement": s.262(1).
"witness": s.307(1).

GENERAL NOTE
This section applies to solemn and summary proceedings and permits the introduction of prior statements, as specified by subs. (2), by a witness in criminal proceedings as evidence of any matter therein of which direct oral evidence from him would have been admissible in the course of those proceedings. In essence the section permits the adoption of earlier statements, suitably authenticated, and is perceptibly influenced by the decision of the High Court in *Jamieson v. H.M. Advocate (No. 2)*, 1995 S.L.T. 666.

Note that the witness has both to acknowledge being the originator of the statement and adopt it as his evidence (subs. (2)(b)), circumstances which did not prevail in either *Muldoon v. Herron*, 1970 J.C. 30; 1970 S.L.T. 228 (a judgment which the court founded upon in *Jamieson*) or in *Smith v. H.M. Advocate*, 1986 S.C.C.R. 135. In both those cases police witnesses' accounts of the witness' evidence replaced the testimony of the witnesses themselves. If a witness can adopt a prior statement as this section provides, *McNee v. Ruxton*, 1997 G.W.D. 13–545 is authority perhaps for the proposition that witness B can adopt the statement of another witness, witness A, as his own. The corollary however surely must be that either witness can have a prior inconsistent statement made by either witness put to him.

The distinction between this section, which in effect enables witnesses to rely upon accurate statements made earlier (but whose details are now forgotten) such that these can form part of the evidence, and section 263 which enables a prior statement to be put as a means, at least initially, only of challenging the credibility or reliability of a witness, can quickly become blurred; see *Ogilvie v. H.M. Advocate*, 1999 S.L.T. 1068. In this case the Crown plainly utilised the (rarely used) power in s.263(2) of the Act to interpose another witness during the witness' evidence, albeit prematurely.

The effect of subs. (4) is to remove the need for a witness to adopt the terms of his precognition on oath (which of course had to be signed as an acknowledgment of its accuracy by the witness at the conclusion of the precognition proceedings) or for him to confirm the accuracy of testimony given in earlier judicial proceedings.

Reference to r.21.4 and Form 21.4 in the 1996 Act of Adjournal indicates that only statements of the type specified in subs. (4) require to be certified with such an authentication docquet;

authentication need not be docquetted by the originator of the statement, the certificate of a party present at the making of the statement would suffice. Note that any prior statement by a witness would be admissible if given as a precognition on oath or in the course of any court proceedings once properly authenticated.

The above certification procedures are not required for any other sort of statement; in such cases it would be sufficient for the witness to assent to the truth of an earlier account which is produced to the court in document form. See s.262(2) and (3) for definitions. It will be noted that nothing in either ss.260 or 262 would permit the use of a precognition.

The different evidential significance of a s.260 and s.263 statement is discussed at p. 355 below.

Statements by accused

261.—(1) Subject to the following provisions of this section, nothing in sections 259 and 260 of this Act shall apply to a statement made by the accused.

(2) Evidence of a statement made by an accused shall be admissible by virtue of the said section 259 at the instance of another accused in the same proceedings as evidence in relation to that other accused.

(3) For the purposes of subsection (2) above, the first mentioned accused shall be deemed—

(a) where he does not give evidence in the proceedings, to be a witness refusing to give evidence in connection with the subject matter of the statement as mentioned in paragraph (e) of subsection (2) of the said section 259; and

(b) to have been, at the time the statement was made, a competent witness in the proceedings.

(4) Evidence of a statement shall not be admissible as mentioned in subsection (2) above unless the accused at whose instance it is sought to be admitted has given notice of his intention to do so as mentioned in subsection (5) of the said section 259; but subsection (6) of that section shall not apply in the case of notice required to be given by virtue of this subsection.

DEFINITIONS
"made": s.262(3).
"statement": s.262(1).
"witness": s.307(1).

GENERAL NOTE
This section applies to solemn and summary proceedings. Its effect is to exclude a statement made by the accused from the provisions of ss.259 and 260. However, statements made by an accused, which are hearsay, may become admissible against that accused when introduced by another accused in the same proceedings. Use of this procedure will normally require a Notice in terms of s.259(5) prior to trial (see notes to s.259 above).

Construction of sections 259 to 261

262.—(1) For the purposes of sections 259 to 261 of this Act, a "statement" includes—

(a) any representation, however made or expressed, of fact or opinion; and

(b) any part of a statement,

but does not include a statement in a precognition other than a precognition on oath.

(2) For the purposes of the said sections 259 to 261 a statement is contained in a document where the person who makes it—

(a) makes the statement in the document personally;

(b) makes a statement which is, with or without his knowledge, embodied in a document by whatever means or by any person who has direct personal knowledge of the making of the statement; or

(c) approves a document as embodying the statement.

(3) In the said sections 259 to 261—

"criminal proceedings" include any hearing by the sheriff of an application made under Chapter 3 of Part II of the Children (Scotland) Act 1995 for a finding as to whether grounds for the referral of a child's case to a children's hearing are established, in so far as the application relates to the commission of an offence by the child, or for a review of such a finding;

"document" includes, in addition to a document in writing—

    (a) any map, plan, graph or drawing;

    (b) any photograph;

    (c) any disc, tape, sound track or other device in which sounds or other data (not being visual images) are recorded so as to be capable (with or without the aid of some other equipment) of being reproduced therefrom; and

    (d) any film, negative, tape, disc or other device in which one or more visual images are recorded so as to be capable (as aforesaid) of being reproduced therefrom;

"film" includes a microfilm;

"made" includes allegedly made.

(4) Nothing in the said sections 259 to 261 shall prejudice the admissibility of a statement made by a person other than in the course of giving oral evidence in court which is admissible otherwise than by virtue of those sections.

DEFINITIONS

    "child": s.307(1).

    "indictment": s.307(1).

    "sheriff": ss.4(4) and 5(1).

GENERAL NOTE

The section makes provision for the construction of ss.259 to 261 of the Act. Subsection (4) enacts that the section's provisions do not prejudice any other rule allowing the admissibility of statements in the course of giving oral evidence in court; see for example s.263(4) which deals with prior inconsistent statements in solemn and summary proceedings. See *Rollo v. H.M. Advocate*, 1997 S.L.T. 958, a prosecution under the Misuse of Drugs Act 1971 (c. 23) in which, for the purposes of search under that Act, an electronic personal organiser was held to be "a document".

Witnesses

Examination of witnesses

263.—(1) In any trial, it shall be competent for the party against whom a witness is produced and sworn *in causa* to examine such witness both in cross and *in causa*.

(2) The judge may, on the motion of either party, on cause shown order that the examination of a witness for that party ("the first witness") shall be interrupted to permit the examination of another witness for that party.

(3) Where the judge makes an order under subsection (2) above he shall, after the examination of the other witness, permit the recall of the first witness.

(4) In a trial, a witness may be examined as to whether he has on any specified occasion made a statement on any matter pertinent to the issue at the trial different from the evidence given by him in the trial; and evidence may be led in the trial to prove that the witness made the different statement on the occasion specified.

(5) In any trial, on the motion of either party, the presiding judge may permit a witness who has been examined to be recalled.

DEFINITIONS
"judge": s.307(1).
"trial": s.307(1).
"witness": s.307(1).

GENERAL NOTE
This section applies to solemn and summary proceedings. Subsections (2) and (3) which permit the interruption of a witness' testimony to allow evidence to be taken from another of the party's witnesses was introduced by the Criminal Justice (Scotland) Act 1980 (c. 62), Sched. 6, para. 54. By implication such a motion could only be made during the examination or re-examination of the first witness, not during cross-examination.

Subsection (4) repeats the familiar terms of ss.147 and 349 of the 1975 Act in relation to prior inconsistent statements by witnesses. This rule does not apply to precognitions which cannot, of course, be put to witnesses unless they are precognitions on oath (see *Kerr v. H.M. Advocate*, 1958 J.C. 14; *K.J.C. v. H.M. Advocate*, 1994 S.C.C.R. 560). See also *Coll, Petr*, 1977 S.L.T. 58, a petition to the nobile officium by a witness to order destruction of his precognition on oath before giving evidence at the trial proceedings.

The second part of subs. (4) does not become operative until the witness has been specifically asked whether he made the statement (*McTaggart v. H.M. Advocate*, 1934 J.C. 33) and that it was made on a specified occasion (*Paterson v. H.M. Advocate*, 1998 S.L.T. 117). Subsection (4) has to be read in conjunction with s.269(1) and (2); with leave of the court it is competent to lead additional evidence (to prove the making of the prior statement) by way of productions and witnesses' evidence even if no notice has been given of them in the trial indictment. It is competent to examine a witness upon the terms of another witness' statement where the former witness has previously adopted that statement, or its terms, as his own; see *McNee v. Ruxton* 1998 S.L.T. 140. In *H.M. Advocate v. Hislop*, 1994 S.L.T. 333 a Crown witness, who claimed to be unable to recall events, stated that she had told the police what had happened. The prosecutor put her account to her by means of her earlier tape-recorded interview and a transcript of it, both of which were listed as productions. Objections to this use of the section's provisions were repelled. See also the notes to s.260 at p. 352 above. The distinction between the admission of a prior statement by means of s.263 and s.260 is vital: a s.263 statement used in the course of proceedings does not itself constitute evidence against the accused but serves only as a test of the credibility and reliability of the maker of the statement once its provenance has been proved; by contrast a s.260 statement (or indeed a *Jamieson* statement) will be primary evidence but only once it has been adopted by the witness as his evidence (see *Ogilvie*, 1999 G.W.D. 14–632).

In *Hemming v. H.M. Advocate*, 1998 S.L.T. 213, H was charged with attempted murder and petitioned the High Court for a commission and diligence to recover witness statements. The object was to attack the credibility of Crown witnesses by demonstrating variations in their accounts as the police investigation proceeded. In the instant case the Court held there to be compelling grounds for overriding the public interest objections raised by the Crown. Compare the approach taken by a court of five judges in *McLeod, Petr*, 1998 S.L.T. 234 (at 244J–L) in which the parameters to be met by an accused seeking a diligence to recover documents are formulated.

Refer also to the discussion of *Ogilvie v. H.M. Advocate*, 1999 S.L.T. 1068 in the Notes to s.260 above.

It is well understood that a *socius criminis* once called to give evidence for the Crown, enjoys immunity from prosecution in relation to the matter. The defence are entitled to criticise the witness' testimony on the grounds of that immunity and, if they do so, it is generally proper for the trial judge to direct attention to this immunity; see generally *Docherty v. H.M. Advocate*, 1987 S.L.T. 784. In *Mason v. H.M. Advocate*, 2000 S.L.T. 1004 no such criticism of a witness' evidence had been voiced by the defence and it was held that there was no automatic duty incumbent upon the trial judge to give such directions; indeed it might be risky to do so without an appreciation of the considerations giving rise to the defence approach.

In *H.M. Advocate v. Megrahi (No. 2)*, 2000 S.L.T. 1399 a transcript of evidence given by a witness before a magistrate in a foreign jurisdiction (in this instance, Malta) was admitted as evidence, the Scottish Court in the Netherlands rejecting defence objections that the statement being put to the witness was akin to a precognition.

Spouse of accused a competent witness

264.—(1) The spouse of an accused may be called as a witness—
(a) by the accused;
(b) by a co-accused or by the prosecutor without the consent of the accused.
(2) Nothing in this section shall—
(a) make the spouse of an accused a compellable witness for a co-accused or for the prosecutor in a case where such spouse would not be so compellable at common law;
(b) compel a spouse to disclose any communication made between the spouses during the marriage.
(3) The failure of the spouse of an accused to give evidence shall not be commented on by the defence or the prosecutor.
(4) The spouse of a person charged with bigamy may be called as a witness either for the prosecution or the defence and without the consent of the person charged.

DEFINITIONS
"prosecutor": s.307(1).
"witness": s.307(1).

GENERAL NOTE
The term "spouse" can only be applied to persons married to each other, not to those who simply co-habit (*Casey v. H.M. Advocate*, 1993 S.L.T. 33). A spouse is a compellable witness for the accused to whom she is married, and is competent but not compellable when called by any other party in proceedings (*Hunter v. H.M. Advocate*, 1984 S.L.T. 434); once she elects to give evidence, she must answer all relevant questions and cannot refrain from answering on the grounds that they might incriminate her spouse (see *Hunter* above and *Bates v. H.M. Advocate*, 1989 S.L.T. 701; 1989 S.C.C.R. 338).
This rule also applies to an estranged spouse who, unless she is the complainer, must be advised that she is not a compellable witness (see *Hay v. McClory*, 1993 S.C.C.R. 1040; 1994 S.L.T. 520).
In *McCulloch v. H.M. Advocate,* 2000 G.W.D. 1357 an extension of the 12 month time-bar was allowed to enable the Crown to re-indict after the trial diet had been deserted, *pro loco et tempore,* by the sheriff following his ruling that the Crown had, in ignorance, commented upon the failure of the spouse to give evidence. It is of note that the sheriff had balanced the public interest in the prosecution of a serious offence against the rights of the accused and had been persuaded by the lack of any prejudice to the accused were the extension to be granted.

Witnesses not excluded for conviction, interest, relationship, etc.

265.—(1) Every person adduced as a witness who is not otherwise by law disqualified from giving evidence, shall be admissible as a witness, and no objection to the admissibility of a witness shall be competent on the ground of—
(a) conviction of or punishment for an offence;
(b) interest;
(c) agency or partial counsel;
(d) the absence of due citation to attend; or
(e) his having been precognosced subsequently to the date of citation.
(2) Where any person who is or has been an agent of the accused is adduced and examined as a witness for the accused, it shall not be competent for the accused to object, on the ground of confidentiality, to any question proposed to be put to such witness on matter pertinent to the issue of the guilt of the accused.
(3) No objection to the admissibility of a witness shall be competent on the ground that he or she is the father, mother, son, daughter, brother or sister, by consanguinity or affinity, or uncle, aunt, nephew or niece, by consanguinity of any party adducing the witness in any trial.
(4) It shall not be competent for any witness to decline to be examined and

give evidence on the ground of any relationship mentioned in subsection (3) above.

DEFINITIONS
  "conviction": s.307(5).
  "witness": s.307(1).

GENERAL NOTE
  This section permits parties' evidence to be heard irrespective of their character or interest or relationship. See generally *Dow v. McKnight*, 1949 J.C. 38. Subsection (2) provides that the accused's solicitor, or former solicitor, can be adduced as a witness by the accused; the agent cannot be objected to on the grounds that he has been present in court (*Campbell v. Cochrane*, 1928 J.C. 25).

Accused as witness

266.—(1) Subject to subsections (2) to (8) below, the accused shall be a competent witness for the defence at every stage of the case, whether the accused is on trial alone or along with a co-accused.

(2) The accused shall not be called as a witness in pursuance of this section except upon his own application or in accordance with subsection (9) or (10) below.

(3) An accused who gives evidence on his own behalf in pursuance of this section may be asked any question in cross-examination notwithstanding that it would tend to incriminate him as to the offence charged.

(4) An accused who gives evidence on his own behalf in pursuance of this section shall not be asked, and if asked shall not be required to answer, any question tending to show that he has committed, or been convicted of, or been charged with, any offence other than that with which he is then charged, or is of bad character, unless—

(a) the proof that he has committed or been convicted of such other offence is admissible evidence to show that he is guilty of the offence with which he is then charged; or

(b) the accused or his counsel or solicitor has asked questions of the witnesses for the prosecution with a view to establishing the accused's good character or impugning the character of the complainer, or the accused has given evidence of his own good character, or the nature or conduct of the defence is such as to involve imputations on the character of the prosecutor or of the witnesses for the prosecution or of the complainer; or

(c) the accused has given evidence against any other person charged in the same proceedings.

(5) In a case to which paragraph (b) of subsection (4) above applies, the prosecutor shall be entitled to ask the accused a question of a kind specified in that subsection only if the court, on the application of the prosecutor, permits him to do so.

(6) An application under subsection (5) above in proceedings on indictment shall be made in the course of the trial but in the absence of the jury.

(7) In subsection (4) above, references to the complainer include references to a victim who is deceased.

(8) Every person called as a witness in pursuance of this section shall, unless otherwise ordered by the court, give his evidence from the witness box or other place from which the other witnesses give their evidence.

(9) The accused may—

(a) with the consent of a co-accused, call that other accused as a witness on the accused's behalf; or

(b) ask a co-accused any question in cross-examination if that co-accused gives evidence, but he may not do both in relation to the same co-accused.

(10) The prosecutor or the accused may call as a witness a co-accused who has pleaded guilty to or been acquitted of all charges against him which remain before the court (whether or not, in a case where the co-accused has pleaded guilty to any charge, he has been sentenced) or in respect of whom the diet has been deserted; and the party calling such co-accused as a witness shall not require to give notice thereof, but the court may grant any other party such adjournment or postponement of the trial as may seem just.

(11) Where, in any trial, the accused is to be called as a witness he shall be so called as the first witness for the defence unless the court, on cause shown, otherwise directs.

DEFINITIONS
"diet": s.307(1).
"offence": s.307(1).
"prosecutor": s.307(1).
"trial": s.307(1).
"witness": s.307(1).

GENERAL NOTE
The accused cannot be compelled to give evidence on his own behalf in his own trial, but his failure to do so can be the subject of comment, with restraint, by the trial judge in solemn proceedings when charging the jury (see *Scott (A.T.) v. H.M. Advocate*, 1946 J.C. 90; *Brown v. Macpherson*, 1918 J.C. 3; *McIntosh v. H.M. Advocate*, 1997 S.L.T. 1320): s.32 of the Criminal Justice (Scotland) Act 1995 removed the long-standing general prohibition against comment by the prosecutor upon such a failure to give evidence, which was found in the 1975 Act, s.141(1)(b) (*Dempsey v. H.M. Advocate*, 1995 S.C.C.R. 431 is a rare example of convictions being set aside on account of such improper comment by a prosecutor).

There was previous authority that in some cases, the proved facts may raise a presumption that the accused committed the crime libelled, and failure by the accused to put forward an explanation sufficient to raise a reasonable doubt in the minds of the jury could occasion comment legitimately (see *H.M. Advocate v. Hardy*, 1938 J.C. 144; *McIlhargey v. Herron*, 1972 J.C.).

Barnes v. H.M. Advocate, 2000 G.W.D. 35–1330 demonstrates the sort of complex issues which can arise when an accused is exposed to cross-examination by others' counsel. It is one thing for a prior record to be revealed inadvertently in the course of questioning but in *Barnes*, the Appeal Court held that his counsel had expressly questioned a co-accused about *Barnes'* involvement in the assault libelled (a fact clearly evident from earlier evidence) solely as a means of drawing out the co-accused's criminal history. Such a tactic flew in the face of the section's purpose, and during the trial, *Barnes'* counsel had been refused the right to cross-examine on record; (*Murdoch v. H.M. Advocate*, 1978 S.L.T. 10 distinguished).

Hanlin v. McFadyen, 2000 S.C.C.R. 428 confirms that no witness citation is necessary when it is intended to call a co-accused upon whom the court has already deferred sentence. In *Hanlin* the sheriff had declined an accused's motion to adjourn trial founded upon the failure of the co-accused to appear for sentence, no witness citation having been served.

38; *Deacons v. H.M. Advocate*, 1994 G.W.D. 11–636). With regard to the reform which became s.32 of the Criminal Justice (Scotland) Act 1995, during the Committee Stage of the Bill (*Hansard*, H.L. Vol. 560, col. 416), the Lord Advocate observed: "Where the law itself only allows comment with restraint, and only for inferences to be drawn in narrow circumstances, it would be a foolish prosecutor indeed who went further than that."

Subss. (2) and (3)
No other party can compel an accused person to give evidence in any trial unless he has already been convicted or acquitted of all charges libelled. The accused may give evidence on his own behalf but ordinarily should do so before leading any other evidence (s.263(2) permits application to be made only for the interruption of evidence to enable the examination of another witness). Once he elects to give evidence the accused can be cross-examined on any issue subject only to the limitations imposed upon the prosecutor by subs. (4); these restrictions do not apply to co-accused who are entitled to cross-examine an accused as to his criminal record if the accused, directly or impliedly, gives evidence against them (*McCourtney v. H.M.*

Advocate, 1978 S.L.T. 10; *Burton v. H.M. Advocate*, 1979 S.L.T. (Notes) 59). Much of the case law originates from the problems created by cross-incrimination of accused (see *Sandlan v. H.M. Advocate*, 1983 S.L.T. 519 which involved prejudicial evidence against first accused elicited in cross-examination of Crown witnesses by second accused without adequate opportunity for first accused to examine anew; in *H.M. Advocate v. Ferrie*, 1983 S.C.C.R. 1 the use, by the Crown, as a witness of an accused who tendered partial pleas during trial was upheld; *Dodds v. H.M. Advocate*, 1987 S.C.C.R. 678; 1988 S.L.T. 194; an accused who had had his partial pleas accepted, then gave evidence in relation to the outstanding charge and was cross-examined by the co-accused in relation to all charges libelled, unsuccessfully appealed.

If in the conduct of his defence, either in cross-examination of prosecution witnesses or in his own evidence, the accused attacks the character of the complainer, impugns the conduct of the prosecutor or represents himself falsely to be of good character, the accused is liable to lose the customary protection of subs. (4). As subs. (5) makes clear, that protection can only properly be withdrawn by the court after the prosecutor has made that motion outwith the presence of any jury. The court must consider the motion (see *Leggate v. H.M. Advocate*, 1988 S.L.T. 665; 1988 S.C.C.R. 391).

The prosecutor has to exercise care to avoid breaching the statutory provisions, particularly in the heat of cross-examination: in *Cordiner v. H.M. Advocate*, 1993 S.L.T. 2; 1991 S.C.C.R. 652 the prosecutor challenged the accused that he had sought to instigate another witness to pervert the course of justice by false testimony, a crime not charged. No objection had been taken at the time and the Court of Appeal held that while the section had been breached technically, the appellant had waived compliance.

Note that subs. (7) has the effect of extending the protection given to the character of the complainer by subs. (4)(b) to deceased victims; it is not necessary that the deceased died as a result of being the victim of the crime charged. A curious variation upon subs. (4)(c) is found in *Marshall v. H.M. Advocate*, 1996 G.W.D. 27–1577 where the jury was provided a copy of a co-accused's 22 page police interview transcript which made reference to M having previously being released from jail. M's appeal against conviction was refused, it being noted that the relevant passage had not been referred to in evidence and the sheriff had consciously decided not to draw attention to it or issue directions. See also *Sinclair v. MacDonald*, 1996 S.C.C.R. 466 where defence cross-examination had gone too far and amounted to attacks on character.

Witnesses in court during trial

267.—(1) The court may, on an application by any party to the proceedings, permit a witness to be in court during the proceedings or any part of the proceedings before he has given evidence if it appears to the court that the presence of the witness would not be contrary to the interests of justice.

(2) Without prejudice to subsection (1) above, where a witness has, without the permission of the court and without the consent of the parties to the proceedings, been present in court during the proceedings, the court may, in its discretion, admit the witness, where it appears to the court that the presence of the witness was not the result of culpable negligence or criminal intent, and that the witness has not been unduly instructed or influenced by what took place during his presence, or that injustice will not be done by his examination.

DEFINITION
"witness": s.307(1).

GENERAL NOTE
It is a matter for the court whether the evidence of a witness present in court during the trial should be taken into account. The court should consider whether there has been any criminative intent or wilful neglect on the part of the witness, the likely effect upon his testimony of his earlier presence in court and the likelihood of injustice being done by the exclusion of that evidence in the case.

See *MacDonald v. Mackenzie*, 1947 J.C. 169; it is the task of the party tendering the witness' evidence to satisfy the court that the evidence should be admitted notwithstanding the improper presence in court. The evidence of a solicitor engaged in the case cannot be objected to on the ground of his earlier presence in court (*Campbell v. Cochrane*, 1928 J.C. 25).

Additional evidence, etc.

Additional evidence

268.—(1) Subject to subsection (2) below, the judge may, on a motion of the prosecutor or the accused made—
   (a) in proceedings on indictment, at any time before the commencement of the speeches to the jury;
   (b) in summary proceedings, at any time before the prosecutor proceeds to address the judge on the evidence,
permit him to lead additional evidence.
   (2) Permission shall only be granted under subsection (1) above where the judge—
   (a) considers that the additional evidence is *prima facie* material; and
   (b) accepts that at the commencement of the trial either—
             (i) the additional evidence was not available and could not reasonably have been made available; or
             (ii) the materiality of such additional evidence could not reasonably have been foreseen by the party.
   (3) The judge may permit the additional evidence to be led notwithstanding that—
   (a) in proceedings on indictment, a witness or production concerned is not included in any list lodged by the parties and that the notice required by sections 67(5) and 78(4) of this Act has not been given; or
   (b) in any case, a witness must be recalled.
   (4) The judge may, when granting a motion in terms of this section, adjourn or postpone the trial before permitting the additional evidence to be led.
   (5) In this section "the commencement of the trial" means—
   (a) in proceedings on indictment, the time when the jury is sworn; and
   (b) in summary proceedings, the time when the first witness for the prosecution is sworn.

DEFINITIONS
   "commencement of proceedings": s.268(5).
   "indictment": s.307(1).
   "judge": s.307(1).
   "prosecutor": s.307(1).

GENERAL NOTE
   Additional evidence can be led in both solemn or summary proceedings provided that the criteria in subs. (2) are satisfied. In solemn proceedings such evidence can be received notwithstanding that the relevant productions or witnesses have not been specified in the indictment (subs. (3)(a)); in either solemn or summary trials the additional evidence can be taken from witnesses whose evidence has already been heard.
   In *Cushion v. H.M. Advocate*, 1994 S.L.T. 410; 1993 S.C.C.R. 356 a review of the trial judge's refusal to admit additional evidence was appealed under the explanation that the court had not been given a full background, and that the judge's decision might have been more favourable to the application; the Appeal Court declined to review the application under s.149(1) of the 1975 Act.

Evidence in replication

269.—(1) The judge may, on a motion of the prosecutor made at the relevant time, permit the prosecutor to lead additional evidence for the purpose of—
   (a) contradicting evidence given by any defence witness which could not reasonably have been anticipated by the prosecutor; or
   (b) providing such proof as is mentioned in section 263(4) of this Act.
   (2) The judge may permit the additional evidence to be led notwithstanding that—

(a) in proceedings on indictment, a witness or production concerned is not included in any list lodged by the parties and that the notice required by sections 67(5) and 78(4) of this Act has not been given; or
(b) in any case, a witness must be recalled.

(3) The judge may when granting a motion in terms of this section, adjourn or postpone the trial before permitting the additional evidence to be led.

(4) In subsection (1) above, "the relevant time" means—
(a) in proceedings on indictment, after the close of the defence evidence and before the commencement of the speeches to the jury; and
(b) in summary proceedings, after the close of the defence evidence and before the prosecutor proceeds to address the judge on the evidence.

DEFINITIONS
"indictment": s.307(1).
"judge": s.307(1).
"prosecutor": s.307(1).
"relevant time, the": s.269(4).

GENERAL NOTE
Evidence in replication may be led with leave of the court to contradict defence evidence which could not be anticipated by the prosecutor, or for the purpose of proving a prior statement of a witness whose evidence is now at variance (s.263(4)).

In assessing whether the prosecutor could have expected the testimony led by the defence, the court may well enquire about the preparations for trial; in both *MacGillivray v. Johnston (No. 2)*, 1994 S.L.T. 1012 and *Neizer v. Johnston*, 1993 S.C.C.R. 772 a decisive factor in refusing such a motion in each case was the Crown's awareness of the existence of witnesses who had been precognosced but had not been led in evidence.

Note that replication can only be used to counter defence evidence and cannot be used by the Crown to contradict earlier prosecution evidence (see *Campbell v. Allan*, 1988 S.C.C.R. 47).

Evidence of criminal record and character of accused

270.—(1) This section applies where—
(a) evidence is led by the defence, or the defence asks questions of a witness for the prosecution, with a view to establishing the accused's good character or impugning the character of the prosecutor, of any witness for the prosecution or of the complainer; or
(b) the nature or conduct of the defence is such as to tend to establish the accused's good character or to involve imputations on the character of the prosecutor, of any witness for the prosecution or of the complainer.

(2) Where this section applies the court may, without prejudice to section 268 of this Act, on the application of the prosecutor, permit the prosecutor to lead evidence that the accused has committed, or has been convicted of, or has been charged with, offences other than that for which he is being tried, or is of bad character, notwithstanding that, in proceedings on indictment, a witness or production concerned is not included in any list lodged by the prosecutor and that the notice required by sections 67(5) and 78(4) of this Act has not been given.

(3) In proceedings on indictment, an application under subsection (2) above shall be made in the course of the trial but in the absence of the jury.

(4) In subsection (1) above, references to the complainer include references to a victim who is deceased.

DEFINITIONS
"prosecutor": s.307(1).
"witness": s.307(1).

GENERAL NOTE
The purpose of this section is to provide a balanced picture where the defence, as a matter of tactics, elects to present the accused as being of good character or brings out the faults of witnesses or a deceased person. A cursory examination might suggest that subs. (2) is very

similar to the more familiar terms of s.266(4)(b) and (c). Section 266 only enables the prosecutor or other accused to question the accused as to his history and character where such defence tactics have been pursued by the accused and the prosecutor, at least, may only do so with leave of the court (s.266(5)). It is important to note that s.266(4) is limited in scope: it is only activated when the accused gives evidence on his own behalf.

By contrast, subs. (2) is much more radical and enables the prosecution to lead evidence (without prior notice but with leave of the court) in rebuttal to demonstrate the history and character of the accused, if the defence has led evidence of his good character, or attacked the character of Crown witnesses or the prosecutor. The introduction of this provision in the Criminal Justice (Scotland) Act 1995, s.24 was not without controversy, given its nature, but it is clear that the conduct of the defence case in the future may require a good deal more circumspection than was necessary hitherto, even where the accused does not give evidence. It may also be said that subs. (1)(b) by its reference to "the nature or conduct of the defence" lacks both the familiarity and clarity of subs. (1)(a).

While the accused may found upon the previous convictions of Crown witnesses, it is clear that only in exceptional circumstances will the court permit scrutiny of, or questioning about, the factual circumstances giving rise to a previous conviction (see *Brady v. H.M. Advocate*, 1986 S.C.C.R. 191): only when the previous conviction relates directly to the circumstances of the current trial can questioning be extended.

Evidence of children

Evidence of vulnerable persons: special provisions

[1]**271.**—(1) Subject to subsections (7) and (8) below, where a vulnerable person has been or could be cited to give evidence in a trial the court may appoint a commissioner to take the evidence of that person if—

    (a) in solemn proceedings, at any time before the oath is administered to the jury;

    (b) in summary proceedings, at any time before the first witness is sworn;

    (c) in exceptional circumstances in either solemn or summary proceedings, during the course of the trial,

application is made in that regard; but to be so appointed a person must be, and for a period of five years have been, a member of the Faculty of Advocates or a solicitor.

(2) Proceedings before a commissioner appointed under subsection (1) above shall be recorded by video recorder.

(3) An accused shall not, except by leave of the commissioner, be present in the room where such proceedings are taking place but shall be entitled by such means as seem suitable to the commissioner to watch and hear the proceedings.

(4) Subsections (2) to (6), (8) and (9) of section 272 of this Act shall apply to an application under subsection (1) above and evidence taken by a commissioner appointed under that subsection as those subsections apply to an application under subsection (1) of that section and evidence taken by a commissioner appointed on such an application.

(5) Subject to subsections (7) and (8) below, where a vulnerable person has been or is likely to be cited to give evidence in a trial, the court may, on an application being made to it, authorise the giving of evidence by that person by means of a live television link.

(6) Subject to subsections (7) and (8) below, where a vulnerable person has been or is likely to be cited to give evidence in a trial, the court may, on application being made to it, authorise the use of a screen to conceal the accused from the sight of that person while that person is present to give evidence; but arrangements shall be made to ensure that the accused is able to watch and hear as the evidence is given by the vulnerable person.

(7) The court may grant an application under subsection (1), (5) or (6) above only on cause shown having regard in particular to—

(a) the possible effect on the vulnerable person if required to give evidence, no such application having been granted;
(b) whether it is likely that the vulnerable person would be better able to give evidence if such an application were granted; and
(c) the views of the vulnerable person.

(8) In considering whether to grant an application under subsection (1), (5) or (6) above the court may take into account, where appropriate, any of the following—
(a) the nature of the alleged offence;
(b) the nature of the evidence which the vulnerable person is likely to be called upon to give;
(c) the relationship, if any, between the person and the accused; and
(d) where the person is a child, his age and maturity.

(9) Where a sheriff to whom an application has been made under subsection (1), (5) or (6) above would have granted the application but for the lack of accommodation or equipment necessary to achieve the purpose of the application, he may by order transfer the case to any sheriff court which has such accommodation and equipment available, being a sheriff court in the same sheriffdom.

(10) The sheriff court to which a case has been transferred under subsection (9) above shall be deemed to have granted an application under, as the case may be, subsection (1), (5) or (6) above in relation to the case.

(11) Where a court has or is deemed to have granted an application under subsection (1), (5) or (6) above in relation to a vulnerable person, and the vulnerable person gives evidence that he recalls having identified, prior to the trial, a person alleged to have committed an offence, the evidence of a third party as to the identification of that person by the vulnerable person prior to the trial shall be admissible as evidence as to such identification.

(12) In this section—
"child" means a person under the age of 16 years;
"court" means the High Court or the sheriff court;
"trial" means a trial under solemn or under summary procedure; and
"vulnerable person" means—
(a) any child; and
(b) any person of or over the age of 16 years—
(i) who is subject to an order made in consequence of a finding of a court in any part of the United Kingdom that he is suffering from mental disorder within the meaning of section 1(2) of the Mental Health (Scotland) Act 1984, section 1(2) of the Mental Health Act 1983, or Article 3(1) of the Mental Health (Northern Ireland) Order 1986 (application of enactment); or
(ii) who is subject to a transfer direction under section 71(1) of the 1984 Act, section 47 of the 1983 Act, or Article 53 of the 1986 Order (transfer directions); or
(iii) who otherwise appears to the court to suffer from significant impairment of intelligence and social functioning.

DEFINITIONS
"commissioner": s.271(1) of the 1995 Act as now inserted by s.29 of the 1997 Act.
"court": s.271(12) of the 1995 Act as now inserted by s.29 of the 1997 Act.
"solemn proceedings": s.3 of the 1995 Act.
"summary proceedings": s.5 of the 1995 Act.
"trial": s.271(12) of the 1995 Act as now inserted by s.29 of the 1997 Act.
"vulnerable person": s.271(12) of the 1995 Act as now inserted by s.29 of the 1997 Act.

NOTE
[1]Substituted by the Crime and Punishment (Scotland) Act 1997 (c. 48) s.29 with effect from August 1, 1997 in terms of the Crime and Punishment (Scotland) Act 1997 (Conmmencement and Transitional Provisions) Order 1997 (S.I. 1997 No. 1712) para. 3.

GENERAL NOTE

This section re-enacts s.271 of the 1995 Act, which contained special provisions in relation to the taking of evidence from child witnesses, but now with two important additions: first, the provisions extend to "vulnerable" persons, a definition which includes children and those over 16 years suffering significant intellectual and behavioural impairment; secondly, the court can consider an application even before the witness has been cited to attend the trial. The procedures enacted operate only in the Sheriff and the High Courts, not in District Courts or in courts presided over by stipendiary magistrates. In the discussion below, references are to s.271 of the Act, as now amended by s.29 of the 1997 Act.

Section 271 of the 1995 Act was a restatement of ss.33 to 35 of the Prisoners and Criminal Proceedings (Scotland) Act 1993 (c. 9), introduced with the general intention of protecting vulnerable child witnesses from the need to have to confront the accused in court. As has been mentioned, these provisions now also extend to witnesses over 16 years where it can be established that they suffer from both significant degrees of intellectual and behavioural impairment (s.271(12)) and the general tests set out in subss. (7) and (8) are met. In the main these provisions have been utilised in cases of a sexual nature but they can be applied to a crime of any sort (subject to the general tests above being satisfied) and it is not necessary that the vulnerable witness should be the complainer in the case.

Three special methods of taking evidence from a vulnerable witness are set out in this section: the witness's evidence may be taken by a court-appointed commissioner (subs. (1)) whose examination of the witness has to be recorded on video and be witnessed at a remove by the accused; the witness can give evidence via a closed circuit television link relayed live into the court during the trial (subs. (5)); or the witness may give evidence from behind a screen out of line of sight of the accused who can view the witness on a closed circuit television link (subs. (6)).

It is a matter for the judge, after hearing parties in relation to an application, to decide whether or not it should be granted having regard to the tests in subss. (7) and (8), and then to consider whether the necessary facilities are available at the court for a live television link or screens, failing which, the case can be transferred to a more suitable court elsewhere in the sheriffdom (subs. (9)). Once a case has been transferred the application will not be required to be reconsidered by the second court, though it is submitted, it would not be incompetent to consider a fresh application should there be a change of circumstances.

The mechanics of each of the three forms of application differ; applications for appointment of a commissioner proceeding under s.272 of the 1995 Act and Chap. 24 of the 1996 Act of Adjournal (using Forms 24.1–A before indictment and 24.1–B after), and television links being governed by Chap. 22 of the 1996 Act of Adjournal, which also sets out the procedures for transfer of cases. Note that r. 22.1 stipulates that application for television links should ordinarily be made not less than 14 days prior to trial, following which a hearing has to be fixed and intimated to other parties. See *H.M. Advocate v. Birkett*, 1992 S.C.C.R. 850 however where only one of several applications was granted, the rest being refused *in hoc statu*, the court having concluded that grounds had not been sufficiently established, but leaving the petition live for the trial court should the need arise; it will be observed that a CCTV link had been authorised and thus there would be no logistical problems in using the equipment for other witnesses if necessary. Understandably applications to use these provisions generally are made by the Crown, but it is equally competent for the defence to make them; in *H.M. Advocate v. Dempsey* (High Court of Justiciary, (1995) 222 Scolag 51) a defence application to receive the evidence of a seven-year-old child, who was related to the accused, was granted without any supporting reports and without debate. The incident libelled was a charge of culpable homicide following an incident in the family home. In the event, when the case proceeded to trial the child's evidence was taken in the ordinary way. Nonetheless it is submitted that impact statements in support of a s.271 application should certainly be the norm where CCTV facilities are sought.

No time limits apply either to applications for appointment of a commissioner or for the use of screens albeit, in the former case, it would be expected that such an application could be considered in advance of trial and only exceptionally thereafter; in the case of a screen application, the issue could be considered at any time once proceedings are live, even during the trial itself subject to fulfilling the requirements of subss. (7) and (8). There may be some difficulty in properly ascertaining the views of some vulnerable witnesses who are not children; curiously consideration of the "maturity" of the witness only comes into play where the witness is a child (subs. (8)(d)).

In placing any application before the court the applicant will have to be able to address the court upon the impact of the case to date upon the vulnerable witness, the likely effect of having to give evidence in the customary manner, and justify the method being sought for presentation of the person's evidence. Experience indicates that applications have almost invariably centred on the evidence of Crown witnesses, as complainers in cases of a sexual nature but there is no bar on applications being made to cover the evidence of vulnerable defence witnesses.

Subsection (11) repeats the previous provision in relation to identification of the accused, extending it to apply to the evidence of any vulnerable witness. It will be appreciated that this apparent evidential concession only comes into play after a s.271 application has been granted. The *raison d'être* of these special provisions is to obviate the need for dock identification of the accused by the witness by statutorily permitting the witness to adopt an earlier identification and leading evidence in support. Given the decision in *Muldoon v. Herron*, 1970 J.C. 20 and decisions following on that case, and the terms of s.260 of the 1995 Act, the main value of subs. (11) is in its explicit statement of law. It will be noted that it is necessary that the vulnerable witness has to attest to having identified the offender previously, failing which reliance would have to be placed instead on a *de recenti* statement and other means of indirect identification of the accused.

The fact that a petition for a CCTV link or the use of screens has been granted does not irrevocably commit the applicant to lead evidence in that manner, but it is patent that careful consideration of two factors—the circumstances of the vulnerable witness, and the strength of available identification evidence, is vital before initiating a s.272 application. Following the Lord Justice-General's judgment in *Brotherston v. H.M. Advocate*, 1995 S.C.C.R. 613, it is clear that once evidence is being adduced by way of s.272 it is not open to a party to switch to conventional testimony in the hope of eliciting a dock identification of the accused. Still, in *Brotherston*, a CCTV case, the camera in court panned around and enabled the child witness sitting in a separate room to pick out the accused; it was notable that there was no suggestion that the camera "lead" the witness and that the jury was directed to attach less weight to that unequivocal identification solely because of technical defects in picture quality, a factor which may well have to be considered in the judge's charge when such remote evidence is led. A similar condition, which ruled out switching from screen testimony to conventional evidence to obtain a dock identification was fixed in *H.M. Advocate v. McGrattan*, 1997 G.W.D. 10–407 largely on account of the undue burden this would place on a cross-examiner.

Once a trial is proceeding great care has to be exercised by Officers of the Court to ensure that witnesses, and particularly vulnerable witnesses, are dealt with appropriately by the court; see *McKie v. H.M. Advocate*, 1997 S.L.T. 1018, where, on appeal, objection was taken both to the manner in which the sheriff sought to comfort the child witness and to the actions of the prosecutor in speaking to the child when her evidence was interrupted, the defence not having been advised of the prosecutor's intention. In response to defence complaints that such actions must prejudice any future proceedings, the sheriff deserted the indictment *pro loco et tempore* (not simpliciter) and extended the twelve month time bar, steps which the Appeal Court held to be entirely appropriate.

Evidence on commission and from abroad

Evidence by letter of request or on commission

272.—(1) In any criminal proceedings in the High Court or the sheriff court the prosecutor or the defence may, at an appropriate time, apply to a judge of the court in which the trial is to take place (or, if that is not yet known, to a judge of the High Court) for—

(a) the issue of a letter of request to a court, or tribunal, exercising jurisdiction in a country or territory outside the United Kingdom, Channel Islands and Isle of Man for the examination of a witness resident in that country or territory; or

(b) the appointment of a commissioner to examine, at any place in the United Kingdom, Channel Islands, or Isle of Man, a witness who—

　(i) by reason of being ill or infirm is unable to attend the trial diet; or

　(ii) is not ordinarily resident in, and is, at the time of the trial diet, unlikely to be present in, the United Kingdom, Channel Islands or the Isle of Man.

(2) A hearing, as regards any application under subsection (1) above by a party, shall be conducted in chambers but may be dispensed with if the application is not opposed.

(3) An application under subsection (1) above may be granted only if the judge is satisfied that—
- (a) the evidence which it is averred the witness is able to give is necessary for the proper adjudication of the trial; and
- (b) there would be no unfairness to the other party were such evidence to be received in the form of the record of an examination conducted by virtue of that subsection.

(4) Any such record as is mentioned in paragraph (b) of subsection (3) above shall, without being sworn to by witnesses, be received in evidence in so far as it either accords with the averment mentioned in paragraph (a) of that subsection or can be so received without unfairness to either party.

(5) Where any such record as is mentioned in paragraph (b) of subsection (3) above, or any part of such record, is not a document in writing, that record or part shall not be received in evidence under subsection (4) above unless it is accompanied by a transcript of its contents.

(6) The procedure as regards the foregoing provisions of this section shall be prescribed by Act of Adjournal; and without prejudice to the generality of the power to make it, such an Act of Adjournal may provide for the appointment of a person before whom evidence may be taken for the purposes of this section.

(7) In subsection (1) above, "appropriate time" means as regards—
- (a) solemn proceedings, any time before the oath is administered to the jury;
- (b) summary proceedings, any time before the first witness is sworn,

or (but only in relation to an application under paragraph (b) of that subsection) any time during the course of the trial if the circumstances on which the application is based had not arisen, or would not have merited such application, within the period mentioned in paragraph (a) or, as the case may be, (b) of this subsection.

(8) In subsection (3) and (4) above, "record" includes, in addition to a document in writing—
- (a) any disc, tape, soundtrack or other device in which sounds or other data (not being visual images) are recorded so as to be capable (with or without the aid of some other equipment) of being reproduced therefrom; and
- (b) any film (including microfilm), negative, tape, disc or other device in which one or more visual images are recorded so as to be capable (as aforesaid) of being reproduced therefrom.

(9) This section is without prejudice to any existing power at common law to adjourn a trial diet to the place where a witness is.

DEFINITIONS
"appropriate time": s.272(7).
"High Court": s.307(1).
"judge": s.307(1).
"prosecutor": s.307(1).
"record": s.272(8).
"trial": s.307(1).
"witness": s.307(1).

GENERAL NOTE
This section applies to solemn and summary proceedings and can apply in circumstances in which the court might otherwise have to convene elsewhere in order to hear a witness' testimony. Chapters 23 and 24 of the 1996 Act of Adjournal regulates the form in which applications for Letters of Request of the taking of evidence on Commission are to be made. The procedures only operate in the Sheriff and High Courts.

Subsection (7) stipulates that such applications can normally only be made before trial proceedings have begun (although see the exceptional provisions available for applications which of necessity need to be made in the course of the trial). As subs. (1) states, any application should be made to a judge within whose jurisdiction the trial is due to take place, or, if no trial diet has been assigned, to a High Court judge. This requirement will be of limited applicability to summary cases since it would only rarely be necessary to seek Letters or a Commission once a trial had been fixed. The application in terms of Rule 23.1.–(4) has to be intimated to other parties and any hearing will occur in chambers if the application is opposed.

The classes of witness in relation to whom applications can be made are set out in subs. (1) but the judge has to be satisfied that the factors stipulated in subs. (3) are met before the application is allowed. Furthermore the granting of the application does not of itself mean that the testimony obtained has to be admitted as evidence: the court on receipt of the record (which must be accompanied by a written transcript) still has to consider whether its contents can be fairly admitted in accordance with the rules of evidence.

In considering the grant of an application, the court has to consider the test set out in subs. (3). It is essential that due weight is given to the potential unfairness to those in the trial who are deprived of the opportunity of oral cross-examination should Letters or a Commission be permitted (see *Muirhead v. H.M. Advocate*, 1983 S.C.C.R. 133). In *Land, Petr*, 1991 S.L.T. 931; 1991 S.C.C.R. 138 while an application by the Crown to take the evidence on commission of a 91-year old witness was granted, and it was conceded that the sheriff's discretion was not subject to review, it was held that the issue of fairness to the accused still fell to be considered at the trial and, if necessary, on appeal.

See also *H.M. Advocate v. Lesacher*, 1982 S.C.C.R. 418 where the trial had to be delayed to allow for the presentation of Letters of Request to West Germany through diplomatic channels.

Refer to Chap. 23 of the 1996 Act of Adjournal for provisions as to expenses, transmission of Letters and custody of documents. Note in particular that Rule 23.6. specifies that such evidence cannot be led or referred to in trial proceedings until a motion to that effect has been made and granted.

It will be observed that requests for live television links for evidence to be taken contemporaneously from abroad during proceedings (s.273 below) are initiated by way of the Letter of Request procedures described above.

Television link evidence from abroad

273.—(1) In any solemn proceedings in the High Court or the sheriff court a person other than the accused may give evidence through a live television link if—

(a) the witness is outside the United Kingdom;

(b) an application under subsection (2) below for the issue of a letter of request has been granted; and

(c) the court is satisfied as to the arrangements for the giving of evidence in that manner by that witness.

(2) The prosecutor or the defence in any proceedings referred to in subsection (1) above may apply to a judge of the court in which the trial is to take place (or, if that court is not yet known, to a judge of the High Court) for the issue of a letter of request to—

(a) a court or tribunal exercising jurisdiction in a country or territory outside the United Kingdom where a witness is ordinarily resident; or

(b) any authority which the judge is satisfied is recognised by the government of that country or territory as the appropriate authority for receiving requests for assistance in facilitating the giving of evidence through a live television link,

requesting assistance in facilitating the giving of evidence by that witness through a live television link.

(3) An application under subsection (2) above shall be granted only if the judge is satisfied that—

(a) the evidence which it is averred the witness is able to give is necessary for the proper adjudication of the trial; and

(b) the granting of the application—

(i) is in the interests of justice; and

(ii) in the case of an application by the prosecutor, is not unfair to the accused.

<small>Definitions</small>
"High Court": s.307(1).
"judge": s.307(1).

"prosecutor": s.307(1).
"sheriff": s.307(1).
"trial": s.307(1).
"witness": s.307(1).

GENERAL NOTE

In solemn proceedings only, application by way of the Letter of Request procedure outlined in s.272 above can be made for a live television link to take the evidence of witnesses who are outwith the United Kingdom. The factors determining whether such an application should be allowed by the court are laid out in subs. (2).

Evidence relating to sexual offences

Restrictions on evidence relating to sexual offences

274.—(1) In any trial of a person on any charge to which this section applies, subject to section 275 of this Act, the court shall not admit, or allow questioning designed to elicit, evidence which shows or tends to show that the complainer—

(a) is not of good character in relation to sexual matters;

(b) is a prostitute or an associate of prostitutes; or

(c) has at any time engaged with any person in sexual behaviour not forming part of the subject matter of the charge.

(2) This section applies to a charge of committing or attempting to commit any of the following offences, that is to say—

(a) rape;

(b) sodomy;

(c) clandestine injury to women;

(d) assault with intent to rape;

(e) indecent assault;

(f) indecent behaviour (including any lewd, indecent or libidinous practice or behaviour);

(g) an offence under section 106(1)(a) or 107 of the Mental Health (Scotland) Act 1984 (unlawful sexual intercourse with mentally handicapped female or with patient); or

(h) an offence under any of the following provisions of the Criminal Law (Consolidation) (Scotland) Act 1995—

(i) sections 1 to 3 (incest and related offences);

(ii) section 5 (unlawful sexual intercourse with girl under 13 or 16);

(iii) section 6 (indecent behaviour toward girl between 12 and 16);

(iv) section 7(2) and (3) (procuring by threats etc.);

(v) section 8 (abduction and unlawful detention);

(vi) section 13(5) (homosexual offences).

(3) In this section "complainer" means the person against whom the offence referred to in subsection (2) above is alleged to have been committed.

(4) This section does not apply to questioning, or evidence being adduced, by the Crown.

DEFINITIONS

"complainer": s.274(3).
"offences": s.307(1).
"trial": s.307(1).

GENERAL NOTE

This section which applies equally to summary and solemn proceedings incorporates the provisions concerning sexual offences now found in the Criminal Law (Consolidation) (Scotland) Act 1995 (c. 39). Where charges of a sexual nature as specified in subs. (2) are libelled, questions by the defence as to the sexual history or sexual preferences of the complainer are generally prohibited. The exceptions to this general rule are contained in s.275 below, where any such questioning proceeds at the discretion of the court which has the power to limit the scope of such cross-examination. In solemn proceedings any motion must be made outwith the presence of the jury.

The provisions of s.274 do not only apply to the complainer; efforts to adduce such evidence by the back door in cross-examination of other witnesses is equally prohibited. The grant or refusal of such an application rests in the discretion of the trial judge (see *Bremner v. H.M. Advocate*, 1992 S.C.C.R. 476).

Exceptions to restrictions under section 274

275.—(1) Notwithstanding section 274 of this Act, in any trial of an accused on any charge to which that section applies, where the court is satisfied on an application by the accused—

(a) that the questioning or evidence referred to in subsection (1) of that section is designed to explain or rebut evidence adduced, or to be adduced, otherwise than by or on behalf of the accused;

(b) that the questioning or evidence referred to in paragraph (c) of that subsection—

   (i) is questioning or evidence as to sexual behaviour which took place on the same occasion as the sexual behaviour forming the subject matter of the charge; or

   (ii) is relevant to the defence of incrimination; or

(c) that it would be contrary to the interests of justice to exclude the questioning or evidence referred to in that subsection,

the court shall allow the questioning or, as the case may be, admit the evidence.

(2) Where questioning or evidence is or has been allowed or admitted under this section, the court may at any time limit as it thinks fit the extent of that questioning or evidence.

(3) Any application under this section shall be made in the course of the trial but in the absence of the jury, the complainer, any person cited as a witness and the public.

DEFINITION
"trial": s.307(1).

GENERAL NOTE
See the notes to s.274 above.

Biological material

Evidence of biological material

276.—(1) Evidence as to the characteristics and composition of any biological material deriving from human beings or animals shall, in any criminal proceedings, be admissible notwithstanding that neither the material nor a sample of it is lodged as a production.

(2) A party wishing to lead such evidence as is referred to in subsection (1) above shall, where neither the material nor a sample of it is lodged as a production, make the material or a sample of it available for inspection by the other party unless the material constitutes a hazard to health or has been destroyed in the process of analysis.

GENERAL NOTE
This section dispenses with the need to produce in court certain biological materials in relation to which evidence is to be led in proceedings. Ordinarily in solemn proceedings the accused is entitled to inspect any productions (see s.68(2)); no such provision is found in summary proceedings given their character. Section 276 arises from considerations of public health and constitutes an exception to the authority that allows an accused to see productions.

Transcripts and records

Transcript of police interview sufficient evidence

277.—(1) Subject to subsection (2) below, for the purposes of any criminal proceedings, a document certified by the person who made it as an accurate transcript made for the prosecutor of the contents of a tape (identified by means of a label) purporting to be a recording of an interview between—

(a) a police officer and an accused person; or

(b) a person commissioned, appointed or authorised under section 6(3) of the Customs and Excise Management Act 1979 and an accused person,

shall be received in evidence and be sufficient evidence of the making of the transcript and of its accuracy.

(2) Subsection (1) above shall not apply to a transcript—

(a) unless a copy of it has been served on the accused not less than 14 days before his trial; or

(b) if the accused, not less than six days before his trial, or by such later time before his trial as the court may in special circumstances allow, has served notice on the prosecutor that the accused challenges the making of the transcript or its accuracy.

(3) A copy of the transcript or a notice under subsection (2) above shall be served in such manner as may be prescribed by Act of Adjournal; and a written execution purporting to be signed by the person who served the transcript or notice, together with, where appropriate, the relevant post office receipt shall be sufficient evidence of such service.

(4) Where subsection (1) above does not apply to a transcript, if the person who made the transcript is called as a witness his evidence shall be sufficient evidence of the making of the transcript and of its accuracy.

GENERAL NOTE

This section permits the admission as evidence of a transcript of any interview conducted by the police or Customs officers with the accused on tape. The transcript, prepared by a person appointed by the procurator fiscal, has to be certified by that person and a copy of it has to be served (subs. (3)) on the accused not less than 14 days before trial (subs. (2)(a)). Any challenge to the accuracy of the transcript has to be intimated to the prosecutor not less than six days before trial normally, or later on cause shown. It appears that a challenge to the accuracy of the transcript can be met conclusively by calling the person who prepared it but this would not preclude the alternative of playing the tape, provided its contents did not breach ss.101(1) and 166(3) and disclose previous convictions or contain other inadmissible material. These factors explain why the prosecution will often prepare and lodge an edited transcript deleting any such untoward references: in that event the jury, or the judge in summary proceedings, should only be referred to the edited transcript in the course of evidence.

Note that, unlike the transcript of any judicial examination, which must be lodged in solemn proceedings (see the notes to ss.36 and 37), this section does not oblige the prosecutor to lodge a transcript of taped interview.

Record of proceedings at examination as evidence

278.—(1) Subject to subsection (2) below, the record made, under section 37 of this Act (incorporating any rectification authorised under section 38(1) of this Act), of proceedings at the examination of an accused shall be received in evidence without being sworn to by witnesses, and it shall not be necessary in proceedings on indictment to insert the names of any witnesses to the record in any list of witnesses, either for the prosecution or for the defence.

(2) On the application of either an accused or the prosecutor—

(a) in proceedings on indictment, subject to sections 37(5) and 72(1)(b)
(iv) of this Act, the court may determine that the record or part of the
record shall not be read to the jury; and

(b) in summary proceedings, subject to the said section 37(5) and to
subsection (4) below, the court may refuse to admit the record or
some part of the record as evidence.

(3) At the hearing of an application under subsection (2) above, it shall be
competent for the prosecutor or the defence to adduce as witnesses the
persons who were present during the proceedings mentioned in subsection
(1) above and for either party to examine those witnesses upon any matters
regarding the said proceedings.

(4) In summary proceedings, except on cause shown, an application under
subsection (2)(b) above shall not be heard unless notice of at least 10 clear
days has been given to the court and to the other parties.

(5) In subsection (2) above, the "record" comprises—

(a) as regards any trial of an indictment, each record included, under
section 68(1) of this Act, in the list of productions; and

(b) as regards a summary trial, each record which it is sought to have
received under subsection (1) above.

DEFINITIONS
"indictment": s.307(1).
"prosecutor": s.307(1).
"record": s.278(5).
"witness": s.307(1).

GENERAL NOTE
Section 278 specifies the principles to be applied to the use of transcripts of judicial
examination at trial. Section 38(1) allows for rectification of the transcript after which
procedure the accuracy of the transcript is settled conclusively (see s.38(4)): s.279 is concerned
with the admissibility, or otherwise, of material in the transcript. On the motion of any party, the
court has to determine which parts of the transcript may be read to the jury or court in the
subsequent trial. See also Chap. 25 of the 1996 Act of Adjournal in relation to the use of
transcripts in evidence.

Any motion to restrict the material in a judicial examination has to be made in compliance
with subs. (2), at a first or preliminary diet in solemn procedure (see s.72(1)(b)), or not less than
10 clear days before a summary trial (it is not essential that the issue be raised at the
intermediate diet (see s.148) but this would obviously be a sensible time for it to be considered).
Since it cannot be certain in a summary case whether the Crown intends to found upon the
transcript of judicial examination until trial proceeds, there is obviously an element of
anticipation involved in making such a motion.

Note that in *Hendry v. H.M. Advocate*, 1985 S.C.C.R. 275, a Five Bench decision, it was held
to be illegitimate to use a self-serving statement made in a judicial examination as a substitute
for parole evidence on oath. See *Robertson v. H.M. Advocate*, 1996 S.C.C.R. 243 discussed at
A4.88. The case of *McEwan v. H.M. Advocate*, 1990 S.C.C.R. 401 gives directions as to how the
contents of a judicial examination should be presented to a jury.

In considering whether a transcript of judicial examination should be admitted as evidence, a
relevant factor is likely to be the similarity or otherwise between the petition charges, which
formed the basis of the examination, and the charges ultimately libelled. Similar considerations
will apply to any alleged admissions put to the accused at examination and their fairness and
admissibility in the light of evidence. The prosecutor is now required to lodge a certified copy of
the petition (and by implication any transcript of alleged admissions put to the accused at the
judicial examination) as well as any transcript of judicial examination as a production.

Documentary evidence

Evidence from documents

279. Schedule 8 to this Act, which makes provision regarding the
admissibility in criminal proceedings of copy documents and of evidence
contained in business documents, shall have effect.

Schedule 8 to the Act restates the terms of Sched. 3 to the Prisoners and Criminal Proceedings (Scotland) Act 1993 which provides for the certification of documentary evidence, particularly business documents, and validates the use of certified copies of documents (as defined in Sched. (8)), which may in some instances contain hearsay material, as best evidence in criminal proceedings. It will be noted that the provisions of this section would not preclude use of the Bankers' Books Evidence Act 1879 (c. 11) in suitable circumstances; there are two means of proving entries in bankers' books though it has to be said that generally the Sched. 8 provisions are more widely drafted (see *Lord Advocate's Reference No. 1 of 1996*, 1996 G.W.D. 21–1189).

Act of Adjournal
Forms 26.1–A to 26.1–C are provided in the 1996 Act of Adjournal for authentication of documents, and setting up business documents, and providing a means for certification of evidence which is not to be found in business documents. This last class of certificate can be tendered in proceedings without the need for the person certifying to attend court as a witness.

Evidence from certain official documents

[1]**279A.**—[2](1) Any letter, minute or other official document issuing from the office of or in custody of any of the departments of state or government in the United Kingdom or any part of the Scottish Administration which—
    (a) is required to be produced in evidence in any prosecution; and
    (b) according to the rules and regulations applicable to such departments may competently be so produced,
shall when so produced be *prima facie* evidence of the matters contained in it without being produced or sworn to by any witness.
    (2) A copy of any such document as is mentioned in subsection (1) above bearing to be certified by any person having authority to certify it shall be treated as equivalent to the original of that document and no proof of the signature of the person certifying the copy or of his authority to certify it shall be necessary.
    [2](3) Any order made by any of the departments of state or government or the Scottish Parliament or any local authority or public body made under powers conferred by any statute or a print or a copy of such order, shall when produced in a prosecution be received as evidence of the due making, confirmation, and existence of the order without being sworn to by any witness and without any further or other proof.
    (4) Subsection (3) above is without prejudice to any right competent to the accused to challenge any order such as is mentioned in that subsection as being *ultra vires* of the authority making it or any other competent ground.
    (5) Where an order such as is mentioned in subsection (3) above is referred to in the indictment or, as the case may be, the complaint, it shall not be necessary to enter it in the record of the proceedings as a documentary production.
    (6) The provisions of this section are in addition to, and not in derogation of, any powers of proving documents conferred by statute or existing at common law.

DEFINITIONS
    "document": s.279 and Sched. 8, para. 8 to the 1995 Act.
    "order": s.307(1) of the 1995 Act.
    "United Kingdom": s.5 of and Sched. 1 to the Interpretation Act 1978 (c. 30).

NOTES
    [1]Inserted by the Crime and Punishment (Scotland) Act 1997 (c. 48) s.28(2); commenced with effect from August 1, 1997 in terms of the Crime and Punishment (Scotland) Act 1997 (Commencement and Transitional Provisions) Order 1997 (S.I. 1997 No. 1712) para. 3.
    [2]As amended by the Scotland Act 1998 (Consequential Modifications) (No. 2) Order 1999 (S.I. 1999 No. 1820) art. 4 and Sched. 2, para.122(4) (effective July 1, 1999).

General Note

This section supercedes s.154 of the 1995 Act and makes provisions for the admissibility of official documents as evidence in any criminal proceedings. Apart from minor rewording, and associated renumbering of subsections, the new provision is all but identical to the old but, importantly, extends to solemn proceedings.

Either the original document or a certified copy of it can be used in proceedings without the need for it to be listed as a production or set up by parole evidence: the only proviso is that there must be valid certification of the document or a copy of it. These specific evidential concessions go beyond the provisions found in Schedule 8 to the 1995 Act; particularly note that there is no requirement to lodge the relevant Order, Local Government Order or Statutory Instrument as a production in proceedings. Reference should also be made to the statutory presumptions found in Sched. 3, para. 12 of the 1995 Act.

The procedure to be followed when a challenge is made to the validity of an Order was discussed in *Johnston v. McGillivray*, 1993 S.L.T. 120 and in *Neizer v. Johnston*, 1993 S.C.C.R. 772.

Routine evidence

Routine evidence

280.—(1) For the purposes of any proceedings for an offence under any of the enactments specified in column 1 of Schedule 9 to this Act, a certificate purporting to be signed by a person or persons specified in column 2 thereof, and certifying the matter specified in column 3 thereof shall, subject to subsection (6) below, be sufficient evidence of that matter and of the qualification or authority of that person or those persons.

(2) The Secretary of State may by order—

(a) amend or repeal the entry in Schedule 9 to this Act in respect of any enactment; or

(b) insert in that Schedule an entry in respect of a further enactment.

(3) An order under subsection (2) above may make such transitional, incidental or supplementary provision as the Secretary of State considers necessary or expedient in connection with the coming into force of the order.

(4) For the purposes of any criminal proceedings, a report purporting to be signed by two authorised forensic scientists shall, subject to subsection (5) below, be sufficient evidence of any fact or conclusion as to fact contained in the report and of the authority of the signatories.

(5) A forensic scientist is authorised for the purposes of subsection (4) above if—

(a) he is authorised for those purposes by the Secretary of State; or

(b) he—

(i) is a constable or is employed by a police authority under section 9 of the Police (Scotland) Act 1967;

(ii) possesses such qualifications and experience as the Secretary of State may for the purposes of that subsection by order prescribe; and

(iii) is authorised for those purposes by the chief constable of the police force maintained for the police area of that authority.

(6) Subsections (1) and (4) above shall not apply to a certificate or, as the case may be, report tendered on behalf of the prosecutor or the accused—

(a) unless a copy has been served on the other party not less than fourteen days before the trial; or

[1](b) where the other party, not more than seven days after the date of service of the copy on him under paragraph (a) above or by such later time as the court may in special circumstances allow, has served notice on the first party that he challenges the matter, qualification or authority mentioned in subsection (1) above or as the case may be the fact, conclusion or authority mentioned in subsection (4) above.

(7) A copy of a certificate or, as the case may be, report required by subsection (6) above, to be served on the accused or the prosecutor or of a

notice required by that subsection or by subsection (1) or (2) of section 281 of this Act to be served on the prosecutor shall be served in such manner as may be prescribed by Act of Adjournal; and a written execution purporting to be signed by the person who served such certificate or notice, together with, where appropriate, the relevant post office receipt shall be sufficient evidence of service of such a copy.

(8) Where, following service of a notice under subsection (6)(b) above, evidence is given in relation to a report referred to in subsection (4) above by both of the forensic scientists purporting to have signed the report, the evidence of those forensic scientists shall be sufficient evidence of any fact (or conclusion as to fact) contained in the report.

(9) At any trial of an offence it shall be presumed that the person who appears in answer to the complaint is the person charged by the police with the offence unless the contrary is alleged.

(10) An order made under subsection (2) or (5)(b)(ii) above shall be made by statutory instrument.

(11) No order shall be made under subsection (2) above unless a draft of the order has been laid before, and approved by a resolution of, each House of Parliament.

(12) A statutory instrument containing an order under subsection (5)(b)(ii) above shall be subject to annulment pursuant to a resolution of either House of Parliament.

DEFINITIONS
  "complaint": s.307(1).
  "constable": s.307(1) and s.51(1) of the Police (Scotland) Act 1967 (c. 77).
  "offence": s.307(1).
  "prosecutor": s.307(1).
  "trial": s.307(1).

NOTE
[1]Amended by the Crime and Punishment (Scotland) Act 1997 (c. 48) s.62(1) and Sched. 1, para. 21(32) with effect from August 1, 1997 in terms of the Crime and Punishment (Scotland) Act (Commencement and Transitional Provisions) Order 1997 (S.I. 1997 No. 1712), para. 3.

GENERAL NOTE
  Unlike s.26(2) of the Criminal Justice (Scotland) Act 1980 which applied only to summary proceedings, the effect of subs. (4) is to apply these provisions relating to routine evidence prepared by authorised forensic scientists to both summary and solemn proceedings. The provisions of s.281 are equally available to prosecution and defence alike provided the authors of the report are authorised scientists.
  It will be noted that subs. (5) broadens the definition of "forensic scientist" to include police constables or police employees appointed by their Chief Constable. The provisions in regard to service of forensic reports are repeated in subs. (6) and the form of certificate, as provided by Chap. 27 of the 1996 Act of Adjournal, may broadly follow the style of Form 27.2.
  Challenges to the contents of a report must be by notice served on the other party not more than seven days after service of the report (note that by contrast, s.26(3) of the 1980 Act allowed challenge up to six days before the trial). Failing such challenge, the contents of the report shall be received as sufficient evidence. Much of the case law generated by s.26 of the 1980 Act related to attacking certificated evidence, which had not been formally challenged, on the basis that the facts contained in the reports did not themselves satisfy the statutory requirements. See *Normand v. Wotherspoon*, 1994 S.L.T. 487; 1993 S.C.C.R. 912; *Straker v. Orr*, 1994 S.C.C.R. 251; *McCrindle v. Walkingshaw*, 1994 S.C.C.R. 299; *O'Brien v. McCreadie*, 1994 S.C.C.R. 516. For more recent discussion of the presumptions as to service of such reports see *Lawrence v. Vannet*, 1998 G.W.D. 40–2041. Objection to the contents of a forensic report served under s.280 (on the basis that the authors had not stated that they had analysed the drugs identified) without having intimated a challenge under subs.(6)(b) was repelled on appeal in *Meek v. H.M. Advocate*, 2000 G.W.D. 9–323.
  The section makes various other provisions intended to reduce the unnecessary attendance of

witnesses at court. The Secretary of State may add to the list of matters which may be introduced into evidence by certificate, by way of subordinate legislation. This will enable suitable matters to be added to the list as they are identified without the need to wait for a suitable opportunity to incorporate them in primary legislation (subss. (2) and (3)).

This section puts it beyond doubt that the facts and conclusions as to facts spoken to either in the report or in subsequent oral evidence based on the report, are sufficient for the purpose of proving those facts. Such evidence can still be attacked on the grounds of credibility or unreliability.

Subsection (9) repeats the terms of s.26(5) and enacts a presumption that the party answering the complaint is the person charged by the police. Unless a challenge is intimated on behalf of the accused before a plea has been tendered, the presumption will hold good and it then becomes unnecessary to identify the accused in the course of the trial, always provided that it has been established that the person responsible for the offence had been charged. See *Rollo v. Wilson*, 1988 S.C.C.R. 312 where the sheriff recalled a police witness to confirm evidence of identification; on appeal it was held that the s.26(5) presumption had in any event rendered the recall unnecessary: in *Hamilton v. Ross*, 1992 S.L.T. 384; 1991 S.C.C.R. 165 the Appeal Court raised the issue of the presumption in response to a Crown appeal against a no case to answer motion; the issue had not been aired before that time but the Crown was still entitled to benefit from the provision.

Routine evidence: autopsy and forensic science reports

281.—(1) Where in a trial an autopsy report is lodged as a production by the prosecutor it shall be presumed that the body of the person identified in that report is the body of the deceased identified in the indictment or complaint, unless the accused not less than six days before the trial, or by such later time before the trial as the court may in special circumstances allow, gives notice that the contrary is alleged.

(2) At the time of lodging an autopsy or forensic science report as a production the prosecutor may intimate to the accused that it is intended that only one of the pathologists or forensic scientists (whom the prosecutor shall specify) purporting to have signed the report shall be called to give evidence in respect thereof; and the evidence of that pathologist or forensic scientist shall be sufficient evidence of any fact or conclusion as to fact contained in the report and of the qualifications of the signatories, unless the accused, not less than six days before the trial or by such later time before the trial as the court may in special circumstances allow, serves notice on the prosecutor that he requires the attendance at the trial of the other pathologist or forensic scientist also.

(3) Where, following service of a notice by the accused under subsection (2) above, evidence is given in relation to an autopsy or forensic science report by both of the pathologists or forensic scientists purporting to have signed the report, the evidence of those pathologists or forensic scientists shall be sufficient evidence of any fact (or conclusion as to fact) contained in the report.

DEFINITIONS
"indictment": s.307(1).
"complaint": s.307(1).
"prosecutor": s.307(1).
"trial": s.307(1).

GENERAL NOTE
It is presumed, unless a challenge is notified to the prosecutor not less than six days before any trial (or later on cause shown), that the person referred to in any autopsy report founded upon in the proceedings is the same person as specified in the libel. Subsection (2) entitles the prosecutor to serve notice that he will call only one of the joint authors of a forensic of autopsy report, a concession designed to minimise inconvenience to such witnesses if their evidence is not in dispute. Again, a challenge to such a notice has to be intimated not less than six days

before trial (or later on cause shown). Rule 27.1 in the 1996 Act of Adjournal requires that such notice will be in writing.

The practice has developed in solemn cases of incorporating the subs. (2) notice to the accused in the List of Productions incorporated in the indictment.

Sufficient evidence

Evidence as to controlled drugs and medicinal products

282.—(1) For the purposes of any criminal proceedings, evidence given by an authorised forensic scientist, either orally or in a report purporting to be signed by him, that a substance which satisfies either of the conditions specified in subsection (2) below is—

(a) a particular controlled drug or medicinal product; or

(b) a particular product which is listed in the British Pharmacopoeia as containing a particular controlled drug or medicinal product,

shall, subject to subsection (3) below, be sufficient evidence of that fact notwithstanding that no analysis of the substance has been carried out.

(2) Those conditions are—

(a) that the substance is in a sealed container bearing a label identifying the contents of the container; or

(b) that the substance has a characteristic appearance having regard to its size, shape, colour and manufacturer's mark.

(3) A party proposing to rely on subsection (1) above ("the first party") shall, not less than 14 days before the trial diet, serve on the other party ("the second party")—

(a) a notice to that effect; and

(b) where the evidence is contained in a report, a copy of the report,

and if the second party serves on the first party, not more than seven days after the date of service of the notice on him, a notice that he does not accept the evidence as to the identity of the substance, subsection (1) above shall not apply in relation to that evidence.

(4) A notice or copy report served in accordance with subsection (3) above shall be served in such manner as may be prescribed by Act of Adjournal; and a written execution purporting to be signed by the person who served the notice or copy together with, where appropriate, the relevant post office receipt shall be sufficient evidence of such service.

(5) In this section—

"controlled drug" has the same meaning as in the Misuse of Drugs Act 1971; and

"medicinal product" has the same meaning as in the Medicines Act 1968.

DEFINITIONS

"controlled drug": s.282(5) and s.2(1)(a) of the Misuse of Drugs Act 1971 (c. 38).

"medicinal product": s.282(5) and s.130(1) of the Medicines Act 1968 (c. 67).

"trial": s.307(1).

GENERAL NOTE

This section, introduced by the Criminal Justice (Scotland) Act 1995, s.25, enables evidence to be given, in certain circumstances, by an authorised forensic scientist in any criminal proceedings to the effect that a substance is listed in British Pharmacopoeia as being, or containing, a controlled drug or medicinal product. Instead of demanding the conduct of a chemical examination to establish identification, s.282 allows forensic identification to be achieved by reference either to the label on a sealed container or, as is more common, to the size, colour, shape and markings on the substance; this latter method is commonplace in medical practice and in the pharmaceutical industry and there seems little virtue in requiring a higher standard than that in criminal proceedings particularly when subs. (3)(b) preserves the rights of the other party to give formal notice of challenge to that evidence.

Any such forensic report can be served in accordance with subs. (3) not less than 14 days prior to trial may broadly follow the style of Form 27, and must be challenged within seven days of the date of service, not receipt. Such a report must be served on all other parties in the proceedings.

Evidence as to time and place of video surveillance recordings

283.—(1) For the purposes of any criminal proceedings, a certificate purporting to be signed by a person responsible for the operation of a video surveillance system and certifying—
  (a) the location of the camera;
  (b) the nature and extent of the person's responsibility for the system; and
  (c) that visual images recorded on a particular video tape are images, recorded by the system, of events which occurred at a place specified in the certificate at a time and date so specified,
shall, subject to subsection (2) below, be sufficient evidence of the matters contained in the certificate.

(2) A party proposing to rely on subsection (1) above ("the first party") shall, not less than 14 days before the trial diet, serve on the other party ("the second party") a copy of the certificate and, if the second party serves on the first party, not more than seven days after the date of service of the copy certificate on him, a notice that he does not accept the evidence contained in the certificate, subsection (1) above shall not apply in relation to that evidence.

(3) A copy certificate or notice served in accordance with subsection (2) above shall be served in such manner as may be prescribed by Act of Adjournal; and a written execution purporting to be signed by the person who served the copy or notice together with, where appropriate, the relevant post office receipt shall be sufficient evidence of such service.

(4) In this section, "video surveillance system" means apparatus consisting of a camera mounted in a fixed position and associated equipment for transmitting and recording visual images of events occurring in any place.

DEFINITION
"video surveillance systems": s.283(4).

GENERAL NOTE
This section provides for evidence as to certain matters to be given by certificate by a person who is responsible for the operation of a video surveillance system, and was adopted from s.26 of the Criminal Justice (Scotland) Act 1995. The evidential matters which may be dealt with in the certificate are specified in subs. (1), and any such certificate shall be sufficient evidence of the matters stated. The form of certificate is stipulated in Chap. 27 of the 1996 Act of Adjournal (see Form 27.2). As elsewhere in Pt. XII of the Act, any certificate must be served not less than 14 days prior to trial and any challenge to the sufficiency of the evidence certified must be intimated within seven days of service.
The prime purpose of this provision is to provide a convenient means of leading the evidence of operators of city centre surveillance systems without requiring the unnecessary attendance at court of personnel. If the accused wishes to challenge this video evidence, the operator can be called upon to attend court.

Evidence in relation to fingerprints

284.—[1](1) For the purposes of any criminal proceedings, a certificate purporting to be signed by a person authorised in that behalf by a chief constable and certifying that relevant physical data (within the meaning of section 18(7A) of this Act) was taken from or provided by thereon were taken from a person designated in the certificate at a time, date and place specified therein shall, subject to subsection (2) below, be sufficient evidence of the facts contained in the certificate.

[2](2) A party proposing to rely on subsection (1) above ("the first party") shall, not less than 14 days before the trial diet, serve on any other party to the proceedings a copy of the certificate, and such other party shall not be

entitled to challenge the sufficiency of the evidence contained within the certificate.

²(2A) Where the first party does not serve a copy of the certificate on any other party as mentioned in subsection (2) above, he shall not be entitled to rely on subsection (1) above as respects that party.

(3) A copy certificate or notice served in accordance with subsection (2) above shall be served in such manner as may be prescribed by Act of Adjournal; and a written execution purporting to be signed by the person who served the copy or notice together with, where appropriate, the relevant post office receipt shall be sufficient evidence of such service.

DEFINITIONS
"constable": s.307(1) and s.51(1) of the Police (Scotland) Act 1967.
"relevant physical data": s.18(7A) of the 1995 Act.

NOTES
¹Substituted by the Crime and Punishment (Scotland) Act 1997 s.47(4)(a) with effect from August 1, 1997 in terms of the Crime and Punishment (Scotland) Act 1997 (Commencement and Transitional Provisions) order 1997 (S.I. 1997 No. 1712) para. 3.
²Substituted by s.47(4)(b) of the 1997 Act and effected by the Order specified above.

GENERAL NOTE
The reforms to s.284 introduced by the Crime and Punishment (Scotland) Act 1997 s.47(4) further abbreviates the procedures for presentation of fingerprint evidence in the Scottish criminal courts. Formerly certificates signed by two police constables on any fingerprint report, giving details of the obtaining of the prints from the person named in the certificate, provided a sufficiency of evidence unless challenged timeously: from August 1, 1997 certification of the taking of relevant physical data can be made by one authorised person, a role which can obviously be undertaken by nominated civilian staff. Ultimately the aim seems to be for a member of staff at the database end, rather than the officers present with the person being fingerprinted, to certify the form produced by the Livescan equipment.

Subsections (2) and (2A) require the party relying upon this provision to serve a copy of the signed certificate on the affected party to the proceedings and, once served, the evidence in the copy shall be sufficient, cannot be challenged and will be conclusive as to its contents. Note that the right to challenge (previously in s.284(2) of the 1995 Act) ceases from August 1, 1997.

A party relying upon this provision (almost invariably the Crown) will need to retain and be able to produce executions of service to the court.

Proof of previous convictions

Previous convictions: proof, general

285.—(1) A previous conviction may be proved against any person in any criminal proceedings by the production of such evidence of the conviction as is mentioned in this subsection and subsections (2) to (6) below and by showing that his fingerprints and those of the person convicted are the fingerprints of the same person.

¹(2) A certificate purporting to be signed by or the Secretary of State or by a person authorised by him to sign such a certificate or the Commissioner of Police of the Metropolis, containing particulars relating to a conviction extracted from the criminal records kept in pursuance of a service provided and maintained by the Secretary of State under or by virtue of Section 36 of the Police (Scotland) Act 1967 or by or on behalf of the Commissioner of Police of the Metropolis, and certifying that the copies of the fingerprints contained in the certificate are copies of the fingerprints appearing from the said records to have been taken in pursuance of rules for the time being in force under sections 12 and 39 of the Prisons (Scotland) Act 1989, or regulations for the time being in force under section 16 of the Prison Act 1952, from the person convicted on the occasion of the conviction or on the occasion of his last conviction, shall be sufficient evidence of the conviction

or, as the case may be, of his last conviction and of all preceding convictions and that the copies of the fingerprints produced on the certificate are copies of the fingerprints of the person convicted.

(3) Where a person has been apprehended and detained in the custody of the police in connection with any criminal proceedings, a certificate purporting to be signed by the chief constable concerned or a person authorised on his behalf, certifying that the fingerprints produced thereon were taken from him while he was so detained, shall be sufficient evidence in those proceedings that the fingerprints produced on the certificate are the fingerprints of that person.

(4) A certificate purporting to be signed by or on behalf of the governor of a prison or of a remand centre in which any person has been detained in connection with any criminal proceedings, certifying that the fingerprints produced thereon were taken from him while he was so detained, shall be sufficient evidence in those proceedings that the fingerprints produced on the certificate are the fingerprints of that person.

²(5) A certificate purporting to be signed by the Secretary of State or by a person authorised by him to sign such a certificate, and certifying that the fingerprints, copies of which are certified as mentioned in subsection (2) above by the Secretary of State or by a person authorised by him to sign such a certificate or by or on behalf of or the Commissioner of Police of the Metropolis to be copies of the fingerprints of a person previously convicted and the fingerprints certified by or on behalf of a chief constable or a governor as mentioned in subsection (3) or (4) above, or otherwise shown, to be the fingerprints of the person against whom the previous conviction is sought to be proved, are the fingerprints of the same person, shall be sufficient evidence of the matter so certified.

(6) An extract conviction of any crime committed in any part of the United Kingdom bearing to have been issued by an officer whose duties include the issue of extract convictions shall be received in evidence without being sworn to by witnesses.

(7) It shall be competent to prove a previous conviction or any fact relevant to the admissibility of the conviction by witnesses, although the name of any such witness is not included in the list served on the accused; and the accused shall be entitled to examine witnesses with regard to such conviction or fact.

(8) An official of any prison in which the accused has been detained on such conviction shall be a competent and sufficient witness to prove its application to the accused, although he may not have been present in court at the trial to which such conviction relates.

(9) The method of proving a previous conviction authorised by this section shall be in addition to any other method of proving the conviction.

³(10) In this section "fingerprint" includes any record of the skin of a person's finger created by a device approved by the Secretary of State under section 18(7B) of this Act.

DEFINITION
  "conviction": s.307(5).

NOTES
  ¹Substituted by the Crime and Punishment (Scotland) Act 1997 (c. 48) s.59(2) with effect from August 1, 1997 as enacted by the Crime and Punishment (Scotland) Act 1997 (Commencement and Transitional Provisions) Order 1997 (S.I. 1997 No. 1712) para. 3.
  ²Substituted by the 1997 Act s.59(3) and enacted from August 1, 1997 by the above Order.
  ³Inserted by the 1997 Act s.47(5) and enacted from August 1, 1997 by the above Order.

GENERAL NOTE
  This section carries over the provisions relating to proof of previous convictions by use of proved fingerprints. This procedure can be deployed to prove previous convictions which have

been disputed by the accused or, in limited circumstances, as evidence in support of a substantive charge (see also s.286 below). Use is made of the fingerprint forms completed at the time of the accused's admission to a prison (subs. (4)) or when routinely detained in police custody in relation to the charges libelled (subs. (3)).

It is not necessary to list as witnesses those prison officials or court officers whose only role is to speak to the fact of a previous conviction or extract conviction.

Certification was previously the responsibility of the Chief Constable of Strathclyde Police but, following amendments to the Police (Scotland) Act 1967 (c. 77) made by s.46 of the 1997 Act, responsibility for this core service now lies with the Scottish Secretary.

The development of "livescan" electronic fingerprinting is reflected in subs. (10). See the discussion at A4.49 above. The Electronic Fingerprinting etc. Device Approval (Scotland) Order 1997 S.I. 1939 approved the use of the Digital Biometrics Corporation (D.B.I.) Tenprinter 1133S with effect from August 8, 1997.

Previous convictions: proof in support of substantive charge

286.—(1) Without prejudice to section 285(6) to (9) or, as the case may be, section 166 of this Act, where proof of a previous conviction is competent in support of a substantive charge, any such conviction or an extract of it shall, if—

    (a) it purports to relate to the accused and to be signed by the clerk of court having custody of the record containing the conviction; and

    (b) a copy of it has been served on the accused not less than 14 days before the trial diet,

be sufficient evidence of the application of the conviction to the accused unless, within seven days of the date of service of the copy on him, he serves notice on the prosecutor that he denies that it applies to him.

(2) A copy of a conviction or extract conviction served under subsection (1) above shall be served on the accused in such manner as may be prescribed by Act of Adjournal, and a written execution purporting to be signed by the person who served the copy together with, where appropriate, the relevant post office receipt shall be sufficient evidence of service of the copy.

DEFINITIONS
"previous conviction": s.307(5).
"trial": s.307(1).

GENERAL NOTE
Where it is necessary to lead evidence of a conviction in support of a substantive charge, this section provides for the use in evidence, of a relevant certified extract conviction. A copy of the extract conviction has to be served on the accused not less than 14 days before trial and any challenge to it must be intimated within seven days of service. Use of a s.286 certificate may well serve to pre-empt any such challenge. In solemn proceedings the completed execution of service should be lodged as a production.

See generally the discussion on the admissibility of evidence of previous convictions in the notes to ss.101 and 166 above.

PART XIII

MISCELLANEOUS

Lord Advocate

Demission of office by Lord Advocate

287.—(1) All indictments which have been raised by a Lord Advocate shall remain effective notwithstanding his subsequently having died or demitted office and may be taken up and proceeded with by his successor.

(2) During any period when the office of Lord Advocate is vacant it shall

be lawful to indict accused persons in name of the Solicitor General then in office.

(3) The advocates depute shall not demit office when a Lord Advocate dies or demits office but shall continue in office until their successors receive commissions.

(4) The advocates depute and procurators fiscal shall have power, notwithstanding any vacancy in the office of Lord Advocate, to take up and proceed with any indictment which—

(a) by virtue of subsection (1) above, remains effective; or
(b) by virtue of subsection (2) above, is in the name of the Solicitor General.

(5) For the purposes of this Act, where, but for this subsection, demission of office by one Law Officer would result in the offices of both being vacant, he or, where both demit office on the same day, the person demitting the office of Lord Advocate shall be deemed to continue in office until the warrant of appointment of the person succeeding to the office of Lord Advocate is granted.

[1](6) The Lord Advocate shall enter upon the duties of his office immediately upon the grant of his warrant of appointment.

DEFINITIONS
"indictment": s.307(1).
"procurator fiscal": s.307(1).

NOTE
[1]As amended by the Scotland Act 1998 (Consequential Modifications) (No.1) Order 1999 (S.I. 1999 No. 1042) art 4 and Sched.2, para.11 and Sched. 2, Pt III.

GENERAL NOTE
The Lord Advocate has the universal and exclusive title to prosecute on indictment. This section is concerned with the consequences of the decession of office by Lord Advocate. This section puts into statutory form a variety of authorities that have evolved or been passed over the years: see Macdonald *Criminal Law of Scotland* (5th ed.) (W. Green, Edinburgh) at p. 212. In short, the section provides for the continuity of Crown business notwithstanding a change of Lord Advocate.

Two points are worth noting. First, during any period when the office of Lord Advocate is vacant it shall be lawful to indict accused persons in the name of the Solicitor General then in office: subs. (2). It is clear that such indictments may be taken up by the new Lord Advocate on his appointment: *H.M. Solicitor General v. Lavelle* (1913) 7 Adam 255. Secondly, the Lord Advocate shall enter upon the duties of his office immediately upon the grant of his warrant: subs. (6). Before this provision the Lord Advocate could not act until the Royal Warrant appointing him reached Crown Office, he was not entitled to act merely on notice of his appointment appearing in the Edinburgh Gazette: *Halliday v. Wilson* (1891) 3 White 38.

Intimation of proceedings in High Court to Lord Advocate

288.—(1) In any proceeding in the High Court (other than a proceeding to which the Lord Advocate or a procurator fiscal is a party) it shall be competent for the court to order intimation of such proceeding to the Lord Advocate.

(2) On intimation being made to the Lord Advocate under subsection (1) above, the Lord Advocate shall be entitled to appear and be heard in such proceeding.

DEFINITIONS
"High Court": s.307(1).
"procurator fiscal": s.307(1).

GENERAL NOTE
This section is probably concerned with Bill of Criminal letters which have not been presented to the Lord Advocate for concurrence or with petitions to the *Nobile Officium* of the High Court of Justiciary. The ordinary practice would be to intimate to the Lord Advocate but

individuals proceeding without legal representation, for example, might not know of that practice.

Devolution issues

Rights of appeal for Advocate General: devolution issues

[1]**288A.**—(1) This section applies where—
(a) a person is acquitted or convicted of a charge (whether on indictment or in summary proceedings), and
(b) the Advocate General for Scotland was a party to the proceedings in pursuance of paragraph 6 of Schedule 6 to the Scotland Act 1998 (devolution issues).

(2) The Advocate General for Scotland may refer any devolution issue which has arisen in the proceedings to the High Court for their opinion; and the Clerk of Justiciary shall send to the person acquitted or convicted and to any solicitor who acted for that person at the trial, a copy of the reference and intimation of the date fixed by the Court for a hearing.

(3) The person may, not later than seven days before the date so fixed, intimate in writing to the Clerk of Justiciary and to the Advocate General for Scotland either—
(a) that he elects to appear personally at the hearing, or
(b) that he elects to be represented by counsel at the hearing,
but, except by leave of the Court on cause shown, and without prejudice to his right to attend, he shall not appear or be represented at the hearing other than by and in conformity with an election under this subsection.

(4) Where there is no intimation under subsection (3)(b), the High Court shall appoint counsel to act at the hearing as amicus curiae.

(5) The costs of representation elected under subsection (3)(b) or of an appointment under subsection (4) shall, after being taxed by the Auditor of the Court of Session, be paid by the Advocate General for Scotland out of money provided by Parliament.

(6) The opinion on the point referred under subsection (2) shall not affect the acquittal or (as the case may be) conviction in the trial.

NOTE
[1]Inserted by the Scotland Act 1998 (c. 46) Sched. 8, para. 32 and brought into force by the Scotland Act 1998 (Commencement) Order 1998, Art. 2, Sched. 3 (S.I. 1998 No. 3178: effective May 6, 1999).

GENERAL NOTE
The Advocate General for Scotland is to be the new law officer with the responsibility for Scottish legal matters in regard to the United Kingdom. Where questions arise as to the competency of legislation, or the actings of some members of the Scottish Executive or related questions, the Advocate General may institute proceedings for the determination of such a devolution issue. It follows then that there requires to be a mode of appeal and that is provided for by s.288A and s.288B of the 1995 Act.

Appeals to Judicial Committee of the Privy Council

[1]**288B.**—(1) This section applies where the Judicial Committee of the Privy Council determines an appeal under paragraph 13(a) of Schedule 6 to the Scotland Act 1998 against a determination of a devolution issue by the High Court in the ordinary course of proceedings.

(2) The determination of the appeal shall not affect any earlier acquittal or earlier quashing of any conviction in the proceedings.

(3) Subject to subsection (2) above, the High Court shall have the same powers in relation to the proceedings when remitted to it by the Judicial Committee as it would have if it were considering the proceedings otherwise than as a trial court.

NOTE

¹Inserted by the Scotland Act 1998 (c. 46) Sched. 8, para. 32 and brought into force by the Scotland Act 1998 (Commencement) Order 1998, Art. 2, Sched. 3 (S.I. 1998 No. 3178: effective May 6, 1999).

Treason trials

Procedure and evidence in trials for treason

289. The procedure and rules of evidence in proceedings for treason and misprision of treason shall be the same as in proceedings according to the law of Scotland for murder.

GENERAL NOTE

It has been the rule in England since the Treason Act 1800 (see now the Criminal Law Act 1967, s.12(7)) that trials for treason and misprision should be governed by the rules applicable to trials for murder. This section restates the position in Scotland which was clarified in s.39 of the 1980 Act. The substantive law of trespass remains English, but the Treason Acts of 1800 and 1945 were repealed by s.83(3) of and Sched. 8 to the 1980 Act, along with what remained of the Treason Act 1708.

Certain rights of accused

Accused's right to request identification parade

290.—(1) Subject to subsection (2) below, the sheriff may, on an application by an accused at any time after the accused has been charged with an offence, order that, in relation to the alleged offence, the prosecutor shall hold an identification parade in which the accused shall be one of those constituting the parade.

(2) The sheriff shall make an order in accordance with subsection (1) above only after giving the prosecutor an opportunity to be heard and only if—

(a) an identification parade, such as is mentioned in subsection (1) above, has not been held at the instance of the prosecutor;
(b) after a request by the accused, the prosecutor has refused to hold, or has unreasonably delayed holding, such an identification parade; and
(c) the sheriff considers the application under subsection (1) above to be reasonable.

DEFINITIONS
"offence": s.307(1).
"prosecutor": s.307(1).
"sheriff": s.4(1) and (4).

GENERAL NOTE

This section re-enacts the provisions of s.10 of the Criminal Justice (Scotland) Act 1980. It is open to the accused to make an application for an identification parade to be held by the prosecutor; (i) where no such parade has been conducted; (ii) where the prosecutor has refused a request by the accused for such a parade, or else been dilatory in organising the parade, and (iii) where the application appears reasonable to the sheriff. An application under s.290 can only be made after charges have been preferred against the accused and once the sheriff has heard the prosecutor on the merits of the charge.

The style of application is found in the 1996 Act of Adjournal, Chap. 28; note that the style applies to circumstances where either an indictment has been served or summary proceedings have begun.

In *Wilson v. Tudhope*, 1985 S.C.C.R. 339 two Crown attempts to hold an identification parade failed because witnesses were unwilling to attend. The defence craved, and were granted, an identification parade, the sheriff opining that it would be competent to cite witnesses to attend such a parade.

See *Beattie v. Hingston*, 1999 S.C.C.R. 362, where the Appeal Court suspended the sheriff's refusal of B's petition for a parade, the s.290 hearing having had to be fixed too early (in view of the imminent trial diet) for intimation to be given to B. Consequently B. was not present and, more importantly, the local agent who had been instructed to lodge the application had only slight knowledge of the factual background to the case. Note that the Appeal Court reserved opinion upon defence submissions that the s.290 hearing should have been held in open court; it is submitted that given that identification of an accused is plainly to be an issue at trial, there would be little to be gained (and much to be risked) by arguing the merits of an application in open court.

Precognition on oath of defence witnesses

291.—(1) The sheriff may, on the application of an accused, grant warrant to cite any person (other than a co-accused), who is alleged to be a witness in relation to any offence of which the accused has been charged, to appear before the sheriff in chambers at such time or place as shall be specified in the citation, for precognition on oath by the accused or his solicitor in relation to that offence, if the court is satisfied that it is reasonable to require such precognition on oath in the circumstances.

(2) Any person who, having been duly cited to attend for precognition under subsection (1) above and having been given at least 48 hours notice, fails without reasonable excuse to attend shall be guilty of an offence and shall be liable on summary conviction to a fine not exceeding level 3 on the standard scale or to imprisonment for a period not exceeding 21 days; and the court may issue a warrant for the apprehension of the person concerned, ordering him to be brought before a sheriff for precognition on oath.

(3) Any person who, having been duly cited to attend for precognition under subsection (1) above, attends but—

  (a) refuses to give information within his knowledge or to produce evidence in his possession; or

  (b) prevaricates in his evidence,

shall be guilty of an offence and shall be liable to be summarily subjected forthwith to a fine not exceeding level 3 on the standard scale or to imprisonment for a period not exceeding 21 days.

DEFINITIONS
  "enactment": s.307(1).
  "imprisonment": ss.307(6) and 309.
  "indictment": s.307(1).
  "offence": s.307(1).

GENERAL NOTE
  A warrant to cite a witness for precognition on oath may be craved by the defence once charges have been preferred and cause can be shown to justify the use of this *compulsitor*; the power should be exercised with caution (*Low v. MacNeill*, 1981 S.C.C.R. 243).

  In *Drummond, Petr*, 1998 S.L.T. 757 where an unrepresented accused petitioned the *nobile officium* for authority to interview police witnesses on tape, the High Court observed, in refusing the application, that the appropriate course would have been to make an application under s.291.

  It is not competent to make an application of this sort prior to full committal on petition, since, in the period between committal for further examination and full committal the Crown are still completing enquiries; see *Cirignaco, Petr*, 1985 S.C.C.R. 157 where precognition on oath of the complainer was sought with a view to secure early release on bail. Refusal on the part of potential witnesses to assist defence investigations, even after joint approaches by both the defence and the Crown, resulted in the grant of warrant to cite for precognition (*Brady v. Lockhart*, 1985 S.C.C.R. 349). It is likely that an application for precognition on oath without first having sought the assistance of the Crown will be treated as premature.

  A warrant for precognition on oath can only be sought prior to the trial (and conviction or acquittal) of the accused (see *Gilmour, Petr*, 1994 S.C.C.R. 872). In *Campbell v. H.M. Advocate*, 1997 S.L.T. 577 the Appeal Court, with some hesitation, refused Crown advocation of a warrant to precognose a police officer who was not a witness in a murder trial, in relation to earlier dealings with a Crown witness; the broad intention was to undermine the credibility of the Crown witness. It is of note that the original warrant was entirely unqualified, and that the warrant for precognition was upheld by the Appeal Court largely on the basis of the case being a murder trial and of undertakings given by counsel to the court.

Failure to attend for precognition after lawful citation, prevarication, or failure to furnish information is an offence liable to peremptory punishment (subs. (3)); in such circumstances the court is not obliged to obtain social enquiry or other reports before sentencing such misconduct.

Pleas of legal privilege will not necessarily be conclusive where application is made to precognosce an accused's solicitor on oath; see *Kelly v. Vannet*, 1999 G.W.D. 4–175. Crown applications proceed as incidental applications in terms of s.134 of the 1995 Act.

Refer to Chap. 29 of the 1996 Act of Adjournal for directions on procedures and styles.

Mode of trial

Mode of trial of certain offences

292.—(1) Subject to subsection (6) below, the offences mentioned (and broadly described) in Schedule 10 to this Act shall be triable only summarily.

(2) An offence created by statute shall be triable only summarily if—

(a) the enactment creating the offence or any other enactment expressly so provides (in whatever words); or

(b) subject to subsections (4) and (5)(a) below, the offence was created by an Act passed on or before 29 July 1977 (the date of passing of the Criminal Law Act 1977) and the penalty or maximum penalty in force immediately before that date, on any conviction of that offence, did not include any of the following—

   (i) a fine exceeding £400;

   (ii) subject to subsection (3) below, imprisonment for a period exceeding 3 months;

   (iii) a fine exceeding £50 in respect of a specified quantity or number of things, or in respect of a specified period during which a continuing offence is committed.

(3) In the application of paragraph (b)(ii) of subsection (2) above, no regard shall be paid to the fact that section 5(3) of this Act permits the imposition of imprisonment for a period exceeding 3 months in certain circumstances.

(4) An offence created by statute which is triable only on indictment shall continue only to be so triable.

(5) An offence created by statute shall be triable either on indictment or summarily if—

(a) the enactment creating the offence or any other enactment expressly so provides (in whatever words); or

(b) it is an offence to which neither subsection (2) nor subsection (4) above applies.

(6) An offence which may under any enactment (including an enactment in this Act or passed after this Act) be tried only summarily, being an offence which, if it had been triable on indictment, could competently have been libelled as an additional or alternative charge in the indictment, may (the provisions of this or any other enactment notwithstanding) be so libelled, and tried accordingly.

(7) Where an offence is libelled and tried on indictment by virtue of subsection (6) above, the penalty which may be imposed for that offence in that case shall not exceed that which is competent on summary conviction.

DEFINITIONS
   "enactment": s.307(1).
   "fine": s.307(1).
   "imprisonment": s.307(6).
   "indictment": s.307(1).
   "offence": s.307(1).

Offences triable summarily only are listed in Sched. 10 and in subs. (2) and can extend to offences defined in s.5(3) notwithstanding the fact that these create liability to a sentence of six months' imprisonment on a second or subsequent conviction in the sheriff court. It will be recalled that s.136(2) enacts that the six-month time limit for the commencement of statutory offences applies only to offences triable summarily only.

Offences which by statute may only be prosecuted summarily can be libelled along with other charges on an indictment but, in that event, any sentence which may be imposed on conviction of that offence shall be restricted to that which could have been passed summarily (subs. (6)).

Art and part and attempt

Statutory offences: art and part and aiding and abetting

293.—(1) A person may be convicted of, and punished for, a contravention of any enactment, notwithstanding that he was guilty of such contravention as art and part only.

(2) Without prejudice to subsection (1) above or to any express provision in any enactment having the like effect to this subsection, any person who aids, abets, counsels, procures or incites any other person to commit an offence against the provisions of any enactment shall be guilty of an offence and shall be liable on conviction, unless the enactment otherwise requires, to the same punishment as might be imposed on conviction of the first-mentioned offence.

DEFINITIONS
"enactment": s.307(1).
"offence": s.307(1).

GENERAL NOTE
Art and part guilt can apply equally to common law and statutory offences. See *Vaughan v. H.M. Advocate*, 1979 S.L.T. 49 where the accused though not himself within the forbidden degrees, was convicted under the Incest Act 1567 as an actor.

Attempt at crime

294.—(1) Attempt to commit any indictable crime is itself an indictable crime.

(2) Attempt to commit any offence punishable on complaint shall itself be an offence punishable on complaint.

Legal custody

Legal custody

295. Any person required or authorised by or under this Act or any other enactment to be taken to any place, or to be detained or kept in custody shall, while being so taken or detained or kept, be deemed to be in legal custody.

DEFINITION
"enactment": s.307(1).

GENERAL NOTE
The definition of legal custody applies to the status of persons either detained or arrested under the Act or other statutory powers. The anomalous position of a person suspected of committing an offence and required to remain where found by police officers (see s.13(1) and (2) above) has already been discussed; such an individual is not then in legal custody.

Warrants

Warrants for search and apprehension to be signed by judge

296. Any warrant for search or apprehension granted under this Act shall be signed by the judge granting it, and execution upon any such warrant may proceed either upon the warrant itself or upon an extract of the warrant issued and signed by the clerk of court.

DEFINITION
    "judge": s.307(1).

GENERAL NOTE
    This section applies to the grant of warrants of apprehension or search by a justice of the peace, sheriff or High Court judge. Ordinarily such warrants are craved from judges in the lower courts. See s.135 of the Act and the notes thereto.

Execution of warrants and service of complaints, etc.

297.—(1) Any warrant granted by a justice may, without being backed or endorsed by any other justice, be executed throughout Scotland in the same way as it may be executed within the jurisdiction of the justice who granted it.

    (2) Any complaint, warrant, or other proceeding for the purposes of any summary proceedings under this Act may without endorsation be served or executed at any place within Scotland by any officer of law, and such service or execution may be proved either by the oath in court of the officer or by production of his written execution.

    (3) A warrant issued in the Isle of Man for the arrest of a person charged with an offence may, after it has been endorsed by a justice in Scotland, be executed there by the person bringing that warrant, by any person to whom the warrant was originally directed or by any officer of law of the sheriff court district where the warrant has been endorsed in like manner as any such warrant issued in Scotland.

    (4) In subsection (3) above, "endorsed" means endorsed in the like manner as a process to which section 4 of the Summary Jurisdiction (Process) Act 1881 applies.

    (5) The Indictable Offences Act Amendment Act 1868 shall apply in relation to the execution in Scotland of warrants issued in the Channel Islands.

DEFINITIONS
    "justice": s.307(1).
    "offence": s.307(1).
    "officer of law": s.307(1).

GENERAL NOTE
    This section reflects the reform introduced by s.9 of the Criminal Justice (Scotland) Act 1995 and applies to all warrants granted in Scotland. It removes the need for a warrant, granted by a justice for execution outwith his jurisdiction, to be "backed" by another justice. A degree of caution is necessary since this reform does not extend to warrants granted in Scotland for execution in England and Wales.
    Historically, a warrant granted for execution within the jurisdiction of a justice could always be executed without further ado, but matters were less straightforward when the warrant was granted for execution elsewhere in Scotland, and thoroughly byzantine when the warrant had to be executed in England and Wales: these are discussed in turn below.
    Warrants craved for execution outwith the jurisdiction of the court, but in Scotland, included a crave requesting the concurrence of judges in that other place in the granting of the warrant. This necessitated application to be made to two courts before the warrant could be executed, an anachronistic, time-consuming, and invariably unnecessary, procedure. Following *Shields v. Donnelly*, 2000 S.L.T. 147; 2000 S.C.C.R. 890 it is now established that the warrant has to be granted within the territorial jurisdiction of the court.

Warrants craved in Scotland for execution in England and Wales require to be "backed" and "endorsed" in accordance with the Summary Jurisdiction (Process) Act 1881 (c. 24): in these circumstances the warrant obtained from a Scottish court has to be docquetted in compliance with the 1881 Act and then be presented to the relevant magistrates' court having jurisdiction. However warrant procedures in England and Wales are regulated by Pt. II of the Police and Criminal Evidence Act 1984 (c. 60) and the court competent to grant warrants under PACE is determined by whether it is "special procedure" material, a situation which requires a Crown Court warrant, or not. In the latter situation it is submitted that application as described earlier should be made to the magistrates court for endorsement.

The position in relation to the cross—border execution of search warrants has been clarified considerably in *R. v. Manchester Stipendiary Magistrate, ex p. Granada Television Ltd* [2000] 2 W.L.R. 1, H.L.(E) by the judgment of Lord Hope of Craighead. This case concerned the use of a Scottish common law search warrant, endorsed in accordance with the 1881 Act by the Manchester Stipendiary Magistrate, to search a broadcaster's premises there for evidential materials arising from a television programme. In England and Wales, materials of this sort are defined as privileged materials in terms of PACE, Sched. I and can only be recovered by means of application to a circuit judge. Nonetheless, it was held that the 1881 Act did prevail for the execution of Scottish search warrants south of the border since the 1984 Act itself made no express provision. By the same token *Granada* emphasises that it is the 1881 Act (not PACE) which regulates the execution of English or Welsh search warrants in Scotland. Thus, in *H.M. Advocate (for Duncan Hodge)* 2000 S.C.C.R. 439 where the Crown took a bill of advocation against the sheriff's refusal to endorse a special procedure production order made by an English circuit judge for such materials in Scotland, the Appeal Court ruled that only an order made by a court of summary jurisdiction in England could be so endorsed. Notably the Appeal Court reserved opinion on whether a petition to the *nobile officium* could have been used instead to resolve the *impasse*. It is submitted that matters could be dealt with satisfactorily in most circumstances by means of a common law warrant obtained by the procurator fiscal for the public interest.

It is suggested that a warrant craved in England and Wales from a magistrates' court for search and recovery of materials held in Scotland is still competent provided that the backing and endorsation procedures have been followed; nevertheless there is an attendant risk that such a search might by chance reveal material which could be regarded as "special procedure" material; thus it may be felt prudent for the local Procurator Fiscal to seek a common law warrant instead.

Trial judge's report

Trial judge's report

298.—(1) Without prejudice to sections 113 and 186(3)(b) of this Act, the High Court may, in relation to—

[1](a) an appeal under section 106(1), 108, 108A or 175(2) to (4) of this Act;

(b) an appeal by way of bill of suspension or advocation; or

(c) a petition to the nobile officium,

at any time before the appeal is finally determined or, as the case may be, petition finally disposed of, order the judge who presided at the trial, passed sentence or otherwise disposed of the case to provide to the Clerk of Justiciary a report in writing giving the judge's opinion on the case generally or in relation to any particular matter specified in the order.

[2](2) The Clerk of Justiciary shall send a copy of a report provided under subsection (1) above to the convicted person or his solicitor, the Crown Agent and, in relation to cases referred under Part XA of this Act, the Commission.

(3) Subject to subsection (2) above, the report of the judge shall be available only to the High Court, the parties and, on such conditions as may be prescribed by Act of Adjournal, such other persons or classes of persons as may be so prescribed.

DEFINITIONS
  "Clerk of Justiciary": s.307(1).
  "judge": s.307(1).

Criminal Procedure (Scotland) Act 1995

Notes
[1] Inserted by the Crime and Punishment (Scotland) Act 1997 (c. 48), Sched. 1, para. 21(33)(a) with effect from October 20, 1997 in terms of the Crime and Punishment (Scotland) Act 1997 (Commencement No. 2 and Transitional and Consequential Provisions) Order 1997 (S.I. 1997 No. 2323) Art. 3 and Sched. 1.
[2] As amended by the Crime and Punishment (Scotland) Act 1997 (c. 48), Sched. 1, para. 21(33)(b) (effective April 1, 1999: SI. 1999 No 652).

General Note
This new provision reinforces the statutory duty on judges at first instance to provide a report in the event of an appeal: the section allows the High Court of Justiciary to order further reports of a general or specific nature. This may be necessary because, for example, the note of appeal may not contain, as is required by s.110(3)(b), a full statement of all the grounds of appeal. Alternatively, difficulty or uncertainty in relation to a material point may have arisen at the hearing of the appeal and the trial judge's opinion may be thought necessary in the circumstances. In *Brady v. Barbour*, 1994 S.C.C.R. 890 the sheriff, for whatever reason, did not produce a draft stated case and thus placed the High Court of Justiciary in some difficulty. This provision allows further orders to be made for reports.

Correction of entries

Correction of entries

299.—(1) Subject to the provisions of this section, it shall be competent to correct any entry in—
(a) the record of proceedings in a prosecution; or
(b) the extract of a sentence passed or an order of court made in such proceedings,
in so far as that entry constitutes an error of recording or is incomplete.
(2) An entry mentioned in subsection (1) above may be corrected—
(a) by the clerk of the court, at any time before either the sentence or order of the court is executed or, on appeal, the proceedings are transmitted to the Clerk of Justiciary;
(b) by the clerk of the court, under the authority of the court which passed the sentence or made the order, at any time after the execution of the sentence or order of the court but before such transmission as is mentioned in paragraph (a) above; or
(c) by the clerk of the court under the authority of the High Court in the case of a remit under subsection (4)(b) below.
(3) A correction in accordance with paragraph (b) or (c) of subsection (2) above shall be intimated to the prosecutor and to the former accused or his solicitor.
(4) Where during the course of an appeal, the High Court becomes aware of an erroneous or incomplete entry, such as is mentioned in subsection (1) above, the court—
(a) may consider and determine the appeal as if such entry were corrected; and
(b) either before or after the determination of the appeal, may remit the proceedings to the court of first instance for correction in accordance with subsection (2)(c) above.
(5) Any correction under subsections (1) and (2) above by the clerk of the court shall be authenticated by his signature and, if such correction is authorised by a court, shall record the name of the judge or judges authorising such correction and the date of such authorisation.

Definitions
"clerk of Court": s.114 of the Criminal Justice (Scotland) Act 1995.
"Clerk of Justiciary": s.307(1).
"High Court": s.307(1).

389

"judge": s.307(1).
"order": s.307(1).
"sentence": s.307(1).

GENERAL NOTE
See *Heywood, Petr*, 1998 G.W.D. 13–639. An unauthenticated correction has no effect (see *Fitzgerald v. Vannet*, 2000 S.C.C.R. 422) where corrections made in error, but not initialled, were disregarded. The Appeal Court utilised its power under s.299(4)(a) to remit the complaint back to the court of first instance having directed correction of defective minutes.

Amendment of records of conviction and sentence in summary proceedings

300.—(1) Without prejudice to section 299 of this Act, where, on an application in accordance with subsection (2) below, the High Court is satisfied that a record of conviction or sentence in summary proceedings inaccurately records the identity of any person, it may authorise the clerk of the court which convicted or, as the case may be, sentenced the person to correct the record.

(2) An application under subsection (1) above shall be made after the determination of the summary prosecution and may be made by any party to the summary proceedings or any other person having an interest in the correction of the alleged inaccuracy.

(3) The High Court shall order intimation of an application under subsection (1) above to such persons as it considers appropriate and shall not determine the application without affording to the parties to the summary proceedings and to any other person having an interest in the correction of the alleged inaccuracy an opportunity to be heard.

(4) The power of the High Court under this section may be exercised by a single judge of the High Court in the same manner as it may be exercised by the High Court, and subject to the same provisions.

DEFINITIONS
"clerk of Court": s.114(1) of the Criminal Justice (Scotland) Act 1995.
"Clerk of Justiciary": s.308(1).

Rights of audience

Rights of audience

301.—(1) Without prejudice to section 103(8) of this Act, any solicitor who has, by virtue of section 25A (rights of audience) of the Solicitors (Scotland) Act 1980, a right of audience in relation to the High Court of Justiciary shall have the same right of audience in that court as is enjoyed by an advocate.

(2) Any person who has complied with the terms of a scheme approved under section 26 of the Law Reform (Miscellaneous Provisions) (Scotland) Act 1990 (consideration of applications made under section 25) shall have such rights of audience before the High Court of Justiciary as may be specified in an Act of Adjournal made under subsection (7)(b) of that section.

Fixed penalties

Fixed penalty: conditional offer by procurator fiscal

302.—(1) Where a procurator fiscal receives a report that a relevant offence has been committed he may send to the alleged offender a notice under this section (referred to in this section as a conditional offer); and where he issues a conditional offer the procurator fiscal shall notify the clerk of court specified in it of the issue of the conditional offer and of its terms.

(2) A conditional offer—

(a) shall give such particulars of the circumstances alleged to constitute the offence to which it relates as are necessary for giving reasonable information about the alleged offence;

(b) shall state—
  (i) the amount of the appropriate fixed penalty for that offence;
  (ii) the amount of the instalments by which the penalty may be paid; and
  (iii) the intervals at which such instalments should be paid;

(c) shall indicate that if, within 28 days of the date on which the conditional offer was issued, or such longer period as may be specified in the conditional offer, the alleged offender accepts the offer by making payment of the fixed penalty or of the first instalment thereof to the clerk of court specified in the conditional offer at the address therein mentioned, any liability to conviction of the offence shall be discharged;

(d) shall state that proceedings against the alleged offender shall not be commenced in respect of that offence until the end of a period of 28 days from the date on which the conditional offer was issued, or such longer period as may be specified in the conditional offer; and

(e) shall state that acceptance of the offer in the manner described in paragraph (c) above by the alleged offender shall not be a conviction nor be recorded as such.

(3) A conditional offer may be made in respect of more than one relevant offence and shall, in such a case, state the amount of the appropriate fixed penalty for all the offences in respect of which it is made.

(4) Where payment of the appropriate fixed penalty or of the first instalment has not been made to the clerk of court, he shall, upon the expiry of the period of 28 days referred to in subsection (2)(c) above or such longer period as may be specified in the conditional offer, notify the procurator fiscal who issued the conditional offer that no payment has been made.

(5) Proceedings shall not be brought against any person for the offence to which a conditional offer relates until the procurator fiscal receives notification from the clerk of court in accordance with subsection (4) above.

(6) Where an alleged offender makes payment of the appropriate fixed penalty or of the first instalment to the clerk of court specified in the conditional offer no proceedings shall be brought against the alleged offender for the offence.

(7) The Secretary of State shall, by order, prescribe a scale of fixed penalties for the purpose of this section, the amount of the maximum penalty on the scale being a sum not exceeding level 1 on the standard scale.

(8) An order under subsection (7) above—
(a) may contain provision as to the payment of fixed penalties by instalments; and
(b) shall be made by statutory instrument, which shall be subject to annulment in pursuance of a resolution of either House of Parliament.

(9) In this section—
(a) "a relevant offence" means any offence in respect of which an alleged offender could competently be tried before a district court, but shall not include a fixed penalty offence within the meaning of section 51 of the Road Traffic Offenders Act 1988 nor any other offence in respect of which a conditional offer within the meaning of sections 75 to 77 of that Act may be sent; and
(b) "the appropriate fixed penalty" means such fixed penalty on the scale prescribed under subsection (7) above as the procurator fiscal thinks fit having regard to the circumstances of the case.

DEFINITIONS
"appropriate fixed penalty": s.302(9).
"offence": s.307(1).

"procurator fiscal": s.307(1).
"relevant offence": s.302(9).
"standard scale": s.225(1).

GENERAL NOTE

This section extends the range of fixed penalties which the procurator fiscal can offer to persons reported to him for offences other than Road Traffic offences. The "fiscal fine" was introduced by the Criminal Justice (Scotland) Act 1987 and then permitted procurator fiscals to use the offer of a £25 fixed fine to alleged offenders as an alternative to prosecution. Payment or part-payment of such a fine brought an end to the procurator fiscal's involvement and was not recorded as a criminal conviction. In 1987 the £25 fine, fixed by statutory instrument, equalled half the Level 1 fine on the standard scale; Level 1 is now a sum of £200. Section 302 permits the Secretary of State by statutory instrument, to set a range of fixed penalty bands from which the procurator fiscal can choose, according to the circumstances of the case as reported, when offering the option of a fiscal fine. Subsection (7) enacts that the bands must not exceed Level 1 on the standard scale.

One of the difficulties identified in the operation of the earlier fiscal fine system was that where several offences were reported against an accused as a result of an incident, the fiscal, if he chose to offer the option of such a fine, had to select one charge only from those reported. In the event of non-payment only the single charge selected previously could later be libelled against the accused; subs. (3) statutorily permits the offer of more than one fiscal fine against an accused following an incident and, hence, in the event of refusal of the offer it will be open to the prosecutor to libel several charges, not just one as before.

The administration and collection of fines remains the responsibility of the clerk of court. Whereas the old fiscal fine system required payment of the entire £25 fine within 28 days, and to an extent limited the range of offenders who could be offered that option, subs. (1)(c) enacts that payment of the full amount or a pre-determined instalment is to be made within 28 days, or a specified longer period. Once either sort of payment is received, the prosecutor is barred from prosecuting those offences. It is then the task of the clerk of court to enforce collection of any unpaid balance (see s.303 below).

It will be appreciated that the thrust of s.302 is to extend the use of fiscal fines as an alternative to prosecution. If successful, the broadened fixed penalty conditional offer scheme may reduce the pressure of criminal business in the lower courts. Failure to pay a fixed penalty timeously can be expected to result in a prosecution for the offence highlighted in the notice. The court convicting of that offence should reach its own view upon the appropriate sentence and need not take account of the fine level stipulated in the unpaid fixed penalty; see *Fyfe v. Walker*, 1998 G.W.D. 16–828.

Fixed penalty: enforcement

303.—(1) Subject to subsection (2) below, where an alleged offender accepts a conditional offer by paying the first instalment of the appropriate fixed penalty, any amount of the penalty which is outstanding at any time shall be treated as if the penalty were a fine imposed by the court, the clerk of which is specified in the conditional offer.

(2) In the enforcement of a penalty which is to be treated as a fine in pursuance of subsection (1) above—

(a) any reference, howsoever expressed, in any enactment whether passed or made before or after the coming into force of this section to—

(i) the imposition of imprisonment or detention in default of payment of a fine shall be construed as a reference to enforcement by means of civil diligence;

(ii) the finding or order of the court imposing the fine shall be construed as a reference to a certificate given in pursuance of subsection (3) below;

(iii) the offender shall be construed as a reference to the alleged offender;

(iv) the conviction of the offender shall be construed as a reference to the acceptance of the conditional offer by the alleged offender;

(b) the following sections of this Act shall not apply—

section 211(7);
section 213(2);
section 214(1) to (6);
section 216(7);
section 219, except subsection (1)(b);
section 220;
section 221(2) to (4);
section 222(8); and
section 224.

(3) For the purposes of any proceedings in connection with, or steps taken for, the enforcement of any amount of a fixed penalty which is outstanding, a document purporting to be a certificate signed by the clerk of court for the time being responsible for the collection or enforcement of the penalty as to any matter relating to the penalty shall be conclusive of the matter so certified.

(4) The Secretary of State may, by order made by statutory instrument subject to annulment in pursuance of a resolution of either House of Parliament, make such provision as he considers necessary for the enforcement in England and Wales or Northern Ireland of any penalty, treated in pursuance of subsection (1) above as a fine, which is transferred as a fine to a court in England and Wales or, as the case may be, Northern Ireland.

DEFINITIONS
"appropriate fixed penalty: s.302(9)(b).
"enactment": s.307(1).
"fine": s.307(1).
"impose detention": s.307(1).
"impose imprisonment": s.307(1).

GENERAL NOTE
The collection of fiscal fines remains the responsibility of the clerk of court. In the event of only partial payment of the instalments due to meet such a fine, subs. (2) allows recovery of the balance due by way of civil diligence. Subsection (3) provides that for the purpose of such enforcement the clerk of court is empowered to certify conclusively the sums due.

Subsection (2) has the effect of removing criminal sanctions for the enforcement of unpaid fiscal fines.

Transfer of rights of appeal of deceased person

[1]**303A.**—(1) Where a person convicted of an offence has died, any person may, subject to the provisions of this section, apply to the High Court for an order authorising him to institute or continue any appeal which could have been or has been instituted by the deceased.

(2) An application for an order under this section may be lodged with the Clerk of Justiciary within three months of the deceased's death or at such later time as the Court may, on cause shown, allow.

(3) Where the Commission makes a reference to the High Court under section 194B of this Act in respect of a person who is deceased, any application under this section must be made within one month of the reference.

(4) Where an application is made for an order under this section and the applicant—
(a) is an executor of the deceased; or
(b) otherwise appears to the Court to have a legitimate interest,
the Court shall make an order authorising the applicant to institute or continue any appeal which could have been instituted or continued by the deceased; and, subject to the provisions of this section, any such order may include such ancillary or supplementary provision as the Court thinks fit.

(5) The person in whose favour an order under this section is made shall from the date of the order be afforded the same rights to carry on the appeal

as the deceased enjoyed at the time of his death and, in particular, where any time limit had begun to run against the deceased the person in whose favour an order has been made shall have the benefit of only that portion of the time limit which remained unexpired at the time of the death.

(6) In this section "appeal" includes any sort of application, whether at common law or under statute, for the review of any conviction, penalty or other order made in respect of the deceased in any criminal proceedings whatsoever.

NOTE
[1]Inserted by the Crime and Punishment (Scotland) Act 1997 (c.48), s.20 with effect from August 1, 1997 in terms of the Crime and Punishment (Scotland) Act 1997 (Commencement and Transitional Provisions) Order 1997 (S.I. 1997 No. 1712) para. 3.

PART XIV

GENERAL

Criminal Courts Rules Council

304.—(1) There shall be established a body, to be known as the Criminal Courts Rules Council (in this section referred to as "the Council") which shall have the functions conferred on it by subsection (9) below.

(2) The Council shall consist of—

(a) the Lord Justice General, the Lord Justice Clerk and the Clerk of Justiciary;

(b) a further Lord Commissioner of Justiciary appointed by the Lord Justice General;

(c) the following persons appointed by the Lord Justice General after such consultation as he considers appropriate—

(i) two sheriffs;

(ii) two members of the Faculty of Advocates;

(iii) two solicitors;

(iv) one sheriff clerk; and

(v) one person appearing to him to have a knowledge of the procedures and practices of the district court;

(d) two persons appointed by the Lord Justice General after consultation with the Lord Advocate, at least one of whom must be a procurator fiscal;

(e) two persons appointed by the Lord Justice General after consultation with the Secretary of State, at least one of whom must be a person appearing to the Lord Justice General to have—

(i) a knowledge of the procedures and practices of the courts exercising criminal jurisdiction in Scotland; and

(ii) an awareness of the interests of victims of crime and of witnesses in criminal proceedings; and

(f) any persons appointed under subsection (3) below.

(3) The Lord Justice General may appoint not more than two further persons, and the Secretary of State may appoint one person, to membership of the Council.

(4) The chairman of the Council shall be the Lord Justice General or such other member of the Council, being a Lord Commissioner of Justiciary, as the Lord Justice General may nominate.

(5) The members of the Council appointed under paragraphs (b) to (f) of subsection (2) above shall, so long as they retain the respective qualifications mentioned in those paragraphs, hold office for three years and be eligible for reappointment.

(6) Any vacancy in the membership of the Council by reason of the death

or demission of office, prior to the expiry of the period for which he was appointed, of a member appointed under any of paragraphs (b) to (f) of subsection (2) above shall be filled by the appointment by the Lord Justice General or, as the case may be, the Secretary of State, after such consultation as is required by the paragraph in question, of another person having the qualifications required by that paragraph, and a person so appointed shall hold office only until the expiry of that period.

(7) The Council shall meet—

(a) at intervals of not more than 12 months; and

(b) at any time when summoned by the chairman or by three members of the Council,

but shall, subject to the foregoing, have power to regulate the summoning of its meetings and the procedure at such meetings.

(8) At any meeting of the Council six members shall be a quorum.

(9) The functions of the Council shall be—

(a) to keep under general review the procedures and practices of the courts exercising criminal jurisdiction in Scotland (including any matters incidental or relating to those procedures or practices); and

(b) to consider and comment on any draft Act of Adjournal submitted to it by the High Court, which shall, in making the Act of Adjournal, take account to such extent as it considers appropriate of any comments made by the Council under this paragraph.

(10) In the discharge of its functions under subsection (9) above the Council may invite representations on any aspect of the procedures and practices of the courts exercising criminal jurisdiction in Scotland (including any matters incidental or relating to those procedures or practices) and shall consider any such representations received by it, whether or not submitted in response to such an invitation.

DEFINITIONS

"Lord Commissioner of Justiciary": s.307(1).
"procurator fiscal": s.307(1).

GENERAL NOTE

This innovation established a Rules Council for criminal court proceedings with functions broadly comparable to the existing Scottish Rules Council for civil court proceedings. The new body will assist the High Court of Justiciary in the discharge of its existing court procedural rule-making functions.

Acts of Adjournal

305.—(1) The High Court may by Act of Adjournal—

(a) regulate the practice and procedure in relation to criminal procedure;

(b) make such rules and regulations as may be necessary or expedient to carry out the purposes and accomplish the objects of any enactment (including an enactment in this Act) in so far as it relates to criminal procedure;

(c) subject to subsection (5) below, to fix and regulate the fees payable in connection with summary criminal proceedings; and

(d) to make provision for the application of sums paid under section 220 of this Act and for any matter incidental thereto.

(2) The High Court may by Act of Adjournal modify, amend or repeal any enactment (including an enactment in this Act) in so far as that enactment relates to matters with respect to which an Act of Adjournal may be made under subsection (1) above.

(3) No rule, regulation or provision which affects the governor or any other officer of a prison shall be made by Act of Adjournal except with the consent of the Secretary of State.

(4) The Clerk of Justiciary may, with the sanction of the Lord Justice

General and the Lord Justice Clerk, vary the forms set out in an Act of Adjournal made under subsection (1) above or any other Act whether passed before or after this Act from time to time as may be found necessary for giving effect to the provisions of this Act relating to solemn procedure.

(5) Nothing in paragraph (c) of subsection (1) above shall empower the High Court to make any regulation which the Secretary of State is empowered to make by the Courts of Law Fees (Scotland) Act 1895.

DEFINITIONS
"governor": s.307(1).
"High Court": s.307(1).
"officer of a prison": s.307(1).

GENERAL NOTE
The High Court of Justiciary is best placed to know how to regulate its own procedure and it does so by Act of Adjournal on statutory authority. The previous powers of ss.282 and 457 of the 1975 Act have been combined in this single provision which relates to "criminal procedure". Variations in the wording of these sections have been removed. Differences as between other statutory powers to make Acts of Adjournal have been removed with this single provision: see, *e.g.* s.32A of the 1980 Act which allowed provisions the court thought "necessary and expedient", a wider power than that of necessity under the 1975 Act. In *H.M. Advocate v. Gourlay* (High Court of Justiciary, September 10, 1999), on the initiative of the trial judge a court of three judges was convened to consider defence objections to documentary evidence the Crown sought to lead. A defence submission that Rule 40.2(1) of the Act of Adjournal (Devolution Issues Rules) (S.I. 1999 No. 1346) which required advance written notice where a devolution issue was to be argued, was *ultra vires* was repelled by the court.

Information for financial and other purposes

306.—(1) The Secretary of State shall in each year publish such information as he considers expedient for the purpose of—
   (a) enabling persons engaged in the administration of criminal justice to become aware of the financial implications of their decisions; or
   (b) facilitating the performance by such persons of their duty to avoid discriminating against any persons on the ground of race or sex or any other improper ground.

(2) Publication under subsection (1) above shall be effected in such manner as the Secretary of State considers appropriate for the purpose of bringing the information to the attention of the persons concerned.

Interpretation

307.—(1) In this Act, unless the context otherwise requires—
   "appropriate court" means a court named as such in pursuance of section 228(4) of this Act or of Schedule 6 to this Act in a probation order or in an amendment of any such order made on a change of residence of a probationer;
   "bail" means release of an accused or an appellant on conditions, or conditions imposed on bail, as the context requires;
   "chartered psychologist" means a person for the time being listed in the British Psychological Society's Register of Chartered Psychologists;
   "child", except in section 46(3) of and Schedule 1 to this Act, has the meaning assigned to that expression for the purposes of Chapters 2 and 3 of Part II of the Children (Scotland) Act 1995;
   "children's hearing" has the meaning assigned to it in Part II of the Children (Scotland) Act 1995;
   "Clerk of Justiciary" shall include assistant clerk of justiciary and shall extend and apply to any person duly authorised to execute the duties of Clerk of Justiciary or assistant clerk of justiciary;
   "commit for trial" means commit until liberation in due course of law;

"community service order" means an order made under section 238 of this Act;

"complaint" includes a copy of the complaint laid before the court;

"constable" has the same meaning as in the Police (Scotland) Act 1967;

"court of summary jurisdiction" means a court of summary criminal jurisdiction;

"court of summary criminal jurisdiction" includes the sheriff court and district court;

"crime" means any crime or offence at common law or under any Act of Parliament whether passed before or after this Act, and includes an attempt to commit any crime or offence;

[6]"devolution issue" has the same meaning as in Schedule 6 to the Scotland Act 1988;

"diet" includes any continuation of a diet;

[5]"drug treatment and testing order" has the meaning assigned to it in section 234B(2) of this Act;

"enactment" includes an enactment contained in a local Act and any order, regulation or other instrument having effect by virtue of an Act;

"examination of facts" means an examination of facts held under section 55 of this Act;

"existing" means existing immediately before the commencement of this Act;

"extract conviction" and "extract of previous conviction" include certified copy conviction, certificate of conviction, and any other document lawfully issued from any court of justice of the United Kingdom as evidence of a conviction;

"fine" includes—

    (a) any pecuniary penalty, (but not a pecuniary forfeiture or pecuniary compensation); and

    (b) an instalment of a fine;

"governor" means, in relation to a contracted out prison within the meaning of section 106(4) of the Criminal Justice and Public Order Act 1994, the director of the prison;

"guardian", in relation to a child, includes any person who, in the opinion of the court having cognizance of any case in relation to the child or in which the child is concerned, has for the time being the charge of or control over the child;

"guardianship order" has the meaning assigned to it by section 58 of this Act;

"High Court" and "Court of Justiciary" shall mean "High Court of Justiciary" and shall include any court held by the Lords Commissioners of Justiciary, or any of them;

"hospital" means—

    (a) any hospital vested in the Secretary of State under the National Health Service (Scotland) Act 1978;

    [1](aa) any hospital managed by a National Health Service Trust established under section 12A of that Act;

    (b) any private hospital registered under Part IV of the Mental Health (Scotland) Act 1984; and

    (c) any State hospital;

[2]"hospital direction" has the meaning assigned to it by section 59A(1) of this Act.

"hospital order" has the meaning assigned to it by section 58 of this Act;

"impose detention" or "impose imprisonment" means pass a sentence of detention or imprisonment, as the case may be, or make an order for committal in default of payment of any sum of money or for contempt of court;

"indictment" includes any indictment whether in the sheriff court or the High Court framed in the form set out an Act of Adjournal or as nearly as may be in such form;

"judge", in relation to solemn procedure, means a judge of a court of solemn criminal jurisdiction and, in relation to summary procedure, means any sheriff or any judge of a district court;

"justice" includes the sheriff and any stipendiary magistrate or justice of the peace;

"justice of the peace" means any of Her Majesty's justices of the peace for any commission area in Scotland within such commission area;

"legalised police cells" has the like meaning as in the Prisons (Scotland) Act 1989;

"local authority" has the meaning assigned to it by section 1(2) of the Social Work (Scotland) Act 1968;

"Lord Commissioner of Justiciary" includes Lord Justice General and Lord Justice Clerk;

"offence" means any act, attempt or omission punishable by law;

"officer of law" includes, in relation to the service and execution of any warrant, citation, petition, indictment, complaint, list of witnesses, order, notice, or other proceeding or document—

(a) any macer, messenger-at-arms, sheriff officer or other person having authority to execute a warrant of the court;

(b) any constable;

[3](ba) any person commissioned by the Commissioners of Customs and Excise;

(c) any person who is employed under section 9 of the Police (Scotland) Act 1967 for the assistance of the constables of a police force and who is authorised by the chief constable of that police force in relation to service and execution as mentioned above;

(d) where the person upon whom service or execution is effected is in prison at the time of service on him, any prison officer; and

[4](e) any person or class of persons authorised in that regard for the time being by the Lord Advocate or by the Secretary of State;

"order" means any order, byelaw, rule or regulation having statutory authority;

"patient" means a person suffering or appearing to be suffering from mental disorder;

"place of safety", in relation to a person not being a child, means any police station, prison or remand centre, or any hospital the board of management of which are willing temporarily to receive him, and in relation to a child means a place of safety within the meaning of Part II of the Children (Scotland) Act 1995;

"the prescribed sum" has the meaning given by section 225(8) of this Act;

"prison" does not include a naval, military or air force prison;

"prison officer" and "officer of a prison" means, in relation to a contracted out prison within the meaning of section 106(4) of the Criminal Justice and Public Order Act 1994, a prisoner custody officer within the meaning of section 114(1) of that Act;

"probationer" means a person who is under supervision by virtue of a probation order or who was under such supervision at the time of the commission of any relevant offence or failure to comply with such order;

"probation order" has the meaning assigned to it by section 228 of this Act;

"probation period" means the period for which a probationer is placed under supervision by a probation order;

"procurator fiscal" means the procurator fiscal for a sheriff court district, and includes assistant procurator fiscal and procurator fiscal depute and any person duly authorised to execute the duties of the procurator fiscal;

"prosecutor"—

    (a) for the purposes of proceedings other than summary proceedings, includes Crown Counsel, procurator fiscal, any other person prosecuting in the public interest and any private prosecutor; and

    (b) for the purposes of summary proceedings, includes procurator fiscal, and any other person prosecuting in the public interest and complainer and any person duly authorised to represent or act for any public prosecutor;

"remand" means an order adjourning the proceedings or continuing the case and giving direction as to detention in custody or liberation during the period of adjournment or continuation and references to remanding a person or remanding in custody or on bail shall be construed accordingly;

"remand centre" has the like meaning as in the Prisons (Scotland) Act 1989;

"residential establishment" means an establishment within the meaning of that expression for the purposes of the Social Work (Scotland) Act 1968 or, as the case may be, of Part II of the Children (Scotland) Act 1995;

"responsible medical officer" has the meaning assigned to it by section 59 of the Mental Health (Scotland) Act 1984;

"restriction order" has the meaning assigned to it by section 59 of this Act;

"sentence", whether of detention or of imprisonment, means a sentence passed in respect of a crime or offence and does not include an order for committal in default of payment of any sum of money or for contempt of court;

"sheriff clerk" includes sheriff clerk depute, and extends and applies to any person duly authorised to execute the duties of sheriff clerk;

"sheriff court district" extends to the limits within which the sheriff has jurisdiction in criminal matters whether by statute or at common law;

"State hospital" has the meaning assigned to it in Part VIII of the Mental Health (Scotland) Act 1984;

"statute" means any Act of Parliament, public general, local, or private, and any Provisional Order confirmed by Act of Parliament;

"supervision requirement" has the meaning assigned to it in Part II of the Children (Scotland) Act 1995;

"training school order" has the same meaning as in the Social Work (Scotland) Act 1968;

"witness" includes haver;

"young offenders institution" has the like meaning as in the Prisons (Scotland) Act 1989.

(2) References in this Act to a court do not include references to a court-martial; and nothing in this Act shall be construed as affecting the punishment which may be awarded by a court-martial under the Naval Discipline Act 1957, the Army Act 1955 or the Air Force Act 1955 for a civil offence within the meaning of those Acts.

(3) For the purposes of this Act, except section 228(6), where a probation order has been made on appeal, the order shall be deemed to have been made by the court from which the appeal was brought.

(4) Any reference in this Act to a previous sentence of imprisonment shall be construed as including a reference to a previous sentence of penal servitude; any such reference to a previous sentence of Borstal training shall be construed as including a reference to a previous sentence of detention in a Borstal institution.

(5) Any reference in this Act to a previous conviction or sentence shall be construed as a reference to a previous conviction by a court in any part of the United Kingdom and to a previous sentence passed by any such court.

(6) References in this Act to an offence punishable with imprisonment shall be construed, in relation to any offender, without regard to any prohibition or restriction imposed by or under any enactment, including this Act, upon the imprisonment of offenders of his age.

(7) Without prejudice to section 46 of this Act, where the age of any person at any time is material for the purposes of any provision of this Act regulating the powers of a court, his age at the material time shall be deemed to be or to have been that which appears to the court, after considering any available evidence, to be or to have been his age at that time.

(8) References in this Act to findings of guilty and findings that an offence has been committed shall be construed as including references to pleas of guilty and admissions that an offence has been committed.

NOTES
[1] Inserted by the Crime and Punishment (Scotland) Act 1997 (c. 48), s.62(1) and Sched. 1, para. 21(34)(b) with effect from August 1, 1997 in terms of the Crime and Punishment (Scotland) Act 1997 (Commencement and Transitional Provisions) Order 1997 (S.I. 1997 No. 1712) para. 3.
[2] Inserted by the Crime and Punishment (Scotland) Act 1997 (c. 48), s.6(5) with effect from January 1, 1998 in terms of the Crime and Punishment (Scotland) Act 1997 (Commencement No. 2 and Transitional and Consequential Provisions) Order 1997 (S.I. 1997 No. 2323) Sched. 2.
[3] Inserted by the Crime and Disorder Act 1998 (c. 37), Sched. 8, para. 124 (effective September 30, 1998: S.I. 1998 No. 2327).
[4] Amended as above.
[5] Inserted by the Crime and Disorder Act 1998 (c. 37), s.95.
[6] Inserted by the Scotland Act 1998 (c. 46), s.125(1) and Sched. 8, para. 31(3).

Construction of enactments referring to detention etc.

308. In any enactment—
(a) any reference to a sentence of imprisonment as including a reference to a sentence of any other form of detention shall be construed as including a reference to a sentence of detention under section 207 of this Act; and
(b) any reference to imprisonment as including any other form of detention shall be construed as including a reference to detention under that section.

Short title, commencement and extent

309.—(1) This Act may be cited as the Criminal Procedure Act 1995.
(2) This Act shall come into force on 1 April 1996.
(3) Subject to subsections (4) and (5) below, this Act extends to Scotland only.
(4) The following provisions of this Act and this section extend to England and Wales—
section 44;
section 47;
section 209(3) and (7);
section 234(4) to (11);
section 244;
section 252 for the purposes of the construction mentioned in subsection (1) of that subsection;

400

section 303(4).

(5) The following provisions of this Act and this section extend to Northern Ireland—

section 44;

section 47;

section 244;

section 252 for the purposes of the construction mentioned in subsection (1) of that subsection;

section 303(4).

(6) Section 297(3) and (4) of this Act and this section also extend to the Isle of Man.

SCHEDULES

SCHEDULE 1

OFFENCES AGAINST CHILDREN UNDER THE AGE OF 17 YEARS TO WHICH SPECIAL PROVISIONS APPLY

1. Any offence under Part I of the Criminal Law (Consolidation) (Scotland) Act 1995.

2. Any offence under section 12, 15, 22 or 33 of the Children and Young Persons (Scotland) Act 1937.

3. Any other offence involving bodily injury to a child under the age of 17 years.

4. Any offence involving the use of lewd, indecent or libidinous practice or behaviour towards a child under the age of 17 years.

Sections 34 & 64(2)   SCHEDULE 2

EXAMPLES OF INDICTMENTS

"A.B. (*name and address, that given in the declaration being sufficient*), you are indicted at the instance of A. F. R. (*name of Lord Advocate*), Her Majesty's Advocate, and the charge against you is that on 20th 199, in a shop in George Street, Edinburgh, occupied by John Cruikshank, draper, you did steal a shawl and a boa."

"...You did rob Charles Doyle, a cattle dealer, of Biggar, Lanarkshire, of a watch and chain and £36 of money..."

"...You did break into the house occupied by Andrew Howe, banker's clerk, and did there steal twelve spoons, a ladle, and a candlestick..."

"...You did force open (*or* attempt to force open) a lockfast cupboard and did thus attempt to steal therefrom..."

"...You did place your hand in one of the packets of Thomas Kerr, commercial traveller, 115 Main Street, Perth, and did thus attempt to steal..."

"...You did assault Lewis Mann, station-master of Earlston, and compress his throat and attempt to take from him a watch and chain..."

"...You did, while in the employment of James Pentland, accountant in Frederick Street, Edinburgh, embezzle £4,075 of money..."

"...You did, while acting as commercial traveller to Brown and Company, merchants in Leith, at the times and places specified in the inventory hereto subjoined, receive from the persons therein set forth the respective sums of money therein specified for the said Brown and Company, and did embezzle the same (*or* did embezzle £470 of money, being part thereof)..."

"...You did pretend to Norah Omond, residing there, that you were a collector of subscriptions for a charitable society, and did thus induce her to deliver to you £15 of money as a subscription thereto, which you appropriated to your own use..."

"...You did reset a watch and chain, pocket book and £15.55 of money, the same having been dishonestly appropriated by theft or robbery..."

"...You did utter as genuine a bill, on which the name of John Jones bore to be signed as acceptor, such signature being forged by (*here describe in general terms how the bill was uttered, and add where the bill is produced*), and said bill of exchange is No. of the productions lodged herewith..."

"...You did utter as genuine a letter bearing to be a certificate of character of you, as a domestic servant, by Mary Watson, of 15 Bon Accord Street, Aberdeen, what was written above the signature of Mary Watson having been written there by some other person without her authority by handing it to Ellen Chisholm of Panmore Street, Forfar, to whom you were applying for a situation (*here add when the letter is produced*), and said letter is No. of the productions lodged herewith…"

"…You did utter a cheque signed by Henry Smith for £8 sterling, which had been altered without his authority by adding the letter Y to eight and the figure 0 to figure 8, so as to make it read as a cheque for XC11,480 sterling, by presenting such altered cheque for payment to Allen Brown, Cashier of the Bank of Scotland at Callander (*here add when the cheque is produced*), and said cheque is No. of the productions lodged herewith…"

"…You did, when examined under section 45 of the Bankruptcy (Scotland) Act 1985 before Hubert Hamilton Esquire, sheriff of the Lothians and Borders, depone (*here state the general nature of the false statement*), in order to defraud your creditors…"

"…You did, sequestration having been awarded on your estate on the 20th March 1991, conceal property consisting of (*here state generally the property concealed*), falling under your sequestration, in order to defraud your creditor, by burying it in the garden of your house in Troon Street, Kilmarnock (*or* by removing it to the house of James Kidd, your son, No. 17 Greek Street, Port-Glasgow)…"

"…You did set fire to a warehouse occupied by Peter Cranston in Holly Lane, Greenock, and the fire took effect on said warehouse, and this you did wilfully (*or* culpably and recklessly)…"

"…You did set fire to the shop in Brown Street, Blairgowrie, occupied by you, with intent to defraud the Liverpool, London, and Globe Insurance Company, and the fire took effect on said shop…"

"…You did assault Theresa Unwin, your wife, and did beat her and did murder her…"

"…You did stab Thomas Underwood, baker, of Shiels Place, Oban, and did murder him…"

"…You did administer poison to Vincent Wontner, your son, and did murder him…"

"…You did strangle Mary Shaw, mill-worker, daughter of John Shaw, residing at Juniper Green, in the county of Midlothian, and did murder her…"

"…You were delivered of a child now dead or amissing, and you did conceal your pregnancy and did not call for or use assistance at the birth, contrary to the Concealment of Birth (Scotland) Act 1809…"

"…You did assault Hector Morrison, carter, of 20 Buccleuch Street, Dalkeith, and did beat him with your fists and with a stick, and did break his arm…"

"…You did ravish Harriet Cowan, mill-worker, of 27 Tweed Row, Peebles…"

"…You did attempt to ravish Jane Peters, servant, at Glen House, near Dunbar…"

"…You did, when acting as railway signalman, cancel a danger signal and allow a train to enter on a part of the line protected by the signals under your charge, and did cause a collision, and did kill William Peters, commercial traveller, of Brook Street, Carlisle, a passenger in said train…"

"…You formed part of a riotous mob, which, acting of common purpose, obstructed A. B., C. D., and E. F., constables of the Northern constabulary on duty, and assaulted them, and forcibly took two persons whom they had arrested from their custody…"

"…You did, being the lawful husband of Helen Hargreaves, of 20 Teviot Row, Edinburgh, and she being still alive, bigamously marry Dorothy Rose, a widow, of 7 Blacks Row, Brechin, and did cohabit with her as her husband…"

"…You being sworn as a witness in a civil cause, then proceeding in the sheriff court, deponed (*here set forth the statements said to be false*) the truth as you knew being that (*here state the true facts*)…"

"…You did suborn James Carruthers, scavenger, 12 Hercles Street, Edinburgh, to depone as a witness in the sheriff court of Edinburgh, that (*here set forth the statements said to be false*), and he did (*time and place*) depone to that effect, the truth as you knew being (*here state the true facts*)…"

"…You did deforce John Macdonald, a sheriff officer of Renfrewshire, and prevent him serving a summons issued by the sheriff of Renfrewshire upon Peter M'Innes, market gardener in Renfrew…"

Sections 64(6) and 138(4)   SCHEDULE 3

INDICTMENTS AND COMPLAINTS

1. An accused may be named and designed—
(a) according to the existing practice; or
(b) by the name given by him and designed as of the place given by him as his residence when he is examined or further examined; or
(c) by the name under which he is committed until liberated in due course of law.
2. It shall not be necessary to specify by any *nomen juris* the offence which is charged, but it shall be sufficient that the indictment or complaint sets forth facts relevant and sufficient to constitute an indictable offence or, as the case may be, an offence punishable on complaint.

3. It shall not be necessary to allege that any act or commission or omission charged was done or omitted to be done "wilfully" or "maliciously", or "wickedly and feloniously", or "falsely and fraudulently" or "knowingly", or "culpably and recklessly", or "negligently", or in "breach of duty", or to use such words as "knowing the same to be forged", or "having good reason to know", or "well knowing the same to have been stolen", or to use any similar words or expressions qualifying any act charged, but such qualifying allegation shall be implied in every case.

4.—(1) The latitude formerly used in stating time shall be implied in all statements of time where an exact time is not of the essence of the charge.

(2) The latitude formerly used in stating any place by adding to the word "at", or to the word "in", the words "or near", or the words "or in the near neighbourhood thereof" or similar words, shall be implied in all statements of place where the actual place is not of the essence of the charge.

(3) Subject to sub-paragraph (4) below, where the circumstances of the offence charged make it necessary to take an exceptional latitude in regard to time or place it shall not be necessary to set forth the circumstances in the indictment, or to set forth that the particular time or the particular place is to the prosecutor unknown.

(4) Where exceptional latitude is taken as mentioned in sub-paragraph (3) above, the court shall, if satisfied that such exceptional latitude was not reasonable in the circumstances of the case, give such remedy to the accused by adjournment of the trial or otherwise as shall seem just.

(5) Notwithstanding sub-paragraph (4) above, nothing in any rule of law shall prohibit the amendment of an indictment or, as the case may be, a complaint to include a time outwith the exceptional latitude if it appears to the court that the amendment would not prejudice the accused.

(6) The latitude formerly used in describing quantities by the words "or thereby", or the words "or part thereof", or the words "or some other quantity to the prosecutor unknown" or similar words, shall be implied in all statements of quantities.

(7) The latitude formerly used in stating details connected with the perpetration of any act regarding persons, things or modes by inserting general alternative statements followed by the words "to the prosecutor unknown" or similar words, shall be implied in every case.

(8) In this paragraph references to latitude formerly used are references to such use before the commencement of—

(a) in the case of proceedings on indictment, the Criminal Procedure (Scotland) Act 1887; and

(b) in the case of summary proceedings, the Summary Jurisdiction (Scotland) Act 1908.

5. The word "money" shall include cheques, banknotes, postal orders, money orders and foreign currency.

6. Any document referred to shall be referred to by a general description and, where it is to be produced in proceedings on indictment, by the number given to it in the list of productions for the prosecution.

7. In an indictment which charges a crime importing personal injury inflicted by the accused, resulting in death or serious injury to the person, the accused may be lawfully convicted of the aggravation that the assault or other injurious act was committed with intent to commit such crime.

8.—(1) In an indictment or a complaint charging the resetting of property dishonestly appropriated—

(a) having been taken by theft or robbery; or

(b) by breach of trust, embezzlement or falsehood, fraud and wilful imposition,

it shall be sufficient to specify that the accused received the property, it having been dishonestly appropriated by theft or robbery, or by breach of trust and embezzlement, or by falsehood, fraud and wilful imposition, as the case may be.

(2) Under an indictment or a complaint for robbery, theft, breach of trust and embezzlement or falsehood, fraud and wilful imposition, an accused may be convicted of reset.

(3) Under an indictment or a complaint for robbery, breach of trust and embezzlement, or falsehood, fraud and wilful imposition, an accused may be convicted of theft.

(4) Under an indictment or a complaint for theft, an accused may be convicted of breach of trust and embezzlement, or of falsehood, fraud and wilful imposition, or may be convicted of theft, although the circumstances proved may in law amount to robbery.

(5) The power conferred by sub-paragraphs (2) to (4) above to convict a person of an offence other than that with which he is charged shall be exercisable by the sheriff court before which he is tried notwithstanding that the other offence was committed outside the jurisdiction of that sheriff court.

9.—(1) Where two or more crimes or acts of crime are charged cumulatively, it shall be lawful to convict of any one or more of them.

(2) Any part of the charge in an indictment or complaint which itself constitutes an indictable offence or, as the case may be an offence punishable on complaint, shall be separable and it shall be lawful to convict the accused of that offence.

(3) Where any crime is charged as having been committed with a particular intent or with particular circumstances of aggravation, it shall be lawful to convict of the crime without such intent or aggravation.

10.—(1) Under an indictment or, as the case may be, a complaint which charges a completed offence, the accused may be lawfully convicted of an attempt to commit the offence.

(2) Under an indictment or complaint charging an attempt, the accused may be convicted of such attempt although the evidence is sufficient to prove the completion of the offence said to have been attempted.

(3) Under an indictment or complaint which charges an offence involving personal injury inflicted by the accused, resulting in death or serious injury to the person, the accused may be lawfully convicted of the assault or other injurious act, and may also be lawfully convicted of the aggravation that the assault or other injurious act was committed with intent to commit such offence.

11. In an indictment or complaint charging a contravention of an enactment the description of the offence in the words of the enactment contravened, or in similar words, shall be sufficient.

12. In a complaint charging a contravention of an enactment—

(a) the statement that an act was done contrary to an enactment shall imply a statement—

(i) that the enactment applied to the circumstances existing at the time and place of the offence;

(ii) that the accused was a person bound to observe the enactment;

(iii) that any necessary preliminary procedure had been duly gone through; and

(iv) that all the circumstances necessary to a contravention existed,

and, in the case of the contravention of a subordinate instrument, such statement shall imply a statement that the instrument was duly made, confirmed, published and generally made effectual according to the law applicable, and was in force at the time and place in question; and

(b) where the offence is created by more than one section of one or more statutes or subordinate instruments, it shall be necessary to specify only the leading section or one of the leading sections.

13. In the case of an offence punishable under any enactment, it shall be sufficient to allege that the offence was committed contrary to the enactment and to refer to the enactment founded on without setting out the words of the enactment at length.

14. Where—

(a) any act alleged in an indictment or complaint as contrary to any enactment is also criminal at common law; or

(b) where the facts proved under the indictment or complaint do not amount to a contravention of the enactment, but do amount to an offence at common law,

it shall be lawful to convict of the common law offence.

15. Where the evidence in a trial is sufficient to prove the identity of any person, corporation or company, or of any place, or of anything, it shall not be a valid objection to the sufficiency of the evidence that any particulars specified in the indictment or complaint relating to such identity have not been proved.

16. Where, in relation to an offence created by or under an enactment any exception, exemption, proviso, excuse, or qualification, is expressed to have effect whether by the same or any other enactment, the exception, exemption, proviso, excuse or qualification need not be specified or negatived in the indictment or complaint, and the prosecution is not required to prove it, but the accused may do so.

17. It shall be competent to include in one indictment or complaint both common law and statutory charges.

18. In any proceedings under the Merchant Shipping Acts it shall not be necessary to produce the official register of the ship referred to in the proceedings in order to prove the nationality of the ship, but the nationality of the ship as stated in the indictment or, as the case may be, complaint shall, in the absence of evidence to the contrary, be presumed.

19. In offences inferring dishonest appropriation of property brought before a court whose power to deal with such offences is limited to cases in which the value of such property does not exceed level 4 on the standard scale it shall be assumed, and it shall not be necessary to state in the charge, that the value of the property does not exceed that sum.

SCHEDULE 4

SUPERVISION AND TREATMENT ORDERS

PART I

PRELIMINARY

1.—(1) In this Schedule "supervision and treatment order" means an order requiring the person in respect of whom it is made ("the supervised person")—

(a) to be under the supervision of a social worker who is an officer of the local authority for the area where the supervised person resides or is to reside (in this Schedule referred to as "the supervising officer") for such period, not being more than three years, as is specified in the order;

(b) to comply during that period with instructions given to him by the supervising officer regarding his supervision; and

(c) to submit during that period to treatment by or under the direction of a medical practitioner with a view to the improvement of his mental condition.

(2) The Secretary of State may by order amend sub-paragraph (1) above by substituting, for the period for the time being specified in that sub-paragraph, such period as may be specified in the order.

(3) An order under sub-paragraph (2) above may make any amendment to paragraph 8(2) below which the Secretary of State considers necessary in consequence of the order.

(4) The power of the Secretary of State to make orders under sub-paragraph (2) above shall be exercisable by statutory instrument subject to annulment in pursuance of a resolution of either House of Parliament.

PART II

MAKING AND EFFECT OF ORDERS

Circumstances in which orders may be made

2.—(1) The court shall not make a supervision and treatment order unless it is satisfied—

(a) that, having regard to all the circumstances of the case, the making of such an order is the most suitable means of dealing with the person; and

(b) on the written or oral evidence of two or more medical practitioners approved for the purposes of section 20 or 39 of the Mental Health (Scotland) Act 1984, that the mental condition of the person—

(i) is such as requires and may be susceptible to treatment; but

(ii) is not such as to warrant the making of an order under paragraph (a) of subsection (2) of section 57 of this Act (whether with or without an order under paragraph (b) of that subsection) or an order under paragraph (c) of that subsection.

(2) The court shall not make a supervision and treatment order unless it is also satisfied—

(a) that the supervising officer intended to be specified in the order is willing to undertake the supervision; and

(b) that arrangements have been made for the treatment intended to be specified in the order.

(3) Subsections (3) to (5) of section 61 of this Act shall have effect with respect to proof of a person's mental condition for the purposes of sub-paragraph (1) above as they have effect with respect to proof of an offender's mental condition for the purposes of section 58(1)(a) of this Act.

Making of orders and general requirements

3.—(1) A supervision and treatment order shall specify the local authority area in which the supervised person resides or will reside.

(2) Before making such an order, the court shall explain to the supervised person in ordinary language—

(a) the effect of the order (including any requirements proposed to be included in the order in accordance with paragraph 5 below); and

(b) that the sheriff court for the area in which the supervised person resides or will reside (in this Schedule referred to as "the relevant sheriff court") has power under paragraphs 6 to

8 below to review the order on the application either of the supervised person or of the supervising officer.

(3) After making such an order, the court shall forthwith give a copy of the order to—

(a) the supervised person;

(b) the supervising officer; and

[1](bb) the medical practitioner by whom or under whose supervision the supervised person is to be treated under the order;

(c) the person in charge of any institution in which the supervised person is required by the order to reside.

(4) After making such an order, the court shall also send to the relevant sheriff court—

(a) a copy of the order; and

(b) such documents and information relating to the case as it considers likely to be of assistance to that court in the exercise of its functions in relation to the order.

(5) Where such an order is made, the supervised person shall comply with such instructions as he may from time to time be given by the supervising officer regarding his supervision and shall keep in touch with that officer and notify him of any change of address.

Obligatory requirements as to medical treatment

4.—(1) A supervision and treatment order shall include a requirement that the supervised person shall submit, during the period specified in the order, to treatment by or under the direction of a medical practitioner with a view to the improvement of his mental condition.

(2) The treatment required by the order shall be such one of the following kinds of treatment as may be specified in the order, that is to say—

(a) treatment as a non-resident patient at such institution or place as may be specified in the order; and

(b) treatment by or under the direction of such medical practitioner as may be so specified; but the nature of the treatment shall not be specified in the order except as mentioned in paragraph (a) or (b) above.

(3) Where the medical practitioner by whom or under whose direction the supervised person is being treated for his mental condition in pursuance of a supervision and treatment order is of the opinion that part of the treatment can be better or more conveniently given at an institution or place which—

(a) is not specified in the order; and

(b) is one at which the treatment of the supervised person will be given by or under the direction of a medical practitioner,

he may, with the consent of the supervised person, make arrangements for him to be treated accordingly.

(4) Where any such arrangements as are mentioned in sub-paragraph (3) above are made for the treatment of a supervised person—

(a) the medical practitioner by whom the arrangements are made shall give notice in writing to the supervising officer, specifying the institution or place at which the treatment is to be carried out; and

(b) the treatment provided for by the arrangements shall be deemed to be treatment to which he is required to submit in pursuance of the supervision and treatment order.

Optional requirements as to residence

5.—(1) Subject to sub-paragraphs (2) to (4) below, a supervision and treatment order may include requirements as to the residence of the supervised person.

(2) Such an order may not require the supervised person to reside as a resident patient in a hospital.

(3) Before making such an order containing any such requirement, the court shall consider the home surroundings of the supervised person.

(4) Where such an order requires the supervised person to reside in any institution, the period for which he is so required to reside shall be specified in the order.

PART III

REVOCATION AND AMENDMENT OF ORDERS

Revocation of order in interests of health or welfare

6. Where a supervision and treatment order is in force in respect of any person and, on the application of the supervised person or the supervising officer, it appears to the relevant sheriff

court that, having regard to circumstances which have arisen since the order was made, it would be in the interests of the health or welfare of the supervised person that the order should be revoked, the court may revoke the order.

Amendment of order by reason of change of residence

7.—(1) This paragraph applies where, at any time while a supervision and treatment order is in force in respect of any person, the relevant sheriff court is satisfied that—

(a) the supervised person proposes to change, or has changed, his residence from the area specified in the order to the area of another local authority;

(b) a social worker who is an officer of the other local authority ("the new supervising officer") is willing to undertake the supervision; and

(c) the requirements of the order as respects treatment will continue to be complied with.

(2) Subject to sub-paragraph (3) below the court may, and on the application of the supervising officer shall, amend the supervision and treatment order by substituting the other area for the area specified in the order and the new supervising officer for the supervising officer specified in the order.

(3) Where a supervision and treatment order contains requirements which, in the opinion of the court, can be complied with only if the supervised person continues to reside in the area specified in the order, the court shall not amend the order under this paragraph unless it also, in accordance with paragraph 8 below, either—

(a) cancels those requirements; or

(b) substitutes for those requirements other requirements which can be complied with if the supervised person ceases to reside in that area.

Amendment of requirements of order

8.—(1) Without prejudice to paragraph 7 above, but subject to sub-paragraph (2) below, the relevant sheriff court may, on the application of the supervised person or the supervising officer, by order amend a supervision and treatment order—

(a) by cancelling any of the requirements of the order; or

(b) by inserting in the order (either in addition to or in substitution for any such requirement) any requirement which the court could include if it were the court by which the order was made and were then making it.

(2) The power of the court under sub-paragraph (1) above shall not include power to amend an order by extending the period specified in it beyond the end of three years from the date of the original order.

Amendment of requirements in pursuance of medical report

9.—(1) Where the medical practitioner by whom or under whose direction the supervised person is being treated for his mental condition in pursuance of any requirement of a supervision and treatment order—

(a) is of the opinion mentioned in sub-paragraph (2) below; or

(b) is for any reason unwilling to continue to treat or direct the treatment of the supervised person,

he shall make a report in writing to that effect to the supervising officer and that officer shall apply under paragraph 8 above to the relevant sheriff court for the variation or cancellation of the requirement.

(2) The opinion referred to in sub-paragraph (1) above is—

(a) that the treatment of the supervised person should be continued beyond the period specified in the supervision and treatment order;

(b) that the supervised person needs different treatment, being treatment of a kind to which he could be required to submit in pursuance of such an order;

(c) that the supervised person is not susceptible to treatment; or

(d) that the supervised person does not require further treatment.

Supplemental

10.—²(1) On the making under paragraph 6 above of an order revoking a supervision and treatment order, the sheriff clerk shall forthwith give a copy of the revoking order to the supervising officer and to the medical practitioner by whom or under whose supervision the supervised person was treated under the supervision and treatment order.

(2) On receipt of a copy of the revoking order the supervising officer shall give a copy to the supervised person and to the person in charge of any institution in which the supervised person was required by the order to reside.

11.—(1) On the making under paragraph 7 or 8 above of an order amending a supervision and treatment order, the sheriff clerk shall forthwith—

[2](a) if the order amends the supervision and treatment order otherwise than by substituting a new area or a new place for the one specified in that order, give a copy of the amending order to the supervising officer and to the medical practitioner by whom or under whose supervision the supervised person has been treated under the supervision and treatment order;

(b) if the order amends the supervision and treatment order in the manner excepted by paragraph (a) above, send to the new relevant sheriff court—

(i) a copy of the amending order; and

(ii) such documents and information relating to the case as he considers likely to be of assistance to that court in exercising its functions in relation to the order;

and in a case falling within paragraph (b) above, the sheriff clerk shall give a copy of the amending order to the supervising officer.

(2) On receipt of a copy of an amending order the supervising officer shall give a copy to the supervised person and to the person in charge of any institution in which the supervised person is or was required by the order to reside.

12. On the making, revocation or amendment of a supervision and treatment order the supervising officer shall give a copy of the order or, as the case may be, of the order revoking or amending it, to the Mental Welfare Commission for Scotland.

NOTE

[1]Inserted by the Crime and Punishment (Scotland) Act 1997 (c. 48), Sched. 1, para. 21(35) with effect from January 1, 1998 as provided by The Crime and Punishment (Scotland) Act 1997 (Commencement No. 2 and Transitional and Consequential Provisions) Order 1997 (S.I. 1997 No. 2323) Art. 4, Sched. 2.

[2]As amended by the above provisions with effect from January 1, 1998.

Section 138(2)   SCHEDULE 5

FORMS OF COMPLAINT AND CHARGES

The following Forms are additional to those contained in Schedule 2 to this Act, all of which, in so far as applicable to charges which may be tried summarily, are deemed to be incorporated in this Schedule:—

You did assault A.L. and strike him with your fists.

You did conduct yourself in a disorderly manner and commit a breach of the peace.

You did threaten violence to the lieges and commit a breach of the peace.

You did fight and commit a breach of the peace.

You did publicly expose your person in a shameless and indecent manner in presence of the lieges.

You did obtain from A.N. board and lodging to the value of £16 without paying and intending not to pay therefor.

You did maliciously knock down 20 metres of the coping of a wall forming the fence between two fields on the said farm.

You did maliciously place a block of wood on the railway line and attempt to obstruct a train.

You did drive a horse and cart recklessly to the danger of the lieges.

You did break into a poultry house and steal three fowls.

You did steal a coat which you obtained from R.O. on the false representation that you had been sent for it by her husband.

having received from D.G. £6 to hand to E.R., you did on (date) at (place) steal the said sum.

having received from G.R. a watch in loan, you did on at, sell it to E.G., and steal it.

having found a watch, you did, without trying to discover its owner, sell it on at, to O.R., and steal it.

You did acquire from K.O., a private in the Third Battalion a military jacket and waist belt, contrary to section 195 of the Army Act 1955.

You, being a person whose estate has been sequestrated, did obtain credit from W.A. to the extent of £260 without informing him that your estate had been sequestrated and that you had not received your discharge, contrary to section 67(9) of the Bankruptcy (Scotland) Act 1985.

You, being the occupier of the said house, did use the same for the purpose of betting with persons resorting thereto, contrary to section 1 of the Betting, Gaming and Lotteries Act 1963.

You did frequent and loiter in the said street for the purpose of betting and receiving bets, contrary to section 8 of the Betting, Gaming and Lotteries Act 1963.

You did assault L.S., a constable of the Police, while engaged in the execution of his duty, and with a stick strike him on the face to the great effusion of blood contrary to section 41 of the Police (Scotland) Act 1967.

You did cruelly ill-treat a horse by causing it to draw a cart while it was suffering from a sore on its back under the saddle, contrary to section 1 of the Protection of Animals (Scotland) Act 1912.

You did wilfully neglect your children K.I., aged seven years; J.I., aged five years; and H.I., aged three years, by failing to provide them with adequate food and clothing, and by keeping them in a filthy and verminous condition, contrary to section 12 of the Children and Young Persons (Scotland) Act 1937.

You are the owner of a dog which is dangerous and not kept under proper control, and which on in did chase a flock of sheep, contrary to section 2 of the Dogs Act 1871, section 2, as amended by section 1 of the Dogs Act 1906, whereby you are liable to be ordered to keep the said dog under proper control or to destroy it.

You, being a parent of D.U., a child of school age, aged, who has attended school, and the said child having failed, between and, without reasonable excuse, to attend regularly at the said school, you are thereby guilty of an offence against section 35 of the Education (Scotland) Act 1980.

being an unauthorised place you did keep for sale 75 kilograms of gunpowder, contrary to the Explosives Act 1875, section 5.

You did keep 78 kilograms of gunpowder, and did not keep it in a fireproof safe, contrary to the Explosives Act 1875, section 22 and section 3, subsection (1), Mode B, of the Order in Council dated 26th October 1896.

You did sell and deliver to N.C. to his prejudice an article of food namely; gallons of sweet milk which was not of the nature, substance and quality of the article demanded by him and was not genuine sweet milk in respect that it was deficient in milk fat to the extent of per cent, or thereby in that it contained only per cent, of milk fat, conform to certificate of analysis granted on (date) by A.N. analytical chemist (address), public analyst for (a copy of which certificate of analysis is annexed hereto) of a sample of the said milk taken (specify time and place) by L.O., duly appointed sampling officer for, acting under the direction of the local authority for the said burgh, while the said milk was in course of delivery to the said N.C. contrary to the Food Act 1984, and the Sale of Milk Regulations 1901.

You did take part in gaming in the street contrary to sections 5 and 8 of the Gaming Act 1968.

You did by night enter on the said land with nets for the purpose of taking game, contrary to section 1 of the Night Poaching Act 1828; or

You did by night unlawfully take six rabbits, contrary to, etc.

You did in the daytime trespass on the said land in search of pursuit of game (*or* rabbits), contrary to section 1 of the Game (Scotland) Act 1832.

You were found in the possession of five hares, a net and six net pins, which hares you had obtained by unlawfully going on land in search or pursuit of game, and which net and nets pins you had used for unlawfully killing or taking game, or you had been accessory thereto, contrary to section 2 of the Poaching Prevention Act 1862.

You did present or cause to be presented to W.E., Assessors for a return in which you falsely stated that the yearly rent of your House. No. Street, was £20, instead of £30, contrary to section 7 of the Lands Valuation (Scotland) Act 1854.

You did sell a half gill of whisky to J.M., who was then a drunken person, contrary to your certificate and section 76 of the Licensing (Scotland) Act 1976.

You were found drunk and incapable of taking care of yourself, and not under the care or protection of some suitable person, contrary to section 74(2) of the Licensing (Scotland) Act 1976.

You did drive a motor car recklessly contrary to section 2 of the Road Traffic Act 1988.

You did act as a pedlar without having obtained a certificate, contrary to section 4 of the Pedlars' Act 1871.

You did place in a Post Office letter box a lighted match, contrary to section 60 of the Post Office Act 1953.

You did travel in a railway carriage without having previously paid your fare, and with intent to avoid payment thereof, contrary to section 5(3)(a) of the Regulation of Railways Act 1889.

Having on within the house No. Street, given birth to a female child, you did fail, within twenty-one days thereafter, to attend personally and give information to C.W., registrar of births, deaths, and marriages for (Registration District), of the particulars required to be registered concerning the birth, contrary to sections 14 and 53 of the Registration of Births, Deaths, and Marriages (Scotland) Act 1965.

You did take two salmon during the annual close time by means of cobles and sweep nets, contrary to section 15 of the Salmon Fisheries (Scotland) Act 1868.

You had in your possession for use for trade a counter balance which was false, and two weights, which were unjust, contrary to the Weights and Measures Act 1985, section 17.

Section 231(1)   SCHEDULE 6

<small>DISCHARGE OF AND AMENDMENT TO PROBATION ORDERS</small>

Discharge

1. A probation order may on the application of the officer supervising the probationer or of the probationer be discharged—
   (a) by the appropriate court; or
   (b) if no appropriate court has been named in the original or in any amending order, by the court which made the order.

Amendment

2.—(1) If the court by which a probation order was made, or the appropriate court, is satisfied that the probationer proposes to change or has changed his residence from the area of a local authority named in the order to the area of another local authority, the court may, and if application is made in that behalf by the officer supervising the probationer shall, by order, amend the probation order by—
   (a) substituting for the area named therein that other area; and
   (b) naming the appropriate court to which all the powers of the court by which the order was made shall be transferred and shall require the local authority for that other area to arrange for the probationer to be under the supervision of an officer of that authority.

(2) Subject to sub-paragraphs (3) and (4) below, the court to be named as the appropriate court in any amendment of a probation order in pursuance of sub-paragraph (1) above shall be a court exercising jurisdiction in the place where the probationer resides or is to reside and shall be a sheriff court or district court according to whether the probation order was made by a sheriff court or district court.

(3) If the probation order was made by a district court and there is no district court exercising jurisdiction in the place mentioned in sub-paragraph (2) above, the court to be named shall be the sheriff court.

(4) If the probation order contains requirements which in the opinion of the court cannot be complied with unless the probationer continues to reside in the local authority area named in the order, the court shall not amend the order as mentioned in sub-paragraph (2) above unless, in accordance with the following provisions of this Schedule, it cancels those requirements or substitutes therefor other requirements which can be so complied with.

(5) Where a probation order is amended under this paragraph, the clerk of the court amending it shall send to the clerk of the appropriate court four copies of the order together with such documents and information relating to the case as the court amending the order considers likely to be of assistance to the appropriate court, and the clerk of that court shall send one copy of the probation order to the local authority of the substituted local authority area and two copies to the officer supervising the probationer, one of which the supervising officer shall give to the probationer.

(6) The foregoing provisions of this paragraph shall, in a case where the probation order was made by the High Court, have effect subject to the following modifications—
   (a) the court shall not name an appropriate court, but may substitute for the local authority named in the order, the local authority for the area in which the probationer is to reside;
   (b) the Clerk of Justiciary shall send to the chief social work officer of that area in which the probationer is to reside three copies of the amending order together with such documents and information relating to the case as is likely to be of assistance to the chief social work officer, and the chief social work officer shall send two copies of the amending order to the officer supervising the probationer, one of which the supervising officer shall give to the probationer.

3.—(1) Without prejudice to paragraph 2 above, the court by which a probation order was made or the appropriate court may, upon application made by the officer supervising the probationer or by the probationer, subject to sub-paragraph (2) below, by order amend a probation order by cancelling any of the requirements thereof or by inserting therein (either in addition to or in substitution for any such requirement) any requirement which could be included in the order if it were then being made by that court in accordance with sections 228 to 230 of this Act.

(2) The court shall not amend a probation order under sub-paragraph (1) above—

(a) by reducing the probation period, or by extending that period beyond the end of three years from the date of the original order;

(b) so that the probationer is thereby required to reside in any institution or place, or to submit to treatment for his mental condition, for any period or periods exceeding 12 months in all;

(c) by inserting in it a requirement that the probationer shall submit to treatment for his mental condition unless the amending order is made within three months after the date of the original order.

4. Where the medical practitioner or chartered psychologist by whom or under whose direction a probationer is being treated for his mental condition in pursuance of any requirement of the probation order is of the opinion—

(a) that the treatment of the probationer should be continued beyond the period specified for that purpose in the order; or

(b) that the probationer needs a different kind of treatment (whether in whole or in part) from that which he has been receiving in pursuance of the probation order, being treatment of a kind which could have been specified in the probation order but to which the probationer or his supervising officer has not agreed under section 230(6) of this Act; or

(c) that the probationer is not susceptible to treatment; or

(d) that the probationer does not require further treatment,

or where the practitioner or psychologist is for any reason unwilling to continue to treat or direct the treatment of the probationer, he shall make a report in writing to that effect to the officer supervising the probationer and the supervising officer shall apply to the court which made the order or to the appropriate court for the variation or cancellation of the requirement.

General

5.—(1) Where the court which made the order or the appropriate court proposes to amend a probation order under this Schedule, otherwise than on the application of the probationer, it shall cite him to appear before the court; and the court shall not amend the probation order unless the probationer expresses his willingness to comply with the requirements of the order as amended.

(2) Sub-paragraph (1) above shall not apply to an order cancelling a requirement of the probation order or reducing the period of any requirement, or substituting a new area of a local authority for the area named in the probation order.

6. On the making of an order discharging or amending a probation order, the clerk of the court shall forthwith give copies of the discharging or amending order to the officer supervising the probationer; and the supervising officer shall give a copy to the probationer and to the person in charge of any institution in which the probationer is or was required by the order to reside.

Section 235　　　　　　　SCHEDULE 7

SUPERVISED ATTENDANCE ORDERS: FURTHER PROVISIONS

1.—(1) A court shall not make a supervised attendance order in respect of any offender unless—

(a) the court has been notified by the Secretary of State that arrangements exist for persons of a class which includes the offender who reside in the locality in which the offender resides, or will be residing when the order comes into force, to carry out the requirements of such an order.

(b) the court is satisfied that provision can be made under the arrangements mentioned in sub-sub-paragraph (a) above for the offender to carry out such requirements.

(2) Before making a supervised attendance order, the court shall explain to the offender in ordinary language—

(a) the purpose and effect of the order and in particular the obligations on the offender as specified in paragraph 3 below;

(b) the consequences which may follow under paragraph 4 below if he fails to comply with any of those requirements; and

(c) that the court has, under paragraph 5 below, the power to review the order on the application either of the offender or of an officer of the local authority in whose area the offender for the time being resides.

(3) The Secretary of State may by order direct that subsection (2) of section 235 of this Act shall be amended by substituting, for any number of hours specified in that subsection such other number of hours as may be specified in the order; and an order under this subsection may in making such amendment specify different such numbers of hours for different classes of case.

(4) An order under sub-paragraph (3) above shall be made by statutory instrument, but no such order shall be made unless a draft of it has been laid before, and approved by a resolution of, each House of Parliament.

2.—(1) A supervised attendance order shall—

(a) specify the locality in which the offender resides or will be residing when the order comes into force; and

(b) require the local authority in whose area the locality specified under sub-sub-paragraph (a) above is situated to appoint or assign a supervising officer.

(2) Where, whether on the same occasion or on separate occasions, an offender is made subject to more than one supervised attendance order, the court may direct that the requirements specified in any of those orders shall be concurrent with or additional to those specified in any other of those orders, but so that at no time shall the offender have an outstanding number of hours during which he must carry out the requirements of these orders in excess of the largest number specified in section 235 of this Act.

(3) Upon making a supervised attendance order the court shall—

(a) give, or send by registered post or by the recorded delivery service, a copy of the order to the offender;

(b) send a copy of the order to the chief social work officer of the local authority in whose area the offender resides or will be residing when the order comes into force; and

(c) where it is not the appropriate court, send a copy of the order (together with such documents and information relating to the case as are considered useful) to the clerk of the appropriate court.

(4) Where a copy of a supervised attendance order has, under sub-paragraph (3)(a) above, been sent by registered post or by the recorded delivery service, an acknowledgement or certificate of delivery of a letter containing the copy order issued by the Post Office shall be sufficient evidence of the delivery of the letter on the day specified in such acknowledgement or certificate.

3.—(1) An offender in respect of whom a supervised attendance order is in force shall report to the supervising officer and notify him without delay of any change of address or in the times, if any, at which he usually works.

(2) Subject to paragraph 5(1) below, instructions given under a supervised attendance order shall be carried out during the period of twelve months beginning with the date of the order; but, unless revoked, the order shall remain in force until the offender has carried out the instructions given under it for the number of hours specified in it.

(3) The instructions given by the supervising officer under the order shall, so far as practicable, be such as to avoid any conflict with the offender's religious beliefs and any interference with the times, if any, at which he normally works or attends a school or other educational establishment.

4.—(1) If at any time while a supervised attendance order is in force in respect of any offender it appears to the appropriate court, on information from the supervising officer, that that offender has failed to comply with any of the requirements of paragraph 3 above or of the order (including any failure satisfactorily to carry out any instructions which he has been given by the supervising officer under the order), the court may issue a warrant for the arrest of that offender, or may, if it thinks fit, instead of issuing a warrant in the first instance issue a citation requiring the offender to appear before that court at such time as may be specified in the citation.

(2) If it is proved to the satisfaction of the court before which an offender is brought or appears in pursuance of sub-paragraph (1) above that he has failed without reasonable excuse to comply with any of the requirements of paragraph 3 above or of the order (including any failure satisfactorily to carry out any instructions which he has been given by the supervising officer under the order) the court may—

(a) revoke the order and impose such period of imprisonment not exceeding—

(i) in the case of a sheriff court, three months; and

(ii) in the case of a district court, 60 days,

as the court considers appropriate; or

412

(b) subject to section 235 of this Act and paragraph 2(2) above, vary the number of hours specified in the order.

(3) The evidence of one witness shall, for the purposes of sub-paragraph (2) above, be sufficient evidence.

5.—(1) Where a supervised attendance order is in force in respect of any offender and, on the application of that offender or of the supervising officer, it appears to the appropriate court that it would be in the interests of justice to do so having regard to circumstances which have arisen since the order was made, that court may—

(a) extend, in relation to the order, the period of twelve months specified in paragraph 3 above;

(b) subject to section 235 of this Act and paragraph 2(2) above, vary the numbers of hours specified in the order;

(c) revoke the order; or

(d) revoke the order and impose such period of imprisonment not exceeding—

      (i) in the case of a sheriff court, three months; and

      (ii) in the case of a district court, 60 days,

as the court considers appropriate.

(2) If the appropriate court is satisfied that the offender proposes to change, or has changed, his residence from the locality for the time being specified under paragraph 2(1)(a) above to another locality and—

(a) that court has been notified by the Secretary of State that arrangements exist for persons who reside in that other locality to carry out instructions under supervised attendance orders; and

(b) it appears to that court that provision can be made under those arrangements for him to carry out instructions under the order,

that court may, and on application of the supervising officer shall, amend the order by substituting that other locality for the locality for the time being specified in the order; and section 235 of this Act and this Schedule shall apply to the order as amended.

(3) Where the court proposes to exercise its powers under sub-paragraph (1)(a), (b) or (d) above otherwise than on the application of the offender, it shall issue a citation requiring him to appear before the court and, if he fails to appear, may issue a warrant for his arrest.

6.—(1) The Secretary of State may make rules for regulating the carrying out of the requirements of supervised attendance orders.

(2) Without prejudice to the generality of sub-paragraph (1) above, rules under this paragraph may—

(a) limit the number of hours during which the requirements of an order are to be met on any one day;

(b) make provision as to the reckoning of time for the purposes of the carrying out of these requirements;

(c) make provision for the payment of travelling and other expenses in connection with the carrying out of these requirements;

(d) provide for records to be kept of what has been done by any person carrying out these requirements.

(3) Rules under this paragraph shall be made by statutory instrument subject to annulment in pursuance of a resolution of either House of Parliament.

7. The Secretary of State shall lay before Parliament each year, or incorporate in annual reports he already makes, a report of the operation of section 235 of this Act and this Schedule.

8. In this Schedule—

"the appropriate court" in relation to a supervised attendance order, means the court having jurisdiction in the locality for the time being specified in the order under paragraph 2(1)(a) above, being a sheriff or district court according to whether the order has been made by a sheriff or district court, but in the case where an order has been made by a district court and there is no district court in that locality, the sheriff court;

"supervising officer" has the same meaning as in section 235 of this Act.

Section 279   SCHEDULE 8

DOCUMENTARY EVIDENCE IN CRIMINAL PROCEEDINGS

Production of copy documents

1.—(1) For the purposes of any criminal proceedings a copy of, or of a material part of, a document, purporting to be authenticated in such manner and by such person as may be prescribed, shall unless the court otherwise directs, be—

(a) deemed a true copy; and

(b) treated for evidential purposes as if it were the document, or the material part, itself, whether or not the document is still in existence.

(2) For the purposes of this paragraph it is immaterial how many removes there are between a copy and the original.

(3) In this paragraph "copy" includes a transcript or reproduction.

Statements in business documents

2.—(1) Except where it is a statement such as is mentioned in paragraph 3(b) and (c) below, a statement in a document shall be admissible in criminal proceedings as evidence of any fact or opinion of which direct oral evidence would be admissible, if the following conditions are satisfied—

(a) the document was created or received in the course of, or for the purposes of, a business or undertaking or in pursuance of the functions of the holder of a paid or unpaid office;

(b) the document is, or at any time was, kept by a business or undertaking or by or on behalf of the holder of such an office; and

(c) the statement was made on the basis of information supplied by a person (whether or not the maker of the statement) who had, or may reasonably be supposed to have had, personal knowledge of the matters dealt with in it.

(2) Sub-paragraph (1) above applies whether the information contained in the statement was supplied directly or indirectly unless, in the case of information supplied indirectly, it appears to the court that any person through whom it was so supplied did not both receive and supply it in the course of a business or undertaking or as or on behalf of the holder of a paid or unpaid office.

(3) Where in any proceedings a statement is admitted as evidence by virtue of this paragraph—

(a) any evidence which, if—

(i) the maker of the statement; or

(ii) where the statement was made on the basis of information supplied by another person, such supplier,

had been called as a witness, would have been admissible as relevant to the witness's credibility shall be so admissible in those proceedings;

(b) evidence may be given of any matter which, if the maker or as the case may be the supplier had been called as a witness, could have been put to him in cross-examination as relevant to his credibility but of which evidence could not have been adduced by the cross-examining party; and

(c) evidence tending to prove that the maker or as the case may be the supplier, whether before or after making the statement or supplying the information on the basis of which the statement was made, made (in whatever manner) some other representation which is inconsistent with the statement shall be admissible for the purpose of showing that he has contradicted himself.

(4) In sub-paragraph (3)(c) above, "representation" does not include a representation in a precognition.

3. A statement in a document shall be admissible in criminal proceedings as evidence of the fact that the statement was made if—

(a) the document satisfies the conditions mentioned in sub-paragraph (1)(a) and (b) of paragraph 2 above;

(b) the statement is made, whether directly or indirectly, by a person who in those proceedings is an accused; and

(c) the statement, being exculpatory only, exculpates the accused.

Documents kept by businesses etc.

4. Unless the court otherwise directs, a document may in any criminal proceedings be taken to be a document kept by a business or undertaking or by or on behalf of the holder of a paid or unpaid office if it is certified as such by a docquet in the prescribed form and purporting to be authenticated, in such manner as may be prescribed—

(a) by a person authorised to authenticate such a docquet on behalf of the business or undertaking by which; or

(b) by, or by a person authorised to authenticate such a docquet on behalf of, the office-holder by whom,

the document was kept.

Statements not contained in business documents

5.—(1) In any criminal proceedings, the evidence of an authorised person that—

(a) a document which satisfies the conditions mentioned in paragraph 2(1)(a) and (b) above does not contain a relevant statement as to a particular matter; or

(b) no document, within a category of documents satisfying those conditions, contains such a statement,

shall be admissible evidence whether or not the whole or any part of that document or of the documents within that category and satisfying those conditions has been produced in the proceedings.

(2) For the purposes of sub-paragraph (1) above, a relevant statement is a statement which is of the kind mentioned in paragraph 2(1)(c) above and which, in the ordinary course of events—

(a) the document; or

(b) a document within the category and satisfying the conditions mentioned in that sub-paragraph,

might reasonably have been expected to contain.

(3) The evidence referred to in sub-paragraph (1) above may, unless the court otherwise directs, be given by means of a certificate by the authorised person in the prescribed form and purporting to be authenticated in such manner as may be prescribed.

(4) In this paragraph, "authorised person" means a person authorised to give evidence—

(a) on behalf of the business or undertaking by which; or

(b) as or on behalf of the office-holder by or on behalf of whom,

the document is or was kept.

Additional evidence where evidence from business documents challenged

6.—(1) This sub-paragraph applies where—

(a) evidence has been admitted by virtue of paragraph 2(3) above; or

(b) the court has made a direction under paragraph 1(1), 4 or 5(3) above.

(2) Where sub-paragraph (1) above applies the judge may, without prejudice to sections 268 and 269 of this Act—

(a) in solemn proceedings, on a motion of the prosecutor or defence at any time before the commencement of the speeches to the jury;

(b) in summary proceedings, on such a motion at any time before the prosecutor proceeds to address the judge on the evidence,

permit him to lead additional evidence of such description as the judge may specify.

(3) Subsections (3) and (4) of section 268 of this Act shall apply in relation to sub-paragraph (2) above as they apply in relation to subsection (1) of that section.

General

7.—(1) Nothing in this Schedule—

(a) shall prejudice the admissibility of a statement made by a person other than in the course of giving oral evidence in court which is admissible otherwise than by virtue of this Schedule;

(b) shall affect the operation of the Bankers' Books Evidence Act 1879;

(c) shall apply to—

    (i) proceedings commenced; or

    (ii) where the proceedings consist of an application to the sheriff by virtue of section 42(2)(c) of the Social Work (Scotland) Act 1968, an application made,

before this Schedule comes into force.

For the purposes of sub-paragraph (1)(c)(i) above, solemn proceedings are commenced when the indictment is served.

8. In this Schedule—

"business" includes trade, profession or other occupation;

"criminal proceedings" includes any hearing by the sheriff under section 62 of the Children (Scotland) Act 1995 of an application for a finding as to whether grounds for the referral of a child's case to a children's hearing are established, in so far as the application relates to the commission of an offence by the child;

"document" includes, in addition to a document in writing—

    (a) any map, plan, graph or drawing;

    (b) any photograph;

    (c) any disc, tape, sound track or other device in which sounds or other data (not being visual images) are recorded so as to be capable, with or without the aid of some other equipment, of being reproduced therefrom; and

    (d) any film, negative, tape, disc or other device in which one or more visual images are recorded so as to be capable (as aforesaid) of being produced therefrom;

"film" includes a microfilm;

"made" includes allegedly made;

"prescribed" means prescribed by Act of Adjournal;

"statement" includes any representation (however made or expressed) of fact or opinion, including an instruction, order or request, but, except in paragraph 7(1)(a) above, does not include a statement which falls within one or more of the following descriptions—

    (a) a statement in a precognition;

    (b) a statement made for the purposes of or in connection with—

        (i) pending or contemplated criminal proceedings; or

        (ii) a criminal investigation; or

    (c) a statement made by an accused person in so far as it incriminates a co-accused;

and

"undertaking" includes any public or statutory undertaking, any local authority and any government department.

Section 280

SCHEDULE 9

CERTIFICATES AS TO PROOF OF CERTAIN ROUTINE MATTERS

Enactment	Persons who may purport to sign certificates	Matters which may be certified
The Parks Regulations Acts 1872 to 1974.	An officer authorised to do so by the Secretary of State.	That, on a date specified in the certificate— (a) copies of regulations made under those Acts, prohibiting such activity as may be so specified, were displayed at a location so specified; (b) in so far as those regulations prohibited persons from carrying out a specified activity in the park without written permission, such permission had not been given to a person so specified.
The Wireless Telegraphy Act 1949 (c. 54) Section 1 in so far as it relates to the installation or use of a television receiver (within the meaning of that Act); and section 1A in so far as it relates to an intended such use.	A person authorised to do so by the British Broadcasting Corporation.	In relation to an address specified in the certificate, whether on a date so specified any television licence (within the meaning of that Act) was, in records maintained on behalf of the Corporation in relation to such licences, recorded as being in force; and, if so, particulars so specified of such record of that licence.
The Building (Scotland) Act 1959 (c. 24) Section 6(1) (prohibition of construction, demolition or change of use of building without warrant).	An officer of a local authority authorised to do so by the authority.	In relation to a building specified in the certificate, that on a date so specified, there had not been obtained a warrant under section 6 of that Act for construction, demolition or, as the case may be, change of use.
Section 9(5) (offence of occupying or using a building before certificate of completion issued).	An officer of a local authority authorised to do so by the authority.	That, on a date specified in the certificate— (a) a certificate of completion under section 9 of that Act had not been issued in respect of a building so specified; and (b) written permission for occupation or use of the building so specified, had not been granted under subsection (6) of that section by the local authority.

417

Enactment	Persons who may purport to sign certificates	Matters which may be certified
The Firearms Act 1968 (c. 27).	[1] As respects the matters specified in paragraph (a) of column 3, a constable or a person employed by a police authority, if the constable or person is authorised to do so by the chief constable of the police force maintained for the authority's area; and as respects the matters specified in paragraph (b) of column 3, an officer authorised to do so by the Secretary of State or a member of staff of the Scottish Administration who is authorised to do so by the Scottish Ministers.	In relation to a person identified in the certificate, that on a date specified therein— (a) he held, or as the case may be did not hold, a firearm certificate or shotgun certificate (within the meaning of that Act); [1] (b) he possessed, or as the case may be did not possess, an authority (which as regards a possessed authority, shall be described in the certificate) given under section 5 of that Act by the Secretary of State or, by virtue of provision made under section 63 of the Scotland Act 1998, the Scottish Ministers.
The Misuse of Drugs Act 1971 (c. 38) Sections 4, 5, 6, 8, 9, 12, 13, 19 and 20 (various offences concerning controlled drugs).	Two analysts who have analysed the substance and each of whom is either a person possessing the qualifications (qualifying persons for appointments as public analysts) prescribed by regulations made under section 76 of the Food Act 1984 (c. 30), or section 30 of the Food Safety Act 1990 (c. 16), or a person authorised by the Secretary of State to make analyses for the purposes of the provisions of the Misuse of Drugs Act 1971 mentioned in column 1.	The type, classification, purity, weight and description of any particular substance identified in the certificate by reference to a label or otherwise, which is alleged to be a controlled drug within the meaning of section 2 of the Act referred to in column 1.

NOTE
[1] As amended by the Scotland Act 1998 (Consequential Modifications) (No. 2) Order 1999 (S.I. 1999 No. 1820) art. 4 and Sched. 2, para.122(5) (effective July 1, 1999).

Enactment	Persons who may purport to sign certificates	Matters which may be certified
The Immigration Act 1971 (c. 77) Section 24(1)(a) in so far as it relates to entry in breach of a deportation order, section 24(1)(b) and section 26(1)(f) in so far as it relates to a requirement of regulations (various offences concerning persons entering, or remaining in, the United Kingdom).	An officer authorised to do so by the Secretary of State.	In relation to a person identified in the certificate— (a) the date, place or means of his arrival in, or any removal of him from, the United Kingdom; (b) any limitation on, or condition attached to, any leave for him to enter or remain in the United Kingdom; (c) the date and method of service of any notice of, or of variations of conditions attached to, such leave.
The Control of Pollution Act 1974 (c. 40) [1]Section 30F (pollution offences), 32(1) (permitting trade effluent or sewage effluent to be discharged into such waters, etc.) or 49(1)(a) (causing accumulated deposit to be carried away in suspension in inland waters) or regulations under section 31(4) (prohibition on carrying on without consent certain activities likely to pollute waters in designated areas).	[1]Two persons authorised to do so by the Scottish Environment Protection Agency.	That they have analysed a sample identified in the certificate (by label or otherwise) and that the sample is of a nature and composition specified in the certificate.
The Licensing (Scotland) Act 1976 (c. 66).	A person authorised to do so by the Secretary of State.	In relation to a person identified in the certificate, that on a date specified therein he held, or as the case may be did not hold, a licence granted under that Act.
Customs and Excise Management Act 1979 The following provisions in so far as they have effect in relation to the prohibitions contained in sections 20 and 21 of the Forgery and Counterfeiting Act 1981 namely— Sections 50(2) and (3) Section 68; and Section 170 (various offences committed in connection with contraventions of prohibitions on the import and export of counterfeits or currency notes or protected coins).	Two officials authorised to do so by the Secretary of State, being officials of the authority or body which may lawfully issue the currency notes or protected coins referred to in column 3 hereof.	That the coin or note identified in the certificate by reference to a label or otherwise is a counterfeit of a currency note or protected coin; where "currency note" has the meaning assigned to it by section 27(1)(a) of the Forgery and Counterfeiting Act 1981, and "protected coin" means any coin which is customarily use as money in the United Kingdom, any of the Channel Islands, the Isle of Man or the Republic of Ireland.

Enactment	Persons who may purport to sign certificates	Matters which may be certified
The Forgery and Counterfeiting Act 1981 Sections 14 to 16 (certain offences relating to counterfeiting).	Two officials authorised to do so by the Secretary of State, being officials of the authority or body which may lawfully issue the currency notes or protected coins referred to in column 3 hereof.	That the coin or note identified in the certificate by reference to a label or otherwise is a counterfeit of a currency note or protected coin; where "currency note" has the meaning assigned to it by section 27(1)(a) of the Forgery and Counterfeiting Act 1981, and "protected coin" means any coin which is customarily used as money in the United Kingdom, any of the Channel Islands, the Isle of Man or the Republic of Ireland.
The Wildlife and Countryside Act 1981 (c. 69) Sections 1, 5, 6(1) to (3), 7, 8, 9(1), (2), (4) and (5), 11(1) and (2), 13(1) and (2) and 14 (certain offences relating to protection of wild animals or wild plants).	An officer of the appropriate authority (within the meaning of section 16(9) of that Act) authorised to do so by the authority.	In relation to a person specified in the certificate that, on a date so specified, he held, or as the case may be did not hold, a licence under section 16 of that Act and, where he held such a licence— (a) the purpose for which the licence was granted; and (b) the terms and conditions of the licence.
The Civic Government (Scotland) Act 1982 (c. 45).	A person authorised to do so by the Secretary of State.	In relation to a person identified in the certificate, that on a date specified therein he held, or as the case may be, did not hold, a licence under a provision so specified of that Act.
The Road Traffic Regulation Act 1984 (c. 27).	Two police officers who have tested the apparatus.	The accuracy of any particular— (a) speedometer fitted to a police vehicle; (b) odometer fitted to a police vehicle; (c) radar meter; or (d) apparatus for measuring speed, time or distance, identified in the certificate by reference to its number or otherwise.

Enactment	Persons who may purport to sign certificates	Matters which may be certified
The Video Recordings Act 1984 (c. 39) Sections 9 to 14 (offences relating to the supply and possession of video recordings in contravention of that Act).	[1]A person authorised to do so by the Secretary of State, being a person who has examined the record maintained in pursuance of arrangements made by the designated authority and in the case of a certificate in terms of— (a) sub-paragraph (a) in column 3, the video work mentioned in that sub-paragraph; (b) sub-paragraph (b) in that column, both video works mentioned in that sub-paragraph.	[1]That the record shows any of the following— (a) in respect of a video work (or part of a video work) contained in a video recording identified by the certificate, that by a date specified no classification certificate has been issued; (b) in respect of a video work which is the subject of a certificate under sub-paragraph (a) above, that the video work differs in a specified way from another video work contained in a video recording identified in the certificate under this sub-paragraph and that, on a date specified, a classification certificate was issued in respect of that other video work; (c) that, by a date specified, no classification certificate had been issued in respect of a video work having a particular title; (d) that, on a date specified, a classification certificate was issued in respect of a video work having a particular title and that a document which is identified in the certificate under this sub-paragraph is a copy of the classification certificate so issued; expressions used in column 2, or in this column, of this entry being construed in accordance with that Act; and in each of sub-paragraphs (a) to (d) above "specified" means specified in the certificate under that sub-paragraph.

NOTE

[1]Substituted by the Crime and Punishment (Scotland) Act 1997 (c. 48), s.30 with effect from August 1, 1997 in terms of the Crime and Punishment (Scotland) Act 1997 (Commencement and Transitional Provisions) Order 1997 (S.I. 1997 No. 1712) para. 3.

Enactment	Persons who may purport to sign certificates	Matters which may be certified
The Road Traffic Act 1988 (c. 52) Section 165(3) (offence of failure to give name and address and to produce vehicle documents when required by constable).	A constable.	In relation to a person specified in the certificate, that he failed, by such date as may be so specified, to produce such documents as may be so specified at a police station so specified.
The Control of Pollution (Amendment) Act 1989 (c. 14) Section 1 (offence of transporting controlled waste without registering).	An officer of a regulation authority within the meaning of that Act authorised to do so by the authority.	In relation to a person specified in the certificate, that on a date so specified he was not a registered carrier of controlled waste within the meaning of that Act.
The Environmental Protection Act 1990 (c. 43) Section 33(1)(a) and (b) (prohibition on harmful depositing, treatment or disposal of waste).	An officer of a waste regulation authority within the meaning of that Act authorised to do so by the authority.	In relation to a person specified in the certificate that, on a date so specified, he held, or as the case may be he did not hold, a waste management licence.
Section 34(1)(c) (duty of care as respects transfer of waste).	An officer of a waste regulation authority within the meaning of that Act authorised to do so by the authority.	In relation to a person specified in the certificate, that on a date so specified he was not an authorised person within the meaning of section 34(3)(b) or (d) of that Act.
[1] The Social Security Administration Act 1992 (c. 5) Section 112(1) (false statements etc. to obtain payments).	Any officer authorised to do so by the Secretary of State.	In relation to a person identified in the certificate— (a) the assessment, award, or nature of any benefit applied for by him; (b) the transmission or handing over of any payment to him.

NOTE
[1] Amended by the Criminal Procedure and Investigations Act 1996 (c. 25) s.73(4).

Enactment	Persons who may purport to sign certificates	Matters which may be certified
The Criminal Justice and Public Order Act 1994 (c. 33)		
Paragraph 5 of Schedule 6 (offence of making false statements to obtain certification as prisoner custody officer).	An officer authorised to do so by the Secretary of State.	That— (a) on a date specified in the certificate, an application for a certificate under section 114 of that Act was received from a person so specified; (b) the application contained a statement so specified; (c) a person so specified made, on a date so specified, a statement in writing in terms so specified.
This Act		
Sections 24(3) to (8), 25 and 27 to 29	The Clerk of Justiciary or the clerk of court.	In relation to a person specified in the certificate, that— (a) an order granting bail under that Act was made on a date so specified by a court so specified; (b) the order or a condition of it so specified was in force on a date so specified; (c) notice of the time and place appointed for a diet so specified was given to him in a manner so specified; (d) as respects a diet so specified, he failed to appear.
Section 150(8) (offence of failure of accused to appear at diet after due notice).	The clerk of court.	That, on a date specified in the certificate, he gave a person so specified, in a manner so specified, notice of the time and place appointed for a diet so specified.

"SCHEDULE 9A

THE COMMISSION: FURTHER PROVISIONS

Membership

1. Her Majesty shall, on the recommendation of the Secretary of State, appoint one of the members of the Commission to be the chairman of the Commission.

2.—(1) Subject to the following provisions of this paragraph, a person shall hold and vacate office as a member of the Commission, or as chairman of the Commission, in accordance with the terms of his appointment.

(2) An appointment as a member of the Commission may be full-time or part-time.

(3) The appointment of a person as a member of the Commission, or as chairman of the Commission, shall be for a fixed period of not longer than five years.

(4) Subject to sub-paragraph (5) below, a person whose term of appointment as a member of the Commission, or as chairman of the Commission, expires shall be eligible for re-appointment.

(5) No person may hold office as a member of the Commission for a continuous period which is longer than ten years.

(6) A person may at any time resign his office as a member of the Commission, or as chairman of the Commission, by notice in writing addressed to Her Majesty.

(7) Her Majesty may at any time remove a person from office as a member of the Commission if satisfied—

(a) that he has without reasonable excuse failed to discharge his functions as a member for a continuous period of three months beginning not earlier than six months before that time;

(b) that he has been convicted of a criminal offence;

(c) that a bankruptcy order has been made against him, or his estate has been sequestrated, or he has made a composition or arrangement with, or granted a trust deed for, his creditors; or

(d) that he is unable or unfit to discharge his functions as a member.

(8) If the chairman of the Commission ceases to be a member of the Commission he shall also cease to be chairman.

Members and employees

3.—(1) The Commission shall—

(a) pay to members of the Commission such remuneration;

(b) pay to or in respect of members of the Commission any such allowances, fees, expenses and gratuities; and

(c) pay towards the provisions of pensions to or in respect of members of the Commission any such sums,

as the Commission are required to pay by or in accordance with directions given by the Secretary of State.

(2) Where a member of the Commission was, immediately before becoming a member, a participant in a scheme under section 1 of the Superannuation Act 1972, the Minister for the Civil Service may determine that his term of office as a member shall be treated for the purposes of the scheme as if it were service in the employment or office by reference to which he was a participant in the scheme; and his rights under the scheme shall not be affected by sub-paragraph (1)(c) above.

(3) Where—

(a) a person ceases to hold office as a member of the Commission otherwise than on the expiry of his term of appointment; and

(b) it appears to the Secretary of State that there are special circumstances which make it right for him to receive compensation,

the Secretary of State may direct the Commission to make to him a payment of such amount as the Secretary of State may determine.

4.—(1) The Commission may appoint a chief executive and such other employees as the Commission think fit, subject to the consent of the Secretary of State as to their number and terms and conditions of service.

(2) The Commission shall—

(a) pay to employees of the Commission such remuneration; and

(b) pay to or in respect of employees of the Commission any such allowances, fees, expenses and gratuities,

as the Commission may, with the consent of the Secretary of State, determine.

(3) Employment by the Commission shall be included among the kinds of employment to which a scheme under section 1 of the Superannuation Act 1972 may apply.

5. The Commission shall pay to the Minister for the Civil Service, at such times as he may direct, such sums as he may determine in respect of any increase attributable to paragraph 3(2) or 4(3) above in the sums payable out of money provided by Parliament under the Superannuation Act 1972.

Procedure

6.—(1) The arrangements for the procedure of the Commission including the quorum for meetings) shall be such as the Commission may determine.

(2) The arrangements may provide for the discharge, under the general direction of the Commission, of any function of the Commission—

(a) in the case of the function specified in sub-paragraph (3) below, by a committee consisting of not fewer than three members of the Commission; and

(b) in any other case, by any committee of, or by one or more of the members or employees of, the Commission.

(3) The function referred to in sub-paragraph (2)(a) above is making a reference to the High Court under section 194B of this Act.

(4) The validity of any proceedings of the Commission (or of any committee of the Commission) shall not be affected by—

(a) any vacancy among the members of the Commission or in the office of chairman of the Commission; or

(b) any defect in the appointment of any person as a member of the Commission or as chairman of the Commission.

(5) Where—

(a) a document or other material has been produced to the Commission under section 194I of this Act, or they have been given access to a document or other material under that section, and the Commission have taken away the document or other material (or a copy of it); and

(b) the person who produced the document or other material to the Commission, or gave them access to it, has notified the Commission that he considers that its disclosure to others may be contrary to the interests of national security,

the Commission shall, after consulting that person, deal with the document or material (or copy) in a manner appropriate for safe-guarding the interests of national security.

Evidence

7. A document purporting to be—
(a) duly executed under the seal of the Commission; or
(b) signed on behalf of the Commission,
shall be received in evidence and, unless the contrary is proved, taken to be so executed or signed.

Annual reports and accounts

8.—(1) As soon as possible after the end of each financial year of the Commission, the Commission shall send to the Secretary of State a report on the discharge of their functions during that year.
(2) Such a report may include an account of the working of the provisions of Part XA of this Act and recommendations relating to any of those provisions.
(3) The Secretary of State shall lay before each House of Parliament, and cause to be published, a copy of every report sent to him under sub-paragraph (1).
9.—(1) The Commission shall—
(a) keep proper accounts and proper records in relation to the accounts; and
(b) prepare a statement of accounts in respect of each financial year of the Commission.
²(2) The statement of accounts shall contain such information and shall be in such form as the Secretary of State may direct.
³(3) The Commission shall send the statement of accounts to the Secretary of State within such period after the end of the financial year to which the statement relates as the Secretary of State may direct.
⁴(3A) The Scottish Ministers shall send the statement of accounts to the Auditor General for Scotland for auditing.
(4) [*Repealed by the Public Finance and Accountability (Scotland) Act (asp 1), s.26 and Sched. 4, para. 14(c).*]
10. For the purposes of this Schedule the Commission's financial year shall be the period of twelve months ending with 31st March; but the first financial year of the Commission shall be the period beginning with the date of establishment of the Commission and ending with the first 31st March which falls at least six months after that date.

Expenses

11. The Secretary of State shall defray the expenses of the Commission up to such amount as may be approved by him.".

NOTES
¹Inserted by s.25 of the Crime and Punishment (Scotland) Act 1997 with effect from April 1, 1999 as provided by the Crime and Punishment (Scotland) Act 1997 (Commencement No. 5 and Transitional Provisions and Savings) Order 1999 (S.I. 1999 No. 652).
²As amended by the Scotland Act 1998 (Consequential Modifications) (No. 2) Order 1999 (S.I. 1999 No. 1820) art. 4 and Sched. 2, para.122(3) (effective July 1, 1999).
³As amended by the Public Finance and Accountability (Scotland) Act (asp 1), s.26 and Sched. 4, para. 14(a).

[4]As inserted by the Public Finance and Accountability(Scotland) Act (asp 1), s.26 and Sched. 4, para. 14(b).

Section 292(1)   SCHEDULE 10

Certain Offences Triable only Summarily

Night Poaching Act 1828 (c. 69)

1. Offences under section 1 of the Night Poaching Act 1828 (taking or destroying game or rabbits by night or entering land for that purpose).

Public Meeting Act 1908 (c. 66)

2. Offences under section 1(1) of the Public Meeting Act 1908 (endeavour to break up a public meeting).

Post Office Act 1953 (c. 36)

3. Offences under section 56 of the Post Office Act 1953 (criminal diversions of letters from addressee).

Betting, Gaming and Lotteries Act 1963 (c. 2)

4. Offences under the following provisions of the Betting, Gaming and Lotteries Act 1963—
(a) section 7 (restriction of betting on dog racecourses);
(b) section 10(5) (advertising licensed betting offices);
(c) section 11(6) (person holding bookmaker's or betting agency permit employing a person disqualified from holding such a permit);
(d) section 18(2) (making unauthorised charges to bookmakers on licensed track);
(e) section 19 (occupiers of licensed tracks not to have any interest in bookmaker thereon);
(f) section 21 (betting with young persons); and
(g) section 22 (betting circulars not to be sent to young persons).

Theatres Act 1968 (c. 54)

5. Offences under section 6 of the Theatres Act 1968 (provocation of breach of the peace by means of public performance of play).

Criminal Law (Consolidation) (Scotland) Act 1995 (c. 39)

6. Offences under section 12(1) of the Criminal Law (Consolidation) (Scotland) Act 1995 (allowing child under 16 to be in brothel).

TABLE OF DERIVATIONS

Notes: 1. This Table shows the derivation of the provisions of the Bill.
2. The following abbreviations are used in the Table:

Acts of Parliament

1975	= Criminal Procedure (Scotland) Act 1975 (c. 21)
1977	= Criminal Law Act 1977 (c. 45)
1978	= Community Service by Offenders (Scotland) Act 1978 (c. 49)
1980B	= Bail (Scotland) Act 1980 (c. 4)
1980LR	= Law Reform (Miscellaneous Provisions) (Scotland) Act 1980 (c. 55)
1980CJ	= Criminal Justice (Scotland) Act 1980 (c. 62)
1982	= Criminal Justice Act 1982 (c. 48)
1983	= Mental Health (Amendment) (Scotland) Act 1983 (c. 39)
1984	= Mental Health (Scotland) Act 1984 (c. 36)
1985	= Law Reform (Miscellaneous Provisions) (Scotland) Act 1985 (c. 73)
1987	= Criminal Justice (Scotland) Act 1987 (c. 41)
1988	= Criminal Justice Act 1988 (c. 33)
1990	= Law Reform (Miscellaneous Provisions) (Scotland) Act 1990 (c. 40)
1991	= Criminal Justice Act 1991 (c. 53)
1993P	= Prisoners and Criminal Proceedings (Scotland) Act 1993 (c. 9)
1993CJ	= Criminal Justice Act 1993 (c. 36)
1994	= Criminal Justice and Public Order Act 1994 (c. 33)
1995	= Criminal Justice (Scotland) Act 1995 (c. 20)
1995C	= Children (Scotland) Act 1995 (c. 36)

Provision	Derivation
1(1)	Court of Session (Scotland) Act 1830 (11 Geo 4 & 1 Will 4 c. 69) s. 18.
(2)	1975 s.113(1).
(3)	1975 s.113(2).
(4), (5)	1975 s.113(4).
2	1975 s.114; 1987 s.57(2).
3(1)	1975 s.2(1).
(2)	1975 s.112; 1987 s.57(1).
(3) to (5)	1975 s.2(2) to (4); 1987 s.58(1).
(6)	1975 s.8; Drafting.
4(1)	1975 ss.3(1), 288(1).
(2)	1975 ss.3(4), 288(5); 1990 s.60; drafting.
(3)	1975 ss.3(2), 288(2).
(4)	1975 s.288(4); drafting.
5(1)	Drafting.
(2)	1975 s.289; 1977 Sch. 11 §44.
(3)	1975 s.290.
(4)	1975 s.291(2), (3); 1980 s.38.
6(1)	District Courts (Scotland) Act 1975 (1975 c. 20) s.2(1), (1A).
(2)	District Courts (Scotland) Act 1975 (1975 c. 20) s.2(2).
(3)	District Courts (Scotland) Act 1975 (1975 c. 20)(1) (part).
(4)	District Courts (Scotland) Act 1975 (1975 c.20) s.6(2) (part), (3) (part).
(5)	District Courts (Scotland) Act 1975 (1975 c. 20) s.6(9).
(6)	Drafting.
7(1)	District Courts (Scotland) Act 1975 (1975 c. 20) s.3(1).
(2)	District Courts (Scotland) Act 1975 (1975 c. 20) s.3(4).
(3)	1980CJ s.7(1); 1995 s.60.
(4)	1980CJ s.7(3); 1982 Sch. 7 §14.
(5)	District Courts (Scotland) Act 1975 (1975 c. 20) s.3(2).
(6)	1975 s.284; 1977 Sch. 11 §3; 1982 Sch. 7 §§4, 5.
(7)	1980CJ s.7(1A); 1995 s.60.
(8)	1975 c.285; 1980CJ s.7(3); 1982 Sch. 7 §6.
(9), (10)	1975 s.286.
8	1980B s.10; 1985 s.21.
9(1)	1975 ss.4(1), 3(3), 287(1).
(2)	1975 ss.4(2), 287(2).
(3)	1975 ss.4(3), 287(3).
(4), (5)	1975 ss.4(4), (5), 287(4), (5).
10	1975 s.5; 1987 Sch. 1 §4.
11(1), (2)	1975 s.6(1), (2).
(3)	1975 s.6(3); 1995 Sch. 6 §7.
(4)	1975 ss.7(1), (2), 292(1), (2).
12	1975 ss.9, 293.
13	1980CJ s.1.
14(1)	1980CJ s.2(1); 1994 s.129(1).
(2)	1980CJ s.2(2); 1987 Sch. 1 §16(a), (b), 1993P Sch. 7.
(3)	1980CJ s.2(3).
(4)	1980CJ s.2(3A); 1987 Sch. 1 §16(c); 1994 Sch. 10 §47; 1995 s.59.
(5)	1980CJ s.2(3B); 1994 Sch. 10 §47.
(6)	1980CJ s.2(4); 1994 s.129(2).
(7) to (9)	1980CJ s.2(5) to (7).
15(1), (2)	1980CJ s.3(1); 1994 s.129(3).
(3) to (5)	1980CJ s.3(2) to (4).
(6)	1980CJ s.3(5); 1985 Sch. 2 §23.
16	1980CJ s.5.

Provision	Derivation
17(1)	1975 ss.19(1), 305; 1980CJ Sch. 7 §25; 1995 Sch. 6 §§11, 106.
18(1), (2)	1993P s.28(1), (2).
(3)	1993P s.28(3); 1995 s.58(2), Sch. 6 §179(5).
(4)	1993P s.28(3A), (3C); 1995 s.58(3).
(5)	1993P s.28(3B); 1995 s.58(3).
(6)	1993P s.28(4); 1995 s.58(4).
(7), (8)	1993P s.28(5), (6).
19	1993P s.28A; 1995 s.58(5).
20	1993P s.28B; 1995 s.58(5).
21(1)	1975 ss.18(1), 294(1).
(2) to (5)	1975 ss.18(2) to (5), 294(2) to (5); 1980B s.7(1), (2).
22(1) to (3)	1975 s.295(1), (2); 1980B s.8.
(4), (5)	1975 ss.294(4), (5), 295(3); 1980B ss.7(2), 8.
23(1)	1975 s.26(2); 1995 Sch. 6 §15(a).
(2)	1975 s.26(3); 1995 Sch. 6 §15(b).
(3)	1975 s.26(4).
(4)	1975 s.27.
(5)	1975 s.28(1).
(6)	1975 s.298(1) (part).
(7)	1975 ss.28(2), 298(2).
(8)	1975 ss.28(3), 298(3); 1980CJ Sch. 7 §§26, 51.
24(1)	1975 ss.26(1), 298(1) (part).
(2)	1975 s.35.
(3)	1980B s.1(1); drafting.
(4) to (8)	1980B s.1(2) to (5); 1995 s.1.
25	1980B s.2.
26	1975 s.28A; 1995 s.3.
27(1), (2)	1980B s.3(1), (2); 1995 s.2(2), (3).
(3) to (6)	1980B s.3(2A) to (2D); 1995 s.2(4).
(7) to (10)	1980B s.3(3) to (6).
(11)	1980B s.3(12).
28	1980B s.3(7) to (11).
29	1980B s.4.
30(1)	1975 ss.30(1), 299(1); 1980B s.1(4).
(2)	1975 ss.30(2), 299(2); 1980B Sch. 1 §§4, 6.
(3)	1975 ss.30(3), 299(3).
(4)	1975 ss.30(4), 299(4); 1980B s.1(4).
31	1975 ss.30A, 299A; 1995 s.4.
32(1)	1975 ss.31(1), 300(1) (part).
(2)	1975 ss.31(2), 300(1) (part); 1987 s.62(4)(a).
(3), (4)	1975 ss.31(3), (4), 300(2), (3).
(5)	1975 ss.31(4A), 300(3A); 1995 Sch. 6 §§16, 105(a).
(6)	1975 ss.31(5), 300(6) (part).
(7), (8)	1975 ss.33(1), 300(4); 1995 Sch. 6 §§17(a), 105(b).
(9)	1975 s.300(4A); 1987 s.62(4)(b).
(10)	1975 s.33(2); 1995 Sch.6 §17(b).
33	1975 s.32, 300(6)(part).
34(1)	1975 s.12.
(2)	1975 s.74(7).
35(1), (2)	1975 s.19(2) (part), (3), s.305(3).
(3)	1975 s.20(1); 1980CJ s.6(1).
(4)	1975 s.20(3); 1980CJ s.6(1).
(5) to (7)	1975 s.20(3A) to (3C); 1980CJ s.6(1).
(8)	1975 s.20(4).
36(1) to (4)	1975 s.20A(1); 1980CJ s.6(2); 1995 s.10(2).

Provision	Derivation
(5)	1975 s.20A(2); 1980CJ s.6(2).
(6)	1975 s.20A(3), (3A); 1980CJ s.6(2); 1995 s.10(3).
(7)	1975 s.20A(4); 1980CJ s.6(2).
(8)	1975 s.20A(5); 1980CJ s.6(2).
(9)	1975 s.20A(6); 1980CJ s.6(2).
(10), (11)	1975 s.20A(7), (8); 1995 s.10(4).
37(1)	1975 s.20B(1); 1980CJ s.6(2); 1993P Sch. 6 §1(2).
(2) to (4)	1975 s.20B(1A) to (1C); 1993P Sch. 5 §1(2).
(5)	1975 s.20B(2); 1993P Sch. 5 §1(2).
(6)	1975 s.20B(3); 1980CJ s.6(2).
(7), (8)	1975 s.20B(5); 1980CJ s.6(2).
(9)	1975 s.20B(6); 1980CJ s.6(2).
(10)	1975 s.20B(9); 1980CJ s.6(2); 1995 Sch. 6 §13.
38	1975 s.20B(4), (7) and (8); 1980CJ s.6(2).
39	1975 s.21.
40	1975 s.22.
41	1975 ss.170, 369.
42(1)	Social Work (Scotland) Act 1968 (1968 c. 49) s.31(1); Health and Social Services and Social Security Adjudications Act 1983 (1983 c. 41) Sch. 2 §7.
(2) to (4)	1975 ss.39(1) to (3), 307(1) to (3).
(5), (6)	1975 ss.39(4), (5), 307(4), (5); 1995C Sch. 4 §24(5), (11).
(7), (8)	1975 ss.40(1), (2), 308(1), (2).
(9), (10)	1975 ss.38, 306.
43(1) to (3)	1975 s.296(1); 1980B s.9(a); 1995 Sch. 6 §104.
(4)	1975 s.296(2); 1995 Sch. 6 §104.
(5), (6)	1975 s.296(3), (4); 1995C Sch.4 §24(9).
(7), (8)	1975 s.296(5), (6); 1980B s.9(b).
44(1)	1975 s.413(1); 1987 s.59(1); 1993P Sch. 5 §1(32); 1995 Sch. 6 §141; 1995C Sch. 4 §24(17).
(2)	1975 s.413(2); 1987 s.59(1).
(3), (4)	1975 s.413(3A), (4); 1987 s.59(1); 1995C Sch. 4 §24(17).
(5)	1975 s.413(5); 1993P s.8.
(6) to (8)	1975 s.413(6A) to (6C); 1993P s.8; 1995C Sch. 4 §24(17).
(9)	1975 s.413(7); 1987 s.59(1); 1993P Sch.5 §1(32).
(10)	1975 s.413(8); 1987 s.59(1).
45(1) to (4)	1975 ss.37(1) to (3), 304(1) to (3).
(5)	1975 ss.37(4), 304(4); 1995C Sch. 4 §24(4), (10).
46(1), (2)	1975 ss.171(1), (2), 368(1), (2); 1995C Sch. 4 §24(7), (15); drafting.
(3)	1975 ss.171(3), 368(3); Sexual Offences (Scotland) Act (c. 67) Sch. 1; Incest and Related Offences (Scotland) Act 1986 (c. 36) Sch. 1 §§1, 3; 1988 Sch. 15 §48.
(4)	1975 ss.171(4), 368(4).
(5), (6)	1975 ss.171(1), (2), 368(1), (2); 1995C Sch. 4 §24(7), (15).
(7)	1975 ss.171(6), 368(6).
47(1) to (3)	1975 ss.169(1), 374(1), 1980CJ s.22.
(4)	1975 ss.169(2), 374(2); 1980CJ s.22; Cable and Broadcasting Act 1986 (c. 46) Sch. 5 §30; Broadcasting Act 1990 (c. 42) Sch. 20 §21.
(5), (6)	1975 ss.169(3), (4), 374(3), (4); 1980CJ s.22.
48	1975 ss.168, 364; 1980CJ Sch. 7 §§34, 57; 1995C Sch. 4 §24(6), (14).
49(1)	1975 ss.173(1), 372(1); Local Government etc. (Scotland) Act 1994 (c. 39) Sch. 13 §97(2).
(2)	1975 ss.173(2), 372(2).
(3)	1975 ss.173(3), 372(3); 1980CJ Sch. 7 §35; Local Government etc. (Scotland) Act 1994 (c. 39) Sch. 13 §97(2).
(4), (5)	1975 ss.173(4), (5), 372(4), (5).

Provision	Derivation
(6), (7)	1975 s.373; Local Government etc. (Scotland) Act 1994 (c. 39) Sch. 13 §97(2).
50(1), (2)	1975 ss.165, 361.
(3), (4)	1975 ss.166(1), (2), 362(1), (2); 1995 Sch. 6 §64.
(5)	1975 ss.167, 363.
(6)	1975 ss.172, 371.
51(1)	1975 ss.23(1), s.329(1); 1987 s.62(2); 1995 Sch. 6 §14; 1995C Sch. 4 §24(13).
(2) to (4)	1975 ss.23(2) to (4), 329(2) to (4); 1995 Sch. 6 §14; 1995C Sch. 4 §24(13).
52(1)	1975 ss.175(2), 376(5).
(2)	1975 ss.25(1), 330(1).
(3)	1975 ss.25(2), 330(2); 1984 Sch. 3 §§24, 31.
(4), (5)	1975 ss.25(3), (4), 330(3), (4).
(6), (7)	1975 ss.25(5), (6), 330(5), (6); 1995 s.53.
53(1)	1974 ss.174A(1) (part), 375A(1) (part); 1983 s.34(a); 1984 Sch. 3 §§25, 32.
(2) to (10)	1975 ss.174A(2) to (10), 375A(3) to (11); 1983 s.34(a).
(11), (12)	1975 ss.174A(1) (part), 375A(1) (part), (2); 1983 s.34(a).
54(1) to (4)	1975 ss.174(1) to (1C), 375(2) to (2C); 1995 s.47(1).
(5)	1975 ss.174(5), 375(4).
(6)	1975 ss.174(2), 375(3A); 1995 s.48, Sch. 6 §65.
(7)	1975 s.375(3); 1995 Sch. 6 §132.
(8)	Drafting.
55	1975 ss.174ZA, 375ZA; 1995 s.49(1), (2).
56	1975 ss.174ZB, 375ZB; 1995 s.49(1), (2).
57(1) to (4)	1975 ss.174ZC, 375ZC; 1995 s.50(1), (2).
(5)	Drafting.
58(1), (2)	1975 ss.175(1), 376(1); 1983 Sch. 2 §§31, 34(a); 1984 Sch. 3 §§26, 33.
(3)	1975 s.376(3); 1995 Sch. 6 §133(b).
(4)	1975 ss.175(3), 376(6).
(5)	1975 ss.175(4), 376(7).
(6)	1975 ss.175(5), 376(8); 1983 Sch. 2 §§31, 34.
(7)	1975 ss.175(6), 376(9); 1983 Sch. 2 §§31, 34.
(8)	1975 ss.175(7), 376(10); 1983 Sch. 2 §§31, 34.
(9)	1975 ss.177, 378; 1995C Sch. 4 §24(8), (16).
(10)	1975 s.376(4).
59(1)	1975 ss.178(1), 379(1); 1983 s.22(2); 1984 Sch. 3 §§28, 35; 1995 s.54.
(2)	1975 ss.178(2), 379(2); 1983 Sch. 2 §§33, 36; 1984 Sch. 3 §§28, 35.
(3)	1975 ss.178(3), 379(3); 1983 Sch. 2 §§33, 36; 1984 Sch. 3 §§28, 35; 1995 Sch. 6 §§67, 135.
60	1975 ss.280, 443; 1980CJ Sch. 2 §32, Sch. 3 §2; 1983 s.34(b), (d).
61(1)	1975 ss.176(1), 377(1); 1983 Sch. 2 §§32, 35; 1984 Sch. 3 §§27, 34; 1995 Sch. 6 §§66(a), 134(a).
(2)	1975 ss.176(1A), 377(1A); 1983 s.35(a), (b).
(3)	1975 ss.176(2), 377(2); 1995 Sch. 6 §§66(b), 134(b).
(4)	1975 ss.176(3), 377(3).
(5)	1975 ss.176(4), 377(4); 1995 Sch. 6 §§66(c), 134(c).
62	1975 ss.174ZD, 375ZD, 1995 s.51.
63(1) to (5)	1975 ss.174ZE, 375ZE; 1995 s.52.
(6)	Drafting.
64(1) to (4)	1975 s.41.
(5)	1975 s.57.
(6)	Drafting.
65(1) to (3)	1975 s.101(1); 1980CJ s.14(1).
(4) to (9)	1975 s.101(2) to (6); 1980CJ s.14(1).
(10)	1975 s.101(1A); 1995 s.15.
66(1), (2)	1975 s.69(1); 1980CJ Sch. 4 §2; 1995 Sch. 6 §26(a).
(3)	1975 s.69(2); 1995 Sch. 6 §26(b).

Provision	Derivation
(4)	1975 s.70.
(5)	1975 s.78(1); 1980CJ Sch. 4 §8; 1995 Sch. 6 §30.
(6)	1975 s.75; 1980CJ Sch. 4 §4; 1995 s.13(1).
(7)	1975 s.71; 1980CJ Sch. 7 §27.
(8)	1975 s.73(1); 1995 Sch. 6 §28.
(9)	1975 s.72(1); 1995 Sch. 5 §27(a), (b).
(10)	1975 s.72(2); 1995 Sch. 6 §27(c).
(11)	1975 s.73(2).
(12) to (14)	1975 s.58; 1995 Sch. 6 §22.
67(1)	1975 s.79(1) (part); 1995 Sch. 6 §31.
(2)	1975 s.79(2).
(3)	1975 s.80(1); 1980CJ Sch. 4 §9; 1995 Sch. 6 §32.
(4)	1975 s.80(2); 1980CJ Sch. 4 §9.
(5)	1975 s.81; 1980CJ Sch. 7 §28; 1995 Sch. 6 §33.
(6)	1975 s.82A; 1980CJ s.27.
68(1)	1975 s.78(2); 1980CJ Sch. 4 §8.
(2)	1975 s.83; 1980CJ Sch. 4 §11.
(3), (4)	1975 s.84; 1980CJ Sch. 4 §12; 1995 s.23.
69(1)	1975 s.68(1).
(2)	1975 s.68(2); 1995 Sch. 6 §25.
(3)	1975 s.68(3) (part); 1980CJ Sch. 4 §1.
(4)	1975 s.68(4) (part); 1995 Sch. 6 §25.
(5)	1975 s.68(3) (part) and (4) (part); 1980CJ Sch. 4 §1; 1995 Sch. 6 §25.
70(1)	Drafting.
(2), (3)	1975 s.74(1).
(4)	1975 s.74(2).
(5)	1975 s.74(4); 1980CJ Sch. 4 §3(b).
(6)	1975 s.74(5).
(7)	1975 ss.74(6), 103(4).
(8)	1975 s.74(8).
71	1975 s.75A; 1995 s.13(2).
72(1)	1975 s.76(1) (part) and (2), s.108(1) (part); 1980CJ Sch. 4 §5, §19; 1985 Sch. 2 §18; 1993P s.39(2), Sch. 5 §1(3); 1995 s.13(3)(a), Sch. 6 §39.
(2)	1975 s.76(1) (part); 1980CJ Sch. 4 §5.
(3) to (6)	1975 s.76(3) to (5), (7).
73(1), (2)	1975 s.76(6) (part).
(3) to (6)	1975 s.76(6A) to (6D); 1995 s.13(3)(b).
(7)	1975 s.109 (part).
(8)	1975 s.76(6) (part); drafting.
74	1975 s.76A; 1980CJ Sch. 4 §5; 1995 s.13(4).
75	1975 s.111A; 1980CJ Sch. 7 §31.
76	1975 s.102; 1980CJ s.16.
77(1)	1975 s.103(1) and (4), s.124 (part); 1980CJ Sch. 4 §14; 1995 Sch. 6 §38.
(2), (3)	1975 s.103(2), (3); 1980CJ Sch. 4 §14.
78(1)	1975 s.82(1) (part); Act of Adjournal (Consolidation) 1988 (S.I. 1988/110) s.68 (part); 1980CJ s.13; 1995 Sch. 6 §34(a).
(2)	1975 s.82(1A); 1995 s.11.
(3)	1975 s.82(1) (part); Act of Adjournal (Consolidation) 1988 (S.I. 1988/110) s.68 (part); 1980CJ s.13; 1995 Sch. 6 §34(a).
(4)	1975 s.82(2); 1980CJ Sch. 4 §10; 1995 Sch. 6 §34(b).
(5)	1975 s.82(3); 1980CJ Sch. 4 §10.
79(1)	1975 s.108(1) (part) and (2); 1980CJ Sch. 4 §19; 1985 Sch. 2 §18; 1995 Sch. 6 §39.
(2)	1975 s.108(1) (part); 1980CJ Sch. 4 §19; 1985 Sch. 2 §18; 1995 Sch. 6 §39.
80(1)	1975 s.77; 1980CJ Sch. 4 §6; 1995 Sch. 6 §29.
(2) to (4)	1975 s.77A(1) to (3); 1980CJ Sch. 4 §7.

Provision	Derivation
(5), (6)	1975 s.77A(4), drafting; 1980CJ Sch. 4 §7.
81(1)	1975 s.127(1); 1980CJ Sch. 4 §27; 1995 Sch. 6 §44(a).
(2)	1975 s.127(1ZA); 1995 Sch. 6 §44(b).
(3)	1975 s.127(1A); 1980CJ s.18(1).
(4) to (6)	1975 s.127(2) to (4); 1995 Sch. 6 §44(c).
(7)	1975 s.127(5); 1995 Sch. 6 §44(d).
82	1975 s.111.
83	1975 s.114A; 1995 Sch. 6 §41.
84(1)	1975 s.85; 1995 Sch. 6 §35.
(2)	1975 s.86(1); 1987 Sch. 1 §5.
(3)	1975 s.86(2); 1987 Sch. 1 §5.
(4)	1975 s.89; 1985 Sch. 2 §16.
(5)	1975 s.90; 1985 Sch. 2 §16.
(6)	1975 s.91; 1980LR Sch. 2 §6; 1985 Sch. 2 §16.
(7)	1975 s.92.
(8)	1975 s.93; 1995 Sch. 6 §36.
(9)	1975 s.94.
(10)	1975 s.95.
85(1)	1975 s.96(1); 1980CJ Sch. 4 §13.
(2)	1975 s.96(2).
(3)	1975 s.97.
(4), (5)	1975 s.98; 1980CJ Sch. 7 §29; 1985 Sch. 2 §17.
(6), (7)	1975 s.99; 1980LR s.2(3).
(8)	1975 s.100(1); 1995 Sch. 6 §37.
86(1)	1975 s.130(3A); 1995 s.8.
(2)	1975 s.130(4).
(3)	1975 s.130(5); 1980LR Sch. 2 §7.
(4)	1975 s.130(6).
87	1975 s.128; 1995 s.30(2), (3).
88(1)	1975 s.125; 1995 Sch. 6 §43.
(2)	1975 s.129 (part); 1987 Sch. 1 §7; 1995 Sch. 6 §45.
(3)	1975 s.131, drafting.
(4)	1975 s.132(1).
(5), (6)	1975 s.135(1); 1995 Sch. 6 §48(a), (b); drafting.
(7)	1975 s.133.
(8)	1975 s.137.
89	1975 s.135(2) to (4); 1995 Sch. 6 §48(c).
90	1975 s.134; 1995 Sch. 6 §47.
91	1975 s.136.
92(1), (2)	1975 s.145(1); 1980CJ s.21.
(3)	1975 s.145(3).
93	1975 s.274; 1980CJ Sch. 8; 1995 Sch. 6 §98.
94	1975 s.275; 1993P Sch. 5 §1(27).
95	1975 s.137A; 1993P Sch. 1 §1(5).
96	1975 s.123.
97(1)	1975 s.140A(1); 1980CJ s.19(1); 1995 Sch.6 §49.
(2), (3)	1975 s.140A(3), (4); 1980CJ s.19(1).
(4)	1975 s.140A(2); 1980CJ s.19(1).
98	1975 s.152.
99(1)	1975 s.153(2); 1980CJ s.24(1).
(2), (3)	1975 s.153(3); 1980CJ s.24(1); 1995 Sch. 6 §57(b).
(4)	1975 s.153(3A); 1980CJ s.24(1).
(5)	1975 s.153(4).
(6)	1975 s.155A; 1993P s.40(1).
100(1), (2)	1975 s.154; 1980CJ s.24(2).

Provision	Derivation
(3)	1975 s.155 (part); drafting.
101(1)	1975 s.160(1).
(2)	1975 ss.160(2), 161(5); 1995 s.24(3).
(3)	1975 s.161(1).
(4), (5)	1975 s.161(2).
(6)	1975 s.161(4).
(7)	1975 s.159(2)
(8)	1975 s.161(3).
102(1)	1975 s.156(1) and (2); 1995 Sch. 6 §58.
(2)	1975 s.157(1); 1995 Sch. 6 §59.
(3)	1975 ss.156(3) and 157(3).
(4)	1975 s.156(6).
(5)	1975 s.158.
103(1)	1975 s.245(2); 1987 Sch. 1 §13(2); drafting.
(2)	1975 s.245(1); 1987 Sch. 1 §13(1); 1995 s.43(1).
(3)	1975 s.245(1A); 1995 s.43(1).
(4)	1975 s.245(3); 1980CJ Sch. 8.
(5)	1975 ss.247 (part), 248; 1980CJ Sch. 2 §15, Sch. 8.
(6)	1975 s.247 (part); 1980CJ Sch. 2 §15, Sch. 8.
(7)	1975 s.249.
(8)	1975 s.250.
104(1)	1975 s.252; 1980CJ Sch. 2 §16; 1993P Sch. 5 §1(18).
(2), (3)	1975 s.253; 1980CJ Sch. 8.
105(1) to (4)	1975 s.251(1) to (4).
(5)	1975 s.251(5); 1980CJ Sch. 7 §44.
(6)	1975 s.251(6).
106(1), (2)	1975 s.228(1); 1980CJ Sch. 2 §1; 1993CJ s.68(1); 1995 s.42(1).
(3)	1975 s.228(2); 1980CJ Sch. 2 §1.
(4)	1975 s.270(1).
(5) to (9)	1975 s.270(2) to (4); 1980CJ Sch. 2 §26; 1995 Sch. 6 §96.
107	1975 s.230A; 1995 s.42(2).
108	1975 s.228A; 1993P s,42(1); 1993CJ s.68(2).
109(1)	1975 s.231(1) (part) and (2); 1980CJ Sch. 2 §3; 1987 s.45(6)(a).
(2)	1975 s.231(1) (part); 1980CJ Sch. 2 §3; 1987 s.45(6)(a).
(3)	1975 s.231(3); 1980CJ Sch. 2 §3.
(4), (5)	1975 s.231(4); 1987 s.45(6)(b).
(6)	1975 s.231(5); 1987 s.45(6)(c).
110(1), (2)	1975 s.233(1); 1980CJ Sch. 2 §5; 1993P Sch. 5 §1(9); 1993CJ Sch. 5 §2(4).
(3), (4)	1975 s.233(2), (3); 1980CJ Sch. 2 §5.
(5)	1975 s.233(3A); 1995 s.42(3).
(6)	1975 s.233(4); 1980CJ Sch. 2§5; 1993CJ Sch. 5 §2(4).
111	1975 s.236B; 1980CJ Sch. 2 §8; 1993P Sch. 5 §1(11).
112(1)	1975 s.238(1); 1993CJ Sch. 5 §2(5); 1995 s.5(2).
(2)	1975 s.2338(1A); 1995 s.5(3).
(3), (4)	1975 s.238(2); 1980CJ Sch. 2 §10(a); 1995 Sch. 6 §81.
(5)	1975 s.238(3); 1980CJ Sch. 2 §10(b).
113	1975 s.236A; 1980CJ Sch. 2 §8; 1995 Sch. 6 §78.
114	1975 s.235; 1995 Sch. 6 §77.
115(1), (2)	1975 s.234(1); 1980CJ Sch. 8.
(3), (4)	1975 s.234(2), (3); 1980CJ Sch. 8.
116(1)	1975 s.244(1); 1980CJ Sch. 2 §13.
(2)	1975 s.244(2); 1980CJ Sch. 2 §13; 1993CJ Sch. 5 §2(6).
117(1), (2)	1975 s.241; 1980CJ Sch. 7 §41.
(3)	1975 s.240; 1993P Sch. 5 §1(15); 1995 Sch. 6 §83.
(4), (5), (6)	1975 s.242; 1980CJ Sch. 7 §42.

Provision	Derivation
(7)	1975 s.242A; 1993P Sch. 5 §1(16).
(8)	1975 s.243; 1980CJ Sch. 7; 1993P Sch. 5 §1(17).
(9)	1975 s.239(1); 1980CJ Sch. 2 §11; 1993 Sch. 5 §1(14); 1995 Sch. 6 §82.
118(1), (2)	1975 s.254(1); 1980CJ Sch. 2 §18; 1993CH Sch. 5 §2(7).
(3)	1975 s.254(2); 1993CJ Sch. 5 §2(7).
(4)	1975 s.254(3), (4A); 1993CJ Sch. 5 §2(7).
(5)	1975 s.254(4); 1993CJ Sch. 5 §2(7); 1995 Sch. 6 §85.
(6)	1975 s.254(5); 1995 Sch. 6 §85.
(7)	1975 s.254A(1); 1995 s.34(1).
(8)	1975 s.254B; 1995 Sch. 6 §86.
119(1)	1975 s.255(1) (part); 1980CJ Sch. 2 §19; 1995 s.46(1).
(2)	1975 s.255(1A); 1995 s.46(1).
(3)	1975 s.255(1) (part), 1980CJ Sch. 2 §19; 1995 s.46(1).
(4)	1975 s.255(2); 1980CJ Sch. 2 §19.
(5)	1975 s.255(3) (part); 1980 Sch. 2 §19.
(6)	1975 s.255(1B); 1995 s.46(1).
(7)	1975 s.255(1C); 1995 s.46(1).
(8)	1975 s.255(3) (part); 1980CJ Sch. 2 §19.
(9)	1975 s.255(4); 1980CJ Sch. 2 §19.
(10), (11)	1975 s.255(5), (6); 1995 s.46(1)(c)
120(1)	1975 s.257; 1980CJ Sch. 8; 1995 Sch. 6 §88.
(2)	1975 s.258; 1993P Sch. 5 §1(19).
(3)	1975 s.260.
(4)	1975 s.261; 1980CJ Sch. 7 §45; 1993P Sch. 5 §1(20).
121(1), (2)	1975 s.264(1), (2); 1980CJ Sch. 2 §23; 1995 Sch. 6 §92(a).
(3)	1975 s.264(3); 1987 s.68(3).
(4)	1975 s.264(4); 1995 Sch. 6 §92(b).
122(1), (2)	1975 s.265(1), (2); 1995 Sch. 6 §93.
(3)	1975 s.265(4).
(4)	1975 s.265(4A); 1993P Sch. 5 §1(22).
123	1975 s.263A; 1980CJ s.37; 1995 Sch. 6 §91.
124(1)	1975 s.263(1) (part); 1980CJ Sch. 2 §22.
(2)	1975 ss.262, 281.
(3)	1975 s.263(1) (part); 1980CJ Sch. 2 §22.
(4)	1975 s.263(2); 1987 Sch. 2.
(5)	1975 s.263(3); 1995 Sch. 6 §90.
125(1)	1975 s.268(1); 1987 Sch. 1 §14(1); 1993P Sch. 5 §1(23); 1993CJ Sch. 5 §2(8).
(2)	1975 s.268(2); 1987 Sch. 1 §14(2); 1993P Sch. 5 §1(23); 1993CJ Sch. 5 §2(8).
(3)	1975 s.268(3); 1987 Sch. 1 §14(3); 1993P Sch. 5 §1(23).
(4)	1975 s.268(4); 1980CJ Sch. 7 §46; 1995 Sch. 6 §94.
126	1975 s.269; 1980CJ Sch. 2 §25; 1993P Sch. 5 §1(24); 1995 Sch. 6 §95.
127	1975 s.271; 1980CJ Sch. 2 §27; 1985 Sch. 2 §19.
128	1975 ss.266, 267.
129(1), (2)	1975 s.277(1); 1980CJ Sch. 8.
(3)	1975 s.277(2); 1980 CJ Sch. 2 §31, Sch. 8; 1995 Sch. 6 §100.
(4)	1975 s.277(1) (part).
130	1975 s.230.
131	1975 s.280A; 1980CJ s.35.
132	1975 s.279.
133(1)	1975 s.283(1); 1995 Sch. 6 §102.
(2)	1975 s.283(1A); 1995 Sch. 6 §102.
(3)	1975 s.283(2) (part).
(4)	1975 s.283(3); drafting.
(5)	1975 s.310A; 1995 s.63.
134	1975 s.310; 1995 Sch. 6 §108; drafting.

Provision	Derivation
135(1)	1975 s.321(1); 1995 Sch. 6 §117(a).
(2)	1975 s.321(2).
(3), (4)	1975 s.321(3); 1980B Sch. 1 §7; 1995 Sch. 6 §117(b).
(5)	1975 s.321(4).
136	1975 s.331; Incest and Related Offences (Scotland) Act 1986 (1986 c. 36) Sch. 1 §2; 1995 s.62.
137(1)	1975 s.314(3); 1980CJ Sch. 8.
(2)	1975 s.314(4); 1980CJ s.11.
(3)	1975 s.314(4A); 1995 Sch. 6 §111(b).
(4), (5)	1975 s.314(5), (6); 1980CJ s.11.
138(1)	1975 s.311(1) (part) & (2); 1995 Sch. 6 §109; drafting.
(2)	1975 s.312 (part); drafting.
(3)	1975 s.311(3).
(4)	1975 s.312(a)–(z), drafting.
139(1)	1975 s.314(1); 1995 Sch. 6 §111(a).
(2)	1975 s.314(2); 1980CJ s.11.
140	1975 s.315; 1995 Sch. 6 §112.
141(1)	1975 s.316(1) & (2) (part).
(2)	1975, s.316(2) (part).
(3), (4)	1975 s.316(3); 1995 Sch. 6 §113.
(5)	1975 s.316(4).
(6), (7)	1975 s.319; 1995 Sch. 6 §115; drafting.
142(1)	1975 s.366(1); 1995 Sch. 6 §131.
(2) to (4)	1975 s.367.
(5)	1975 s.370; 1980CJ Sch. 7 §58.
143	1975 s.333.
144(1)	1975 s.334(1) (part); 1980CJ Sch. 7 §54(a); 1993P Sch. 5 §1(30).
(2), (3)	1975 s.334(3).
(4), (5)	1975 s.334(1) (part) & (2) (part); 1980CJ Sch. 7 §54(b).
(6) to (8)	1974 s.334(4) to (6).
(9)	1975 s.334(1) (part); 1980CJ Sch. 7 §54(a); drafting.
145	1975 s.333A; 1993P s.38(1).
146(1)	1975 s.337 (part).
(2)	1975 s.337(a); 1980B Sch. 2.
(3)	1975 s.337(b).
(4), (5)	1975 s.337(c).
(6)	1975 s.337(d); 1980B Sch. 1 §8; 1987 s.62(3).
(7) to (9)	1975 s.337(f) to (h).
147	1975 s.331A; 1980CJ s.14(2).
148	1975 s.337A; 1980CJ s.15; 1995 s.14; drafting.
149	1975 s.339; 1995 Sch. 6 §121.
150(1)	1975 s.338(1) (part); 1995 Sch. 6 §120.
(2)	1975 s.338(1)(a) (part).
(3)	1975 s.338(1)(c).
(4)	1975 s.338(1)(a) (part).
(5), (6), (7)	1975 s.338(1)(b).
(8), (9), (10)	1975 s.338(2) to (4); 1980CJ s.17.
151	1975 s.331B; 1995 s.30(4).
152	1975 s.338A; 1980CJ s.18(2).
153	1975 s.337B; 1995 s.31.
154	1975 s.353.
155(1)	1975 s.344(1); 1980CJ s.46(1)(c); 1982 Sch. 7 §7; 1995 Sch. 6 §122.
(2), (3)	1975 s.344(2), (3).
(4)	1975 s.344(4); 1980CJ Sch. 7 §55.
156(1), (2)	1975 s.320; 1995 Sch. 6 §117.

Provision	Derivation
(3), (4)	1975 s.321(5), (6); 1995 Sch. 6 §117.
157	1975 s.359; 1995 Sch. 6 §128.
158	1975 s.360A(1); 1993P s.40(2); 1995 Sch. 6 §130.
159	1975 s.335; 1995 Sch. 6 §118.
160	1975 345A; 1980CJ s.19(2).
161	1975 s.351.
162	1975 s.355.
163(1)	1975 s.440; 1995 Sch. 6 §145.
(2)	1975 s.441; 1995 Sch. 6 §146.
164	1975 s.427.
165	1975 s.429.
166(1) to (6)	1975 s.357(1); 1980CJ s.40; 1995 Sch. 6 §127(a).
(7)	1975 s.356(2).
(8)	1975 s.357(5); 1995 s.24(6).
167(1)	1975 s.433.
(2), (3), (4)	1975 s.430(1); 1995 Sch. 6 §142(a).
(5), (6)	1975 s.430(2), (3).
(7)	1975 s.430(4); 1995 Sch. 6 §142(b).
(8)	1975 s.434.
168	1975 s.303(1).
169	1975 s.424; 1980CJ Sch. 7 §68.
170	1975 s.456.
171	1975 s.332.
172(1)	1975 s.309(1); 1995 Sch. 6 §107.
(2), (3)	1975 s.309(2) (part), (3).
173	1975 s.451A; 1995 s.43(2).
174	1975 s.334(2A) to (2D); 1980CJ s.36.
175(1) to (4)	1975 s.442(1); 1980 Sch. 3 §1; 1993CJ s.68(3); 1995 s.42(4).
(5), (6)	1974 s.442(2), (3); 1980 Sch. 3 §1.
(7), (8)	1975 s.442A(1), (2); 1980CJ Sch. 3 §1.
(9)	1975 s.442B; 1980CJ Sch. 3 §1; 1993CJ Sch. 5 §2(1).
(10)	1975 s.283(2) (part).
176(1)	1975 s.444(1); 1980CJ Sch. 3 §3; 1993CJ Sch. 5 §2(12); 1995 Sch. 6 §148.
(2)	1975 s.444(1A); 1980CJ Sch. 3 §3.
(3)	1975 s.444(1B); 1980CJ Sch. 3 §3.
(4)	1975 s.444(2).
(5)	1975 s.450; 1980CJ Sch. 3 §9; drafting.
177(1)	1975 s.446(1); 1980CJ Sch. 3 §5.
(2), (3)	1975 S.446(2).
(4)	1975 s.446(3).
(5) to (7)	1975 s.446(4) to (6); 1995 Sch. 6 §149.
178(1)	1975 s.447(1); 1980CJ Sch. 3 §6; 1985 Sch. 2 §20.
(2)	1975 s.447(2); 1980CJ Sch. 8.
179	1975 s.448(1)–(5); 1980CJ Sch. 3 §7; 1985 Sch. 4.
180	1975 s.442ZA; 1995 s.42(5).
181(1), (2)	1975 ss.444(3), (4), 448(6), (7); 1980CJ Sch. 3 §7.
(3)	1975 ss.444(5), 448(8); 1980B Sch. 1 §10, §12; 1980CJ Sch. 3 §3, §7.
182	1975 s.452; 1980CJ Sch. 3 §11; 1995 s.42(6).
183(1), (2)	1975 s.452A(1); 1980CJ Sch. 3 §11; 1993P Sch. 5 §1(35).
(3)	1975 s.452A(2) (part); 1980CJ Sch. 3 §11; 1993P Sch. 5 §1(35)(b); 1993CJ Sch. 5 §2(13).
(4)	1975 s.452A(3); 1980CJ Sch. 3 §11.
(5)	1975 s.452A(2) (part); 1980CJ Sch. 3 §11; 1993P Sch. 5 §1(35)(b); 1993CJ Sch. 5 §2(13).
(6), (7)	1975 s.452A(7); 1980CJ Sch. 3 §11.
(8)	1975 s.452A(4A); 1993CJ Sch. 5 §2(13).

Provision	Derivation
(9)	1975 s.452A(5); 1980CJ Sch. 3 §11.
(10)	1975 s.452A(6); 1980CJ Sch. 3 §11.
184	1975 s.449; 1980CJ Sch. 3 §8.
185(1)	1975 s.452B(1) (part); 1980CJ Sch. 3 §11; 1995 s.46(2).
(2)	1975 s.452B(1A); 1995 s.46(2).
(3)	1975 s.452B(1) (part); 1980CJ Sch. 3 §11.
(4)	1975 s.452B(2); 1980CJ Sch. 3 §11.
(5)	1975 s.452B(3) (part); 1980CJ Sch. 3 §11.
(6), (7)	1975 s.452B(1B), (1C); 1995 s.46(2).
(8)	1975 s.452B(3) (part); 1980CJ Sch. 3 §11.
(9)	1975 s.452B(4); 1980CJ Sch. 3 §11.
(10)	1975 s.452B(5); 1995 s.46(2)(c).
186(1), (2)	1975 s.453B(1), (2); 1980CJ Sch. 3 §13; 1993P Sch. 5 §1(36); 1993CJ Sch. 5 §2(14).
(3)	1975 s.453B(3); 1980CJ Sch. 3 §13; 1993CJ Sch. 5 §2(14).
(4), (5)	1975 s.453B(4); 1980CJ Sch. 3 §13; 1993CJ Sch. 5 §2(14); 1995 s.45(2).
(6)	1975 s.453B(4A); 1995 Sch. 6 §152.
(7)	1975 s.453B(5); 1980CJ Sch. 3 §13; 1993P Sch. 5 §1(36).
(8), (9)	1975 s.453B(6), (7); 1980CJ Sch. 3 §13; 1993P Sch. 5 §1(36); 1993CJ Sch. 5 §2(14).
(10)	1975 s.453B(8); 1980CJ Sch. 3 §13.
187	1975 s.453AA; 1995 s.42(7).
188(1)	1975 s.453(1); 1993P s.43; 1995 Sch. 6 §151(2).
(2), (3)	1975 s.453 (2), (3); 1993P s.43.
(4)	1975 s.453(4); 1993P s.43; 1995 Sch. 6 §151(3).
(5). (6), (7)	1975 s.453(5), (6), (7); 1993P s.43.
189(1), (2)	1975 s.453C(1); 1980CJ Sch. 3 §13.
(3)	1975 s.453C(2); 1980 Sch. 3 §13.
(4)	1975 s.453C(3); 1980CJ Sch. 3 §13; 1993P Sch. 5 §1(37); 1993CJ Sch. 5 §2(15).
(5), (6)	1975 s.453C(4), (5); 1993CJ Sch. 5 §2(15).
(7)	1975 s.455A(1); 1995 s.34(2).
190	1975 s.453D; 1980CJ Sch. 3 §13; 1995 Sch. 6 §153.
191(1), (2)	1975 s.453A(1); 1980CJ Sch. 3 §13.
(3), (4)	1975 s.453A(2), (3); 1980CJ Sch. 3 §13.
192(1), (2)	1975 s.453E; 1980CJ Sch. 3 §13.
(3)	1975 s.454(1); 1995 Sch. 6 §154.
(4), (5)	1975 s.455(1), (2).
193(1), (2)	1975 s.443A(1), (2); 1987 s.68(1); 1993CJ Sch. 5 §2(11).
(3)	1975 s.443A(3); 1995 Sch. 6 §147.
194(1)	1975 s.451(1); 1980CJ Sch. 3 §10.
(2)	1975 s.451(2); 1980CJ Sch. 3 §10; 1995 s.45(1).
(3)	1975 s.451(3); 1980CJ Sch. 3 §10; 1995 Sch. 6 §150.
195(1)	1975 s.104(1); 1980CJ Sch. 4 §15.
(2)	1975 s.104(1A); 1987 s.58(2).
(3), (4)	1975 s.104(2), (3); 1980CJ Sch. 4 §15.
196	1975 ss.217A, 430A; 1995 s.33.
197	1975 ss.254A(2), 455A(2); 1995 s.34.
198(1)	1975 s.217(1) (part); drafting.
(2), (3)	1975 s.217(2), (3); drafting.
199	1975 ss.193, 394; 1977 Sch. 13 §7; 1980CJ s.46(2), Sch. 8; 1982 Sch. 7 §10; drafting.
200(1), (2)	1975 ss.180(1) (part), 381(1) (part); 1995 s.55(2).
(3), (4), (5)	1975 ss.180(1A) to (1C), 381(1A) to (1C); 1995 s.55(3).
(6)	1975 ss.180(2), 381(2); 1980B Sch. 1 §5, Sch. 2.
(7)	1975 ss.180(4), 381(4); 1995 s.55(4).

Provision	Derivation
(8)	1975 ss.180(4A), 381(4A); 1995 s.55(5).
(9)	1975 ss.180(5), 381(5); 1980B s.6(b); 1995 s.55(6).
(10), (11)	1975 ss.180(6), (7), 381(6), (7); 1995 s.55(7).
201(1) to (3)	1975 ss.179(1), 380(1); 1980B s.5(a); 1980CJ Sch. 7 §36(a), §59(a); 1995 Sch. 6 §68.
(4)	1975 s.179(2), s.380(2); 1980B s.5(b); 1980CJ Sch. 7 §36(b), §59(b).
202	1975 ss.219, 432; 1980CJ s.54; 1995 Sch. 6 §143.
203(1)	1975 ss.179A, 380A(1); 1995 s.37.
(2)	1975 s.380A(2); 1995 s.37(2).
(3)	1975 ss.192 (part), 393 (part); 1995 Sch. 6 §74.
204(1)	1980CJ s.41(1).
(2)	1980 s.42(1).
(3)	1980CJ s.42(2).
(4)	1980CJ ss.41(2), 42(3) (part); 1987 Sch. 1 §17; 1988 Sch. 9 §5.
(5)	1980CJ ss.41(3), 42(3) (part).
(6)	1980CJ s.41(4).
205(1) to (3)	1975 s.205(1) to (3); 1980CJ s.43.
(4) to (6)	1975 s.205A(1) to (3); 1980CJ s.43.
206	1975 s.425.
207(1) to (4)	1975 ss.207(1) to (4), 415(1) to (4); 1980CJ s.45(1).
(5)	1975 ss.207(5), 415(5); 1980CJ ss.45(1); 1985 s.43(a); 1988 s.124.
208	1975 s.206; 1980CJ s.44; Prisons (Scotland) Act 1989 (1989 c.45) Sch. 2 §12.
209(1)	1975 s.212A(1); 1993P s.14(1).
(2)	1975 s.212A(1A); 1995 s.36.
(3), (4)	1975 s.212A(2), (3); 1993P s.14(1); 1995 s.132.
(5) to (7)	1975 s.212A(4) to (6).
(8)	1975 s.212A(7); 1993CJ s.69.
210(1)	1975 ss.218(1), 431(1); 1980 Sch. 7 §70, Sch. 8; 1993P s.41.
(2), (3)	1975 ss.218(2), (3), 431(2), (3); 1993P s.41.
211(1)	1975 s.193A(1); 1977 Sch. 11 §1; 1980CJ Sch. 7 §37; 1982 Sch. 15 §17.
(2)	1975 s.193A(2); 1982 Sch. 15 §17.
(3)	1975 ss.196(1), 402; 1995 Sch. 6 §75.
(4)	1975 s.196(2); 1980CJ s.48.
(5)	1975 s.203.
(6)	1975 s.412.
(7)	1975 ss.194, 395(1).
212(1), (2)	1975 s.395(2) (part); 1980CJ Sch. 7 §60.
(3) to (7)	1975 s.395(3) to (7).
(8), (9)	1975 s.395(2) (part); 1980CJ Sch. 7 §60.
213	1975 ss.194, 395A(1) to (3); 1980CJ ss.47, 49.
214(1) to (6)	1975 ss.194, 396(1) to (6); 1980CJ s.47; drafting.
(7)	1975 ss.194, 396(7); 1980CJ s.47; 1995 Sch. 6 §137.
(8)	1975 ss.194, 399(1); 1980CJ s.47.
(9)	1975 ss.194, 399(2) & (3); 1980CJ s.47, Sch. 7 §62(b).
215(1), (2)	1975 ss.194, 397; 1977 Sch. 11 §8; Magistrates' Courts Act 1980 (1980 c.43) Sch. 7 §136; 1980CJ s.47.
(3), (4)	1975 ss.194, 397(2), (3); 1980CJ s.47.
216(1), (2)	1975 ss.194, 398(1); 1980CJ s.47, Sch. 7 §61; 1995 Sch. 6 §138.
(3)	1975 ss.194, 398(2); 1980CJ s.47.
(4)	1975 ss.194, 398(3); 1980CJ s.47.
(5)	1975 ss.194, 318(1); 1980CJ s.47.
(6)	1975 ss.194, 318(2) & (3), 398(4) & (5); 1980CJ s.47; 1995 Sch. 6 §114.
(7)	1975 ss.194, 406; 1980CJ s.47; 1995 Sch. 6 §139.
217	1975 ss.194, 400; 1980CJ s.47.
218(1), (2)	1975 ss.194, 401(1), (2); 1980CJ s.47.
(3)	1975 ss.194, 401(3); 1980CJ s.47, Sch. 7 §63.

Provision	Derivation
219(1)	1975 ss.194, 407(1); 1980CJ ss.47, 50; 1990 Sch. 7 §27(3).
(2)	1975 ss.194, 407(1A); 1980CJ ss.47, 50; 1985; 1987 s.67(1); 1991 s.23(2).
(3) to (5)	1975 ss.194, 407(1B) to (1D); 1980CJ s.47, 50.
(6)	1975 ss.194, 407(2); 1980CJ s.47.
(7)	1975 ss.194, 407(4); 1980CJ s.47.
(8)	1975 ss.194, 407(5); 1980CJ s.47; 1987 s.67(2).
220(1), (2)	1975 ss.194, 409(1); 1980CJ s.47, Sch. 7 §65.
(3)	1975 s.194, Sch. 7; 1980CJ s.47.
(4)	1975 ss.194, 409(2); 1980CJ s.47.
221(1)	1975 ss.194, 411(1); 1980CJ s.47; Debtors (Scotland) Act 1987 (1987 c. 18) Sch. 6 §18.
(2), (3)	1975 ss.194, 411(3); 1980CJ s.47.
(4)	1980CJ s.52 (part).
222(1)	1975 ss.194, 403(1); 1977 Sch. 7 §2; 1980CJ s.47.
(2)	1975 ss.194, 403(2); 1980CJ s.47.
(3)	1975 ss.194, 403(3); 1980CJ s.47; 1995 s.67(2).
(4)	1975 ss.194, 403(3A); 1980CJ s.47; 1995 s.67(3).
(5)	1975 ss.194, 403(3B); 1980CJ s.47; 1995 s.67(3).
(6)	1975 ss.194, 403(4); 1977 Sch. 7 §2; 1980CJ s.47.
(7)	1975 ss.194, 403(4A); 1980CJ s.47; 1994 s.47(4).
(8)	1975 ss.194, 403(6); 1977 Sch. 7 §2; 1980CJ s.47.
223	1975 s.404.
224	1975 ss.194, 408; 1980CJ s.47; 1995 Sch. 6 §140.
225(1)	1975 s.289G(1); 1982 s.54.
(2)	1975 s.289G(2); 1982 s.54; S.I. 1984/526; 1991 s.17(1).
(3)	1975 s.289G(3); 1982 s.54.
(4)	1975 s.289D(1); 1977 Sch. 11 §5; 1982 s.53(a).
(5)	1975 s.289D(1A); 1982 s.53(a); 194 s.157(7).
(6)	1975 s.289D(1B); 1982 s.53(a); drafting.
(7)	1975 s.289D(4); 1977 Sch. 11 §5; 1987 Sch. 2.
(8)	1975 s.289B(6) (part); drafting.
226	1975 s.289GB; 1987 s.66(2).
227	1975 s.182A; 1995 Sch. 6 §69.
228(1)	1975 ss.183(1), 384(1); 1980CJ s.53(1); 1987 Sch. 1 §10; 1990 s.61(1); 1995 s.38(3)(a).
(2)	1975 ss.183(1A), 384(1A); 1990 s.61; 1991 Sch. 3 §7(2).
(3), (4)	1975 ss.183(2), 384(2).
(5)	1975 ss.183(6), 384(6); 1987 s.65(4); 1995 s.38(3)(c).
(6)	1975 ss.183(7), 384(7); 1995 Sch. 6 §70.
229(1)	1975 ss.183(4), 384(4); 1978 s.7; 1987 s.65(3); 1990 s.61(1).
(2), (3)	1975 ss.183(5), 384(5).
(4), (5)	1975 ss.183(5A), 384(5A); 1978 s.7; 1982 Sch. 13 §3; 1995 s.38(1), (3)(b); drafting.
(6), (7)	1975 ss.183(5B), (5C), 384(5B), (5C); 1987 s.65.
230(1)	1975 ss.184(1), 385(1); 1984 Sch. 3 §§29, 36; 1995 s.39(1).
(2)	1975 ss.184(2), 385(2); 1984 Sch. 3 §§29, 36; 1995 s.39(1).
(3)	1975 ss.184(3), 385(3).
(4)	1975 ss.184(5), 385(5); 1983 s.36(2); 1995 s.39(1).
(5)	1975 ss.184(5A), 385(5A); 1983 s.36(2).
(6)	1975 ss.184(5B), 385(5B); 1983 s.36(2); 1995 s.39(1).
(7)	1975 ss.184(6), 385(6); 1983 s.36(3).
(8), (9)	1975 ss.184(7), (8), 385(7), (8).
231	1975 ss.185, 386.
232(1)	1975 ss.186(1), 387(1); 1978 s.8; 1990 s.61(2); Local Government etc. (Scotland) Act 1994 (c. 39) Sch. 13 §97(3); 1995 Sch. 6 §671.

Provision	Derivation
(2)	1975 ss.186(2), 387(2); 1978 s.8; 1980CJ s.46(1); 1982 Sch. 7 §§3, 9; 1987 s.65(5); 1995 s.38(2).
(3)	1975 ss.186(2A), 387(2A); 1993P Sch. 5 §1(7).
(4) to (6)	1975 ss.186(3) to (5), 387(3) to (5).
(7)	1975 s.317.
233(1), (2)	1975 ss.187(1), (2), 388(1), (2).
(3) to (5)	1975 ss.187(3) to (5), 388(3) to (5); 1995 s.40(1), (2).
234(1), (2)	1975 ss.188(1), 389(1); 1978 Sch. 2 §2, 3; 1991 Sch. 3 §7(3).
(3) to (10)	1975 ss.188(2) to (8), 389(2) to (8); 1991 Sch. 3 §7(3).
(11)	Drafting.
235	1990 s.62; 1995 s.35(2) to (7).
236	1975 s.412A; 1995 s.35(11).
237	1975 s.412B; 1995 s.35(11).
238(1)	1978 s.1(1); 1990 s.61(3).
(2) to (7)	1978 s.1(2) to (7).
(8), (9)	1978 s.2(1), (2).
(10), (11)	1978 s.2(3), (4); 1995 Sch. 6. §161.
239(1) to (3)	1978 s.3(1) to (3).
(4)	1978 s.4(1); 1995 Sch. 6 §162.
(5)	1978 s.4(2); 1982 Sch. 7 §12.
(6)	1978 s.4(3); 1990 Sch. 8 §28.
240	1978 s.5.
241	1978 s.5A; 1995 s.40(3).
242	1978 s.6; 1982 Sch. 13 §4.
243(1)	1978 s.6A(1); 1982 Sch. 13 §5.
(2)	1978 s.6A(2); 1982 Sch. 13 §5; S.I. 1989/1345.
(3)	1978 s.6A(3); 1982 Sch. 13 §5.
244	1978 s.6B; 1982 Sch. 13 §5.
245(1) to (3)	1978 s.10(1) to (3).
(4)	1978 s.11.
(5)	1978 s.12(1).
246(1)	1975 ss.181, 382; 1993CJ Sch. 5 §2(2).
(2)	1975 s.182.
(3)	1975 s.383.
247(1)	1975 ss.191(1) (part), 392(1) (part).
(2)	1975 ss.191(2), 392(2).
(3)	1975 ss.191(3) (part), 392(3) (part), 392(3); 1993CJ Sch. 5 §2(3), (9).
(4)	1975 ss.191(4), 392(5); 1995 Sch. 6 §§73, 136.
(5)	1975 s.392(4); 1995 Sch. 6 §136.
(6)	1975 ss.191(1) (part), 392(1) (part).
248(1) to (4)	1975 ss.223A, 436A; Road Traffic Act 1991 (c. 40) s.39.
249(1), (2)	1980CJ s.58(1).
(3), (4)	1980CJ s.58(2), (3).
(5), (6)	1980CJ s.59(1).
(7), (8)	1980CJ s.59(2), (3).
(9), (10)	1980CJ s.60(1), (2).
250(1)	1980CJ s.61.
(2)	1980CJ s.62.
(3), (4)	1980CJ s.63(1), (2).
251	1980CJ s.64.
252	1980CJ s.66.
253	1980CJ s.67; Armed Forces Act 1991 (c. 62) Sch. 2) Sch. 2 §9(2).
254	1975 ss.224, 437.
255	1975 ss.67, 312(x); drafting.
256(1)	1975 ss.150(1), 354(1); 1995 Sch. 6 §§55(a), 126; drafting.
(2)	1975 ss,150(2), 354(2) (part); 1995 Sch. 6 §55(b).

Provision	Derivation
(3)	1975 ss.150(3), 354(2) (part); drafting.
257	1975 ss.84A, 333B; 1995 s.12.
258	1995 s.16.
259	1995 s.17.
260	1995 s.18.
261	1995 s.19.
262	1995 s.20.
263(1) to (3)	1975 ss.148(1) to (3), 340(1) to (3); 1995 Sch. 6 §54.
(4)	1975 ss. 147, 349.
(5)	1975 ss.148A, 349A; 1982 s.73(1), (2).
264(1) to (3)	1975 ss.143(1) to (3), 348(1) to (3); 1980CJ s.29.
(4)	Criminal Justice Administration Act 1914 (c. 58) s.28(3).
265(1)	1975 ss.138(1), (2), 341(1), (2).
(2)	1975 ss.138(4), 341(4).
(3), (4)	1975 ss.139, 342.
266(1)	1975 ss.141(1) (part), 346(1) (part); Criminal Evidence Act 1979 (1979 c. 16) s.1(1); 1980CJ s.28, Sch. 7 §56; 1995 s.24.
(2)	1975 ss.141(1)(a), 346(1)(a).
(3)	1975 ss.141(1)(e), 346(1)(e).
(4)	1975 ss.141(1)(f), 346(1)(f); Criminal Evidence Act 1979 (c. 16) s.1(1); 1995 s.24(1)(a), (4)(a).
(5)	1975 ss.141(1A), 346(1A): 1995 s.24(1)(b), (4)(b).
(6)	1975 s.141(1B); 1995 s.24(1)(b).
(7)	1975 ss.141(1C), 346(1B); 1995 s.24(1)(c), (4)(b).
(8)	1975 ss.141(1)(g), 346(1)(g).
(9)	1975 ss.141(2), 346(2); 1980CJ s.28.
(10)	1975 ss.141(3), 346(3); 1980CJ s.28.
(11)	1975 ss.142, 347; 1995 Sch. 6 §§50, 124.
267(1)	1975 ss.139A, 342A; 1987 s.63.
(2)	1975 ss.140, 343.
268(1), (2)	1975 ss.149(1), 350(1); 1980CJ s.30; 1985 s.37; 1987 Sch. 1 §9; 1993P Sch. 5 §1(31).
(3), (4)	1975 ss.149(2), (3), 350(2), (3); 1980CJ s.30.
(5)	Drafting.
269(1)	1975 ss.149A(1), 350A(2); 1980CJ s.30; 1985 s.37.
(2), (3)	1975 ss.149A(2), (3), 350A(2), (3); 1980CJ s.30.
(4)	Drafting.
270(1), (2)	1975 ss.141ZA(1), (2), 346ZA(1), (2); 1995 s.24(2), (5).
(3)	1975 s.141ZA(3); 1995 s.24(2).
(4)	1975 ss.141ZA(4), 346ZA(3); 1995 s.24(2), (5).
271(1) to (3)	1993P s.33(1) to (3).
(4)	1993P s.33(4); 1995 Sch. 6 §179(6).
(5)	1990 s.56(1); 1995 Sch. 6 §175(a).
(6)	1993P s.34; 1995 Sch. 6 §179(7).
(7)	1990 s.56(2); 1995 Sch. 6 §175(b).
(8)	1990 s.56(3).
(9)	1990 s.57(1).
(10)	1990 s.57(2).
(11)	1990 s.58; 1995 Sch. 6 §176.
(12)	1990 s.59.
272(1)	1980CJ s.32(1); 1987 s.61.
(2), (3)	1980CJ s.32(2).
(4)	1980CJ s.32(3).
(5)	1980CJ s.32(3A); 1993P s.30.
(6)	1980CJ s.32(4); 1987 s.61.
(7)	1980CJ s.32(5).

Provision	Derivation
(8)	1980CJ s.32(5A); 1993P s.30
(9)	1980CJ s.32(6).
273	1980CJ s.32A; 1993P s.32.
274(1)	1975 ss.141A(1), 346A(1); 1985 s.36.
(2)	1975 ss.141A(2), 346A(2); 1985 s.36; 1995 s.28.
(3), (4)	1975 ss.141A(3), (4), 346A(3), (4); 1985 s.36.
275	1975 ss.141B, 346B; 1985 s.36.
276	1995 s.21.
277(1)	1987 s.60(1); 1993P s.31.
(2)	1987 s.60(2).
(3)	1987 s.60(3); 1995 Sch. 6 §170.
(4)	1987 s.60(4).
278(1)	1975 ss.151(1), 352(1); 1980CJ s.6.
(2), (3)	1975 ss.151(2), 352(2); 1995 Sch. 6 §§56, 125.
(4)	1975 s.352(4).
(5)	1975 ss.151(3), 352(3).
279	1993P s.29.
280(1)	1980CJ s.26(1).
(2), (3)	1980 s.26(1A), (1B); 1995 s.22(2).
(4)	1980 CJ s.26(2); 1995 s.22(3).
(5)	1980CJ s.26(2A); 1995 s.22(4).
(6)	1980CJ s.26(3); 1995 s.22(5).
(7)	1980CJ s.26(4); 1995 s.22(6), Sch. 6 §163.
(8)	1980CJ s.26(4A); 1995 s.22(7).
(9)	1980CJ s.26(5); 1995 s.22(8).
(10) to (12)	1980 s.26(7B) to (7D); 1995 s.22(9).
281(1), (2)	1980CJ s.26(6), (7).
(3)	1980CJ s.26(7A); 1995 s.22(9).
282	1995 s.25.
283	1995 s.26.
284	1995 s.27.
285(1) to (5)	1975 ss.164(1) to (5) 358(1) to (5).
(6)	1975 ss.162(1), 357(2) (part).
(7)	1975 s.162(2).
(8)	1975 ss.162(3), 357(2) (part); 1995 Sch. 6 §§62, 127(b).
(9)	1975 ss.164(6), 357(2) (part), 358(6).
286	1975 ss.162(4), (5), 357(6), (7); 1995 s.29.
287	1975 s.42; 1995 Sch. 6 §18.
288(1)	1975 s.10.
(2)	1975 s.11.
289	1980CJ s.39.
290	1980CJ s.10(1), (2).
291(1)	1980CJ s.9(1).
(2)	1980CJ s.9(2); 1982 Sch. 6 §64.
(3)	1980CJ s.9(3); 1982 Sch. 7.
292(1)	1975 ss.283A(1), (2); 1977 Sch. 11 §2; 1980CJ Sch. 7 §49.
(2) to (7)	1975 s.457A(1) to (4); 1982 s.55(1).
293	1975 ss.216, 428; 1987 s.64(1).
294(1)	1975 s.63(1) (part).
(2)	1975 s.312(o) (part).
295	1975 ss.215, 426; 1980CJ Sch. 7 §§39, 69; 1987 Sch. 1 §12.
296	1975 ss.15A, 309(2) (part); 1995 Sch. 6 §9.
297(1)	1975 ss.15, 327; 1995 s.9.
(2)	1975 s.326(1) (part).
(3), (4)	1975 ss.16(1), (2), 324(1), (2).

Provision	Derivation
(5)	1975 s.326(1) (part).
298	1995 s.44.
299	1975 ss.227A, 439; 1980CJ s.20.
300	1975 s.439A; 1995 s.41.
301(1)	1975 s.282A; 1990 Sch. 8 §27.
(2)	1975 s.282B; 1990 Sch. 8 §27.
302(1)	1987 s.56(1).
(2)	1987 s.56(3); 1995 s.61(3).
(3)	1987 s.56(3A); 1995 s.61(4).
(4) to (6)	1987 s.56(4) to (6); 1995 s.61(5).
(7), (8)	1987 s.56(7), (7A); 1995 s.61(6).
(9)	1987 s.56(2), (2A); Road Traffic (Consequential Provisions) Act 1988 (1988 c. 54) Sch. 3 §34; 1995 s.61(2).
303(1) to (4)	1987 s.56(8) to (11); 1995 s.61(8).
304	1995 s.56(1) to (10).
305(1)	1975 ss.409(3), 457ZA(1) (part); Summary Jurisdiction (Scotland) Act 194 (c. 48) s.76(1)(d); 1995 Sch. 6 §156.
(2)	1975 s.457ZA(2); 1995 Sch. 6 §156.
(3)	1975 s.457ZA(1) (part); 1995 Sch. 6 §156.
(4)	1975 s.278.
(5)	Summary Jurisdiction (Scotland) Act 1954 (1954 c. 48) s.76(3).
306	1995 s.57.
307(1)	1975 s,462(1); 1977 Sch. 11 §10; National Health Service (Scotland) Act 1978 (1978 c. 29) Sch. 16 §41; 1980B Sch. 1 §14; 1980CJ s.25, Sch. 7 §76; 1982 Sch. 15 §19; 1983 Sch. 2 §37; 1984 Sch. 3 §37; National Health Service and Community Care Act 1990 (c. 19) Sch. 9 §14; 1995 s.39(2), Sch. 6 §157; 1995C Sch. 4 §24(18).
(2)	1975 s.462(2).
(3) to (8)	1975 s.462(4) to (9).
308	1975 ss.458, 459; 1980CJ Sch. 7 §§73, 74.
309	Drafting.
Sch. 1	1975 Sch. 1; Sexual Offences (Scotland) Act 1976 (1976 c. 67) Schs. 1, 2; 1988 Sch. 15 §§50, 51.
Sch. 2	Criminal Procedure (Scotland) Act 1887 (c. 35) Sch. 1
Sch. 3	
§1	1975 ss.43 (part), 312(a).
§2	1975 ss.44, 312(b).
§3	1975 ss.48, 312(e).
§4(1)	1975 ss.50(1), 312(f) (part).
(2)	1975 ss.50(2), 312(f) (part).
(3)	1975 ss.50(3) (part), 312(f) (part).
(4)	1975 ss.50(3) (part), 312(f) (part).
(5)	1975 ss.50(4), 312(f) (part); 1995 Sch. 6 §§20, 110(a).
(6)	1975 ss.51 (part), 312(g) (part).
(7)	1975 ss.51 (part), 312(g) (part).
(8)	Drafting.
§5	1975 ss.54, 312(j); 1995 Sch. 6 §§21, 110(b).
§6	1975 ss.55, 312(k).
§7	1975 s.63(2).
§8(1)	1975 ss.59 (part), 312(l) (part).
(2)	1975 ss.60(1), 312(m) (part).
(3)	1975 ss.60(2), 312(m) (part).
(4)	1975 ss.60(3), 312(m) (part).
(5)	1975 ss.60(4), 312(m) (part).
§9(1)	1975 ss.61(l), 312(n) (part).
(2)	1975 ss.61(2), 312(n) (part).

Provision	Derivation
(3)	1975 ss.61(3), 312(n) (part).
§10(1)	1975 ss.63(1) (part), 312(o) (part).
(2)	1975 ss.63(1) (part), 312(o) (part).
(3)	1975 ss.63(2), 312(o) (part).
§11	1975 ss.48B, 312(p); 1995 Sch. 6 §19.
§12	1975 s.312(q), (r).
§13	1975 ss.49, 312(s).
§14	1975 ss.64, 312(t).
§15	1975 ss.65, 312(u).
§16	1975 ss.66, 312(v).
§17	1975 ss.48A, 312(w); 1995 Sch. 6 §19.
§18	1975 ss.60A, 312(y); 1995 Sch. 6 §23.
§19	1975 s.312(z); 1977 Sch. 11 §6; 1980CJ s.46(b); 1982 Sch. 7 §7.
Sch. 4	1975 Sch. 5A; 1995 Sch. 2.
Sch. 5	Summary Jurisdiction (Scotland) Act 1954 (c. 48) Sch. 2 Part II.
Sch. 6	
§1	1975 Sch. 5 §1.
§2	1975 Sch. 5 §2.
§3	1975 Sch. 5 §3.
§4	1975 Sch. 5 §4; 1983 s.36(4); 1995 Sch. 6 §158.
§5	1975 Sch. 5 §5.
§6	1975 Sch. 5 §6.
Sch. 7	
§1	1990 Sch. 6 §1; 1995 s.35(8)(a).
§2	1990 Sch. 6 §2; 1995 Sch. 6 §177(a).
§3	1990 Sch. 6 §3.
§4	1990 Sch. 6 §4; 1995 s.35(8)(b), Sch. 6 §177(b).
§5	1990 Sch. 6 §5; 1995 s.35(8)(c).
§6	1990 Sch. 6 §6.
§7	1990 Sch. 6 §7.
§8	1990 Sch. 6 §9.
Sch. 8	1993P Sch. 3; 1995 Sch. 6 §179(8).
Sch. 9	1980CJ Sch. 1; Forgery and Counterfeiting Act 1981 (1981 c. 45) s.26; Road Traffic Regulation Act 1984 (1984 c. 27) Sch. 13 §37; Video Recording Act 1984 (1984 c. 39) s.20; 1987 Sch. 1 §18(2); 1993P Sch. 4; 1995 Sch. 1.
Sch. 10	1975 Sch. 7A; 1977 Sch. 11 §11.

TABLE OF DESTINATIONS

COURT OF SESSION (SCOTLAND) ACT 1830
(11 GEO. 4 & 1 WILL. 4 C.69)

1830	1995
s.18	s.1(1)

CRIMINAL PROCEDURE (SCOTLAND) ACT 1887
(C.35)

1887	1995
Sched.A	Sched.2

CRIMINAL JUSTICE ADMINISTRATION ACT 1914
(C.58)

1914	1995
s.28(3)........	s.264(4)

SUMMARY JURISDICTION (SCOTLAND) ACT 1954
(C.48)

1954	1995
s.76(1)(d).....	s.305(1)
76(3)........	305(5)
Sched.2, Pt.II .	Sched.5

SOCIAL WORK (SCOTLAND) ACT 1968
(C.49)

1968	1995
s.31(1)........	s.42(1)

DISTRICT COURTS (SCOTLAND) ACT 1975
(C.20)

1975	1995
s.2(1).........	s.6(1)
(1A).......	6(1)
(2)........	6(2)
3(1)........	7(1)
(2)........	7(5)
(4)........	7(2)
6(1) part	6(3)
(2) part	6(4)
(3) part	6(4)
(9)........	6(5)

1975	1995	1975	1995	1975	1995
s.2(1).........	s.3(1)	s.30(4)........	s.30(4)	s.63(1) part ...	s.294(1)
(2)–(4).....	(3)–(5)	30A	31		Sched. 3,
3(1).........	4(1)	31(1).......	32(1)		para. 10(1)
(2).........	4(3)	(2)........	32(2)		para. 10(2)
(3).........	9(1)	(3), (4)....	32(3), (4)	(2)........	Sched. 3,
4(1)........	9(1)	(4a)	32(5)		para. 7
(2).........	9(2)	(5)........	32(6)		para. 10(3)
(3).........	9(3)	32	33	64	Sched. 3,
(4), (5).....	9(4), (5)	33(1)........	32(7), (8)		para. 14
5	10	(2)........	32(10)	65	Sched. 3,
6(1), (2).....	11(1), (2)	35	24(2)		para. 15
(3).........	11(3)	37(1)–(3)....	45(1)–(4)	66	Sched. 3,
7(1), (2).....	11(4)	(4)........	45(5)		para. 16
8	3(6)	38	42(9), (10)	67	255
9	12	39(1)–(3)....	42(2)–(4)	68(1)........	69(1)
10	288(1)	(4), (5)....	42(5), (6)	(2)........	69(2)
11	288(2)	40(1), (2)....	42(7), (8)	(3) part ...	69(3), (5)
12	34(1)	41	64(1)–(4)	(4) part ...	69(4), (5)
15	297(1)	42	287	69(1)........	66(1), (2)
15A	296	43 part......	Sched. 3,	(2)........	66(3)
16(1), (2)....	297(3), (4)		para. 1	70	66(4)
18(1)........	21(1)	44	Sched. 3,	71	66(7)
(2)–(5)....	21(2)–(5)		para. 2	72(1)........	66(9)
19(1)........	17(1)	48	Sched. 3,	(2)........	66(10)
(2)........	17(2)		para. 3	73(1)........	66(8)
(2) part) ..	35(1), (2)	48A	Sched. 3,	(2)........	66(11)
(3)........	35(1), (2)		para. 17	74(1)........	70(2), (3)
20(1)........	35(3)	48B.........	Sched. 3,	(2)........	70(4)
(3)........	35(4)		para. 11	(4)........	70(5)
(3A)–(3C)	35(5)–(7)	49	Sched. 3,	(5)........	70(6)
(4)........	35(8)		para. 13	(6)........	74(7)
20A(1).....	36(1)–(4)	50(1).......	Sched. 3,	(7)........	34(2)
(2)......	36(5)		para. 4(1)	(8)........	70(8)
(3), (3A)	36(6)	(2)........	Sched. 3,	75	66(6)
(4)......	36(7)		para. 4(2)	75A	71
(5)......	36(8)	(3) part ...	Sched. 3,	76(1) part ...	72(1), (2)
(6)......	36(9)		para. 4(3)	(2)........	72(1)
(7), (8)..	36(10), (11)		para. 4(4)	(3)–(5)....	72(3)–(6)
20B(1)	37(1)	(4)........	Sched. 3,	(6) part ...	73(1), (2), (8)
(1A)–(1C)	37(2)–(4)		para. 4(5)	(6A)–(6D)	73(3)–(6)
(2)......	37(5)	51 part......	Sched. 3,	(7)........	72(3)–(6)
(3)......	37(6)		para. 4(6)	76A	74
(4)......	38		para. 4(7)	77	80(1)
(5)......	37(7), (8)	54	Sched. 3,	77A(1)–(3)..	80(2)–(4)
(6)......	37(9)		para. 5	(4).....	80(5), (6)
(7), (8)..	38	55	Sched. 3,	78(1)........	66(5)
(9)......	37(10)		para. 6	(2)........	68(1)
21	39	57	64(5)	79(1) part ...	67(1)
22	40	58	66(12)–(14)	(2)........	67(2)
23(1)........	51(1)	59 part......	Sched. 3,	80(1)........	67(3)
(2)–(4)....	51(2)–(4)		para. 8(1)	(2)........	67(4)
25(1)........	52(2)	60(1).......	Sched. 3,	81	67(5)
(2)........	52(3)		para. 8(2)	82(1) part ...	78(1), (3)
(3), (4)....	52(4), (5)	(2)........	Sched. 3,	(1A)......	78(2)
(5), (6)....	52(6), (7)		para. 8(3)	(2)........	78(4)
26(1)........	24(1)	(3)........	Sched. 3,	(3)........	78(5)
(2)........	23(1)		para. 8(4)	82A	67(6)
(3)........	23(2)	(4)........	Sched. 3,	83	68(2)
(4)........	23(3)		para. 8(5)	84	68(3), (4)
27	23(4)	60A	Sched. 3,	84A	257
28(1)........	23(5)		para. 18	85	84(1)
(2)........	23(7)	61(1)........	Sched. 3,	86(1)........	84(2)
(3)........	23(8)		para. 9(1)	(2)........	84(3)
28A	26	(2)........	Sched. 3,	89	84(4)
30(1)........	30(1)		para. 9(2)	90	84(5)
(2)........	30(2)	(3)........	Sched. 3,	91	84(6)
(3)........	30(3)		para. 9(3)	92	84(7)
				93	84(8)

1975	1995	1975	1995	1975	1995
s.94	s.84(9)	s.141A(1).....	s.274(1)	s.173(4), (5)...	s.49(4), (5)
95	84(10	(2).....	274(2)	174(1)–(1C) .	54(1)–(4)
96(1).......	85(1)	(3), (4).	274(3), (4)	(2)	54(6)
(2).......	85(2)	141B........	275	(5)	54(5)
97	85(3)	141ZA(1), (2)		174A(1) part	53(11), (12)
98	85(4), (5)		270(1), (2)	(2)–(10)	53(2)–(10)
99	85(6), (7)	(3) ...	270(3)	174ZA......	55
100(1)	85(8)	(4) ...	270(4)	174ZB	56
101(1)	65(1)–(3)	142	266(11)	174ZC	57(1)–(4)
(1A).....	65(10)	143(1)–(3)...	264(1)–(3)	174ZD	62
(2)–(6)...	65(4)–(9)	145(1)	97(1), (2)	174ZE	63(1)–(5)
102	76	(3)	97(3)	175(1)	58(1), (2)
103(1)	77(1)	147	263(4)	(2)	52(1)
(2), (3)...	77(2), (3)	148(1)–(3)...	263(1)–(3)	(3)	58(4)
(4)	ss.70(7), 77(1)	148A	263(5)	(4)	58(5)
s.104(1)	195(1)	149(1)	268(1), (2)	(5)	58(6)
(1A).....	195(2)	(2)	268(2), (3)	(6)	58(7)
(2), (3)...	195(3), (4)	149A(1).....	269(1)	(7)	58(8)
108(1) part..	ss.72(1), 79(1),	(2), (3).	269(2), (3)	176(1)	61(1)
	(2)	150(1)	256(1)	(1A).....	61(2)
(2)	79(1)	(2)	256(2)	(2)	61(3)
109 part.....	73(7)	(3)	256(3)	(3)	61(4)
111	82	151(1)	278(1)	(4)	61(5)
111A	75	(2)	278(2), (3)	177	58(9)
112	3(2)	(3)	278(5)	178(1)	59(1)
113(1)	1(2)	152	98	(2)	59(2)
(2)	1(3)	153(2)	99(1)	(3)	59(3)
(4)	1(4), (5)	(3)	99(2), (3)	179(1)	201(1)–(3)
114	2	(3A)	99(4)	(2)	201(4)
114A	83	(4)	99(5)	179A	203(1)
123	96	154	100(1), (2)	180(1) part ..	200(1), (2)
124 part.....	78(1)	155 part.....	100(3)	(1A)–(1C)	200(3)–(5)
125	88(1)	155A	99(6)	(2)	200(6)
127(1)	81(1)	156(1)	102(1)	(4)	200(7)
(1A).....	81(3)	(2)	102(1)	(4A).....	200(8)
(1ZA)...	81(2)	(3)	102(3)	(5)	200(9)
(2)–(4)...	81(4)–(6)	(6)	102(4)	(6), (7)...	200(10, (11)
(5)	81(7)	157(1)	102(2)	181	246(1)
128	87	(3)	102(4)	182	246(2)
129 part.....	88(2)	158	102(5)	A	227
130(3A).....	86(1)	159(2)	101(7)	183(1)	228(1)
(4)	86(2)	160(1)	101(1)	(1A).....	228(2)
(5)	86(3)	(2)	101(2)	(2)	228(3), (4)
(6)	86(4)	161(1)	101(3)	(4)	229(1)
131	88(3)	(2)	101(4), (5)	(5)	229(2), (3)
132(1)	88(4)	(3)	101(8)	(5A).....	229(4), (5)
133	88(7)	(4)	101(6)	(5B),	
134	90	(5)	101(2)	(5C).....	229(6), (7)
135(1)	88(5), (6)	162(1)	285(6)	(6)	228(5)
(2)–(4)...	89	(2)	285(7)	(7)	228(6)
136	91	(3)	285(8)	184(1)	230(1)
137	88(8)	(4), (5)...	286	(2)	230(2)
137A	95	164(1)–(5)...	285(1)–(5)	(3)	230(3)
138(1), (2)...	265(1)	(6)	285(9)	(5)	230(4)
(4)	265(2)	165	50(1), (2)	(5A).....	230(5)
139	265(3), (4)	166(1), (2)...	50(3), (4)	(5B)	230(6)
139A	267(1)	167	50(5)	(6)	230(7)
140	267(2)	168	48	(7), (8)...	230(8), (9)
140A(1).....	97(1)	169(1)	47(1)–(3)	185	231
(2).....	97(4)	(2)	47(4)	186(1)	232(1)
(3), (4).	97(2), (3)	(3), (4)...	47(5), (6)	(2)	232(2)
141(1) part ..	266(1)	170	41	(2A).....	232(3)
(1)(a)....	266(2)	171(1), (2)...	46(1), (2), (5),	(3)–(5)...	232(4)–(6)
(e)....	266(3)		(6)	187(1)	233(1), (2)
(f)....	266(4)	(3)	46(3)	(3)–(5)...	233(3)–(5)
(g)....	266(8)	(4)	46(4)	188(1)	234(1), (2)
(1A)....	266(5)	(6)	46(7)	(2)–(8)...	234(3)–(10)
(1B)	266(6)	172	50(6)	191(1) part) .	247(1), (6)
(1C)	266(7)	173(1)	49(1)	(2)	247(3)
(2)	266(9)	(2)	49(2)	(3) part ..	247(3)
(3)	266(10)	(3)	49(3)	(4)	247(4)

1975	1995	1975	1995	1975	1995
s.192 part	s.203(3)	s.242A	s.117(7)	s.283(1)	s.133(1)
193	199	243	117(8)	(1A)	133(2)
193A(1)	211(1)	244(1)	116(1)	(2) part	ss.133(3), 175(10)
(2)	211(2)	(2)	116(2)	(3)	133(4)
194	ss.211(7), 213, 214(1)–(6), (7), (8), (9), 215(1), (2), (3), (4), 216(1), (2), (3), (4), (5), (6), (7), 217, 218(1), (2), (3), 219(1), (2), (3)–(5), (6), (7), (8), 220(1), (2), (3), (4), 221(1), (2), (3), 222(1), (2), (3), (4), (5), (6), (7), (8), 224	245(1)	103(2)	283A(1), (2)	292(1)
		(1A)	103(3)	284	7(6)
		(2)	103(1)	285	(8)
		(3)	103(4)	286	(9), (10)
		247 part	103(5), (6)	287(1)	9(1)
		248	103(5)	(2)	9(2)
		249	103(7)	(3)	9(3)
		250	103(8)	(4), (5)	9(4), (5)
		251(1)–(4)	105(1)–(4)	288(1)	4(1)
		(5)	105(5)	(2)	4(3)
		(6)	105(6)	(4)	4(4)
		252	104(1)	(5)	4(2)
		253	104(2), (3)	289	5(2)
		254(1)	118(1), (2)	289B(6) part	225(8)
196(1)	211(3)	(2)	118(3)	289D(1)	(4)
(2)	211(4)	(3)	118(4)	(1A)	225(5)
203	211(5)	(4)	118(5)	(1B)	225(6)
205(1)–(3)	205(1)–(3)	(4A)	118(4)	(4)	225(7)
205A(1)–(3)	205(4)–(6)	(5)	118(6)	289G(1)	225(1)
206	208	254A(1)	118(7)	(2)	225(2)
207(1)–(4)	207(1)–(4)	(2)	197	(3)	225(3)
(5)	207(5)	254B	118(8)	289GB	226
212A(1)	209(1)	255(1) part	119(1), (3)	290	5(3)
(1A)	209(2)	(1A)	119(2)	291(2), (3)	5(4)
(2), (3)	209(3), (4)	(1B)	119(6)	292(1), (2)	11(4)
(4)–(6)	209(5)–(7)	(1C)	119(7)	293	12
(8)	209(8)	(2)	119(4)	294(1)	21(1)
215	295	(3) part	119(5), (8)	(2)–(5)	21(2)–(5)
216	293	(4)	119(9)	(4), (5)	22(4), (5)
217(1) part	198(1)	(5), (6)	119(10), (11)	295(1), (2)	22(1)–(3)
(2), (3)	198(2), (3)	257	120(10)	(3)	22(4), (5)
217A	196	258	120(2)	296(1)	43(1)–(3)
218(1)	210(1)	260	120(3)	(2)	43(4)
(2), (3)	210(2), (3)	261	120(4)	(3), (4)	43(5), (6)
219	202	262	124(2)	(5), (6)	43(7), (8)
223A	248(1)–(4)	263(1) part	124(1), (3)	298(1) part	ss.23(6), 24(1)
224	254	(2)	124(4)	(2)	23(7)
227A	299	(3)	124(5)	(3)	23(8)
228(1)	106(1), (2)	263A	123	299(1)	30(1)
(2)	106(3)	264(1), (2)	121(1), (2)	(2)	30(2)
228A	108	(3)	121(3)	(3)	30(3)
230	130	(4)	121(4)	(4)	30(4)
230A	107	265(1), (2)	122(1), (2)	299A	31
231(1) part	109(1), (2)	(4)	122(3)	300(1) part	32(1), (2)
(2)	109(1)	(4A)	122(4)	(2), (3)	32(3), (4)
(3)	109(3)	266	128	(3A)	32(5)
(4)	109(4), (5)	267	128	(4)	32(7), (8)
(5)	109(6)	268(1)	125(1)	(4A)	32(9)
233(1)	110(1), (2)	(2)	125(2)	(6) part	ss.32(6), 33
(2), (3)	110(3), (4)	(3)	125(3)	303(1)	168
(3A)	110(5)	(4)	125(4)	304(1)–(3)	45(1)–(4)
(4)	110(6)	269	126	(4)	45(5)
234(1)	115(1), (2)	270(1)	106(4)	305	17(1), (2)
(2)	115(3), (4)	(2)–(4)	106(5)–(9)	(3)	35(1), (2)
235	114	271	127	306	42(9), (10)
236A	113	274	93	307(1)–(3)	42(2)–(4)
236B	111	275	94	(4), (5)	42(5), (6)
238(1)	112(1)	277(1) part	129(1), (2), (4)	308(1), (2)	42(7), (8)
(1A)	112(2)	(2)	129(3)	309(1)	172(1)
(2)	112(3), (4)	278	305(4)	(2) part	ss.172(2), (3), 296
(3)	112(5)	279	132	(3)	172(2), (3)
239(1)	117(9)	280	60	310	134
240	117(3)	280A	131	310A	133(5)
241	117(1), (2)	281	124(2)	311(1) part	138(1)
242	117(4)–(6)	282A	301(1)	(2)	138(1)
		282B	301(2)		

449

451

Criminal Procedure (Scotland) Act 1995

1975	1995
s.453C(4), (5)	s.189(5), (6)
453D	190
453E	192(1), (2)
453AA	187
454(1)	192(3)
455(1), (2)	192(4), (5)
455A(1)	189(7)
(2)	197
456	170
457A(1)–(4)	292(2)–(7)
457ZA(1) part	305(1), (3)

1975	1995
s.457ZA(2)	s.305(2)
458	308
459	308
462(1)	307(1)
(2)	307(2)
(4)–(9)	307(3)–(8)
Sched.1	Sched.1
Sched.5, para.1	Sched.6, para.1
para.2	Sched.6, para.2

1975	1995
Sched.5—*cont.*	
para.3	Sched.6, para.3
para.4	Sched.6, para.4
para.5	Sched.6, para.5
para.6	Sched.6, para.6
Sched.5A	Sched.4
Sched.7	s.220(3)
Sched.7A	Sched.10

SEXUAL OFFENCES (SCOTLAND) ACT 1976
(c.67)

1976	1995
Sched.1	s.46(3), Sched.1
Sched.2	Sched.1

CRIMINAL LAW ACT 1977
(c.45)

1977	1995
Sched.7, para.2	s.222(1), (6), (8)
Sched.11, para.1	211(1)
para.2	292(1)
para.3	7(6)
para.4	5(2)
para.5	225(4), (7)
para.6	Sched.3, para.19
para.8	s.215(1), (2)
para.10	307(1)
para.11	Sched.10
Sched.13, para.7	s.199

NATIONAL HEALTH SERVICE (SCOTLAND) ACT 1978
(c.29)

1978	1995
Sched.16, para.41	s.307(1)

452

Criminal Procedure (Scotland) Act 1995

COMMUNITY SERVICE BY OFFENDERS (SCOTLAND) ACT 1978
(c.49)

1978	1995	1978	1995	1978	1995
s.1(1)	s.238(1)	s.5A	s.241	s.10(1)–(3)	s.245(1)–(3)
(2)–(7)	238(2)–(7)	6	242	11	245(4)
2(1), (2)	238(8), (9)	6A(1)	243(1)	12(1)	245(5)
(3), (4)	238(10), (11)	(2)	243(2)	Sched.2,	
3(1)–(3)	239(1)–(3)	(3)	243(3)	para.2	234(1), (2)
4(1)	239(4)	6B	244	para.3	234(1), (2)
(2)	239(5)	7	229(1), (4), (5)		
(3)	239(6)	8	232(1), (2)		
5	240				

CRIMINAL EVIDENCE ACT 1979
(c.16)

1979	995
s.1(1)	s.266(1), (4)

BAIL (SCOTLAND) ACT 1980
(c.4)

1980	1995	1980	1995	1980	1995
s.1(1)	s.24(3)	s.4	s.29	Sched.1,	
1(2)–(3)	24(4)–(8)	5(a)	201(1)–(3)	para.4	s.30(2)
1(4)	24(4)–(8), 30(1), (4)	5(b)	201(4)	para.5	200(6)
1(5)	24(4)–(8)	6(b)	200(9)	para.6	30(2)
2	25	7(1)	21(2)–(5)	para.7	135(3), (4)
3(1), (2)	27(1), (2)	7(2)	21(2)–(5), 22(4), (5)	para.8	146(6)
3(2A)–(2D)	27(3)–(6)	8	22(1)–(3), (4), (5)	para.10	181(3)
3(3)–(6)	27(7)–(10)	9(a)	43(1)–(3)	para.12	181(3)
3(7)–(11)	28	9(b)	43(7)–(8)	para.14	307(1)
3(12)	27(11)	10	8	Sched.2	ss.146(2), 200(6)

MAGISTRATES' COURTS ACT 1980
(c.43)

1980	1995
Sched.7,	
para.136	s.215(1), (2)

LAW REFORM (MISCELLANEOUS PROVISIONS) (SCOTLAND) ACT 1980
(c.55)

1980	1995
s.2(3)	s.85(6), (7)
Sched.2,	
para.6	84(6)
para.7	86(3)

CRIMINAL JUSTICE ACT (SCOTLAND) ACT 1980
(c.62)

1980	1995
Sched.7—*cont.*	
para.42	s.117(4)–(6)
para.44	105(5)
para.45	120(4)
para.46	125(4)
para.49	292(1)
para.51	23(1)
para.54(a)	144(1), (9)
para.54(b)	144(4), (5)
para.55	155(4)
para.56	266(1)

1980	1995
Sched.7—*cont.*	
para.57	s.48
para.58	142(5)
para.59(a)	201(1)–(3)
para.59(b)	201(4)
para.60	212(1), (2), (8), (9)
para.61	216(1), (2)
para.62(b)	214(9)
para.63	218(3)
para.65	220(1), (2)

1980	1995
Sched.7—*cont.*	
para.68	s.169
para.69	295
para.73	308
para.74	308
para.76	307(1)
Sched.8	ss.93, 103(4)–(6), 104(2), (3), 115(1)–(4), 120(1), 129(1)–(3), 137(1), 178(2), 199

FORGERY AND COUNTERFEITING ACT 1981
(c.45)

1981	1995
s.26	Sched.9

CRIMINAL JUSTICE ACT 1982
(c.48)

1982	1995
s.53(a)	s.225(4)–(6)
54	225(1)–(3)
55(1)	292(2)–(7)
73(1), (2)	263(5)
Sched.6	
para.64	291(2)
Sched.7	291(3)
para.4	7(6)
para.3	232(2)

1982	1995
Sched.7—*cont.*	
para.5	s.7(6)
para.6	7(8)
para.7	155(1), Sched.3, para.19
para.9	232(2)
para.10	199
para.12	239(5)
para.14	7(4)

1982	1995
Sched.13	
para.3	s.229(4), (5)
para.4	242
para.5	ss.243(1)–(3), 244
Sched.15,	
para.17	211(1), (2)
para.19	307(1)

MENTAL HEALTH (AMENDMENT) (SCOTLAND) ACT 1983
(c.39)

1983	1995
s.22(2)	s.59(1)
34(a)	53(1), (2)–(10), (11), (12), 58(1), (2)
34(b), (d)	60
35(a), (b)	61(2)
36(2)	230(4)–(6)

1983	1995
s.36(3)	s.230(7)
36(4)	Sched.6, para.4
Sched.2	
para.31	58(1), (2), (6)–(8)
para.32	61(1)

1983	1995
Sched. 2—*cont.*	
para.33	s.59(2), (3)
para.34	58(6)–(8)
para.35	61(1)
para.36	59(2), (3)
para.37	307(1)

HEALTH AND SOCIAL SERVICES AND SOCIAL SECURITIES AJUDICATIONS ACT 1983
(c.41)

1983	1995
Sched.2	
para.7	42(1)

ROAD TRAFFIC REGULATION ACT 1984
(C.27)

1984	1995
Sched.13,	
para.37	Sched.9

MENTAL HEALTH (SCOTLAND) ACT 1984
(C.36)

1984	1995
Sched.3,	
para.24	52(3)
para.25	53(1)
para.26	58(1)
para.27	61(1)
para.28	59(1)–(3)
para.29	230(1), (2)
para.31	52(3)
para.32	53(1)
para.33	58(1)
para.34	61(1)
para.35	59(1)–(3)
para.36	230(1), (2)
para.37	307(1)

VIDEO RECORDING ACT 1984
(C.39)

1984	1995
s.20	Sched.9

LAW REFORMS (MISCELLANEOUS PROVISIONS) (SCOTLAND) ACT 1985
(C.73)

1985	1995
s.21	s.8
36	ss.274(1), (2), (3), (4), 275
s.37	ss.268(1), (2), 269(1)
43(a)	s.207(5)
Sched.2,	
para.16	84(4)–(6)
para.17	85(4), (5)
para.18	ss.72(1), 79(1), (2)
para.19	s.127
para.20	178(1)
para.23	15(6)
Sched.4	179

INCEST AND RELATED OFFENCES (SCOTLAND) ACT 1986
(C.36)

1986	1995
Sched.1,	
para.1	s.46(3)
para.2	136
para.3	46(3)

CABLE AND BROADCASTING ACT 1986
(c.46)

1986	1995
Sched.5,	
para.30	s.47(4)

DEBTORS (SCOTLAND) ACT 1987
(c.18)

1987	1995
Sched.6,	
para.18	s.221(1)

CRIMINAL JUSTICE (SCOTLAND) ACT 1987
(c.41)

1987	1995	1987	1995	1987	1995
s.45(6)(a)	s.109(1), (2)	s.60(4)	s.277(4)	Sched. 1—*cont.*	
(6)(b)	109(4), (5)	61	272(1), (6)	para.7	s.88(2)
(6)(c)	109(6)	62(3)	146(6)	para.9	268(1), (2)
56(1)	302(1)	(4)(a)	32(2)	para.10	228(1)
(2), (2A)	302(9)	(4)(b)	32(9)	para.12	295
(3)	302(2)	63	267(1)	para.13(1)	103(2)
(3A)	302(3)	64(1)	293	para.13(2)	103(1)
(4)–(6)	302(4)–(6)	65	229(6), (7)	para.14(1)	125(1)
(7), (7A)	302(7), (8)	(3)	229(1)	para.14(2)	125(2)
(8)–(11)	303(1)–(4)	(4)	228(5)	para.14(3)	125(3)
57(1)	3(2)	(5)	232(2)	para.16(a),	
(2)	2	66(2)	226	(b)	14(2)
58(1)	3(3)–(5)	67(1)	219(2)	para.16(c)	14(4)
(2)	195(2)	(2)	219(8)	para.17	204(4)
59(1)	44(1)–(4), (9),	68(1)	193(1), (2)	para.18(2)	Sched.9
	(10)	(3)	121(3)	Sched.2	ss.124(4),
60(1)	277(1)	Sched.1,			225(7)
(2)	277(2)	para.4	10		
(3)	277(3)	para.5	84(2), (3)		

CRIMINAL JUSTICE ACT 1988
(c.33)

1988	1995
s.124	s.207(5)
Sched.9,	
para.5	204(4)
Sched.15,	
para.48	46(3)
para.50	Sched.1
para.51	Sched.1

ROAD TRAFFIC (CONSEQUENTIAL PROVISIONS) ACT 1988
(c.54)

1988	1995
Sched.3,	
para 34	s.302(9)

PRISONS (SCOTLAND) ACT 1989
(c.45)

1989	1995
Sched.2,	
para.12	s.208

NATIONAL HEALTH SERVICE AND COMMUNITY CARE ACT 1990
(c.19)

1990	1995
Sched.9,	
para.14	s.307(1)

LAW REFORM (MISCELLANEOUS PROVISIONS) (SCOTLAND) ACT 1990
(c.40)

1990	1995	1990	1995	1990	1995
s.56(1)	s.271(5)	s.61(1)	s.229(1)	Sched.6—*cont.*	Sched.7—*cont.*
(2)	271(7)	(2)	232(1)	para.5	para.5
(3)	271(8)	(3)	238(1)	para.6	para.6
57(1)	271(9)	62	235	para.7	para.7
(2)	271(10)	Sched.6,	Sched.7	para.9	para.8
58	271(11)	para.1	para.1	Sched.8,	
59	271(12)	para.2	para.2	para.27	s.301(1), (2)
60	4(2)	para.3	para.3	para.27(3)	219(1)
61	228(1), (2)	para.4	para.4	para.28	239(6)

BROADCASTING ACT 1990
(c.42)

1990	1995
Sched.20,	
para.21	47(4)

ROAD TRAFFIC ACT 1991
(c.40)

1991	1995
s.39	s.248(1)–(4)

CRIMINAL JUSTICE ACT 1991
(c.53)

1991	1995
s.17(1)	s.225(2)
23(2)	219(2)
Sched.3,	
para.7(2)	228(2)
para.7(3)	234(1)–(10)

ARMED FORCES ACT 1991
(c.62)

1991	1995
Sched.2,	
para.9(2)	253

PRISONERS AND CRIMINAL PROCEEDINGS (SCOTLAND) ACT 1993
(c.9)

1993	1995	1993	1995	1993	1995
s.8	s.44(5), (6)–(8)	s.39(2)	s.72(1)	Sched.5—cont.	
14(1)	209(1), (3),	40(1)	99(6)	para.1(17)	s.117(8)
	(4)	(2)	158	para.1(18)	104(1)
28(1), (2)	18(1), (2)	41	210(1), (2),	para.1(19)	120(2)
(3)	18(3)		(3)	para.1(20)	120(4)
(3A), (3C)	18(4)	42(1)	108	para.1(22)	122(4)
(3B)	18(5)	43	188(1)–(7)	para.1(23)	125(1), (2),
(4)	18(6)	Sched.3	Sched.8		(3)
(5), (6)	18(7), (8)	Sched.4	Sched.9	para.1(24)	126
28A	19	Sched.5,		para.1(27)	94
28B	20	para.1(2)	37(1), (2)–(4),	para.1(30)	144(1)
29	279		(5)	para.1(31)	268(1), (2)
30	272(5), (8)	para.1(3)	72(1)	para.1(32)	44(1), (9)
31	277(1)	para.1(5)	95	para.1(35)	183(1), (2)
(1)–(3)	271(1)–(3)	para.1(7)	232(3)	para.1(35)(b)	183(3), (5)
32	273	para.1(9)	110(1), (2)	para.1(36)	186(1), (2),
33(4)	271(4)	para.1(11)	111		(7), (8), (9)
34	271(6)	para.1(15)	117(3)	para.1(37)	189(4)
38(1)	145	para.1(16)	117(7)	Sched.7	14(2)

CRIMINAL JUSTICE ACT 1993
(c.36)

1993	1995	1993	1995	1993	1995
s.68(1)	s.106(1), (2)	Sched.5—cont.		Sched.5—cont.	
(2)	108	para.2(4)	s.110(1), (2),	para.2(11)	s.193(1), (2)
(3)	175(1)–(4)		(6)	para.2(12)	176(1)
69	209(8)	para.2(5)	112(1)	para.2(13)	183(3), (5),
Sched.5,		para.2(6)	116(2)		(8)
para.2(1)	175(9)	para.2(7)	118(1)–(5)	para.2(14)	186(1)–(5),
para.2(2)	246(1)	para.2(8)	125(1), (2)		(8), (9)
para.2(3)	247(3)	para.2(9)	247(3)	para.2(15)	189(4)–(6)

CRIMINAL JUSTICE AND PUBLIC ORDER ACT 1994
(c.33)

1994	1995
s.47(4)	s.222(7)
129(1)	14(1)
(2)	14(6)
(3)	15(1), (2)
132	209(3), (4)
157(7)	225(5)
Sched.10,	
para.47	14(4), (5)

LOCAL GOVERNMENT ETC. (SCOTLAND) ACT 1994
(c.39)

1994	1995
Sched.13,	
para.97(2)	s.49(1), (3), (6), (7)
para.97(3)	232(1)

Criminal Procedure (Scotland) Act 1995

CRIMINAL JUSTICE (SCOTLAND) ACT 1995
(C.20)

CHILDREN (SCOTLAND) ACT 1995
(c.36)

INCREASE OF CRIMINAL PENALTIES ETC. (SCOTLAND) ORDER 1984
(S.I. 1984/526)

ACT OF ADJOURNAL (CONSOLIDATION) 1988
(S.I. 1988/110)

COMMUNITY SERVICE ORDERS (NORTHERN IRELAND CONSEQUENTIAL AMENDMENTS) ORDER 1989
(S.I. 1989/1345)

INDEX

References are to page

Index

Index

Index

Index

Index

Index

Index

Index

Index